D1597090

BUSINESS PLANNING

LEXISNEXIS LAW SCHOOL ADVISORY BOARD

Lenni B. Benson
Professor of Law &
Associate Dean for Professional Development
New York Law School

Raj Bhala
Rice Distinguished Professor
University of Kansas, School of Law

Charles P. Craver
Freda H. Alverson Professor of Law
The George Washington University Law School

Richard D. Freer
Robert Howell Hall Professor of Law
Emory University School of Law

Craig Joyce
Andrews Kurth Professor of Law &
Co-Director, Institute for Intellectual Property and Information Law
University of Houston Law Center

Ellen S. Podgor
Professor of Law &
Associate Dean of Faculty Development and Electronic Education
Stetson University College of Law

Paul F. Rothstein
Professor of Law
Georgetown University Law Center

Robin Wellford Slocum
Professor of Law & Director,
Legal Research and Writing Program
Chapman University School of Law

David I. C. Thomson
LP Professor & Director, Lawyering Process Program
University of Denver, Sturm College of Law

BUSINESS PLANNING

Scott B. Ehrlich
Professor of Law & Chair, J.D./M.B.A. Dual Degree Program
California Western School of Law

Douglas C. Michael
Edward T. Breathitt Professor of Law & Associate Dean for Academic Affairs
University of Kentucky College of Law

Library of Congress Cataloging-in-Publication Data

Ehrlich, Scott B.
  Business planning / Scott B. Ehrlich, Douglas C. Michael.
     p. cm.
  Includes index.
  ISBN 978-1-4224-1196-4 (hardbound)
  1. Business enterprises--Law and legislation--United States. 2. Commercial law--United States. I. Michael, Douglas
C., 1957- II. Title
  KF1355.E367 2009
  346.73'065--dc22

                                                                                              2009016879

This publication is designed to provide accurate and authoritative information in regard to the subject matter covered. It is sold with the understanding that the publisher is not engaged in rendering legal, accounting, or other professional services. If legal advice or other expert assistance is required, the services of a competent professional should be sought.

LexisNexis and the Knowledge Burst logo are registered trademarks and Michie is a trademark of Reed Elsevier Properties Inc., used under license. Matthew Bender and the Matthew Bender Flame Design are registered trademarks of Matthew Bender Properties Inc.

Copyright © 2009 Matthew Bender & Company, Inc., a member of the LexisNexis Group.
All Rights Reserved.

No copyright is claimed in the text of statutes, regulations, and excerpts from court opinions quoted within this work. Permission to copy material exceeding fair use, 17 U.S.C. § 107, may be licensed for a fee of 25¢ per page per copy from the Copyright Clearance Center, 222 Rosewood Drive, Danvers, Mass. 01923, telephone (978) 750-8400.

NOTE TO USERS
To ensure that you are using the latest materials available in this area, please be sure to periodically check the LexisNexis Law School web site for downloadable updates and supplements at www.lexisnexis.com/lawschool.

Editorial Offices
744 Broad Street, Newark, NJ 07102 (973) 820-2000
201 Mission St., San Francisco, CA 94105-1831 (415) 908-3200
www.lexisnexis.com

MATTHEW⬥BENDER

ACKNOWLEDGMENTS

I want to acknowledge the following people for their assistance, guidance and inspiration. First, many thanks to my domestic partner of 22 years, Frank DiPalermo, whose warmth and support helped to sustain me during the three years of writing this book. Second, Professor Tom Barton and his wife, Professor Sharon Foster. Both Tom and Sharon have been unwavering in their guidance and enthusiasm for this project. Many thanks to Dean Steven Smith who provided me with the motivation, professional support and guidance necessary for an undertaking of this scope. I owe a sincere debt of gratitude to two other people: Professor Walter Schwidetzky for his gracious and invaluable input with respect to the tax aspects of business entity formation and operation; and my co-author, Douglas Michael, who is a joy to work with. Finally, I must acknowledge the many students in my Business Planning seminars over the last 15 years. I have learned so much from them.

Scott B. Ehrlich

I would like to acknowledge the help of many professional colleagues and mentors: Martin J. McMahon, Jr., who first introduced me to this subject and encouraged my neophyte teaching efforts; Richard A. Westin, who continued in that fashion and provided helpful commentary for some of the tax materials; Rutheford "Biff" Campbell, who did similarly for the securities materials; and mostly Scott Ehrlich, who convinced me that Business Planning is a subject which can be suitable for and valuable to every law student. If these materials can convey even a small portion of his energy and passion for this subject, I will consider them a success. I also want to credit two decades of my Business Planning students who have endured various classroom experiments, successes, and failures and thus have, directly and indirectly, contributed their valuable experiences. Finally, this work would not have been possible without the guidance and patience of my wife Susan and my children Stuart and Amanda, who provided encouragement, persevered with me through long hours of work and episodes of grumpy writer's block, and deserve the credit for much which is right herein.

Douglas C. Michael

TABLE OF CONTENTS

TABLE OF CONTENTS

TABLE OF CONTENTS

TABLE OF CONTENTS

TABLE OF CONTENTS

TABLE OF CONTENTS

TABLE OF CONTENTS

Chapter 7	MANAGEMENT AND CONTROL 333

TABLE OF CONTENTS

TABLE OF CONTENTS

TABLE OF CONTENTS

TABLE OF CONTENTS

TABLE OF CONTENTS

Chapter 1

INTRODUCTION TO BUSINESS PLANNING

A. INTRODUCTION

These materials take both an analytical and practical approach to the formation, operation and dissolution of business enterprises. We will look at doctrinal, statutory and regulatory foundations that attorneys use to draft documents, advise clients, and make strategic decisions regarding the formation, operation and dissolution of business entities.

One chapter of these materials focuses on the necessity of finding an exception from the securities registration requirements of the Securities Act of 1933 (the "Securities Act"). Under the Securities Act, the offer or sale of "securities"[1] must be registered with the Securities and Exchange Commission (the "SEC") unless an exemption can be found. Registration is a time-consuming and expensive process that is intended primarily for companies whose securities will be publicly traded. Most non-public business entities are formed without registration by fulfilling the requirements for an exemption from registration. An important part of the formation of *every* business entity is making sure that an appropriate exemption from registration can be found for the company's investment interests or, in the alternative, that the entity has complied with registration requirements for those investment interests. These materials concentrate on the formation of business entities that will *not* be registering their securities with the SEC. In this regard, the focus of this book is on the formation, operation and dissolution of non-publicly traded business entities that can satisfy the requirements for exemption from registration. In preparing the materials on securities registration and exemption, we have oriented the readings, explanatory text and exercises so that they can be understood by students who have not already taken a securities regulation course.

Similarly, taxation issues play a major role in connection with the formation, operation, sale and dissolution of all business entities and we will be devoting significant attention to these tax issues. In this regard, we recognize that many students will not have had advanced courses in partnership and corporate taxation. We have organized the materials to provide all upper level law students with the background they need to understand the primary tax considerations and concerns that arise, regardless of whether they have taken taxation courses.

---

[1] When a business entity is formed, ownership of the entity is allocated to its owners in some way: shares of stock in the case of a corporation, membership interests in the case of limited liability companies, or partnership interests in the case of general or limited partnerships. Any of these means of allocating ownership can constitute "securities" as that term is used in Section 2 of the Securities Act. See Chapter 4 for an in-depth analysis of when a participation interest in an entity constitutes a security.

B. THE CONSTITUENTS IN BUSINESS ENTITY FORMATION AND OPERATION

Our first task is to fully understand the role of the attorney in transactions involving the formation and operation of business entities. Before we can undertake that task, we first need to understand the interests of each of the constituents typically involved in business entity formation and operation. Who is involved, what is his or her role, and does the constituent need a lawyer?

1. The Promoters

The promoters are the people who generate the idea to form a business venture and bring it into existence. They have studied the market, consulted with specialists and begun to formulate a business plan that they can present to potential investors and lenders. Most of the time, to adequately fund the business entity, the promoters will be using investment capital contributed by investors, as well as arranging for loans from lenders.[2]

The promoters will probably participate as equity holders[3] in the business entity but this is not *always* the case. Promoters often extract a fee for putting the deal together and, following formation, receipt of the fee may be the end of the promoters' participation. However, most promoters also seek an equity interest in the entity to assure that they participate in profits of the business and any enhanced capital value of the entity.

Payment of a fee to the promoters is fair. Promoters are performing the valuable service of generating the business concept, finding investors, organizing the business entity, making contractual arrangements, purchasing property, consulting with accountants, lawyers and lenders. These pre-formation activities are costly and time consuming. They are also risky since the deal may never come to fruition.[4] The fee charged by promoters might be a fixed fee but, more commonly, is based on some percentage of the investment funds raised for capitalization of the entity. In addition, promoters may sometimes receive a "promotional share" of the equity in the venture for no cost or at some favorable price.[5] In a properly constructed business transaction, all of the promotional consideration received by the promoters will be disclosed to investors. There is a built-in incentive impelling the promoters to be fair, since informed investors won't participate if the promotional consideration is excessive.

---

[2] The difference between capital contributions and debt financing is discussed later in this chapter. Sometimes the promoters will be relying entirely on their own economic contributions to fund the business without capital contributions from investors or debt financing from a lender. This is a relatively rare occurrence for most business enterprises.

[3] An "equity holder" is an owner of the business. In a corporation, the equity holders are shareholders. In a partnership, the equity holders are the general or limited partners. In a limited liability company, the equity holders are the members.

[4] In many cases, if the entity is eventually formed, the capital of the entity will be used to reimburse the promoters for the pre-formation costs and expenses. This reimbursement is separate from any compensation or fees received by the promoters for their services.

[5] For instance, suppose the business entity will have ten owners (seven investors and three promoters). Each of the investors will be contributing $100,000 for a one-tenth equity share in the business. The promoters will each receive a one-tenth share but might only have to contribute $75,000 each.

2.   The Equity Holders

The equity holders are the *owners* of the business entity. In the case of corporations they are the shareholders, in partnerships they are the partners, in limited liability companies they are the members. Being an "owner" has different meanings depending on the type of entity, the nature of the ownership interest, and the rights granted in the original documents creating the entity. In general, ownership means that the equity holders get to participate in: (i) the financial profits of the business entity,[6] and, (ii) control and management of the business entity.[7]

One of the primary benefits of equity ownership is that, in addition to profits, the equity holders are entitled to any appreciation of *value* of their ownership interests in the entity. An ownership interest in a business entity is personal property that can be sold. Like any other property, it may rise or fall in value. Many investors are looking for a capital investment that will rise in value, as well as generate income from profits.

One of the primary *risks* of equity ownership, is that the equity holders are primarily responsible for the *losses* of the business entity. Upon termination or liquidation of the business entity, the owners get paid last, after all of the assets of the business entity have been used to pay secured and unsecured debt.[8] Every owner who invests in a business enterprise as an equity holder faces the prospect of unlimited "upside" (an increase in the value of the owner's share of the business entity) and a "downside" (the decrease in value or complete loss of the owner's share).

A serious issue for any equity holder is whether or not there is liability beyond the amount invested in the business entity. What if the entity is dissolved or bankrupt and the creditors seek to collect from the owners of the entity? Imagine investing $100 to purchase one share of the stock of a genetic bioengineering company, Xsilicon Corp. Six months after purchasing the stock, Xsilicon incurs debt equivalent to $100,000 per share, as a result of the unintended release of a dangerous biological agent. Unless there is liability shield for stockholders, each stockholder would be liable for $100,000 per share, in addition to the loss of $100 per share.

Without limited liability, potential investors would shy away from capital investment. After all, if owning a few shares of stock of a corporation placed the investor at risk of unlimited personal liability for the debts of the corporation, the

---

[6] The profits of a business entity are the net income from the operations of that entity's regular business, as compared to the liquidation or sale of assets of the business. The degree of entitlement to participate in profits is laid out in the formation documents and can vary widely. Even though an equity holder might own the right to some proportion of the profits, there may be no guarantee of receiving a profit *distribution*, even in a profitable year. The managers of the business entity may elect to retain annual profits for reinvestment in the business, or as a reserve against future contingencies.

[7] The degree of control exercised by equity holders vary's widely. Even in the traditional corporate form of business entity, the degree to which shareholders can vote on matters of control may vary depending on the class of stock they hold and the rights granted to the shareholders in the formation documents. In the case of general and limited partnerships as well as limited liability companies, the statutes that control formation of these entities allow the parties to freely customize the degree of control granted to equity holders (except for a few matters).

[8] See the discussion of unsecured creditors in Section 4 of this chapter.

outcome could be catastrophic — an unacceptable risk to a casual equity holder. The rise of limited liability investment mechanisms, such as corporate stock ownership, can be seen as one of the greatest contributors to the economic growth of the United States in the late nineteenth and twentieth centuries.[9] More recently, limited liability companies have begun to supplant corporations and limited partnerships as a powerful mechanism that allows for flexible control and financial structures while limiting liability for all investors.[10]

When a company is being formed, or seeking to expand its business, the promoters may finance the formation or expansion from their own savings. However, in most cases, the promoters will seek outside investors to raise the necessary capital. Outside investors may include friends and business acquaintances, or the promoters may use brokers or agents to help find potential investors. Sometimes, the promoters will seek capital financing from established "venture capital" firms.

Although not a legal term, "venture capital" is often used to describe financing by wealthy pools of investors that regularly invest large amounts of money in exchange for equity interests, often in high-risk startup or growth ventures that might have trouble obtaining financing using other sources. Professionally managed venture capital firms are private partnerships, closely-held corporations or limited liability companies, funded by private and public pension funds, endowment funds, foundations, corporations, wealthy individuals, foreign investors, and the venture capitalists themselves. Venture capital firms have played a major role in the recent startup and growth of companies in the areas of biotechnology, computer software, and internet enterprises. According to statistics published by the National Venture Capital Association, venture capital provides a significant amount of recent financing in the U.S.:[11]

Year	Funds	Venture Capital ($ millions)
2002	172	$3,767
2003	147	$10,622
2004	205	$18,566
2005	218	$27,957
2006	212	$30,260

These venture capital firms specialize in financing risky companies with a potential for high value growth and profit. This type of financing comes with a heavy price tag and the venture capital firms will use their bargaining power to maximize the return on their investment in several ways. First, they will seek a substantial equity interest in exchange for providing the startup or growth capital. They will

---

[9] Halpern, Trebilcock & Turnbull, *An Economic Analysis of Limited Liability in Corporation Law*, 30 U. TORONTO L.J. 117 (1980). *See also* Vandervoot, *Piercing the Veil of Limited Liability Companies: The Need for a Better Standard*, 3 DePAUL BUS. & COMM. L.J. 51(2004).

[10] The first Limited Liability Company Act was enacted in Wyoming in 1977. Other states were slow to adopt LLC Acts until the mid 1990s. Since changes in the tax laws in 1997, there has been widespread adoption of Limited Liability Company Acts, so that all states have now enacted them. See Section A.5. and Chapter 3 for a detailed discussion of the rise of LLCs and the importance of tax law considerations in the development and usefulness of LLCs.

[11] *See* http://www.nvca.org/.

often insist on a large percentage of the equity ownership, giving them substantial control over management of the company, as well as a large financial stake.

Second, they will structure the transaction to get their capital investment returned to them as soon as possible, while retaining their original equity position in the venture. This allows the venture capitalists to more quickly re-invest the money in a new venture, thereby increasing the return on the original capital contributed to the venture. To accomplish this goal, venture capitalists may insist on a priority of distribution from profits of the business. This priority scheme may require that the venture capitalists be repaid some substantial portion of their original investment before other equity holders receive distributions.

3.   The Business Entity

Following formation, a business entity is a "person"[12] with an independent legal existence.[13] It is vested with legal rights and burdened by legal obligations that are separate from those of the promoters who created the entity and the equity holders who own it. As a separate person, the business entity will enter into contracts, own and convey property, incur debts, hire employees, sue and be sued, and be subject to the usual range of criminal and civil liabilities. Unfortunately, in smaller business entities, it is not unusual for the promoters and equity holders to neglect the essential distinction that the newly formed business organization is a separate legal entity, leading to troublesome problems discussed later in these materials.

4.   Unsecured Creditors

When a business entity is formed, it exists as a fictional person with rights and obligations independent of its equity holders. Debts and obligations will arise on the basis of contractual, and non-contractual, activities of the entity. The persons entitled to collect those debts are creditors. Unless these creditors have obtained some kind of lien interest to secure payment of the debt, they are "unsecured" creditors. Common unsecured creditors are lenders (loans), employees (wages and benefits), suppliers (goods and utilities), consultants (accounting, management, legal and other services), tort claimants (parties injured by the activities of the entity) and government (taxes and fees). The business entity is responsible for paying these creditors *prior* to the rights of any equity holders to distribution of profits or liquidated assets. One essential difference between equity holders and creditors is their relative priority with regard to payment from the profits or liquidation of the entity. The equity holders take a greater risk with respect to the

---

[12] As used in these materials, the term "person" includes individuals, business entities and governmental units. It is used expansively to describe any legal person that is entitled to own property or is otherwise vested with legal rights and obligations. You will discover, as you read federal and state statutes, that the term "person" is nearly always used in this expansive manner.

[13] Whether the entity is a general partnership, limited partnership, corporation or limited liability company, the entity has a separate legal existence. At one time this wasn't fully true for general partnerships, which were conceived of as separate for some limited purposes only. However, since the widespread adoption of the Revised Uniform Partnership Act of 1994 ("RUPA"), even general partnerships are now conceived of as separate entities, having an existence independent from the general partners. Section 201 of RUPA provides, simply: "A partnership is an entity distinct from its partners."

fiscal failure of the business entity and their interests are subordinated to the interests of creditors.[14]

5.   Secured Creditors

In the event that the business entity is unable, or unwilling, to pay its debts, ordinary unsecured creditors are in a difficult position. To obtain satisfaction of a claim, an unsecured creditor must commence a law suit in state or federal court, obtain a judgment and then, if the judgment remains unpaid, find valuable assets of the business entity that can be seized to satisfy the claim. The process is expensive, time-consuming and inherently unreliable. Even if the creditor rigorously pursues relief, the creditor must compete with many other creditors who are also seeking to obtain satisfaction of their claims. Each unsecured creditor will be racing to the courthouse to be the first to obtain a judgment and seize any of the entity's available assets. Unfortunately, even the winner of this race often finds that the business entity has no "equity" in any assets worth seizing.[15]

The collection efforts of unsecured creditors may also be impeded by the intercession of a bankruptcy proceeding.[16] In the event the business entity files bankruptcy, unsecured creditors are entitled to be paid prior to equity holders but, nevertheless, they often fare poorly. In a liquidating bankruptcy the company will go out of business and its assets will be sold by the bankruptcy trustee. If there is any equity remaining following the liquidation, the unsecured creditors will be paid only after administrative expenses (which can be very high) and after the payment of claims of secured and priority creditors. The list of priority claimants is extensive and includes tax claimants, employees and others.[17] What this means for the ordinary unsecured claimant in bankruptcy is that chances of payment in a liquidation are very low. Chances of repayment of unsecured debt in a chapter 11 bankruptcy *reorganization* may be somewhat improved but general, non-priority unsecured creditors are still likely to receive far less than they are owed if the debtor files any type of bankruptcy.[18]

It is for these reasons that risk-averse contractual creditors will often seek to boost their position to that of a secured creditor by requiring that some of the business entity's assets be pledged as collateral. These risk-averse creditors will insist on consensual liens, commonly referred to as "security interests" to secure

---

[14] In every jurisdiction there are limits on the ability of business entities to pay dividends or make liquidating distributions to equity holders unless there are sufficient assets remaining to satisfy the creditors of the business entity. Distribution limitations are discussed in Chapters 6 and 10.

[15] "Equity" is the value of the debtor's interest in property in excess of the interest of others in that property. Even if the debtor owns a valuable asset, such as a building, it may be subject to a prior consensual lien in favor of a secured lender such as a mortgagee. For instance, if the debtor owns an office building worth $500,000 but subject to a valid first mortgage securing a debt of $480,000, there is only $20,000 worth of equity available for seizure by any judgment creditors. There may also be nonconsensual liens such as tax liens, or prior judgment liens. If the debtor is deeply in debt, it is unlikely that the debtor will have substantial equity in property.

[16] The impact of the Bankruptcy Code on business entities is discussed in detail in Chapter 10.

[17] 11 U.S.C. § 507(a).

[18] 11 U.S.C. § 1101 *et. seq.* In a reorganization chances of substantial payment to unsecured claimants is enhanced since confirmation of the plan requires creditor approval or a finding by the court that the creditors are receiving more than they would in a chapter 7 liquidation. See Chapter 10 for an explanation of how reorganizations produce greater distributions to creditors.

the claims of those creditors. A security interest grants the secured creditor the right to use the collateral to satisfy the creditor's claim — to the exclusion of other junior creditors. In the case of real property, this is accomplished by the business entity's execution of a mortgage or deed of trust. In the case of personal property, this is accomplished by the debtor's execution of a security agreement.[19] In either case, a security interest is an interest in property that, in the event of a default, entitles the holder of the security to seize the collateral and have it sold at a foreclosure sale. The proceeds of the sale will be used to satisfy the secured creditor's claim. Secured creditors are in the enviable position of having a quick and relatively inexpensive mechanism for satisfying their claims in the event of default.

To assure that there is plenty of collateral to cover the collection of both principal and interest, most secured lenders will carefully assess the value of the collateral *prior* to extending credit or making a loan to the debtor, in order to assure a favorable "loan-to-value ratio." For example, a risk-averse real property secured lender will usually loan only 80 percent of the value of the collateral. If the land and improvements are worth $100,000, the lender will loan only $80,000 and require a first-lien position. If the debtor defaults, there will be enough collateral to satisfy the lender's claims for principal and accruing interest — and, most likely, to cover the costs of conducting the foreclosure.

In commercial lending transactions, the secured lender will also monitor the collateral during the life of the loan to make sure the collateral retains its value. For instance, a secured lender who makes a loan to a manufacturing company may be relying on a security interest in inventory collateral, which can fluctuate in value as inventory is sold off. Many secured lenders will have a default provision in the loan documents allowing them to demand repayment of the loan if the loan-to-equity ratio falls below a certain percentage (let's assume 80%). The lender will require monthly or quarterly reports to assure that the inventory remains at least 20% higher in value than the remaining outstanding balance, plus accrued interest.

Let's consider another example where a risk averse secured lender wants to assure a debt to equity ratio sufficient to cover any default in the payment of principal or interest. Suppose a bank is willing to loan $1 million to an automobile dealership, and insists on a security interest in all of the inventory (the automobiles held for sale), valued at $1.4 million at the time of the loan. The bank will have a loan to equity ratio of about 75%, assuring plenty of equity to cover any defaults. A prudent lender will require that if the value of the inventory falls below $1.2 million (the amount necessary to sustain an 80% loan to value ratio), then the dealer must either: (i) repay a portion of the loan or (ii) acquire additional inventory.

Sometimes, secured lenders are *inadequately* secured. If, at the time of foreclosure, the collateral is insufficient to cover the full amount of the debt (principal and interest),[20] the remaining deficiency owed by the borrower will be unsecured. In such cases, the lender will have a mere unsecured claim for the

---

[19] Creation and perfection of security interests in personal property are governed by Article 9 of the Uniform Commercial Code. Creation and perfection of security interests in real property are governed by state "mortgage" or "deed of trust" statutes.

[20] Most of the time, well drafted loan documents will create a security interest to secure the lender's principal, interest and costs of collection/foreclosure.

deficiency. For instance, if the amount of the lender's claim was $105,000 (principal and accrued interest) and the collateral was sold for $95,000, the unsecured deficiency claim would be $10,000.

6.   Managers (Corporate Boards, General Partners, Managing Members)

Because all business entities are fictional persons, some individuals must be vested with control of the business entity. Traditionally, in a corporate organization, control is vested in a board of directors elected by the shareholders.[21] In a general partnership, the general partners are vested with control. In a limited partnership, there will be one or more general partners vested with control and, in a limited liability company, the equity holders may elect either an all-member manager model or a central-manager model.[22]

Although it is common for some or all of the equity holders to participate in control and management, this is not always the case. In many publicly held corporations the boards of directors do not necessarily own shares of stock in the entity they are managing. In general partnerships and limited liability companies, only one partner or member (or a committee of partners or members) may be in charge of managing the affairs of the business entity despite the default rule that all partners or members are entitled to participate in control.[23]

Whether or not they have an equity stake in the entity, the manager(s) are burdened with the task of directing the affairs of the organization and operation of its business. In this capacity, they must act in good faith and are held to duties of loyalty and care that are distinct from, and must be exercised independently of, any equity interest they may hold in the entity.

7.   Operating Officers, Managers and Employees

These are the people who are responsible for the day-to-day management and operation of the entity. They will be paid wages and receive benefits in compensation for their efforts on behalf of the organization. They may range from mail room clerks to the chief executive officer and chief financial officer. As employees, their efforts are oriented towards the operation and success of the entity. Extensive federal, state and local laws will govern the nature of this employment relationship but the company and each employee are likely to memorialize the terms of employment in an employment agreement. In addition, many companies will adopt rules and regulations to govern the relationship between employer and employees.

---

[21] This may not always be the case. In California, for instance, in the case of a statutory close corporation, all of the rights to control may be allocated in a shareholder agreement, with the right to vote completely eliminated. See California Corporations Code §§ 158(a), 300(b).

[22] Section 407(a) of the Uniform Limited Liability Company Act ("ULLCA") provides that the business and affairs of the company shall be managed by all of its members, *unless* the articles of organization vest management in a single manager or group of managers.

[23] Section 401(f) of RUPA provides: "Each partner has equal rights in the management and conduct of the partnership business." Nevertheless, § 103 allows the partners to vary the control mechanism by agreement among the partners. In many general partnership law firms, for instance, control over many partnership matters is delegated to a managing partner or a managing committee.

In a closely-held business entity, it is common practice for some of the early promoters and investors to serve as employees of the company. In a properly run business, the fact that the managers and employees are also large equity holders impels them to work hard for the success of the business since, in addition to their compensation, the value of their equity interests improves with the success of the company.

As the company grows, many employees (especially non-management employees) will have only an employment relationship with the entity, without any equity interest. These employees are motivated by standard incentives such as salary, bonuses, skills training and resume-building. In many companies, some of the compensation package might include shares of stock or "stock options" in the business entity.[24] Stock options give employees the right to purchase shares of the employer-corporation at a fixed price, usually the market value at the time the options are issued. If the market value of the shares rises, then the employee can purchase the shares at the option price and resell the shares at market price, reaping a profit from the transaction. Of course, if the value of the shares declines, the employee will simply hold onto the options and wait for the value to rise again. This type of compensation is often attractive to potential employees since it gives them a stake in the success of the entity and has some beneficial income tax implications. It's also attractive to the company, since there is no need to pay cash in the year that the stock options are issued and the cost of this portion of the compensation package can be deferred to some future date when the options are exercised.

Regardless of whether or not employees have financial interests in the form of stock or equity, these constituents have a deeply rooted interest in the operation and success of the business venture. Their wages, bonuses and professional careers will be tied to the fortunes of the company.

C. THE ROLE OF ATTORNEYS IN BUSINESS TRANSACTIONS

Transactional attorneys earn their living and establish their reputations by providing legal services to constituents in business transactions. As *advisors*, lawyers provide clients with an accurate and informed understanding of each client's legal rights and obligations, and the practical implications of those rights and obligations. As *negotiators*, lawyers pursue each client's objectives as advocates seeking to maximize their client's position, while acting consistently with the requirements of honest and professional dealings with others. As *drafters*, lawyers seek to memorialize their client's rights, obligations and objectives into the transactional documents to preserve and protect the clients with regard to predictable future events.

The tasks of the transactional lawyer are to: (i) identify the objectives, interests and concerns of the client; (ii) gather relevant factual information necessary to

---

[24] The term "stock" is used here for purposes of simplicity and assumes that the business entity is a corporation. This type of compensation is common in business ventures operating as corporations because of the well-established practice of authorizing and issuing large numbers of shares of stock for this purpose. Theoretically, equity participation interests or options could be offered as compensation for other forms of business entities, such as limited liability companies, although this would require some creative drafting.

advise and guide the client; (iii) ascertain controlling statutory, regulatory and common law, including tax, non-tax and securities laws; (iv) analyze the client's rights, obligations and interests in light of the controlling laws; (v) advise the clients and guide them with regard to the client's decisions and plans; and (vi) implement the decisions and plans of the clients through negotiation, document preparation and regulatory compliance.

Considering the constituents we've discussed, two intriguing questions arise about the role of attorneys in the formation and operation of business entities: (i) which of the constituents needs legal advice and representation?; and, (ii) who does the attorney represent when forming a business entity?

1.   Legal Representation — Promoters

The *promoters* will need legal assistance with regard to virtually all aspects of forming and financing the business entity. They will also need lawyers to assist them in either complying with the requirements for registering the securities or obtaining an exemption from securities registration. The lawyers for the promoters will have to incorporate into the legal documents the business deal being proposed by the promoters and make sure that the objectives of the promoters are reflected in the formation documents. Some of the primary documents the lawyers will work on include:

1. Subscription Agreements: Contracts executed by investors that govern the amount and conditions of the investors' contributions.
2. Investment Certificates: Documents executed by each potential investor. Investor certificates are used to ascertain whether a sale to an investor is in compliance with the requirements for the entity's exemption from registration of its securities.
3. Formation Documents: Articles of incorporation and bylaws for corporations, articles of organization and operating agreements for limited liability companies, partnership agreements for general partnerships and certificates of limited partnership and limited partnership agreements for limited partnerships. These documents form the heart of the business entity and will govern the valuation of contributions, allocation of control, and allocation of financial interests.
4. Buyout Agreements: Contracts between equity holders regarding the option or obligation to buy the investment units of other equity holders upon the happening of certain triggering events.[25]
5. Third-party Documents: Leases, loan agreements, employment agreements, management agreements and real property contracts of sale.

---

[25] Buyout agreements are important in many closely held business entities. If three individuals are forming a new entity, they may be very concerned about who is an equity owner in this venture. If, following formation, one of the three equity holders voluntarily or involuntarily transfers his or her interest, the other two might want to the right to buy out the selling party's interest, rather than having a stranger join in the ownership and control of the entity. On the other hand, older equity holders might want the ability to force the other equity holders to buy out his or her interest if he or she retires. In the absence of such an obligation, the aging equity holder might have a hard time finding a buyer for his or her interest in the entity. The events that trigger an optional or mandatory buy out, the mechanisms for determining the price of the buy out, and the process for accomplishing the buy out, make these complex agreements. The equity holders entering into a buyout agreement will often have serious conflicts of interest at the time the agreement is negotiated. Buyout agreements are discussed in depth in Chapter 8.

6. Disclosure Documents: Written representations by the promoters disclosing all of the material risks and information that investors need to make an informed decision about investing in the business entity.

There are many other matters that the lawyers may assist the promoters with, such as obtaining regulatory approvals and securing intellectual property interests.

Keep in mind that each of the promoters may need separate legal representation. Despite their common interest in forming the entity, the promoters may have substantially conflicting interests. For instance, one promoter may be making a large capital contribution, while another promoter may be contributing expertise and services. Yet another promoter may be contributing personal or real property. Each promoter will have different objectives and concerns that conflict with the objectives and concerns of the other promoters.[26]

In most entity formations, the promoters will surely have conflicting interests when it comes to determining the allocation of the financial profits and losses from the business venture. In addition, the promoters may have different long-term investment plans[27] and different tax situations.[28] Finally, the promoters may have different perspectives on the allocation of control once the business entity is formed.

It would be difficult for a single attorney to fairly and fully represent the conflicting interests of the promoters. In many sophisticated transactions, each promoter will wisely choose his or her own legal counsel to represent the promoter in putting the deal together. However, in some cases, in order to reduce the amount of attorneys' fees, the promoters may want to use a single attorney or firm to represent all of the promoters in connection with the formation of the entity and related matters. This creates some serious potential for conflicts for the lawyer representing these multiple clients. The problem may be compounded if the promoters want to use the same lawyer to represent the business entity following its formation.

2.   Legal Representation — Equity Holders

Investors who will be equity holders in the venture will need lawyers to evaluate the formation documents and inform the investors about the stability of the entity and the rights and/or obligations of the investors. For example, assume a potential investor is contemplating signing a subscription agreement to purchase a $100,000 equity interest in a newly formed business entity. Many questions will arise regarding the protection of the investor's interest. Will the investor be obligated to contribute *additional* funds if there is a need for more capital? Will the investor

---

[26] A promoter contributing property may want a high valuation for the property, while the promoters contributing money will want a low valuation for the property. A promoter contributing cash may want a priority of distribution to assure that the cash is repaid before other promoters receive distributions from profits. Another promoter contributing services will want a favorable employment contract and a high valuation for those services. Many of these conflicts of interest are discussed later in these materials.

[27] Some promoters, particularly the cash contributors, may want to withdraw their capital investment as early as possible and put it to use in another investment. Other promoters, who are contributing primarily services and/or property, may have a much longer-term viewpoint.

[28] See Chapter 3 for a discussion of the tax implications impacting the promoters and equity holders.

have the right to freely sell the investment unit or will there be limitations on the conveyance of the investment unit? Will the investor have the right to participate in management and control of some or all aspects of the business entity? What are the tax consequences of investing in this entity?

Only a foolish and unsophisticated investor would fail to obtain a legal review of the documents prior to an investment of this size. After all, the formation, subscription and operating documents will have been carefully drafted by lawyers to protect the interests of the constituencies who hired them. Most often, the drafters will be the lawyers for the *promoters* — parties that may have fundamentally different interests in the transaction than the investors.

Sophisticated lawyers for the promoters will usually anticipate the needs and interests of potential investors and draft the documents to fairly accommodate those needs and interests. If the documents don't protect the interests of investors, it will be hard to market the investment units. Nevertheless, no investor should risk a large investment without having the documents reviewed by a skilled business lawyer to make sure that the investor's expectations about rights, obligations and objectives are properly reflected in the documents.

3. Legal Representation — The Business Entity

The business entity, once it's formed, will have its own legal needs. Lawyers will be involved in advising the business entity regarding matters such as: maintaining the entity as a valid legal person, operating the entity, complying with regulatory requirements, executing contracts, obtaining and protecting intellectual property, complying with employment and tax laws, and all of the other civil and criminal rights and obligations of the business entity. Since the business entity has a separate legal identity, it may have different lawyers than the lawyers who represented the promoters during the formation stage. Nevertheless, it is quite common for the same lawyers who assisted in the formation of the business entity to then be employed as the lawyers for the business entity. If the same lawyers are retained, difficult conflict issues may arise if the lawyers continue to represent the promoters or others involved in the business venture.[29]

4. Legal Representation — Other Constituents

The remaining constituents (unsecured creditors, secured lenders, managers, operating officers and employees) will also want to seek the advice of lawyers regarding the protection of their interests in the business venture. Their objectives and interests are clearly different from those of the promoters, equity holders and the business entity. Commercial lenders will always have attorneys advising them about their loan transactions and drafting the necessary documents, such as

---

[29] The ABA Model Rules of Professional Conduct (2009) provide:

Rule 1.13 Organization as Client:

(a) A lawyer employed or retained by an organization represents the organization acting through its duly authorized constituents.

* * *

(f) In dealing with an organization's directors, officers, employees, members, shareholders or other constituents, a lawyer shall explain the identity of the client when the lawyer knows or reasonably should know that the organization's interests are adverse to those of the constituents with whom the lawyer is dealing.

promissory notes, security agreements and mortgages. Executive officers and managers will almost certainly hire lawyers to negotiate their employment or management agreements. The rank-and-file employees may have union representatives who will hire lawyers to deal with employment contracts and other employment issues.

D. THE ETHICAL CONSTRAINTS ON TRANSACTIONAL LAWYERS

We can reach two broad conclusions about the role of the "business" lawyer in the formation and operation of business entities: (i) lawyers serve many different constituents in the formation and operation of business entities and (ii) many of the constituents in the formation and operation of a business enterprise have inherently conflicting positions. As lawyers, it is important to identify exactly who the client *is* and, on the other hand, who the client is not. As the next part of this chapter stresses, lawyers must exercise considerable care in making sure that they comply with professional restrictions on representing clients with conflicting interests.

Ethical obligations to clients are prescribed in the ABA Model Rules of Professional Conduct (the "ABA Model Rules") and similar state professional rules and statutes.[30] The ABA Model Rules are based on the fundamental concept that lawyers and clients have a relationship of mutual respect and trust, as well as openness and honestly about options and objectives.

E. THE PROBLEM OF MULTIPLE CLIENT REPRESENTATION

As a cost-cutting measure, promoters may want to have a single lawyer[31] to represent all of the promoters and, possibly, the business entity as well. Experienced lawyers understand that the cost-efficiency of using a single lawyer may create problems for the clients — and the lawyer. From the client's perspective, each of the promoters may have fundamentally different objectives, rights and obligations in connection with the proposed venture, making it difficult for a single lawyer to fully represent their individual interests. From the perspective of the lawyer, he or she will sometimes face a near-insurmountable task of exercising the critical duties of loyalty and independent judgment with respect to each of the clients while balancing the interests of all of them.

The ABA Model Rules recognize the practical necessity of balancing the economic need for multiple representation and concurrently representing clients

---

[30] The ABA adopted the original Canons of Professional Ethics in 1908. The Canons were replaced by the Model Code of Professional Responsibility in 1969 and widely adopted by many state and federal jurisdictions. In 1983, the Model Code was superceded by the ABA Model Rules of Professional Conduct. The 1983 Model Rules have been adopted, often with state-specific amendments, in 46 states (as well as the District of Columbia and the Virgin Islands). The four states that have not adopted the Model Rules are California, Maine, New York and Ohio.

[31] As used in this book, the term "lawyer" includes law firms with more than one lawyer. Under the ABA Model Rules, law firms are treated as a single "lawyer" for purposes resolving conflicts of interest in cases of multiple client representation. See Rule 1.10 *Imputation of Conflicts of Interest General Rule*, which states: "(a) While lawyers are associated in a firm, none of them shall knowingly represent a client when any one of them practicing alone would be prohibited from doing so . . . "

with different interests in the same transaction. At the heart of this balance are the requirements of adequate disclosure of information by the lawyer, and "informed consent" from each of the clients, before beginning multiple representation. Under the Rules, if clients *fully* understand the implications of multiple representation, then they can freely consent to having a single lawyer represent them. At a minimum, informed consent requires that the *lawyer*:

— Disclose to each of the clients, in writing, the potential conflicts of interest. This requires that the lawyer spend some time and effort determining the reasonably foreseeable conflicts that might arise between the clients. To do so, the lawyer will have to inquire into some of the basic objectives and circumstances of each of the clients.

— Explain to the clients that the duty of undivided loyalty that the attorney would exercise, if representing the client separately, might be compromised in order to balance and serve the needs of the co-represented clients.

— Inform the clients that the traditional privilege of lawyer-client confidentiality will be partially compromised. In a possible subsequent lawsuit between these parties, the lawyer-client privilege of confidentiality will not apply as to matters disclosed to the lawyer by one or more of the multiple clients in connection with the transaction.

— Disclose that, if an actual controversy develops among the clients, the attorney cannot continue to represent *any* of the clients unless there is a new informed consent executed by *all* of the clients, after full disclosure of the actual conflict that has arisen.[32]

— Recommend that it is in the best interests of each client to seek independent legal representation.

— Obtain a written informed consent from each of the clients after making the above written disclosures and explanations.

The existence of potential conflicts poses some serious risks for the lawyer agreeing to represent two or more clients concurrently. Clients have successfully sued for disgorgement of fees, malpractice, and disqualification or removal of the lawyer from representing any of the clients, and other remedies.[33] Even non-clients, such as a partner in a general partnership, or a shareholder in a corporation, can bring actions against a lawyer who concurrently represents the entity as well as some of the other equity holders.[34]

---

[32] This might result in each of the multiple clients having to hire new, independent counsel.

[33] In *In re Sedor*, 245 N.W.2d 895 (Wis. 1976), an attorney was suspended for eight months when he represented himself and two clients in a joint business matter. The court held that representing clients with interests adverse to each other was inappropriate where the joint representation: (i) could impair the attorney's independent professional judgment, or (ii) there was not full disclosure with informed written consent prior to agreeing to the multiple representation. In *Eriks v. Denver*, 824 P.2d 1207 (Wash. 1992), an attorney was required to disgorge all fees paid in connection with multiple representation of both investors and promoters in a tax shelter venture. The court held that the inherent conflicts violated the applicable Code of Professional Responsibility of Washington. *See also* Douglas R. Richmond, *Choosing Sides: Issue or Positional Conflicts of Interest*, 51 FLA. L. REV. 383 (1999).

[34] In *Griva v. Davison*, 637 A.2d 830 (D.C. Ct. App. 1994), it was held that a general partner may sue for access to the records of the partnership's lawyer, and for disgorgement of fees, when the lawyer represented the partnership and some of the general partners without informed written consent by the partnership. The plaintiff, Rose Griva was a minority partner in a general partnership with her brother and sister. A single lawyer, Dennis Davison, represented the partnership, as well as Ms. Griva's brother and sister but not Ms. Griva. Acting as a general partner, Ms. Griva sought copies of the lawyer's files pertaining to the partnership. When the lawyer refused, Ms. Griva sued, seeking access to the files,

To fully understand the problems of multiple representation, imagine that both the seller and buyer of a $20 million office building want to use the same lawyer as a way of reducing the costs of the sale and purchase. The positions of the seller and the buyer are fundamentally opposed on virtually every aspect of the transaction such as the price, financing, warranties, tax allocations, title, improvements and many more matters. Theoretically, the Model Rules allow for joint representation under these circumstances if there is disclosure by the lawyer of all of the possible conflicts of interest, followed by informed consent of both parties. The likelihood of strong conflicts arising during the course of the sale is so great that such concurrent representation is almost guaranteed to end in acrimony.[35]

1. Potential Conflicts of Interest Between Multiple Clients

What are some of the possible conflicts in the context of multiple clients who will be forming a business entity? We can broadly divide the conflicts into four areas: (i) financial matters, (ii) tax matters, (iii) control and management of the entity, and (iv) dispositions and buyouts of equity interests.

a. Financial Matters

Each client may have widely different objectives regarding the allocations and/or distributions of profits and losses, as well as valuation of non-cash property contributed to the entity, as well as compensation for services to the entity. Each client has a natural inclination to seek a larger share of the equity interests and profits in exchange for that client's capital contribution or post-formation services. Clients who are *cash* investors may also want to assure that they receive a priority of distribution as compared to participants who are contributing property or services. If represented separately, the attorneys for investors would vigorously pursue these interests on behalf of their investor-clients.

Some clients may be rendering *services* to the business entity in exchange for equity interests. Whether the distribution of equity is received upon organization or the entity, or at a later time,[36] the client contributing services will be motivated to seek a high equity-for-services ratio. Clients who will be regular employees of the entity will pursue favorable employment agreements in terms of total compensation, work conditions, competition agreements, vacation, retirement, dismissal and much more.

---

disqualification of the lawyer, and a refund of any legal fees paid by the partnership to the lawyer because the lawyer had failed to adequately disclose conflicts of interest in the joint representation and obtain informed written consent from the partnership. The D.C. Court of Appeals held that such an action viable under these circumstances. Similarly, in *In re Disciplinary Proceedings against Usow*, 349 N.W.2d 480 (Wis. 1984), an attorney was found guilty of unprofessional conduct and suspended from the practice of law when he continued to represent both a corporation and one of its stockholders despite the existence of a conflict of interest. Wisconsin Supreme Court held that the lawyer knowingly disregarded "an elemental rule of professional ethics that a lawyer may not represent two parties whose interests were conflicting" in the absence of disclosure and informed consent.

[35] In *In re Boivin*, 533 P.2d 171 (Or. 1975), the Oregon state bar brought disciplinary action against a lawyer who had represented both the buyer and the seller in the sale of a business. The Oregon supreme court affirmed the disciplinary action and held that it was improper for the lawyer to represent both the buyer and the seller in the absence of express consent, after full disclosure.

[36] Compensation packages for executives will often include compensation in the form of "stock options" or similar equity interests for non-corporate entities, discussed later in this book.

Clients who are receiving equity interests or other compensation for their services must pay state and federal income taxes and, consequently, will have compelling reasons for structuring the transactions to produce favorable tax consequences that may not be favorable for the other participants or the business entity. If represented separately, attorneys for clients like these would seek to maximize the compensation for services, as well as the other terms of any employment agreements. Of course, attorneys for the other equity participants and the business entity would want to carefully review and negotiate the terms of these agreements from the perspectives of their own clients.

Clients contributing *property* will want a high value attributed to the property, while other clients would be better served if the property was appraised at a lower value. For instance, suppose that three individuals agree to contribute $100,000 each in equity to form a new business entity. One of the individuals is going to contribute land together with an existing building on the land. If sold on the open market, the land and building would fetch $90,000. If represented separately, the landowner's lawyer would assert that the land should be valued at $100,000 for purposes of assuring that his client does not have to contribute any cash to the entity. On the other hand, independent lawyers for the other two investors would insist on a value of $90,000. The positions of the parties are fundamentally in conflict. The parties would also be in possible conflicting positions with regard to the allocation of the purchase price between the land and the improvements on the land.[37]

b. Tax Considerations

Depending on each client's financial situation, sources of income, estate plan and other tax considerations, there may be conflicting positions regarding the optimum tax strategy in choosing the type of entity to be formed and the allocation of profits and losses by the entity.[38] There also may be conflicting positions with respect to the nature and valuation of capital contributions by the investors. If represented separately, each client's lawyer would seek to maximize the tax consequences for his or her client, even if this had a negative effect on the impact of the other investors.

c. Control and Management

The key to success of any business entity is the management of financial and operational activities of the business. The managers will be making crucial decisions about hiring employees, manufacturing or acquisition of goods, provision of services, financing, investing, sales, acquisitions of property, mergers, divestments and many other essential matters. Differences and disputes may arise regarding the proper decisions for the success of the business and, over time, the participants may have different views of how the business should be run.

At the formation stage of a business, control and management of the entity are often hotly contested areas of negotiation among the initial investors. Some of those investors will be actively participating in management, while others will be

---

[37] See the discussion of tax implications of contributing property in Chapter 3, Section H.

[38] There are many tax considerations for investors in business entities that will be discussed in greater detail in Chapter 3.

only minimally participating or not participating at all.

Lawyers representing clients who are seeking to actively participate in management will energetically endeavor to structure the entity so that their individual clients have substantial rights to manage the business.

On the other hand, some investors may be partially active in management. They may not be interested in managing the day-to-day affairs of the business. Nevertheless they, may wish to retain a right to vote on important organic decisions, as well as the right to remove and/or replace managers.[39]

There may be passive investors who are interested only in a financial return on their investment with little or no participation in management.[40] These investors will want to make certain they do *not* have to participate in day-to-day management. Attorneys for passive investors will want to assure that the management structure places control of the business in the hands of trusted and talented managers and that the objectives and interests of their passive investor will be protected.

Many potential conflicts may exist with regard to management and control. Among the investors seeking active participation in management, each be seeking to maximize his or her rights to direct the affairs of the business. They may also be seeking compensation based on a share of profits, or salaries, or fees for services. The awarding of such compensation is not necessarily in the interests of partially active or passive investors, who are depending on their share of the profits, and/or an increase in the value of their equity interest, for a return on their investment.

d.   Disposition and Buyouts of Equity Interests

Participants in the formation of a business venture, particularly a closely held one, may be concerned about future changes in the proportions of equity ownership, sales of equity interests to outsiders or other changes in the ownership structure of the business.

Equity ownership often includes rights to manage and control the business. A change in the *proportion* of ownership among the equity holders, might have an impact on the voting rights of the parties with regard to management and control. For example, suppose there are four original equity holders of a business, Ann, Bob, Carol and Dave. Each has a 25% share of the business and management is dependent on the percentage of equity ownership. If Ann sells all or part of her 25% interest to Bob, Bob would then have larger equity interest and greater rights to manage and control the business.

In many closely held businesses, the identity, personality and skills of each of the equity holders may be essential to the success of the enterprise. If one of those

---

[39] This is a very common arrangement in corporations, limited partnerships and some limited liability companies. Even in general partnerships, the participants may agree that only some of the general partners (or a committee of general partners) handles the day-to-day affairs of the partnership, while the complete cadre of general partners retain control over major decisions and the appointment of managing partners or committees.

[40] Passive investors may not be interested in the day-to-day management of the business nor even in the occasional oversight of the business. They are purchasing an equity interest in the business enterprise in reliance on the manager's ability to return profits and/or enhance the value of their equity interests.

participants sells his or her interest to an outsider, the remaining equity holders may find the value of their interests sharply reduced, the viability of the business diminished and management impeded by the appearance of a new equity holder.

Because of these and other concerns, it is common for early investors to bargain for rights of first refusal as well as mandatory buy out provisions.[41] Investors will have inherently conflicting positions regarding the events that trigger the buy-out, the mandatory or optional nature of the buy-out, the procedures to be followed, the value to be paid and the method of payment. Buy-sell agreements may impact the liquidity of the equity interests and investors may have different concerns about the ability to freely transfer their interests.

e.   Conclusion — Potential Conflicts of Interest Between Multiple Clients

Under the ABA Model Rules (2009), to obtain the required *informed* written consent from clients for multiple representation, the attorney must spend significant time and effort to determine the potential conflicts and disclose them to the clients. As we have seen above, there are many potential conflicts that need to be explored with, and explained to, the clients at the start of legal representation. Moreover, the duty to obtain informed consent is a continuing obligation. If actual conflicts between the clients develop later in the representation, the attorney must, once again, obtain informed written consent before continuing to represent *any* of the clients in the matter.[42]

2.   Organizations as Clients

Following the formation of an entity, the organization will have legal needs regarding it's operations, contracts, rights and obligations, as well as regular legal help properly maintaining its formal legal identity and satisfying regulatory requirements. When an attorney represents an organization, the client is the entity and not the constituents who created, own, manage or are employed by the entity.[43] This sometimes creates confusion because the lawyer interacts with the organization through its duly authorized constituents but often does not represent the constituents themselves. Individual constituents may not realize that their communications to lawyers are not privileged and that the lawyer owes them no duty of loyalty.[44] Attorneys should be careful in their communications with both

---

[41] See Chapter 8 regarding Buy-Sell Agreements and some additional justifications for negotiating buy-sell agreements.

[42] A new informed consent would also have to be obtained if a new client joins the existing clients in connection with the business. In addition, any new client would be entitled to material information that was disclosed by the original clients in connection with the business formation and operation — a point that would need to be carefully disclosed in the informed consent document.

[43] See Model Rule 1.13 later in this chapter.

[44] Model Rule 1.13(b) imposes a duty on the lawyer to act in the best interests of the organization and not that of its constituents. See *Responsible Citizens v. Superior Court*, 16 Cal. App. 4th 1717 (1993), holding that an attorney representing a general partnership does not have an attorney-client relationship with an individual partner for purposes of applying conflict of interest rules. Whether such a relationship exists turns on the totality of the circumstances, including the type and size of the partnership and the existence of an agreement, express or implied, that the attorney also represents the partner. See also *Rice v. Strunk*, 670 N.E.2d 1280 (Ind. 1996), where the court held that the relationship between a lawyer and the managing partner of a general partnership did not give rise to an

the entity, it's owners and its managers to clearly identify who the client is. It is only fair that non-clients understand that the lawyer's loyalties, and the confidentiality privilege, serve only to protect the entity-client unless there is a dual client agreement. It is also in the best interests of the *lawyer* to be crystal clear about who is the intended beneficiary of legal services. A lawyer who represents only the entity but provides advice to individual owners or managers might be found to be in a lawyer-client relationship with that individual, unless it is clear that no attorney client relationship exists.[45]

It sometimes happens that lawyers are asked to represent individual constituents (such as promoters, investors or managers) as well as the business entity. Where such multiple representation exists, written informed consent is, of course, required from both the individual constituent and the entity.[46] All of the usual problems of ongoing multiple representation rise to the surface and, in the case of an actual conflict, the attorney will have to withdraw from representing any of the clients unless there are renewed informed consents from the clients.

EXERCISE 1-1: REPRESENTING MULTIPLE CLIENTS CONCURRENTLY

This exercise focuses on issues arising from concurrent multiple representation and the steps a lawyer must take before agreeing to such representation. Carefully read the factual scenario, and the excerpts from the ABA Model Rules of Professional Conduct, set forth below. Your tasks in this exercise are: (i) identify any ethical issues that may arise for the lawyer from the representation of the clients in the factual scenario; and, (ii) identify areas of potential conflicts between the clients; (iii) prepare a "Disclosure Statement and Informed Consent" letter for the clients. The letter should adequately disclose the issues and potential conflicts that may arise as a result of multiple representation of the clients.[47]

Factual Scenario

You are a lawyer with a local law firm that specializes in formation and operation of business entities. Yesterday, you met with three potential clients, Ann, Bev and Carl (the "Promoters"). The Promoters intend to form a business entity that will construct and operate a large restaurant in your city. They want to employ your firm to represent them with respect to the formation of the business entity and related matters, including the drafting of employment contracts, real estate leases and/or real estate purchase agreements, loan agreements and buy-sell agreements. They came to your law firm because you have represented Bev in prior business transactions.

---

attorney-client relationship with the managing partner, since that partner was merely the "duly authorized constituent" for purposes of New Hampshire's equivalent of Model Rule 1.13.

[45] See *Johnson v. Superior Court*, 38 Cal. App. 4th 463 (1995), where an attorney was found to represent limited partners.

[46] Where informed consent is required, it must be given by an appropriate authorized person acting on behalf of the entity *other* than the constituent who is to be jointly represented.

[47] The letter should be typed in a professional format and ready to submit to the clients. See the Sample Form of Informed Consent, *infra*, that can be used in this drafting assignment.

The Business Concept

Carl is the "idea man" and is proposing to open a large restaurant in your city called "Carl's Digital Fish House." Carl operates an existing restaurant by the same name in a major city about 400 miles away. The restaurant is highly computerized with computer monitors built into each table (flush with the surface). Patrons can view on the video monitors the process of preparing their food from live "fish cams" on the fishing boats through "cook cams" in the kitchen. The menu is a video game that is highly interactive, with PlayStation type graphics.

The food is copious and delicious. Carl has been in the fish-restaurant business for 37 years and has owned, in succession, six different restaurants. The existing Carl's Digital Fish House was opened two years ago has been wildly successful. The local restaurant will be modeled on the existing restaurant.

The venture will require approximately $4.6 million in capital investment. After formation, the plan is to borrow additional funds in the form of loans from local banks. The three Promoters will be contributing $1.6 million ($1.2 million in cash and $400,000 in services and personal property). The remainder of the capital, $3 million, will be raised by selling equity interests to investors. The three promoters have the following backgrounds and objectives:

Ann is a single woman who has accumulated a significant net worth in her career. She is retired and travels extensively. Ann owns a $2 million home and the remainder of her wealth is in the form of stable and low-risk investments. Ann is willing to contribute $400,000 to the project. She is a long-term friend of the proposed chef and manager, Carl. Ann sees this venture as an opportunity to help a friend while increasing the usual return that she gets on her investments. Ann will be a "passive" investor and will not be actively participating in the management of the business entity nor its operations. Her proposed $400,000 investment is approximately 10% of her net worth.[48] Ann wants to invest her money for a reasonable period but would like to be able to withdraw her original contribution as quickly as possible once the restaurant operations become profitable.

Bev is married with teenage children. She is a successful businesswoman and has accumulated a personal net worth in excess of $20 million, with many investments. She has been involved in numerous business ventures and has always taken an active and controlling role in the management and

---

[48] "Net worth" is a term used to identify the value of all of a person's assets, less that all of that person's liabilities. In the example in the following chart, note that even though Ann has assets worth almost $4 million, her net worth would be $2.5 million:

Assets	Value	Liabilities		Net
Home	$2,000,000	Mortgage debt	($1,200,000)	$800,000
Auto	$50,000	Auto loan	($40,000)	$10,000
Retirement Account	$1,000,000			$1,000,000
Stock Mutual Funds	$450,000	Margin loan	($160,000)	$290,000
Furnishings	$100,000			$100,000
Certificates of Deposit & Cash	$300,000			$300,000
Totals	$3,900,000		($1,400,000)	$2,500,000

operation of the business. Bev will be contributing $800,000 to the venture. Bev wants to be able to protect her capital investment to the fullest extent possible and assure a priority of distribution from profits of the restaurant operation.

Carl is 55 years old and a successful restaurant operator. Over the years, he has acquired a succession of ever-larger restaurants. Most of his assets are wrapped up in his existing restaurant, which he does not intend to sell. He has abundant monthly income from the restaurant but has little money for a new venture. Carl will be contributing his services, expertise, good will, recipes, designs and intellectual property.[49] Years ago, Carl purchased a local parcel of real estate that is a perfect location for the restaurant. At this stage, Carl is proposing to sell the real estate to the business entity or, in the alternative, lease it to the business entity.

Carl sees the new restaurant venture as a long-term investment that will provide him with additional income into his retirement years. He expects to have a long-term employment contract with the business entity, as well as a comfortable retirement plan. Depending on his health and age, he may want the right to sell his interest in the business. He is also concerned about assuring that his interest can be sold for a fair value in the event of his death or disability.

3.   Excerpts: ABA Model Rules of Professional Conduct (2009)

The Preamble to the ABA Model Rules of Professional Conduct states:

Preamble: A Lawyer's Responsibilities

* * *

[2] As a representative of clients, a lawyer performs various functions. As advisor, a lawyer provides a client with an informed understanding of the client's legal rights and obligations and explains their practical implications. As advocate, a lawyer zealously asserts the client's position under the rules of the adversary system. As negotiator, a lawyer seeks a result advantageous to the client but consistent with requirements of honest dealings with others. As an evaluator, a lawyer acts by examining a client's legal affairs and reporting about them to the client or to others.

Rule 1.0   Terminology

(a) "Belief" or "believes" denotes that the person involved actually supposed the fact in question to be true. A person's belief may be inferred from circumstances.

(b) "Confirmed in writing," when used in reference to the informed consent of a person, denotes informed consent that is given in writing by the person or a writing that a lawyer promptly transmits to the person confirming an oral informed

---

[49] Carl owns the rights to use valuable tradenames, trademarks and good will associated with his current restaurant. He also owns copyrights on computer software that assists him in operating the restaurant. Carl will retain ownership of these items of intellectual property but will license the property to the proposed venture at a nominal cost.

consent. See paragraph (e) for the definition of "informed consent." If it is not feasible to obtain or transmit the writing at the time the person gives informed consent, then the lawyer must obtain or transmit it within a reasonable time thereafter.

(c) "Firm" or "law firm" denotes a lawyer or lawyers in a law partnership, professional corporation, sole proprietorship or other association authorized to practice law; or lawyers employed in a legal services organization or the legal department of a corporation or other organization. * * *

(e) "Informed consent" denotes the agreement by a person to a proposed course of conduct after the lawyer has communicated adequate information and explanation about the material risks of and reasonably available alternatives to the proposed course of conduct.

(f) "Knowingly," "known," or "knows" denotes actual knowledge of the fact in question. A person's knowledge may be inferred from circumstances.

(h) "Reasonable" or "reasonably" when used in relation to conduct by a lawyer denotes the conduct of a reasonably prudent and competent lawyer.

(i) "Reasonable belief" or "reasonably believes" when used in reference to a lawyer denotes that the lawyer believes the matter in question and that the circumstances are such that the belief is reasonable.

(j) "Reasonably should know" when used in reference to a lawyer denotes that a lawyer of reasonable prudence and competence would ascertain the matter in question.

(k) "Screened" denotes the isolation of a lawyer from any participation in a matter through the timely imposition of procedures within a firm that are reasonably adequate under the circumstances to protect information that the isolated lawyer is obligated to protect under these Rules or other law.

(l) "Substantial" when used in reference to degree or extent denotes a material matter of clear and weighty importance. * * *

(n) "Writing" or "written" denotes a tangible or electronic record of a communication or representation, including handwriting, typewriting, printing, photostating, photography, audio or video-recording and e-mail. A "signed" writing includes an electronic sound, symbol or process attached to or logically associated with a writing and executed or adopted by a person with the intent to sign the writing.

Rule 1.6   Confidentiality of Information

(a) A lawyer shall not reveal information relating to the representation of a client unless the client gives informed consent . . .

Rule 1.7   Conflict of Interest: Current Clients

(a) Except as provided in paragraph (b), a lawyer shall not represent a client if the representation involves a concurrent conflict of interest. A concurrent conflict of interest exists if:

(1) the representation of one client will be directly adverse to another client; or

(2) there is a significant risk that the representation of one or more clients will be materially limited by the lawyer's responsibilities to another client, a former client or a third person or by a personal interest of the lawyer.

(b)   Notwithstanding the existence of a concurrent conflict of interest under paragraph (a), a lawyer may represent a client if:

(1)   the lawyer reasonably believes that the lawyer will be able to provide competent and diligent representation to each affected client;

(2)   the representation is not prohibited by law;

(3)   the representation does not involve the assertion of a claim by one client against another client represented by the lawyer in the same litigation or other proceeding before a tribunal; and

(4)   each affected client gives informed consent, confirmed in writing.

Comment

General Principles

[1] Loyalty and independent judgment are essential elements in the lawyer's relationship to a client. Concurrent conflicts of interest can arise from the lawyer's responsibilities to another client, a former client or a third person or from the lawyer's own interests. . . .

[2] Resolution of a conflict of interest problem under this Rule requires the lawyer to: 1) clearly identify the client or clients; 2) determine whether a conflict of interest exists; 3) decide whether the representation may be undertaken despite the existence of a conflict, i.e., whether the conflict is consentable; and 4) if so, consult with the clients affected under paragraph (a) and obtain their informed consent, confirmed in writing. The clients affected under paragraph (a) include both of the clients referred to in paragraph (a)(1) and the one or more clients whose representation might be materially limited under paragraph (a)(2).

[3] A conflict of interest may exist before representation is undertaken, in which event the representation must be declined, unless the lawyer obtains the informed consent of each client under the conditions of paragraph (b). . .

[4] If a conflict arises after representation has been undertaken, the lawyer ordinarily must withdraw from the representation, unless the lawyer has obtained the informed consent of the client under the conditions of paragraph (b) . . . Where more than one client is involved, whether the lawyer may continue to represent any of the clients is determined both by the lawyer's ability to comply with duties owed to the former client and by the lawyer's ability to represent adequately the remaining client or clients, given the lawyer's duties to the former client . . .

*   *   *

Identifying Conflicts of Interest: Directly Adverse

*   *   *

[7] Directly adverse conflicts can also arise in transactional matters. For example, if a lawyer is asked to represent the seller of a business in negotiations with a buyer represented by the lawyer, not in the same transaction but in another, unrelated matter, the lawyer could not undertake the representation without the informed consent of each client.

Identifying Conflicts of Interest: Material Limitation

[8] Even where there is no direct adverseness, a conflict of interest exists if there is a significant risk that a lawyer's ability to consider, recommend or carry out an appropriate course of action for the client will be materially limited as a result of the lawyer's other responsibilities or interests. For example, a lawyer asked to represent several individuals seeking to form a joint venture is likely to be materially limited in the lawyer's ability to recommend or advocate all possible positions that each might take because of the lawyer's duty of loyalty to the others. The conflict in effect forecloses alternatives that would otherwise be available to the client. The mere possibility of subsequent harm does not itself require disclosure and consent. The critical questions are the likelihood that a difference in interests will eventuate and, if it does, whether it will materially interfere with the lawyer's independent professional judgment in considering alternatives or foreclose courses of action that reasonably should be pursued on behalf of the client.

* * *

Prohibited Representations

[14] Ordinarily, clients may consent to representation notwithstanding a conflict. However, as indicated in paragraph (b), some conflicts are non-consentable, meaning that the lawyer involved cannot properly ask for such agreement or provide representation on the basis of the client's consent. When the lawyer is representing more than one client, the question of consentability must be resolved as to each client.

[15] Consentability is typically determined by considering whether the interests of the clients will be adequately protected if the clients are permitted to give their informed consent to representation burdened by a conflict of interest. Thus, under paragraph (b)(1), representation is prohibited if in the circumstances the lawyer cannot reasonably conclude that the lawyer will be able to provide competent and diligent representation . . .

Informed Consent

[18] Informed consent requires that each affected client be aware of the relevant circumstances and of the material and reasonably foreseeable ways that the conflict could have adverse effects on the interests of that client . . . The information required depends on the nature of the conflict and the nature of the risks involved. When representation of multiple clients in a single matter is undertaken, the information must include the implications of the common representation, including possible effects on loyalty, confidentiality and the attorney-client privilege and the advantages and risks involved . . .

[19] Under some circumstances it may be impossible to make the disclosure necessary to obtain consent. For example, when the lawyer represents different clients in related matters and one of the clients refuses to consent to the disclosure necessary to permit the other client to make an informed decision, the lawyer cannot properly ask the latter to consent. In some cases the alternative to common representation can be that each party may have to obtain separate representation with the possibility of

incurring additional costs. These costs, along with the benefits of securing separate representation, are factors that may be considered by the affected client in determining whether common representation is in the client's interests.

Consent Confirmed in Writing

[20] Paragraph (b) requires the lawyer to obtain the informed consent of the client, confirmed in writing. Such a writing may consist of a document executed by the client or one that the lawyer promptly records and transmits to the client following an oral consent . . . See also Rule 1.0(n) (writing includes electronic transmission). If it is not feasible to obtain or transmit the writing at the time the client gives informed consent, then the lawyer must obtain or transmit it within a reasonable time thereafter. . . . The requirement of a writing does not supplant the need in most cases for the lawyer to talk with the client, to explain the risks and advantages, if any, of representation burdened with a conflict of interest, as well as reasonably available alternatives, and to afford the client a reasonable opportunity to consider the risks and alternatives and to raise questions and concerns. Rather, the writing is required in order to impress upon clients the seriousness of the decision the client is being asked to make and to avoid disputes or ambiguities that might later occur in the absence of a writing.

Revoking Consent

[21] A client who has given consent to a conflict may revoke the consent and, like any other client, may terminate the lawyer's representation at any time. Whether revoking consent to the client's own representation precludes the lawyer from continuing to represent other clients depends on the circumstances, including the nature of the conflict, whether the client revoked consent because of a material change in circumstances, the reasonable expectations of the other client and whether material detriment to the other clients or the lawyer would result.

Consent to Future Conflict

[22] Whether a lawyer may properly request a client to waive conflicts that might arise in the future is subject to the test of paragraph (b). The effectiveness of such waivers is generally determined by the extent to which the client reasonably understands the material risks that the waiver entails. The more comprehensive the explanation of the types of future representations that might arise and the actual and reasonably foreseeable adverse consequences of those representations, the greater the likelihood that the client will have the requisite understanding. Thus, if the client agrees to consent to a particular type of conflict with which the client is already familiar, then the consent ordinarily will be effective with regard to that type of conflict. If the consent is general and open-ended, then the consent ordinarily will be ineffective, because it is not reasonably likely that the client will have understood the material risks involved. On the other hand, if the client is an experienced user of the legal services involved and is reasonably informed regarding the risk that a conflict may arise, such consent is more likely to be effective, particularly if, e.g., the client is independently represented by other counsel in giving consent and the

consent is limited to future conflicts unrelated to the subject of the representation. In any case, advance consent cannot be effective if the circumstances that materialize in the future are such as would make the conflict nonconsentable under paragraph (b).

*   *   *

Nonlitigation Conflicts

*   *   *

[28] Whether a conflict is consentable depends on the circumstances. For example, a lawyer may not represent multiple parties to a negotiation whose interests are fundamentally antagonistic to each other, but common representation is permissible where the clients are generally aligned in interest even though there is some difference in interest among them. Thus, a lawyer may seek to establish or adjust a relationship between clients on an amicable and mutually advantageous basis; for example, in helping to organize a business in which two or more clients are entrepreneurs, working out the financial reorganization of an enterprise in which two or more clients have an interest or arranging a property distribution in settlement of an estate. The lawyer seeks to resolve potentially adverse interests by developing the parties' mutual interests. Otherwise, each party might have to obtain separate representation, with the possibility of incurring additional cost, complication or even litigation. Given these and other relevant factors, the clients may prefer that the lawyer act for all of them.

Special Considerations in Common Representation

[29] In considering whether to represent multiple clients in the same matter, a lawyer should be mindful that if the common representation fails because the potentially adverse interests cannot be reconciled, the result can be additional cost, embarrassment and recrimination. Ordinarily, the lawyer will be forced to withdraw from representing all of the clients if the common representation fails. In some situations, the risk of failure is so great that multiple representation is plainly impossible. For example, a lawyer cannot undertake common representation of clients where contentious litigation or negotiations between them are imminent or contemplated. Moreover, because the lawyer is required to be impartial between commonly represented clients, representation of multiple clients is improper when it is unlikely that impartiality can be maintained. Generally, if the relationship between the parties has already assumed antagonism, the possibility that the clients' interests can be adequately served by common representation is not very good. Other relevant factors are whether the lawyer subsequently will represent both parties on a continuing basis and whether the situation involves creating or terminating a relationship between the parties.

[30] A particularly important factor in determining the appropriateness of common representation is the effect on client-lawyer confidentiality and the attorney-client privilege. With regard to the attorney-client privilege, the prevailing rule is that, as between commonly represented clients, the privilege does not attach. Hence, it must be assumed that if litigation

eventuates between the clients, the privilege will not protect any such communications, and the clients should be so advised.

[31] As to the duty of confidentiality, continued common representation will almost certainly be inadequate if one client asks the lawyer not to disclose to the other client information relevant to the common representation. This is so because the lawyer has an equal duty of loyalty to each client, and each client has the right to be informed of anything bearing on the representation that might affect that client's interests and the right to expect that the lawyer will use that information to that client's benefit. . . The lawyer should, at the outset of the common representation and as part of the process of obtaining each client's informed consent, advise each client that information will be shared and that the lawyer will have to withdraw if one client decides that some matter material to the representation should be kept from the other. In limited circumstances, it may be appropriate for the lawyer to proceed with the representation when the clients have agreed, after being properly informed, that the lawyer will keep certain information confidential. For example, the lawyer may reasonably conclude that failure to disclose one client's trade secrets to another client will not adversely affect representation involving a joint venture between the clients and agree to keep that information confidential with the informed consent of both clients.

[32] When seeking to establish or adjust a relationship between clients, the lawyer should make clear that the lawyer's role is not that of partisanship normally expected in other circumstances and, thus, that the clients may be required to assume greater responsibility for decisions than when each client is separately represented. Any limitations on the scope of the representation made necessary as a result of the common representation should be fully explained to the clients at the outset of the representation . . .

[33] Subject to the above limitations, each client in the common representation has the right to loyal and diligent representation and the protection of Rule 1.9 concerning the obligations to a former client. The client also has the right to discharge the lawyer as stated in Rule 1.16.

Rule 1.8   Conflict of Interest: Current Clients: Specific Rules
* * *

(b)   A lawyer shall not use information relating to representation of a client to the disadvantage of the client unless the client gives informed consent, except as permitted or required by these Rules.

. . .

(g)   A lawyer who represents two or more clients shall not participate in making an aggregate settlement of the claims of or against the clients, . . . unless each client gives informed consent, in a writing signed by the client. The lawyer's disclosure shall include the existence and nature of all the claims . . . involved and of the participation of each person in the settlement.

. . .

(k)   While lawyers are associated in a firm, a prohibition in the foregoing paragraphs (a) through (i) that applies to any one of them shall apply to all of them.

Rule 1.9   Duties to Former Clients

(a)   A lawyer who has formerly represented a client in a matter shall not thereafter represent another person in the same or a substantially related matter in which that person's interests are materially adverse to the interests of the former client unless the former client gives informed consent, confirmed in writing.

(b)   A lawyer shall not knowingly represent a person in the same or a substantially related matter in which a firm with which the lawyer formerly was associated had previously represented a client

(1)   whose interests are materially adverse to that person; and

(2)   about whom the lawyer had acquired information protected by Rules 1.6 and 1.9(c) that is material to the matter;

unless the former client gives informed consent, confirmed in writing.

(c)   A lawyer who has formerly represented a client in a matter or whose present or former firm has formerly represented a client in a matter shall not thereafter:

(1)   use information relating to the representation to the disadvantage of the former client except as these Rules would permit or require with respect to a client, or when the information has become generally known; or

(2)   reveal information relating to the representation except as these Rules would permit or require with respect to a client.

Rule 1.10   Imputation of Conflicts of Interest General Rule

(a)   While lawyers are associated in a firm, none of them shall knowingly represent a client when any one of them practicing alone would be prohibited from doing so by Rules 1.7 or 1.9, unless the prohibition is based on a personal interest of the prohibited lawyer and does not present a significant risk of materially limiting the representation of the client by the remaining lawyers in the firm.

* * *

(c)   A disqualification prescribed by this rule may be waived by the affected client under the conditions stated in Rule 1.7.

* * *

Rule 1.13   Organization as Client

(a)   A lawyer employed or retained by an organization represents the organization acting through its duly authorized constituents.

(b)   If a lawyer for an organization knows that an officer, employee or other person associated with the organization is engaged in action, intends to act or refuses to act in a matter related to the representation that is a violation of a legal obligation to the organization, or a violation of law that reasonably might be imputed to the organization, and that is likely to result in substantial injury to the organization, then the lawyer shall proceed as is reasonably necessary in the best interest of the organization. Unless the lawyer reasonably believes that it is not necessary in the best interest of the organization to do so, the lawyer shall refer the matter to higher authority in the organization, including, if warranted by the circumstances to the highest authority that can act on behalf of the organization as determined by applicable law.

(c)   Except as provided in paragraph (d), if

(1)   despite the lawyer's efforts in accordance with paragraph (b) the highest authority that can act on behalf of the organization insists upon or fails to address in a timely and appropriate manner an action, or a refusal to act, that is clearly a violation of law, and

(2)   the lawyer reasonably believes that the violation is reasonably certain to result in substantial injury to the organization,

then the lawyer may reveal information relating to the representation whether or not Rule 1.6 permits such disclosure, but only if and to the extent the lawyer reasonably believes necessary to prevent substantial injury to the organization.

(d)   Paragraph (c) shall not apply with respect to information relating to a lawyer's representation of an organization to investigate an alleged violation of law, or to defend the organization or an officer, employee or other constituent associated with the organization against a claim arising out of an alleged violation of law.

(e)   A lawyer who reasonably believes that he or she has been discharged because of the lawyer's actions taken pursuant to paragraphs (b) or (c), or who withdraws under circumstances that require or permit the lawyer to take action under either of those paragraphs, shall proceed as the lawyer reasonably believes necessary to assure that the organization's highest authority is informed of the lawyer's discharge or withdrawal.

(f)   In dealing with an organization's directors, officers, employees, members, shareholders or other constituents, a lawyer shall explain the identity of the client when the lawyer knows or reasonably should know that the organization's interests are adverse to those of the constituents with whom the lawyer is dealing.

(g)   A lawyer representing an organization may also represent any of its directors, officers, employees, members, shareholders or other constituents, subject to the provisions of Rule 1.7. If the organization's consent to the dual representation is required by Rule 1.7, the consent shall be given by an appropriate official of the organization other than the individual who is to be represented, or by the shareholders.

Rule 1.16   Declining or Terminating Representation

(a)   Except as stated in paragraph (c), a lawyer shall not represent a client or, where representation has commenced, shall withdraw from the representation of a client if:

(1)   the representation will result in violation of the rules of professional conduct or other law;

* * *

(d)   Upon termination of representation, a lawyer shall take steps to the extent reasonably practicable to protect a client's interests, such as giving reasonable notice to the client, allowing time for employment of other counsel, surrendering papers and property to which the client is entitled and refunding any advance payment of fee or expense that has not been earned or incurred. The lawyer may retain papers relating to the client to the extent permitted by other law.

Rule 1.18   Duties to Prospective Client

(a)   A person who discusses with a lawyer the possibility of forming a client-lawyer relationship with respect to a matter is a prospective client.

(b)   Even when no client-lawyer relationship ensues, a lawyer who has had discussions with a prospective client shall not use or reveal information learned in the consultation, except as Rule 1.9 would permit with respect to information of a former client.

(c)   A lawyer subject to paragraph (b) shall not represent a client with interests materially adverse to those of a prospective client in the same or a substantially related matter if the lawyer received information from the prospective client that could be significantly harmful to that person in the matter, except as provided in paragraph (d). If a lawyer is disqualified from representation under this paragraph, no lawyer in a firm with which that lawyer is associated may knowingly undertake or continue representation in such a matter, except as provided in paragraph (d).

(d)   When the lawyer has received disqualifying information as defined in paragraph (c), representation is permissible if:

(1)   both the affected client and the prospective client have given informed consent, confirmed in writing, or:

(2)   the lawyer who received the information took reasonable measures to avoid exposure to more disqualifying information than was reasonably necessary to determine whether to represent the prospective client; and

(i)   the disqualified lawyer is timely screened from any participation in the matter and is apportioned no part of the fee therefrom; and

(ii)   written notice is promptly given to the prospective client.

Rule 2.1   Advisor

(2)   In representing a client, a lawyer shall exercise independent professional judgment and render candid advice. In rendering advice, a lawyer may refer not only to law but to other considerations such as moral, economic, social and political factors, that may be relevant to the client's situation.

4.   Sample Informed Consent to Multiple Representation

Andrews & Bender
Attorneys at Law
225 Cedar St.
Springfield, XX

When two or more potential clients seek to have the firm of Andrews and Bender (hereinafter, the "Firm") represent the clients jointly in a business matter, the Firm is required by professional rules of conduct to obtain "informed consent" from each client, in writing, after disclosing adequate information for the clients to make an informed decision regarding joint representation.

This document will provide you with the information you need to make an informed judgment about the Firm representing you jointly. Please read this document carefully and, if you consent to joint representation, sign and return a copy of this document.

Issues Arising From Joint Representation

General Issues

When a lawyer represents a single client, the lawyer is a partisan advocate for that client, exercising loyalty and independent judgment solely for that client. In many business transaction each person will have his or her own attorney, who can vigorously pursue the objectives of that person.

Nevertheless, the cost of separate legal representation can be high and cause complications and delays. Given these and other relevant factors, when multiple clients are generally aligned in interest, they may prefer that a single lawyer act for all of them in pursuing a common business venture or transaction, even though there are some differences in their objectives and interests in the proposed venture.

Instead of vigorously asserting any individual client's interests or objectives, the Firm will attempt to balance the objectives and interests of all of the clients, possibly leading to results less favorable (from an individual perspective) than might be obtained if each client was represented separately.

It is also possible that the common representation may fail in the future because adverse interests cannot be reconciled, or a dispute might develop between the clients. In either case, the Firm would have to withdraw from representing any client unless all of the clients newly agreed to an informed written consent, which is unlikely. Ordinarily in such situations, the Firm will be forced to withdraw from representing all of the clients. In such an event, there could be additional expenses and inconvenience.

Confidentiality

Normally, when the Firm represents only one client, communications made in confidence by the client to the Firm are protected by the attorney-client privilege. The Firm will not reveal the communications to anyone except employees, affiliates or consultants for the Firm who are working on the client's behalf. Similarly, in most circumstances, the Firm cannot be compelled to reveal the confidential information in subsequent litigation against the client.

However, when the Firm represents clients jointly, confidential communications made by one client to the Firm in the course of common representation are not confidential as *between* the clients. The Firm may disclose these matters to the other clients because the Firm has an equal duty of loyalty to each client, and each client has the right to be informed of anything bearing on the representation that might affect that client's interests and the right to expect that the lawyer will use that information to that client's benefit. If one client decides that some information material to the representation should be kept from the others, the Firm will have to withdraw from the representation unless the clients, after being properly informed, consent to the Firm keeping that information confidential.

Also, in the event of subsequent litigation between jointly represented clients, the Firm can be compelled by one client to disclose information that was delivered in confidence by another client in connection with the common transaction.

Potential Conflicts of Interest[50]

1.   Each client may have different objectives regarding the allocations of profits, losses and liquidating distributions. Cash investors will have

---

[50] This segment of the document should set forth the potential conflicts that arise from the particular

different economic concerns with regard to allocations and distributions than investors who contribute property or services.

2. If a client is contributing property or services in exchange for an ownership interest, the clients may have significantly different interests in determining the amount of the valuation of the property and/or services and the terms of the transfer of ownership interests to the contributing client.

3. Each client's tax situation may be different from other clients, which may influence the client's choices regarding the transaction.

4. It may be advantageous for one client's to bargain for a mandatory buy out provision, while it may be an advantage to another client to bargain for an optional buy out. In negotiating a buy-sell agreement, clients may have substantially different interests regarding the valuation of interests, the method of paying for interests, and the procedures to be followed. Clients may also have different objectives with respect to the liquidity of their investments.

5. Potential conflicts may exist between clients who will be active managers and other clients who will be passive investors. Clients actively managing the business may seek to receive compensation based on a share of profits, as well as salaries or fees for specific services, while passive investors depend solely on their share of the profits for a return on their investment.

Prior Representation of a client

The Firm previously represented one of the clients, _____, in connection with a prior matter. The Firm may have obtained information regarding that client that is confidential and cannot be disclosed to the other clients.

Recommendation: Separate Legal Representation

It is the Firm's professional obligation to recommend that each client consult independently with other counsel to review his or her personal objectives and whether it is in each client's individual interests to consent to having the Firm represent them jointly.

Consent to Multiple Representation

By signing this document, each client acknowledges that:

1. He or she has been informed of the potential conflicts associated with multiple representation in this matter.

2. He or she has been advised to consult with, and had the opportunity to consult with, independent legal counsel regarding this Informed Consent to Multiple Representation; and,

3. He or she consents to multiple representation by the Firm in this matter.

Executed this _____ day of _____, 20_____.

_____
[Client Name]

---

objectives and circumstances of the clients who are seeking multiple representation. Some general areas of potential conflict are listed here but will need to be narrowed to reflect the potential conflicts that arise in any particular case of multiple representation.

[Client Name]
_____

[Client Name]
_____

F. THE ATTORNEY CLIENT AGREEMENT

1. The Importance of a Written Attorney Client Agreement

Many states _require_ that the attorney enter into a written agreement with his or her client(s) and, even if not required by statute or state bar rules, a written agreement is always a good idea. What purposes can the attorney client agreement serve?

a. Charges for Legal Services, Fees and Costs

The agreements clearly set forth the contractual obligation of the clients to pay for legal services, fees incurred on the client's behalf and the costs associated with performing services for the clients. Clients may not always be fully aware of the nature of the charges for legal services, fees and costs. By including these matters fully and clearly in the agreement, the attorney can avoid future frustrations and disputes when the client is presented with a bill. If fees for services are charged on an hourly basis, the agreement should lay out the hourly fees of the attorneys and paralegals working on the case. If there is a different rate for partners and associates, that should be indicated as well. It's also important to lay out the fact that charges will accrue whenever the attorney or paralegal is working on the case, including conferences, consultations with accountants or other experts, or telephone calls with the client. If the firm bills in 10-minute intervals,[51] this should be explained in the agreement.

Fees for services in transactional matters may also be set on a "fixed fee" basis. For instance, the attorney may be charging $2,500 to assist the clients in forming a corporation. If the fee is fixed, would you want to make sure that the exact _scope_ of the services to be provided are clearly stated in the agreement? Can you see the danger in setting a "fixed fee"? What if you expected to draft only three documents (the Articles of Incorporation, the Bylaws, and Minutes of the Organizational Meeting of the Board of Directors) and the clients expected that you would also be preparing a complicated buyout agreement, governing their rights and obligations to buy out their co-shareholder's interests if certain events (such as death) occur?[52]

In the formation of business entities, there are often filing or other fees that must be paid on behalf of the entity. For instance, the successful filing of the Articles of Organization for a limited liability company might require a $100 filing fee paid to the Secretary of State and an additional tax pre-payment of $800 paid to the state taxing authority. The attorney client agreement should make clear that

---

[51] The client is billed for each 10-minute interval or part thereof. For instance, if an attorney works for 11 minutes, the client will be charged with two intervals. To be fair, some law firms bill in smaller intervals.

[52] Buyout agreements are a complicated matter and the subject of extensive discussion in Chapter 8.

these additional fees are the client's responsibility, even if the firm advances the fees on behalf of the clients.

The attorney may expect that certain costs incurred on behalf of the client are not part of the fee for services but will be separately charged to the clients. For instance, in the formation of a business entity, there may be significant printing costs incurred to duplicate the subscription agreements, investor questionnaires, disclosure and other documents.[53] Or, if the firm charges for long-distance telephone calls, in-house duplication, travel or other costs, these should be set forth in the agreement.

b.   Billing

How often will the client be billed and how quickly does the attorney expect those bills to be paid? A well drafted attorney-client agreement will include these expectations and will also inform multiple clients that each is liable for the full amount billed, unless the attorney is expecting only certain clients will be liable for paying the bill.

c.   Client's Obligations

The obligations of the *clients* should be set forth as well. Keep in mind that the agreement is a contract and the attorney will want to be able to terminate the relationship with the client in the event that the client is in material breach of the agreement. Unless the client's obligations are expressed in the agreement, the attorney may have a hard time exiting the attorney client relationship.[54] What are the client's obligations? Some standard client obligations are: pay bills in a timely manner; be honest, truthful and cooperative with the attorney; and respond within a reasonable time to requests for information.

d.   Scope of Work Undertaken

As mentioned above, the scope of work undertaken by the attorney can be extremely important when a fixed fee is charged for services. Is it equally important when the lawyer is charging an hourly fee? In a transactional setting, the answer is probably yes. Suppose the client has related tax issues that require resolution in litigation before the U.S. Tax Court? What if the client's business is based on technology and the client is sued for patent infringement? Perhaps some of the clients have complex estate planning needs in connection with the formation of the business entity? While these additional matters might be welcomed by a large law firm with the expertise to handle them, a smaller "boutique" law firm dealing with business entity formation may lack the competence or desire to provide these types of legal services. If the firm is contemplating that the scope of services is limited to matters related directly to the formation and operation of the business entity, it is best to be crystal clear about those expectations in the attorney client agreement.

---

[53] These costs can run into thousands of dollars as the size of the documentation grows and the number of investors increases. A professionally composed prospectus will often be scores or hundreds of pages in bound form and will be sent to many potential investors.

[54] *See* ABA Model Rule 1.16; California Rules of Professional Conduct Rule 3-700 (2005).

e.   Conflicts of Interest and Informed Consent

As discussed in detail earlier in this chapter, it is essential that "informed consent" be obtained when representing multiple clients. The adequate disclosure and informed consent can be included in the attorney client agreement or as a separate document bundled with the attorney client agreement.

f.   Summary — The Attorney Client Agreement

The relationship between attorneys and clients can be productive and mutually satisfying, particularly in business entity formation. The lawyer provides the client with the legal advice and guidance to get the business formed and fulfill the objectives of the clients. However, a good relationship is based on a mutual set of expectations regarding the nature of the attorney's services, the charges related to those services, the scope of the attorney's work, the obligations of the clients and other matters discussed above. In the case of new clients or the renewal of a relationship with former clients, it is *always* best to put those expectations in writing. The submission of the attorney client agreement to the clients creates an opportunity to double-check that the parties expectations are in synch. If those expectations are not in synch, the written documenet will help to flush out any areas of the relationship that need to be discussed, negotiated and resolved *prior* to the commencement of the relationship. As you will see below, once entered into, the relationship is not easily terminated, even though the lawyer is losing money or the client is causing frustration and stress for the attorney.

The ABA Model Rules of Professional Conduct do not expressly *require* a written attorney client agreement, although the Rules recommend that the agreement between lawyer and clients be in writing. Many states require, by statute or professional rule, that the agreement be in writing in many circumstances. Below are some excerpts from the Model Rules, as well as California statutes, that will help to understand the importance and preferred contents of an attorney client agreement.

ABA Model Rules of Professional Conduct (2009)

Rule 1.2   Scope Of Representation And Allocation Of Authority Between Client And Lawyer

(a)   Subject to paragraphs (c) and (d), a lawyer shall abide by a client's decisions concerning the objectives of representation and, as required by Rule 1.4, shall consult with the client as to the means by which they are to be pursued. A lawyer may take such action on behalf of the client as is impliedly authorized to carry out the representation . . .

(2)   * * *

(c)   A lawyer may limit the scope of the representation if the limitation is reasonable under the circumstances and the client gives informed consent.

(d)   A lawyer shall not counsel a client to engage, or assist a client, in conduct that the lawyer knows is criminal or fraudulent, but a lawyer may discuss the legal consequences of any proposed course of conduct with a client and may counsel or assist a client to make a good faith effort to determine the validity, scope, meaning or application of the law.

Rule 1.3 Diligence

A lawyer shall act with reasonable diligence and promptness in representing a client.

Rule 1.4 Communication

(a) A lawyer shall:

(1) promptly inform the client of any decision or circumstance with respect to which the client's informed consent, as defined in Rule 1.0(e), is required by these Rules;

(2) reasonably consult with the client about the means by which the client's objectives are to be accomplished;

(3) keep the client reasonably informed about the status of the matter;

(4) promptly comply with reasonable requests for information; and

(5) consult with the client about any relevant limitation on the lawyer's conduct when the lawyer knows that the client expects assistance not permitted by the Rules of Professional Conduct or other law.

Rule 1.5 Fees

(a) A lawyer shall not make an agreement for, charge, or collect an unreasonable fee or an unreasonable amount for expenses. The factors to be considered in determining the reasonableness of a fee include the following:

(1) the time and labor required, the novelty and difficulty of the questions involved, and the skill requisite to perform the legal service properly;

(2) the likelihood, if apparent to the client, that the acceptance of the particular employment will preclude other employment by the lawyer;

(3) the fee customarily charged in the locality for similar legal services;

(4) the amount involved and the results obtained;

(5) the time limitations imposed by the client or by the circumstances;

(6) the nature and length of the professional relationship with the client;

(7) the experience, reputation, and ability of the lawyer or lawyers performing the services; and

(8) whether the fee is fixed or contingent.

(b) The scope of the representation and the basis or rate of the fee and expenses for which the client will be responsible shall be communicated to the client, preferably in writing, before or within a reasonable time after commencing the representation, except when the lawyer will charge a regularly represented client on the same basis or rate. Any changes in the basis or rate of the fee or expenses shall also be communicated to the client.

* * *

(e)   A division of a fee between lawyers who are not in the same firm may be made only if:

(1)   the division is in proportion to the services performed by each lawyer or each lawyer assumes joint responsibility for the representation;

(2)   the client agrees to the arrangement, including the share each lawyer will receive, and the agreement is confirmed in writing; and

(3)   the total fee is reasonable.

Rule 1.16   Declining Or Terminating Representation

(a)   Except as stated in paragraph (c), a lawyer shall not represent a client or, where representation has commenced, shall withdraw from the representation of a client if:

(1)   the representation will result in violation of the rules of professional conduct or other law;

(2)   the lawyer's physical or mental condition materially impairs the lawyer's ability to represent the client; or

(3)   the lawyer is discharged.

(b)   Except as stated in paragraph (c), a lawyer may withdraw from representing a client if:

(1)   withdrawal can be accomplished without material adverse effect on the interests of the client;

(2)   the client persists in a course of action involving the lawyer's services that the lawyer reasonably believes is criminal or fraudulent;

(3)   the client has used the lawyer's services to perpetrate a crime or fraud;

(4)   the client insists upon taking action that the lawyer considers repugnant or with which the lawyer has a fundamental disagreement;

(5)   the client fails substantially to fulfill an obligation to the lawyer regarding the lawyer's services and has been given reasonable warning that the lawyer will withdraw unless the obligation is fulfilled;

(6)   the representation will result in an unreasonable financial burden on the lawyer or has been rendered unreasonably difficult by the client; or

(7)   other good cause for withdrawal exists.

* * *

(d)   Upon termination of representation, a lawyer shall take steps to the extent reasonably practicable to protect a client's interests, such as giving reasonable notice to the client, allowing time for employment of other counsel, surrendering papers and property to which the client is entitled and refunding any advance payment of fee or expense that has not been earned or incurred. The lawyer may retain papers relating to the client to the extent permitted by other law.

California Business and Professions Code
Division 3. Professions and Vocations Generally

Chapter 4   Attorneys

Article 8.5   Fee Agreements

§ 6148.   Contracts for services in cases not coming within § 6147;[55] bills rendered by attorney; contents; failure to comply

(a)   In any case not coming within Section 6147 in which it is reasonably foreseeable that total expense to a client, including attorney fees, will exceed one thousand dollars ($1,000), the contract for services in the case shall be in writing. At the time the contract is entered into, the attorney shall provide a duplicate copy of the contract signed by both the attorney and the client, or the client's guardian or representative, to the client or to the client's guardian or representative. The written contract shall contain all of the following:

(1)   Any basis of compensation including, but not limited to, hourly rates, statutory fees or flat fees, and other standard rates, fees, and charges applicable to the case.

(2)   The general nature of the legal services to be provided to the client.

(3)   The respective responsibilities of the attorney and the client as to the performance of the contract.

(b)   All bills rendered by an attorney to a client shall clearly state the basis thereof. Bills for the fee portion of the bill shall include the amount, rate, basis for calculation, or other method of determination of the attorney's fees and costs. Bills for the cost and expense portion of the bill shall clearly identify the costs and expenses incurred and the amount of the costs and expenses. Upon request by the client, the attorney shall provide a bill to the client no later than 10 days following the request unless the attorney has provided a bill to the client within 31 days prior to the request, in which case the attorney may provide a bill to the client no later than 31 days following the date the most recent bill was provided. The client is entitled to make similar requests at intervals of no less than 30 days following the initial request. In providing responses to client requests for billing information, the attorney may use billing data that is currently effective on the date of the request, or, if any fees or costs to that date cannot be accurately determined, they shall be described and estimated.

(c)   Failure to comply with any provision of this section renders the agreement voidable at the option of the client, and the attorney shall, upon the agreement being voided, be entitled to collect a reasonable fee.

(d)   This section shall not apply to any of the following:

(1)   Services rendered in an emergency to avoid foreseeable prejudice to the rights or interests of the client or where a writing is otherwise impractical.

(2)   An arrangement as to the fee implied by the fact that the attorney's services are of the same general kind as previously rendered to and paid for by the client.

(3)   If the client knowingly states in writing, after full disclosure of this section, that a writing concerning fees is not required.

---

[55] Section 6147 covers contingency fee agreements.—Eds.

(4)   If the client is a corporation. * * *

EXERCISE 1-2: DRAFTING AN ATTORNEY CLIENT AGREEMENT

Prepare a draft of an attorney-client agreement for the clients described in Exercise 1-1 of this chapter. Imagine that you are drafting the standard form of attorney-client agreement to be used by your law firm in this and future transactions. You can be creative and contact a local lawyer to obtain a copy of the lawyer's standard agreement for transactional clients. The agreement will be based on hourly charges and the fees for legal services for you and other lawyers in your firm are $250 per hour ($150 per hour for paralegals). Your firm charges in six minute units. Make sure that you check the statutes and professional rules for your state to make sure that your draft agreement complies with the requirements in your state.

Other resources for forms are:

1.   California State Bar Sample Fee Agreement Forms: http://www.calbar.ca.gov/calbar/pdfs/MFA/Sample-Fee-Agreement-Forms.pdf

2. Forming and Operating California Limited Liability Companies § 2.16 (2d ed Cal CEB 2008) available online on lexis.com.[56]

---

[56] From the main search page follow this hierarchy: States Legal — U.S./California/Search Analysis & CLE Materials/Continuing Education of the Bar (CEB), CA/Treatises and Practice Guides.

Chapter 2

CHOOSING AND FORMING THE ENTITY

The fundamental skill in business planning is getting started: helping your clients choose the right form of business entity from the many which are available, and acting as the legal "midwife" in the birth of that entity. Section A of this chapter describes the history and development of each of the basic business entity forms available in most states today, and Section B reviews the "birthing process" for each of these entities. Section C deals with the remaining "life cycle" issues the entity faces: management, compensation, liability, transfer of interests, and dissolution.

As you read through this chapter and discuss the problems, you should consider how the attributes of each type of business entity discussed here will either further or prevent attainment of your client's business objectives. There is always room for a good business lawyer to add value to the deal. The choice-of-entity decision is not one based on simple algorithms or check-lists, for at least three different reasons. First, many of the attributes of an entity may be changed to achieve the particular needs and objectives of your client; but not always in the same ways. Second, the types of entities we use today, and the statutory foundations for those entities, will surely evolve over your professional lifetime.[1] Finally, each of the constituents to the business "deal" discussed in chapter 1 will have different objectives, needs and demands, and these are likely to change from one transaction to the next.

A. TYPES OF BUSINESS ENTITIES

This section describes the development of each of the basic business entities available in most states today. We proceed generally in chronological order, so that the descriptions will in turn give you a sense of the historical pattern of development of business entities.

1. The Sole Proprietorship

The sole proprietorship is nothing more or less than a business conducted without using any separate legal entity at all. By definition, it is the oldest of the business entities, for it has been around as long as humankind's entrepreneurial spirit. All of the attributes discussed in this section will be indistinguishable from the owner in his or her personal (non-business) capacity.

The law will not distinguish between property owned by the sole proprietor for business use or personal use; each is owned in the same fashion and subject to the same rules. Nor will the law distinguish between the income from the business and

---

[1] For a good modern chronology of the dizzying development of business entities, see Harry J. Haynsworth, *The Unified Business Organizations Code: The Next Generation*, 29 DEL. J. CORP. L. 83, 84–89, 85–86 (2004) ("The increase in the number of business forms is bewildering to practicing lawyers, judges, law professors, and legislators. Almost every year, a new type of entity or a major revision to an existing business organization statute is promulgated or enacted.").

the proprietor's other sources of income. Finally, the law will not distinguish between business and personal property when dealing with business or personal creditors of the proprietor; all of his or her property will be equally available to satisfy the debts of any creditor.

The sole proprietorship is often referred to as the entity which results "by default." This "default" only means that an entrepreneur who "goes into business" alone and without doing more has probably formed a sole proprietorship. It does not mean that a sole proprietorship would never be the best choice of business entity. On the contrary, the ease of formation (by doing nothing) and operation (nothing required) may make this the superior choice for a new small business.

2. The (General) Partnership

When lawyers refer to "partnerships," without more, they are probably referring to *general* partnerships, as the caption of this section indicates. The adjective "general" is used to distinguish this entity from a "limited" partnership, a "limited liability" partnership, or a "limited liability limited" partnership, each of which will be discussed shortly. We will follow this convention, and if the term "partnership" is used without specific reference to a particular form of partnership, we are referring to a general partnership.

If the sole proprietorship is the oldest form of business entity, the partnership cannot be far behind, for it is "as old as cooperative activity."[2] This business entity is different from the sole proprietorship only in that it requires an *associate in the business activity*.[3] No further formalities are required in either case. Indeed, your client or clients might have a sole proprietorship or general partnership without even knowing it.

Because partnerships are old, they have a long history of development. The partnership originated by the custom of merchants dealing as associates, and the form — and the custom — was recognized by medieval courts. This common-law development gave way to partnership statutes in the early twentieth century, first in England and then in the United States.[4]

In the United States, partnership law is based on the Uniform Partnership Act (UPA), which was first adopted as a uniform law in 1914 and was completely revised and adopted in revised form in 1994. Technically, both statutes are known by the "UPA" abbreviation; the first as UPA (1914) and the second as UPA (1994). To make things simpler, we will here (as do most other texts and lawyers) refer to the second statute as the Revised Uniform Partnership Act (RUPA). RUPA is now the governing statute in most states (38 at the latest count), with the others (save Louisiana) using the older UPA.[5] In general, RUPA follows the same basic rules of UPA, but modernizes and updates default provisions in several areas:

---

[2] I Alan R. Bromberg & Larry E. Ribstein, Bromberg and Ribstein on Partnership § 1.02(a) at p. 1:19 (1996) (hereinafter cited without reference to volume number).

[3] Indeed, the partnership statutes we discuss shortly define a partnership in accord with these distinctions, as "an association of two or more persons to carry on as co-owners a business for profit." UPA § 6(1), RUPA § 202(a).

[4] For a brief history of partnership law and further references, see Bromberg & Ribstein, *supra* note 2, at 1:20 to 1:21; J. William Callison & Maureen A. Sullivan, Partnership Law & Practice 1–8 (2004); Robert D. Cooter, *Decentralized Law for a Complex Economy: The Structural Approach to Adjudi-*

- departure of a partner, replacing the unclear UPA concepts of "dissolution" with "dissociation" of a partner which does not necessarily end the partnership, thus improving the stability of the partnership form;

- the nature and extent of fiduciary duties owed by each partner to each other partner and to the partnership, replacing a generalized high standard of good faith and disclosures with specified and limited duties of loyalty and care;

- the existence of the partnership as an entity separate from the partners, so that departure of a partner does not end the partnership. Under the UPA every departure of a partner ended the partnership, creating potential for unintended and unnecessary defaults on loans, leases, and other contracts.

- the contribution, recording, and transfer of partnership property, making more clear the ability of the partnership to file a "statement of authority" relating to acts of a partner in general and the authority to transfer real property in particular.

EXERCISE 2-1

Find your state's partnership law. If it is a UPA jurisdiction, have there been efforts made to introduce RUPA? You can find some information at www.nccusl.org. If it is a RUPA jurisdiction, what happens to old partnerships? Are they governed by the new law immediately, never, or at some "phase-in" date? You may want to consult your jurisdiction's version of RUPA § 1006.[6]

3.   The Limited Partnership

The limited partnership is nearly as old as the general partnership, both having begun in medieval times and developed as part of the law merchant.[7] In the United States, the law of limited partnerships developed in much the same fashion as the law of general partnerships, with an initial uniform act and later revisions. The Uniform Limited Partnership Act (ULPA) was promulgated in 1916 and was revised in 1976 and again in 1985, the first revision known as the Revised Uniform Limited Partnership Act (RULPA), and the second as RULPA with 1985 amendments.

The distinguishing feature of the limited partnership is, the limited partner, who differs from the other (general) partners. A limited partnership must have at least one general and one limited partner, but the nature of the distinction between a general and limited partner has changed over the years. Generally speaking, a limited partner has limited liability, but also limited authority. A limited partner who asserted "too much" authority in running the partnership risked having unlimited liability as well. Because of this Draconian consequence, one of the major refinements from ULPA to RULPA was to clarify the scope of the limited

---

cating the New Law Merchant, 144 U. PA. L. REV. 1643, 1647 & n.14 (1996).

[5] *See* www.nccusl.org/Update/uniformact_factsheets/uniformacts-fs-upa9497.asp for the latest updates. This is the website of the National Conference of Commissioners on Uniform State Laws, the drafters of all of the uniform non-corporate statutes we discuss in this part.

[6] *See also* Bromberg & Ribstein, *supra*, § 1.04(e), p. 1:77 (retroactive application of RUPA).

[7] *See supra* note 3; Bromberg & Ribstein, *supra*, § 11.02(a), pp. 11:19 to 11:21.

partner's permitted participation in the management of the limited partnership.[8] The other major differences between general and limited partnerships are those relating to the limited partners: their admission, withdrawal, and the like. The limited partnership was for many years treated as a "subspecies" of partnership; most state laws provided that, where nothing in a state's limited partnership law applied, the state's general partnership law would control.[9]

A revolution in business entity law took place with the development of the limited liability company and limited liability partnership, discussed in Sections A.6 and A.7 below. One collateral casualty of that revolution was the limited partnership. Until the revolution, the limited partnership was very useful, and was often the preferred choice of business planners, because it provided the key combination of limited liability for investors with "pass-through" tax treatment. (There is much more about tax treatment of business entities in Chapter 3.) After the revolution, there arose simpler and more effective ways of doing the same thing. It seemed that the days of the limited partnership were numbered.[10]

To the rescue came the uniform-law writers. Reluctant to throw the limited partnership on the trash heap, they reinvented the form for the twenty-first century. The new act, entitled the Uniform Limited Partnership Act (2001) but known as "Re-RULPA," has recognized the small but clear niche which limited partnerships now occupy in the universe of business entities in the United States.[11] Re-RULPA has been adopted in thirteen states so far.[12]

EXERCISE 2-2

C and L want to go into business together operating a small retail store. C has no business expertise, and will be providing only the start-up funds for the store. L has business expertise, but little money to invest and will be providing the labor (L's own and employees L might hire) for the store. L will want protections in order to avoid being taken advantage of by C, particularly to avoid C's abrupt withdrawal of funding. C will want protections to guarantee the security of C's capital investment, that is, to make sure that L operates the store in a prudent fashion, and to avoid any liabilities which may arise in the operation of the store.

---

[8] Bromberg & Ribstein, *supra*, § 11.02(c) at p. 11:27.

[9] *Id.* § 11.02(b), p. 11:25. This is referred to as "linkage" of the general partnership and limited partnership acts. The statutes were "un-linked" with RUPA and Re-RULPA. *See generally* Elizabeth S. Miller, *Linkage and Delinkage: A Funny Thing Happened to Limited Partnerships When the Revised Uniform Partnership Act Came Along*, 37 Suffolk Univ. L. Rev. 891 (2004); Prefatory Note to Re-RULPA ("The Decision to "De-Link" and Create a Stand Alone Act").

[10] Except, perhaps, where an old limited partnership had been created and could not be converted into something simpler without substantial costs in tax or liability.

[11] The prefatory note to Re-RULPA states in part:

> The new Act has been drafted for a world in which limited liability partnerships and limited liability companies can meet many of the needs formerly met by limited partnerships. This Act therefore targets two types of enterprises that seem largely beyond the scope of LLPs and LLCs: (i) sophisticated, manager-entrenched commercial deals whose participants commit for the long term, and (ii) estate planning arrangements (family limited partnerships). This Act accordingly assumes that, more often than not, people utilizing it will want:
> - strong centralized management, strongly entrenched, and
> - passive investors with little control over or right to exit the entity.

The Act's rules, and particularly its default rules, have been designed to reflect these assumptions.

[12] *See* www.nccusl.org/Update/uniformact_factsheets/uniformacts-fs-ulpa.asp.

Both will of course want some protection for their investment in "the business," should they choose to sell it. Could C and L get what they want if:

(1) C lends the money to L who operates the store as a sole proprietorship? Recall particularly the "inadvertent partnership" doctrine.[13]

(2) C and L form a general partnership? In particular, suppose L agrees to indemnify C against any liabilities?

(3) C and L form a limited partnership with C as the limited partner?

4.   The Corporation

The ancestor of the modern corporation in the United States probably first appeared in England about 500 years ago.[14] An early form of corporation was used in England primarily for business ventures of great public importance. "Ordinary commercial enterprises" were organized as unincorporated joint stock companies.[15] In the United States, however:

> [W]e proceeded to use the corporate instrument on a scale unmatched in England. In that development we built public policy toward the corporation almost wholly out of our own wants and concerns, shaped primarily by our own institutions.[16]

Corporation law in the United States developed first as a cacophony of special charter laws, where the legislature would grant "X Co." the privilege of incorporated status, subject to unique terms and conditions. This practice ended by the late nineteenth century, as most states had by then passed general purpose corporation laws. This change was fueled in most instances by the perception that special interests were favored over the public interest in these individual corporate charters.[17]

After states turned to general-purpose incorporation statutes, they next began to move from restrictive general laws to more permissive general incorporation laws.[18] Different states attempted to encourage businesses to incorporate in their jurisdictions by writing statues which would be perceived as favorable to management. Although originally characterized as a "race of laxity;"[19] the exact nature of this "race" as it was run over the years has been hotly debated. Some have

---

[13] *See, e.g.*, Martin v. Peyton, 246 N.Y. 213, 158 N.E. 77 (1927); Bromberg & Ribstein, *supra*, § 2.05(c), pp. 2:60–2:61 & n.29.

[14] James W. Hurst, The Legitimacy of the Business Corporation in the Law of the United States 1780–1970 2 (1970).

[15] James D. Cox & Thomas Lee Hazen, Cox & Hazen on Corporations § 2.02 at p. 84 (2d ed. 2003).

[16] Hurst, *supra*, at 8.

[17] The perception of special favor from special statutes was probably not accurate, since the businesses in which the corporations wished to engage would require special state regulation in any event: railroads, banks, turnpike or canal companies, and the like. *Id.* at 39.

[18] Hurst sets this period of change from restrictive to permissive general incorporation laws as running from about the mid-1880s to the 1930s. *Id.* at 69–70.

[19] "Laxity" was the term coined by Justice Brandeis dissenting in *Louis K. Liggett Co. v. Lee*, 288 U.S. 517, 549 (1933). Professor Conard describes the competition more as one of liberality than laxity. *See* Alfred F. Conard, Corporations in Perspective 13 (1976).

considered it a "race to the bottom," others a "race to the top."[20] But the results — race or no race — are crystal clear in two respects. First of all, the race is over for the most part. Most state corporation laws are very similar in essential respects, and most are of the "enabling" or "liberal" type. Second, Delaware is the clear winner of the race.[21] This remains so today, even though the statute laws of most states are very similar.[22]

The triumph of state law in this area is a result of a conflict-of-laws rule known as the "internal affairs doctrine."[23] This doctrine requires a court to apply the law of the corporation's jurisdiction of incorporation in deciding matters relating to the governance of a corporation and the rights and duties of its constituents (share-holders, officers, and directors).

The primacy of state law is limited in two important respects. First, as far as publicly-traded corporations are concerned, the Sarbanes-Oxley Act[24] imposes many requirements upon the corporation and its governance as a matter of federal law.[25] Second, some states have provided exceptions to the internal affairs doctrine for foreign corporations with a substantial presence in the state.[26]

Unlike the partnership and limited partnership statutes, which developed with the guidance of NCCUSL uniform acts, corporation law has been illuminated by a slightly different lodestar: the Model Business Corporation Act (MBCA).[27] The MBCA is developed not by the uniform law commissioners, but by the Section on Business Law of the American Bar Association (ABA). As a "model" act rather than a "uniform" act, it does not stress uniformity. Therefore, while the MBCA constitutes, in large part, the corporation law of thirty-two states and the District of Columbia,[28] it is not the same in any of them. The MBCA is constantly amended

---

[20] For an excellent discussion, see Cox & Hazen, *supra*, § 2.05 at p. 91 n. 10 (collecting sources) and § 2.06 at pp. 92–96.

[21] New Jersey was the early winner of the race, indeed it was this state to which Justice Brandeis referred. *See Liggett Co., supra*, 288 U.S. at 549 n.37. However, New Jersey governor Woodrow Wilson championed legislation returning New Jersey law to its more restrictive version.

> Consequences followed quickly. Corporations flocked to Delaware, which had a statute very much like the old New Jersey statute. . . . In 1917, with Woodrow Wilson in the White House, the New Jersey legislature again amended its corporation statute, this time to undo the Wilson-era reforms. By 1917, however, large corporations had come to like their home in Delaware, and they had no interest in moving back to New Jersey.

Larry D. Soderquist & A.A. Sommer, Jr., Understanding Corporation Law 16 (1990).

[22] *See* Cox & Hazen, *supra*, § 2.06 at pp. 96–97 (discussing factors still favoring Delaware incorporation for public companies).

[23] *See id.* § 2.13 at pp. 112–13.

[24] Pub. L. No. 107-204, 116 Stat. 745 (2002).

[25] *See, e.g., id.* at § 301 (independent directors required on audit committees), § 407 (disclosure of existence of "financial expert" on audit committee), § 404 (management assessment of adequacy of internal controls). "Publicly-traded" generally means a corporation which has more than $10 million in assets and whose shares are held of record by more than 500 persons or traded on a national securities exchange. *See* Securities Exchange Act of 1934, § 12(a), (g).

[26] *See, e.g.*, Cal. Corp. Code § 2119; N.Y. Bus. Corp. Law § 1319.

[27] In fact, there were early efforts by NCCUSL on a Uniform Business Corporation Act, but it was not widely adopted. *See* Cox & Hazen, *supra*, § 2.05 at p. 90.

[28] 1 Model Bus. Corp. Act Ann. at xxvii. It is easier to list the states which are *not* "Model Act" states: California, Colorado, Delaware, Illinois, Kansas, Louisiana, Maryland, Michigan, Minnesota, Montana, Nevada, New Jersey, New York, North Dakota, Ohio, Oklahoma, Pennsylvania, and Texas.

by the ABA, and therefore the MBCA-based corporation law of your state may not include all of the modern updates which have been made to the MBCA itself.

Importantly for business planners, modern incorporation statutes do not have as many affirmative requirements as did the early statutes. Rather, they typically offer options for governance structures in two areas. First, many statutes provide for a general rule but permit modification of that rule as the corporation might provide in its articles or bylaws. For example, sections of the MBCA permit super-majority rules for director action or shareholder action, preemptive rights, cumulative voting, removal of directors only for cause, and other arrangements if the corporation's articles so provide.[29] Second, most states provide more liberal rules for closely-held corporations. This liberality is provided in three different formats. Eighteen states have special statutes applicable to such entities.[30] Twenty-one states have adopted § 7.32 of the Model Business Corporation Act, which authorizes shareholder agreements to provide for virtually any type of corporate governance arrangement in a closely-held corporation.[31] And judicial decisions in many states have provided a broad but more indeterminate rule of leniency for the governance of the closely-held corporation.[32]

EXERCISE 2-3

Find and become familiar with your state's corporation law. Which of the special arrangements for closely-held corporations does your law provide? Do you think it is acceptable to use your state as the default jurisdiction when you are a lawyer advising a new business on where to incorporate?

5.   The Limited Liability Company

The limited liability company ("LLC") has been around for about 30 years, and has been available in every state for at least ten years, so it is hard to still speak of it as a "new" form of business entity. However, the story of creation of the LLC is worth repeating for two important lessons to be learned. First, business lawyers can create value for their clients when they "think outside the box" and create innovative solutions.[33] Second, nothing about the law will remain static in your professional lifetime, so it is just as important to obtain a larger understanding of your clients' issues and objectives, because the tools at hand will surely change over the years.

For many years, lawyers struggled to give their clients three important attributes in their businesses: limited liability, the ability to participate in business

---

[29] *See* MBCA § 8.24(c) (supermajority for director action), § 7.25(c) (supermajority for shareholder action), § 6.30(a) (preemptive rights), § 7.28(b) (cumulative voting), § 8.08(a) (removal of directors only for cause).

[30] 4 Model Bus. Corp. Act Ann. CC-71 to CC-72.

[31] 2 Model Bus. Corp. Act Ann. 7-249 to 7-251 (five of these states have made substantial changes in their versions of § 7.32).

[32] *See, e.g.,* Galler v. Galler, 32 Ill.2d 16, 203 N.E.2d 577(1965); *Long Park v. Trenton-New Brunswick Theatres Co.,* 297 N.Y. 174, 77 N.E.2d 633 (1948). For a good summary of the judicial and legislative developments and motives relating to close corporations, see Hurst, *supra,* at 76–82.

[33] "The explanation behind the LLC's birth boils down to innovative professionals creating solutions when the current legal system fails to meet client needs." Susan Pace Hamill, *The Origins Behind the Limited Liability Company,* 59 Ohio St. L.J. 1459, 1463 (1998).

management, and favorable income tax treatment.[34] The corporation could provide the first two but not the third.[35] The partnership could provide the second two but not the first.[36] The limited partnership could provide the first and third, but not the second.[37] The key to business lawyering was therefore to select a type of entity and try to bend it as far as possible without breaking it. For example, a corporation could meet all three of these requirements if its income could be "zeroed out" so that it had no taxable income, which could be done only under the watchful eye of a revenue agent assessing the reasonableness of deductible expenses. A limited partnership could meet all three of these requirements if the limited partners had some basic management rights, so long as it didn't go too far to risk either unlimited liability under state law or classification as a corporation for tax purposes. And the general partnership could attempt to contractually limit liabilities, but this was often unsuccessful for a small, new business which is typically at the mercy of its major creditors.

It was not until 1977 that lawyers finally realized the problem was that they did not have the right kind of business entity tools. Was there any inherent reason that "limited" partners must forfeit management rights? Or why general partners must be liable for all the debts of a partnership while the opposite is the rule for shareholders in corporations? Or, indeed, why must there be general partners in a limited partnership at all? The answer to all of these questions was simply that state law required that outcome; but no one had seriously tried to change the law. In 1977, in Wyoming, lawyers in a business transaction did just that, lobbying the Wyoming legislature to pass the first limited liability company statute.[38] The LLC was modeled after similar entities which were in common use in most civil law countries.[39] The wonder is really that we didn't think of it sooner.

The victory for the LLC was sealed when the IRS conceded in 1988 that a Wyoming LLC would be classified as a partnership for federal income tax purposes. The cascade of LLC laws then began, with some important modifications made by some states along the way. In 1997, the IRS threw in the towel and repealed the "Kintner Regulations,"[40] thus according all LLCs favorable federal

---

[34] We have not said much about the income tax treatment of business entities. This is a critical issue, one which drives much of the development of LLCs. The technical details await in Chapter 3, Section A. This list of business attributes usually includes a fourth: free transferability of interests. These four attributes were those used by the Internal Revenue Service in its infamous "Kintner Regulations" to distinguish corporations which were liable for a separate income tax from other associations which were not. We have not focused on transferability of interests here in order to keep the discussion more simple. We will consider that issue in detail in Section F of this chapter.

[35] This is because a corporation pays a separate income tax under federal and most state laws, whereas a partnership (whether general or limited) does not. Congress provided a partial solution in 1957 with the "Subchapter S corporation," which provides for partnership-like tax treatment of small corporations which meet certain restrictions in size and structure.

[36] This is because general partners are liable for the obligations of the partnership.

[37] This is because limited partners are not liable for the obligations of the partnership but only so long as they do not "participate in control" of the partnership. The time period about which we speak is before the 1976 amendments to ULPA, which ameliorated this problem slightly.

[38] For a good summary of the story, see Carter G. Bishop & Daniel S. Kleinberger, Limited Liability Companies: Tax and Business Law ¶ 1.01[3][a] & n. 30 (2005) (citing Bradley J. Sklar & W. Todd Carlisle, *The Alabama Limited Liability Company Act*, 45 ALA. L. REV. 145 (1997)).

[39] *See* Sklar & Carlisle, *id.* at 153–58.

[40] Classification of Certain Business Entities, 61 Fed. Reg. 66,584 (1996), *codified at* Treas. Reg.

income tax treatment. NCCUSL's Uniform Limited Liability Company Act (ULLCA) appeared on the scene in 1994, too late to be useful as a prototype for new statutes, but it is now becoming a useful model as states turn to refining their LLC statutes.[41] In 2006, NCCUSL adopted a new modern statute, dubbed "Re-ULLCA," and self-described as a "second generation" statute. It dispenses with many of the formalities which were required in the LLCs' early years, for example, regarding number of members and choice of management and operation.

Because LLC statutes have developed in this fashion, they exist today more like corporation statutes than partnership statutes. They are not uniform, but they are similar, and most are of an "enabling" variety. All LLC statutes provide for limited liability for the members of the LLC, in a fashion similar to that provided for shareholders of a corporation.[42] Beyond that, an LLC is permitted to have almost any assortment of attributes which the organizers desire.[43] It can have "corporate" attributes: centralized management, free transferability of interests, and unlimited life. It can have "partnership" attributes: equal management in every owner, no transferability of interests, and automatic dissolution upon the request of any one member. Or it can have whichever mix of these attributes the organizers desire.

Obviously, the LLC provides the best of all possible worlds for the business planner. You may wonder only why there is anything else ever used today. Many reformers have called for an "omnibus" business entity law which combines all these different types into one LLC-like format. Many reformers have also called upon Congress to repeal Subchapter S, which they say is no longer needed now that LLCs have pass-through income tax treatment. However, the old ways have proven durable. Corporations continue to be used for small business start-ups, and partnerships have proven durable as well.

But you needn't fear that this is an irrational arrangement. Indeed, it is a good lesson in how business planners (lawyers) respond to change. They are risk averse. Entrepreneurs are *not* risk averse, indeed, profit lies only in taking carefully-managed risks. But no lawyer wants to run the risk of *legal* uncertainty if it can be avoided. And the one drawback which everyone recognizes in the LLC is that it is still a relatively new form of organization. This means that the common law has not begun to develop the robustness which exists in most states for small corporation law and in Delaware for public corporation law. In addition, the partnership remains a necessary alternative because the law must provide a set of default rules for those who do not consult a lawyer but simply go into business. So good lawyers continue to need the other forms of business organization. They need partnership law because they may face an existing business which is in fact a partnership by default. They need limited partnership law because they may have an existing

---

§ 301.7701-3. Intermediate guidance in the spirit of the Kintner Regulations had been provided in Rev. Proc. 95-10, 1995-1 C.B. 501.

[41] *See generally* Cox & Hazen, *supra*, § 1.11[1] at pp. 40–42.

[42] *Compare* ULLCA § 303(a) ("the debts, obligations, and liabilities of a limited liability company, whether arising in contract, tort, or otherwise, are solely the debts, obligations, and liabilities of the company. A member or manager is not personally liable for a debt, obligation, or liability of the company solely by reason of being or acting as a member or manager."), *with* MBCA § 6.22(b) ("a shareholder of a corporation is not personally liable for the acts or debts of the corporation except that he may become personally liable by reason of his own acts or conduct.").

[43] In fact, the limited liability could be waived as well, but it is hard to imagine a situation in which the organizers would do so outside a contractual arrangement with a particular creditor.

client organized as a limited partnership which cannot be reorganized without great cost, or a new entity which fits into the 21st century LP niche. They need corporation law, even for the start-up business, because they are be comfortable with the clear answers which statutes and settled decisions provide for many questions: the extent of limited liability, fiduciary duties, duties to creditors, the status of investments as securities, just to name a few.

Although this arrangement is rational, it lacks permanence. The LLC is definitely on the rise. In many states it has easily eclipsed the corporation as the form of choice for new businesses. As time passes, judicial precedent will become more secure. Lawyers may see the wisdom of a single default omnibus business entity law and an "enabling" LLC law for all other situations. But that day may be a long time coming. In the meantime, we must be comfortable with the diversity which has grown up around us.[44]

EXERCISE 2-4

Find your state's limited liability company law. Has it been amended since the "Kintner" regulations were repealed by the IRS in 1997? What are the default arrangements for agency authority, dissolution, and transferability of interests? Is it allowed to have only one member? What is the scope of the liability shield: torts, contracts, other liabilities?

6.   The Limited Liability Partnership

The Limited Liability Partnership (LLP) developed as a corollary to the LLC for businesses (such as law and accounting firms) which are required by the rules governing their professions to be organized in partnership form.[45] First used in Texas, it spread as quickly as did the LLC, so that it is now law in all states and the District of Columbia.

The LLP is simply a general partnership in which the rule of general partner unlimited liability is reversed. The scope of this reversal — or "shield" — differs among the states. Because the initial concern which gave rise to the LLP was the liability of "innocent partners" in a law firm for the malpractice of their colleagues, the LLP shield initially extended only to tort liability. But this shield was soon recognized as imperfect, and in any event more limited than the broader shield available to everyone else who could form an LLC. Most state laws now provide partners in an LLP with a liability limitation identical to that for members in an LLC.[46] Because the LLP is a modification to the general partnership statutes, it is typically incorporated in the state's partnership law, and the uniform law writers did the same in 1996, adding the LLP to RUPA.

There were occasional tussles with regulators once the use of LLPs became widespread. In the law firm arena, the conflict was obvious between (1) the desire of an "innocent partner" in a law firm to avoid crushing liability on account of the

---

[44] *See generally* Comment, Tara J. Wortman, *Unlocking Lock-In: Limited Liability Companies and the Key to Underutilization of Close Corporation Statutes,* 70 N.Y.U. L. REV. 1362 (1995).

[45] For the story relating to development of the first LLP as a response to perceived liability of Texas law firms in the savings and loan crisis of the 1980s, see Robert W. Hamilton, *Registered Limited Liability Partnerships: Present at the Birth (Nearly),* 66 COLORADO L. REV. 1065 (1995).

[46] *See* Callison & Sullivan, *supra,* § 32.3, pp. 32-5 to 32-10.

malpractice of other partners and (2) the ethical obligation of a lawyer to not limit his or her malpractice liability to his or her clients. The compromise reached in most states was to permit law firms to organize as LLPs, but they were required to maintain specific amounts of liability insurance or liquid assets available to malpractice creditors.[47]

The mechanics of the LLP are very simple. All that is required is for an "ordinary" general partnership to elect LLP status, which is done by a filing (and fee).[48] The LLP is otherwise identical to the partnership which it was before. The general partnership with unlimited liability for partners would continue to be used only by those partners who have gone into business without competent legal advice or could not afford the (modest) LLP filing fee.

EXERCISE 2-5

Find your state's limited liability partnership law. (Note: typically, it is found as a portion of the general partnership law.) What must a partnership do to become an LLP? What is the scope of the liability shield? Is it the same as your state's LLC liability shield?

7. The Limited Liability Limited Partnership

The Limited Liability Limited Partnership (LLLP) developed as yet another corollary to the LLC for business which were already organized as *limited* partnerships and could not be reorganized without serious adverse consequences, or for business which meet the narrow criteria to be organized as modern limited partnerships in the Re-RULPA era.[49] If you can follow a simple analogy (with confusing acronyms), you will understand everything perfectly. The LLLP is to the LP what the LLP is to the general partnership. The LLLP removes all general-partner liability from the LP, just as the LLP did for general partnerships.[50] It operates in a similar structural fashion as well. An LP which chooses to file and pay a fee may become LLLP, which is the same as the LP except that the general partners no longer have unlimited liability for partnership obligations. Because fewer entities are organized as LPs to begin with, the LLLP has not proved as popular as either the LLC or the LLP.

8. The Special-Purpose Regulated Entity

There are many regulated industries, entities and professions. The rules for each may significantly impact the choice of entity decision. A few of the major areas are discussed in this subsection.

---

[47] Robert W. Hillman, *Organizational Choices of Professional Service Firms: An Empirical Study*, 58 Bus. Law. 1387, 1400 & n.72 (2003).

[48] *See, e.g.*, RUPA § 1001 (statement of qualification).

[49] *See supra* Section A.3.

[50] *See* Re-RULPA § 404(c) ("An obligation of a limited partnership incurred while the limited partnership is a limited liability limited partnership, whether arising in contract, tort, or otherwise, is solely the obligation of the limited partnership. A general partner is not personally liable, directly or indirectly, by way of contribution or otherwise, for such an obligation solely by reason of being or acting as a general partner.").

One type of entity available to lawyers and members of many other professions in some states is a professional corporation (PC) or a professional limited liability company (PLLC). The differences between these "professional entities" and the ordinary varieties are usually that membership or ownership is restricted to individuals who are licensed in the relevant profession. The list of professions permitted to so organize varies from state to state. Typically, the PC or PLLC statute provides for restricted transfer of ownership and automatic buyout or dissolution if ownership interests should fall into the hands of an individual who is not a licensed professional.

Regulated industries often have the particulars of organization dictated for them. In most states, for example, banks and insurance companies must be organized as corporations. Public utilities, common carriers, other financial intermediaries, health care providers and the like, may also have their business structures and operations limited, sometimes severely, by particular regulatory statutes. If your client is engaging in one of these regulated businesses, the regulatory law should be the *first* thing the lawyer consults in determining the choice of business entity.

9.   The Business Trust and other Variations

A trust is a separate legal person with which you will become familiar in other courses in law school. It is the major non-business association which is given the attributes of legal personhood: the abilities to own property, sue, make contracts, and the like. You might therefore conclude that a trust is yet another option to consider when forming a business. And you would be right. The business trust, an ancient form of organization, is enjoying a vigorous renaissance,[51] particularly as a vehicle for "securitizing" real estate and financial assets,[52] at least in some parts of the country. There are other variations too, such as a joint stock company. "To a large extent, these [other variations] are simply partnerships, one or more aspects of which have been altered from the standard form."[53]

Our introductory survey of the various types of entities is now complete. The discussions and exercises which follow concentrate on discerning the important differences among the most important types of entities in areas most relevant to business planners. We proceed in chronological fashion, with the "life cycle" of the business entity, from birth (formation) to death (dissolution, merger, or other amalgamation).

B.   BIRTH OF AN ENTITY

The main value of any business entity is that it exists as a legal person apart from the other constituents described in Chapter 1: the promoters, the owners, the managers, and the employees (we'll put aside creditors for the moment). The

---

[51]   Cox & Hazen, *supra*, § 1.15 at pp. 61–64, note a "resurgence of interest in business trusts."

[52]   *See generally* Steven L. Schwarcz, *Commercial Trusts as Business Organizations: Unravelling the Mystery*, 58 Bus. Law. 559 (2003); John H. Langbeinn, *The Secret Life of the Trust: The Trust as an Instrument of Commerce*, 107 Yale L.J. 165 (1997); Robert H. Sitkoff, *Trust as "Uncorporation": A Research Agenda*, 2005 Ill. L. Rev. 31.

[53]   Bromberg & Ribstein, *supra*, § 1.01(b)(6) at p. 1:9.

entities begin in various ways; we will survey them from the simplest to the most complicated.

The sole proprietorship is probably the easiest to form. Suppose Bill Gates has a computer repair service. He uses a room in the basement, his own tools and equipment, training he has acquired over the years, and advertises in the local paper. Bill has probably created a sole proprietorship. He can probably conduct business in this form without having to do anything more.[54]

EXERCISE 2-6

What would be the consequences, if any, to Bill or his business, if it were a "sole proprietorship" as opposed to a "nothing," that is, no separate entity at all?

What distinguishes a sole proprietorship from a partnership is, obviously, that there are two people[55] instead of one. And the people must have a particular relationship: "carry[ing] on as co-owners a business for profit."[56] This distinguishes a partnership from some other relationship, most likely a sole proprietor and an employee, creditor, lessor, or some other contractual relationship. Indeed, partnership law expressly permits such individuals to receive profit shares as their compensation without thereby becoming partners.[57] The trap for the unwary here is for the business planner to make sure that the legal result follows the intent of the parties; everyone who intends to be a partner is a partner, and everyone who does not intend to be a partner is not.

EXERCISE 2-7

Barnum is in business as a talent agent for entertainers. Barnum hires Bailey to help with the business. Bailey is generally supervised by Barnum, but otherwise has discretion to seek out new business, set rates, and make contracts with new clients and venues. Bailey's salary is a fixed amount per month plus a 2% share of the business' net profits. Barnum has granted to Bailey an option to buy into the business after two years at a price to be determined. Who owns the valuable lists of clients and contacts which Bailey has developed over years of work for Barnum? Who is liable to the bank which extends credit to the talent agency? Who is liable to the disgruntled actor who claims that Bailey acted with a conflict of interest and sues for damages?

The previous exercise dealt with the issue of unintended or inadvertent partners. When it is clear who intends to be partners, the prudent lawyer memorializes the arrangement in a partnership agreement. The agreement does not necessarily create the partnership; the partnership is created when the two partners begin to "carry on as co-owners a business for profit." Nonetheless, the sooner the essentials of the agreement are reduced to writing, the better off everyone is. The negotiating

---

[54] If Bill conducts business under any name other than his own, he would be required to file a "fictitious business name" (FBN) statement with local officials. *See, e.g.*, Cal. Bus. & Prof. Code §§ 17900, 17910. *See generally* 65 C.J.S. *Names* § 16. The FBN requirement applies generally to any business entity not using its legal name.

[55] We use "people" here in the broadest sense, as a partner can be a human or another entity: a partnership, a corporation, a trustee, for example.

[56] UPA § 6(1); RUPA § 202(a).

[57] UPA § 7(4); RUPA § 202(c)(3). UPA covers wages only; RUPA extends coverage to independent contractors.

and planning which underlies the drafting of the agreement assures that expectations are clear and all important contingencies have been addressed.

All other entities save for a sole proprietorship and a partnership are brought into being by filing an organizational document with a state official, usually the Secretary of State. The usual titles of these documents are indicated below.

Entity	Organizational document
Limited partnership (including LLLP)	Certificate of limited partnership
Limited liability company	Articles of organization
Corporation	Articles of incorporation or Charter
Limited liability partnership	Statement of qualification

Legal issues may arise when entrepreneurs attempt to file these documents themselves, and there is some failure in the filing process. In the case of the corporation, there are well developed legal doctrines relating to the liability of "promoters" who purport to act on behalf of a corporation which is not yet organized, and participants in a defectively-organized corporation. There are similar rules in many states relating to LLCs, and probably the same types of rules apply to LLPs as well. Good lawyers know better than to take any chances with the filings. They will await proof of acceptance of filing before advising their clients to commence business.

Normally, the organizational document is short. The information required by modern statutes is limited to basic identifying information. Nonetheless, additional items might be included in the organizational document for three reasons. First, state law may stipulate that certain provisions are binding only if contained in the organizational document. Second, clients may wish to place certain fundamental agreements (limited purpose or location of business, term or termination of business or the entity) in the organizational document because it is often more difficult to amend. And third, the normal hierarchy of the documents places the organizational document at the top, that it to say, its provisions will "trump" contrary rules in bylaws or owners' agreements.

Once the organizational documents have been filed, the work of the business planner must continue. There is more to be done to complete the basic governance structure of the entity, usually in the form of an agreement among the owners. The usual titles of these documents are indicated below.

Entity	Agreement among owners
Partnership (all types)	Partnership agreement
Limited liability company	Operating agreement
Corporation	Shareholders' agreement / Bylaws

None of these agreements is required to be in writing to have legal effect, although it is always wise to have them in writing and signed by the owners. The statute of frauds may require a writing, or in some cases, an agreement may have to be reduced to writing to have a statutory presumption of validity.[58]

---

[58] *See, e.g.*, MBCA § 7.32(b)(1) (shareholder agreements).

In the case of a corporation, bylaws may be required by statute,[59] but a shareholders' agreement typically is not required. The distribution of corporate governance arrangements between the bylaws and a shareholders' agreement is largely a matter of custom. The important point for the lawyer is to assure that the desired legal consequences of the arrangement are obtained. This is not difficult, it only requires that you know the rules.

In *Blount v. Taft*,[60] an agreement among the shareholders on a particular matter (the "Section 7" referred to in the quote below) had been inserted into a draft of new bylaws, which was then approved by all the directors. The bylaws elsewhere provided (in the "Section 4" referred to in the quote below) for amendment by a majority of the board. A later amendment to Section 7 was challenged by dissident shareholders, who claimed that, as a shareholder agreement, it could be amended only with the unanimous consent of the shareholders. The court held otherwise:

> Had Section 7 been a "side agreement" signed by all the stockholders, and not been made a part of the bylaws, it is plausible to argue that absent an internal provision governing its amendment it could be amended only by unanimous consent of all the stockholders. As the Court of Appeals noted in its opinion, "a shareholders' agreement may not be altered or terminated except as provided by the agreement, or by all parties, or by operation of law." Had Section 4 been omitted from the bylaws, the directors would have been precluded from amending Section 7 since it is a bylaw adopted by the shareholders. In the absence of a valid provision in the charter or bylaws controlling amendment, statutory or common law norms governing amendment apply. Similarly, when parties to a shareholders' agreement choose to embody it in the charter or bylaws, it must be concluded that they intended for these norms to apply absent an expressed intention to deviate from them.[61]

The key is to be precise about the "hats" your clients wear, even in a close corporation, where it is common for each individual to be a shareholder, officer and director. Action as shareholders will be respected as such, likewise action as directors. Therefore, each must meet the requirements for that action in the statute, bylaw, or agreement.

Finally, once you have prepared the organizational document(s) and the agreement(s) among the owners, there is the matter of funding. The details of how to choose what funding sources and the proper amount of funds are discussed in Chapter 5. Here we are concerned with bringing those decisions into proper form. In the case of a partnership or LLC, the agreement among owners can simply recite the consideration paid by each partner or member for his or her interest in the entity.[62] In the case of a corporation, the payment for stock issued is slightly more

---

[59] MBCA § 2.06(a) requires that a corporation adopt bylaws. Section 2.06(b) provides that the bylaws "may contain any provision for managing the business and regulating the affairs of the corporation that is not inconsistent with law or the articles of incorporation."

[60] 246 S.E.2d 763 (N.C. 1978). The case is reprinted and discussed more fully in Chapter 7, Section C.3.

[61] *Id.* at 772.

[62] If the individuals anticipate problems with the ability of each owner to make the required payments, rather than recite amounts paid, the agreement could provide for a date certain by which payment must be received.

complicated. Some states limit the types of consideration which may be received for stock. In addition, most states require that the consideration received must be at least equal to the "par value" of the shares, which is an arbitrary dollar amount set by the corporation's directors or in the articles of incorporation.[63] Additionally, whatever the actual consideration received, it must be approved by the directors as adequate and the shares should be declared as "fully paid and nonassessable."[64]

In general, the choreography of incorporation is more complicated than organizing any other business entity. One must first form a corporation before it can have directors; it must have directors before it can adopt bylaws and thus have offices or officers, and it must have directors before it can sell shares in order to have shareholders; and obviously it must have shareholders before they can sign a shareholders' agreement.[65]

EXERCISE 2-8

You represent three individuals who wish to form a corporation. You will include in the articles of incorporation only the items required by law. Your clients have agreed on the following basic rules for their business:

(1)   They will each be a director, officer and a one-third shareholder.
(2)   They would like to limit director liability.
(3)   They would like to require unanimity for all decisions.
(4)   They would like to require a shareholder who wishes to leave the corporation to sell his or her shares back to the corporation at a specified price.

Should each of these provisions be contained in articles, bylaws or in a shareholder agreement? What difference does it make under the law of your state? How will you go about having these documents prepared and executed so that everything is done in the correct order and the corporation is not "stillborn"?

Suppose instead that the three individuals wished to form a member-managed LLC, with each as a manager and member. They would like requirements similar to those specified above. Should each of these provisions be contained in the articles of organization, operating agreement, or some other document?

---

[63] The full story of lawful consideration is told in Chapter 5, Section D.1.b. The full story of par value is told in Chapter 6, as it serves more to regulate dividends than to regulate payments for shares. If your state's corporation laws recognize or require par value, you can avoid any problems if the par value is set at a low but non-zero value, and in any event is lower than the consideration actually paid by each shareholder.

[64] *See, e.g.*, MBCA § 6.21(c) ("Before the corporation issues shares, the board of directors must determine that the consideration received or to be received for shares to be issued is adequate. That determination by the board of directors is conclusive insofar as the adequacy of consideration for the issuance of shares relates to whether the shares are validly issued, fully paid, and nonassessable."), § 6.21(d) ("When the corporation receives the consideration for which the board of directors authorized the issuance of shares, the shares issued therefor are fully paid and nonassessable."). It will be important to have established in the record that the shares are fully paid, because this will facilitate later offerings of additional shares.

[65] It is possible that an agreement signed "as shareholders" before shares are issued would nonetheless be binding, but it's a simple matter of timing to execute the agreement after the shares are issued and avoid this problem altogether.

C. OPERATIONAL ISSUES IN CHOICE AND FORMATION

We now presume that you have solved knotty problems of ownership, and in this part we move on to the business' daily life: profits, management, liability, transfer of interests, and dissolution.[66]

1.   Allocations and Payments to Owners

Entrepreneurs go into business to make money. Once the business has been organized and capitalized, your clients will proceed to begin their business operations. The plan, of course, is to make more money selling goods or providing services than those goods and services cost to produce and deliver. The excess is "profit" in the ordinary non-technical sense. At the end of the business day, the owners expect this profit to inure to them in their capacity *as owners*. This is our sole topic in this section, although it is surely not the only way the owners may receive money from the corporation. They can be employees and receive a salary; they could lend the business money or goods or rent it property and be a creditor or lessor; or there could be some other arrangement whereby the payment to the owner is not made *because* he or she is an owner.

We put aside those other payments for the moment, because the legal issues involved are by and large the same whether the arrangement is with an owner or a disinterested third party. To be sure, there will be additional complications created by the appearance of impropriety when an owner deals with his or her business. But getting assets out of the business to the owners *as owners* is a good deal more complicated. We will discuss first the mechanics of allocation, then the mechanics of actual payments, and then consider when or whether we might want to distribute these disproportionately to the owners' interests.

a.   Mechanics of Allocation

In a general partnership, profit and loss are allocated equally among all the partners unless the partnership agreement provides otherwise.[67] In a limited partnership, the agreement likewise governs, but the default is not equal allocation, but rather allocation based on value of contributions.[68] In addition, particular types of income, expense, or other items can be allocated among the partners for federal income tax purposes.[69] If no such allocation is made, the default rule under tax law is similar to that for limited partnerships.[70] This is necessary because a partnership's income is calculated in part at the partnership level according to some simplified rules, and in part at the level of each partner.[71]

---

[66] Indeed, these are the subjects of Chapters 5–10 of the book, so this Section C serves as an overview of those topics, with an emphasis on the differences among the types of entities.

[67] UPA § 18(a); RUPA § 401(b). Regarding the ability of the partnership agreement to override the Act's default provisions, see UPA § 18 (introductory language) and RUPA § 103(a).

[68] ULPA § 503.

[69] IRC § 704(a). More on this ability to allocate different tax treatment in Section C.1.c below.

[70] IRC § 704(b) provides as a default rule that the partner's distributive share "shall be determined in accordance with the partner's interest in the partnership."

[71] *See* IRC § 703(a) (calculation of partnership's income on which a partner's share is based), § 702(a) (items which must be separately calculated by each partner).

Allocation of profits in a corporation is much simpler for two reasons. First, since a corporation calculates and pays its own federal income tax, it is not necessary to allocate particular items of gain, loss, deduction or credit among the shareholders. Second, under state law, "all shares of a class or series must have terms, including preferences, rights and limitations, that are identical with those of other shares of the same class or series."[72]

Allocation in all other entities follows one of these models. In general, state law permits a limited liability company to allocate profits and losses according to the operating agreement among the members.[73] Federal income tax law has two major additional rules here. First, tax law permits LLCs and their members to be taxed as partnerships. Second, tax law provides for "Subchapter S" corporations or "S Corporations." An S Corporation is an ordinary corporation for state law purposes and subject to the usual state law rules discussed above, but it is treated very much like a partnership for federal income tax purposes.[74]

b.   The Difference between Allocation and Payments

Allocation is very different from payment. Allocation, discussed above, is the process by which profits, losses, or other items are apportioned among owners. Payment is nothing more (or less) than the receipt of cash or other assets by the owners in their capacity as owners. It is the critical final step in the conversion of business profit or individual profit to economic gain. It is a critical step because it is impossible for your business clients to pay for desired goods and services with "book income" of a corporation or partnership.

Payments from the business entity can be of two different types. Both result in the receipt of cash or other assets by the owner, but one is a payment *on account of* or *because of* that ownership interest, and the other is a payment *in exchange for all or part of* that interest. We will consider payments on account of an interest in Chapter 6 and payments in exchange for an interest in Chapter 8.

c.   Disproportionate Profit and Ownership Interests

The above discussion assumed that the investor's ownership interest would be the same as the investor's interest in the profits (or losses) of the business. In many situations, however, your clients may plan to share profits disproportionately to their investment shares. The most typical example is one in which two entrepreneurs will be undertaking a business venture with one of them supplying the capital and the other supplying the labor.

Example. Consider C and L, each of whom desires to be one-half owners of an enterprise. C will invest $100,000 in cash and L will invest L's full-time efforts in managing the business.[75] If the business were to liquidate tomorrow, it is likely

---

[72] MBCA § 6.01(a).

[73] *See* ULLCA § 103(a). The default arrangement in the ULLCA is that all distributions must be made equally. *See id.* § 405(a).

[74] See Chapter 3 for a more detailed discussion of federal income tax treatment of the entities discussed here, and Chapter 6, Section G, for specific discussion of the tax treatment of allocations and payments.

[75] This fact situation is a common real-life scenario, as demonstrated by the number of classic cases dealing with just this setup. *See, e.g.*, Kessler v. Antinora, 653 A.2d 579 (N.J. Super. Ct. 1995); Koestner

that C and L intended that C receive C's $100,000 back and L receive nothing. However, C and L may desire to divide the future profits equally. Thus, we could have the arrangement where C and L are partners with equal profits interests but unequal capital interests.

There are three basic questions for the business planner to address. First, can the chosen business entity support different ownership and profit shares? Second, what will happen if the venture is not profitable? Finally, will it be possible to allocate profits differently from losses?

First, let's reconsider the choice-of-entity problem. Not all business entities adapt well to this arrangement. A partnership works nicely here, because it permits capital investments to differ from profit (or loss) shares. A corporation cannot meet these investors' needs if each gets the same amount and type of stock, because of the requirement that each share of stock be treated alike regarding profit share and ownership interest.[76] And each time we as business planners try to solve the problem, we end up creating another. For example, suppose we give C and L each different kinds of stock (perhaps agreeing that L can pay some nominal amount for L's stock). We have made it impossible for the corporation to receive the favorable partnership-like tax treatment of a Subchapter-S Corporation, because such corporations can only have one class of stock, or classes which differ from each other only in voting rights.[77] As a second example, if we have C and L make nominal payments for the same kinds of stock and then have C lend the bulk of the capital to the entity, we may have created a "thin" corporation. The result may be that C would not be treated on parity with the corporation's other creditors, and might have his "debt" recast as stock by tax authorities in any event.[78] In most states, an LLC will be able to provide C and L with their desired treatment, as the capital and profit — and loss-sharing arrangements in an LLC normally need not be equivalent.[79] And because the LLC can elect to be taxed as a partnership, it will not face the S-Corporation restrictions.[80]

Second, what happens when the partnership or LLC venture is unprofitable? The reported cases[81] attest to the fact that courts have difficulty with this problem. The difficulty stems from the fact that normally the law's default situation is clear but it leads to inequitable results. Under partnership law and many LLC laws, in such a situation the "labor" partner or member must reimburse the "capital" partner or member for one-half the capital losses.[82] This seems inequitable to many courts because the "labor" partner typically does not have any such extra funds, while the "capital" partner does have such funds; indeed, that's why he or

---

v. Wease & Koestner Jewelers, Inc., 381 N.E.2d 11 (Ill. App. Ct. 1978); Richert v. Handly, 330 P.2d 1079 (Wash. 1958); Kovacik v. Reed, 315 P.2d 314 (Cal. 1957); Collins v. Lewis, 283 S.W.2d 258 (Tex. Civ. App. Ct. 1955).

[76]　MBCA § 6.01(a).

[77]　IRC § 1361(b)(1)(D), (c)(4).

[78]　*See* Franklin A. Gevurtz, Corporation Law § 2.3.3 at pp. 147–52 (2000) (discussing both tax and insolvency law aspects of "thin" incorporation).

[79]　*See* ULLCA § 103(a).

[80]　For a general discussion of the limitations of an "S" Corporation, see Chapter 3, Section D. For a detailed discussion of the financing options and problems discussed in this paragraph, see Chapter 5, Section D.1.

[81]　See the cases cited at the beginning of this section for a representative sample.

[82]　UPA §§ 18, 40; RUPA § 807; ULLCA § 806.

she was an investor in the first place. It is virtually impossible to harmonize the many reported cases in this area, but the important lesson for the business planner lies elsewhere; the cases arose in the first place because *the parties simply did not consider the possibility* that the business would not be profitable. If counsel had helped them with their planning, they would have agreed upon a result which would be respected by the courts. In the absence of such planning, many courts find the default rules unfair and strain to avoid them.[83]

Finally, suppose C and L decide that it might be prudent for C to be allocated an equal share of the profits but be allocated all of the losses. Before you dismiss the idea out of hand, consider why it might make economic sense. As we have defined our business venture, C has assets to contribute and L does not. If there are losses, it is likely C who could use the tax benefit of those losses against other income, whereas L would likely have little or no other income. This can be done in a partnership or LLC but not in a corporation (again because of the "one class of stock" requirement), but is subject to a host of other complicated tax rules to assure that C is not receiving a tax benefit (deduction of losses) without a real economic cost.[84]

2.   Authority and Agency

If you have created a business entity other than a sole proprietorship, it is a separate legal person. It can sue and be sued, hold title to real and personal property, make contracts, commit torts, and engage in criminal activities and virtually any other type of activity that a natural person can. The only problem is that it has no hands, legs, or even willpower to do any of these things. Thus the law of business entities is intimately connected with the law of agency, for without agents, most business entities would be powerless.

We begin with a general review of agency principles. Then we survey each of the different types of agents present in the various business entities presented in Section A. This provides the tools for you as a prudent business planner to choose the right agent for the job at hand.

a.   General Principles of Agency

Agency is a deep and rich subject worth of separate study. We sketch here only the basic principles necessary for an overall understanding of agency in the context of business planning. Agency is the power of one individual to affect the legal relations of another. The "one" is called the "agent," and the "other" is the "principal." Agency is a consensual relationship; it begins only when both principal and agent consent so to act, and ends whenever either of them desires it to end, regardless of promises to the contrary. The scope of the agent's power to affect the legal status of the principal is known as the agent's "authority." An agent with authority who contracts on behalf of his or her principal binds only the principal. An agent with authority who commits torts binds both himself or herself and the

---

[83] See the more detailed discussion in Chapter 5, Section D.2.

[84] These are known as the "substantial economic effect" regulations, discussed in detail in Chapter 5, Section D.2 and Chapter 6, Section G.1.

principal. Authority is the key agency concept involved in business entities.[85]

b.   Types of Agents

Given these general principles, we will now examine the constituents of the business from Chapter 1 in our search for the agents involved. We can begin with basic principles applicable to two key constituencies: owners and employees. Owners are *not* agents by virtue of ownership alone. Unlike owners, employees are *always* agents. Next we consider some of the unique aspects of agency in each of the basic types of business entities.

* *Partnership.* There are two basic agency concepts important in the partnership: the general and the limited partner.

→ *General partners.* Every partnership has one or more general partners. A general partner is unique because he or she has, by simple virtue of being a partner, authority to act for the partnership "for the purpose of its business" and in "carrying on in the usual way the business of the partnership."[86] Although the partners might agree to limit the authority of some, or all, of the partners, such an agreement is not binding on contractual third parties without notice. The fact that each and every general partner has such broad authority to act as an agent, binding the partnership to contract obligations and tort liabilities, is a source of serious problems in partnerships.[87] The authority of a general partner is the same whether the entity is a general or limited partnership.[88]

→ *Limited partners.* Limited partners, by contrast, have no authority arising from their status as limited partners. If a limited partner has any authority, it will arise only from the explicit creation of an agency relationship by the limited partnership which it could have done with anyone, limited partner or not. The rub, of course, is that a limited partner who does in fact exercise "too much" control risks losing his or her limited liability.[89] It is in this odd fashion that the law describes the scope of authority of a limited partner. Modern limited partnership law provides that a limited partner may become an agent of the limited partnership without losing his or her limited liability for that reason alone.[90]

* *Corporation.* By contrast, in a traditional corporation, although there are three constituencies — shareholders, officers, and directors — there is only one source of agency authority.

---

[85] Excellent readable references on agency are William A. Gregory, Agency and Partnership (3d ed. 2001) and the Restatement (Third) of Agency.

[86] UPA § 9(1); RUPA § 301(1).

[87] This concept is discussed fully in Chapter 7, Section B.

[88] In RULPA jurisdictions, the matter is this simple, because the statute simply refers to UPA/RUPA partners, *see* RULPA § 403, hence the "linkage" of the general- and limited-partnership statutes. In Re-RULPA jurisdictions, the two statutes are not linked, but the same result obtains from explicit language in Re-RULPA § 403(a).

[89] RULPA § 303(a). This rule has been eliminated in Re-RULPA § 303(a). The official comment to Re-RULPA § 303(a) observes that it "eliminates the so-called 'control rule' with respect to personal liability for entity obligations and brings limited partners into parity with LLC members, LLP partners and corporate shareholders."

[90] RULPA § 303(b)(1).

→ *Shareholders.* We stated above that owners are not agents, and this is true of the owners of a corporation — its shareholders. The shareholders' direct authority is mainly limited to calling a special shareholders' meeting. In publicly-held corporations, federal law provides a shareholder the right of "initiative," that is, to put certain matters before a vote the shareholders' meeting.[91] Shareholders also have indirect authority in that they typically elect directors and vote on fundamental changes when put to them by the directors.

→ *Officers.* In addition to its owners (shareholders), a corporation typically has officers and directors. Officers are *employees* of the corporation and are vested with agency authority by statute, bylaws or resolutions of the board of directors. Typical examples are presidents, treasurers and secretaries. The extent of each officer's actual authority to act on behalf of the corporation will be dependent on the statute, bylaw or resolution creating the position. They may owe additional fiduciary duties to the corporation by virtue of their office,[92] but such duties are not well defined and are probably very similar to duties owed by other high-level employees.

→ *Directors.* Directors are a unique species. They are not agents of the corporation.[93] A single director cannot act on behalf of the corporation by virtue of his or her directorship. The directors may act together, whether at a meeting or by written consent,[94] but when they do so, the more accurate description is that they are acting *as* the corporation, rather than *for* the corporation.[95] In large corporations, directors cannot manage every business decision or even every major business decision; rather, they hire top management and delegate the remainder of the management functions, subject to general oversight through reporting, records, and internal controls.[96] In a closely-held corporation, the directors may mostly or completely overlap with the officers and the shareholders. In this case, much confusion can result if the actors (with the lawyer as their "director" in the theatrical sense) are not careful which role they play.[97]

• *Limited liability company* If you are familiar with the basic rules of partnership authority in a general partnership, and with director and shareholder authority in a corporation, you will understand the management structure choices for a limited liability company. In short, the business planner may choose between management of the LLC by its members (a member-managed LLC) and management by managers chosen by the members (a manager-managed LLC).[98]

---

[91] Professor Clark refers to these rights collectively as "voting rights," to distinguish them from the other two types of shareholder rights: the right to sue, and the right to receive certain reports and information. *See* Robert C. Clark, Corporate Law 94 (1986). The right of "initiative" exists under Rule 14a-8 of the Securities Exchange Act of 1934.

[92] *See, e.g.*, MBCA § 8.42.

[93] Clark, *supra*, at 22 & n. 65.

[94] *See* MBCA §§ 8.20–8.21; Cox & Hazen, *supra*, §§ 9.05–9.06, pp. 414–20.

[95] " 'The directors are the chosen representatives of the corporation, and constitute, . . . to all purposes of dealing with others, *the corporation.* What they do within the scope of the objects and purposes of the corporation, the corporation does.' " Cox & Hazen, *supra*, § 9.04 at p. 410 (quoting Maynard v. Fireman's Fund Ins. Co., 34 Cal. 48, 57 (1857)).

[96] See Clark, *supra*, at 108, Cox & Hazen, *supra* note 15, § 9.02, pp. 392–408.

[97] See *supra* notes 38–39 and the accompanying text, the story of *Blount v. Taft*, and the legal consequences of acting in the proper role.

[98] Most state LLC statutes require the LLC to choose in its articles. Others set a statutory default

→ *Analogies to partnerships and corporations.* The analogies are obvious. The member-managed LLC operates much like (if not identically to) a general partnership. Each member has full management rights and agency powers, just as do general partners.[99] Similarly, the manager-managed LLC operates much like a corporation or a limited partnership. Each member has the right to vote in selecting the managers and to vote on certain other fundamental matters.[100] Beyond those rights, however, the management authority of the members is limited and the agency rights (based on membership alone) are nonexistent, just as with limited partners in a limited partnership or shareholders in a corporation.

→ *Agency and authority consequences.* The management analogies are a consequence of the preexisting structures blended to make the LLC. General partners have full management and agency rights; limited partners and shareholders have very few management or agency rights. It is simply historical coincidence that the two attributes — agency and authority — are linked together.[101]

EXERCISE 2-9

Arthur and Murray plan to be the sole investors in a local dance studio. Arthur is the business type who will concentrate on finding a location, advertising, and legal and financial matters. Murray, a former professional dancer, is the creative genius who will hire and supervise instructors and determine the content of the studio's dance courses, arrange contests, social dances, and the like. Which business form will best allow these two to divide their responsibilities cleanly, with no ambiguity or overlap? Can you think of other matters which might arise in the course of the business about which they haven't yet planned? How should they take unforeseen matters or disagreements into account?[102]

3.   Liability for Debts

As we continue to deal with the life cycle of this business entity, we have now arranged for each investor's contribution and settled the management responsibilities and the financial rewards and consequences. However, the financial consequence of unintended losses is one which the investors perhaps have not considered in great detail.

---

of member management which can be changed in the articles. Still newer statutes, following the lead of Re-ULLCA (see *supra* Section A.5) have dispensed with the member-manager control issue as an organizational concept. *See* Chapter 7, Section D.3.

[99] *See, e.g.,* ULLCA § 4.04(a).

[100] *See, e.g.,* ULLCA § 4.04(b)(3)(i), (c). The list in § 4.04(c) of matters requiring unanimous consent of members applies to member- and manager-managed LLCs alike.

[101] "The linkage between default agency and default management structures in the LLC has existed since the inception of the structure, appears in nearly all of the extant statutes, and is derived from the general and limited partnership laws that combined to create the LLC, a hybrid of the two." Thomas E. Rutledge, *The Lost Distinction Between Agency And Decisional Authority: Unfortunate Consequences Of The Member-Managed Versus Manager-Managed Distinction In The Limited Liability Company*, 93 KY. L.J. 737, 738 (2004). Although Mr. Rutledge believes this "linkage" is an historical accident, he notes that "there is little (if any) likelihood that the linkage between agency and decisional authority will be eliminated from LLC law any time soon (if ever)." *Id.* at 739.

[102] This problem is intended to invoke introductory planning discussion regarding concerns and strategies. The details, including drafting these provisions, are covered in Chapter 7, Section A.

a. Liability in Tort or Contract

The general rules are straightforward. In a partnership, the general partners are liable for all the obligations of the partnership. Limited liability is available by forming a limited partnership, LLP, LLC, LLLP, or a corporation. However, the general rules need some real-world qualification. In many cases, these rules do not provide much protection for a business' owners and managers.

First, consider tort liability. An individual is liable for his or her negligence (or other torts) regardless of the presence of a limited liability entity. Such torts committed in the course and scope of employment will make the employer (usually the entity) liable as well. The other owners or managers may escape liability,[103] but the business might suffer the loss of business assets. Insurance provides some measure of protection for most anticipated injuries from negligence. Indeed, because business assets are important to protect, it is true that even limited liability entities buy casualty insurance.

Second, consider contract liability. A loan or lease entered into by a manager on behalf of the entity binds only the entity. However, the business assets are still at risk, just as with tort liability. In addition, most small business lenders or landlords require individual guarantees (often with security) from the owners and managers of the business.

So, as a practical matter, a limited liability entity will provide insulation only from unanticipated, uninsured (or uninsurable) catastrophic events, and perhaps from contract liability to unsecured creditors, provided the dealing was not tainted with fraud. Still, creating a limited liability entity is nonetheless a worthwhile endeavor, because the cost is very low (the filing and annual fees for the documents discussed in Section B above) and there will be some benefit.

b. Judicial Disregard of a Limited Liability Entity

In addition to liability based on contractual assumption, direct liability, or statutory liability, in some cases courts will simply refuse to recognize the statutory protection provided to the limited liability entity. In the context of corporation law, this refusal is typically known as "piercing the corporate veil" or "disregard of the corporate entity." The doctrine is used by courts to make corporate shareholders liable for corporate obligations despite the general statutory rule to the contrary.[104]

There is very little certainty in judicial doctrines of veil piercing, which means that there is very little which can be done by a business planner to avoid this liability. The doctrine is usually clearly stated by courts: the corporate entity can be disregarded when there is complete control by the individual shareholders of the corporate entity, this control is used to commit fraud or wrong, and this fraud or wrong causes injury to another.[105] Regardless of exactly how the doctrine

---

[103] This conclusion is not at all certain. They might be personally liable under some failure-to-supervise theory for the torts of their partners, employees, or coworkers. There is also the possibility of indirect liability under the "veil-piercing" theory discussed in Subsection 3.b below.

[104] *See, e.g.,* MBCA § 6.22(b) ("Unless otherwise provided in the articles of incorporation, a shareholder of a corporation is not personally liable for the acts or debts of the corporation except that he may become personally liable by reason of his own acts or conduct.").

[105] There are different variations of this test to be sure, but results do not typically turn on the

stated, courts typically examine several factors which are considered relevant in deciding whether the veil should be pierced. The most common are: undercapitalization, lack of observance of corporate formalities, removal of assets from the corporation leaving it unable to pay creditors, personal use and commingling of funds.[106] So really, the best the business planner can do is to advise his or her clients to avoid conduct which arouses the equitable suspicion of courts. In other words, your clients should invest initial capital which appears sufficient given the nature and risks of the business,[107] respect corporate formalities, deal with the corporation as a separate entity, and not remove assets from the corporation leaving it insolvent.[108]

The concept of veil piercing is being expanded from corporation law to the newer forms of limited liability entities: LLCs and LLPs.[109] The analogy is not perfect, however, because these entities are generally understood to have a larger degree of informality "built in" to their structures. It is more difficult disregard formalities in an entity such as an LLC or LLP which is intentionally informal to begin with. But this reasoning might be dangerously inverted upon the unlucky LLC or LLP owner, by a court finding that the entity is almost inherently informal and thus prone to piercing.[110]

"Substantive consolidation" refers to the treatment of a group of related corporations together as one debtor. A corporation which has a wholly-owned subsidiary may find itself liable for the obligations of the subsidiary under this theory. This is much like "veil piercing," but some of the concepts and the judicial reasoning may be different when the shareholder to be held liable is itself another corporation.[111] As a term of art, "substantive consolidation" ordinarily refers to this concept being used in a bankruptcy proceeding where one of the corporations is the debtor, yet the court considers the assets of all the corporations as available for repayment.[112]

---

specific test announced by the court. See Cox & Hazen, supra, § 7.08 at p. 279 ("On close scrutiny, none of the . . . variants of 'piercing the veil' offers precision or a characteristic that distinguishes it from the other[s] . . . .").

[106] There are many other factors; the record for the longest list currently stands at nineteen. Cox & Hazen, supra, § 7.08 at 280–81 & n. 30.

[107] That, of course, is a very difficult call to make. Initially, your clients will be motivated to invest capital based on the financial needs of the business and the desires of the investors for oversight, control, and perhaps even favorable tax treatment. Furthermore, your clients are not likely to want to invest more in the business than is necessary based on your legal conclusion that it would be more "just" to do so. What is important is to avoid the appearance of bad faith, or even lack of good faith, which is what inadequate capitalization is probably trying to indirectly measure. Id. § 7.11 at p. 291.

[108] This last one, of course, is already covered in large part by the law of fraudulent conveyances. See generally Clark, supra, § 2.4 at pp. 71–81 ("Some piercing cases . . . are simply substitutes for fraudulent conveyance actions.").

[109] For an excellent recent summary of judicial decisions and academic commentary and analysis, see Jeffrey K. Vandervoort, Piercing the Veil of Limited Liability Companies: The Need for a Better Standard, 3 DePaul Bus. & Comm'l L.J. 51 (2004).

[110] See Cox & Hazen, supra, § 7.09 at p. 285 ("Limited liability companies pose a greater risk that the entity's veil will be pierced because one characteristic most LLC statutes attempt to accommodate is the greater informality the LLC members seek within that business form over that provided by a corporation."). The same would be true of an LLP, of course, because it is grounded on the even more informal arrangement of a general partnership.

[111] See Cox & Hazen, supra, § 7.16 at pp. 299–308.

[112] We cover bankruptcy planning in Chapter 10.

EXERCISE 2-10

Clyde plans to use a large portion of his personal wealth to buy and operate a Dairy-Freeze franchise. First National Bank will lend some money to the business, but insists upon a personal guarantee from Clyde secured by his personal assets. Clyde will also purchase casualty and liability insurance. Does Clyde put his personal assets more at risk if he runs the Dairy-Freeze as a sole proprietorship, a corporation, or an LLC? What are the benefits and costs of each form to Clyde with respect to avoiding unanticipated liabilities?

4.   Transfer of Interests

The next event which typically occurs in the life of the business entity is a transfer of an interest in the entity from one of the original entrepreneurs. In this area, the business entities differ dramatically from each other, so we must consider first the nature of the interests which owners have in these entities. Next we will consider the default rules governing these transfers. Finally, we will consider how these arrangements might be contractually altered.

a.   The Nature of the Interests in the Entity

In general, an owner has three types of interests in the entity. First, an owner has an interest in receiving payments on account of profits and, to a lesser extent, an interest in being allocated losses. This is the interest which we discussed in Section D above. Second, an owner has an interest in his or her rightful share of the net assets of the entity should it be liquidated. Finally, an owner has an interest in how the entity is managed. Each of these varies in depth and presumption between a partnership and a corporation.

In a partnership, statutes explicitly recognize the right of a partner to share in profits (and losses),[113] to receive a share of the net assets in liquidation,[114] and to participate in the management of the partnership.[115] In the UPA, each partner had certain identified (but small) rights in individual partnership property, but this concept of "tenancy by the partnership" was eliminated in RUPA.[116]

In a corporation, statutes require that there exists a class of stock which holds the right to receive net assets in liquidation, and the right to vote whenever voting is permitted or required.[117] In these respects, the interests of a shareholder are similar to the interests of a partner. However, the interest in profits (or losses) and distributions is less clear in a corporation. Profit and loss shares are not allocated

---

[113] RUPA § 401(b) ("Each partner is entitled to an equal share of the partnership profits and is chargeable with a share of the partnership losses in proportion to the partner's share of the profits."); *accord* UPA § 18(a), ULPA §§ 503–504.

[114] RUPA § 807(a). Much less clear but to the same effect are UPA §§ 18(a) and 40. For the similar rules in a limited partnership, see ULPA § 804.

[115] RUPA § 401(f); UPA § 27(3). As discussed in Section A.3 above, a limited partner typically has more limited management rights than a general partner. *See* ULPA § 303.

[116] *Compare* UPA § 25(1) ("A partner is co-owner with his partners of specific partnership property, holding as a tenant in partnership"), *with* RUPA § 501 ("A partner is not co-owner of partnership property and has no interest in partnership property which can be transferred, either voluntarily or involuntarily").

[117] MBCA § 6.01(b).

to each shareholder in corporations (as discussed in Section C.1 above). And distributions of corporate assets to shareholders are *permitted* but not required.[118]

You might wonder, therefore, how a shareholder expects a return on his or her investment if not through dividends or other periodic payments. In the case of publicly-traded shares, a shareholder may or may not receive dividends,[119] but he or she can always receive payment by selling his or her shares in the market. But publicly-traded corporations are not our concern as business planners. During the initial (non-publicly-held) phase of a business in corporate form, the corporation will be closely-held, meaning that there is no reliable market for the shares. Therefore, providing for distributions by dividends (or other payments to shareholders, such as salaries) will be vital to each shareholder. Without such payments, the shares will have little or no value unless the corporation is liquidated.

An LLC will likely have interests similar to those of a partnership, as the LLC will likely elect to be treated as a partnership for tax purposes. Thus, it needs a method of allocation of profits and losses to each member.[120] It may provide for distributions to members,[121] and the members are entitled to the net assets of the LLC upon liquidation.[122]

b.   Default Rules on Transfer

The statutory default rules vary significantly. In a partnership, the only transferable interest is the partner's "interest in the partnership" which consists of the partner's right to be allocated profits and losses and the right to receive distributions.[123] In a corporation, the share is transferable, which includes (as discussed above) the entire ownership interest: the right to vote and the right to receive distributions (whether periodic or in liquidation). In an LLC, the default arrangement is typically that the member's interest in the LLC follows partnership or partnership-like rules. The ULLCA calls this interest the member's "distributional interest" and provides that only that interest is transferable.[124]

It appears that the partnership and corporation default rules are at two different ends of the spectrum of transferability. On the one hand, shares in a corporation are freely transferable in whole; the recipient "steps into the shoes" of the transferor. On the other hand, partners may not so easily relinquish their status; they may transfer only their right to be allocated profits or losses and to

---

[118]   MBCA § 6.40(a).

[119]   An investor's preference for dividends or no dividends is a matter of individual judgment. Modern finance theory suggests that an investor should be indifferent to the dividend policy of a firm in which he or she invests, because the specific cash return can always be replicated by the investor through sales of all or part of his or her investment in the market.

[120]   *See* Chapter 3 Section E.

[121]   *See* ULLCA § 405.

[122]   *See* ULLCA § 806.

[123]   RUPA § 502. UPA § 26 provides a similar definition of the partner's "interest in the partnership," although it does not include the right to allocation of losses. The UPA does not say that this is the only transferable right, but provides instead that all the other property rights of a partner are *not* transferable. *See* UPA §§ 25(2)(b) (prohibiting transfer of interest in specific partnership property), 18(e) (providing that only partners have management rights).

[124]   *See* ULLCA §§ 502–503; Re-ULLCA § 502.

receive distributions. Membership interests in an LLC could be anywhere along this spectrum. Under the ULLCA the default rules are akin to those governing partnerships. However, these default rules are not particularly important to a good business planner because, in each case, the partners, shareholders or members can agree to modify those rules. The prudent lawyer will discuss with his or her business clients how to handle transfer of interests by agreement. We next consider the limits on contractual modifications to these default rules.

c.   Prohibiting Transfers Otherwise Permitted

First consider whether your clients might want to make *not* transferable an interest which is otherwise freely transferable. Sometimes even the innocuous transfer of a partnership interest could be objectionable. It is true under partnership law that the transferee does not become a partner, nor is the transferor partner relieved of his or her powers or duties. But consider what is left in the hands of the transferee partner after such a transfer. What motivates a partner who has transferred away his or her right to receive profits and other distributions? Perhaps that partner still receives some salary or bonus, but much of the owner's motivation has disappeared. If that is important to the other partners, they might want to prohibit transfer of any partnership interest. The transfer of corporate stock, on the other hand, results in a new owner replacing the old completely. There is no "lame duck" owner without profits interest as there is in the partnership. However, your clients might want to prohibit transfer even of corporate stock to an entirely new investor. A new small business is often a deeply personal commitment by the entrepreneurs. In a small corporation, even shareholders typically have pivotal roles in management, as the lines between shareholder, officer and director are not often carefully drawn. So we see that, in either entity, a good case might be made for prohibiting or restricting transfer of otherwise transferable interests.

Turning first to the partnership interest, can its transfer be prohibited? There is no blanket prohibition of such limitations, but there are reasons why transfer restrictions might be disfavored by a court. A court might, for example, invoke the general common law disfavor of restraints on alienation, or perhaps wonder about the purpose for the restriction since a transferee has limited rights in any event.[125] However, since a partner retains the power to leave the partnership and be paid for his or her interest at any time,[126] there seems to be little reason not to enforce an absolute prohibition on transfer of a partnership interest.

Second, consider corporate stock. Can its transfer be prohibited? In general, the MBCA permits such restrictions if "not manifestly unreasonable."[127] Courts are unlikely to frown on such restrictions, although opinions can be found showing concern about restraints on alienation and overall fairness.[128] In the corporate context, the more important issue is not whether transfer can be prohibited outright, but rather the conditions under which transfer will be permitted. Owners of shares are unlikely to want to prohibit transfer outright, as might be the case in a partnership, because they have no partner-like ability to demand liquidation of

---

[125] Bromberg & Ribstein, *supra*, § 3.05(c)(3)(i) at p. 3:77.

[126] *See infra* Section C.5.

[127] MBCA § 6.27(d).

[128] *See* Clark, *supra*, § 18.2 at p. 764; Cox & Hazen, *supra*, § 14.10, at pp. 844–45.

the entity and payment for their shares. Even if a court would enforce an absolute prohibition, the shareholders are left with an illiquid investment and thus with limited ways to realize a return on that investment. This is an arrangement to which few shareholders would agree. The real problem, ironically, is that even with a *legal* rule of free transferability, there is little or no *practical* ability for the shareholder to sell his or her shares, a problem we deal with in the next subsection.

Finally, consider the LLC. Recall that statutes typically provide for default partnership-type arrangement but permit broader flexibility. Normally only the member's economic interest (like the partnership interest) is transferable, but full transferability of membership and all other rights (just as with corporate stock) can be provided in the operating agreement.[129]

d.   Permitting Transfers Otherwise Prohibited

Next, consider whether your clients would want to make transferable an interest which is ordinarily *not* transferable. Lack of transferability means lack of liquidity. Again, because the default rules differ markedly in each type of entity, we will look at them in turn.

In a partnership, would your clients want to agree to admit the transferee of a partner's interest as a new partner in place of the old? It would be legally possible; the statute requires only unanimous consent of the partners for admission of a new partner.[130] But the partnership's default rules limiting transfer seem to fit the desires of most new small businesses.

In a corporation, would your clients want to change the default rule of free transferability of the entire interest? At first blush, it seems like this rule already provides for the desired liquidity. However, recall that there are likely few if any buyers for shares in a closely-held corporation. These sorts of problems can be handled in court with doctrines prohibiting unjust "freezing out" shareholders, or by creating and enforcing fiduciary duties owed by shareholders in closely-held corporations. But a good lawyer and business planner anticipates these issues and handles the problem ahead of time with a well-thought-out transfer (or "buy-sell") agreement.

Well-written transfer agreements cover all of the following terms:

- Event(s) which trigger the obligation to purchase or sell;
- Purchaser(s);
- Whether the purchase is mandatory or optional;
- Purchase/sale price; and
- Payment terms.[131]

The *events* are typically the voluntary or mandatory departure of a shareholder from his or her position as officer or director, the shareholder's death, or even a desire by the shareholder to sell his or her shares. The *purchaser* may be some or all of the other shareholders, the corporation, or a third party identified by the

---

[129] ULLCA §§ 502–503. Many states have more severe, partnership-like, limitations on transfer. *See* Bishop & Kleinberger, *supra*, § 8.06[2][a][i], pp. 8-102 to 8-103.

[130] *See* RUPA § 401(i)

[131] Each of these options, and the legal rules and strategic considerations, will be discussed in Chapter 8, Section D. There are obviously important considerations in each part of these agreements.

selling shareholder. The obligation is usually either *mandatory* repurchase obligation on the part of the corporation or other shareholders, or a *right* of first refusal (an option to buy) before the shareholder chooses to sell to a third party. These arrangements typically bind the shareholder to sell or to offer the shares first to the corporation, the other shareholders, or both (usually the corporation first). The *price* for the shares can be a stipulated sum, an amount determined by the parties periodically (usually once a year), a formula for a price (based on earnings or some other verifiable number), or an amount determined by a third-party valuator. In the case of a right of first refusal, the price is ordinarily the price at which the third party has offered to pay to the selling shareholder. And finally, the *payment terms* are important to stipulate. It is quite common for the sale to involve a large portion of the stock of the company. Obviously no purchaser is likely to have such a large amount of cash on hand; the sale will need to be financed. Transfer agreements can be combined with a prohibition on transfer otherwise than through these methods,[132] so that the agreement serves as a comprehensive treatment of any disposition of shares.

The transfer of shares in a corporation is further complicated by the many "hats" which the entrepreneurs may wear. In the previous paragraph, we discussed whether a shareholder should be obligated to sell his or her shares if he or she leaves (voluntarily or otherwise) a position of employment or a directorship. The reverse may need to be considered as well: should a shareholder be permitted to retain his or her shares if he or she leaves an office or directorship?

Turning to the LLC, we have the familiar arrangement in most states of statutory default to the partnership rules, but permission to make any other arrangement in the agreement among the LLC members. A member's right in an LLC consists of economic rights and management rights (even in a manager-managed LLC). As with a partnership, the transfer of the economic rights does not presume the transfer of the management rights. However, the operating agreement can reverse this presumption and make the transfer of all economic rights presumably the transfer of management rights as well, substituting a new member for the old.

5.   Dissolution

Finally, we consider the last phase of the entity's life. Unfortunately, we cannot be more precise with the terminology, although we have used "dissolution" in the caption. We caution that you must be unyieldingly precise here. The words "dissolution" and "liquidation" can mean different things under your state's partnership or LLC laws. Those laws may introduce yet another term — "dissociation" — and each of these may differ still from the termination of the partnership under federal income tax law. Again, the rules are different for each type of entity.[133]

---

[132] It will be important, of course, to consider *involuntary* transfer (other than on the shareholder's death, which was mentioned above), which may not be preventable but should be planned for nonetheless. Again, fuller treatment is coming in Chapter 8, Section D.

[133] Further coverage of these topics are in Chapter 8 regarding departure of an owner and the continuation of the business, which is the sense in which "dissolution" is discussed here. The liquidation of the business apart from departure of one or more owners is a different topic covered in Chapter 10.

A partnership is a tenuous thing. The default rule is that any partner may, at any time, dissolve the partnership and demand liquidation of the business.[134] A partner can agree not to exercise these rights. Indeed, since liquidation can be severely disruptive to a nascent business, it is common for partnership agreements to provide that a partner who leaves agrees not to call for liquidation.[135] And although a partner can agree not to leave the partnership, such agreements are *not* specifically enforceable, though damages may be assessed for breach. The Official Comments to RUPA summarize these concepts.

> Section 602(a) provides that a partner has the power to withdraw at any time. The power to withdraw is immutable under Section 103(b)(6), with the exception that the partners may agree the notice must be in writing. This continues the present rule that a partner has the power to withdraw at will, even if not the right. See UPA Section 31(2).[136]

The disruption in a partnership can thus be minimized by a carefully-written partnership agreement, but it cannot be eliminated.

In a limited liability entity, the presumptions are very different. Even in a limited partnership, for example, only the general partner has the rights referred to above. A limited partner's right to withdraw is limited by the partnership agreement.[137] In a corporation, the presumption in favor of continued existence is even stronger. A corporation has perpetual existence unless its articles state otherwise,[138] and dissolution of a corporation ordinarily requires approval by the directors and the shareholders.[139] These presumptions can be reversed, of course. A corporation's articles could provide for a fixed term.[140] More commonly, the shareholders could agree that the corporation will dissolve upon certain occurrences or votes.[141]

The LLC provisions in this area vary significantly.[142] Many states have partnership-like provisions, giving members the right to leave the LLC at any time and cause dissolution. Others, especially those which are based on the ULLCA, permit the members' interests to be made very much like shares in a corporation, that is, no member has any right to dissolve, and the members' interests are

---

[134] This results from the combined work of two different sections. RUPA § 601(1) allows a partner to "dissociate" from the partnership at any time by "express will." RUPA § 801(1) provides that, in this situation, the "partnership is dissolved, and its business must be wound up." For the same rules, see UPA §§ 31(1)(b) and 38(1).

[135] Typically, such language provides that in the event of a partner's departure "the business of the partnership shall be continued by the remaining partners."

[136] Comment to RUPA § 601.

[137] *See* ULPA §§ 602 (withdrawal of general partner), 801(4) (right to continue business of partnership if general partner withdraws), 603 (withdrawal of limited partner).

[138] MBCA § 3.02 (introductory language).

[139] *See* MBCA § 14.02(b).

[140] The danger of such a provision, of course, is that the parties will forget about or ignore it, and will be conducting business as a dissolved corporation, always a risky business because it may result in personal liability for what they thought were "corporate" obligations.

[141] This rather remarkable power is provided explicitly by MBCA § 7.32(a)(7).

[142] Even the terminology is inconsistent; three states use the term "resign," four use the term "withdraw," others, including those patterned on the ULLCA, use "dissociate." Bishop & Kleinberger, *supra*, §8.03[1][a] at pp. 8-16 to 8-17. "Members of California LLCs may either 'withdraw,' 'resign,' or 'retire,' although the terms appear interchangeable." *Id.* at 8-17.

transferable with the recipients becoming members and the transferor no longer a member.[143]

Alternatively, the end of the entity's life may not be an end at all, but rather a new beginning. Even a technical "liquidation" can result in the continuation of the business by some or all of the remaining entrepreneurs who purchase the business assets in the liquidation. And the entity may be reorganized or merged with another entity.[144]

EXERCISE 2-11

A, B, and C agree to enter into a business together. You have worked out the arrangements for management, compensation, and profit-sharing, but the three have other requirements. They would like to promise to stay in business together for three years. They believe it will take this long for the business to "gel" and become profitable, and any departure or rearrangement before then could prove fatal to the nascent enterprise. Thereafter, they would like to require that, if any of them wants to "sell out," that the entity will purchase the interest of that person at a price to be determined by a neutral third party (assume they all agree on who that party should be). Answer the following questions either (a) according to the statutes in your jurisdiction, or (b) using the RUPA, MBCA and ULLCA.

(1)   Will you be able to meet the requirements of these three using a general partnership or LLP? A corporation? An LLC?

(2)   Suppose instead that the three wanted to provide that any one of them could retire at any time and require either (a) a liquidation or (b) the entity to purchase their interest at a price determined by the third party. Will you be able to meet these requirements with an LLP? A corporation? An LLC?

COMPREHENSIVE EXERCISE: CHOICE AND FORMATION OF ENTITY

This exercise focuses on issues relating to the choice from among the many entities discussed in this chapter, and the drafting of documents required to begin business in each form. You represent the client(s) identified in Chapter 1, Exercise 1: Ann, Bev, Carl, the entity which they will form or have already formed, or some or all of the above. Let us assume that the ethical issues have been solved as neatly as possible. We are now ready to consider which type of business entity would likely be the best arrangement to meet the needs identified by each of the parties.[145]

(1)   Prepare a memorandum for a partner in your firm discussing which entity

---

[143] *Id.* at pp. 8-18 to 8-19; *see* ULLCA § 602(a) & Official Comment ("An operating agreement may eliminate a member's power to withdraw by express will to promote the business continuity of an at-will company by removing member's right to force the company to purchase the member's distributional interest.").

[144] *See, e.g.*, UPA Art. 9 (merger of partnerships); MBCA §§ 9.50 (conversion of corporations or other entities into corporations), 11.02 (merger of corporations with other corporations or other entities). In the case of an entity treated as a partnership for federal income tax purposes, reorganization will be governed by those provisions, and tax rules may govern the treatment of a corporate merger or reorganization as well. In addition, reorganizations occur under the federal bankruptcy law. Reorganizations and conversions are covered in detail in Chapters 9 and 10.

[145] *See* Chapter 1.

available in your jurisdiction (*see* Section A of this chapter) would be best suited for the restaurant. Briefly explain why the entity you have chosen is the best and the major disadvantages of the other major candidates.[146]

(2)   Prepare the organizational documents (*see* Section B of this chapter) necessary to begin the operation of the restaurant as a distinct business (if not a separate legal entity). An important part of this exercise is to find and identify good sources of draft documents.

(3)   Prepare a summary of the arrangements to be made among the three investors regarding:

  • *contributions:* what will be "paid" for each investment interest, and how will that consideration be made and valued;

  • *management:* who will have particular duties and responsibilities regarding the business, the finances, the hiring, and so forth, and how disputes will be resolved;

  • *profit sharing (and loss sharing if a partnership or LLC):* what will be the profit and loss shares; how will these be calculated; what will be the result if these are different from the proportionate contributions made by each investor.

  • *transferability:* will any of these rights be transferable? Under what conditions? At what prices?

(4)   Prepare a memorandum for Ann, Bev and Carl explaining the choices you have made in (1) and (3) and describing other decisions they need to make.[147]

---

[146] This is a memo to another lawyer and should therefore contain citations and other legal materials as appropriate.

[147] This is a memo to lay individuals and should be carefully written but devoid of technical legal terms and citations.

Chapter 3

TAXATION AND BUSINESS ENTITIES

A. INTRODUCTION TO TAX CONSIDERATIONS

To fully comprehend the formation, operation, restructuring and dissolution of business enterprises, it is essential to understand the tax consequences that flow from these events. All attorneys who engage in business planning must have, at a minimum, a basic understanding of the tax consequences, even if they are relying on tax experts to advise them. In practice, attorneys who are not experts in tax law will consult with tax professionals to assist in understanding the tax implications of the transactions. Following these consultations, the attorneys are then in a position to advise clients and structure the transactions so as to maximize the tax outcome for their clients. An essential skill of a competent business planning lawyer is *the ability to recognize the need to consult with experts* when he or she lacks sufficient expertise to properly represent his or her clients.

One objective of this chapter is to assist students in gaining an elemental understanding of the tax considerations that arise at the point in time of formation of a business entity. Another objective is to sensitize students to some of the tax pitfalls and problems that confront the participants in forming and operating business entities, so that students recognize common tax-related "red flag warnings" that often arise in these types of transactions. After completing this chapter, students should be able to: (i) recognize some of the common tax issues that arise in business entity formation and operation; (ii) talk intelligently about tax consequences with a tax expert about the tax aspects of the transaction; and, (iii) be in a position to advise clients and draft documents to reflect the tax objectives that are determined following consultation with experts and consulting with clients.

The discussion in this chapter will be divided into two major segments: (i) taxation of income at the entity and equity holder levels; and, (ii) the tax consequences to equity holders when they contribute money, services or property to a business entity, in exchange for equity interests.

Federal taxation of income is governed by the Internal Revenue Code of 1986, as amended, and set forth in Title 26 of the United States Code (sometimes referred to in these materials as the "IRC").[1] The history of modern income tax law starts with the 1916 adoption of the 16th Amendment to the U.S. Constitution, which states: "The Congress shall have power to lay and collect taxes on incomes, from whatever source derived, without apportionment among the several States, and without regard to any census or enumeration."

Prior to the adoption of the 16th Amendment, the ability of the Congress to enact "direct taxes," such as income taxes, was constrained by the Apportionment Clause

---

[1] 26 U.S.C. § 101, *et seq.* There are a few tax matters, such as taxation in bankruptcy, that are partially governed by other titles, such as Title 11.

of Article 1 of the Constitution, which provides: "Representatives and direct taxes shall be apportioned among the several states which may be included within this union, according to their respective numbers, which shall be determined by . . . "[2]

In 1895, the U.S. Supreme Court invalidated tax laws intended to impose a federal tax on income arising from real estate rents, and income from personal property (including dividend income), because of the failure of the federal laws to evenly apportion the collected taxes in accordance with the requirements of the Apportionment Clause.[3] In 1916, approximately 20 years later, on the cusp of the United States entry into World War I, the 16th Amendment was adopted, freeing congress from the constraints of the Apportionment Clause and allowing the implementation of an income tax.

Following the adoption of the 16th Amendment, Congress was free to tax *income* from all sources, including wages, real property, personal property and dividends received from corporate distributions.[4]

Since the implementation of federal income taxation in 1916, corporations and corporate-like entities[5] are commonly taxed as separate legal entities, paying taxes on income at rates set forth in the IRC. In addition, corporations have been subject to *state* income tax liability if the corporation resides or does business within one or more U.S. states.[6] Most states mimic the federal laws governing taxation, although there are significant and multitudinous differences among the 50 states, and the rates of taxation are usually far lower than federal rates. Notwithstanding the existence of state taxation laws, the primary tax considerations for corporations and individuals usually focus on federal taxation, with state income tax implications a secondary consideration. Therefore, we will limit our discussion to the federal tax laws, keeping in mind that a full understanding of the tax issues in real-life transactions requires examination of both federal *and* state tax implications.

Every business entity in the United States that is not a trust[7] (or subject to special treatment under the IRC) is treated, for tax purposes, as either a sole

---

[2] U.S. Constitution, Article 1, Section 2, Clause 3.

[3] *Pollock v. Farmers' Loan & Trust Co.*, 158 U.S. 601 (U.S. 1895).

[4] The 16th Amendment limits Congress taxing authority to *income* taxes, regardless of the source of income:

> [T]he power of the Congress to lay and collect taxes on income is confined to that which is actually and essentially income; and income, as thus used, means the gain derived from capital, from labor, or from both combined. The taxing power in respect to income cannot by legislative definition be extended beyond that scope. That which is not actually and essentially income cannot by definition be subjected to such a tax.

Nicholas v. Fifteenth Street Inv. Co., 105 F.2d 289, 290 (10th Cir. 1939). Income has been defined for tax purposes " . . . as the gain derived from capital, from labor, or from both combined . . . ." Stratton's Independence v. Howbert, 231 U.S. 399, 415 (1913).

> Whatever difficulty there may be about a precise and scientific definition of "income," it imports, as used here, something entirely distinct from principal or capital either as a subject of taxation or as a measure of the tax; conveying rather the idea of gain or increase arising from corporate activities.

Doyle v. Mitchell Brothers Co., 247 U.S. 179, 185 (1918).

[5] Some entities, such as limited partnerships and limited liability companies are subject to being taxed as "C Corporations" under certain conditions. See the discussion of the "check-the-box" rules in Section F.1.a of this chapter.

[6] There may be additional layers of taxation at the municipal or regional level.

[7] *See* 26 CFR § 301.7701-4. Trusts generally do not have equity holders nor an objective to carry on

proprietorship, a corporation or a partnership.[8] This distinction between corporation and partnership taxation is extremely important and can have dramatic financial consequences for the entity and its equity holders.

B. SOME BASIC TAX CONCEPTS

Before we can discuss taxes professionally, we need to understand a few basic tax concepts: (i) income taxes; (ii) capital gains taxes; and (iii) basis.

1.   Income Taxes

All individuals and corporations must pay taxes on the net income earned during the tax year. The rates vary depending upon whether the taxpayer is an individual or a corporation, and the amount of net income earned. As of 2008, the income tax rates for individuals were as follows:[9]

If taxable income is over:	But not over:	The Marginal Tax Rate is:	Effective Tax Rate for Top of Range
Individual Single Filer Tax Rates 2008			
$0	$22,100	15% of taxable income over $0	15%
$22,100	$53,500	$3,315, plus 28% of the excess over $22,100	22.6%
$53,500	$115,000	$12,107, plus 31% of the excess over $53,500.	27%
$115,000	$250,000	$31,172, plus 36% of the excess over $115,000.	32%
$250,000		$79,772, plus 39.6% of the excess over $250,000.	See below

Note that the *effective* tax rate is lower than the marginal tax rate because only the amounts above the threshold for each income range are taxed at that rate. For instance, a single individual with a net income of $150,000 is in the 36% income bracket for all net income over $115,000 (the individual will pay 36% in taxes on each new net income dollar above $115,000). However, that individual will face a *total* tax liability of $43,772,[10] which is only *29%* of the net income of $150,000. As incomes

---

business for profit. IRS Rule 301.7701-4 defines a trust as

> an arrangement whereby trustees take title to property for the purpose of protecting or conserving it for the beneficiaries under the ordinary rules applied in chancery or probate courts . . . Generally speaking, an arrangement will be treated as a trust under the Internal Revenue Code if it can be shown that the purpose of the arrangement is to vest in trustees responsibility for the protection and conservation of property for beneficiaries who cannot share in the discharge of this responsibility and, therefore, are not associates in a joint enterprise for the conduct of business for profit.

[8] *See* 26 CFR § 301.7701-2(a), which states in relevant part:

> [A] business entity is any entity recognized for federal tax purposes . . . that is not properly classified as a trust under § 301.7701-4 or otherwise subject to special treatment under the Internal Revenue Code. A business entity with two or more members is classified for federal tax purposes as either a corporation or a partnership.

[9] IRC § 1. The chart shows the rates only for unmarried taxpayers with no dependents. The rates are different for married couples or individual "head of households" with dependents.

[10] $31,172 plus $12,600 (36% of the amount over $115,000 up to $150,000)

reach around $600,000, the marginal tax rate and effective tax rate become similar. For instance, an individual earning $600,000 pays $218,372 in taxes (an effective tax rate of 36.39%)[11]

Below we will be talking about the impact of income distributions, or the realization of income, by individuals who are equity holders in business entities. *To ease the discussion of the tax implications, we will sometimes assume that all individual taxpayers are in the 33% income tax bracket — so that each new dollar of recognized income will be taxed at 33%.* This will allow us to calculate the impacts by simply assuming that the after-tax cash available to an equity holder who receives income is reduced by approximately one-third. In other words, a taxpayer receiving a distribution of income in the amount of $300,000 will have an income tax obligation of $100,000, leaving the taxpayer with $200,000 in after-tax cash.

As of 2008, the income tax rates for corporations were as follows:[12]

Corporate Tax Rates 2008			
If taxable income is over:	But not over:	The Marginal Tax Rate is:	Effective Tax Rate for Top of Range
$0	$50,000	15%	15%
$50,000	$75,000	$7,500, plus 25% of the excess over $50,000	18%
$75,000	$10,000,000	$13,750 plus 34% of the excess over $75,000	33.88%
$10,000,000		$3,388,250 plus 35% of the excess over $115,000.	about 35%

The effective tax rate for corporations with higher incomes is slightly different than that for individuals. Similar to individuals, corporations pay lower tax rates on the first $50,000 of income (15%) than they do on the next $25,000 of income (25%), etc. However, for corporations with high income, there is a "phase out" of the lower tax rates. As a result corporations with taxable income between $335,000 and $10 million effectively face a flat 34 percent rate, and those with income above $18.3 million are effectively subject to a flat 35 percent rate.

Once again, for ease of our following discussions, we will sometimes assume *that all corporate taxpayers are in the 33% income tax bracket — so that each new dollar of recognized income will be taxed at 33%.* This will allow us to calculate income tax consequences for corporations by assuming that one out of three net income dollars is paid in federal income taxes.

2.　Capital Gains Taxes

When an individual taxpayer disposes of many types of *property* known as "capital assets," capital gains taxes must be paid on any gain realized by the taxpayer. Most types of property in the hands of an individual taxpayer are capital assets. IRC § 1221(a) describes capital assets as "property held by the taxpayer

---

[11] $79,772 plus 39.6% of the amount over $250,000.

[12] IRC § 11(b). There are some surtaxes and exclusions in § 11 that we not be including in our discussions.

(whether or not connected with his trade or business)" and then adds a list of some excluded items. Publication 544 of the IRS states the concept simply:

> Capital Assets. Almost everything you own and use for personal purposes or investment is a capital asset. For exceptions, see Noncapital Assets, later.

> The following items are examples of capital assets.

> Stocks and bonds.

> A home owned and occupied by you and your family.

> Timber grown on your home property or investment property, even if you make casual sales of the timber.

> Household furnishings.

> A car used for pleasure or commuting.

> Coin or stamp collections.

> Gems and jewelry.

> Gold, silver, and other metals.

> Personal-use property. Property held for personal use is a capital asset. Gain from a sale or exchange of that property is a capital gain . . .

> Investment property. Investment property (such as stocks and bonds) is a capital asset, and a gain or loss from its sale or exchange is a capital gain or loss. This treatment does not apply to property used to produce rental income . . .[13]

When an individual sells a capital asset, he or she will have a gain or loss. In the event of a net capital gain for that tax year, the taxpayer will have to pay a capital gains tax on the difference between the value received and the taxpayer's "basis" in the property.[14] For the moment, we can consider the taxpayer's basis to be the amount he or she paid for the property. For instance, an individual who bought stock in Google for $100,000 and later sells that asset for $400,000 would have a $300,000 capital gain. Fortunately for the taxpayer, the capital gains rate is significantly lower than the rate paid on net *income*. As of 2008, the capital gains tax rate for individuals for long-term capital gains (gains on assets held for over one year) was only 15%, compared to approximately 33% for net income.[15]

---

[13] IRS Publication 544, Part 2 (2007). Capital assets are assets held for personal use, not business assets or property used in trade or business.

[14] In the event of a net capital loss, some of the loss may be deductible. In most cases, individuals are limited to $3,000 in *net* capital losses for the year but can carry over any excess loss. That means, if a taxpayer has a $7,000 capital loss and no offsetting capital gains for that year, the taxpayer is limited to $3,000 in deductions this year, but may be able to deduct another $3,000 the following year — or offset the remaining $4,000 loss against future capital gains. In most of our business transaction scenarios, we will be dealing with the impact of capital *gains*, not losses.

[15] Appreciated capital assets that are sold by an individual after being held more than one year (long-term capital gain) will be taxed at a maximum rate of 15%. For the sale of collectibles and small business stock, the rate of taxation for individuals is a maximum of 28%. Appreciated capital assets that are sold by individuals after being held less than one year (short-term capital gain) will be taxed as ordinary income.

Although the capital gains tax rate is significantly lower than the income tax rate, it is a tax to be reckoned with when there is a large difference between the cost of the property and its value at the time of disposition. We will see that this causes some serious problems when equity holders are contributing low-basis property in exchange for their equity interests in a business entity. For example, assume a shareholder contributes property worth $500,000 for stock in a C corporation. The shareholder's basis was $100,000. If the disposition of the property is considered a sale of a capital asset, the shareholder will have to pay approximately $60,000 in capital gains taxes (15% of $400,000). We will discuss this issue in greater detail later in this chapter.

Corporations, on the other hand, receive no preferential treatment for the profits made when capital assets are disposed of. The gain from any sale of capital assets will be taxed at the same rate as income.

3. Basis and Adjusted Basis

"Basis" is the amount of a taxpayer's investment in property for tax purposes and is used to figure to figure gain or loss on the sale or other disposition of property. Adjusted basis is the taxpayer's cost of acquiring the property, increased by certain additional improvements to the property, and decreased by certain deductions taken by the taxpayer. The adjusted basis will always be important in the case of capital assets when trying to determine whether, upon disposition of the asset, there is gain or loss from the transaction.

The computation of basis is simple if the taxpayer pays cash for the asset. The basis will be the purchase price of the asset (including related costs to close the transaction). However, in non-cash or mixed-cash acquisitions, the basis will be more difficult to determine. It will be computed by adding the sum of any cash paid, plus the equity value of any property exchanged, plus the value of any services given in exchange, plus the value of any obligation incurred, plus any other value given in exchange for the ownership interest in the asset. There may be times where capital assets are acquired in non-purchase transactions, such as *inter vivos* gifts, testate or intestate succession or employment bonuses.[16] In such cases the basis is usually determined by the fair market value of the asset at the time the taxpayer receives it. There are also some special situations where the new owner's basis in the capital asset is *not* adjusted to fair market value but remains the previous owner's adjusted basis in the asset. Can you see why the new owner would not be happy if the basis isn't readjusted to current fair market value?

In the case of publicly traded stocks and bonds, the basis is usually the purchase price plus the costs associated with the purchase, such as commissions and recording or transfer fees. In the case of non-publicly traded business investment units, such as corporate shares, partnership interests, limited liability company membership interests or similar equity investments, the basis is the sum of cash, plus the equity value of any property contributed, plus the value of any services, plus the value of any obligation incurred or other source of value transmitted to the

---

[16] For instance, at the end of the calendar year, a company gives an employee a brand new car. If the car is later sold by the employee, there will be gain or loss depending upon the price received and the employee's basis.

entity in exchange for the ownership interest. In the case of real property, it's the cost of acquiring the property, including many of the costs and fees paid by the buyer as part of the acquisition.

In the case of intangible assets, such as goodwill, patents, copyrights, trademarks, and trade names, the basis is usually the cost to buy or create it. This may result in a very low basis for the *creator* of many types of intangible property. An individual or entity that develops a business with multi-million dollar good will, trademark recognition or copyrights may have done so at relatively low cost. A sale of that intellectual property may result in a large gain.

Before figuring gain or loss on disposition of property there may be adjustments to the basis of the property. Increases will result from additional costs of adding to physical improvements or maintaining intangible property. In the case of investment interests in business entities, the basis may be increased by additional amounts paid to the entity as capital contributions (not loans to the entity). Decreases may result from deductions that the taxpayer has taken with regard to the capital asset, such as depreciation, and casualty losses. In the context of business investments, the basis may be decreased by some of the amounts of cash or property transferred to the investor by the entity. For now, we just need to simply understand that the taxpayer's "basis" may be increased or decreased by the occurrence of certain events. The essential importance of knowing the adjusted basis is determining whether or not there is a gain or loss upon disposition of the asset.

C. C CORPORATION ENTITY LEVEL TAXATION

1. The Problem of Double Taxation

Taxation of *corporations* is governed by IRC § 301 *et. seq.* (commonly referred to as "Subchapter C") which treats corporations as independent tax paying entities, separate from the corporation's stockholders.[17] This means that *profits* earned by the corporation will be taxed twice: (i) once when the corporation earns profits, and (ii) again when after-tax profits of the corporation are distributed to shareholders as dividends.

An example can help to fully understand the problem of double taxation of C corporations. Imagine a corporation with 650 shareholders[18] that has net earnings of $100 million during it's fiscal year. As a tax-paying entity, the corporation will be required to pay federal income taxes of approximately $33 million, leaving $67 million for distribution to its stockholders after payment of corporate income taxes.[19]

---

[17] 26 USC § 301. Subchapter C is nested in the following hierarchy within the IRC: Subtitle A: Income Taxes → Chapter 1: Normal Taxes and Surtaxes → Subchapter C: Corporate Distributions and Adjustments. Corporations taxed under Subchapter C are commonly referred to as "C Corporations."

[18] To simplify the discussion, assume that all of the shareholders are individuals, rather than a mix of individuals and legal entities (such as trusts, corporations, partnerships, etc.)

[19] We are using a 33% income tax rate throughout this chapter for the sake of simplicity. The actual rates paid by a corporation are set forth in 26 U.S.C. § 11(a) which provides: "[a] tax is hereby imposed for each taxable year on the taxable income of every corporation." The tax rates for corporations as of 2007 were the sum of: (A) 15 percent of so much of the taxable income as does not exceed $50,000, (B) 25 percent of so much of the taxable income as exceeds $50,000 but does not exceed $75,000, (C) 34

When the corporation distributes some or all of the remaining profits (the "after-tax" profits) to its shareholders as dividends, the distribution constitutes income for the *shareholders*. Each shareholder must include the dividend income on his or her tax return and pay appropriate taxes.[20]

In our example, the 650 individual shareholders, will each receive income of about $100,000, if all of the after-tax earnings are distributed.[21] Each shareholder will then have to pay income taxes on these distributions. Assuming individual tax rates of about 33%, that means that each shareholder must pay taxes of about $33,000, leaving each shareholder with about $67,000 after taxes. From the perspective of each shareholder, after adding together the taxes paid by the corporation and the taxes paid by the shareholder, the combined tax rate on his or her share of the earnings of the corporation is a stunningly high 56%.[22]

As we will see, if the shareholders had operated the business as a partnership, limited liability company, limited liability partnership or limited partnership, this double level of taxation could be easily avoided and the effective tax rate dramatically reduced, leaving each equity holder with about $108,000 after taxes. That's $41,000 more than they would receive if the entity is taxed as a C corporation.

The double taxation problem appears again when C corporations sell assets, or distribute them to shareholders upon liquidation of the corporation. The sale or disposition of assets is a taxable event and the corporation must pay taxes on any increased value of the assets above the cost basis of the assets. Because there is no preferential tax treatment for *corporate* capital gains, as compared to income, the corporation will pay taxes at the rate of approximately 33%. Shareholders will then have to pay taxes on any of the gain distributed or received by them. If, for example, a corporation acquired real property assets for $1 million and sold the property for $4 million, the corporation would pay taxes on the gain of $3 million (at the tax rate of 33%). When the after-tax gains are then distributed to shareholders, the shareholders will also pay taxes on their share of the distribution. This can have a devastating impact on the amount of after-tax value to shareholders.

---

percent of so much of the taxable income as exceeds $75,000 but does not exceed $10,000,000, and (D) 35 percent of so much of the taxable income as exceeds $10,000,000. 26 U.S.C. § 11(b).

[20] Every individual and corporate entity must file a tax return. Individuals file a Form 1040 or 1040A, reporting dividend income on Schedule B.

[21] The corporation may elect not to distribute *all* of the after-tax earnings. It is common for a corporation to retain a portion for use in future operations, capital acquisitions, or as a reserve for future contingencies.

[22] Dividend tax rates have been temporarily reduced to alleviate some of this double taxation problem for C corporations. See the next section of this chapter. In this hypothetical, the corporation had pre-tax income of $100 million ($154,000 per shareholder). After payment of taxes by both the corporation and the individual shareholder, each shareholder ends up with only $67,000. The effective tax rate, from the perspective of the shareholders, was about 56%.

2.   Some Temporary Relief from the Double Taxation Problem

In 2003, The Jobs and Growth Tax Relief Reconciliation Act of 2003[23] provided capital gains and dividends tax relief to individual taxpayers by lowering rates on most capital gains and dividends. The Tax Increase Prevention and Reconciliation Act of 2005[24] extended these lower rates to 2010. Together, the Acts accomplished two goals. First, the capital gains tax rates for individuals were dramatically reduced to 15% for most long-term capital gains.[25] In addition, there was a temporary reduction in the tax rate applied to dividends distributed by corporations. Rather than paying taxes at the normal income tax rates for individuals, the rates for dividends received from domestic corporations and certain qualified foreign corporations were substantially reduced. Rather than dividends being taxed at the ordinary income rates (as high as 39.6% by 2008) the *maximum tax* rate for qualifying dividends was reduced to 15% most people — and less for individuals in the lower income brackets.

The reduction of the rate of taxes paid on dividends has caused a substantial reduction in the "double-taxation problem." Nevertheless, the problem is not eliminated and remains worthy of discussion for several reasons. First and foremost, the 15% dividend rate merely *reduces* the impact of double taxation but does not eliminate it. If the corporation has substantial income, it will be taxed at the rate of 35% prior to distribution and taxed again at the 15% rate when distributed to individual stockholders. The double taxation will still cause the taxpayer to end up with less after-tax cash in his or her pocket than if the income was taxed only once (as it is in partnership type entities or Subchapter S corporations). In addition, there are other impediments to taking advantage of the reduced dividend rate:

(i) Sunset provisions: The lower tax rates on dividend income will expire at the end of 2011.[26] Unless made permanent by some future Congress, these new provisions will fade into the sunset, and the rules on the taxation of dividends will revert back to the old rules (ordinary income taxed at normal tax rates).

(ii) Qualifying Dividends: To receive the lower tax rate, the dividends must be received from a domestic corporation or a qualified foreign corporation.[27] Dividends paid to policyholders by insurance companies don't qualify, nor do dividends paid by several other types of entities such as dividends paid by cooperatives to their patrons, dividends taxpayers elect to take into account as investment income, dividends received from charitable, religious and scientific organizations exempt from tax IRC § 501, dividends paid by a mutual savings bank, dividends paid and held by

---

[23] 108 P.L. 27 (2003).

[24] 109 P.L. 222 (2005).

[25] There are several rates for capital gains, ranging from 5% for lower income taxpayers, to 28% for certain "collectibles and some other properties. However, the 15% rate is the most common rate for middle class and upper class taxpayers disposing of long-term capital assets.

[26] The 2003 Act originally had a sunset date of 2008. The date was extended to 2011 by the 2005 Act.

[27] A qualified foreign corporation is incorporated in a U.S. possession or in a country that has a current tax treaty with the U.S., and meets several other qualifications.

an employee stock plan. Dividends received from mutual funds can be passed along to taxpayers at the lower dividend rate only to the extent received by the mutual fund from qualifying dividends from stock held by the mutual fund.

(iii) <u>Holding period</u>: To qualify for the lower rates on dividends, individuals must hold the stock for more than 60 days during the 120-day period that begins 60 days before the ex-dividend date. The ex-dividend date is the last date on which a shareholder of record is entitled to receive the upcoming dividend.

In summary, the double taxation problem has been partially reduced but not eliminated by the Jobs and Growth Tax Relief Reconciliation Act of 2003.

3.   C-Corporation Taxation — Reducing the Impact of Double Taxation

Are there ways of reducing the impact of double taxation of C corporations? Lawyers and accountants have worked hard on this issue and have come up with some strategies to respond to the problem: (i) accumulate earnings without paying dividends; (ii) distribute earnings to shareholders in the form of payments for services; (iii) distribute earnings in the form of rents, or installment contract payments, for the lease or sale of property by the stockholder to the corporation; or (iv) file for "Subchapter S" status.[28]

a.   Accumulating Earnings Without Paying Dividends

One possible solution is to simply avoid the payment of dividends to shareholders in profitable years by retaining the profits within the corporation and not making dividend distributions to stockholders. Although the *corporation* will have to pay income taxes for profits earned during the year, shareholders will not be receiving any dividend income and won't be liable for taxes. The retained profits can be used for capital projects, future operations or simply held by the corporation in bank or investment accounts. Of course, the shareholders will have to forego the cash income until a dividend is paid but at least the profits are being used productively by the corporation without a second level of taxation diminishing the available funds. This strategy of retaining cash in the corporate coffers has the added benefit of tending to increase the value of the shares of the corporation, since the retained cash increases the overall assets of the corporation. Shareholders can reap the benefit of this added value by selling their shares of stock. *Capital gains* taxes will have to be paid on the difference between the sales price and the shareholder's basis in the stock (usually the cost of acquisition). This can be advantageous since the capital gains rate is usually far lower than the rate

---

28 26 U.S.C. § 1361 *et. seq.* The common reference to "Subchapter S" arises from the following chain within the structure of the IRC: Subtitle A (Income Taxes) → Chapter 1 (Normal Taxes and Surtaxes) → Subchapter S (Tax Treatment of S Corporations and Their Shareholders). If a corporation and its shareholders meet the requirements for a Subchapter S election, and all of the shareholders consent, the shareholders may elect to be treated more like a partnership with only one level of taxation at the individual level, rather than an additional level of taxation at the corporate-entity level. There are several requirements to qualify for Subchapter S status. Three of those requirements often prevent S elections for many corporations: (i) there can be no more than 75 shareholders, (ii) there can only be one class of stock (including non-conventional loans by equity holders); and (iii) all shareholders must be individuals. S elections are discussed in greater detail in Section D of this chapter.

paid on dividend income. Currently the dividend and capital tax rates are the same (15% in most cases). However, if the 15% dividend rates expire in 2010, there is a considerable advantage to receiving value from the corporate investment in the form of capital gains (taxed at 15%) rather than income (usually taxed at much higher rates).

The strategy can backfire by triggering the IRC "accumulated earnings" tax penalties. The IRC imposes a penalty surcharge (plus interest) on earnings retained "for the purpose of avoiding the income tax with respect to its shareholders . . . by permitting earnings and profits to accumulate instead of being divided or distributed," rather than being retained for the reasonable needs of the business.[29] There is no limit on the amount of profits that a corporation may retain for legitimate needs such as expanding the business, funding operations and capital acquisitions but to the extent that the retention is part of a scheme to avoid double taxation, the accumulated earnings tax may be assessed against the corporation.

The IRC and Treasury Regulations treat accumulations of $250,000 or less as within the reasonable needs of most businesses ($150,000 for service businesses)[30] and not subject to the accumulated earnings tax. However, for overall accumulations in excess of these amounts, the absence of a *bona fide* business reason for a corporation's accumulated earnings may be indicated by many different circumstances, such as a lack of regular distributions to its shareholders or withdrawals by the shareholders classified as personal loans.

The bottom line is that the decision to retain earnings in excess of the actual and reasonable needs of the business is an imperfect strategy for avoiding double taxation of profits and may subject the corporation to the unexpected and unpleasant imposition of an accumulated earnings tax. The adoption of a retained earnings strategy must be carefully analyzed by tax specialists to assess the possible adverse tax consequences.

b.   Salaries vs. Dividends: Distributing Earnings to Shareholders in the Form of Salaries for Services

Another strategy for avoiding double taxation is to pay profits to stockholders in the form of salaries and bonuses for services rendered by the stockholder as an *employee* of the corporation. Corporations pay income taxes only on the *net* taxable income earned by the corporation, after deduction of expenses.[31] In general terms, the taxable income of the corporation is computed by deducting ordinary operating expenses from the gross income derived from sales, services or other earnings of the business. Deductible expenses include items such as the cost of acquiring inventory, manufacturing costs and employee salaries. To the extent that expenses

---

[29] IRC §§ 531–37. The rate of the penalty is keyed to the corporate dividend rate. The dividend rate is *temporarily* fixed at 15%. However, the rate may rise dramatically in the event that the current 15% dividend rate expires in 2010

[30] Corporations performing services in the fields of accounting, actuarial science, architecture, consulting, engineering, health (including veterinary services), law, and the performing arts.

[31] IRC § 162(a)(1) provides that: "[t]here shall be allowed as a deduction all the ordinary and necessary expenses paid or incurred during the taxable year in carrying on any trade or business, including — (1) a reasonable allowance for salaries or other compensation for personal services actually rendered . . . "

are deducted, the overall profits of the corporation will be reduced and the tax obligations will be reduced proportionally. Assuming a corporation is taxed at approximately 33%, every $3 worth of deductions will reduce the taxes of the corporation by about $1.

A corporation that sells $1 million in goods but has operating expenses of $800,000 will have taxable income of $200,000 and will pay taxes of approximately $60,000, leaving $140,000 for post-tax distribution to shareholders in the form of dividends. This $140,000 will be taxed *again* when distributed to shareholders. What if just prior to the end of the tax year, the corporation paid two of its employees a bonus of $100,000 each? This additional $200,000 expense would reduce the net income of the corporation to $0, since it would have total expenses of $1 million, equal to the amount of its gross income. The corporation would pay no income taxes. Now, suppose that the recipients were the two primary shareholders of the corporation, Ann and Bob. Ann and Bob would have received $100,000 each in income from their earnings as "employees" of the corporation and they will have to pay income taxes on those earnings. However, the corporation will not, eliminating the entity level of taxation.

Payments to stockholders in the form of salaries and bonuses are often legitimate expenses of a closely held corporation, paid in exchange for services rendered by the stockholders in their role as employees of the corporation. However, there are times that the IRS will treat excessive payments of salaries or bonuses paid to stockholders as *constructive* dividends intended to avoid the entity level of corporate taxation.[32] Distinguishing between legitimate employee expenses and constructive dividends to employee-stockholders is a factual question, that is determined in light of all of the circumstances.[33] The essential question is whether the payments to employees are reasonable and are, in fact, payments purely for services.[34] Seven factors that tend to indicate the payments are constructive dividends, and not deductible, are:

— whether the corporation has only a few shareholders, practically all of whom draw salaries.
— the employee's qualifications
— the size and complexity of the business
— whether the shareholder actually rendered services to the corporation that normally draw that level of compensation
— whether the payments are in excess of those paid to employees in other companies for similar services
— whether the payments correspond or bear a close relationship to the stockholdings of the employees (are the salaries paid in proportion to stock ownership)
— whether salaries in prior years fluctuate in relation to profits.[35]

---

[32] Treas. Reg. § 1.162-8. A "constructive dividend" is any payment made by a corporation to a shareholder, even if no formal dividend has been declared. Truesdell v. Commissioner, 89 T.C. 1280, 1295 (1987).

[33] Pacific Grains, Inc. v. Commissioner, 399 F.2d 603 (9th Cir. 1968); Hoffman Radio Corp. v. Commissioner, 177 F.2d 264 (9th Cir. 1949) Owensby & Kritikos, Inc. V. Commissioner, 819 F.2d 1315 (2d Cir. 1987).

[34] Treas. Reg. § 1.162-7(a); Botany Worsted Mills v. U.S., 287 U.S. 282 (1929).

[35] Elliotts, Inc. v. Commissioner, 716 F.2d 1241 (9th Cir. 1983); Mayson Mfg. Co. v. Commissioner, 178 F.2d 115 (6th Cir. 1949).

The Seventh Circuit Court of Appeals took a different, minority viewpoint in *Exacto Spring Corp. v. Commissioner.*[36] In a well known but controversial opinion authored by Judge Posner, the court refused to apply the seven-point test. In *Exacto*, a closely held corporation paid its cofounder, chief executive, and principal owner a total of $2.3 million in salary over a two year period. The IRS reduced it by more than half, adding the difference to the corporation's income, and assessed a tax deficiency. The Tax Court found that the maximum *reasonable* compensation was about halfway between his $2.3 million and the IRS's amount. The Seventh Circuit reversed, applied an "independent investor" test that resulted in the $2.3 million salary being held *presumptively* reasonable:

> When, notwithstanding the CEO's "exorbitant" salary (as it might appear to a judge or other modestly paid official), the investors in his company are obtaining a far higher return than they had any reason to expect, his salary is presumptively reasonable. We say "presumptively" because we can imagine cases in which the return, though very high, is not due to the CEO's exertions. Suppose Exacto had been an unprofitable company that suddenly learned that its factory was sitting on an oil field, and when oil revenues started to pour in its owner raised his salary from $50,000 a year to $1.3 million. The presumption of reasonableness would be rebutted. There is no suggestion of anything of that sort here and likewise no suggestion that Mr. Heitz was merely the titular chief executive and the company was actually run by someone else, which would be another basis for rebuttal.
>
> The government could still have prevailed by showing that while [the CEO's] salary may have been no greater than would be reasonable in the circumstances, the company did not in fact intend to pay him that amount as salary, that his salary really did include a concealed dividend though it need not have. This is material (and the "independent investor" test, like the multifactor test that it replaces, thus incomplete, though invaluable) because any business expense to be deductible must be, as we noted earlier, a bona fide expense as well as reasonable in amount. The fact that [his] salary was approved by the other owners of the corporation, who had no incentive to disguise a dividend as salary, goes far to rebut any inference of bad faith here, which in any event the Tax Court did not draw and the government does not ask us to draw.[37]

Under either test, when paying salaries and bonuses to shareholder-employees, the question is whether or not the compensation is the same as that which the corporation would have agreed to pay for like services by non-shareholder employees at the time that the contract for services was entered into. Bonuses and contingent payments (such as commissions) are deductible so long as the compensation is paid pursuant to a bargain between the parties made before the services are rendered and not influenced by considerations on the part of the corporation other than that of securing, on fair and advantageous terms, the services of the individual.[38]

---

[36] 196 F.3d 833 (7th Cir. 1999).

[37] *Id.* at 839.

[38] Treas. Reg. §§ 1.162–7(b), 1.162–9.

Keep in mind that reasonable salaries, benefits and bonuses paid to stockholder-employees for actual services rendered to the corporation are fully deductible by the corporation and will reduce the tax burden at the entity level. In this regard, it makes sense to structure appropriate salary plans for stockholders who will be employees of the corporation. To the extent that payments to employees are truly compensation for services rendered, the payments are deductible by the corporation. However, schemes to avoid double taxation by re-categorizing dividends as employee salaries will subject the corporation to adverse tax consequences.[39]

c. Rent vs. Dividends: Distributing Earnings to Shareholders in the Form of Rent

Another strategy that reduces taxable income at the entity level is to pay rent to shareholders for real or personal property that is leased to the corporation. Legitimate rental payments at *reasonable* market rates will avoid the problem of double taxation.[40] Rental payments to a shareholder in the form of rent will constitute taxable income to the shareholder but will be deducted as an expense by the corporation, reducing the corporation's income by a commensurate amount.

There may be a temptation to funnel profits of the corporation to some shareholders, and avoid double taxation, by having the corporation lease property from shareholders and distribute earnings to the shareholders in the form of excessive "rent." For instance, a corporation leasing retail space from a shareholder might enter into a percentage rent lease under which the corporation will pay a higher rent when the business of the corporation is profitable and less when the business is unprofitable. This would accomplish the objective of avoiding double taxation by linking rental payments to the earnings of the corporation. However, the IRS is cognizant of these types of attempts to avoid corporate taxes. To the extent that the rental payments under the lease exceed fair market rental value and do not reflect reasonable rental terms that would be negotiated in an arms-length commercial transaction, the excess payments can be determined by the IRS to be non-deductible, constructive dividends.[41]

d. Interest vs. Dividends: Distributing Income to Shareholders in the Form of Debt Payments

Interest on debts paid by a C corporation is deductible as an ordinary and necessary expense of the corporation.[42] So long as the payments are categorized as interest, they will reduce the net income of the corporation, thereby reducing the entity level of taxation. However, if the interest payments are merely part of a

---

[39] It makes sense to plan for the possibility of the IRS recharacterizing excessive payments to a stockholder-employee as a constructive dividend. Many closely held corporations have provisions in their bylaws, or other documents, that obligate shareholder-employees to repay any excess amount to the corporation in the event of an adverse determination by the IRS. The repayment is deductible by the shareholder in the year of repayment. Oswald v. Commissioner, 49 T.C. 645 (1968).

[40] IRC § 162(a)(3) allows the deduction of: "rentals or other payments required to be made as a condition to the continued use or possession, for purposes of the trade or business, of property to which the taxpayer has not taken or is not taking title or in which he has no equity."

[41] *Id.; see also* Treas. Reg. § 1.162-11. Common methods for establishing the reasonableness of the rent would be the use of appraisers and market comparisons. Sparks Nugget, Inc. v. Commissioner, 458 F.2d 631 (9th Cir. 1972); Audano v. U.S., 428 F.2d 251 (5th Cir. 1970).

[42] IRC § 163.

scheme to avoid double taxation, they may be characterized by the IRS as constructive dividends, the deduction is lost and the corporation must pay taxes on the amounts paid out as "interest."

When interest is paid to a commercial lender there is little doubt that the interest can be deducted from gross income, reducing the taxable income of the corporation. This would be equally true if the lender happened to be a stockholder of the corporation, so long as the loan from the stockholder was on normal commercial terms and not contingent on profits of the corporation or otherwise keyed to factors other than normal commercial loan payment terms.

Investors often structure their initial contributions to a C corporation in the form of *both* equity and debt. By doing so, the investors seek to avoid double taxation of amounts paid to them by the corporation in the form of interest. In addition, repayments of *principal* to lenders by the corporation *do not constitute a taxable event* for the lender-shareholder. Rather, repayments are merely a return of principal. This allows investors to obtain, in addition to interest on their loans, a return of some of the funds that they used to capitalize the corporation, without payment of income or capital gains taxes.

For example, suppose three investors each have $100,000 to contribute to the startup of a new corporation. The investors are planning to contribute $25,000 in exchange for shares of stock and *loan* $75,000 to the corporation. The promissory notes evidencing the loans will provide for interest at market rates of 10% and the notes will be self-amortizing over a 10 year period, with monthly payments of principal and interest of $991.[43] The corporation will be funded with a total of $75,000 in equity and $225,000 in debt. If the debt was owed to a commercial lender, there is no doubt that the interest payments would be deductible by the corporation. Should the outcome be the same if the debt is owed to the three shareholders in proportion to their equity investments? If the answer is yes, then this might be a legitimate way to pass some corporate earnings to the shareholders without double income taxation, as well as return some of the invested funds without capital gains tax. Over the course of ten years, the $75,000 in principal will be repaid, without any taxes due by the investor, and each investor will be paid a total of $43,935.66 in interest. Although taxes will be paid by the investor on the *interest* received, the corporation will deduct the interest payments as expenses, reducing its taxable income by the same amount and thereby avoid double taxation.

The starting point for answering the question of whether interest payments are legitimate, or constructive dividends, is whether or not the debt is structured as normal commercial debt, with terms similar to what the corporation would obtain in the outside lending marketplace. If payments are contingent on profits (or if the corporation makes payments only when there are profitable periods but fails to do so at other times), then the debt is probably a disguised form of equity investment

---

[43] Self-amortizing means that payments of principal and interest will, over the period of the loan, reduce the loan balance to zero. Note that the monthly payment of $991 exceeds the interest due for the first month of $625 (10% of $75,000, divided by 12 months). The difference, $366, is a repayment of principal. The second month, the balance of the loan will be reduced by $366 to $74,634. Monthly interest on this amount is only $623, so a larger proportion of the $991 payment will be credited towards principal. Over the 10 year term of the loan, the proportions will continue to change until, on the date of the last payment, principal will be reduced to zero.

and interest payments may be determined by the IRS to be constructive dividends.[44]

When will the IRS honor stockholder loans as debt and, on the other hand, when will the IRS treat stockholder loans as equity contributions?Section 385 of the IRC, aptly titled "Treatment of certain interests in corporations as stock or indebtedness," helps to answer this question by granting the IRS the authority to prescribe regulations to help determine whether a debtor-creditor relationship exists or a corporation-shareholder relationship exists, based on factors including the following:

1. whether there is a written unconditional promise to pay on demand or on a specified date a sum certain in money in return for an adequate consideration in money or money's worth, and to pay a fixed rate of interest,
2. whether there is subordination to or preference over any indebtedness of the corporation,
3. the ratio of debt to equity of the corporation,
4. whether there is convertibility into the stock of the corporation, and
5. the relationship between holdings of stock in the corporation and holdings of the interest in question.[45]

In the early 1980s, proposed regulations were released by the IRS, but eventually withdrawn.[46] Nevertheless, the five factors listed in IRC § 385 and explained in the proposed regulations have evolved into generally accepted guidelines for answering the question of when debt owed to shareholders might be considered equity. No single factor is determinative or relevant in every case. One court explained the nature of the inquiry:

> The identified factors are neither equally significant nor is any single factor determinative or relevant in each case . . . The "real issue for tax purposes has long been held to be the extent to which the transaction complies with arm's length standards and normal business practice." *Estate of Mixon v. United States*, 464 F.2d 394, 403 (5th Cir. 1972). "The various factors * * * are only aids in answering the ultimate question whether the investment, analyzed in terms of its economic reality, constitutes risk capital entirely subject to the fortunes of the corporate venture or represents a strict debtor-creditor relationship." *Fin Hay Realty Co. v. United States*, 398 F.2d 694, 697 (3d Cir. 1968). We have stated that the ultimate question is, "was there a genuine intention to create a debt, with a reasonable expectation of repayment, and did that intention comport with the economic reality of creating a debtor-creditor relationship?" *Litton Business Systems, Inc. v. Commissioner*, 61 T.C. 367, 377 (1973).[47]

Cases are "all over the map" on when debt will be considered equity. However, looking at the five factors in § 385, for shareholder loans to survive scrutiny by the IRS, at a minimum the terms of the loans must be similar to those that would be

---

[44] Even if the face terms of the promissory notes are "straight" in format, if the debt is convertible into equity or otherwise part of a direct or indirect plan to tie payments to equity interests, the "interest" is generally not deductible. IRC § 163(l).

[45] IRC § 385(b).

[46] The proposed regulations can be found at 47 F.R. 163 (Jan. 5, 1982).

[47] Calumet Industries, Inc. v. Commissioner, 95 T.C. 257, 286 (1990).

obtained from a commercial lender and payments must not be conditioned on earnings.

One serious consideration, particularly when the debt is proportional to the equity holdings of the shareholders, is the degree of debt funding compared to the amount of equity capitalization. A *high* debt to equity ratio tends to make the loan look like equity financing, particularly if the payment of the debt obligations is unrealistic for the corporation. The proposed regulations set forth a "safe harbor" test that has become a standard among tax professionals. If the corporation's debt owed to shareholders does not exceed three times equity, and the overall debt of the corporation to all lenders (including shareholders) does not exceed ten times equity, then the debt to equity ratio will not be considered excessive and the debt is less likely to be considered equity. Prudent planners and tax professionals will, therefore, make sure that the debt to equity ratio for funds contributed by shareholders won't exceed three to one: 75% debt and 25% equity.

In summary, it is advantageous for investors in C corporations to structure their contributions so that some or all of the stockholders loan money to the corporation, in addition to purchasing shares in the corporation. When doing so, it is important to keep certain key factors in mind: (i) the terms of the loans must be evidenced by standard commercial promissory notes, with terms of payment that reflect market conditions; (ii) the corporation and shareholders must actually treat the loans as debt, making payments on time regardless of profits; (iii) the debt to equity ratio for funds received from shareholders should not exceed three-to-one; and (iv) the debt should be as straight as possible, without tying arrangements to convertibility. Keep in mind that the ultimate test is whether there was a genuine intention to create a debtor-creditor relationship, with the corporation obligated to pay the debt, or a corporation-shareholder relationship, with distributions intended to be keyed to corporate profits.

4.   C Corporations and the Problem of Losses

Subchapter C corporations are taxed as separate entities with respect to both profits *and* losses. If the corporation suffers a loss of income during the tax year, it cannot pass the loss to its shareholders as a deduction for the *shareholder*. This makes sense since, ultimately, the shareholders are not at risk for this loss of income and don't really suffer a "loss" of income that they can deduct on their tax returns.[48]

The inability to pass along losses from a C corporation to its shareholders is a serious tax consideration. Many business entities incur losses during the early years of operations and, in the realm of taxation, these losses can be valuable and desirable assets for the equity holders *if* they can be "passed-through" by the business entity to the equity holders. For a taxpayer who is being taxed on income

---

[48] The corporation's losses may affect the *value* of the shares of stock held by the shareholders but the shareholders cannot deduct this decrease in value on their tax returns unless they dispose of their stock interest and suffer a loss (if the stock is sold for less than the stockholder's basis in the stock). Ultimately, if the shareholder sells the shares and suffers a loss from the sale, the shareholder will have a *capital* loss that the shareholder can offset against capital gains or deduct on the shareholder's tax return.

at the rate of approximately 33%, every $3 of deductible[49] passed-through losses results in $1 in *after-tax* cash in the pocket of the taxpayer. Here's an example:

> Imagine that Jane, an individual, earned $300,000 last year from her employment and investment income. Assuming a tax rate of about 33%, Jane's federal tax liability will be $100,000, leaving Jane with after-tax cash of $200,000. Suppose that Jane also had a *loss* of $60,000 from an Internet business that Jane runs as a sole proprietor. Jane is the sole operator of the business and devotes significant amounts of effort to operating the business. If Jane could deduct this loss on her income tax return, it would reduce her tax liability by about $20,000, resulting in a federal tax liability of only $80,000 rather than $100,000.[50] Notice that this means Jane would have $220,000 in after-tax cash. Compare the following two outcomes:
>
> a. Jane earns $300,000 and has no deductible losses: Jane has taxable income of $300,000 and must pay $100,000 in taxes. Jane will be left with $200,000 in cash after she pays her taxes.
>
> b. Jane earns $300,000 and has deductible losses of $60,000: Jane has taxable income of only $240,000 and will pay only $80,000 in taxes. Jane received $300,000 in actual income, so she will have $220,000 in cash after she pays her taxes.

Jane's loss in this scenario was a result of her operating an Internet business as a sole proprietor who actively managed the business and, therefore, there will be no serious impediments to her deducting the loss on her tax return. However, what if the loss of income was Jane's proportional share of an Internet business operating as a *C corporation*? Jane would be unable to deduct the loss on her tax return and would have lost $20,000 in after-tax cash. This would be an unnecessary sacrifice that could easily be avoided. If losses were foreseeable when Jane was planning her Internet business, it should have occurred to her, and/or her lawyer, that it would be best to structure the business in a way that would allow losses to be passed through to Jane, such as a partnership, limited liability company or a Subchapter S corporation.

What if Jane's lawyer advised her to form a C corporation to operate the Internet business so that Jane could avoid personal liability for the debts of the corporation — and failed to warn Jane about the adverse tax consequences?[51] A lawyer of ordinary competence engaged in the formation of business enterprises should be well aware of this basic tax consideration and advise his or her client regarding the matter. It would surely be malpractice for Jane's lawyer to fail to advise her about these tax considerations in connection with choosing the form of entity to operate the business.

In the realm of business investments, losses are valuable assets that form part of the financial calculations that investors will consider when deciding whether or

---

[49] Not all business losses are fully deductible in the year incurred. See the discussion of passive activity loss limits and at-risk loss limitations in Section G of this chapter.

[50] If Jane earned $300,000 but lost $60,000, her net taxable income for the year would be $240,000. In the 33% tax bracket, her tax obligation would be $80,000 (a savings of $20,000 as compared to a tax obligation of $100,000).

[51] Interestingly, as a single shareholder, Jane can easily form a corporation and avoid the pitfalls of Subchapter C taxation by electing Subchapter S status. See the discussion of Subchapter S in Section D of this chapter.

not to invest in a business entity. High-income investors, particularly investors with *income* from other investments,[52] will be searching for investment opportunities that provide them with deductible *losses* that can be used to offset some of their income and reduce their tax obligations. Sometimes, investments that will generate loss deductions will be referred to as "tax shelters," and a significant part of the marketing scheme for sale of investment units in these types of businesses may be the availability of loss deductions for investors. The term "tax shelter" has neither a positive nor a negative connotation. It simple describes investment in a business enterprise that will generate deductible losses for an investor.[53]

Consider, on a larger scale, a proposed venture with 150 individual equity holders. The financial plan for the business predicts losses in the first five years of approximately $15 million ($100,000 per equity holder). If this business is organized as a C corporation, no investor will be able to use the deductions to offset income and increase his or her after-tax cash position. This constitutes an after-tax cash loss of about $30,000 per shareholder during the five year period. With proper foresight and planning, this entity might have been structured as a partnership or limited liability company which, as we shall see, can pass through these losses to the equity holders so that they can be used as deductions on the equity holders tax returns — putting more after tax cash in the investors' pockets.

D. SUBCHAPTER S CORPORATIONS

Operating a business enterprise as a C corporation can have seriously negative tax consequences. One solution to the tax problems is to form a general partnership, limited partnership or limited liability company and achieve the preferable tax goal of passing through profits and losses. However, *non-tax* considerations relating to financing, control, management, transferability, continuity of life and unlimited liability may weigh in favor of choosing a corporate business entity. In addition, prior to 1997, it was not always clear that the election of partnership pass-through taxation for a limited partnership or LLC would be honored by the IRS.[54]

There is another method to achieve the goal of pass-through taxation for closely held "small business" corporations. Under some circumstances, a small business corporation and its shareholders can elect tax treatment under Subchapter S of the IRC.[55] Subchapter S offers some of the advantages of partnership taxation, while allowing the equity holders to operate the business as a corporate entity. Profits and

---

[52] The deduction of passed-through losses is always available when the income being offset is from other investment-type activities known as "passive" activities. However, the deductibility of passed-through losses may be postponed to future years if the income being offset is from wages and some other sources. See the discussion of passive activity loss limits in Section H of this chapter.

[53] The Tax Reform Act of 1986, instituted significant changes that restricted the use of tax shelter investments to generate loss deductions. Pub. L. 99-514, 100 Stat. 2085 (1986). These and other restrictions (passive activity loss limitations and at-risk loss limitations), are discussed later in this chapter.

[54] See the discussion of limited partnership and LLC taxation later in this chapter. Until the check-the-box rules were adopted in 1997, it was unclear whether or not pass through taxation was available to limited partnerships with corporate general partners, or to LLCs that did not meet the inflexible, bulletproof restraints of Wyoming-type LLC statutes.

[55] 26 USC § 1361 *et. seq.* Subchapter S is nested in the following hierarchy within the IRC: Subtitle A: Income Taxes → Chapter 1: Normal Taxes and Surtaxes → Subchapter S — tax Treatment of S Corporations and Their Shareholders.

losses will be passed through without taxation at the entity level.[56]

The qualifications and procedural requirements for S corporation status are particular and exacting. Great care must be taken to assure that all the requirements for the election are satisfied and that the election is made in a timely manner for the first tax year. In future years, the qualifications for the election must be monitored to make sure that S corporation status is not lost through inadvertent changes in the stockholders or stock structure that disqualify the entity's S corporation status.

Before examining the requirements, it's worth emphasizing the potentially catastrophic consequences if the corporation is operated as a pass-through entity under Subchapter S but the election is invalid, or terminated, because of a failure to meet the qualification and filing requirements. Suppose that a business was incorporated on January 1st of this year. The financial plan for the corporation was to elect Subchapter S status but, unfortunately, the Subchapter S election was improperly made, or some of the qualification requirements were not satisfied, although all of the stockholders and corporate management believed the election was valid. If the business of the corporation is successful, profits will be passed through without payment of income taxes at the corporate entity level. If the business in unprofitable, losses will be passed through to the stockholders. Suppose that one or two years later, the IRS determines that the S election was not valid. What would the result be? In the case of profits, the *corporation* will owe past-due income taxes (plus interest and penalties) for the prior years. In the case of losses, the *shareholders* will owe past-due income taxes (plus interest and penalties) on the income that was offset by the deduction of the losses on their tax returns. In either case, there may be substantial sums of money due to the IRS.[57]

When planning the organization of a Subchapter S corporation, the lawyer and accountant must make sure that all of the highly restrictive requirements for the Subchapter S election are satisfied, and that the strict timing requirements of the IRC are observed.

1.   The Requirements for Subchapter S Status

The requirements for making and retaining a Subchapter S election are set forth in § 1361 and § 1362 of the IRC. They are listed briefly below then discussed more fully in the following pages:

(1)   the corporation cannot have more than 100 shareholders,

(2)   all shareholders must be individuals, although there are some exceptions for estates and certain types of tax-exempt organizations, estates, pension plans and family trusts,[58]

---

[56] IRC § 1366. Prior to the rise of LLCs, S corporation status was highly appealing to closely held businesses, since it offered investors the advantages of a corporation (continuity of life, limited liability, centralized management and transferability of investor interests) while allowing investors to take advantage of many attributes of partnership pass-through taxation.

[57] The IRS has adjusted its stance on the consequences of a late or imperfect S election. As of 2007, there is a simpler process for requesting relief for late elections under a change instituted by Revenue Procedure 2007-62. There are also procedures for dealing with "inadvertent" terminations and avoiding the adverse consequences of the unintended loss of S corporation status. See the more in depth discussions of these matters later in this chapter.

[58] *See* IRC § 1361(b)(1)(B).

(3)   the corporation cannot have a nonresident alien as a shareholder,

(4)   the corporation may have only one economic class of stock (differences in voting rights are allowed but there must be identical rights to distribution),

(5)   *all* shareholders must consent to the election in writing at the time of the election, and

(6)   a timely filing of the S election must be filed with the IRS.

a.   The Shareholders of S Corporations

The first three requirements are not as simple as they first appear. At the time of the election, the attorney or accountant handling the case must carefully count the number of shareholders and make sure that they are all individuals (none of whom are nonresident aliens), or an estate of an individual, or one of the permissible types of tax-exempt organizations, or trusts, allowed by the IRC. When counting to determine whether the 100 person limit is satisfied, individuals spouses and their estates can be treated as "one" shareholder, as can lineal family members and their estates.[59]

Following the election, transfers of shares by any means, whether voluntary, involuntary, testamentary or intestate, must be monitored to assure that the number of shareholders does not exceed 100, and that there are no transfers to unqualified shareholders. When there are close to 100 shareholders,[60] this monitoring may be difficult. What would the result be if there are 100 shareholders and one of them: (i) voluntarily conveys one half of his or her shares to a buddy? (ii) dies, leaving his or her shares to two nieces? (iii) dies and leaves his or her shares to a non-qualified organization? (iv) involuntarily has his or her shares seized as part of a debt collection action and the shares are sold to an incorporated, for-profit collection agency? or (vi) shares are sold to a non-resident alien?

If there are 101 shareholders at any time, or if a single share is transferred to a non-resident alien or an unqualified non-individual, the exemption will be terminated, converting the tax status of the corporation from partnership type taxation under Subchapter S to Subchapter C. Fortunately, Treasury Regulations allow for the possibility of relief for such inadvertent termination of S corporation status:

Treas. Reg. § 1.1362-4   Inadvertent terminations.

(a)   In general. A corporation is treated as continuing to be an S corporation during the period specified by the Commissioner if —

(1)   The corporation made a valid election . . . and the election terminated;

(2)   The Commissioner determines that the termination was inadvertent;

(3)   Steps were taken by the corporation to return to small business corporation status within a reasonable period after discovery of the terminating event; and

---

[59] IRC § 1361(c)(1)–(2).

[60] Counting is not a problem in the vast majority of S corporations. It has been estimated that 88% of S corporations have two or fewer shareholders.

(4) The corporation and shareholders agree to adjustments that the Commissioner may require for the period.

Nevertheless, Subchapter S status needs to be vigilantly monitored and proper precautions taken when drafting the original formation documents to assure against inadvertent transfers to unqualified stockholders. For instance, the formation documentation should limit the ability of shareholders to freely transfer shares without first obtaining review and approval from the company's management (who will consult with a lawyer or accountant), to assure against inadvertent loss of S status *before* the transfer is completed.

b. One Class of Stock

A major constraint imposed on S Corporations is that they may have only one class of stock. While differences in *voting* rights are allowed, the financial structure of the corporation cannot directly or indirectly give some shareholders preferential rights to payments from the profits or assets of the corporation.[61]

Since many closely held corporations have only one class of common stock, this may not seem like much of a concern but, in fact, this is a difficult requirement to satisfy if some of the capitalization of the corporation is in the form of debt financing. Typically, problems arise when a shareholder has loaned money to the corporation and, as a creditor, is entitled to receive a priority of payment from the profits of the business. For instance, suppose three people form a corporation and each contributes $100,000 in exchange for shares of stock. In addition, one of the shareholders loans the corporation $250,000 and the corporation signs a promissory note agreeing to repay this debt. The note is drafted so that payments by the corporation are to be paid only if the corporation has earned enough profits to make the payment. Under such circumstances, the promissory note is really a mechanism for giving the lending shareholder a preferential distribution for the $250,000 he or she has made available to the corporation. The IRS will treat such a preferential right to payment as a second class of stock and the S election will be retroactively invalidated. Since this can occur years after the election was made, the potential for a large assessment for past due taxes is likely.

Note that a loan to the corporation would *not* be considered a second class of stock if it was ordinary, "straight" debt from a bank or commercial lender that was unrelated to the profitability of the corporation.[62] The terms of a standard, commercial promissory note would require payment of interest and principal at

---

[61] See Treas. Reg. § 1.1361-1(l)(1), which states:

. . . [A] corporation is treated as having only one class of stock if all outstanding shares of stock of the corporation confer identical rights to distribution and liquidation proceeds. Differences in voting rights among shares of stock of a corporation are disregarded in determining whether a corporation has more than one class of stock . . .

[62] IRC § 1361(c)(5)(B) defines "straight debt" as:

[A]ny written unconditional promise to pay on demand or on a specified date a sum certain in money if —

(i) the interest rate (and interest payment dates) are not contingent on profits, the borrower's discretion, or similar factors,

(ii) there is no convertibility (directly or indirectly) into stock, and

(iii) the creditor is an individual (other than a nonresident alien), an estate, a trust described

specific times, regardless of whether the corporation was profitable or not. For instance, a bank might loan the corporation $250,000, for a term of ten years, at an interest rate of 10%, with monthly payments of principle and interest of $3,304. Such a true loan is not a mechanism for preferring one shareholder over another but merely a debt of the corporation that must be paid, unrelated to the sharing of profits.

This would also be true if the loan was from a shareholder, rather than a bank if, but only if, debt repayment is structured along terms similar to a standard commercial loan and, in fact, payments are made by the corporation as though it was a standard commercial loan.[63] If, during the lifetime of the corporation, there is evidence that payments are made only when there are profits, the loan will be treated as a second class of stock, even if the paperwork mimics traditional commercial loan terms.

The one-class-of-stock requirement will often block the use of Subchapter S when one or more of the equity holders are moneyed investors who are contributing large amounts of cash and expect to be given priority over other equity holders if there are profits, or upon sale or liquidation of the corporation's assets. Any attempt to set up a preferential payment scheme in favor of those moneyed investors will constitute a second class of stock and invalidate the S election. This would be true regardless of the direct or indirect nature of the distributional preference, if the effect is to give preferential treatment to an investor based upon the presence or absence of profits, or the sale or liquidation of the corporate assets. Buy-sell agreements among the shareholders, or stock redemption agreements between the corporation and shareholders, do not necessarily create a preferential right to payment. However, the Treasury Regulations make clear that if these types of agreements are structured to create preferential economic distributions among shareholders based on corporate profits or liquidations, they will be viewed as a second class of stock and the S election will be invalidated.[64]

Similarly, the S election would be lost if an employment agreement with a shareholder was intended to shift cash or assets to that shareholder in the form of "wages" or "bonuses" based on profits, or sale/liquidation of corporate assets, rather than in exchange for actual services rendered to the corporation. The Treasury Regulations state that *any* type of agreement will be viewed as creating a second class of stock if the "principal purpose of issuing or entering into the instrument, obligation, or arrangement is to circumvent the rights to distribution or liquidation proceeds conferred by the outstanding shares of stock."[65]

One situation that commonly arises with regard to the viability of an S election is the proportional financing of a corporation with both debt and equity. What would the outcome be if the corporation was structured so that three shareholders each contributed $10,000 in exchange for shares of stock and, in addition, each

---

in paragraph (2), or a person which is actively and regularly engaged in the business of lending money.

[63] Bargained for variations from commercial loans, such as lower interest rates, don't impact the determination so long as the debt is not conditioned on profits.

[64] Treas. Reg. § 1.1361-1(l)(2).

[65] Treas. Reg. § 1.1361-1(l)(4)(ii)(A)(2).

loaned the corporation $70,000?[66] Theoretically, there would be two classes of stock in the highly-likely event that the debt obligations were not "straight" debt. However, this type of debt, if held solely by the stockholders in the same proportion as the outstanding stock of the corporation, is not treated as a second class of stock by the IRS, since all shareholders are receiving the same share of profits and are liable for the same proportional extent of losses.[67] The objective of the one-class-of-stock requirement is to assure that there are no preferential rights to economic treatment among the shareholders.

c.   Timing and Shareholder Consents

In the case of a newly formed corporation, the election must be made within two and one-half months following the beginning of the corporation's taxable year which commences at the earliest of: (a) the date the corporation first had shareholders; (b) the date the corporation first had assets, or (c) the date the corporation (entity) began doing business. For instance, if the articles of incorporation are filed on March 1st and shares are issued on March 4th, the election must be made no later than May 19th. All shareholders must consent in writing at the time of the election on May 19th.

In the case of an existing corporation, the election must be made prior to the commencement of the corporation's current tax year or within the first two months and fifteen days of the current tax year (March 15th for corporations with a calendar based tax year)

A failure to make the election in a timely fashion will result in the election being effective for the *following* tax year, not the current one. This means that the lawyers and accountants must be vigilant to make sure that the normal formation procedures are quickly followed by the filing of the S election with the appropriate shareholder consents. Fortunately, there is now readily available relief for late elections under IRC § 1362(b)(5) if there was "reasonable cause for the failure to timely make such election . . . " In 2007, the IRS adopted Revenue Procedure 2007-62, which allows small businesses that missed filing the S election form to file the form contemporaneously with the corporate income tax return, although the taxpayer must technically justify the establish "reasonable cause" for making a late election.

Despite the ready availability of relief for negligently failing to file the S election on time, no lawyer or accountant wants to *rely* on potentially excusable neglect as an antidote to the failure to timely make the election.

d.   The Stability of Subchapter S Elections — Disqualification in Future Years

Following a successful S corporation election, the restrictive requirements of Subchapter S must be observed consistently or the S election will be lost.[68] As discussed earlier, if there are changes such that the number of stockholders

---

[66] This type of debt-to-equity funding of the corporation may have some advantages for the equity holders of C Corporation, as discussed earlier in in this chapter.

[67] Treas. Reg. § 1.1361-1(l)(4)(ii)(B)(2).

[68] IRC § 1362(d)(2).

exceeds 100, or a second class of stock is issued,[69] or shares are sold to a nonqualifying stockholder, the S corporation status will be lost as of the date of the disqualifying event. If disqualification occurs, and the corporation does not succeed in reversing the inadvertent termination within a reasonable time, the corporation is not be eligible to make another S election for five years.[70] In view of the potential economic losses if the election is lost, it is important that lawyers and accountants properly advice clients about the need to avoid changes in corporate structure or ownership that might trigger the disqualification of the S election.

E.   TAXATION OF PARTNERSHIPS

Unlike corporations, which are taxed under Subchapter C, partnerships are governed by Subchapter K of the IRC and are not treated as entities for purposes of taxation. IRC § 701 states:

Partners, not partnership, subject to tax

§ 701   Partners, not partnership, subject to tax

A partnership as such shall not be subject to the income tax imposed by this chapter. Persons carrying on business as partners shall be liable for income tax only in their separate or individual capacities.[71]

This is known as "pass through" or "conduit" taxation. The business entity is considered a mere conduit, with both income and losses being passed through to the partners. In profitable years, each partner reports his or her allocable share of income on his or her income tax return. In unprofitable years, losses are allocated to the partners, who will each seek to use the losses on his or her tax return to offset income from other sources. The partnership pays no taxes, and receives no loss deductions, but will file an annual information return,[72] reporting the allocations of income, losses and other tax attributes.

1.   Partnership Income

With respect to partnership *income*, the partners avoid the problem of double taxation since there is no tax at the entity level. However, the partners must pay income tax on profits that are *allocated* to them, regardless of the amount of cash actually *distributed* to them.[73] This can cause serious problems for cash-strapped

---

[69] Keep in mind the broad definition of "one class of stock" discussed earlier in this chapter.

[70] IRC § 1362(g). Under some circumstances, another S election might be allowed in less than five years following an inadvertent termination, if consent is obtained from the IRS. However, the corporation has the burden of establishing that under the relevant facts and circumstances, the Commissioner should consent to a new election. Consent ordinarily is denied unless the corporation shows that the event causing termination was inadvertent and not reasonably within the control of the corporation or shareholders having a substantial interest in the corporation. Treas. Reg. § 1362-5(a).

[71] 26 U.S.C. § 701 *et. seq.* Subchapter K appears in the following chain within the IRC: Subtitle A (Income Taxes) → Chapter 1 (Normal Taxes and Surtaxes) → Subchapter K (Partners and Partnerships).

[72] The partnership's tax return is I.R.S. Form 1065, "U.S. Return of Partnership Income," which computes the overall profits or losses for the partnership's fiscal year. Attached to Form 1065 are Schedule K-1's for each of the partners, containing the allocational share of profit or loss for that partner. The partnership then furnishes a copy the relevant Form K-1 to each partner.

[73] IRC § 702.

partners. Suppose a general partnership has ten partners and net income of $1 million during the first year of operations, which was last year. Rather than distributing the profits to the partners, the money has been placed in reserve for this year's operations or used to purchase equipment and inventory. Despite the fact that there was cash profit of $1 million, there is no actual *money* being distributed to the partners from last year's profits. Nevertheless, the partners will be allocated a proportional share of the profits. Each partner will have to report $100,000 in income on his or her income tax return and pay approximately $30,000 in taxes, even though the partner received no actual cash distribution from the partnership. This can be a serious problem for partners who don't have $30,000 sitting around when taxes are due on April 15th. For these reasons, when drafting partnership agreements, it is common to provide some procedural mechanism for assuring that in profitable years, sufficient cash distributions are made to cover the taxes that each partner will incur by virtue of the pass through of profit. In our example, it is important that each partner receive $30,000 in distributions to cover the income tax liability each partner will incur as a result of being allocated $100,000 of income.

2. Partnership Losses

Partnership *losses* are passed through to the partners, who may then deduct the losses on their tax returns.[74] As discussed earlier, this will have beneficial tax consequences for partners with income to offset. In general, for each $3 of losses allocated to a partner, the partner will receive $1 of after-tax cash in his or her pocket. This is one of the great advantages of partnership taxation as compared to taxation of C corporations. The pass-through of losses by a partnership can be valuable assets when used by investors to reduce their tax obligations for income they have earned from other sources during the tax year. A passed-through loss of $100,000 would be worth approximately $30,000 to a partner able to deduct the loss on his or her tax return.

The pass-through of partnership profits and losses makes conceptual sense when viewed from the perspective of the Uniform Partnership Act of 1914, which characterized a general partnership as an "aggregate" of the individual partners, rather than as a separate tax-paying entity.[75] From a tax perspective (prior to adoption of RUPA in 1997), general partnerships are conceptually different from corporations in four essential ways:

---

[74] There may be limits on the amount of a partner's loss deduction. See 26 U.S.C. § 465 and the discussion of "at risk loss limitations" in Section G of this chapter. Under the at-risk loss limitations, losses can only be deducted to the extent that a partner is actually at risk for the losses suffered. The total of all losses deducted by a partner over the term of his or her participation in the partnership cannot exceed the amount of the partner's basis in the partnership, measured by the partner's capital contributions and share of the debts of the partnership as allocated by the partnership agreement. See also 26 U.S.C. § 469 and the discussion of "passive activity loss limitations." To the extent that a partner is not actively participating in the management of the partnership, the losses deducted in any tax year may be limited and postponed to future tax years.

[75] The Uniform Partnership Act of 1914 was promulgated by the National Conference of Commissioners on Uniform State Laws ("NCCUSL") and adopted by 49 states (not Louisiana). A new Act was adopted by NCCUSL in 1992 and amended in 1993, 1994, 1996 and 1997. The final 1997 version is known as the Revised Uniform Partnership Act (RUPA) and has been adopted in about 35 states, according to the NCCUSL. In its original form the UPA did not classify general partnerships as separate legal entities.

<u>Continuity of Life:</u> Corporations have perpetual continuity of existence, unrelated to the lives of the stockholders of the corporation. General partnerships, on the other hand, are voluntary associations of partners who join together to operate a business and are dissolved if there are changes in the composition of the general partners such as death, withdrawal or transfer of a partner's interest.

<u>Centralized Management:</u> Corporations are centrally managed by a board of directors, who might or might not be composed of stockholders. Although shareholders retain some rights to remove or elect board members, and to vote on major changes in the fundamental structure of the entity, corporations are managed independently from the ownership interests of the stockholders. On the other hand, general partnerships are managed by all of the general partners and *only* by the general partners.

<u>Transferability of Equity Interests:</u> Corporate shares of stock are freely transferable. Ownership can be shifted from one stockholder to another, without interrupting the legal existence of the corporate entity. In general partnerships, a transfer of a general partner's ownership interest without the consent of the other partners will trigger a dissolution. The partnership and the composition of its partners are inseparable.

<u>Limited Liability:</u> A corporation's stockholders are insulated from liability for the corporation's debts, compared to a general partnership where the general partners are, ultimately, fully liable for all of the debts of the partnership.

These four essential distinctions highlight the traditional distinctions between a corporation, which is an independent legal entity that is subject to entity-level taxation, and a general partnership, which lacks an identity and characteristics of an entity that is separate and distinct from its equity holders. As we shall see, for a substantial period of time, these four distinctions played an important role in taxation of some business entities.

F.   TAXATION OF LIMITED PARTNERSHIPS AND LIMITED LIABILITY COMPANIES

While it was undisputed that *general* partnerships were entitled to freedom from entity-level taxation, the outcome was not always so clear with regard to *limited partnerships* and *limited liability companies.* These hybrid type entities could, depending on their characteristics in particular cases, be seen as having more of the characteristics of a corporation than a general partnership. Until 1997, it was possible that the IRS might treat a limited partnership or limited liability company as a *C corporation,* subject to double taxation, despite the expectations of the promoters and investors that the entity be taxed as a partnership.

A limited partnership or LLC may have been planned by its promoters, and marketed to investors, based on the financial advantages of being taxed as a partnership. However, years later, the IRS might *retroactively* re-classify the entity as a C corporation. Such a reclassification could have devastating consequences for the limited partnership, or LLC, as years of unpaid "corporate" taxes would become due, together with interest and penalties. Such an unexpected re-classification could put a company out of business.

1. Limited Partnerships

To fully understand the problem, suppose a limited partnership, "Iconics L.P.", was formed on January 1, 1995, with one general partner and nine limited partners, each sharing equally in the profits and losses of the limited partnership. The general partner was a corporation organized in the same state as the limited partnership. The investment strategy for the formation and operation of Iconics L.P. was based on the intention of the constituents to be taxed as a partnership under Subchapter K. During 1995 and 1996, Iconics L.P. earned profits of $1.5 million each year and paid no tax at the entity level. For each of those two years, the partners were allocated $150,000 in profit and all of the partners reported that income in their tax returns (filed in April 1996 and April 1997 respectively). For tax years 1995 and 1996, each partner would have paid income taxes of about $50,000 on the income the partner was allocated. Iconics L.P. paid no taxes and merely filed an appropriate partnership information return.

In May 1997, for reasons discussed below, the IRS made a determination that the election by Iconics L.P. to be taxed as a partnership was improper and, in retrospect, the entity should have been paying taxes as a Subchapter C corporation. This would mean that, as of May, 1997, Iconics L.P. would owe entity-level, past-due federal taxes of approximately $1 million, plus substantial interest and penalties.[76] What would the outcome be if, in May 1997, Iconics L.P. didn't have the cash to pay the tax debt or had to use cash reserves that were needed for future operations or acquisitions? Such a large, unplanned for expense could destroy the viability of the venture.

The adverse effects of being retroactively reclassified as a C corporation would have equally disturbing impacts even if Iconics L.P. suffered *losses*, rather than profits, prior to the reclassification. Suppose that during 1995 and 1996 Iconics L.P. suffered losses of $1.5 million in each year. Operating as a Subchapter K partnership, the losses would have been passed along to the partners who, in turn, would have deducted their proportional share of those losses on their income tax returns for the 1995 and 1996 tax years. This means that each of the ten partners would have retained after-tax cash of $50,000 in 1995 and another $50,000 in 1996.[77] If, in May 1997, it was determined by the IRS that the entity should be taxed as a C corporation, then the earlier pass-through and deduction of losses by the partners was improper. As of May, 1997, each partner would owe a total $100,000 in past-due taxes for 1995 and 1996, plus interest and penalties. Imagine the reaction of the limited partners when they discover in May 1997 that they each must immediately come up with well over $100,000 in cash to pay these tax obligations.

---

[76] Iconic L.P. earned *profits* of $3 million during 1995 and 1996. Assuming a federal tax rate of about 33%, Iconic L.P. would owe close to $1 million in entity-level taxes.

[77] Assuming a tax bracket of about 33%, each equity holder receives $1 of after-tax cash benefit for each $3 of deduction. Since the ten partners are sharing equally in profits and losses, each partner would have received an allocation of $150,000 in loss deductions in both 1995 and 1996 ($1.5 million divided by 10). The after-tax cash benefit over two years would be $100,000 for each partner. For purposes of this discussion, assume that all ten equity holders can deduct the full amount of their share of the losses. Passive activity loss limitations, discussed later in this chapter, may restrict the ability of some investors to fully deduct the loss in the year that it occurs.

Why might the IRS determine that a limited partnership such as Iconics L.P. should be taxed as a corporation under Subchapter C, rather than a partnership under Subchapter K? Prior to January 1, 1997, the answer to this question was dependent on whether or not the entity, even though technically a partnership, had too many characteristics of a corporation. After all, at the heart of *general* partnership taxation was the concept that the general partners were fully liable for the debts of the partnership and the entity itself lacked the kind of solid, independent existence that was the hallmark of a corporation. In the case of *limited* partnerships, the IRC was willing to treat all of the partners, general or limited, as entitled to pass through taxation, so long as the limited partnership had *at least one general* partner who was at risk for the debts of the entity. When, however, the general partner was a corporation, the limited partnership entity could be seen as the equivalent of a corporation in substance, regardless of its form.

In our example, Iconics L.P. was formed with a corporation serving as the general partner of the limited partnership. This was a common technique to insulate the individual promoters who put together the limited partnership would be acting as the general partner after formation. Liability for the debts of the limited partnership would stop at the shield of the corporation and no *person* would be liable for the debts of the limited partnership. Only the assets of the limited partnership, and the assets of the corporate general partner, would be at risk. If the corporate general partner was an independent corporation with substantial assets, then the corporation could be perceived as a general partner liable for the debts of the partnership and the partnership would be taxed as a Subchapter K partnership. On the other hand, if the corporate general partner lacked substantial independent assets, and was formed primarily to serve as a liability shield, then it was possible the IRS might assert that there really was no general partner at risk for the debts of the partnership.

For tax purposes, limited partnerships with *individual* general partners would not face the risk of being taxed as a corporation, since there was no shield against liability for at least one general partner. However, if a limited partnership was formed with a corporate general partner, there some serious risk of the IRS reclassifying the tax status from Subchapter K to Subchapter C. This uncertainty about tax classifications placed some constraints on the use of limited partnerships as investment vehicles when limited liability was an important objective. The financial advantages of pass-through taxation could be achieved only if there was an individual at risk, or if there was a well-funded, independent corporation acting as the general partner. There are few individuals (or business entities) willing to put their life savings (or corporate wealth) at risk to serve as the general partner of a potentially risky, start-up investment venture.

Prior to January 1, 1997, it was unclear whether or not a limited partnership might be reclassified as a corporation by the IRS if the entity had more than two of the four classic characteristics of a corporation (continuity of existence, centralization of management, liability for entity debts limited to entity property, and free transferability of interests).[78] If it did, then, on balance, the entity might

---

[78] 26 CFR 301.7701-2(a)(1)–(2) (1996). Treas. Reg. § 301.7701-2(a)(1) (prior to revisions in 1997). These regulations were commonly referred to as the "Kintner Regulations" and are discussed in Section A.5 of Chapter 2. The Kintner Regulations also provided, in part: "Whether a particular organization is

be taxed as a corporation. We will see later in this chapter that this problem was eliminated by the adoption of the "check the box" rules, effective January 1, 1997.

2. Taxation of Limited Liability Companies

The quest for limiting liability for *all* of the investors in a venture influences the structuring of many business entities. While this is easily accomplished by forming a corporation, the unappetizing tax implications have pushed promoters and their lawyers to come up with creative ideas to accomplish a perfect synergy of limited liability and pass through taxation. This synergy was achieved during the 1990s as lawyers began to widely utilize limited liability companies.

LLCs are the obvious choice to achieve the objectives of limited liability, flexibility of management and pass-through taxation. Even though the first LLC statute was enacted in 1977, this form of business entity languished on the back burner for many years before exploding in popularity in the late 1990s and the new millennium. The story of the rise of LLCs can only be understood by a review of the tax history between 1977 and 1997.

In 1977, Wyoming adopted the first LLC statute, intending to provide a new form of business entity with the desirable characteristics of a corporation (limited liability and the choice of centralized management), as well as the desirable characteristics of a partnership (flexibility and the choice of decentralized management). If such an entity could properly elect Subchapter K pass-through taxation, it would be an ideal investment mechanism for many business ventures. Lawyers and entrepreneurs waited for some confirmation from the IRS that an LLC could qualify for partnership type taxation. In 1980, the IRS issued an unpopular proposed regulation, indicating an intention to tax LLCs as C corporations, based on the presence of unlimited liability, as well as other classic C-corporate characteristics.[79]

The proposed regulation was withdrawn in 1983 but its chilling effect caused the use of LLCs to languish on a back burner during much of the 1980's. Between the adoption of the LLC statute in Wyoming in 1977 and 1990, only Florida bothered to enact an LLC statute in 1983. However, in 1988, after years of studying the issue, the IRS adopted a new Revenue Ruling concluding that a company formed pursuant to Wyoming's LLC statute was a Subchapter K partnership for federal tax purposes, because the entity had no more than two of the four classic C corporation characteristics.[80]

The ruling was based on the "bullet-proof" nature of the Wyoming statute which assured that LLCs in Wyoming could not have continuity of life or free transferability. The LLC in question had centralized management (only three of the twenty-five individual members managed the LLC) and limited liability (no

---

to be classified as an association must be determined by taking into account the presence or absence of each of these corporate characteristics. The presence or absence of these characteristics will depend upon the facts in each individual case . . . An organization will be treated as an association if the corporate characteristics are such that the organization more nearly resembles a corporation than a partnership or trust. *See, Morrissey et al. v. Commissioner* (1935) 296 U.S. 344."

[79]   Prop. Reg 301.7701-2, 45 Fed. Reg. 75709 (Nov. 17, 1980)

[80]   Rev. Rul. 88-76, 1988-2 C.B. 360.

member or manager was liable for LLC debts beyond his or her capital contribution). However, like all LLCs in Wyoming, the entity lacked two other corporate characteristics:

— Membership interests were not freely transferable. Under Wyoming law, the interests could be transferred only with the unanimous written consent of remaining members. Without that consent, only the economic interest would pass without rights of management or ownership.

— The LLCs did not have continuity of life. Under Wyoming law, the LLC would dissolve upon the occurrence of several different events: (i) when its term (not to exceed 30 years) expired; (ii) by the unanimous written consent of all the members; (iii) by the death, retirement, resignation, expulsion, bankruptcy, or dissolution of a member; or (iv) termination of the membership of a member.

The 1988 revenue ruling enabled the LLC bandwagon to gain some momentum. Within the next four years, 20 states enacted LLC statutes. Nevertheless, the pace of growth of LLCs was slow for two reasons. First, the restrictive nature of the Wyoming "bullet-proof" LLC statute limited the flexibility and usefulness of LLCs. LLCs formed under these statutes lacked ease of transferability of equity interests and were unstable with regard to continuity. For many investors these are limitations that make investments in the entity less attractive, since membership interests cannot be easily sold and the entity may be confronted with dissolution upon the happening of many different events.

Some states adopted more flexible statutes that allowed LLCs to be formed with less restrictions on transferability of membership interests and allowing more stable continuity of life. However, the 1988 revenue ruling left substantial uncertainties about the taxation of LLCs formed under these flexible statutes, since it was possible that the IRS might determine the LLC to have more than two classic C corporation characteristics.

The uncertainty about tax classifications created serious constraints on the use of limited liability companies as investment vehicles. During much of the 1990s, formation of new LLCs was inhibited — but that changed on January 1, 1997, when a new IRS Regulations triggered a meteoric rise in the use of LLC entities.

Beginning January 1, 1997, the I.R.S. rules governing classification of corporations, partnerships and limited liability companies were radically altered.[81] Under the changes to the IRS rules, limited partnerships, LLPs and LLCs with at least two members were given the simple option to choose whether to be classified as a Subchapter C or Subchapter K entity.[82] Indeed, the new regulations provided that the *default* classification for limited partnerships, LLPs and LLCs was Subchapter K pass-through partnership taxation, since that is the most common expectation of the investors when forming these types of companies. If the limited partnership, LLP or LLC wanted to elect to be taxed as a corporation under Subchapter C, it could elect to do so by "checking the box" on the IRS form. These

---

[81] Final IRS Rules 301.7701(1) through (4) were adopted on December 18, 1996, effective January 1, 1997. 61 FR 66584, 66588, Dec. 18, 1996. The publication of the new rule in the Federal Register was aptly titled "Simplification of Entity Classification Rules."

[82] Single member LLCs are simply disregarded as separate tax paying entities under the regulation.

regulations are known by nearly all business and tax lawyers as the "check-the-box" regulations.

G. LIMITATIONS ON PASS THROUGH TAXATION OF LOSSES

In the context of partnership taxation under Subchapter K, and partnership-type taxation of corporations under Subchapter S, business losses can be passed through to the equity holders and used as deductions on their individual returns. These losses can be valuable assets when used by taxpayers to reduce their tax obligations for income they have earned from other sources during the tax year.

Prior to 1986, there were many tax shelter schemes that were viewed as abusive. These schemes would promise to deliver loss deductions that exceeded the amount of investment at risk and, in some cases, promised deductions that were several times the amount of the investment at risk. Wouldn't it be great if an investor could invest $5,000 to purchase an interest in one of these pre-1986 ventures and receive loss deductions of $30,000? Without ever making a profit, the after tax value of the loss deductions would be worth about $10,000 in after tax cash for investors paying taxes at the rate of about 33%. Some of these tax shelters seemed too good to be true and were, simply, fraudulent. However, many of the tax deductions that were legal under the Internal Revenue Code at the time were perceived as abusive. The Tax Reform Act of 1986,[83] instituted significant changes that restricted the use of tax shelter investments to generate loss deductions. The primary limitations, passive activity loss limitations restrict the ability of equity holders to utilize loss deductions on their individual returns. There are also "at-risk" limitations that preceded the adoption of the 1986 Act and these play a significant role in the ability to use pass-through losses. Set forth below is a general introduction to these two limits on deductibility. There are many sub-rules, exceptions and special provisions dealing with these limitations, so it is always important to consult with tax professionals who fully understand the application of these rules.

1. IRC § 469 — Limitations on Passive Activity Loss Deductions

Losses from certain types of business or trade investments in which the individual does not "materially participate" are characterized as "passive activity losses" and *may* be restricted with regard to the deductibility of the loss. Income and losses from the following activities are generally considered "passive" by the IRS:[84]

1. rental real estate,[85]
2. equipment leasing,
3. sole proprietorship or farm in which the taxpayer does not materially participate (i.e., does not regularly work),
4. limited partnership interests,[86] and

---

[83] Pub. L. 99-514, 100 Stat. 2085 (1986).

[84] IRC § 469(c)(2); Treas. Reg. § 1.469-1T(e)(3).

[85] Except rentals in which a real estate professional materially participates. *See* IRC § 469(c)(7).

[86] There are some exceptions in Treas. Reg. § 1.469-5T(e).

5. partnerships, corporations and limited liability company investments in which the taxpayer does not materially participate.

Passive activity investment losses can be fully deducted against gain from other passive activity investments — but they can *not* be deducted against income from other, non-passive activities and sources. This means that only the only individuals who can utilize a passive activity loss in the year its passed through are those individuals with gains from other investments that are also passive activities.

For instance, suppose an investor, Ann, receives a pass through loss of $25,000 from Investment A, and an allocation of profits from Investment B of $30,000 (both are passive activity investments). Ann can fully deduct the $25,000 loss derived from Investment A against income received from Investment B and benefit from the reduction in taxable income. Another investor, Bob also has a $25,000 pass through loss from Investment A but Bob has no other passive activity income. Bob will not be able to deduct the loss even though he has income such as salary, interest, or active income from businesses in which Bob materially participates. Bob's deduction won't be lost, just postponed. Bob will be allowed to carry over the loss to future tax years and use it to offset future passive activity gains, however Bob will not benefit from any tax deductions during the *current* tax year, although he will eventually be entitled to claim the passive activity deduction in some future year.[87]

The passive activity loss limits will have different impacts on different taxpayers. For those taxpayers with many passive activity investments, the pass through of losses will most likely be fully utilized to offset gains in the current tax year. However, the benefit of the tax deduction will be postponed, perhaps for many years, for investors without other passive activity gains to offset.

Keep in mind that the passive activity loss limits apply only to passive activity investments in which the taxpayer is not "materially participating." What would the result be if Bob "materially participates" in the business of Investment A as a general partner (or the president of a Subchapter S corporation)? If Bob materially participates in the operations of the business, the losses from the investment may be deducted from income from *all* sources (subject to at-risk limitations).[88] The IRC describes a taxpayer as materially participating in a business activity only if the taxpayer is involved in the operations of the activity on a basis which is regular, continuous, and substantial throughout the tax year.[89] There are extensive Temporary Treasury Regulations to help determine when a taxpayer is materially participating that must be carefully consulted by any investor who wants to fully deduct losses from an investment in a business or trade against forms of income other than passive activity income.[90] The Temporary

---

[87] Bob is allowed to "carry over" the deduction and use it in a subsequent year if Bob has passive activity gains from the same investment, or any other passive activity investment. Eventually, when the passive activity investment interest is disposed of, the losses that have been carried over will be fully deductible from *any* type of taxable income. IRC § 469(g).

[88] IRC § 469(e)(2)(3).

[89] IRC § 469(h).

[90] Temp. Treas. Reg. § 1.469-5T. Some examples of "material participation" set forth in the regulation are:

(1) The individual participates in the activity for more than 500 hours during such year;

(2) The individual's participation in the activity for the taxable year constitutes substantially

Regulations provide that the activity level must be quite substantial to lift the investment from the confinement of passive activity to material participation.[91] It is clear that limited partners and S corporation shareholders who are not active in the management of the entity are passive activity investors.

Summary — Passive Activity Loss Limits

Transactional lawyers should be generally familiar with the limits placed on deductibility of losses by the IRC passive activity loss limitations. They should be able to talk intelligently with tax professionals and explain to potential investors the limitations on deductibility of losses that will be passed through under the rules of Subchapter K and Subchapter S. At the risk of oversimplification, the participants in the venture should be aware that: (i) only those investors who materially participate can fully deduct passed through losses against all forms of income; and, (ii) investors for whom the investment is a passive activity will not be able to fully utilize the deduction in the year it's passed through, except to offset gains from other passive investments.

2. Section 465 — At-Risk Loss Limitations

Individuals are taxed only on *net* taxable income from business and trade activities, after taking into account both income and deductible losses. Regardless of whether losses suffered by investors are "passive" or "active," they are losses nonetheless. It's only fair that, at some point, investors be allowed to deduct losses against income in computing the overall taxable income. The at-risk rules were adopted to prevent abusive tax sheltering schemes that were created to allow investors to claim losses that exceeded the amount that the investor actually had at risk in the venture. For instance, an investor in a limited partnership with a capital investment of only $10,000 might end up claiming loss deductions of $25,000. As a limited partner, the investor faced no possibility of loss in excess of the $10,000 at risk. It seemed abusive to allow such a taxpayer to deduct "losses" if the taxpayer was not going to actually suffer a loss of income or property.

Starting in the 1970s, IRC § 465(a) placed limitations on the amounts that taxpayers could claim as losses, regardless of whether those losses were from passive activities or from material participation. Taxpayers cannot claim deductions in excess of the aggregate amount of losses for which the taxpayer is actually "at risk." Generally, the amount at risk is a combination of:

---

all of the participation in such activity of all individuals (including individuals who are not owners of interests in the activity) for such year;

(3) The individual participates in the activity for more than 100 hours during the taxable year, and such individual's participation in the activity for the taxable year is not less than the participation in the activity of any other individual (including individuals who are not owners of interests in the activity) for such year; * * *

[91] There is an exception for an annual deduction of up to $25,000 worth of losses from rental real estate if the investor meets a lesser standard of "active" participation in the venture and owns at least 10% of the venture. Active participation requires only that the taxpayer participate in the rental activities in a significant and bona fide way. IRC § 469(i)(6). Unfortunately for higher income taxpayers, the deduction is "phased-out" based on the amount of the taxpayer's modified adjusted gross income ("MAGI"). The phase out range is normally $100,000 to $150,000 of MAGI — it reduces the $25,000 deduction progressively until it reaches zero.

1. The amount of money and property[92] contributed to the business in exchange for an equity share.
2. Amounts borrowed by the investor on behalf of the business if the investor is personally liable for repayment or has pledged property as security for the loan.
3. Loans directly to the business entity that have been guaranteed or co-signed by the investor, giving rise to personal liability.

In other words, the at-risk limits restrict an investor from deducting more than the investor actually has placed at risk in the venture. If the aggregate amount of deductions exceeds the amount at risk in the venture, then the excessive deductions are not allowed, although they may be carried over to a subsequent year *if* there are additional amounts placed at risk.

3. Increasing At-Risk Basis for Partnership & LLC Debt Liabilities

There is an important source of increasing the amount that a taxpayer has at risk that transactional lawyers must understand. When a general partnership, limited partnership or limited liability company (but not an S corporation) incurs debt at the entity level, there are times that an allocable share of the debt may be used to increase the at-risk amount of some or all of the investors above the amounts that they have invested in the business.

This makes sense, for instance, with respect to *general* partners, since a general partner is personally liable for the debts of the partnership.[93] In a general partnership, as the partnership incurs debt, each of the general partners is ultimately liable for his or her allocable share of the debt and can increase the at-risk basis by the amount that the partner is proportionally liable.[94] It is also possible for general partners to take advantage of qualified non-recourse, mortgage financing discussed in the following paragraph.

In a *limited* partnership, the limited partners are, by definition, not at risk for the debts incurred by the limited partnership. Similarly, in a limited liability company, none of the members are at risk for debts incurred by the entity. However, under special some circumstances, limited partners and LLC members may proportionally share in the increased amounts at risk when a partnership or LLC borrows money. The circumstances are narrow but this mechanism for increasing at-risk basis has fueled the marketing of certain types of investment opportunities. Under IRC § 465(b)(6), partners and members can increase their at-

---

[92] For property contributed by an investor, the amount at risk is not the *value* of the property but the investor's *adjusted basis* in the property. An investor may contribute property valued at $1 million for shares in the entity, but the taxpayer's adjusted basis may only be $750,000. The taxpayer is at risk for only $750,000.

[93] General partners are considered at risk with respect to borrowed amounts only if they are truly liable for the debt. For instance, general partners cannot increase the amount at risk if the debt is non-recourse secured financing (the lender has agreed to use only the collateral to satisfy the debt in the event of default), or the lender has an interest in the activity other than as a creditor.

[94] The partner's share of debt is the portion for which the partner would be legally bound to make payments to the creditor or contribute capital to the partnership to pay the debt. IRC § 752; Treas. Reg. § 1.752-2.

risk basis by their proportional share of qualified "nonrecourse"[95] mortgage financing that is secured by the real property used by the entity. This means that the limited partners and LLC members can use the debt incurred by the *entity* to increase the amounts held to be at risk for the investor (and, therefore, deductible by the investor) beyond the amounts which the investor has invested. To take advantage of this benefit there are some essential qualifications that must be satisfied:

  (i)   the activity of the entity must be the developing and/or leasing of real estate

  (ii) the debt must be mortgage financing secured by the real estate

  (iii) the debt must be nonrecourse with no person personally liable for payment of the debt (the lender must agree to resort only to the collateral for repayment of the loan in the event of a default in payment by the entity)

  (iv) the lender must a qualified, third-party lender such as an institutional mortgage lender.[96]

In the context of a real estate venture, this can be very productive. Suppose a limited partnership or limited liability company has ten investors. Each investor is contributing $50,000 in equity capital, for a total capitalization of $500,000. The entity borrows another $2 million from a commercial bank to purchase an apartment building for approximately $2.5 million. The debt to the bank will be secured by a mortgage lien on the apartment building and the bank has agreed that the loan will be nonrecourse. The nonrecourse debt will result in the at-risk basis for each investor to be increased by one-tenth of the amount of the loan ($250,000) from $50,000 to $300,000.

For *limited liability companies*, the non-recourse aspect of the mortgage loan is easier to establish. All loans to the LLC are nonrecourse since no member is personally liable for the debts incurred by the LLC. There is no need to have the lender specifically agree to make the loan non-recourse. Of course, the lender will *treat* the loan as non-recourse for the very same reasons. So long as no member personally guarantees the loan or offers security for repayment of the loan, the non-recourse nature of the loan is easily satisfied. For limited partnerships, the lender will have to agree in writing to make the loan on a non-recourse basis.

As a result, for general partnerships, as well as limited partnerships and LLCs that meet the qualification requirements, the at-risk basis of *all* partners or members can be increased by the member's allocable share of losses in the partnership or LLC operating agreement.[97]

---

[95] In a "nonrecourse" loan the lender agrees that no person other than the entity will be liable for payment of the debt, including the general partners of a partnership. Normally, nonrecourse loans are made in connection with real estate mortgage loans, with the lender looking to a mortgage lien in the entity's property to satisfy its claim in the event of a default by the entity. Why would a lender be willing to make a mortgage loan on a nonrecourse basis? Prior to forming the entity, the promoters will work closely with the proposed lender to assure the nonrecourse nature of the loan so that the venture can gain the advantages of increased at risk basis for its investors. The lender will agree if it determines that the loan is likely to be repaid by the entity and that there is sufficient equity in the collateral to assure repayment in the event of a default. The lender is likely to charge higher fees and interest as a condition to making the loan on a nonrecourse basis.

[96] IRC § 465(b)(6).

[97] IRC §§ 465(b), 705, 752.

Unfortunately, there is no similar ability to increase at-risk basis for S corporations. Shareholders of S corporations can write off losses only to the extent of their capital investment in shares, or loans made to the corporation. As a result LLCs are almost always the preferred form of business entity where the organizers are pursuing both limited liability and the opportunity to increase the availability of loss deductions for equity holders.

Summary — At-Risk Loss Limits

Transactional lawyers should be generally familiar with the at-risk limits placed on deductibility of losses passed through to investors in partnerships, LLCs and S corporations. The lawyers should also be able to talk intelligently with tax professionals about selecting the optimum type of business entity if there is an intention to provide investors with increases in their at-risk basis as a result of allocation of debt incurred by the entity. After consulting with the tax professionals, the transactional lawyer must make sure that the documents reflect the objectives of their clients.

A basic summary of the at-risk rules is:

(i)   The deduction by investors of passed through losses (passive or not) can not exceed the amount that the investor actually has "at risk" in the entity.

(ii)   There are times that the amount held to be at risk by the Internal Revenue Code can be increased beyond the amount actually at risk, by allocating to the investor a proportionate share of non-recourse debt incurred by real property partnerships or limited liability companies (but not S corporations) thereby allowing the tax-sheltering advantage of increased loss deductions.

H.   TAX CONSEQUENCES: CONTRIBUTING SERVICES OR PROPERTY TO A BUSINESS ENTITY

There are no taxation issues for investors when *cash* is used to purchase ownership interests in an entity, regardless of whether the interest is in the form of shares of stock, partnership interests, or membership interests. The purchase does not produce any gains or losses to the taxpayer purchasing the equity interest if the consideration is cash.

However, when an ownership interest is transferred by an entity to an investor in exchange for *services* or *property* there may be noteworthy tax consequences *to the investor* in the year of the transfer of the equity interest to the investor.

1.   Contributions of Services to Corporations

There are times that promoters, managers and investors may receive ownership shares in a business entity in exchange for the services they have rendered, or promise to render. The value of the property (shares of stock, partnership interests or LLC member interests) received by a taxpayer in exchange for services is a form of compensation that must be included on the taxpayer's tax return and appropriate taxes paid.[98] This can be a serious problem for investors who are contributing services, since the recipient will have to pay taxes on the

---

[98] This outcome would be true regardless of the form of entity is formed, corporation, partnership or

value of the equity interest received. For instance, suppose that three investors are forming a corporation and each will be receiving one-third of the shares of stock upon formation. Two of the investors, Ann and Bob, are each contributing $145,000 in cash in exchange for a one-third interest in the business. The third investor, Carl, is contributing only $10,000 in cash but will be operating and managing the business.

Assume that shortly after the articles of incorporation are filed, the investors make their contributions and the shares are issued, with each of the three investors receiving one-third of the shares of the corporation. Assuming that the value of Carl's shares is $100,000,[99] Carl has received $90,000 worth of property in exchange for his *services*. Carl will have to report this income on his tax return and pay a substantial income tax of about $30,000. Since this tax liability arises in exchange for services, he may also face additional liabilities for social security, medicare and other taxes. In view of the fact that Carl has not received any *cash* from the corporation, Carl will have to dig into his own assets to come up with the cash to pay these taxes. Imagine Carl's surprise when his accountant tells him around April 15 of the next year that he has to produce $30,000 in tax payments.

One of the roles of the transactional lawyer is to assure that when investors are contributing services or property, that the potential tax liability is *disclosed* to the investor — and that a tax reduction strategy is evaluated.

There are some creative mechanisms to defer taxes by making the transfer of equity interests contingent on some future event, rather than issued outright to the taxpayer in the year of formation. Under applicable IRC provisions, the stock interest need not be reported as compensation if it is non-transferable or subject to a substantial risk of forfeiture.[100] Thus, if full vesting or transferability of the shares are conditioned upon Carl remaining in the employ of the corporation for a certain time, and subject to forfeiture if he does not, then Carl does not have to report the compensation until the conditions are removed or satisfied.[101] Of course, Carl may not be willing to put his ownership interest at risk just to avoid the tax

---

LLC, and regardless of form of the equity share that Carl receives. IRC § 83 states:

"Property transferred in connection with performance of services:

(a) . . . If, in connection with the performance of services, property is transferred to any person other than the person for whom such services are performed, the excess of —

(1) the fair market value of such property . . . over

(2) the amount (if any) paid for such property, shall be included in the gross income of the person who performed such services in the first taxable year in which the rights of the person having the beneficial interest in such property are transferable or are not subject to a substantial risk of forfeiture, whichever is applicable . . . "

[99] The outstanding shares of the corporation held by all three shareholders will be worth at least $300,000, since Ann and Bob have contributed a combined total of $290,000 and Carl has contributed $10,000.

[100] *See* IRC § 83(a). Section 83 (c) provides:

(1) Substantial risk of forfeiture — The rights of a person in property are subject to a substantial risk of forfeiture if such person's rights to full enjoyment of such property are conditioned upon the future performance of substantial services by any individual.

(2) Transferability of property — The rights of a person in property are transferable only if the rights in such property of any transferee are not subject to a substantial risk of forfeiture.

See *Campbell v. Commissioner* reproduced later in this chapter.

[101] Note that the shares of stock may be worth far more at that time, with Carl having to report a greater amount of compensation and pay a commensurate amount of taxes at that time. For this reason, it might make sense to space out the expiration dates of the conditions.

consequences but postponing $30,000 in tax liability is a compelling motivator. There is a risk in postponing the vesting of the equity interest. Carl will have to pay the value of the interest received *at the time that the forfeiture conditions terminate.* The value of the capital interest may be considerably higher at that time, forcing Carl to pay a greater sum in taxes at some future time.

Another alternative to reduce the tax impact on a service contributor such as Carl is to restructure the debt and equity contributions of all of the investors. Suppose that Ann, Bob and Carl will all contribute only $10,000 each for the shares of stock of the corporation. However, Ann and Bob will also each *loan* the corporation another $135,000. Under such circumstances, the total capitalization of the corporation would be $30,000 and the corporation would have an additional $270,000 in cash available to begin its operations. Since Carl is receiving shares worth only $10,000 in exchange for his cash contribution, he will not face any income taxes as a result of issuance of shares to him. An employment contract can be entered into between Carl and the corporation to compensate him for his services, and promissory notes will be executed to evidence the debt obligations to Ann and Bob. There's a certain symmetry to this capitalization plan. As creditors, the moneyed investors will receive interest on their loans, and have priority of distribution with regard to repayment of the principal, for the large amounts of cash they are contributing. If the loans are set up on "straight" debt terms that mirror commercial lending conditions, the interest payments will be deductible to the corporation and repayment of principal to Ann and Bob will not constitute taxable income. On the other hand, Carl will be an equal equity holder but will be entitled for compensation for the services he performs for the entity, with that compensation being taxed only in later years, when actually received by Carl.

2.   Contributions of Services to Partnerships

The equity interest in a *partnership* transferred to a partner in exchange for services is also *income* and subject to taxation in the year that the equity interest is received by the service-contributing partner.[102] The value of the partnership interest will be included in the service-contributor's taxable income. What result would this produce if Carl contributes services for his one-third share of a partnership with Ann and Bob who, together, contribute $600,000 in cash? At the instant of the funding of the partnership Carl's share of the partnership would be worth $200,000 (one-third of $600,000). Carl will have to include the $200,000 in value in his gross income and pay approximately $60,000 in taxes.

Could the *value* (and related tax obligation) of Carl's partnership interest be reduced by provisions that give a priority of distribution to Ann and Bob for the first $600,000 of cash received upon dissolution of the partnership but all parties share equally in the profits, including any appreciation in the value of the partnership above $600,000? What would the value of Carl's interest be on the day his "interest" in the partnership is transferred to him? The following case helps to answer these questions.

---

[102] *See* IRC § 83.

CAMPBELL v. COMMISSIONER
United States Court of Appeals, Eighth Circuit
943 F.2d 815 (1991)

BEAM, CIRCUIT JUDGE.

William and Norma Campbell appeal from the tax court's decision affirming, in part, the Commissioner's assessment of deficiencies in their federal income tax for the years 1979 and 1980. The Campbells challenge the tax court's finding that partnership profits interests received by Mr. Campbell constitute income. We affirm in part and reverse in part.

I. BACKGROUND

Prior to and during the years in issue, William Campbell was employed by Summa T. Group, a collection of business entities involved in the formation and syndication of limited partnerships. Campbell served as vice president and director for most members of the Summa T. Group, including Summa T. Realty, Inc., a real estate brokerage and consulting firm. He also served as vice president of Realty Properties Company, another member of Summa T. Group. Most of Campbell's services during these years were performed for Summa T. Realty. *Campbell v. Commissioner*, 59 T.C.M. (CCH) 236, 237 (1990).

In partnership with Jim Nettles, another Summa T. Realty employee, Campbell packaged and sold interests in transactions on behalf of Summa T. Realty. *Id.* Nettles left Summa T. Realty in 1979, and Campbell became responsible "for locating suitable properties for Summa T. Realty, negotiating the acquisition of those properties, obtaining the financing necessary to acquire the properties, organizing the partnerships which would eventually acquire those properties, and assisting in the preparation of offering materials in connection with the syndication of those partnerships." *Id.* Following Nettles's departure, Campbell negotiated a new compensation agreement under which he received fifteen percent of the proceeds from each syndication and, for his services, special limited partnership interests (profits interests) in the partnerships that he helped form and finance. Campbell sought these interests because of the immediate tax benefits he would receive and the residual value they might have. Based on consultation with two tax attorneys, he believed that the receipt of these interests in exchange for services would not be taxable events, at the time of acquisition.

Relevant to this appeal, Campbell performed services in the formation and syndication of three limited partnerships. In 1979, he received a two percent special limited partnership interest in Phillips House Associates, Ltd. Realty Properties was the sole general partner in Phillips House, and David Kane, president of Realty Properties, was also a special limited partner. Phillips House was formed to purchase, renovate and operate a hotel in downtown Kansas City, Missouri. The offering memorandum, which was provided to potential investors in the thirty-five Class A limited partner units available for sale, predicted losses for tax purposes from 1979 to 1985, ninety-four percent allocated to the limited partners and two percent allocated to each special limited partner and the general partner. However, the memorandum warned that an Internal Revenue Service audit was likely. And, it was predicted that the IRS probably would disallow some or all of the deductions and allocations.

Twenty Class A interests were sold by December 31, 1979, and the remaining fifteen were sold by December 31, 1980. Each unit sold for $99,250. Resale of partnership units was subject to approval by the general partner, which could withhold approval arbitrarily. The partnership did not anticipate cash distributions to the Class A limited partners until 1982 and to the special limited partners and the general partner until 1984. became available for distribution, the Class A limited partners were given priority. They were also entitled to return of their capital investment upon the sale or refinancing of the hotel. The first $30,000 of any additional proceeds from such a transaction were allocated to the general partner as return of capital. The special limited partners were each entitled to a share of any remaining proceeds.

Diversified Financial Services, a member of Summa T. Group, received three percent of the Phillips House offering proceeds as reimbursement for expenses incurred in the offering. Realty Properties, and other members of the group, received 42.5 percent of the proceeds for "expense allowances, consulting fees, and management fees." Campbell provided services in the formation and syndication of the partnership. However, the record does not reveal what part of these fees were paid to Summa T. Group for services actually performed by Campbell, nor does it reveal what part of Campbell's partnership interest, if any, was received as compensation for services for which his employer was compensated.

The other two limited partnerships at issue here were formed under similar agreements. Campbell received a one percent interest in The Grand partnership, which was formed in 1980 to purchase and operate the Howard Johnson's Motor Lodge in Myrtle Beach, South Carolina. Also in 1980, the Airport partnership was formed to purchase and operate the Northwest Airport Inn in St. Louis County, Missouri. Campbell received a one percent interest in Airport. As in Phillips House, Realty Properties was the general partner, Campbell and Kane were special limited partners, and thirty-five Class A limited partnerships were sold in both The Grand and Airport. Realty Properties and its affiliates, including Diversified Financial Services and Summa T. Realty, received 30.2 percent of the proceeds of The Grand's offering of limited partnership interests, and 38.5 percent of the proceeds of Airport's offering. These payments were made for expense allowances, consulting fees, management fees and financing fees. Again, Campbell provided some of these services, and the record does not reveal the capacity in which he performed them. The offering memoranda for The Grand and Airport projected taxable losses for the first several years of operations. As with Phillips House, however, the memoranda warned that any of the deductions and credits might be disallowed by the Internal Revenue Service.

On May 10, 1983, the Commissioner issued a notice of deficiency for the tax years 1979 and 1980, alleging that Campbell should have included the value of his interests in these partnerships in ordinary income.[103] The Commissioner valued Campbell's interests in Phillips House, The Grand and Airport at $42,084, $16,968 and $20,683, respectively. amendment to his answer, the Commissioner alleged that Campbell was liable for additions to tax for, *inter alia*, negligently failing to include these interests in his ordinary income.

---

[103] [1] The notice contained other adjustments to Campbell's income. However, the only remaining dispute is in regard to the inclusion of the partnership interests in ordinary income.

The tax court upheld, in part, the Commissioner's assessment of deficiency and addition to tax. The court agreed that the fair market value of the profits interests should have been included in Campbell's income. The court, however, did not fully agree with the Commissioner's valuation of the interests. Upon revaluation, the court sustained the Commissioner's deficiency in regard to The Grand. The court valued Campbell's interest in Airport at $15,000 and his interest in Phillips House at $25,000 and entered an order accordingly.

II. DISCUSSION

Campbell argues on appeal, as he did unsuccessfully in the tax court, that a service partner (i.e., a partner who receives his partnership interest in exchange for services provided to the partnership) who receives a profits interest (i.e., a right to share in profits and losses only, as opposed to an interest in the capital assets of a partnership) in a partnership does not realize income upon receipt of that interest, and, therefore, no taxable event occurs. In the alternative, he argues that the interests he received had no value at the time he received them and, thus, he should not have been taxed.

At this point, the Commissioner concedes that the tax court erred in holding that the receipt of a profits interest in exchange for services to the partnership should be considered ordinary income to the service provider. *See* Brief for Appellee at 13–14. However, for the first time, the Commissioner now asserts that Campbell actually received the partnership interests in exchange for services he provided to his employer, rather than services he provided to the partnerships. According to the Commissioner, the tax court held that Campbell received the interests as compensation from his employer. Thus, he is not a service partner; the principles of partnership taxation do not apply; and Campbell's receipt of compensation from his employer was taxable upon receipt.

A. *Employee or Partner*

We make short work of the Commissioner's alternate argument. We may affirm a trial court's decision on any ground supported by the record, whether or not that ground was addressed by the lower court. *See Brown v. St. Louis Police Dep't*, 691 F.2d 393, 396–97 (8th Cir.1982) (when issue was raised but not addressed by the district court and did not require factual findings, appellate court may affirm based on that issue), *cert. denied*, 461 U.S. 908, 103 S. Ct. 1882, 76 L. Ed.2d 812 (1983). Such action, however, would be inappropriate here. The Commissioner's argument, at best, requires that we resolve a disputed question of fact. Contrary to the Commissioner's belief, the tax court did not hold that Campbell received his partnership interests for services he performed for his employer rather than services performed for the partnerships. In reaffirming *Diamond v. Commissioner*, 492 F.2d 286 (7th Cir.1974), the court held "that section 721(a) and the regulations thereunder are simply inapplicable where, as in the *Diamond* case and *the instant case, a partner receives his partnership interest in exchange for services he has rendered to the partnership*." *Campbell*, 59 T.C.M. at 249. (emphasis added). The court also noted the records of the partnerships indicate that Campbell received the partnership interests after rendering services. The Commissioner tenuously relies on the tax court's statements that Campbell received his partnership interests in connection with services provided for his employer. These statements were made in the discussion of *when* Campbell received his interests. We believe that the court did not specifically hold that the interests were received as payment for services provided to his employer. In any event, we decline to address this factual matter and we disregard the argument.[104]

B. *Taxing Profits Interests*

Although the Commissioner concedes the tax court's error in taxing a service partner's profits interest, the tax court's holding is not without support. In fact, the only circuit court to address the issue arrived at the same conclusion. *See Diamond*, 492 F.2d 286. However, Campbell and several amici curiae[105] strongly argue that the tax court's decision does substantial damage to established principles of partnership tax law. In addition, several commentators have recently analyzed the issue and have come to a variety of conclusions. *Compare, e.g.,* Hortenstine & Ford, *Receipt of a Partnership Interest For Services: A Controversy That Will Not Die*, 65 Taxes 880, 881 (1987) (Generally, the fair market value of a profits interest received by a service partner should be included in income.) *and* C. Bishop & J. Brooks, Federal Partnership Taxation 83–86 (1990) (Perhaps, when partnership income is very speculative, some profits interests should not be included in income.) *with* 1 W. McKee, W. Nelson, & R. Whitmire, Federal Taxation of Partnerships & Partners ¶¶ 5.02[1][b], at 5–14, 5.02[1][c], at S5-2 to -3 (2d ed. 1990 & Supp. 2 1991) (The receipt of a profits interest is not a taxable event.) *and* A. Willis, T. Pennell, & P. Postlewaite, Partnership Taxation § 46.12, at 46-36 (4th ed. 1991) (Although the ultimate result is uncertain, "[t]he preferred tax treatment of the transfer of a profits interest as compensation for services is not to tax it at all."). Thus, we are reluctant to accept the Commissioner's concession without substantive review.

The tax court rejected Campbell's contention that the regulations promulgated under section 721 of the Internal Revenue Code and the general principles of partnership taxation exempt from taxation profits interests received in exchange for services.[106] *Campbell*, 59 T.C.M. at 248–49. The court reaffirmed its holding

---

[104] [2] The details of Campbell's compensation agreement with his employer are not in the record. Campbell apparently agreed to forego compensation from his employer in exchange for the opportunity to receive interests in the partnerships that he helped form. The record does not suggest that he received the interests from his employer.

[105] [3] Two amici curiae briefs were filed in this appeal. Deloitte and Touche, an international accounting firm, filed one. The other was filed jointly by National Venture Capital Association, The American Film Marketing Association, The Coalition of Publicly Traded Partnerships, The International Council of Shopping Centers, The Investment Program Association, the National Association of Industrial and Office Parks, and the Securities Industry Association.

[106] [4] Section 721 provides: "No gain or loss shall be recognized to a partnership or to any of its partners in the case of a contribution of property to the partnership in exchange for an interest in the partnership." I.R.C. § 721(a) (1988). The regulations under section 721 provide:

> To the extent that any of the partners gives up any part of his right to be repaid his contributions (as distinguished from a share in partnership profits) in favor of another partner as compensation for services (or in satisfaction of an obligation), section 721 does not apply. The value of an interest in such partnership capital so transferred to a partner as compensation for services constitutes income to the partner under section 61. The amount of such income is the fair market value of the interest in capital so transferred, either at the time the transfer is made for past services, or at the time the services have been rendered where the transfer is conditioned on the completion of the transferee's future services.

Treas. Reg. § 1.721-1(b)(1) (1956).

that section 721 and its regulations are "inapplicable where, as in the *Diamond* case and the instant case, a partner receives his partnership interest in exchange for services he has rendered to the partnership." Section 721 relates to contributions of property to partnerships, but not to contributions of services, which are not property within the meaning of that section. *Id.* Section 721 was enacted to allow the contribution of property to a partnership without recognition of gain or loss. The rationale for nonrecognition is that no disposition of property has occurred. Rather, the partnership interest represents a change in form of the asset. In the present case, the court held that the receipt of profits interests represented compensation for services, not change in form of assets. court also noted the inconsistency in imposing immediate taxation upon a service partner who receives a capital interest and not upon a service partner who receives a profits interest, as section 721 makes no distinction between the two. Section 721 regulations do not expand the scope of the statute to provide nonrecognition of income to partners who contribute services in exchange for a partnership interest. tax court found no authority to support different treatment for capital and profits interests received in exchange for services and held that Campbell received ordinary income upon receipt of the profits interests.

After finding that Campbell's receipt of the profits interests were taxable events, the court applied section 83 to determine when the income should have been recognized. Section 83 provides rules governing when property received in connection with the performance of services must be recognized as income. I.R.C. § 83(a) (1988).[107] The regulations define property to "include[] real and personal property other than either money or an unfunded and unsecured promise to pay money or property in the future." Treas. Reg. § 1.83-3(e) (1985). *The tax court had no doubt that a profits interest is property rather than a promise to pay money or property in the future. Campbell, 59 T.C.M. at 249–51. Further, the court found no substantial risk of forfeiture. Thus, the interests were taxable upon receipt.*[108]

The tax court's holding was based principally on *Diamond*, and that case is analogous. However, to fully understand the concerns raised, we must review several prior cases and the underlying statutory provisions. When a service partner receives an interest in partnership capital, the cases clearly hold that a taxable event has occurred. The receipt of the capital interest must be included in the service partner's income. *See, e.g. United States v. Frazell*, 335 F.2d 487, 489 (5th Cir.1964), *cert. denied*, 380 U.S. 961, 85 S. Ct. 1104, 14 L. Ed.2d 152 (1965). *See also* W. McKee, *supra*, ¶ 5.01, at 5-2 (transfer of capital interest is taxable). As an interest in intangible personal property, the receipt of a capital interest appears to be taxable under the authority of section 83 of the Internal Revenue Code.[109]

---

[107] [5] The text of section 83(a) provides, in part:

(a) General Rule-If, in connection with the performance of services, property is transferred to any person other than the person for whom such services are performed, the excess of —

(1) the fair market value of such property . . . at the first time the rights of the person having the beneficial interest in such property are transferable or are not subject to a substantial risk of forfeiture, whichever occurs earlier, over

(2) the amount (if any) paid for such property, shall be included in the gross income of the person who performed such services in the first taxable year in which the rights of the person having the beneficial interest in such property are transferable or are not subject to a substantial risk of forfeiture, whichever is applicable.

[108] [Emphasis added.—Eds.]

[109] [6] A proposed amendment to the treasury regulations provides: "(i) If the partnership interest

There is little, if any, dispute that such a transaction involves the recognition of income.

As noted, however, when the service partner receives solely a profits interest, the tax consequences are unclear. In contrast to *Diamond*, the tax court has held, and the Commissioner has conceded in some cases, that receipt of a profits interest by a service partner creates no tax liability. *See National Oil Co. v. Commissioner*, 52 T.C.M. (CCH) 1223, 1228 (1986) (Commissioner conceded that if taxpayer received only profits interest, no taxable event had occurred); *Kenroy, Inc. v. Commissioner*, 47 T.C.M. (CCH) 1749, 1756–59 (1984) (profits interest had no fair market value, thus no tax liability upon receipt); *Hale v. Commissioner*, 24 T.C.M. (CCH) 1497, 1502 n. 3 (1965) ("Under the regulations, the mere receipt of a partnership interest in future profits does not create any tax liability. Sec. 1.721-(1)(b), Income Tax Regs.").

The code does not expressly exempt from taxation a service partner's receipt of a profits interest, and the courts that have held that it is not taxed upon receipt do not appear to have closely analyzed the issue. However, commentators have developed three interrelated theories in support of the proposition that it is not a taxable event: 1) based upon regulation 1-721.1(b), a profits interest is not property for purposes of sections 61 and 83; 2) a profits interest may have no fair market value; and 3) the nonrealization concepts governing transactions between partner and partnership preclude taxation. *See, e.g.*, W. McKee, *supra*, ¶¶ 5.01–.02[1], at 5-3 to -5; 5.02[2], at 5–15 to -18; 5.02[1][c], at 5-2 to -9.

The tax court and the Seventh Circuit rejected at least the first two of these theories in *Diamond*.[110] The tax court found that Diamond's receipt of a partnership profits interest in exchange for services was taxable as ordinary income, did not come within the scope of section 721 and had a readily ascertainable fair market value. The Seventh Circuit affirmed. *Diamond*, 492 F.2d at 286–87, 291. The facts in *Diamond* are very similar to those before us, except in regard to the issue of value. Diamond had arranged the financing of a land

---

is transferred after June 30, 1969 . . . then the transfer of such interest in partnership capital shall be treated as a transfer of property to which section 83 and the regulations thereunder applies." Proposed Treas. Reg. § 1.721-1(b)(1)(i) (1971).

[110] [7] Because section 83 had not been enacted at the time of the *Diamond* transfer, the court's holding was limited to finding that a service partner's receipt of a profits interest was governed by section 61. Although the language of the statute is clear, some question exists as to the applicability of section 83 to a service partner's receipt of a profits interest. Regulation 1.83-1(a) provides the general rule for the inclusion of property transferred in connection with the performance of services in gross income: "Section 83 provides rules for the taxation of property transferred to an *employee or independent contractor* . . . in connection with the performance of services by such employee or independent contractor." Treas. Reg. § 1.83-1(a) (1978) (emphasis added). And, the regulations further provide: "Property transferred to an *employee or an independent contractor* . . . in recognition of the performance of, or the refraining from performance of, services is considered transferred in connection with the performance of services within the meaning of section 83." *Id.* § 1.83-3(f) (emphasis added). A proposed regulation under section 721 states: "If the partnership interest is transferred after June 30, 1969 . . . then the transfer of such interest in *partnership capital* shall be treated as a transfer of property to which section 83 and the regulations thereunder applies." Proposed Treas. Reg. 1.721-1(b)(1)(i) (1971) (emphasis added). Arguably, the section 1.721-1(b)(1) distinction between capital and profits interests and the regulations under section 83 create the implication that a profits interest is not property subject to section 83. *See* W. McKee, *supra*, ¶¶ 5.01–.02, at 5-3 to -5, 5.02[1][c][iii], at 5–7 to -8; A. Willis, *supra*, § 46.08, at 46-22 to -24. *But see* Hortenstine, *supra*, at 903–08 (profits interest not excluded from section 83). Regulation 1.83-3(e), however, includes all personal property within the definition of property for purposes of section 83.

purchase in exchange for a profits interest in the partnership that was to hold title to the land. Diamond arranged the financing and received his partnership profits interest and then, three weeks later, sold his interest to a third party for $40,000. Diamond treated the sale proceeds as short-term capital gain, which he offset by short-term capital loss. Seventh Circuit rejected Diamond's argument that regulation 1-721.1(b)(1), because it distinguishes between receipt of a capital interest and a profits interest and specifically states only that a service partner who receives a capital interest must recognize income, implies that a service partner who receives a profits interest does not recognize income. The court noted that section 721 applies only to those partners who contribute property to the partnership and that the application of the regulation could also be so limited. After considering other published views on the matter, the court declined to interpret the regulation as Diamond proposed. Although it affirmed the tax court, the Seventh Circuit noted the presence of strong views to the contrary, and recognized the limitations of its holding:

> There must be wide variation in the degree to which a profit-share created in favor of a partner who has or will render service has determinable market value at the moment of creation. Surely in many if not the typical situations it will have only speculative value, if any.

Id. at 290.

The commentators generally agree that the nonrecognition principles of section 721 do not apply to a service partner because a service partner does not contribute property in exchange for his partnership interest. *See, e.g.*, W. McKee, *supra*, ¶ 5.01, at 5-2. We also agree. However, the section 721 regulations are relied upon to tax a service partner's receipt of a capital interest. And, as with a profits interest, a service partner who receives a capital interest has not contributed property in exchange for his partnership interest. Thus, the section 721 regulations provide some guidance when reviewing whether general principles of partnership taxation provide for nonrealization in this case.

Section 721 codified the rule that a partner who contributes property to a partnership recognizes no income. And, regulation 1.721-1(b)(1) simply clarified that the nonrecognition principles no longer apply when the right to return of that capital asset is given up by transferring it to another partner. At that time, the property has been disposed of and gain or loss, if realized, must be recognized. As a corollary, section 1.721-1(b)(1) outlines the tax treatment of the partner who receives that capital interest.

A substantial distinction, however, exists between a service partner who receives a capital interest and one who receives a profits interest. When one receives a capital interest in exchange for services performed, a shift in capital occurs between the service provider and the individual partners. *See id.* ¶ 5.02[1][c][i], at 5-4; Hortenstine, *supra*, at 885–87. The same is not true when a service partner receives a profits interest. In the latter situation, prior contributions of capital are not transferred from existing partners' capital accounts to the service provider's capital account. Receipt of a profits interest does not create the same concerns because no transfer of capital assets is involved. That is, the receipt of a profits interest never affects the nonrecognition principles of section 721. Thus, some justification exists for treating service partners who receive profits interests differently than those who receive capital interests.

Probably more relevant to our analysis, however, is section 707 of the Internal Revenue Code, which supports Campbell's argument. *See* I.R.C. § 707 (1988). Generally, a partner receives a distributive share of income instead of compensation from his partnership. *See Pratt v. Commissioner*, 550 F.2d 1023, 1026 (5th Cir.1977) (salary payments to a partner treated as a distributive share of income); *Commissioner v. Moran*, 236 F.2d 595, 598 (8th Cir.1956) ("an individual cannot be his own employee nor can a partner be an employee of his own partnership"); *Lloyd v. Commissioner*, 15 B.T.A. 82, 87 (1929) (same). Except under certain circumstances, "the general statutory policy for treating partnerships for tax purposes contemplated that the income of a partnership would flow through to the individual partners." *Pratt*, 550 F.2d at 1026. Only when the transaction is treated as one between the partnership and a partner acting in a nonpartner capacity is the payment received by the partner not considered a distributive share. *See id.* at 1026–27; I.R.C. § 707(a)(2)(A). Section 707 created an exception to the general rule.

Section 707 provides that when a partner engages in a transaction with a partnership in a nonpartner capacity that transaction will be treated as between the partnership and one who is not a partner. I.R.C. § 707(a)(1). When a partner receives payment for services performed for the partnership, that transaction falls under section 707(a)(1) if "the performance of such services . . . and the allocation and distribution, when viewed together, are properly characterized as a transaction occurring between the partnership and a partner acting other than in his capacity as a member of the partnership." This exception was enacted to prevent partnerships from using direct allocations of income to individuals, disguised as service partners, to avoid the requirement that certain expenses be capitalized. *See* W. McKee, *supra*, ¶ 5.02[1][b], at 5–13. However, it was not intended to apply when a service provider acts within his capacity as a partner. *See* § 707(a)(2)(A)(iii). Arguably, section 707(a) would be unnecessary if compensatory transfers of profits interests were taxable upon receipt because, if so, every such transfer would be taxed without this section. W. McKee, *supra*, ¶ 5.02[1][b], at 5–13 to -14.

In *Diamond*, where the service provider became a partner solely to avoid receiving ordinary income, we have no doubt that the receipt of the profits interest was for services provided other than in a partner capacity. That is, Diamond was likely to (and in fact did) receive money equal to the value of his services and apparently did not intend to function as or remain a partner. Thus, the receipt of his partnership profits interest was properly taxable as easily calculable compensation for services performed. Campbell's case, however, is not so clear. Campbell's interests were not transferable and were not likely to provide immediate returns. Thus, we doubt that the tax court correctly held that Campbell's profits interests were taxable upon receipt.

More troubling, however, is Campbell's argument that the profits interests he received had only speculative, if any, value. We fully agree with this contention and we reverse the tax court. As noted by the tax court, "fair market value is 'the price at which property would change hands in a transaction between a willing buyer and a willing seller, neither being under compulsion to buy nor to sell and both being informed' of all the relevant circumstances." *See Palmer v. Commissioner*, 523 F.2d 1308, 1310 (8th Cir.1975) (quoting *Hamm v. Commissioner*, 325 F.2d 934, 937 (8th Cir.1963), *cert. denied*, 377 U.S. 993, 84 S. Ct. 1920, 12 L. Ed.2d 1046 (1964)). And, while we review de novo the basis of a fair market value determination, the ultimate question of value is one of fact. *See Estate of Palmer v. Commissioner*, 839 F.2d 420, 423 (8th Cir.1988).

Campbell's expert testified that the values of the partnership interests were speculative and not in excess of $1,000. His opinion was based on the present values of the cash distributions projected in the offering memoranda. He discounted these values because of the restrictions on transferability and the lack of participation rights in management of the partnerships. He attached no present value to the projected tax benefits because of the substantial risk of disallowance upon likely audits. The Commissioner used the same basic method of valuation, except that he included the present value of the tax benefits in his calculations and used a much lower discount rate resulting in higher present values.

The tax court accepted the method of valuation proposed by the parties, with some modifications. The court rejected Campbell's expert's opinion that the tax benefits were so speculative that they had no value and rejected the Commissioner's determination of the appropriate discount rate. Then, based on the present value of the tax benefits and future cash payments, reduced by the speculative nature of the the interests as indicated above. *Campbell*, 59 T.C.M. at 254–56. Recognizing that the tax court's determination of value is a factual finding subject to clearly erroneous review, and that the tax court does not have to accept an expert's opinion as to value, *see Palmer*, 523 F.2d at 1310, we are, nonetheless, left with the firm belief that the court's valuation was erroneous.

The tax court relied too heavily on the fact that Class A limited partners were willing to pay substantial sums for their interests at the same time Campbell received his interest.

Because of the difference in the nature of the investments, we believe that this fact is not relevant. The Class A limited partners had superior rights to cash distributions and return of capital, as well as some rights of participation. Further, the court should not have disregarded the expert's belief that the tax benefits were speculative in nature. The partnerships were taking untested positions in regard to deductions and all of them were likely to be challenged and disallowed by the IRS. In fact, many of the deductions were ultimately disallowed. Further, the predictions contained in the offering memoranda were just that-predictions. The partnerships had no track record. Any predictions as to the ultimate success of the operations were speculative. Thus, we hold that Campbell's profits interests in Phillips House, The Grand and Airport were without fair market value at the time he received them and should not have been included in his income for the years in issue.

III. CONCLUSION

The decision of the tax court holding that the Campbells should have included the receipt of profits interests in Phillips House, The Grand and Airport in ordinary income in the year of receipt is reversed. The remainder of the decision, in which Campbell alleges no error in this appeal, is affirmed.

NOTES AND COMMENTS

1. The court in *Campbell* did not wrestle with the issue of whether the "profit interests" received by Campbell were income subject to taxation. Instead, the court wrestled with the question of *when* the income would have to be realized on

Campbell's tax returns. Campbell was trying to postpone the tax realization event from the time that he actually received the property interest in the entity, to some time in the future when the profits were actually paid to him. Campbell and his tax advisors did some smart work. By classifying his interest as a *future* profits interest, rather than a current capital interest in the entity, Campbell argued that although he rendered services to the entities in the year of formation, he didn't receive any compensation until the profits were paid to him. This argument was successful with the court, which relied on IRC § 83(a), Property transferred in connection with performance of services:

> (a) General rule: If, in connection with the performance of services, property is transferred to any person other than the person for whom such services are performed, the excess of —

> > (1) the fair market value of such property . . . at the first time the rights of the person having the beneficial interest in such property are transferable or are not subject to a substantial risk of forfeiture, whichever occurs earlier . . .

Campbell was successful in convincing the court that a "profits interest" was significantly different from a capital interest in the partnership. Unlike partners receiving capital interests, he argued, Campbell had no right to current distributions, nor any right to participate in management or other aspects of owning partnership interest. The court was also swayed by the arguments that Campbell had not really received any transferable property interest because the profits interest lacked transferability and might never be paid if profits weren't received. Therefore, the court concluded that the profits interest lacked any current value.

Was the court correct? Is a "profits interest" really any different than a capital interest in the partnership with regard to its recognition as property capable of valuation? In 2005, the IRS issued proposed regulations that sought to overrule the outcome in *Campbell*.[111] Excerpts from the IRS "Explanation of Provisions" provide some insight as to whether or not there is really a difference between a "profits interest" and some other interest exchanged for services by someone like Campbell:

> The proposed regulations apply section 83 to all partnership interests, without distinguishing between partnership capital interests and partnership profits interests. Although the application of section 83 to partnership profits interests has been the subject of controversy, see, e.g., Campbell v. Commissioner, . . . 943 F.2d 815 (8th Cir. 1991), . . . the Treasury Department and the IRS do not believe that there is a substantial basis for distinguishing among partnership interests for purposes of section 83. All partnership interests constitute personal property under state law and give the holder the right to share in future earnings from partnership capital and labor. Moreover, some commentators have suggested that the same tax rules should apply to both partnership profits interests and partnership capital interests. These commentators have suggested that taxpayers may exploit any differences in the tax treatment of partnership profits interests and partnership capital interests. The Treasury Department and the IRS agree with these comments. Therefore, all of the rules in these proposed

---

[111] 70 F.R. 29675 (2005).

regulations and the accompanying proposed revenue procedure (described below) apply equally to partnership capital interests and partnership profits interests . . .

2. What about *stock options* given to employees of corporations as part of their compensation packages? Can stock options be used to transfer equity interests to service contributors without causing a taxable income event in the year that the services are rendered? Are the stock options *current* income or *future* income under § 83(a)? The technique of awarding stock options is very popular among startup corporations. Employees may accept lower salaries if part of their compensation package is the granting of stock options — the right to purchase stock at a particular price. Imagine that an employee of an Internet startup company is paid $75,000 per year plus, on December 31 of each year, the employee receives stock options to purchase 1,000 shares at the market value of the stock on the date the options are received. Assume the market value on December 31 is $10 per share. If, over time, the shares rise in value to $100 per share, the employee will exercise the options (or sell them) by paying $10 per share for 1,000 shares and then immediately reselling the shares for $100 per share, yielding a profit of $90,000. However, in our hypothetical, the options will not "vest" until the employee works for the company for at least three years. Until the options vest, the employee cannot transfer the options, nor exercise the options. So, even if the stock price rises from $10 to $100, the employee cannot reap the value prior to the stock vesting. If the employee leaves at any time prior to the expiration of the three year period, the stock options will be forfeited. It makes sense in this scenario that § 83(a) provides that the employee need not include the value of the stock options in the employee's income until the stock vests (becomes transferable and is no longer subject to a risk of forfeiture).

However, note that the employee will have a very large income realization event if the options vest when they are worth $100 per share. The $90,000 value of the options will be included in income and taxed at the approximate rate of 33%. Is there some way to reduce this tax obligation? Read § 83:

(b) Election to include in gross income in year of transfer.

(1) In general: Any person who performs services in connection with which property is transferred to any person may elect to include in his gross income for the taxable year in which such property is transferred, the . . . fair market value of such property at the time of transfer (determined without regard to any restriction other than a restriction which by its terms will never lapse) . . .

If such election is made, subsection (a) shall not apply with respect to the transfer of such property, and if such property is subsequently forfeited, no deduction shall be allowed in respect of such forfeiture. * * *

(c) Special rules. For purposes of this section —

(1) Substantial risk of forfeiture: The rights of a person in property are subject to a substantial risk of forfeiture if such person's rights to full enjoyment of such property are conditioned upon the future performance of substantial services by any individual.

(2) Transferability of property: The rights of a person in property are transferable only if the rights in such property of any transferee are not subject to a substantial risk of forfeiture. * * *

In other words, an employee can elect to include the value of the stock options in the year received, even though they may never vest and pay *income* taxes at that time on the actual value of the stock options, which will be quite low if the options are pegged to fair market value.[112] If the options vest and the employee subsequently realizes $90,000 in gain, the gain will be *capital* gains, not *income* gains, and taxed at the much more favorable capital gains rate or 15%. Thus, it may be prudent for employees to exercise their § 83(b) election in the year the stock options are received, even though they won't vest until future years.

Summary — Contribution of Services

The tax consequences of issuing equity interests in exchange for services are sufficiently severe to merit serious attention by the attorneys and tax professionals involved in forming any business entity. This is an area in which practitioners must recognize the need to consult with experts to minimize the tax implications for clients like Carl.

3.   Contributions of Property

When a taxpayer disposes of capital assets,[113] capital gains taxes must be paid on any gain realized by the taxpayer. The current 15% capital gains tax rate for individuals for long-term capital gains (gains on assets held for over one year) is usually significantly lower than the tax rate for *income* earned by the taxpayer[114] but, nonetheless, is a tax to be reckoned with when there is a large difference between the basis of the taxpayer in the property and the property's value at the time of disposition. If one of the investors in a business entity is contributing appreciated property in exchange for an equity interest, the possibility of a hefty capital gains tax must be considered and, if possible, steps taken to avoid the imposition of a tax on that investor.

For instance, suppose that an investor acquired property five years ago for $50,000 and will be contributing the same property, now worth $250,000, to a newly formed business entity. If the taxpayer simply sold the property on the open market and used the proceeds to buy an interest in the business entity, the taxpayer would have to pay taxes of 15% of the capital gains of $200,000.[115] Is the contribution of the property to a business entity in exchange for a $250,000

---

[112] If the stock options give the employee the right to buy shares at $10 and the market price is $10, the options are valueless. Anyone, whether or not an employee, can buy the shares for $10 per share. However, if the option is more favorable and grants the employee the right to buy shares at $6 per share, the options are worth $4 each.

[113] See the discussion of capital assets earlier in this chapter at Section B.

[114] Appreciated capital assets that are sold by an individual after being held more than one year (long term capital gain) will be taxed at a maximum rate of 15%. For the sale of collectibles and small business stock, the rate of taxation for individuals is a maximum of 28%. Appreciated capital assets that are sold by individuals after being held less than one year (short term capital gain) will be taxed as ordinary income, which rises as high as 39.6% in the U.S. progressive tax system as of 2008.

[115] The capital gain is the difference between the sale price and the taxpayer's basis in the property, which is usually the cost of acquisition.

investment interest in the entity the same as a disposition by sale? If the contribution to a business entity constitutes the equivalent of a sale or disposition of the property by the investor, then he or she will have to pay $30,000 in capital gains taxes. Since the investor is not receiving cash in exchange for the asset, he or she will have to find the cash to make the tax payment. Whether or not the contribution of property will trigger a capital gains tax obligation for the contributor depends on whether the asset is being transferred to C corporation or an entity that is treated as a partnership for tax purposes.

a. Contributions of Property to Corporations

Generally, the exchange of property for shares of stock constitutes a disposition of the property by the contributing shareholder and he or she must pay capital gains on any appreciated value in the property. This could be a highly unwelcome event. Just imagine the surprise of an investor who contributed low-basis property when he or she visits an accountant around April of the next year and discovers that he or she owes a whopping capital gains tax. Using our previous example where the taxpayer's basis was $50,000 and the taxpayer received $250,000 worth of stock, the taxpayer will have to somehow come up with $30,000 in cash to pay the tax. Is there some way that this undesirable outcome can be avoided?

It is *possible* for investors to avoid the payment of a capital gains tax under the tax-free exchange provisions of IRC § 351.[116] If the contributor or joint contributors can qualify, the contributing taxpayer(s) can avoid payment of capital gains taxes, and the corporation assumes the taxpayers basis in the property.[117]

To qualify for tax free incorporation, IRC § 351 requires the following:

— the property must be exchanged *solely* for stock in the corporation[118]
— immediately after the exchange, the transferor (or transferors if more than one owner of the property) control the corporation by possessing at least 80 percent of the total combined voting power of all classes of stock entitled to vote and at least 80 percent of the total number of shares of all other classes of stock of the corporation[119]

Tax free incorporation under § 351 is an attractive way for an owner, or co-owners, of property such as an existing business, to transfer assets into a new corporation without having to pay capital gains taxes. For example, Abe and Barb buy an apartment complex for $100,000. Two years later, they organize a corporation and contribute the property, along with additional cash. At the time the property is contributed, it has a fair market value of $300,000. The corporation issues one class of stock, with Abe and Barb receiving 85% of the shares. The

---

[116] IRC § 351 states: "Transfer to corporation controlled by transferor — (a) General rule: No gain or loss shall be recognized if property is transferred to a corporation by one or more persons solely in exchange for stock in such corporation and immediately after the exchange such person or persons are in control . . . of the corporation."

[117] Eventually, if the corporation sells the property, taxes will be paid on the difference between the sales price and the contributing taxpayer's basis. In that sense, capital gains taxes are not avoided, just postponed.

[118] Any cash or debt securities, as well as certain types of preferred stock, are considered as taxable to the transferor(s). The contributors must recognize gain up to the amount of money plus the fair market value of property they receive other than stock.

[119] IRC § 368(c).

remaining 15% is sold to a third investor for cash. Since Abe and Barb "control" the corporation by meeting the 80% rules, no capital gains will be recognized on the transfer of the apartment complex in exchange for their shares of stock.

The tax-free exchange rules apply to exchanges to existing as well as newly formed corporations, so long as the shareholder or shareholders contributing the property control the corporation by meeting the 80% rules following the exchange. There are many pitfalls and considerations when planning an IRC § 351 exchange and, as usual, the role of the transactional lawyer is to recognize the general implications, consult with tax professionals, and properly inform the clients about the pros and cons of pursuing this type of tax-free exchange.

b.   Contribution of Property to Partnerships or Limited Liability Companies

When property is contributed in exchange for an equity interest in a partnership or limited liability company, neither the contributing partner nor the entity recognizes a gain or loss.[120] This applies whether the entity is being formed or is already operating. However, the contributing partner's *adjusted basis* in the property is assumed by the entity for all purposes including matters such as depreciation, gain or loss.[121]

From the perspective of the contributing partner, this is a terrific way of disposing of low-basis property in exchange for a partnership interest without having to pay capital gains tax at the time of the transfer. For instance, suppose a potential partner, Bobby, owns an apartment building worth $100,000. Bobby acquired the land and building several years ago for $35,000 and his current adjusted basis is $25,000 as a result of deducting $10,000 in depreciation. If Bobby was to sell the land for $100,000, he would have to pay capital gains taxes on the $75,000 difference between the sales price and the adjusted basis. The capital gains tax rate would be 15% on the portion of the gain that was not depreciated ($65,000 × 15% = $9,750) and 25% on the portion of the gain that was depreciated ($10,000 × 25% = $2,500), yielding a total tax of $12,250. Instead, by contributing the property directly to the partnership, Bobby avoids the payment of capital gains tax in the year of the transfer, notwithstanding the fact that he is disposing of the property in exchange for a $100,000 equity interest in the partnership. However, as discussed below, Bobby will *eventually* have to pay capital gains taxes on the "built-in gain", if the property is disposed of by the partnership or if Bobby disposes of his equity interest in the partnership.[122]

The contribution of low-basis property creates some problems for the partnership if Bobby owns less than 51% of the partnership interests. The

[120] IRC § 721 provides: "Nonrecognition of gain or loss on contribution — (a) General rule: No gain or loss shall be recognized to a partnership or to any of its partners in the case of a contribution of property to the partnership in exchange for an interest in the partnership."

[121] IRC § 723.

[122] There are other limitations on the ability of a contributing partner to avoid payment of capital gains taxes on the property contributed. IRC § 707(a)(2)(B) excludes "disguised sales" where, following the contribution of property to the partnership, there is a related transfer of money or other property to the partner. IRC § 752 provides that if the partnership assumes the contributing partner's liabilities for debt connected to the property, or the property is subject to a security interest, the contributing partner is treated as receiving a distribution of money equal to the amount of the debt and must pay appropriate taxes.

partnership will assume Bobby's low basis in the property and this will have an impact on the computation of depreciation deductions and, if the property is disposed of, capital gains or losses. For instance, depreciation deductions will be limited to Bobby's low adjusted basis of $25,000. If the property is sold by the partnership for $125,000, the amount of capital gain will be $100,000, using *Bobby's* $25,000 basis in the property, which will mean an increased capital gains burden. Compare this to a scenario in which Bobby contributes $100,000 in cash and the cash is used to *buy* the property. The partnership's basis would be its cost of acquisition — $100,000. This means an enhanced ability to take depreciation deductions. The gain upon sale of the property for $125,000 will be only $25,000 (assuming the adjusted basis remains at $100,000). In the absence of some adjustments in the allocation of these capital gains, it would mean that Bobby has effectively transferred the tax burden for his appreciated property to his partners, since they will all have to share in payment of the capital gains taxes caused by the partnership's assumption of Bobby's low basis.

These problems are handled by IRC § 704(c), and accompanying regulations,[123] which are designed to prevent the shifting of tax consequences among partners with respect to contributed property when the basis of the contributing partner is less than the fair market value of the property. Essentially, IRC § 704(c) establishes the contributing partner's "built in" gain or loss at the time of the partner's contribution and requires partnerships to allocate income, gain, loss, and deductions with respect to property contributed to the partnership "so as to take account of the variation between the basis of the property to the partnership and its fair market value at the time of contribution." The "built in" gain or loss is determined by computing the difference between the fair market value of the property and the contributing partner's adjusted basis *at the time of the contribution.*

In the case of a sale of the property in our example, the large capital gains of $100,000 will be allocated so that Bobby receives the lion's share of the gain of $75,000 and all partners will share in the smaller $25,000 gain that has occurred. IRC § 704(c) and the accompanying Regulations also require adjustments in the allocation of *depreciation* between the parties to reflect the contributing partner's low basis in the property.

Despite the adjustments required by IRC § 704(c) Bobby gains significant advantages by contributing the low-basis property rather than contributing cash, since he will succeed in *postponing* the payment of capital gains taxes to some future date. That future date will occur when the property is sold by the partnership, or Bobby disposes of his partnership interest.

It's important to note that Bobby's basis in his *partnership interest* will be the same as his *basis* in the contributed property ($25,000 in our example), plus any additional cash he contributes, rather than the fair market value of the property he contributed ($100,000 in our example).[124] This makes sense, since Bobby might sell his interest in the partnership, while the partnership still retains the property. If,

---

[123] Treas. Reg. § 1.704-3

[124] IRC § 722, which provides: "The basis of an interest in a partnership acquired by a contribution of property, including money, to the partnership shall be the amount of such money and the adjusted basis of such property to the contributing partner at the time of the contribution increased by the amount (if any) of gain recognized under section 721(b) to the contributing partner at such time."

for instance, he sells his partnership interest for $110,000, his capital gain upon disposition of the *partnership interest* will be computed by deducting from the sale's price his adjusted basis transferred from the property ($25,000) for a capital gain of $85,000. In other words, while Bobby can postpone the obligation to pay capital gains on the contributed low-basis property, he will eventually have to pay capital gains taxes computed by reference to his original basis in the property.

EXERCISE 3-1

Angela and Barry are software designers and entrepreneurs. In the past, they formed two software companies that were highly successful and generated substantial returns for themselves and investors in their companies. Recently, they developed a business plan for a third company, based on their design of an innovative software program. The plan envisions the formation of a business entity that will own, develop, market and license the software program. After much effort, Angela and Barry have lined up some potential investors and lenders, and it is time to consider the tax implications before selecting the form of business entity to own and operate the business. The general parameters of the business plan are:

Capitalization & Financing: There will be fifteen investment units. Thirteen of the units will be sold to investors for $100,000 per unit. Each of these thirteen investors will be obligated to *loan* the company an additional $50,000.

Angela and Barry will each receive one investment unit in exchange for: (i) an assignment of the intellectual property rights to the software; (ii) a non-competition agreement; and (iii) their services in planning and forming the entity.

In addition, the company will be authorized to borrow an additional $1 million from a commercial lender to cover operating costs of the business.

Investors: All of the investors are individuals with significant assets and income.

Employment Contracts: Angela and Barry will have employment contracts for a term of five years, obligating them to manage the affairs of the company.

Financial Forecasts: The company will have substantial losses for the first two years but will likely have a small profit in year three. In subsequent years there will be increasingly large profits.

Angela and Barry are considering whether or not to form a general partnership, limited partnership, limited liability company, C corporation or S corporation. They recognize that their ability to obtain subscription agreements from their investors, and loan commitments from their lenders, will partially depend on the tax consequences of their choice of business entity. They have come to you seeking advice. Prepare a memorandum discussing:

1. The fundamental tax attributes of the different types of business entities.
2. The basic tax advantages and disadvantages of selecting each type of entity for this transaction with regard to the distribution of profits, losses, and return of capital to investors. Identify any areas where it might be prudent to consult with a tax specialist.

3.   The impact on Angela and Barry with regard to their contributions of property, services and non-competition agreements.

EXERCISE 3-2

Suppose that the financial forecasts in the business plan were altered as follows:

Financial Forecasts: The company will have no losses. Profits in the first year will be modest. In subsequent years there will be increasingly large profits. Over a five year period the financial forecasts predict a return on investment of 200%.

What adjustments would you make in your tax considerations memorandum to reflect the changes in financial forecasts?

Chapter 4

SECURITIES LAW CONSIDERATIONS

Lawyers advising businesses must be simultaneous experts in many varied fields of law. Of all of these, there are three subjects important in virtually *every* business transaction, because they are broad based and cut across all different types of deals and problems. The first two are the substantive law of the business entity (whether as a partnership, corporation, limited liability company or some other form) and income tax law. These were the subjects of Chapters 2 and 3.

The third broad area — securities regulation — may seem to be specialized and narrow, not one implicated in most business planning questions. However, the financing of most business entities involves the sale of securities, and every sale of every security is potentially within the reach of federal or state securities law. In Section A of this chapter, we present the two basic provisions of the securities laws which can be problems for a new business: (i) the requirement that securities be registered or exempted from registration, and (ii) the application of antifraud rules to the offer or sale of any security. Section B describes the nature of the beast — a "security" — subject to these laws. Sections C and D provide more details on how to comply with each of these requirements, and Section E discusses the parallel universe of state securities regulation.

A. THE TWO PROBLEMS OF THE SECURITIES LAWS

By the term "securities laws," we refer primarily to two federal[1] statutes: the Securities Act of 1933, and the Securities Exchange Act of 1934.[2] There are two major requirements in these acts which confront the organizer of a new business. First, there is "registration" — every sale of securities not exempt from this rule must follow an expensive and exhaustive set of disclosure requirements. Second, there is "antifraud" — a general requirement to tell the truth when selling securities.

1. Registration

The Securities Act of 1933 requires the "registration" of every sale of securities before that sale takes place. Section 5(c) of that act provides in part that:

---

[1] We will discuss the state law counterparts in Section E below.

[2] The Securities Act of 1933 is codified at 15 U.S.C. § 77 *et seq.* and the Securities Exchange Act of 1934 is codified at 15 U.S.C. § 78 *et seq.* We will follow the custom of nearly all securities lawyers and refer to the statutes in short form: the first as the "Securities Act" or "the '33 Act," and the second as the "Exchange Act" or "the '34 Act." When referring to sections of each act, we will also follow the custom of most securities lawyers and refer to sections of the Acts themselves, not the convoluted codification, e.g. "Securities Act § 5" rather than "15 U.S.C. § 77e" and "Exchange Act § 10(b)" rather than "15 U.S.C. § 78j(b)."

> It shall be unlawful for any person, directly or indirectly, to make use of any means or instruments of transportation or communication in interstate commerce or of the mails to offer to sell or offer to buy through the use or medium of any prospectus or otherwise any security, unless a registration statement has been filed as to such security . . . .[3]

It is apparent that Section 5 "covers the universe."[4] The only "out" obvious from the language of the statute is to somehow avoid the use of interstate commerce.[5]

However, you may have noticed that Section 5 says only that "it shall be unlawful" to sell unregistered securities. The consequences are not immediately apparent.[6] You must read all the way to Section 12(a)(1) for the bad news:

> Any person who . . . offers or sells a security in violation of section 5 . . . shall be liable . . . to the person purchasing such security from him, who may sue either at law or in equity in any court of competent jurisdiction, to recover the consideration paid for such security with interest thereon . . . or for damages if he no longer owns the security.

Stated another way, the main consequence of a violation of Section 5 is to give everyone who purchased a security an opportunity for a refund. This, of course, they will be glad to take if the business has gone badly, in which case there is probably little or no money for your clients to refund to these investors.[7] There is also the prospect of criminal liability for "willful" violations,[8] but we won't dwell on that — the enormous civil liability under Section 12(a)(1) is probably sufficient to focus the attention of you and your client on compliance with the Securities Act.

Returning to Section 5, we see that the way to comply with the Act is to "file" a "registration statement." This is done with the Securities and Exchange Commission.[9] And while the Commission has endeavored to make the process of filing a registration statement simple, the undertaking is breathtakingly complicated. The

---

[3] Section 5(a) of the Act goes further and precludes sales until that registration statement has been "declared effective."

[4] Louis Loss & Joel Seligman, Fundamentals of Securities Regulation 93 (5th ed. 2003). This book began in 1983 as a "student edition" of the most comprehensive multi-volume securities law treatise (which goes by same title shorn of the "Fundamentals of" precursor). Now many years later it is still a very useful distillation of the much longer definitive work by the same authors. Because our coverage here is introductory, we will cite ordinarily to the one-volume version of Professor Loss' and Professor Seligman's work.

[5] It will be difficult to do this, since even intrastate conduct, such as travel, or a phone call, fax or email, which uses interstate "facilities" will meet the jurisdictional requirement of § 5. See Gary M. Brown, Soderquist on the Securities Laws, § 3.2.1 at pp. 3-6 to 3-7 (5th ed. 2007) ("The concept of jurisidictional means . . . is broad. . . . . Lawyers litigating securities cases may sometimes find 'no jurisdictional means' arguments helpful. Others will find such arguments too dangerous to rely on."). Even then, you may have only moved from the frying pan to the fire, that is, from the federal securities law to one of its state-law counterparts. See Section E, this chapter.

[6] Indeed, one difficulty of understanding the Securities Act is to realize that the whole thing revolves around § 5 and its "unlawfulness" declaration. "That scheme of involuted drafting does not facilitate comprehensibility." Loss & Seligman, supra, at 93.

[7] The Act does provide a statute of limitations, but it is an agonizingly long three years from the date "after the security was bona fide offered to the public." Securities Act § 13.

[8] Section 24 of the Act provides in part that "[a]ny person who willfully violates any of the provisions of this title . . . shall upon conviction be fined not more than $10,000 or imprisoned not more than five years, or both."

[9] Hereafter referred to as "the Commission" or "the SEC."

process of registration will require the assistance of specialized securities law counsel, detailed work by a certified public accountant, and even in this electronic age there may be printing expenses; a copy of part of this registration statement (called a "prospectus") must be sent to each purchaser.[10] Each of these experts charges tens or hundreds of thousands of dollars, depending on the complexity of the task.[11] Obviously, a company will have to have in mind raising several million dollars before a registered offering is feasible. And at this level, it is often the case that an investment banking firm must be hired to find investors to buy such a large amount of securities. These firms typically charge ten percent or more of the aggregate offering price,[12] pushing the cost and the minimum practical size of the offering still higher. Finally, the registration statement, once filed, may be subject to detailed review by the staff at the SEC before it can be used to sell securities.[13] This review may include detailed inspection of disclosure by lawyers and accountants, requiring response and redrafting by your client, which may delay the process and further increase the costs. That is not the end of your worries. Although the registration statement is informally cleared by the SEC, the issuer and a host of others, including attorneys and accountants, remain liable for misstatements which appear therein.[14]

Has Congress, in its wisdom, made the offer or sale of securities impossible except in such large amounts as to make financing by small businesses impossible?[15] Not entirely. Section 5 only applies to "securities," a term which might seem self-evident but requires some careful study. Even if the investments *are* securities, many offers and sales of securities are exempt from Section 5's onerous requirements. These are the subjects of Parts B and C below.

2.   Antifraud

The second major requirement in federal securities law relevant to the business planner is the obligation to not commit fraud or make material misstatements in the offer or sale of securities. This requirement is stated in several different places

---

[10] This is courtesy of § 5(b) of the Act.

[11] Brown, *supra*, § 2.2.2 at p. 2–9.

[12] *Id.*

[13] This is courtesy of § 5(a) of the Act, which prohibits sales unless a registration statement is "in effect" for the securities involved. Although § 8(a) of the Act provides that registration statements become effective 20 days after filing, in practice that is never the case; the registration statement becomes effective when the SEC staff is ready to have it become effective. This process "renders the statutory 20 day period largely of historical interest." Loss & Seligman, *supra*, at 129. See Brown, *supra*, § 2:4, pp. 2-18 to 2-22, for a good concise summary of the registration process from filing until effectiveness.

[14] Securities Act § 11. This is only the beginning of life under the securities laws. Normally, a company which makes a public offering is required thereafter to file comprehensive annual and quarterly reports with the SEC which make these professional costs an ongoing expense.

[15] *See generally* Rutheford B Campbell, Jr., *Regulation A: Small Business' Search for "A Moderate Capital,"* 31 DEL. J. CORP. L. 77, 91–92 (2006) ("Registration has never been a viable way for small businesses to raise capital. High transaction costs associated with registered offerings inevitably put registration out of the range of small businesses in search of capital."). On the other hand, it is clear that the alternatives to a registered offering also have their costs, and that a registered offering, once the bitter pill of the high cost is swallowed, can reduce costs for subsequent rounds of financing. For a comprehensive yet concise summary of both the costs and benefits of registered offerings, see Brown, *supra*, §§ 2:2.1 and 2:2.2, pp. 2-2 to 2-14.

in the '33 and '34 Acts, and together these are usually known as "antifraud" requirements. The antifraud requirement most likely to be relevant in the organization of a business is the famous Rule 10b-5, which makes it unlawful to make a false statement or to make a material omission from an otherwise truthful statement "in connection with" the purchase or sale of any security. The breadth of this requirement is discussed in Section D below, along with some background on other antifraud requirements.

There are no significant exemptions from this antifraud requirement. However, like the registration requirement, it applies only to a "security."

B. DEFINITION OF A "SECURITY"

Securities Act § 2(a)(1)

The term "security" means any note, stock, treasury stock, security future, bond, debenture, evidence of indebtedness, certificate of interest or participation in any profit-sharing agreement, collateral-trust certificate, pre-organization certificate or subscription, transferable share, investment contract, voting-trust certificate, certificate of deposit for a security, fractional undivided interest in oil, gas, or other mineral rights, any put, call, straddle, option, or privilege on any security, certificate of deposit, or group or index of securities (including any interest therein or based on the value thereof), or any put, call, straddle, option, or privilege entered into on a national securities exchange relating to foreign currency, or, in general, any interest or instrument commonly known as a "security", or any certificate of interest or participation in, temporary or interim certificate for, receipt for, guarantee of, or warrant or right to subscribe to or purchase, any of the foregoing.

This is obviously quite a list, and the Supreme Court has made clear that each term is subject to its own separate analysis.[16] So perhaps one way to understand what a "security" is would be to work our way down the list.

REVES v. ERNST & YOUNG
United States Supreme Court
494 U.S. 56 (1990)

JUSTICE MARSHALL delivered the opinion of the Court.

This case presents the question whether certain demand notes issued by the Farmers Cooperative of Arkansas and Oklahoma (Co-Op) are "securities" within the meaning of § 3(a)(10) of the Securities Exchange Act of 1934. We conclude that they are.

I

The Co-Op is an agricultural cooperative that, at the time relevant here, had approximately 23,000 members. In order to raise money to support its general business operations, the Co-Op sold promissory notes payable on demand by the

---

[16] Loss & Seligman, *supra*, at 232, *citing* Landreth Timber Co. v. Landreth, 471 U.S. 681, 691 (1985).

holder. Although the notes were uncollateralized and uninsured, they paid a variable rate of interest that was adjusted monthly to keep it higher than the rate paid by local financial institutions. The Co-Op offered the notes to both members and nonmembers, marketing the scheme as an "Investment Program." Advertisements for the notes, which appeared in each Co-Op newsletter, read in part: "YOUR CO-OP has more than $11,000,000 in assets to stand behind your investments. The Investment is not Federal [*sic*] insured but it is . . . Safe . . . Secure . . . and available when you need it." App. 5 (ellipses in original). Despite these assurances, the Co-Op filed for bankruptcy in 1984. At the time of the filing, over 1,600 people held notes worth a total of $10 million.

After the Co-Op filed for bankruptcy, petitioners, a class of holders of the notes, filed suit against Arthur Young & Co., the firm that had audited the Co-Op's financial statements (and the predecessor to respondent Ernst & Young). Petitioners alleged, *inter alia*, that Arthur Young had intentionally failed to follow generally accepted accounting principles in its audit, specifically with respect to the valuation of one of the Co-Op's major assets, a gasohol plant. Petitioners claimed that Arthur Young violated these principles in an effort to inflate the assets and net worth of the Co-Op. Petitioners maintained that, had Arthur Young properly treated the plant in its audits, they would not have purchased demand notes because the Co-Op's insolvency would have been apparent. On the basis of these allegations, petitioners claimed that Arthur Young had violated the antifraud provisions of the 1934 Act as well as Arkansas' securities laws.

Petitioners prevailed at trial on both their federal and state claims, receiving a $6.1 million judgment. Arthur Young appealed, claiming that the demand notes were not "securities" under either the 1934 Act or Arkansas law, and that the statutes' antifraud provisions therefore did not apply. A panel of the Eighth Circuit, agreeing with Arthur Young on both the state and federal issues, reversed. *Arthur Young & Co. v. Reves*, 856 F.2d 52 (1988). We granted certiorari to address the federal issue, 490 U.S. 1105, 109 S.Ct. 3154, 104 L.Ed.2d 1018 (1989), and now reverse the judgment of the Court of Appeals.

II

A

This case requires us to decide whether the note issued by the Co-Op is a "security" within the meaning of the 1934 Act. Section 3(a)(10) of that Act is our starting point:

> "The term 'security' means any note, stock, treasury stock, bond, debenture, certificate of interest or participation in any profit-sharing agreement or in any oil, gas, or other mineral royalty or lease, any collateral-trust certificate, preorganization certificate or subscription, transferable share, investment contract, voting-trust certificate, certificate of deposit, for a security, any put, call, straddle, option, or privilege on any security, certificate of deposit, or group or index of securities (including any interest therein or based on the value thereof), or any put, call, straddle, option, or privilege entered into on a national securities exchange relating to foreign currency, or in general, any instrument commonly known as a 'security'; or any certificate of interest or participation in, temporary or interim certifi-

cate for, receipt for, or warrant or right to subscribe to or purchase, any of the foregoing; but shall not include currency or any note, draft, bill of exchange, or banker's acceptance which has a maturity at the time of issuance of not exceeding nine months, exclusive of days of grace, or any renewal thereof the maturity of which is likewise limited."

48 Stat. 884, as amended, 15 U.S.C. § 78c(a)(10).

The fundamental purpose undergirding the Securities Acts is "to eliminate serious abuses in a largely unregulated securities market." *United Housing Foundation, Inc. v. Forman*, 421 U.S. 837, 849 (1975). In defining the scope of the market that it wished to regulate, Congress painted with a broad brush. It recognized the virtually limitless scope of human ingenuity, especially in the creation of "countless and variable schemes devised by those who seek the use of the money of others on the promise of profits," *SEC v. W.J. Howey Co.*, 328 U.S. 293, 299 (1946), and determined that the best way to achieve its goal of protecting investors was "to define 'the term "security" in sufficiently broad and general terms so as to include within that definition the many types of instruments that in our commercial world fall within the ordinary concept of a security.'" *Forman, supra*, (quoting H.R.Rep. No. 85, 73d Cong., 1st Sess., 11 (1933)). Congress therefore did not attempt precisely to cabin the scope of the Securities Acts.[17] Rather, it enacted a definition of "security" sufficiently broad to encompass virtually any instrument that might be sold as an investment.

Congress did not, however, "intend to provide a broad federal remedy for all fraud." *Marine Bank v. Weaver*, 455 U.S. 551 (1982). Accordingly, "[t]he task has fallen to the Securities and Exchange Commission (SEC), the body charged with administering the Securities Acts, and ultimately to the federal courts to decide which of the myriad financial transactions in our society come within the coverage of these statutes." *Forman, supra*, 421 U.S., at 848. In discharging our duty, we are not bound by legal formalisms, but instead take account of the economics of the transaction under investigation. See, *e.g.*, *Tcherepnin v. Knight*, 389 U.S. 332 (1967) (in interpreting the term "security," "form should be disregarded for substance and the emphasis should be on economic reality"). Congress' purpose in enacting the securities laws was to regulate *investments*, in whatever form they are made and by whatever name they are called.

A commitment to an examination of the economic realities of a transaction does not necessarily entail a case-by-case analysis of every instrument, however. Some instruments are obviously within the class Congress intended to regulate because they are by their nature investments. In *Landreth Timber Co. v. Landreth*, 471 U.S. 681 (1985), we held that an instrument bearing the name "stock" that, among other things, is negotiable, offers the possibility of capital appreciation, and carries the right to dividends contingent on the profits of a business enterprise is plainly within the class of instruments Congress intended the securities laws to cover. *Landreth Timber* does not signify a lack of concern with economic reality; rather, it signals a recognition that stock is, as a practical matter, always an investment if it has the economic characteristics traditionally associated with stock. Even if sparse excep-

---

[17] [1] We have consistently held that "[t]he definition of a security in § 3(a)(10) of the 1934 Act, . . . is virtually identical [to the definition in the Securities Act of 1933] and, for present purposes, the coverage of the two Acts may be considered the same." *United Housing Foundation, Inc. v. Forman*, 421 U.S. 837, 847, n. 12, (1975) (citations omitted). We reaffirm that principle here.

tions to this generalization can be found, the public perception of common stock as the paradigm of a security suggests that stock, in whatever context it is sold, should be treated as within the ambit of the Acts. *Id.*, at 687, 693.

We made clear in *Landreth Timber* that stock was a special case, explicitly limiting our holding to that sort of instrument. *Id.*, at 694. Although we refused finally to rule out a similar *per se* rule for notes, we intimated that such a rule would be unjustified. Unlike "stock," we said, " 'note' may now be viewed as a relatively broad term that encompasses instruments with widely varying characteristics, depending on whether issued in a consumer context, as commercial paper, or in some other investment context." *Ibid.* (citing *Securities Industry Assn. v. Board of Governors of Federal Reserve System*, 468 U.S. 137, 149–153, (1984)). While common stock is the quintessence of a security, *Landreth Timber, supra*, 471 U.S., at 693, and investors therefore justifiably assume that a sale of stock is covered by the Securities Acts, the same simply cannot be said of notes, which are used in a variety of settings, not all of which involve investments. Thus, the phrase "any note" should not be interpreted to mean literally "any note," but must be understood against the backdrop of what Congress was attempting to accomplish in enacting the Securities Acts.[18]

Because the *Landreth Timber* formula cannot sensibly be applied to notes, some other principle must be developed to define the term "note." A majority of the Courts of Appeals that have considered the issue have adopted, in varying forms, "investment versus commercial" approaches that distinguish, on the basis of all of the circumstances surrounding the transactions, notes issued in an investment context (which are "securities") from notes issued in a commercial or consumer context (which are not).

The Second Circuit's "family resemblance" approach begins with a presumption that *any* note with a term of more than nine months is a "security." *See, e.g., Exchange Nat. Bank of Chicago v. Touche Ross & Co.* 544 F.2d 1126, 1137 (CA2 1976). Recognizing that not all notes are securities, however, the Second Circuit has also devised a list of notes that it has decided are obviously not securities. Accordingly, the "family resemblance" test permits an issuer to rebut the presumption that a note is a security if it can show that the note in question "bear[s] a strong family resemblance" to an item on the judicially crafted list of exceptions, *id.*, at 1137–1138, or convinces the court to add a new instrument to the list, *see, e.g., Chemical Bank v. Arthur Andersen & Co.*, 726 F.2d 930, 939 (CA2 1984).

. . . .

The . . . "family resemblance" and "investment versus commercial" tests are really two ways of formulating the same general approach. Because we think the "family resemblance" test provides a more promising framework for analysis, however, we adopt it. The test begins with the language of the statute; because the

---

[18] [2] An approach founded on economic reality rather than on a set of *per se* rules is subject to the criticism that whether a particular note is a "security" may not be entirely clear at the time it is issued. Such an approach has the corresponding advantage, though, of permitting the SEC and the courts sufficient flexibility to ensure that those who market investments are not able to escape the coverage of the Securities Acts by creating new instruments that would not be covered by a more determinate definition. One could question whether, at the expense of the goal of clarity, Congress overvalued the goal of avoiding manipulation by the clever and dishonest. If Congress erred, however, it is for that body, and not this Court, to correct its mistake.

Securities Acts define "security" to include "any note," we begin with a presumption that every note is a security. We nonetheless recognize that this presumption cannot be irrebuttable. As we have said, Congress was concerned with regulating the investment market, not with creating a general federal cause of action for fraud. In an attempt to give more content to that dividing line, the Second Circuit has identified a list of instruments commonly denominated "notes" that nonetheless fall without the "security" category. See *Exchange Nat. Bank, supra,* at 1138 (types of notes that are not "securities" include "the note delivered in consumer financing, the note secured by a mortgage on a home, the short-term note secured by a lien on a small business or some of its assets, the note evidencing a 'character' loan to a bank customer, short-term notes secured by an assignment of accounts receivable, or a note which simply formalizes an open-account debt incurred in the ordinary course of business (particularly if, as in the case of the customer of a broker, it is collateralized)"); *Chemical Bank, supra,* at 939 (adding to list "notes evidencing loans by commercial banks for current operations").

We agree that the items identified by the Second Circuit are not properly viewed as "securities." More guidance, though, is needed. It is impossible to make any meaningful inquiry into whether an instrument bears a "resemblance" to one of the instruments identified by the Second Circuit without specifying what it is about *those* instruments that makes *them* non-"securities." Moreover, as the Second Circuit itself has noted, its list is "not graven in stone," 726 F.2d, at 939, and is therefore capable of expansion. Thus, some standards must be developed for determining when an item should be added to the list.

An examination of the list itself makes clear what those standards should be. In creating its list, the Second Circuit was applying the same factors that this Court has held apply in deciding whether a transaction involves a "security." First, we examine the transaction to assess the motivations that would prompt a reasonable seller and buyer to enter into it. If the seller's purpose is to raise money for the general use of a business enterprise or to finance substantial investments and the buyer is interested primarily in the profit the note is expected to generate, the instrument is likely to be a "security." If the note is exchanged to facilitate the purchase and sale of a minor asset or consumer good, to correct for the seller's cash-flow difficulties, or to advance some other commercial or consumer purpose, on the other hand, the note is less sensibly described as a "security." See, *e.g., Forman,* 421 U.S., at 851 (share of "stock" carrying a right to subsidized housing not a security because "the inducement to purchase was solely to acquire subsidized low-cost living space; it was not to invest for profit"). Second, we examine the "plan of distribution" of the instrument, *SEC v. C.M. Joiner Leasing Corp.,* 320 U.S. 344, 353 (1943), to determine whether it is an instrument in which there is "common trading for speculation or investment," *id.,* at 351. Third, we examine the reasonable expectations of the investing public: The Court will consider instruments to be "securities" on the basis of such public expectations, even where an economic analysis of the circumstances of the particular transaction might suggest that the instruments are not "securities" as used in that transaction. Compare *Landreth Timber,* 471 U.S., at 687, 693 (relying on public expectations in holding that common stock is always a security), with *id.,* at 697–700 (STEVENS, J., dissenting) (arguing that sale of business to single informed purchaser through stock is not within the purview of the Acts under the economic reality test). See also *Forman, supra,* at 851. Finally, we examine whether some factor such as the existence of another regulatory scheme significantly reduces the risk of the instrument, thereby rendering application of the Securities Acts unnecessary. See, *e.g., Marine Bank*, 455 U.S., at 557–559, and n. 7.

We conclude, then, that in determining whether an instrument denominated a "note" is a "security," courts are to apply the version of the "family resemblance" test that we have articulated here: A note is presumed to be a "security," and that presumption may be rebutted only by a showing that the note bears a strong resemblance (in terms of the four factors we have identified) to one of the enumerated categories of instrument. If an instrument is not sufficiently similar to an item on the list, the decision whether another category should be added is to be made by examining the same factors.

B

Applying the family resemblance approach to this case, we have little difficulty in concluding that the notes at issue here are "securities." Ernst & Young admits that "a demand note does not closely resemble any of the Second Circuit's family resemblance examples." Brief for Respondent 43. Nor does an examination of the four factors we have identified as being relevant to our inquiry suggest that the demand notes here are not "securities" despite their lack of similarity to any of the enumerated categories. The Co-Op sold the notes in an effort to raise capital for its general business operations, and purchasers bought them in order to earn a profit in the form of interest.[19] Indeed, one of the primary inducements offered purchasers was an interest rate constantly revised to keep it slightly above the rate paid by local banks and savings and loans. From both sides, then, the transaction is most naturally conceived as an investment in a business enterprise rather than as a purely commercial or consumer transaction.

As to the plan of distribution, the Co-Op offered the notes over an extended period to its 23,000 members, as well as to nonmembers, and more than 1,600 people held notes when the Co-Op filed for bankruptcy. To be sure, the notes were not traded on an exchange. They were, however, offered and sold to a broad segment of the public, and that is all we have held to be necessary to establish the requisite "common trading" in an instrument. See, *e.g., Landreth Timber, supra* (stock of closely held corporation not traded on any exchange held to be a "security"); *Tcherepnin*, 389 U.S., at 337 (nonnegotiable but transferable "withdrawable capital shares" in savings and loan association held to be a "security"); *Howey*, 328 U.S., at 295 (units of citrus grove and maintenance contract "securities" although not traded on exchange).

The third factor — the public's reasonable perceptions — also supports a finding that the notes in this case are "securities." We have consistently identified the fundamental essence of a "security" to be its character as an "investment." The advertisements for the notes here characterized them as "investments," and there were no countervailing factors that would have led a reasonable person to question this characterization. In these circumstances, it would be reasonable for a prospective purchaser to take the Co-Op at its word.

Finally, we find no risk-reducing factor to suggest that these instruments are not in fact securities. The notes are uncollateralized and uninsured. Moreover, unlike

[19] [4] We emphasize that by "profit" in the context of notes, we mean "a valuable return on an investment," which undoubtedly includes interest. . . . .

the certificates of deposit in *Marine Bank, supra,* at 557–558, which were insured by the Federal Deposit Insurance Corporation and subject to substantial regulation under the federal banking laws, and unlike the pension plan in *Teamsters v. Daniel,* 439 U.S. 551, 569–570 (1979), which was comprehensively regulated under the Employee Retirement Income Security Act of 1974, 88 Stat. 829, 29 U.S.C. § 1001 *et seq.* (1982 ed.), the notes here would escape federal regulation entirely if the Acts were held not to apply.

The court below found that "[t]he demand nature of the notes is very uncharacteristic of a security," 856 F.2d, at 54, on the theory that the virtually instant liquidity associated with demand notes is inconsistent with the risk ordinarily associated with "securities." This argument is unpersuasive. Common stock traded on a national exchange is the paradigm of a security, and it is as readily convertible into cash as is a demand note. The same is true of publicly traded corporate bonds, debentures, and any number of other instruments that are plainly within the purview of the Acts. The demand feature of a note does permit a holder to eliminate risk quickly by making a demand, but just as with publicly traded stock, the liquidity of the instrument does not eliminate risk altogether. Indeed, publicly traded stock is even more readily liquid than are demand notes, in that a demand only eliminates risk when, and if, payment is made, whereas the sale of a share of stock through a national exchange and the receipt of the proceeds usually occur simultaneously.

We therefore hold that the notes at issue here are within the term "note" in § 3(a)(10).

. . . .

Accordingly, we reverse the judgment of the Court of Appeals and remand the case for further proceedings consistent with this opinion.

So ordered.

[The concurring opinion of Justice Stevens and the concurring and dissenting opinion of Chief Justice Rehnquist (joined by Justices White, O'Connor, and Scalia) are omitted.]

NOTES AND QUESTIONS

1.   In Chapters 1 and 2, we noted that a business, whether sole proprietorship or large corporation, often raises money by borrowing it. In Chapter 3, we noted that in many instances borrowing provides an advantage in deductibility of interest payments. Suppose a small partnership, corporation, or LLC were to borrow money from an investor. How would you determine if the note given by the business is a "security"?

2.   This case did not involve the registration requirement of Section 5 of the Securities Act. Rather, the disappointed investors were suing Ernst & Young based on the antifraud provisions of the Exchange Act Note here that the definition of "security" is dealt with in virtually identical fashion in both acts, and Justice Marshall notes that the two statutory provisions will be construed as if identical.

3.   Once something is determined to be a "security," there may be other hurdles before deciding it is subject to the provisions of the federal securities laws. In *Reves,* another issue faced by the Court was whether the notes, even if "securities,"

were exempted by another provision with which we deal in Section C below. This exemption is the issue with which the omitted part of the Court's opinion and the dissenting opinions are concerned.

The next item mentioned in the statutory definition of a security is "stock." In *Reves*, the Court indicated that there was really no sophisticated issue here. Stock is almost always a "security." There are exceptions, to be sure. In *United Housing Foundation, Inc. v. Forman*,[20] the Court held that shares in a nonprofit cooperative housing association, although called "stock," were really investments in real estate and not "securities" within the Securities Act or the Exchange Act. However, in *Landreth Timber Co. v. Landreth*,[21] the Court refused to extend such analysis further, holding that the sale of *all* the stock of a corporation was still a sale of "stock" under the Securities Act and the Exchange Act, and was not actually a sale of the corporation's underlying assets, nor an "investment contract." Thus, as the Court made clear in *Reves*, the same "economic substance" doctrine applies to stock as well as notes. But the inquiry is far more abbreviated in the case of stock.

Although the definition of a "security" comprises many terms, our consideration of the list can be limited to only three terms: note, stock and "investment contract." The first two have been covered above, the third by the case which follows. There are many other terms included in the definition of a "security," but these are the main ones which present legal issues with which a business attorney will deal.

SECURITIES AND EXCHANGE COMMISSION v. W.J. HOWEY CO.
United States Supreme Court
328 U.S. 293 (1946)

MR. JUSTICE MURPHY delivered the opinion of the Court.

This case involves the application of § 2(a)(1)[22] of the Securities Act of 1933 to an offering of units of a citrus grove development coupled with a contract for cultivating, marketing and remitting the net proceeds to the investor.

The Securities and Exchange Commission instituted this action to restrain the respondents from using the mails and instrumentalities of interstate commerce in the offer and sale of unregistered and nonexempt securities in violation of § 5(a) of the Act. The District Court denied the injunction, 60 F.Supp. 440, and the Fifth Circuit Court of Appeals affirmed the judgment, 151 F.2d 714. We granted certiorari, 327 U.S. 773, on a petition alleging that the ruling of the Circuit Court of Appeals conflicted with other federal and state decisions and that it introduced a novel and unwarranted test under the statute which the Commission regarded as administratively impractical.

Most of the facts are stipulated. The respondents, W. J. Howey Company and Howey-in-the-Hills Service Inc., are Florida corporations under direct common control and management. The Howey Company owns large tracts of citrus acreage in Lake County, Florida. During the past several years it has planted about 500

---

[20] 421 U.S. 837 (1975).

[21] 471 U.S. 681 (1985).

[22] [Section 2 was amended in 1996 to add letter subdivisions, so former § 2(1) is now § 2(a)(1). We have made this editorial change here and without further notice in the remainder of this opinion.—Eds.]

acres annually, keeping half of the groves itself and offering the other half to the public 'to help us finance additional development.' Howey-in-the-Hills Service, Inc., is a service company engaged in cultivating and developing many of these groves, including the harvesting and marketing of the crops.

Each prospective customer is offered both a land sales contract and a service contract, after having been told that it is not feasible to invest in a grove unless service arrangements are made. While the purchaser is free to make arrangements with other service companies, the superiority of Howey-in-the-Hills Service, Inc., is stressed. Indeed, 85% of the acreage sold during the 3-year period ending May 31, 1943, was covered by service contracts with Howey-in-the-Hills Service, Inc.

The land sales contract with the Howey Company provides for a uniform purchase price per acre or fraction thereof, varying in amount only in accordance with the number of years the particular plot has been planted with citrus trees. Upon full payment of the purchase price the land is conveyed to the purchaser by warranty deed. Purchases are usually made in narrow strips of land arranged so that an acre consists of a row of 48 trees. During the period between February 1, 1941, and May 31, 1943, 31 of the 42 persons making purchases bought less than 5 acres each. The average holding of these 31 persons was 1.33 acres and sales of as little as 0.65, 0.7 and 0.73 of an acre were made. These tracts are not separately fenced and the sole indication of several ownership is found in small land marks intelligible only through a plat book record.

The service contract, generally of a 10-year duration without option of cancellation, gives Howey-in-the-Hills Service, Inc., a leasehold interest and 'full and complete' possession of the acreage. For a specified fee plus the cost of labor and materials, the company is given full discretion and authority over the cultivation of the groves and the harvest and marketing of the crops. The company is well established in the citrus business and maintains a large force of skilled personnel and a great deal of equipment, including 75 tractors, sprayer wagons, fertilizer trucks and the like. Without the consent of the company, the land owner or purchaser has no right of entry to market the crop; thus there is ordinarily no right to specific fruit. The company is accountable only for an allocation of the net profits based upon a check made at the time of picking. All the produce is pooled by the respondent companies, which do business under their own names.

The purchasers for the most part are non-residents of Florida. They are predominantly business and professional people who lack the knowledge, skill and equipment necessary for the care and cultivation of citrus trees. They are attracted by the expectation of substantial profits. It was represented, for example, that profits during the 1943–1944 season amounted to 20% and that even greater profits might be expected during the 1944–1945 season, although only a 10% annual return was to be expected over a 10-year period. Many of these purchasers are patrons of a resort hotel owned and operated by the Howey Company in a scenic section adjacent to the groves. The hotel's advertising mentions the fine groves in the vicinity and the attention of the patrons is drawn to the groves as they are being escorted about the surrounding countryside. They are told that the groves are for sale; if they indicate an interest in the matter they are then given a sales talk.

It is admitted that the mails and instrumentalities of interstate commerce are used in the sale of the land and service contracts and that no registration statement or letter of notification has ever been filed with the Commission in accordance with the Securities Act of 1933 and the rules and regulations thereunder.

Section 2(a)(1) of the Act defines the term 'security' to include the commonly known documents traded for speculation or investment. This definition also includes 'securities' of a more variable character, designated by such descriptive terms as 'certificate of interest or participation in any profit-sharing agreement,' 'investment contract' and 'in general, any interest or instrument commonly known as a "security."' The legal issue in this case turns upon a determination of whether, under the circumstances, the land sales contract, the warranty deed and the service contract together constitute an 'investment contract' within the meaning of § 2(a)(1). An affirmative answer brings into operation the registration requirements of § 5(a), unless the security is granted an exemption under § 3(b). The lower courts, in reaching a negative answer to this problem, treated the contracts and deeds as separate transactions involving no more than an ordinary real estate sale and an agreement by the seller to manage the property for the buyer.

The term 'investment contract' is undefined by the Securities Act or by relevant legislative reports. But the term was common in many state 'blue sky' laws in existence prior to the adoption of the federal statute and, although the term was also undefined by the state laws, it had been broadly construed by state courts so as to afford the investing public a full measure of protection. Form was disregarded for substance and emphasis was placed upon economic reality. An investment contract thus came to mean a contract or scheme for 'the placing of capital or laying out of money in a way intended to secure income or profit from its employment.' *State v. Gopher Tire & Rubber Co.*, 146 Minn. 52, 56, 177 N.W. 937, 938. This definition was uniformly applied by state courts to a variety of situations where individuals were led to invest money in a common enterprise with the expectation that they would earn a profit solely through the efforts of the promoter or of some one other than themselves.

By including an investment contract within the scope of § 2(a)(1) of the Securities Act, Congress was using a term the meaning of which had been crystallized by this prior judicial interpretation. It is therefore reasonable to attach that meaning to the term as used by Congress, especially since such a definition is consistent with the statutory aims. In other words, an investment contract for purposes of the Securities Act means a contract, transaction or scheme whereby a person invests his money in a common enterprise and is led to expect profits solely from the efforts of the promoter or a third party, it being immaterial whether the shares in the enterprise are evidenced by formal certificates or by nominal interests in the physical assets employed in the enterprise. Such a definition necessarily underlies this Court's decision in *Securities Exch. Commission v. C. M. Joiner Leasing Corp.*, 320 U.S. 344 (1943), and has been enunciated and applied many times by lower federal courts. It permits the fulfillment of the statutory purpose of compelling full and fair disclosure relative to the issuance of 'the many types of instruments that in our commercial world fall within the ordinary concept of a security.' H.Rep.No.85, 73rd Cong., 1st Sess., p. 11. It embodies a flexible rather than a static principle, one that is capable of adaptation to meet the countless and variable schemes devised by those who seek the use of the money of others on the promise of profits.

The transactions in this case clearly involve investment contracts as so defined. The respondent companies are offering something more than fee simple interests in land, something different from a farm or orchard coupled with management services. They are offering an opportunity to contribute money and to share in the profits of a large citrus fruit enterprise managed and partly owned by respondents. They are offering this opportunity to persons who reside in distant localities and who lack the equipment and experience requisite to the cultivation, harvesting and marketing of the citrus products. Such persons have no desire to occupy the land or to develop it themselves; they are attracted solely by the prospects of a return on their investment. Indeed, individual development of the plots of land that are offered and sold would seldom be economically feasible due to their small size. Such tracts gain utility as citrus groves only when cultivated and developed as component parts of a larger area. A common enterprise managed by respondents or third parties with adequate personnel and equipment is therefore essential if the investors are to achieve their paramount aim of a return on their investments. Their respective shares in this enterprise are evidenced by land sales contracts and warranty deeds, which serve as a convenient method of determining the investors' allocable shares of the profits. The resulting transfer of rights in land is purely incidental.

Thus all the elements of a profit-seeking business venture are present here. The investors provide the capital and share in the earnings and profits; the promoters manage, control and operate the enterprise. It follows that the arrangements whereby the investors' interests are made manifest involve investment contracts, regardless of the legal terminology in which such contracts are clothed. The investment contracts in this instance take the form of land sales contracts, warranty deeds and service contracts which respondents offer to prospective investors. And respondents' failure to abide by the statutory and administrative rules in making such offerings, even though the failure result from a bona fide mistake as to the law, cannot be sanctioned under the Act.

This conclusion is unaffected by the fact that some purchasers choose not to accept the full offer of an investment contract by declining to enter into a service contract with the respondents. The Securities Act prohibits the offer as well as the sale of unregistered, non-exempt securities. Hence it is enough that the respondents merely offer the essential ingredients of an investment contract.

We reject the suggestion of the Circuit Court of Appeals, 151 F.2d at page 717, that an investment contract is necessarily missing where the enterprise is not speculative or promotional in character and where the tangible interest which is sold has intrinsic value independent of the success of the enterprise as a whole. The test is whether the scheme involves an investment of money in a common enterprise with profits to come solely from the efforts of others. If that test be satisfied, it is immaterial whether the enterprise is speculative or non-speculative or whether there is a sale of property with or without intrinsic value. See *S.E.C. v. C. M. Joiner Leasing Corp., supra.* The statutory policy of affording broad protection to investors is not to be thwarted by unrealistic and irrelevant formulae.

Reversed.

Mr. Justice Jackson took no part in the consideration or decision of this case.

[The dissenting opinion of Justice Frankfurter is omitted.]

Justice Murphy's concise definition of an investment contract as "a contract, transaction or scheme whereby a person invests his money in a common enterprise and is led to expect profits solely from the efforts of the promoter or a third party" is known as the *Howey* test. As the Court noted in *Reves*, the *Howey* test is to be used only in determining if something is an "investment contract," not a "stock" or "note" or something else on the list in § 2(a)(1). The *Howey* test is recognized as having four parts: (1) an investment of money, (2) in a common enterprise, (3) with profits expected (4) solely from the efforts of others.[23] Courts have since relaxed the "solely" language in part four of the test to read "primarily" or "substantially"[24] or that "the efforts made by those other than the investor are the undeniably significant ones, those essential managerial efforts which affect the failure or success of the enterprise."[25]

In *Howey*, unlike *Reves*, the lawsuit involved violation of the registration provision: Section 5 of the Securities Act. Note the difference in litigation strategy. The plaintiff in a § 5 lawsuit (here, the government, but it could be a private investor) need only prove that the security was offered or sold and that no registration statement was in effect. Contrast the antifraud suit, which requires proof of a material or omission misstatement and some sort of knowledge on the part of the defendant.

The fact that § 5 via § 12(a)(1) yields almost "no fault" liability means that many plaintiffs will attempt to make "securities" out of the oddest things. These "esoteric securities" cases include the orange groves in *Howey*, as well as "scotch whiskey, self-improvement courses, cosmetics, earthworms, beavers, muskrats, rabbits, chinchillas, animal feeding programs, cattle embryos, fishing boats, vacuum cleaners, cemetery lots, coin operated telephones, master recording contracts, [and] pooled litigation funds"[26] as well as "Ponzi schemes and . . . gambling."[27] The point, of course, is not that all these things were necessarily free of fraud or misstatements, only that the registration violation is much easier to prove and yields as good or better a recovery for the plaintiff.

The serious lesson here is that we need to use the "investment contract" analysis to cover important items which appear nowhere on the list in § 2(a)(1): interests in non-corporate entities, such as partnerships and LLCs. How do these interests fare under the *Howey* test? Consider first the general partnership interest.

> Although general partners and joint venturers may not individually have decisive control over major decisions, they do have the sort of influence which generally provides them with access to important information and protection against a dependence on others. Moreover, partnership powers are not in the nature of a nominal role in the enterprise which a seller of

---

[23] Loss & Seligman, *supra*, at 250.

[24] Thomas Lee Hazen, The Law of Securities Regulation 44 (4th ed. 2002) (citations omitted). As with the Loss & Seligman treatise, Professor Hazen offers both a "student" and "practitioner's" edition of his work. We cite here to the student edition.

[25] Loss & Seligman, supra at 256 (citing SEC v. Glenn W. Turner Enterprises, Inc., 474 F.2d 476, 482 (9th Cir. 1973)).

[26] Hazen, *supra*, at 37–38 (citations omitted).

[27] *Id.* at 41.

investment contracts would include in order to avoid the securities laws; on
the contrary, one would expect such a promoter to insist on ultimate control
over the investment venture. An investor who is offered an interest in a
general partnership or joint venture should be on notice, therefore, that his
ownership rights are significant, and that the federal securities acts will not
protect him from a mere failure to exercise his rights.

It should be clear from the context of the cases discussed above, however,
that the mere fact that an investment takes the form of a general
partnership or joint venture does not inevitably insulate it from the reach
of the federal securities laws. All of these cases presume that the
investor-partner is not in fact dependent on the promoter or manager for
the effective exercise of his partnership powers. If, for example, the
partner has irrevocably delegated his powers, or is incapable of exercising
them, or is so dependent on the particular expertise of the promoter or
manager that he has no reasonable alternative to reliance on that person,
then his partnership powers may be inadequate to protect him from the
dependence on others which is implicit in an investment contract.

Thus, a general partnership in which some agreement among the partners
places the controlling power in the hands of certain managing partners may
be an investment contract with respect to the other partners. In such a case
the agreement allocates partnership power as in a limited partnership,
which has long been held to be an investment contract. Similarly, one would
not expect partnership interests sold to large numbers of the general public
to provide any real partnership control; at some point there would be so
many partners that a partnership vote would be more like a corporate vote,
each partner's role having been diluted to the level of a single shareholder
in a corporation. Such an arrangement might well constitute an investment
contract.[28]

This general rule suggests that the answer would ordinarily be different for limited
partnerships.

In the case of a limited partnership interest, the [ULPA] requires that, at
least to some extent, the investment be a passive one. Any significant
degree of control or management in the enterprise may transform the
limited partner into a general partner. . . . It follows that unless the
limited partner exercises an unusual amount of control over the business,
his or her limited partnership interest will be a security.[29]

Or, as Professors Loss and Seligman put it succinctly: "In short, it is substance, not
form, that controls here, too."[30]

Although experience with LLC interests under the securities laws is more
limited than with partnerships, in general we would expect the same "form over
substance" rule to apply, and if there exists *de facto* management control through
the membership interest, ordinarily a security will *not* exist, with the converse true

[28] Williamson v. Tucker, 645 F.2d 404, 422–23 (5th Cir. 1981) (citations omitted).

[29] Hazen, *supra*, at 56–57.

[30] Loss & Seligman, *supra*, at 259.

for primarily passive interests.[31]

ROBINSON v. GLYNN
United States Court of Appeals, Fourth Circuit
349 F.3d 166 (2003)

Before Wilkinson and Gregory, Circuit Judges, and Hamilton, Senior Circuit Judge.

Wilkinson, Circuit Judge:

Plaintiff James Robinson filed suit against Thomas Glynn, Glynn Scientific, Inc., and GeoPhone Company, LLC, alleging that Glynn committed federal securities fraud when he sold Robinson a partial interest in GeoPhone Company. The district court found that Robinson's membership interest in GeoPhone was not a security within the meaning of the federal securities laws, and it dismissed Robinson's securities fraud claim. Because Robinson was an active and knowledgeable executive at GeoPhone, rather than a mere passive investor in the company, we affirm. To do otherwise would unjustifiably expand the scope of the federal securities laws by treating an ordinary commercial venture as an investment contract.

I.

Robinson appeals from a grant of summary judgment to Glynn, and accordingly we take the facts in the light most favorable to Robinson. In 1995, Glynn organized GeoPhone Corporation to develop and commercially market the GeoPhone telecommunications system. The GeoPhone system was designed around a signal processing technology, Convolutional Ambiguity Multiple Access (CAMA), that Glynn purportedly designed. Glynn was GeoPhone Corporation's majority shareholder and chairman. In September 1995, GeoPhone Corporation became a limited liability company, GeoPhone Company, LLC. LLCs are noncorporate business entities that offer their members limited liability, tax benefits, and organizational flexibility.

In March 1995, Glynn and his associates contacted James Robinson, a businessman with no prior telecommunications experience, in an effort to raise capital for GeoPhone. Over the next several months, Glynn met and corresponded with Robinson, attempting to convince Robinson to invest in GeoPhone. Glynn described to Robinson the CAMA technology, its centrality to the GeoPhone system, and Geo-Phone's business plan. In July 1995, Robinson agreed to loan Glynn $1 million so that Glynn could perform a field test of the GeoPhone system and the CAMA technology.

In addition to Robinson's loan, in August 1995 Robinson and Glynn executed a "Letter of Intent," in which Robinson pledged to invest up to $25 million in GeoPhone, LLC if the field test indicated that CAMA worked in the GeoPhone system. Robinson's $25 million investment was to be comprised of his initial $1 million loan, an immediate $14 million investment upon successful completion of the field test, and a later $10 million investment. In October 1995, engineers hired by Glynn performed the field test, but, apparently with Glynn's knowledge, they

---

[31] *See* Hazen, *supra,* at 59–60.

did not use CAMA in the test. Nevertheless, Glynn allegedly told Robinson that the field test had been a success.

Consistent with the Letter of Intent, in December 1995 Robinson and Glynn executed an "Agreement to Purchase Membership Interests in GeoPhone" (APMIG). Under the APMIG, Robinson agreed to convert his $1 million loan and his $14 million investment into equity and subsequently to invest the additional $10 million. Robinson and Glynn also entered into an "Amended and Restated GeoPhone Operating Agreement" (ARGOA), which detailed the capital contribution, share ownership, and management structure of GeoPhone.

Pursuant to the ARGOA, Robinson received 33,333 of GeoPhone's 133,333 shares. On the back of the share certificates that Robinson received, the restrictive legend referred to the certificates as "shares" and "securities." It also specified that the certificates were exempt from registration under the Securities Act of 1933, and stated that the certificates could not be transferred without proper registration under the federal and state securities laws.

In addition, the ARGOA established a seven-person board of managers that was authorized to manage GeoPhone's affairs. Two of the managers were to be appointed by Robinson with the remaining five appointed by Glynn and his brother. Finally, the ARGOA vested management of GeoPhone in Robinson and Glynn based on each member's ownership share. Robinson was named GeoPhone's treasurer, and he was appointed to the board of managers and the company's executive committee. Glynn served as GeoPhone's chairman and was intimately involved in the company's operations and technical development.

Trouble first surfaced only a few months later in April 1996, when Robinson sued Glynn in Maryland state court. Robinson alleged breach of fiduciary duty, fraud, and conversion, all due to Glynn's purported mismanagement of GeoPhone funds. In October 1997, Robinson and Glynn settled the state court action, and as part of the settlement in November 1997 they entered into a "Membership Interest Purchase Agreement" (MIPA). Under the MIPA, Robinson purchased all of Glynn's shares in GeoPhone.

Yet in 1998 Robinson allegedly learned for the first time that the CAMA technology had never been implemented in the GeoPhone system-not even in the field test that had provided the basis for Robinson's investment. Robinson then filed suit in federal court, claiming violation of the federal securities laws, specifically § 10(b) of the Securities Exchange Act of 1934 and Rule 10b-5. The district court, however, granted summary judgment to Glynn, because it found that Robinson's membership interest in GeoPhone, LLC did not constitute a security under the federal securities laws. Robinson now challenges the district court's dismissal of his federal securities law claim.

II.

In order to establish a claim under [the federal securities laws], Robinson must prove fraud in connection with the purchase of securities. [Section 2(a)(1) of t]he Securities Act of 1933 and [section 3(a)(10) of] the Securities Exchange Act of 1934 define a "security" broadly as "any note, stock, treasury stock, security future, bond, debenture, . . . , investment contract, . . . , or, in general, any interest or instrument commonly known as a 'security.' "[32] In this case, Robinson claims that his membership interest in GeoPhone, a limited liability company (LLC), qualifies as either an "investment contract" or "stock" under the Securities Acts.

A.

The district court determined that Robinson's interest in GeoPhone was not an investment contract, a question of law that we review de novo. The Supreme Court has defined an investment contract as "a contract, transaction or scheme whereby a person invests his money in a common enterprise and is led to expect profits solely from the efforts of the promoter or a third party." *S.E.C. v. W.J. Howey, Co.*, 328 U.S. 293, 298–99 (1946). The parties agree that Robinson invested his money in a common enterprise with an expectation of profits. Their disagreement concerns whether Robinson expected profits "solely from the efforts" of others, most notably Glynn.

Since *Howey*, however, the Supreme Court has endorsed relaxation of the requirement that an investor rely only on others' efforts, by omitting the word "solely" from its restatements of the *Howey* test. And neither our court nor our sister circuits have required that an investor like Robinson expect profits "solely" from the efforts of others. Requiring investors to rely wholly on the efforts of others would exclude from the protection of the securities laws any agreement that involved even slight efforts from investors themselves. It would also exclude any agreement that offered investors control in theory, but denied it to them in fact. Agreements do not annul the securities laws by retaining nominal powers for investors unable to exercise them.

What matters more than the form of an investment scheme is the "economic reality" that it represents. The question is whether an investor, as a result of the investment agreement itself or the factual circumstances that surround it, is left unable to exercise meaningful control over his investment. *See Williamson v. Tucker*, 645 F.2d 404, 424 (5th Cir.1981). Elevating substance over form in this way ensures that the term "investment contract" embodies "a flexible rather than a static principle, one that is capable of adaptation to meet the countless and variable schemes devised by those who seek the use of the money of others on the promise of profits." *Howey*, 328 U.S. at 299.

B.

In looking at the powers accorded Robinson under GeoPhone's operating agreement, as well as Robinson's activity as an executive at GeoPhone, it is clear that Robinson was no passive investor heavily dependent on the efforts of others like Glynn. Under the ARGOA, management authority for GeoPhone resided in a board of managers. Robinson not only had the power to appoint two of the board members, but he himself assumed one of the board seats and was named as the board's vice-chairman. The board, in turn, delegated extensive responsibility to a four-person executive committee of which Robinson was also a member.

---

[32] [2] The Securities Acts' definitions of "security" differ in wording only slightly and are generally treated as identical in meaning.

In addition, Robinson served as GeoPhone's Treasurer. Among his powers were the ability to select external financial and legal consultants; to consult with GeoPhone's Chief Financial Officer on all financial matters relating to the company; to review status reports from the President and other officers; and to assemble the executive committee in order to discuss variations from GeoPhone's operating plan. Beyond even these fairly extensive powers, the ARGOA forbade GeoPhone from either incurring any indebtedness outside the normal course of business without Robinson's approval or diluting his interest in GeoPhone without first consulting him. In short, Robinson carefully negotiated for a level of control "antithetical to the notion of member passivity" required to find an investment contract under the federal securities laws. *Keith v. Black Diamond Advisors, Inc.*, 48 F.Supp.2d 326, 333 (S.D.N.Y.1999).

None of this, of course, establishes that Robinson could entirely direct the affairs of GeoPhone. He controlled neither the board nor the executive committee, and he lacked the technological expertise of Glynn and others at the company. But Robinson was not interested in sole managerial control of GeoPhone; he was interested instead in sufficient managerial control to ensure that other managers like Glynn could neither harm nor dilute his investment. Through his positions as Treasurer, Vice-Chairman of the Board, and member of GeoPhone's executive committee, Robinson may have lacked "decisive control over major decisions," but he preserved "the sort of influence which generally provide[d][him] with access to important information and protection against a dependence on others." *Rivanna* [Trawlers Unlimited v. Thompson Trawlers, Inc., 840 F.2d 236,] 241 [(4th Cir. 1988)] (internal quotation omitted).

Robinson argues, however, that his lack of technological expertise relative to Glynn prevented him from meaningfully exercising his rights. We faced essentially the same legal argument in *Rivanna*, and found that it assumed too much. *See id.* at 242 n. 10. To the extent that Robinson needed assistance in understanding any particular aspect of the CAMA technology, nothing prevented him from seeking it from outside parties or others at GeoPhone. *See id.* In fact, prior to purchasing all of Glynn's shares in GeoPhone, Robinson asked his accountant to scrutinize the company's financial records, and he hired an outside engineer to study the company's technology and market potential.

Indeed, the record amply supports the district court's conclusion that Robinson exercised his management rights despite his lack of technical expertise. For instance, Robinson reviewed GeoPhone's technology and financial records, as well as weekly status reports from GeoPhone's President, Chief Operating Officer, and Chief Financial Officer covering numerous aspects of GeoPhone's operation. He disapproved disbursements and proposed licenses of the GeoPhone technology. Robinson even expressed to the board of managers problems he perceived with GeoPhone, including the company's technological development, its management, and marketability. In the end, Robinson generally asserts that he lacked technical sophistication, without explaining in any detail what was beyond his ken or why it left him powerless to exercise his management rights.

Moreover, Robinson's argument would work a fundamental and unjustifiable expansion in the securities laws by bringing innumerable commercial ventures within their purview. Business ventures often find their genesis in the different contributions of diverse individuals-for instance, as here, where one contributes his technical expertise and another his capital and business acumen. Yet the securities laws do not extend to every person who lacks the specialized knowledge of his partners or colleagues, without a showing that this lack of knowledge prevents him from meaningfully controlling his investment. Here, Robinson concedes that "nothing of consequence that would affect [his] position adversely could be done without [his] prior expressed approval," thus undermining his claim that his lack of technical expertise left him powerless over his investment. In essence, Robinson was a savvy and experienced businessman who negotiated for formal management rights and actively exercised those rights, only now relying on his lack of technical sophistication to claim the cover of the federal securities laws.

Robinson's opportunity, especially as an executive at GeoPhone, to oversee his interests distinguishes his case from *Bailey v. J.W.K. Properties, Inc.*, 904 F.2d 918 (4th Cir.1990). In *Bailey*, we found that a cattle breeding program was an investment contract, in part because the investors lacked specialized expertise in crossbreeding and cattle breeding selection. *See id.* at 924–25 & n. 13. Yet the *Bailey* investors' lack of specialized knowledge alone did not convert their interest into a security — again, such a result would bring a host of commercial enterprises within the ambit of the securities laws. Rather, the *Bailey* investors lacked the indicia of control-formal and actual — that mark active investors like Robinson. *See id.* at 923–24. And unlike the present case, the *Bailey* investors ran headlong into a coordination problem that heightened their dependence on the breeders: no single investor owned enough cattle to run a breeding program, and so they relied on the breeders to pool their herds and coordinate the process. *See id.* at 924–25; *see also Howey*, 328 U.S. at 300. Robinson was GeoPhone's only major investor, and he was not dependent on the investments or expertise of others.

Finally, Robinson argues that he and Glynn considered his interest in GeoPhone a security, based on language in the APMIG, in the ARGOA, and on the back of Robinson's GeoPhone certificates. For instance, the restrictive legend on the back of Robinson's certificates refers to the certificates as "shares" and "securities." While this may be persuasive evidence that Robinson and Glynn believed the securities laws to apply, it does not indicate that their understanding was well-founded. Just as agreements cannot evade the securities laws by reserving powers to members unable to exercise them, neither can agreements invoke those same laws simply by labelling commercial ventures as securities. It is the "economic reality" of a particular instrument, rather than the label attached to it, that ultimately determines whether it falls within the reach of the securities laws. *See Great Rivers Coop. v. Farmland Indus., Inc.*, 198 F.3d 685, 701 (8th Cir.1999). The "economic reality" here is that Robinson was not a passive investor relying on the efforts of others, but a knowledgeable executive actively protecting his interest and position in the company.

III.

Robinson further claims that his membership interest in GeoPhone was not only an "investment contract" within the meaning of the federal securities laws, but "stock" as well.[33] Congress intended catch-all terms like "investment contract" to encompass the range of novel and unusual instruments whose economic realities

---

[33] [3] The Securities Acts define a "security" as "any note, stock, treasury stock, security future, bond, debenture, . . . , investment contract, . . . , or, in general, any interest or instrument commonly known as a 'security.' " [Securities Act § 2(a)(1), Exchange Act § 3(a)(10)].

invite application of the securities laws; but the term "stock" refers to a narrower set of instruments with a common name and characteristics. *See Landreth Timber Co. v. Landreth*, 471 U.S. 681, 686 (1985). Thus the securities laws apply "when an instrument is both called 'stock' and bears stock's usual characteristics." *Id.* Yet Robinson's membership interest was neither denominated stock by the parties, nor did it possess all the usual characteristics of stock.

The characteristics typically associated with common stock are (i) the right to receive dividends contingent upon an apportionment of profits;(ii) negotiability; (iii) the ability to be pledged or hypothecated; (iv) the conferring of voting rights in proportion to the number of shares owned; and (v) the capacity to appreciate in value. *See id.* Robinson's membership interest in GeoPhone lacked several of these characteristics. Consider *Great Lakes Chemical Corp. v. Monsanto Co.*, 96 F.Supp.2d 376, 387–89 (D.Del.2000) (finding that LLC membership interests do not constitute stock under *Landreth*).

First, as is common with interests in LLCs, GeoPhone's members did not share in the profits in proportion to the number of their shares. *See* Larry E. Ribstein, *Form and Substance in the Definition of a "Security": The Case of Limited Liability Companies*, 51 Wash. & Lee L. Rev. 807, 833 (1994) (noting that "LLC statutes usually do not provide for dividend rights"). Pursuant to the ARGOA, Robinson was to receive 100 percent of GeoPhone's net profits up to a certain amount, only after which were funds to be distributed pro rata to the members in proportion to their relative shares.

Second, like interests in LLCs more generally, Robinson's membership interests were not freely negotiable. *See id.* (observing that LLC statutes "invariably restrict transferability of management rights"). According to the ARGOA, Robinson could only transfer his interests if he first offered other members the opportunity to purchase his interests on similar terms. Moreover, unlike with stock (except some stock in close corporations), anyone to whom Robinson or other members transferred their interests would not have thereby acquired any of the control or management rights that normally attend a stock transfer. *See* Carol R. Goforth, *Why Limited Liability Company Membership Interests Should Not Be Treated as Securities and Possible Steps to Encourage This Result*, 45 Hastings L.J. 1223, 1247 (1994) (discussing ability of corporate stockholders, unlike owners of LLC interests, to convey all attributes of ownership without additional third-party consent). Rather, the ARGOA requires that transferees satisfy several conditions to become members, in addition to receiving the approval of a majority of GeoPhone's managers.

Similarly, Robinson could pledge his interest, but the pledgee would acquire only distribution rights and not control rights. *See id.* ("Unlike stock, however, the pledgee [of a LLC membership interest] acquires no rights to become a substitute owner with rights to participate in control of the entity upon default of the pledgor."). As for the apportionment of voting rights, the parties dispute whether voting rights were conferred in proportion to members' interests in GeoPhone. Even resolving this dispute in Robinson's favor, it remains clear that Robinson's membership interest lacked the ordinary attributes of stock.

Finally, from the very beginning Robinson and Glynn consistently viewed Robinson's investment as a "membership interest," and never as "stock." The purchase and operating agreements that Robinson and Glynn executed, as well as the agreement in which Robinson bought out Glynn's interest in GeoPhone, all termed Robinson's investment as a "membership interest" rather than "stock." Even the shares that Robinson received as a result of his investments declared Robinson the holder of "membership interests in GeoPhone Company, L.L.C., within the meaning of the Delaware Limited Liability Company Act." Robinson thus cannot argue that he was misled into believing that his membership interests were stock whose purchases were governed by the securities laws. *See Landreth*, 471 U.S. at 687, 693, 105 S.Ct. 2297 (finding that calling instruments "stock" justifiably leads purchasers to believe that the federal securities laws apply). And it would do violence to the statutory language of the securities laws to include within the term "stock" an instrument that was neither labelled stock nor like stock.

IV.

The parties have vigorously urged us to rule broadly in this case, asking that we generally classify interests in limited liability companies, or LLCs, as investment contracts (Robinson's view) or non-securities (Glynn's view). LLCs are particularly difficult to categorize under the securities laws, however, because they are hybrid business entities that combine features of corporations, general partnerships, and limited partnerships. As their name indicates, LLCs can limit the liability of their members, which may mean that LLC members are more likely to be passive investors who need the protection of the securities laws. *See, e.g., Ak's Daks Communications, Inc. v. Maryland Sec. Div.*, 138 Md.App. 314, 771 A.2d 487, 497–98 (2001). However, LLC members are also able to actively participate in management without piercing the veil of their liability, which would suggest that LLC members are more likely than limited partners or corporate shareholders to be active investors not in need of the securities statutes. *See, e.g., Great Lakes*, 96 F.Supp.2d at 391–92.

Precisely because LLCs lack standardized membership rights or organizational structures, they can assume an almost unlimited variety of forms. It becomes, then, exceedingly difficult to declare that LLCs, whatever their form, either possess or lack the economic characteristics associated with investment contracts. Even drawing firm lines between member-managed and manager-managed LLCs threatens impermissibly to elevate form over substance. Certainly the members in a member-managed LLC will often have powers too significant to be considered passive investors under the securities laws. And yet even members in a member-managed LLC may be unable as a practical matter to exercise any meaningful control, perhaps because they are too numerous, inexperienced, or geographically disparate. *See, e.g., Nutek Info. Sys., Inc. v. Arizona Corp. Comm'n*, 194 Ariz. 104, 977 P.2d 826, 831–32 (1998); *S.E.C. v. Parkersburg Wireless Ltd. Liability Co.*, 991 F.Supp. 6, 9 n. 3 (D.D.C.1997). By the same token, while interests in manager-managed LLCs may often be securities, their members need not necessarily be reliant on the efforts on their managers. *See, e.g., Great Lakes*, 96 F.Supp.2d at 392.

We decline, therefore, the parties' invitation for a broader holding. On the facts of this case, it is clear that Robinson did not lack the ability to meaningfully exercise the rights granted him under GeoPhone's operating agreement.[34] To the

---

[34] [4] The weaknesses of Robinson's case are highlighted by comparison to *S.E.C. v. ETS Payphones, Inc.*, 300 F.3d 1281 (11th Cir.2002), *cert. granted sub nom, S.E.C. v. Edwards*, 538 U.S. 976 (2003). *ETS*

contrary, Robinson had a significant say in GeoPhone's management. If Robinson, despite his own managerial efforts, was misled by Glynn about his investment, his remedy belongs to another forum. The federal securities laws were not intended to be a substitute for state fraud and breach of contract actions. We therefore affirm the district court's dismissal of the action in this case.

AFFIRMED.

C. EXEMPTIONS FROM REGISTRATION

So far, we have the bad news. The Securities Act has a worrisome registration requirement for the offer or sale of securities, which your clients ignore at grave risk to their financial health. Complying with the requirement is out of the question, unless they are going to raise tens of millions of dollars in capital. And it is going to be difficult to avoid issuing "securities" — that is done in *any* conventional business deal.

Now for the good news. Many transactions and securities are exempt from the registration requirement of the Securities Act. Notice the distinction in the preceding sentence between exempt *transactions* and exempt *securities*. The former depends on the nature of the offer or sale, the latter on the nature of the security being offered. We will consider each in turn.

1. Transaction Exemptions for Initial Sales

There are three main types of initial offers and sales exempt from the registration requirement of Securities Act § 5. First, there are "private" offerings, so denoted because of the statutory language which exempts "transactions by an issuer not involving any public offering."[35] Second, there are "intrastate" offerings, exempt if the issuer, business and purchasers are confined within one state.[36] And finally, there are "limited" offerings, limited either by the size or the nature of the offering, which are made exempt by the SEC under delegated authority from Congress so to do.[37] After we understand each exemption, we will discuss the

---

Payphones involved the sale of pay telephones by a corporation, rather than a limited liability company, to a class of over 10,000 investors. Having purchased the phones, the investors then leased them back to the company for management in exchange for a fixed monthly fee. *See id.* at 1282. While the investors retained limited contractual rights under the lease, they were active in neither the company's management nor operation. Their inexperience, geographical dispersion, and lack of access to important information made the *ETS Payphones* investors practically dependent on the efforts of others in a way that Robinson was not. [In *SEC v. Edwards*, 540 U.S. 389 (2004), the Court held that the interests in that case were investment contracts and thus "securities" under the federal securities laws.—Eds.]

[35] Securities Act § 4(2).

[36] Securities Act § 3(a)(11) exempts "[a]ny security which is a part of an issue offered and sold only to persons resident within a single State or Territory, where the issuer of such security is a person resident and doing business within or, if a corporation, incorporated by and doing business within, such State or Territory." Although § 3(a)(11) speaks of exempt "securities," it is clear that this is a transaction exemption. *See* Loss & Seligman, *supra*, at 341–42; *infra* Section C.3.

[37] Securities Act § 3(b) provides that "[t]he Commission may from time to time by its rules and regulations, and subject to such terms and conditions as may be prescribed therein, add any class of securities to the securities exempted as provided in this section, if it finds that the enforcement of this title with respect to such securities is not necessary in the public interest and for the protection of investors by reason of the *small amount* involved or the *limited character* of the public offering; but no issue of securities shall be exempted under this subsection where the aggregate amount at which such

doctrine of "integration," and how to keep exempt transactions from being combined and their individual exemptions lost.

a.   Private Offerings

SECURITIES AND EXCHANGE COMMISSION v. RALSTON PURINA CO.
United States Supreme Court
346 U.S. 119 (1953)

Mr. Justice Clark delivered the opinion of the Court.

Section [4(2)][38] of the Securities Act of 1933 exempts "transactions by an issuer not involving any public offering" from the registration requirements of § 5. We must decide whether Ralston Purina's offerings of treasury stock to its "key employees" are within this exemption. On a complaint brought by the Commission under § 20(b) of the Act seeking to enjoin respondent's unregistered offerings, the District Court held the exemption applicable and dismissed the suit. The Court of Appeals affirmed. The question has arisen many times since the Act was passed; an apparent need to define the scope of the private offering exemption prompted certiorari. 345 U.S. 903.

Ralston Purina manufactures and distributes various feed and cereal products. Its processing and distribution facilities are scattered throughout the United States and Canada, staffed by some 7,000 employees. At least since 1911 the company has had a policy of encouraging stock ownership among its employees; more particularly, since 1942 it has made authorized but unissued common shares available to some of them. Between 1947 and 1951, the period covered by the record in this case, Ralston Purina sold nearly $2,000,000 of stock to employees without registration and in so doing made use of the mails.

In each of these years, a corporate resolution authorized the sale of common stock "to employees * * * who shall, without any solicitation by the Company or its officers or employees, inquire of any of them as to how to purchase common stock of Ralston Purina Company." A memorandum sent to branch and store managers after the resolution was adopted, advised that "The only employees to whom this stock will be available will be those who take the initiative and are interested in buying stock at present market prices." Among those responding to these offers were employees with the duties of artist, bakeshop foreman, chow loading foreman, clerical assistant, copywriter, electrician, stock clerk, mill office clerk, order credit trainee, production trainee, stenographer, and veterinarian. The buyers lived in over fifty widely separated communities scattered from Garland, Texas, to Nashua, New Hampshire and Visalia, California. The lowest salary bracket of those purchasing was $2,700 in 1949, $2,435 in 1950 and $3,107 in 1951. The record shows

---

issue is offered to the public exceeds $5,000,000" (emphasis added). In addition, a new provision, Securities Act § 28, allows the Commission to exempt by rule or regulation any security or transaction, with the only addition requirement being that the exemption is "necessary or appropriate in the public interest, and is consistent with the protection of investors," This exemptive authority has been used only once so far; see Section C(1)(c)(iii) *infra*.

[38] [At the time of this opinion, the "private offering" exemption was in § 4(1) of the Act, and the Court referred to it as such. We have changed this designation without further notice to the modern citation: § 4(2) of the Act. We will deal with the modern version of § 4(1) later in Section E of this chapter.— Eds.]

that in 1947, 243 employees bought stock, 20 in 1948, 414 in 1949, 411 in 1950, and the 1951 offer, interrupted by this litigation, produced 165 applications to purchase. No records were kept of those to whom the offers were made; the estimated number in 1951 was 500.

The company bottoms its exemption claim on the classification of all offerees as "key employees" in its organization. Its position on trial was that "A key employee * * * is not confined to an organization chart. It would include an individual who is eligible for promotion, an individual who especially influences others or who advises others, a person whom the employees look to in some special way, an individual, of course, who carries some special responsibility, who is sympathetic to management and who is ambitious and who the management feels is likely to be promoted to a greater responsibility." That an offering to all of its employees would be public is conceded.

The Securities Act nowhere defines the scope of § 4(2)'s private offering exemption. Nor is the legislative history of much help in staking out its boundaries. The problem was first dealt with in § 4(1) of the House Bill, H.R. 5480, 73d Cong., 1st Sess., which exempted "transactions by an issuer not with or through an underwriter; * * *." The bill, as reported by the House Committee, added "and not involving any public offering." H.R.Rep. No. 85, 73d Cong., 1st Sess. 1. This was thought to be one of those transactions "where there is no practical need for * * * (the bill's) application or where the public benefits are too remote." Id., at 5. The exemption as thus delimited became law. . . . .

Decisions under comparable exemptions in the English Companies Acts and state "blue sky" laws, the statutory antecedents of federal securities legislation[,] have made one thing clear — to be public, an offer need not be open to the whole world. In Securities and Exchange Comm. v. Sunbeam Gold Mines Co., 9 Cir., 1938, 95 F.2d 699, 701, this point was made in dealing with an offering to the stockholders of two corporations about to be merged. Judge Denman observed that:

> In its broadest meaning the term "public" distinguishes the populace at large from groups of individual members of the public segregated because of some common interest or characteristic. Yet such a distinction is inadequate for practical purposes; manifestly, an offering of securities to all redheaded men, to all residents of Chicago or San Francisco, to all existing stockholders of the General Motors Corporation or the American Telephone & Telegraph Company, is no less "public," in every realistic sense of the word, than an unrestricted offering to the world at large. Such an offering, though not open to everyone who may choose to apply, is none the less "public" in character, for the means used to select the particular individuals to whom the offering is to be made bear no sensible relation to the purposes for which the selection is made. * * * To determine the distinction between "public" and "private" in any particular context, it is essential to examine the circumstances under which the distinction is sought to be established and to consider the purposes sought to be achieved by such distinction.

The courts below purported to apply this test. The District Court held, in the language of the Sunbeam decision, that "The purpose of the selection bears a 'sensible relation' to the class chosen," finding that "The sole purpose of the 'selection' is to keep part stock ownership of the business within the operating personnel of the business and to spread ownership throughout all departments and activities of the business."[39] The Court of Appeals treated the case as involving "an offering, without solicitation, of common stock to a selected group of key employees of the issuer, most of whom are already stockholders when the offering is made, with the sole purpose of enabling them to secure a proprietary interest in the company or to increase the interest already held by them."[40]

Exemption from the registration requirements of the Securities Act is the question. The design of the statute is to protect investors by promoting full disclosure of information thought necessary to informed investment decisions. The natural way to interpret the private offering exemption is in light of the statutory purpose. Since exempt transactions are those as to which "there is no practical need for * * * (the bill's) application," the applicability of § 4(2) should turn on whether the particular class of persons affected need the protection of the Act. An offering to those who are shown to be able to fend for themselves is a transaction "not involving any public offering."

The Commission would have us go one step further and hold that "an offering to a substantial number of the public" is not exempt under § 4(2). We are advised that "whatever the special circumstances, the Commission has consistently interpreted the exemption as being inapplicable when a large number of offerees is involved." But the statute would seem to apply to a "public offering" whether to few or many. It may well be that offerings to a substantial number of persons would rarely be exempt. Indeed nothing prevents the Commission, in enforcing the statute, from using some kind of numerical test in deciding when to investigate particular exemption claims. But there is no warrant for superimposing a quantity limit on private offerings as a matter of statutory interpretation.

The exemption, as we construe it, does not deprive corporate employees, as a class, of the safeguards of the Act. We agree that some employee offerings may come within § 4(2), e.g., one made to executive personnel who because of their position have access to the same kind of information that the act would make available in the form of a registration statement.[41] Absent such a showing of special circumstances, employees are just as much members of the investing "public" as any of their neighbors in the community. . . .

Keeping in mind the broadly remedial purposes of federal securities legislation, imposition of the burden of proof on an issuer who would plead the exemption seems to us fair and reasonable. Agreeing, the court below thought the burden met primarily because of the respondent's purpose in singling out its key employees for stock offerings. But once it is seen that the exemption question turns on the knowledge of the offerees, the issuer's motives, laudable though they may be, fade into irrelevance. The focus of inquiry should be on the need of the offerees for the

---

[39] [8] 102 F.Supp. at pages 968, 969.

[40] [9] 200 F.2d at page 91.

[41] [12] This was one of the factors stressed in an advisory opinion rendered by the Commission's General Counsel in 1935. "I also regard as significant the relationship between the issuer and the offerees. Thus, an offering to the members of a class who should have special knowledge of the issuer is less likely to be a public offering than is an offering to the members of a class of the same size who do not have this advantage. This factor would be particularly important in offerings to employees, where a class of high executive officers would have a special relationship to the issuer which subordinate employees would not enjoy." 11 Fed.Reg. 10952.

protections afforded by registration. The employees here were not shown to have access to the kind of information which registration would disclose. The obvious opportunities for pressure and imposition make it advisable that they be entitled to compliance with § 5.

Reversed.

The CHIEF JUSTICE and MR. JUSTICE BURTON dissent.

MR. JUSTICE JACKSON took no part in the consideration or decision of this case.

NOTES AND QUESTIONS

1. After *Ralston Purina*, how are we to decide if an offering is "public"? More importantly, if we decide that it *is* going to be "public," is there anything we can do before the offering takes place to change that result?

2. Can an offering to one person be a "public" offering? Conversely, would you have taken the Commission's invitation and held that an offering to more than a certain number of offerees is necessarily a "public" offering? What would that number be?

3. The SEC has provided helpful guidance in the interpretation of the statutes it administers, as do many administrative agencies. In many cases, this guidance takes the form of a "safe harbor" rule. The "safe harbor" designation means simply that compliance with such a rule is guaranteed to be compliance with the statute insofar as the agency is concerned. Daring issuers and their counsel may still choose to "sail" outside the safe harbor, risking that the Commission staff or a disgruntled investor and a court might disagree with their analysis. A "safe harbor" rule for private offerings is provided in Rule 506 of "Regulation D" which we will study later in this chapter.[42]

b. Intrastate Offerings

The second major exemption which we will consider is for "intrastate" offerings. We will look first at the statutory language and then consider the helpful guidance the SEC has given, again in a "safe harbor" regulation.

Securities Act § 3(a)(11)

Except as hereinafter expressly provided, the provisions of this title shall not apply to any of the following classes of securities:

. . . .

> (11) Any security which is a part of an issue offered and sold only to persons resident within a single State or Territory, where the issuer of such security is a person resident and doing business within or, if a corporation, incorporated by and doing business within, such State or Territory.

The statutory language is sparse and provides little guidance on at least two important issues: (1) what does "residence" within the state mean, for either the

---

[42] In this respect, Rule 506 is substantively different from the other parts of Regulation D, which are not "safe harbor" rules.

offerees/purchasers or the issuer, and (2) what does "doing business" in the state mean — what is "business" and how much must be "done."[43] This suggests that a business planner relying on the statute alone will face irreducible uncertainty.

> Persons deciding to rely on the exemption have to draw from the relatively scant judicial precedent and SEC interpretive releases and rules available. Because of the close factual questions involved, it became common practice for issuers deciding to rely on the intrastate exemption to request a no action letter from the Commission before proceeding. . . . [R]eliance upon no action letters, which by their very nature are expressly confined to the facts given, provides little precedential value and thus little comfort to the corporate planner trying to tailor the transaction to the exemption.[44]

The Commission, sensitive to this predicament, provided guidance with a "safe harbor" rule set forth below.

Securities Act Rule 147 "Part of an Issue," "Person Resident," and "Doing Business Within" for Purposes of Section 3(a)(11)
17 C.F.R. § 230.147

Preliminary Notes:

1. This rule shall not raise any presumption that the exemption provided by section 3(a)(11) of the Act is not available for transactions by an issuer which do not satisfy all of the provisions of the rule.

2. Nothing in this rule obviates the need for compliance with any state law relating to the offer and sale of the securities.

3. Section 5 of the Act requires that all securities offered by the use of the mails or by any means or instruments of transportation or communication in interstate commerce be registered with the Commission. Congress, however, provided certain exemptions in the Act from such registration provisions where there was no practical need for registration or where the benefits of registration were too remote. Among those exemptions is that provided by section 3(a)(11) of the Act for "transactions in any security which is a part of an issue offered and sold only to persons resident within a single State or Territory, where the issuer of such security is a person resident and doing business within * * * such State or Territory." The legislative history of that Section suggests that the exemption was intended to apply only to issues genuinely local in character, which in reality represent local financing by local industries, carried out through local investment. Rule 147 is intended to provide more objective standards upon which responsible local businessmen intending to raise capital from local sources may rely in claiming the section 3(a)(11) exemption.

All of the terms and conditions of the rule must be satisfied in order for the rule to be available. These are: (i) That the issuer be a resident of and doing business within the state or territory in which all offers and sales are made; and (ii) that

---

[43] There is also the ambiguous "part of an issue" language, but we will consider this separately in Section C.1.d on "integration," and in Section E on resales.

[44] Hazen, *supra*, at 193 (footnotes omitted). The use of "no action letters" is covered in Section G.

no part of the issue be offered or sold to non-residents within the period of time specified in the rule. For purposes of the rule the definition of issuer in section 2(4) of the Act shall apply.

All offers, offers to sell, offers for sale, and sales which are part of the same issue must meet all of the conditions of Rule 147 for the rule to be available. The determination whether offers, offers to sell, offers for sale and sales of securities are part of the same issue (i.e., are deemed to be integrated) will continue to be a question of fact and will depend on the particular circumstances. . . . Subparagraph (b)(2) of the rule, however, is designed to provide certainty to the extent feasible by identifying certain types of offers and sales of securities which will be deemed not part of an issue, for purposes of the rule only.

Persons claiming the availability of the rule have the burden of proving that they have satisfied all of its provisions. However, the rule does not establish exclusive standards for complying with the section 3(a)(11) exemption. The exemption would also be available if the issuer satisfied the standards set forth in relevant administrative and judicial interpretations at the time of the offering but the issuer would have the burden of proving the availability of the exemption. Rule 147 relates to transactions exempted from the registration requirements of section 5 of the Act by section 3(a)(11). Neither the rule nor section 3(a)(11) provides an exemption from . . . the anti-fraud provisions of the federal securities laws, the civil liability provisions of section 12(2) of the Act or other provisions of the federal securities laws.

Finally, in view of the objectives of the rule and the purposes and policies underlying the Act, the rule shall not be available to any person with respect to any offering which, although in technical compliance with the rule, is part of a plan or scheme by such person to make interstate offers or sales of securities. In such cases registration pursuant to the Act is required.

4. The rule provides an exemption for offers and sales by the issuer only. It is not available for offers or sales of securities by other persons. . . .

(a) **Transactions Covered.** Offers, offers to sell, offers for sale and sales by an issuer of its securities made in accordance with all of the terms and conditions of this rule shall be deemed to be part of an issue offered and sold only to persons resident within a single state or territory where the issuer is a person resident and doing business within such state or territory, within the meaning of section 3(a)(11) of the Act.

(b) **Part of an issue.**

(1) For purposes of this rule, all securities of the issuer which are part of an issue shall be offered, offered for sale or sold in accordance with all of the terms and conditions of this rule.

(2) For purposes of this rule only, an issue shall be deemed not to include offers, offers to sell, offers for sale or sales of securities of the issuer pursuant to the exemption provided by section 3 or section 4(2) of the Act or pursuant to a registration statement filed under the Act, that take place prior to the six month period immediately preceding or after the six month period immediately following any offers, offers for sale or sales pursuant to this rule, *Provided*, That, there are during either of said six month periods no offers, offers for sale or sales of securities by or for the issuer of the same or similar class as those offered, offered for sale or sold pursuant to the rule.

(c) **Nature of the issuer.** The issuer of the securities shall at the time of any offers and the sales be a person resident and doing business within the state or territory in which all of the offers, offers to sell, offers for sale and sales are made.

(1) The issuer shall be deemed to be a resident of the state or territory in which:

(i) It is incorporated or organized, if a corporation, limited partnership, trust or other form of business organization that is organized under state or territorial law;

(ii) Its principal office is located, if a general partnership or other form of business organization that is not organized under any state or territorial law;

(iii) His principal residence is located if an individual.

(2) The issuer shall be deemed to be doing business within a state or territory if:

(i) The issuer derived at least 80 percent of its gross revenues and those of its subsidiaries on a consolidated basis. . . .

(ii) The issuer had at the end of its most recent semi-annual fiscal period prior to the first offer of any part of the issue, at least 80 percent of its assets and those of its subsidiaries on a consolidated basis located within such state or territory;

(iii) The issuer intends to use and uses at least 80 percent of the net proceeds to the issuer from sales made pursuant to this rule in connection with the operation of a business or of real property, the purchase of real property located in, or the rendering of services within such state or territory; and

(iv) The principal office of the issuer is located within such state or territory.

(d) **Offerees and purchasers: Person Resident.** Offers, offers to sell, offers for sale and sales of securities that are part of an issue shall be made only to persons resident within the state or territory of which the issuer is a resident. For purposes of determining the residence of offerees and purchasers:

(1) A corporation, partnership, trust or other form of business organization shall be deemed to be a resident of a state or territory if, at the time of the offer and sale to it, it has its principal office within such state or territory.

(2) An individual shall be deemed to be a resident of a state or territory if such individual has, at the time of the offer and sale to him, his principal residence in the state or territory. . . .

(e) **Limitation of resales.** During the period in which securities that are part of an issue are being offered and sold by the issuer, and for a period of nine months from the date of the last sale by the issuer of such securities, all resales of any part of the issue, by any person, shall be made only to persons resident within such state or territory.

(f) **Precautions against interstate offers and sales.**

(1)   The issuer shall, in connection with any securities sold by it pursuant to this rule:

(i)   Place a legend on the certificate or other document evidencing the security stating that the securities have not been registered under the Act and setting forth the limitations on resale contained in paragraph (e) of this section;

(ii)   Issue stop transfer instructions to the issuer's transfer agent, if any, with respect to the securities, or, if the issuer transfers its own securities make a notation in the appropriate records of the issuer; and

(iii)   Obtain a written representation from each purchaser as to his residence.

(2)   The issuer shall, in connection with the issuance of new certificates for any of the securities that are part of the same issue that are presented for transfer during the time period specified in paragraph (e), take the steps required by paragraphs (f)(1)(i) and (ii) of this section.

(3)   The issuer shall, in connection with any offers, offers to sell, offers for sale or sales by it pursuant to this rule, disclose, in writing, the limitations on resale contained in paragraph (e) and the provisions of paragraphs (f)(1)(i) and (ii) and paragraph (f)(2) of this section.

NOTES

1.   Preliminary Note 3 contains a lot of background, including the SEC's reading of the legislative history and the proper scope of § 3(a)(11). It is also one of the earliest references in SEC rules to the "integration" doctrine. We will study this doctrine in detail in Section C.1.d of this chapter.

2.   Rule 147(e) indicates that the Rule is not available for resales. We will study resales in detail in Section C.2 below. The nine-month prohibition on resales outside the state is not an exemption for those resales. It is instead establishing that the issue — remember § 3(a)(11) only exempts securities which are "part of an issue" — was all sold within one state and "came to rest," to use the SEC's terminology.

> It has long been the Commission's position . . . that once securities sold pursuant to the intrastate exemption have finally come to rest in the hands of residents, subsequent isolated resales to nonresidents will not destroy the prior exemptions. In terms of planning such transactions, the nine month safe harbor guidelines of Rule 147 provide a good rule of thumb.[45]

3.   The "part of an issue" concept is a sword as well as a shield. If there is *only one* out-of-state offer or sale, the § 3(a)(11) exemption [whether based on Rule 147 or not] is unavailable, and *none* of the offers or sales which are "part of that issue" will be exempt. That means that even an *intrastate* purchaser could recover under § 12(a)(1). We deal with what constitutes "part of an issue" when we discuss "integration" in Section C.1.d below.

---

[45]   Hazen, *supra*, at 196.

c.   Small or Limited Offerings

The exemptions we study last have nothing in common except that most were created by the SEC pursuant to delegated authority from Congress. That authority is intended for offerings of "small amount" or "limited character."[46] These exemptions are not statutory; rather Congress has left the scope and details of each exemption up to the SEC. Therefore, the limited offering rules are substantively different from the SEC rules we have seen so far. They are not "safe harbor" or even interpretive rules, but the rules themselves create the exemptions.

i.   Regulation A

The first and oldest limited offering exemption is a collection of rules known as "Regulation A."[47] Although technically an exemption from registration, Regulation A requires an "offering circular" to be filed with and qualified by the SEC, much like a registration statement, although without the full costs and liabilities of a registration statement. Regulation A has some features helpful to new businesses, notably the ability to make general advertisements and to "test the waters," that is, to look for preliminary indications of interest in the securities without completing the formal offering documents.[48] Although the SEC has attempted to make Regulation A attractive for small business, this attempt has largely failed.

> Today, Regulation A is essentially unused because it does not have a niche. No matter the size or nature of the offering, the exemption does not provide small issuers with an attractive alternative for capital formation.
>
> On the small offering end of the Regulation A spectrum . . . issuers are discouraged from using Regulation A by the complexities of the filing, disclosure and other requirements and by the difficulties in many instances of meeting state blue sky requirements. Together, the costs of meeting these federal and state requirements overwhelm any benefit a small business would attain from utilizing Regulation A.
>
> As offerings get larger, one might imagine that Regulation A becomes more attractive to businesses in search of capital. . . . It appears, however, that the advantages of a Regulation A offering at such higher levels still do not make up for lingering difficulties. State law compliance problems are probably the most apparent among these problems. . . .
>
> It is unlikely, therefore, that Regulation A as presently constituted, or even if increased in its limit, will have a significant role in the capital formation activities of small businesses. The shame in all this is that the fundamental concepts of Regulation A — providing an exemption from registration through a disclosure tailored to meet the tension between

---

[46] Securities Act §§ 3(b), 28.

[47] Regulation A consists of Securities Act Rules 251 through 263. Various collections of Securities Act rules are grouped by "Regulation" designation in this fashion. Originally they followed an alphabetical order (Regulations A, B, C, etc.), but began departing from this pattern with Regulation S-K in 1980. *See* Loss & Seligman, *supra*, at 153. The Regulations now use mnemonic abbreviations: Regulation SB for small business offerings, Regulation FD for "fair disclosure" rules, and so forth.

[48] See Hazen, *supra*, at 204; Loss & Seligman, *supra*, at 391–95.

capital formation and investor protection — makes perfect sense.[49]

ii.   Regulation D

A far more successful effort by the SEC using its limited offering exemption powers is Regulation D, adopted in 1982. Regulation D consists of eight different rules, five of which we edit[50] and present below.[51] The operative exemptions are in Rules 504–506. Rules 501–502 provide definitions, general rules, and conditions for using Regulation D. Be sure to read the general rules carefully, because not all limitations apply to each Regulation D offering.

Regulation D

Rules Governing the Limited Offer and Sale of Securities Without Registration Under the Securities Act of 1933
17 C.F.R. §§ 230.501 *et seq.*

Preliminary Notes:

1.   The following rules relate to transactions exempted from the registration requirements of section 5 of the Securities Act of 1933 (the Act). Such transactions are not exempt from the anti-fraud, civil liability, or other provisions of the federal securities laws. Issuers are reminded of their obligation to provide such further material information, if any, as may be necessary to make the information required under this regulation, in light of the circumstances under which it is furnished, not misleading.

3.   Attempted compliance with any rule in Regulation D does not act as an exclusive election; the issuer can also claim the availability of any other applicable exemption. For instance, an issuer's failure to satisfy all the terms and conditions of Rule 506 shall not raise any presumption that the exemption provided by section 4(2) of the Act is not available.

4.   These rules are available only to the issuer of the securities and not to any affiliate of that issuer or to any other person for resales of the issuer's securities. The rules provide an exemption only for the transactions in which the securities are offered or sold by the issuer, not for the securities themselves.

6.   In view of the objectives of these rules and the policies underlying the Act, Regulation D is not available to any issuer for any transaction or chain of transactions that, although in technical compliance with these rules, is part of a plan or scheme to evade the registration provisions of the Act. In such cases, registration under the Act is required.

Rule 501   Definitions and Terms Used in Regulation D

As used in Regulation D, the following terms shall have the meaning indicated:

---

49 Campbell, *supra*, at 110–12 (footnotes omitted). *Accord*, Loss & Seligman, *supra*, at 391 (noting the "near total eclipse" of Regulation A).

50 Omissions from the Regulation D rules presented below are not indicated by ellipses or otherwise.

51 We have omitted: Rule 503, which requires filing a "notice of sales" under Regulation D with the SEC; Rule 507, which disqualifies an issuer from using Regulation D if Rule 503 has not been complied with; and Rule 508, which states that "insignificant deviations" from the rules in Regulation D will not result in loss of the exemption.

(a) *Accredited investor. Accredited investor* shall mean any person who comes within any of the following categories, or who the issuer reasonably believes comes within any of the following categories, at the time of the sale of the securities to that person:

(4) Any director, executive officer, or general partner of the issuer of the securities being offered or sold, or any director, executive officer, or general partner of a general partner of that issuer;

(5) Any natural person whose individual net worth, or joint net worth with that person's spouse, at the time of his purchase exceeds $1,000,000;

(6) Any natural person who had an individual income in excess of $200,000 in each of the two most recent years or joint income with that person's spouse in excess of $300,000 in each of those years and has a reasonable expectation of reaching the same income level in the current year . . . .

(c) *Aggregate offering price. Aggregate offering price* shall mean the sum of all cash, services, property, notes, cancellation of debt, or other consideration to be received by an issuer for issuance of its securities. Where securities are being offered for both cash and non-cash consideration, the aggregate offering price shall be based on the price at which the securities are offered for cash.

(e) *Calculation of number of purchasers.* For purposes of calculating the number of purchasers under Rule 505(b) and Rule 506(b) only, the following shall apply:

(1) The following purchasers shall be excluded:

(i) Any relative, spouse or relative of the spouse of a purchaser who has the same principal residence as the purchaser;

(ii) Any trust or estate in which a purchaser and any of the persons related to him as specified in paragraph (e)(1)(i) or (e)(1)(iii) of this section collectively have more than 50 percent of the beneficial interest (excluding contingent interests);

(iii) Any corporation or other organization of which a purchaser and any of the persons related to him as specified in paragraph (e)(1)(i) or (e)(1)(ii) of this section collectively are beneficial owners of more than 50 percent of the equity securities (excluding directors' qualifying shares) or equity interests; and

(iv) Any accredited investor.

(2) A corporation, partnership or other entity shall be counted as one purchaser. If, however, that entity is organized for the specific purpose of acquiring the securities offered and is not an accredited investor under paragraph (a)8 of this section, then each beneficial owner of equity securities or equity interests in the entity shall count as a separate purchaser for all provisions of Regulation D, except to the extent provided in paragraph (e)(1) of this section.

(f) *Executive officer. Executive officer* shall mean the president, any vice president in charge of a principal business unit, division or function (such as sales, administration or finance), any other officer who performs a policy making function, or any other person who performs similar policy making functions for the issuer.

(h) *Purchaser representative. Purchaser representative* shall mean any person who satisfies all of the following conditions or who the issuer reasonably believes satisfies all of the following conditions:

(1)   Is not an affiliate, director, officer or other employee of the issuer.

(2)   Has such knowledge and experience in financial and business matters that he is capable of evaluating, alone, or together with other purchaser representatives of the purchaser, or together with the purchaser, the merits and risks of the prospective investment;

(3)   Is acknowledged by the purchaser in writing, during the course of the transaction, to be his purchaser representative in connection with evaluating the merits and risks of the prospective investment; and

(4)   Discloses to the purchaser in writing a reasonable time prior to the sale of securities to that purchaser any material relationship between himself or his affiliates and the issuer or its affiliates that then exists, that is mutually understood to be contemplated, or that has existed at any time during the previous two years, and any compensation received or to be received as a result of such relationship.

Rule 502   General Conditions to Be Met

The following conditions shall be applicable to offers and sales made under Regulation D:

(a)   *Integration.* All sales that are part of the same Regulation D offering must meet all of the terms and conditions of Regulation D. Offers and sales that are made more than six months before the start of a Regulation D offering or are made more than six months after completion of a Regulation D offering will not be considered part of that Regulation D offering, so long as during those six month periods there are no offers or sales of securities by or for the issuer that are of the same or a similar class as those offered or sold under Regulation D.

(b)   *Information requirements-*

(1)   *When information must be furnished.* If the issuer sells securities under Rule 505 or Rule 506 to any purchaser that is not an accredited investor, the issuer shall furnish the information specified in paragraph (b)(2) of this section to such purchaser a reasonable time prior to sale. The issuer is not required to furnish the specified information to purchasers when it sells securities under Rule 504, or to any accredited investor.

Note: When an issuer provides information to investors pursuant to paragraph (b)1, it should consider providing such information to accredited investors as well, in view of the anti-fraud provisions of the federal securities laws.

(2)   *Type of information to be furnished.*

(i)   If the issuer is not subject to the reporting requirements of section 13 or 15(d) of the Exchange Act, at a reasonable time prior to the sale of securities the issuer shall furnish to the purchaser, to the extent material to an understanding of the issuer, its business and the securities being offered:

(A)   *Non-financial statement information.* If the issuer is eligible to use Regulation A, the same kind of information as would be required in Part II of Form 1-A. If the issuer is not eligible to use Regulation A, the same kind of information as required in Part I of a registration statement filed under the Securities Act on the form that the issuer would be entitled to use.

(B)   *Financial statement information.*

1.   *Offerings up to $2,000,000.* The information required in Item 310 of Regulation S-B, except that only the issuer's balance sheet, which shall be dated within 120 days of the start of the offering, must be audited.

2.   *Offerings up to $7,500,000.* The financial statement information required in Form SB-2. If an issuer, other than a limited partnership, cannot obtain audited financial statements without unreasonable effort or expense, then only the issuer's balance sheet, which shall be dated within 120 days of the start of the offering, must be audited. If the issuer is a limited partnership and cannot obtain the required financial statements without unreasonable effort or expense, it may furnish financial statements that have been prepared on the basis of Federal income tax requirements and examined and reported on in accordance with generally accepted auditing standards by an independent public or certified accountant.

3.   *Offerings over $7,500,000.* The financial statement as would be required in a registration statement filed under the Act on the form that the issuer would be entitled to use. If an issuer, other than a limited partnership, cannot obtain audited financial statements without unreasonable effort or expense, then only the issuer's balance sheet, which shall be dated within 120 days of the start of the offering, must be audited. If the issuer is a limited partnership and cannot obtain the required financial statements without unreasonable effort or expense, it may furnish financial statements that have been prepared on the basis of Federal income tax requirements and examined and reported on in accordance with generally accepted auditing standards by an independent public or certified accountant.

(c)   *Limitation on manner of offering.* Except as provided in Rule 504(b)(1), neither the issuer nor any person acting on its behalf shall offer or sell the securities by any form of general solicitation or general advertising, including, but not limited to, the following:

(1)   Any advertisement, article, notice or other communication published in any newspaper, magazine, or similar media or broadcast over television or radio; and

(2)   Any seminar or meeting whose attendees have been invited by any general solicitation or general advertising.

(d)   *Limitations on resale.* Except as provided in Rule 504(b)(1), securities acquired in a transaction under Regulation D shall have the status of securities acquired in a transaction under section 4(2) of the Act and cannot be resold without registration under the Act or an exemption therefrom.

Rule 504   Exemption for Limited Offerings and Sales of Securities Not Exceeding $1,000,000

(a)   *Exemption.* Offers and sales of securities that satisfy the conditions in paragraph (b) of this Rule 504 by an issuer . . . shall be exempt from the provision of section 5 of the Act under section 3(b) of the Act.

(b)   *Conditions to be met.*

(1)   *General conditions.* To qualify for exemption under this Rule 504, offers and sales must satisfy the terms and conditions of Rule 501 and Rule 502 (a), (c) and

(d), except that the provisions of Rule 502 (c) and (d) will not apply to offers and sales of securities under this Rule 504 that are made:

(i)   Exclusively in one or more states that provide for the registration of the securities, and require the public filing and delivery to investors of a substantive disclosure document before sale, and are made in accordance with those state provisions;

(ii)   In one or more states that have no provision for the registration of the securities or the public filing or delivery of a disclosure document before sale, if the securities have been registered in at least one state that provides for such registration, public filing and delivery before sale, offers and sales are made in that state in accordance with such provisions, and the disclosure document is delivered before sale to all purchasers (including those in the states that have no such procedure); or

(iii)   Exclusively according to state law exemptions from registration that permit general solicitation and general advertising so long as sales are made only to "accredited investors" as defined in Rule 501(a).

(2)   The aggregate offering price for an offering of securities under this Rule 504, as defined in Rule 501(c), shall not exceed $1,000,000, less the aggregate offering price for all securities sold within the twelve months before the start of and during the offering of securities under this Rule 504, in reliance on any exemption under section 3(b), or in violation of section 5(a) of the Securities Act.

Rule 505   Exemption for Limited Offers and Sales of Securities Not Exceeding $5,000,000

(a)   *Exemption.* Offers and sales of securities that satisfy the conditions in paragraph (b) of this section by an issuer that is not an investment company shall be exempt from the provisions of section 5 of the Act under section 3(b) of the Act.

(b)   *Conditions to be met*

(1)   *General conditions.* To qualify for exemption under this section, offers and sales must satisfy the terms and conditions of Rule 501 and Rule 502.

(2)   *Specific conditions*

(i)   *Limitation on aggregate offering price.* The aggregate offering price for an offering of securities under this Rule 505, as defined in Rule 501(c), shall not exceed $5,000,000, less the aggregate offering price for all securities sold within the twelve months before the start of and during the offering of securities under this Rule 505 in reliance on any exemption under section 3(b) of the Act or in violation of section 5(a) of the Act.

(ii)   *Limitation on number of purchasers.* There are no more than or the issuer reasonably believes that there are no more than 35 purchasers of securities from the issuer in any offering under this section.

Rule 506   Exemption for Limited Offers and Sales without Regard to Dollar Amount of Offering

(a)   *Exemption.* Offers and sales of securities by an issuer that satisfy the conditions in paragraph (b) of this Rule 506 shall be deemed to be transactions not involving any public offering within the meaning of section 4 (2) of the Act.

(b)   *Conditions to be met—*

(1) *General conditions.* To qualify for an exemption under this section, offers and sales must satisfy all the terms and conditions of Rule 501 and Rule 502.

(2) *Specific Conditions—*

(i) *Limitation on number of purchasers.* There are no more than or the issuer reasonably believes that there are no more than 35 purchasers of securities from the issuer in any offering under this section.

(ii) *Nature of purchasers.* Each purchaser who is not an accredited investor either alone or with his purchaser representative(s) has such knowledge and experience in financial and business matters that he is capable of evaluating the merits and risks of the prospective investment, or the issuer reasonably believes immediately prior to making any sale that such purchaser comes within this description.

A SHORT QUIZ AND WORKSHEET ON REGULATION D

1. Notice that there are no requirements in Rule 501; it is simply a "dictionary" of terms used elsewhere in Regulation D. Go through the rest of Regulation D now and note where these defined terms are used. This will be important in answering questions on Regulation D later in these exercises.

2. Rule 502 presents four requirements which appear to apply throughout Regulation D: integration, information requirements, limitations on manner of offering, and limitations on resale. But appearances are deceiving. Actually, these rules do *not* apply throughout the Regulation D exemptions. Which of these four requirements of Rule 502 apply to offerings under Rule 504? Rule 505? Rule 506?

3. We said that Regulation D was promulgated under the SEC's delegated authority in § 3(b) of the Securities Act. Actually, this is not completely true. Which Rule is not a § 3(b) rule? (You may think this is picky, but it will be critically important later.) Note that the rule which is not a § 3(b) rule is a "safe harbor" rule.

4. What is the difference between Rule 505 and Rule 506? Or to put it another way, since Rule 505 has a $5 million limit and Rule 506 has no dollar limit, why is Rule 505 even here?

5. Would it be possible to for sales under Rule 504 or 505 to be made to more than 35 people? (Be sure to consult Rule 501 for how to count purchasers; it is trickier than you might think.)

6. Now that you are thoroughly familiar with Regulation D, you can compile your quiz answers in the following table.

| | Statutory authority | Dollar limit on offering | Requirements from Rule 502 (√ if required): | | | Limit on no. of offerees | Purchaser qualification required? |
			Information to offerees	Limits on advertising	Limit on re-sales		
Rule 504							
Rule 505							
Rule 506							

This is a worksheet you will want to keep for future reference in this course and in practice until you have these Regulation D rules committed to memory. And even then, the rules *will* change during your professional lifetime, so maybe you'll want to keep this chart handy all the time and review and update it regularly.[52]

The Aggravation of Aggregation

From the quiz and worksheet above, you determined that Rules 504 and 505 have a dollar limit on the size of the offering, in addition to other requirements. (Note that Rule 506 has no such requirement. Why is that?)

A dollar limit would be pretty meaningless if an issuer could make offers each day (or each hour) up to the full $1 million / $5 million limit under either Rule 504 or Rule 505. Therefore, each rule has a method for calculating when the dollar limit has been reached, phrased similarly in Rule 504(b)(2) and Rule 505(b)(2)(i). Because the rules are for determining the "aggregate" offering price, this requirement is known as "aggregation." In each case, the amount available under the rule is determined by taking the $1 million (Rule 504) or $5 million (Rule 505) limit

> less the aggregate offering price for all securities sold within the twelve months before the start of and during the offering of securities under this Rule . . . in reliance on any exemption under section 3(b) of the Act or in violation of section 5(a) of the Act.[53]

We know that the § 3(b) exemptions include Rule 504 and Rule 505 (but *not* Rule 506) and Regulation A.

Examples

(1) W Corp. sold $500,000 of common stock in a Rule 504 offering yesterday. For the next year, W Corp. can offer only $500,000 under Rule 504, and $4.5 million under Rule 505.

(2) X Corp. sold $2 million of common stock in a Rule 505 offering yesterday. For the next year, X Corp. can offer only $3 million under Rule 505, and *nothing* under Rule 504.

EXERCISE 4-1

For all problems, assume the date is October 1.

(1)   J Corp. sold $500,000 worth of common stock in January in reliance on Rule 504. How much may now be sold under Rule 504? Under Rule 505?

(2)   K Corp. sold $500,000 worth of common stock in January in reliance on Rule 504 *and* $2 million worth of common stock in May in reliance on Rule 505. How much may now be sold under Rule 504? Under Rule 505?

(3)   L Corp. sold $2 million worth of common stock in January in reliance on the § 3(a)(11) "intrastate offering" exemption. How much may now be sold under Rule 504? Under Rule 505?

---

[52] For a head start on your chart, see Brown, *supra*, § 6.5 at pp. 6-31 to 6-33.

[53] A similar requirement for Regulation A offerings is found in Rule 251(b).

iii.   Other small or limited offerings

Regulation D is likely the most useful collection of exemptions for small business engaging in their initial offering of securities. There are two other less well-known exemptions which may be useful parts of the business planner's toolbox.

First, Securities Act Rule 701 exempts offers and sales of securities made pursuant to qualifying employee benefit plans. The rule was initially written pursuant to the Commission's § 3(b) authority and accordingly contained a $5 million limit. However, in 1996, Congress granted the Commission general exemptive authority under the Securities Act.[54] In 1999, the Commission used this authority to remove the dollar limitation from Rule 701 offerings.[55] Rule 701 "is useful because it frequently will exempt sales to employees that are not otherwise qualified purchasers under Section 4(2). Your client can sell at least $1 million of securities under Rule 701, no matter how small the company is."[56]

Second, Congress in 1980 added its own exemption. Section 4(6) of the Securities Act exempts

> transactions involving offers or sales by an issuer solely to one or more accredited investors, if the aggregate offering price of an issue of securities offered in reliance on this paragraph does not exceed the amount allowed under section 3(b), if there is no advertising or public solicitation in connection with the transaction by the issuer or anyone acting on the issuer's behalf, and if the issuer files such notice with the Commission as the Commission shall prescribe.

Section 4(6), although it may appear useful at first glance, has no real advantages over Regulation D offerings.[57]

d.   Integration

Just as a dollar limit on offerings would be pointless if an issuer could make "new" offerings each hour, likewise the registration requirement of § 5 would be gutted if an issuer could similarly parse one offering into sufficiently discrete and exempt portions. The SEC has developed the "integration" doctrine to deal with this problem. Unlike the aggregation rule, the integration doctrine is potentially applicable to *any* offering of securities which is claimed to be exempt from § 5. This doctrine provides the Commission with the ability to combine parts of an offering which were claimed by the issuer to be separate.[58] We consider integration first as

---

[54] Securities Act § 28 provides broad exemptive authority, with the only catch being that the exemption must be "by rule or regulation."

[55] This is the only use to date by the Commission of its § 28 authority. *See* Hazen, *supra*, at 281–82. Other amount limitations still apply. *See* Rule 701(d).

[56] William W. Barker, *Outside Bucks: A Practical Guide to Raising Capital for a Business*, BUSINESS LAW TODAY, vol. 15, no. 9, July/August 2000, at 15, 20.

[57] Section 4(6) offerings are apparently not subject to the "aggregation" rule of Rule 505(b)(2)(ii) or the limitations on resales of Rule 502(d). However, global restrictions on resales will likely still apply to § 4(6) offerings; *see infra* Section C.2.

[58] The integration doctrine thus closely resembles the tax law's "step transaction doctrine" with which you may already be familiar. Hazen, *supra*, at 197. The Internal Revenue Service employs this doctrine to combine what a taxpayer would like to treat as separate transaction into one integrated whole

it might affect two otherwise exempt transactions, and then how it might affect an exempt transaction followed by a registered offering.

i.   Integrating exempt transactions

The integration doctrine was developed in the early 1960s, in the context of the § 3(a)(11) intrastate exemption,[59] and the § 4(2) private offering exemption.[60] The Commission in each context identified five factors to be used in determining whether two apparently separate issues of securities should be "integrated." Those same factors continue in use today; they are presented in similar form[61] in the notes following Rule 502(a) and in the notes preceding Rule 147:

(1) whether the offers or sales are part of a single plan of financing;

(2) whether the offers or sales involve issuance of the same class of securities;

(3) whether the offers or sales have been made at or about the same time;

(4) whether the same type of consideration is or is to be received; and

(5) Whether the offers or sales are made for the same general purpose.

The application of these factors is difficult.[62] The factors "do not provide much certainty in planning transactions. Furthermore, because the . . . doctrine's availability is essentially dependent upon questions of fact varying with the nuances of each situation, it is often difficult to glean any learning from the relatively sparse precedent that exists."[63] It may be safe to say that the first factor ("single plan") and the fifth factor ("same general purpose") have "considerable overlap and are highly important, and that the fourth factor (type of consideration) is probably the least important (since it is almost always cash).[64]

Perhaps recognizing that the integration factors are difficult to apply, the Commission has provided "safe harbors" for many exempt offerings. Rules 147(b)(2) and 502(a) give the issuer a six-month safe harbor — offers made more than six months apart will not be integrated.[65] **Warning:** the language needs to be

---

(or vice versa). *See generally* Boris I. Bittker, Martin J. McMahon, Jr. & Lawrence A. Zelenak, Federal Income Taxation of Individuals ¶ 1.03[5] (3d ed. 2002).

[59] *See* Securities Act Release No. 4434, 26 Fed. Reg. 11,896, 11,896 (1961) ("the exemption should not be relied upon in combination with another exemption for the different parts of a single issue where a part is offered or sold to nonresidents.").

[60] *See* Securities Act Release No. 4552, 27 Fed. Reg. 11,316, 11,317 (1962) ("A person may not separate parts of a series of related transactions, the sum total of which is really one offering, and claim that a particular part is a non-public transaction.").

[61] Securities Act Rule 147, Preliminary Note 3, refers to "offerings," while Securities Act Rule 502(a) refers to "sales," but otherwise the factors are the same. In the summary below, we refer to both offers and sales.

[62] This is probably an understatement. For the full assault on the integration doctrine with citations to the main authorities, see C. Steven Bradford, *Regulation A and the Integration Doctrine: The New Safe Harbor*, 55 Ohio St. L.J. 255, 265–66 (1994).

[63] Hazen, *supra*, at 285.

[64] Loss & Seligman, *supra* at 361–62. Professors Loss and Seligman caution similarly to Professor Hazen that "[n]either the Commission nor the courts have provided express guidance on how to weight these factors when analyzing an integration problem." *Id.* at 362.

[65] This conclusion must be qualified; under Rules 147 and 502, the safe harbor is only "one way." In

read carefully; although the rules appear similar, there are devils in the details. Rule 502(b) looks only at Regulation D offers or sales during the "safe harbor" period.

> Offers and sales that are made more than six months before the start of a Regulation D offering or are made more than six months after completion of a Regulation D offering will not be considered part of that Regulation D offering, so long as during those six month periods there are no offers or sales of securities by or for the issuer that are of the same or a similar class as those offered or sold under Regulation D . . . .

However, Rule 147(b)(2) provides a safe harbor only if there are *no offers* at all in the six-month period:

> For purposes of this rule only, an issue shall be deemed not to include offers, offers to sell, offers for sale or sales of securities of the issuer pursuant to the exemptions provided by Section 3 or Section 4(2) of the Act or pursuant to a registration statement filed under the Act, that take place prior to the six month period immediately preceding or after the six month period immediately following any offers, offers for sale or sales pursuant to this rule, *Provided*, That, there are during either of said six month periods no offers, offers for sale or sales of securities by or for the issuer of the same or similar class as those offered, offered for sale or sold pursuant to the rule.

Examples

(1) Y Corp. sold $2 million of stock in an offering not meeting the requirements of Rules 505 or 506, but in reliance on the intrastate offering exemption under § 3(a)(11). If tomorrow, Y Corp. sells $1 of common stock to someone else in another state, and the offerings are "integrated," there will be no exemption for any of the securities sold!

(2) Any offering made in reliance on § 4(2) will be destroyed if it is integrated with some earlier or later offer to an uninformed or unsophisticated investor.

EXERCISE 4-2

For all problems, assume the date is October 1.

(1)   Q Corp. sold $1 million worth of common stock to its President on July 1. May it now make a $900,000 common stock offering to its employees in reliance on Rule 504?

(2)   Suppose instead that the sale to its President occurred on January 1. Could that offering be integrated with the planned offering to employees?

(3)   R Corp., a New York corporation with all its offices and operations in New

---

Rule 147 it is only for the intrastate offering, in Regulation D it is only for the Regulation D offering. The other offering may still be subject to the five-factor test and may be integrated with the "safe harbor" offering. See Loss & Seligman, *supra*, at 362–63. There are other safe harbors. Rule 251(c) of Regulation A provides a broad safe harbor; *see* Bradford, *supra*, at 272–83. However, as Regulation A is of limited usefulness to small businesses in their initial offerings, *see supra* Section C.1.c.i, the safe harbor is likewise of limited usefulness. Rule 701(f) provides that Rule 701 offerings will not be integrated with any other offerings.

York, sold $10 million worth of common stock to New York residents in reliance on § 3(a)(11).

(a) Suppose R Corp. sells $10 of stock the next week to its President, who is a resident of Connecticut? Is there a problem if these two offerings are integrated?

(b) Suppose instead that one of the original New York resident purchasers resells her shares to a resident of New Jersey? Is there a problem here? *See* Securities Act Rule 147(e).

ii.   Integrating later registered offerings

Most businesses begin by raising capital from private investors, and they may continue by obtaining one or more additional rounds of private financing. But eventually a growing business will need to raise money in such large amounts or from such a large number of investors that a registered public offering is necessary. While coverage of the details of your work in completing such a public offering is beyond the scope of this course, you should keep the eventual public offering in mind during the initial financing stages.

For example, an issuer may offer so-called "piggyback" registration rights to initial purchasers of securities. This means that when or if the issuer proceeds with a registered public offering, it will agree to also register an offering by the initial purchasers of their shares for resale. It is quite common to see this promise taken up; that is, an initial public offering by an issuer often also includes a number of shares being offered by insiders. Some purchasers with significant bargaining power can extract a promise from the issuer to register securities when the purchaser wishes to sell. In either case, filing a registration statement for the resales will avoid the problem of finding an exemption for the resales, discussed in Section C.2 below.[66]

The main problem with this scenario is the danger, again, of integration. If the "exempt" offering and the registered public offering are integrated, it is clear that the formerly "exempt" offering is no longer so. Beginning in the mid-1980s, however, the SEC staff rediscovered a 1937 rule and adapted it for this purpose, effectively permitting non-integration of the completed private offering and the later public offering.[67] In the case of a failed private offering re-started as a registered offering, or vice versa, the SEC adopted a new rule in 2001 permitting the failed offering to avoid being integrated with the later offering.[68]

---

[66] Remember that, to the extent we rely upon an exemption for the *transaction* and not for the *securities* themselves (discussed in Section C.3 below), each transaction must be registered or exempt. The registration obligation of Securities Act § 5 relates to an *offer or sale*, although lawyers sometimes colloquially (and inaccurately) speak of registering "the securities."

[67] Securities Act Rule 152 provides that "[t]he phrase 'transactions by an issuer not involving any public offering' in Section 4(2) shall be deemed to apply to transactions not involving any public offering at the time of said transactions although subsequently thereto the issuer decides to make a public offering and/or files a registration statement." The modern use of Rule 152 took place in a series of SEC staff "no action" letters and is thus informal guidance. It may be beyond the scope of Rule 152, but is nonetheless a modest and probably admirable attempt to adapt the strictures of the '33 Act and particularly the integration doctrine to the realities of small business finance. *See* Lyman Johnson & Steve Patterson, *The Reincarnation of Rule 152: False Hope on the Integration Front*, 46 Wash. & Lee L. Rev. 525 (1989).

[68] *See* Securities Act Rule 155.

2.   Transaction Exemptions for Resales

The treatment of resales — sales of securities by persons other than the issuer — appears straightforward at first glance. When we have completed our initial round of financing, surely the investors can resell their interests to others without worrying about the securities laws.

Indeed, we find that § 4(1) of the Securities Act exempts "transactions by any person other than an issuer, underwriter, or dealer," and therefore seems to take care of the problem. It is obvious that the people we are talking about are not "issuers," but what about the other two terms? A "dealer" is someone who is engaged in the business of dealing or trading in securities,[69] and therefore wouldn't seem to include the original investors in the business entity who turn around and want to sell their interests to someone else. However, determining who is an "underwriter" can be a more complicated inquiry. We begin with the statutory definition.

Securities Act § 2(a)(11)

The term "underwriter" means any person who has purchased from an issuer with a view to, or offers or sells for an issuer in connection with, the distribution of any security, or participates or has a direct or indirect participation in any such undertaking, or participates or has a participation in the direct or indirect underwriting of any such undertaking; but such term shall not include a person whose interest is limited to a commission from an underwriter or dealer not in excess of the usual and customary distributors' or sellers' commission. As used in this paragraph the term "issuer" shall include, in addition to an issuer, any person directly or indirectly controlling or controlled by the issuer, or any person under direct or indirect common control with the issuer.

So, let's review. Our ordinary business owner can rely on the exemption in § 4(1) if he or she is not an "underwriter." (We can summarily dispense with "issuer" or "dealer.") And that person is not an underwriter, according to § 2(a)(11), if he or she does or did not take the securities from the issuer "with a view to . . . distribution." In order to determine that the resales are exempt under § 4(1), therefore, we need to know what is a "distribution" (never mind the "view" requirement).

The consequences of this otherwise technical inquiry can be grave. Suppose, for example, the initial business sells securities to the investors A and B, in reliance on the § 4(2) exemption, clearly appropriate since A and B have all the information about the new issuer which exists at the time. *Ralston Purina* would be good authority here. Then, suppose some time later, B resells to C. If B is considered to be an "underwriter," then the sale from B to C will not be exempt under § 4(1), but that is not the main problem. If B is considered an underwriter, then B is participating in a "distribution," which means the *initial sale* was not complete until the resale to C. Therefore, if C does not meet the *Ralston Purina* requirements, the *initial § 4(2) exemption* will no longer apply.[70] That means that A (and all the other

---

[69] Securities Act § 2(a)(12).

[70] If you thought of using Rule 504 here, on the theory that it requires no investor sophistication, you are congratulated on your recall of the power of Rule 504. However, Rule 504 and the rest of Regulation D provide exemptions only for *issuers* and therefore do not cover resales.

A's if there are more purchasers) would have their § 12(a)(1) right to rescission. Couple this with the fact that you may not even know who C is at the time of the original sales to A and B, and you can appreciate the magnitude of the problem posed by private resales.

However, there is a convenient solution here, known by all securities lawyers as the § 4(1½) exemption. The solution has that designation because it involves using the concepts from § 4(2) — such as *Ralston* Purina — to determine that a resale is exempt under § 4(1). Professors Loss & Seligman provide a concise description of how this exemption works.

> Because the SEC staff often has required such resales to meet some of the *Ralston*-type criteria for § 4(2) offerings by an issuer, this variety of sale has been dubbed a "Section 4(1½)" transaction. But the answer, of course, is simply § 4(1). Section 4(2) with its reference to "transactions by an issuer" can have no application to a resale unless the securities have not yet "come to rest" in the reseller's hands. In that event, it is appropriate for the sophistication and access criteria to be applied, but only for the purpose of ensuring that the issuer's original § 4(2) exemption has not been lost.

> It follows that, if the person who bought from an issuer . . . has held the securities long enough to make credible the assertion that he or she did not take them with a view to distribution — so that, as it used to be said, the securities have "come to rest" in his or her hands — he or she should not be brought within the . . . "underwriter" definition in § 2(a)(11) and his later distribution should be exempted under § 4(1).[71]

This interpretation, meant to be helpful to business planners and their lawyers, can be confusing because it conflates at least three different concepts. First, we need to know whether the initial purchaser has taken the securities "with a view to distribution." There is likely no direct proof of that purchaser's intent, so we use the holding period as a proxy — this is the source of the "come to rest" rule referred to above. Second, it is relevant whether the second purchaser can meet the *Ralston Purina* requirements which normally apply only to issuer exemptions, that is, whether that person has or has access to the information a registration statement would provide. And finally, the rationale of the § 4(1½) exemption is that a person is not an "underwriter" if he or she is not participating in a "distribution" and a "distribution" is understood to be a "public offering" in the *Ralston Purina* sense, all of which is gloss not immediately apparent from the language of § 2(a)(11).[72]

However confusing it might be, this § 4(1½) exemption is probably the best thing we have to use as authority for exemption of resale of securities originally sold to the business' owners, operators, or major investors. There are four other possible sources of authority, but upon closer examination each has faults which will probably keep you from being able to rely on them.

---

[71] Loss & Seligman, *supra*, at 429. You may need to reread this a few times to follow the path through all the statutes. If this is *too* concise, see the seminal article on this exemption, ABA Committee on Federal Regulation of Securities, *The Section "4(1½)" Phenomenon: Private Resales of Restricted Securities*, 34 Bus. Law. 1961 (1979), or Harold S. Bloomenthal, Securities Law Handbook § 10:8 (2006).

[72] See Brown, *supra*, § 7.3.1 at p. 7–8 (" 'Distribution' is not defined in the statute, but it is understood essentially to be synonymous with 'public offering.' ").

First, there is Rule 144, which is itself complicated and something we have not yet considered. Rule 144 is a safe harbor permitting resales of "restricted" securities. But two onerous requirements of that rule are (1) that there be "current *public* information" about the issuer,[73] and (2) that the sales be made through a broker.[74] Although these requirements lapse after one year,[75] they do so only in the case of resales by individuals who are not "affiliates" of the issuer, a condition not likely met by the investors who might now want to use Rule 144 for their resales.[76]

Second, Rule 144A is a "safe harbor" rule for resales, but only for resales to "qualified institutional buyers." These buyers include: insurance companies, investment companies, employee plans, charitable organizations, businesses, and investment advisers. These buyers must be purchasing for their own account or on behalf of other qualified institutional buyers.[77] These restrictions likely make the Rule of limited utility to the occasional seller of small business securities.

Third, Rule 504(b)(1) permits resales of securities, but only if the initial sale registered under at least one state's securities laws.[78] However, registration under state securities laws is not likely a feasible option for many of the same reasons that federal registration was not an option.

Finally, although Rule 147 explicitly notes that it does *not* cover resales,[79] § 3(a)(11) itself does *not* say that in so many words, raising the hope that perhaps the statute will exempt resales where the "safe harbor" rule does not. That hope is dashed by remembering that the statute exempts only securities which are "part of an *issue*," suggesting that the exemption is available only to an issuer.[80]

The generally-accepted solution to the "resale" problem is to have objective evidence of investment intent for the initial sale and evidence of sophistication-or-access for the resale. At the time of the initial sale, you will probably require each purchaser to affirm that he or she is purchasing for investment and not for resale. In addition, you as counsel must have the question of resale brought to you *at the time of the resale*. Only then can evaluate whether the initial purchaser likely did purchase for investment and whether the subsequent purchaser would meet the requirements for § 4(2) to apply. The mechanism for bringing the proposed sale before counsel is a transfer restriction imposed in the *original* sale (through a

---

[73] *See* Securities Act Rule 144(c).

[74] *See* Securities Act Rule 144(f).

[75] *See* Securities Act Rule 144(d)(1)(ii).

[76] A resale *could* come within Rule 144(d)(1)(ii) if, for example, the insider has held the securities for one year, resigns his or her inside position such that he or she is no longer an "affiliate," waits three months, and then sells the securities. There are several problems here; (1) that is a long time to wait, especially the three months after surrender of insider status, and (2) there is no guarantee that such surrender will make the potential seller not an "affiliate." Rule 144(a)(1) defines affiliate in terms of "control," and the SEC resolutely refuses to assist issuers or counsel in determining control. *See generally* Loss & Seligman, *supra*, Ch. 5.

[77] Rule 144A(a)(1).

[78] For the details of state registration, see *infra* Section E.

[79] Rule 147(a) makes clear it is only an issuer exemption. The nine-month prohibition on interstate resales in Rule 147(e) does not exempt those resales, but is relevant only in determining whether the otherwise exempt issue has "come to rest" within the boundaries of the state. *See* Loss & Seligman, *supra*, at 442.

[80] This is the better but not universally-held view. *See* Hazen, *supra*, at 192 & n.3.

shareholder or operating agreement).[81] Both Rules 147(f) and 502(d) provide for such restrictions and restrictive legends.[82]

Finally, it should be noted that the concern about resales extends not only to the *first* resale, but probably to the second as well. This is courtesy of the cryptic second sentence of § 2(a)(11), which provides that "[a]s used in this paragraph the term "issuer" shall include, in addition to an issuer, any person directly or indirectly controlling or controlled by the issuer, or any person under direct or indirect common control with the issuer." Although "control" is not a concept clearly defined in the Securities Act, it is likely that the initial investors in a business are sufficiently few as to likely "control" the issuer.[83] Therefore, the sale from the issuer to A and B probably means that A and B are still considered "issuers" for the sole purpose[84] of making the person who purchases from *them* a "purchaser from an issuer" and thus potentially an underwriter in his or her own right.

EXERCISE 4-3

D, E and F are individuals who are planning to go into business together. They will each contribute $500,000 to their corporation in exchange for 100 shares of common stock each. All three are familiar with the business.

(1)   Eight months later, F wants to sell half of her stock to her mother who meets the "accredited investor" standards for individuals but otherwise knows nothing about F's business and lives in another state. What conditions would you place upon the sale to F's mother in order to protect the original exemption for the sales to D and E?

(2)   Suppose that shortly after F's sale to her mother (which you *did* ultimately approve), the company decides to make a registered public offering of stock? What legal issues are raised by the prior sales to D, E, F and F's mother? How can these issues be best (and most cheaply) resolved?

(3)   Suppose the planned public offering is abandoned after preliminary prospectuses were shown to 15 wealthy individuals meeting the "accredited investor" standards. The company would like nonetheless to sell stock (albeit a lesser amount) to these 15 individuals. How do you recommend that the company proceed?

3.   Exempt securities

Section 3 of the Securities Act provides a list of "exempted securities," and Section 4 provides a list of "exempted transactions." However, things are not as they seem. We have already seen that § 3(a)(11), the "intrastate" exemption, is really a transaction exemption although it is included in Section 3. There are other examples:

---

[81]   *See generally* Loss & Seligman, *supra*, at 423–26. For full details of transfer restrictions, including determinations of validity under state law, see Chapter 8.

[82]   Rule 147(f) appears to be a no-exceptions requirement, while Rule 502(d) indicates that purchaser representations, transfer restrictions and stop-transfer orders are only one way of demonstrating that the issuer has exercised reasonable care to avoid sales to underwriters.

[83]   *See generally* Loss & Seligman, *supra*, Ch. 5.

[84]   Since A and B are considered "issuers" *only* for the purpose of § 2(a)(11), they *cannot* take advantage of issuer exemptions such as Regulation D or § 4(2). *See* Loss & Seligman, *supra*, at 325. (Nice try, though; you wouldn't be the first to think of that.)

A moment's glance at the two Sections [§§ 3 and 4] will reveal that the dichotomy was not carefully considered. The exemptions in §§ 3(a)(2)–(8) and § 3(a)(13) are genuine security exemptions. But there is nothing peculiar about the securities, or the issuers of the securities, that are exempted under §§ 3(a)(9)–(12), 3(b), or 3(c). All those exemptions were created because of the circumstances surrounding the particular *offering*.[85]

Although §§ 3(a)(9)–(11) and (13) are in a section captioned "exempt securities," they are really exempt *transactions*, and their exempted nature ceases when the transaction ends.[86] Conversely, the other subsections of § 3(a) are securities exempt by the very nature of the security or the issuer, and they retain their exemption transaction after transaction so long as the securities retain the requisite exempt features. Of these truly exempt securities, the type most likely to interest the small business planner is so-called "commercial paper" exempted by Securities Act § 3(a)(3), and a similar exemption in Exchange Act § 3(a)(10).

Securities Act § 3(a)(3)

Except as hereinafter expressly provided, the provisions of this title shall not apply to any of the following classes of securities:

> (3) Any note, draft, bill of exchange, or banker's acceptance which arises out of a current transaction or the proceeds of which have been or are to be used for current transactions, and which has a maturity at the time of issuance of not exceeding nine months, exclusive of days of grace, or any renewal thereof the maturity of which is likewise limited . . . .

Securities Exchange Act § 3(a)(10)

The term "security" . . . shall not include currency or any note, draft, bill of exchange, or banker's acceptance which has a maturity at the time of issuance of not exceeding nine months, exclusive of days of grace, or any renewal thereof the maturity of which is likewise limited.

REVES v. ERNST & YOUNG
United States Supreme Court
494 U.S. 56 (1990)

JUSTICE MARSHALL delivered the opinion of the Court.

This case presents the question whether certain demand notes issued by the Farmers Cooperative of Arkansas and Oklahoma (Co-Op) are "securities" within the meaning of § 3(a)(10) of the Securities Exchange Act of 1934. We conclude that they are.

[The facts of the case are presented in Part I of the opinion. In Part II, the Court concludes that the notes are "securities" within the meaning of § 3(a)(10) of the 1934 Act and its near-twin, § 2(a)(1) of the 1933 Act. These portions of the

---

[85] Loss & Seligman, *supra*, at 341 (italics added).

[86] On this all major authorities are in agreement. *See id.*; Hazen, *supra*, at 181; Securities Act Release No. 4434, 26 Fed. Reg. 11,896, 11,896 n.3 (1961). These sections were moved to § 3 by 1934 amendments to the 1933 Act which, in attempting to solve another problem, created this one. Loss & Seligman, *supra*, at 342.

opinion are reprinted in Section B of this chapter.]

III

Relying on the exception in [§ 3(a)(10) of the Exchange Act] for "any note . . . which has a maturity at the time of issuance of not exceeding nine months," respondent contends that the notes here are not "securities," even if they would otherwise qualify. Respondent cites Arkansas cases standing for the proposition that, in the context of the state statute of limitations, " [a] note payable on demand is due immediately." See, *e.g., McMahon v. O'Keefe*, 213 Ark. 105, 106, 209 S.W.2d 449, 450 (1948) (statute of limitations is triggered by the date of issuance rather than by date of first demand). Respondent concludes from this rule that the "maturity" of a demand note within the meaning of § 3(a)(10) is immediate, which is, of course, less than nine months. Respondent therefore contends that the notes fall within the plain words of the exclusion and are thus not "securities."

Petitioners counter that the "plain words" of the exclusion should not govern. Petitioners cite the legislative history of a similar provision of the 1933 Act, [§ 3(a)(3)], for the proposition that the purpose of the exclusion is to except from the coverage of the Acts only commercial paper — short-term, high quality instruments issued to fund current operations and sold only to highly sophisticated investors. Petitioners also emphasize that this Court has repeatedly held that the plain words of the definition of a "security" are not dispositive, and that we consider the economic reality of the transaction to determine whether Congress intended the Securities Acts to apply. Petitioners therefore argue, with some force, that reading the exception for short-term notes to exclude from the Acts' coverage investment notes of less than nine months' duration would be inconsistent with Congress' evident desire to permit the SEC and the courts flexibility to ensure that the Acts are not manipulated to investors' detriment. If petitioners are correct that the exclusion is intended to cover only commercial paper, these notes, which were sold in a large scale offering to unsophisticated members of the public, plainly should not fall within the exclusion.

We need not decide, however, whether petitioners' interpretation of the exception is correct, for we conclude that even if we give literal effect to the exception, the notes do not fall within its terms.

Respondent's contention that the demand notes fall within the "plain words" of the statute rests entirely upon the premise that Arkansas' statute of limitations for suits to collect demand notes is determinative of the "maturity" of the notes, as that term is used in the *federal* Securities Acts. The "maturity" of the notes, however, is a question of federal law. To regard States' statutes of limitations law as controlling the scope of the Securities Acts would be to hold that a particular instrument is a "security" under the 1934 Act in some States, but that the same instrument is not a "security" in others. We are unpersuaded that Congress intended the Securities Acts to apply differently to the same transactions depending on the accident of which State's law happens to apply.

The Chief Justice's argument in partial dissent is but a more artful statement of respondent's contention, and it suffers from the same defect. The Chief Justice begins by defining "maturity" to mean the time when a note becomes due. Because a demand note is "immediately 'due' such that an action could be brought at any time without any other demand than the suit," the Chief Justice concludes that a demand note is due immediately for purposes of the federal securities laws. Even if the Chief Justice is correct that the "maturity" of a note corresponds to the time at which it "becomes due," the authority he cites for the proposition that, as a matter of federal law, a demand note "becomes due" immediately (as opposed to when demand is made or expected to be made) is no more dispositive than is Arkansas case law. The Chief Justice's primary source of authority is a treatise regarding the *state* law of negotiable instruments, particularly the Uniform Negotiable Instruments Law. The quotation upon which the Chief Justice relies is concerned with articulating the general *state*-law rule regarding when suit may be filed. . . . In short, the dissent adds nothing to respondent's argument other than additional authority for what "maturity" means in certain state-law contexts. The dissent provides no argument for its implicit, but essential, premise that state rules concerning the proper method of collecting a debt control the resolution of the federal question before us.

Neither the law of Arkansas nor that of any other State provides an answer to the federal question, and as a matter of federal law, the words of the statute are far from "plain" with regard to whether demand notes fall within the exclusion. . . . In light of Congress' broad[] purpose in the Acts of ensuring that investments of all descriptions be regulated to prevent fraud and abuse, we interpret the exception not to cover the demand notes at issue here. Although the result might be different if the design of the transaction suggested that both parties contemplated that demand would be made within the statutory period, that is not the case before us.

IV

For the foregoing reasons, we conclude that the demand notes at issue here fall under the "note" category of instruments that are "securities" under the 1933 and 1934 Acts. We also conclude that . . . these demand notes do not fall within the exclusion. Accordingly, we reverse the judgment of the Court of Appeals and remand the case for further proceedings consistent with this opinion.

So ordered.

JUSTICE STEVENS, concurring.

While I join the Court's opinion, an important additional consideration supports my conclusion that these notes are securities notwithstanding the statute's exclusion for currency and commercial paper that has a maturity of no more than nine months. The Courts of Appeals have been unanimous in rejecting a literal reading of that exclusion. They have instead concluded that "when Congress spoke of notes with a maturity not exceeding nine months, it meant commercial paper, not investment securities." *Sanders v. John Nuveen & Co.*, 463 F.2d 1075, 1080 (CA7), cert. denied, 409 U.S. 1009 (1972). . . .

In my view such a settled construction of an important federal statute should not be disturbed unless and until Congress so decides. . . .

Indeed, the agreement among the Courts of Appeals is made all the more impressive in this case because it is buttressed by the views of the Securities and Exchange Commission. See Securities Act Release No. 33-4412, 26 Fed.Reg. 9158 (1961) (construing § 3(a)(3) of the Securities Act of 1933, the 1933 Act's counterpart to § 3(a)(10) of the 1934 Act).

. . . .

For these reasons and those stated in the opinion of the Court, I conclude that the notes issued by respondents are securities within the meaning of the 1934 Act.

CHIEF JUSTICE REHNQUIST, with whom JUSTICE WHITE, JUSTICE O'CONNOR, and JUSTICE SCALIA join, concurring in part and dissenting in part.

I join Part II of the Court's opinion, but dissent from Part III and the statements of the Court's judgment in Parts I and IV. In Part III, the Court holds that these notes were not covered by the statutory exemption for "any note . . . which has a maturity at the time of issuance of not exceeding nine months." Treating demand notes as if they were a recent development in the law of negotiable instruments, the Court says "if it is plausible to regard a demand note as having an immediate maturity because demand *could* be made immediately, it is also plausible to regard the maturity of a demand note as being in excess of nine months because demand *could* be made many years or decades into the future. Given this ambiguity, the exclusion must be interpreted in accordance with its purpose."

But the terms "note" and "maturity" did not spring full blown from the head of Congress in 1934. Neither are demand notes of recent vintage. "Note" and "maturity" have been terms of art in the legal profession for centuries, and a body of law concerning the characteristics of demand notes, including their maturity, was in existence at the time Congress passed the 1934 Act.

In construing any terms whose meanings are less than plain, we depend on the common understanding of those terms at the time of the statute's creation. . . . Pursuant to the dominant consensus in the case law, instruments payable on demand were considered immediately "due" such that an action could be brought at any time without any other demand than the suit. See, *e.g.*, M. Bigelow, Law of Bills, Notes, and Checks § 349, p. 265 (3d ed. W. Lile rev. 1928); 8 C.J., Bills and Notes § 602, p. 406, and n. 83 (1916). . . .

To be sure, demand instruments were considered to have "the peculiar quality of having two maturity dates — one for the purpose of holding to his obligation the party primarily liable (*e.g.* maker), and the other for enforcing the contracts of parties secondarily liable (*e.g.* drawer and indorsers)." Bigelow, *supra*, § 350, at 266 (emphasis omitted). But only the rule of immediate maturity respecting makers of demand notes has any bearing on our examination of the exemption; the language in the Act makes clear that it is the "maturity at time of issuance" with which we are concerned. Accordingly, in the absence of some compelling indication to the contrary, the maturity date exemption must encompass demand notes because they possess "maturity at the time of issuance of not exceeding nine months."[87]

Petitioners and the lower court decisions cited by Justice Stevens rely, virtually exclusively, on the legislative history of § 3(a)(3) of the 1933 Act for the proposition that the term "any note" in the exemption in § 3(a)(10) of the 1934 Act encompass

---

87 [*] Reference to the state common law of negotiable instruments does not suggest that "Congress intended the Securities Acts to apply differently to the same transactions depending on the accident of which State's law happens to apply." Rather, in the absence of a *federal* law of negotiable instruments or other alternative sources for discerning the applicability of the statutory term "maturity" to demand notes, we are dependent on the state common law at the time of the Act's creation as a basis for a nationally uniform answer to this "federal question." . . .

only notes having the character of short-term "commercial paper" exchanged among sophisticated traders. I am not altogether convinced that the legislative history of § 3(a)(3) supports that interpretation even with respect to the term "any note" in the exemption in § 3(a)(3), and to bodily transpose that legislative history to another statute has little to commend it as a method of statutory construction.

The legislative history of the 1934 Act — under which this case arises — contains nothing which would support a restrictive reading of the exemption in question. Nor does the legislative history of § 3(a)(3) of the 1933 Act support the asserted limited construction of the exemption in § 3(a)(10) of the 1934 Act. . . .

. . . . Although I do not doubt that both the 1933 and 1934 Act exemptions encompass short-term commercial paper, the expansive language in the statutory provisions is strong evidence that, in the end, Congress meant for commercial paper merely to be a subset of a larger class of exempted short-term instruments.

The plausibility of imputing a restrictive reading to § 3(a)(10) from the legislative history of § 3(a)(3) is further weakened by the imperfect analogy between the two provisions in terms of both phraseology and nature. Section 3(a)(10) lacks the cryptic phrase in § 3(a)(3) which qualifies the class of instruments eligible for exemption as those arising " out of . . . current transaction[s] or the proceeds of which have been or are to be used for current transactions. . . . " While that passage somehow may strengthen an argument for limiting the exemption in § 3(a)(3) to commercial paper, its absence in § 3(a)(10) conversely militates against placing the same limitation thereon.

The exemption in § 3(a)(3) excepts the short-term instruments it covers solely from the registration requirements of the 1933 Act. The same instruments are not exempted from the 1933 Act's antifraud provisions. . . . By contrast, the exemption in § 3(a)(10) of the 1934 Act exempts instruments encompassed thereunder from the entirety of the coverage of the 1934 Act including, conspicuously, the Act's antifraud provisions.

In sum, there is no justification for looking beyond the plain terms of § 3(a)(10), save for ascertaining the meaning of " maturity" with respect to demand notes. That inquiry reveals that the Co-Op's demand notes come within the purview of the section's exemption for short-term securities. I would therefore affirm the judgment of the Court of Appeals, though on different reasoning.

NOTES AND QUESTIONS

1. In footnote 1 of the Court's opinion (reprinted in Section A of this chapter), it was noted that the virtually identical definitions of "security" in the 1933 and 1934 Acts would be construed together. However, the "short-term note" exemptions in the two acts have several important differences, as Chief Justice Rehnquist pointed out. First, comparing the language of the two, reprinted before this excerpt from *Reves*, we see that the 1933 Act includes the qualifying language "which arises out of a current transaction or the proceeds of which have been or are to be used for current transactions" absent from the 1934 Act. A second important difference, also noted by Chief Justice Rehnquist, is that the 1933 Act exemption is an exemption from the registration provisions of § 5, and not from the antifraud provisions of the Act. The 1934 Act exemption, on the other hand, is an exemption from the *definition*

of a security, meaning that *none* of the 1934 Act, even the antifraud provisions, would apply to exempt short-term notes.

2. Is it likely that an initial investor will demand that he or she receive a short-term note in return? Consider Ann in our continuing restaurant example. She is considering investing $400,000 but would like to withdraw her investment "as quickly as possible" after the restaurant becomes profitable. Another possibility is an investor who is providing "seed money" to fund the expenses of a planned public offering, who would like to be paid out of the proceeds of the public offering. Would you construct these notes to be "demand" notes? Would that provide an exemption from either the 1933 or 1934 Acts according to *Reves*?

D. ANTIFRAUD

The second major requirement in federal securities law relevant to the business planner is the obligation to not commit fraud or make material misstatements or omissions in the offer or sale of securities. This requirement is stated in several different places in the '33 and '34 Acts, and together these are usually known as "antifraud" requirements.

The antifraud rules of the '33 Act are likely inconsequential in the case of a small business issuing securities in a private offering. We will briefly consider each of two '33 Act provisions in turn.

First, § 12(a)(2) imposes liability on an offeror or seller who does so "by means of a prospectus or oral communication, which includes an untrue statement of a material fact or omits to state a material fact necessary in order to make the statements, in the light of the circumstances under which they were made, not misleading." In a controversial case, the Supreme Court held that the use of the term "prospectus" limits § 12(a)(2)'s applicability to registered offerings.[88] This is so, said the majority, because the term "prospectus" refers to materials in a registration statement and should be read to refer to registered offerings. So § 12(a)(2) poses little danger in an unregistered exempt offering.

Second, § 17(a) makes it unlawful:

> for any person in the offer or sale of any securities . . . by the use of any means or instruments of transportation or communication in interstate commerce or by use of the mails, directly or indirectly —
>
> (1) to employ any device, scheme, or artifice to defraud, or
>
> (2) to obtain money or property by means of any untrue statement of a material fact or any omission to state a material fact necessary in order to make the statements made, in light of the circumstances under which they were made, not misleading; or
>
> (3) to engage in any transaction, practice, or course of business which operates or would operate as a fraud or deceit upon the purchaser.

This seems to be a more inclusive provision than § 12(a)(2). It is clearly not limited to registered offerings; § 17(c) explicitly states that the exemptions in § 3 do not apply here. However, making something "unlawful" and providing for private

---

[88] Gustafson v. Alloyd Co., Inc., 513 U.S. 561, 569 (1995).

recovery are very different things. While implied private rights of action have fared well under other provisions of the federal securities laws,[89] that is not the case here. "Will § 17(a) of the 1933 Act support a private right of action? If *anything* in the 1933 Act can be stated categorically, the answer is no."[90]

We then turn to the '34 Act which does not provide specific antifraud provisions regarding purchasers or sellers of securities as does the '33 Act. Congress did, however, delegate to the SEC the authority to so provide.

Securities Exchange Act § 10(b)
Manipulative and Deceptive Devices

It shall be unlawful for any person, directly or indirectly, by the use of any means or instrumentality of interstate commerce or of the mails, or of any facility of any national securities exchange —

(b) To use or employ, in connection with the purchase or sale of any security . . . , any manipulative or deceptive device or contrivance in contravention of such rules and regulations as the Commission may prescribe as necessary or appropriate in the public interest or for the protection of investors.

Pursuant to this delegated authority, the SEC adopted Rule 10b-5. The rule was written by the Commission in 1942 to reach the fraudulent *purchase* of securities. Purchases are not mentioned in § 17(a) of the '33 Act which speaks only about misstatements in *offers* and *sales*. However, the language of the rule does not reveal its modest heritage, and Rule 10b-5 has become the most far-reaching federal securities antifraud provision. You will notice the parallels to § 17(a) of the '33 Act, as the rule was modeled on that statutory provision.[91]

Securities Exchange Act Rule 10b-5
Employment of Manipulative and Deceptive Devices
17 C.F.R. § 240.10b-5

It shall be unlawful for any person, directly or indirectly, by the use of any means or instrumentality of interstate commerce, or of the mails or of any facility of any national securities exchange,

(a) to employ any device, scheme, or artifice to defraud,

(b) to make any untrue statement of a material fact or to omit to state a material fact necessary in order to make the statements made, in the light of the circumstances under which they were made, not misleading, or

---

[89] Most importantly, the one to which we turn next, Rule 10b-5.

[90] Loss & Seligman, *supra*, at 1297 (italics in original). However, the Supreme Court has not spoken on the matter, and the circuits have mostly but not entirely denied private recovery under § 17(a). The trend is however clearly against private liability. Hazen, *supra*, at 682–83; Brown, *supra*, at § 8.3.4, pp. 8-26 to 8-33.

[91] For a colorful description of the humble origins of one of the most far-reaching rules in securities regulation, see Loss & Seligman, *supra*, at 936–39. The story is made more authentic by the fact that Professor Loss was himself present at the birth of Rule 10b-5. *See* Conference on Codification of the Federal Securities Laws, 22 Bus. Law. 793, 921–23 (1967).

(c) to engage in any act, practice, or course of business which operates or would operate as a fraud or deceit upon any person,

in connection with the purchase or sale of any security.

The Basics of Rule 10b-5

First, although the rule was taken largely from § 17(a) of the '33 Act, there has been no similar reluctance by the courts to imply a private right of action under the rule. It has long been clear that there is such a private right.

Second, the rule applies to *any* security, whether in a '33 Act registered offering or not. The only way to avoid the rule's reach is to not have a "security" in the first place.[92] Even an isolated transaction in securities will be within the Rule's reach.

Finally, the '34 Act (unlike the '33 Act) provides for exclusive federal jurisdiction and nationwide service of process,[93] which in turn can make federal cases out of the smallest, most ordinary transactions if misstatements are involved.

WHARF (HOLDINGS) LTD. v. UNITED INTERNATIONAL HOLDINGS, INC.
United States Supreme Court
532 U.S. 588 (2001)

JUSTICE BREYER delivered the opinion of the Court.

This securities fraud action focuses upon a company that sold an option to buy stock while secretly intending never to honor the option. The question before us is whether this conduct violates § 10(b) of the Securities Exchange Act of 1934, which prohibits using "any manipulative or deceptive device or contrivance . . . in connection with the purchase or sale of any security." We conclude that it does.

I

Respondent United International Holdings, Inc., a Colorado-based company, sued petitioner The Wharf (Holdings) Limited, a Hong Kong firm, in Colorado's Federal District Court. United said that in October 1992 Wharf had sold it an option to buy 10% of the stock of a new Hong Kong cable television system. But, United alleged, at the time of the sale Wharf secretly intended not to permit United to exercise the option. United claimed that Wharf's conduct amounted to a fraud "in connection with the . . . sale of [a] security," prohibited by § 10(b), and violated numerous state laws as well. A jury found in United's favor. The Court of Appeals for the Tenth Circuit upheld that verdict. 210 F.3d 1207 (2000). And we granted certiorari to consider whether the dispute fell within the scope of § 10(b).

The relevant facts, viewed in the light most favorable to the verdict winner, United, are as follows. In 1991, the Hong Kong Government announced that it would accept bids for the award of an exclusive license to operate a cable system in Hong Kong. Wharf decided to prepare a bid. Wharf's chairman, Peter Woo,

---

[92] This is why the difference between § 3(a)(3) of the '33 Act (an exemption from registration) and § 3(a)(10) (an exception from the definition of "security") was important in *Reves v. Ernst & Young*, *supra*.

[93] *See* Securities Exchange Act § 27.

instructed one of its managing directors, Stephen Ng, to find a business partner with cable system experience. Ng found United. And United sent several employees to Hong Kong to help prepare Wharf's application, negotiate contracts, design the system, and arrange financing.

United asked to be paid for its services with a right to invest in the cable system if Wharf should obtain the license. During August and September 1992, while United's employees were at work helping Wharf, Wharf and United negotiated about the details of that payment. Wharf prepared a draft letter of intent that contemplated giving United the right to become a co-investor, owning 10% of the system. But the parties did not sign the letter of intent. And in September, when Wharf submitted its bid, it told the Hong Kong authorities that Wharf would be the system's initial sole owner, although Wharf would also " consider" allowing United to become an investor.

In early October 1992, Ng met with a United representative, who told Ng that United would continue to help only if Wharf gave United an enforceable right to invest. Ng then orally granted United an option with the following terms: (1) United had the right to buy 10% of the future system's stock; (2) the price of exercising the option would be 10% of the system's capital requirements minus the value of United's previous services (including expenses); (3) United could exercise the option only if it showed that it could fund its 10% share of the capital required for at least the first 18 months; and (4) the option would expire if not exercised within six months of the date that Wharf received the license. The parties continued to negotiate about how to write documents that would embody these terms, but they never reduced the agreement to writing.

In May 1993, Hong Kong awarded the cable franchise to Wharf. United raised $66 million designed to help finance its 10% share. In July or August 1993, United told Wharf that it was ready to exercise its option. But Wharf refused to permit United to buy any of the system's stock. Contemporaneous internal Wharf documents suggested that Wharf had never intended to carry out its promise. For example, a few weeks before the key October 1992 meeting, Ng had prepared a memorandum stating that United wanted a right to invest that it could exercise if it was able to raise the necessary capital. A handwritten note by Wharf's Chairman Woo replied, "No, no, no, we don't accept that." In September 1993, after meeting with the Wharf board to discuss United's investment in the cable system, Ng wrote to another Wharf executive, "How do we get out?" In December 1993, after United had filed documents with the Securities and Exchange Commission (SEC) representing that United was negotiating the acquisition of a 10% interest in the cable system, an internal Wharf memo stated that "[o]ur next move should be to claim that our directors got quite *upset* over these representations. . . . Publicly, we *do not* acknowledge [United's] opportunity" to acquire the 10% interest. In the margin of a December 1993 letter from United discussing its expectation of investing in the cable system, Ng wrote, "[B]e careful, must deflect this! [H]ow?" Other Wharf documents referred to the need to " back ped[al]" and " stall."

These documents, along with other evidence, convinced the jury that Wharf, through Ng, had orally sold United an option to purchase a 10% interest in the future cable system while secretly intending not to permit United to exercise the option, in violation of § 10(b) of the Securities Exchange Act and various state laws. . . .

II

Section 10(b) of the Securities Exchange Act makes it " unlawful for any person . . . [t]o use or employ, in connection with the purchase or sale of any security . . . , any manipulative or deceptive device or contrivance in contravention of such rules and regulations as the [SEC] may prescribe." . . . Pursuant to this provision, the SEC has promulgated Rule 10b-5. . . . To succeed in a Rule 10b-5 suit, a private plaintiff must show that the defendant used, in connection with the purchase or sale of a security, one of the four kinds of manipulative or deceptive devices to which the Rule refers . . . .

In deciding whether the Rule covers the circumstances present here, we must assume that the "security" at issue is not the cable system stock, but the option to purchase that stock. That is because the Court of Appeals found that Wharf conceded this point. 210 F.3d, at 1221 ("Wharf does not contest on appeal the classification of the option as a security"). That concession is consistent with the language of the Securities Exchange Act, which defines "security" to include both "any . . . option . . . on any security" and "any . . . right to . . . purchase" stock. [§ 3(a)(10)] . . . .

[There is no] convincing reason to interpret the Act to exclude oral contracts as a class. The Act itself says that it applies to "any contract" for the purchase or sale of a security. § 3(a)(13), (14) Oral contracts for the sale of securities are sufficiently common that the Uniform Commercial Code and statutes of frauds in every State now consider them enforceable. See U.C.C. § 8-113 ("A contract . . . for the sale or purchase of a security is enforceable whether or not there is a writing signed or record authenticated by a party against whom enforcement is sought") . . . . Any exception for oral sales of securities would significantly limit the Act's coverage, thereby undermining its basic purposes.

Wharf makes a related but narrower argument that the Act does not encompass oral contracts of sale that are unenforceable under state law. But we do not reach that issue. The Court of Appeals held that Wharf's sale of the option was not covered by the then-applicable Colorado statute of frauds, Colo.Rev.Stat. § 4-8-319 (repealed 1996), and hence was enforceable under state law. Though Wharf disputes the correctness of that holding, we ordinarily will not consider such a state-law issue, and we decline to do so here.

Second, Wharf argues that a secret reservation not to permit the exercise of an option falls outside § 10(b) because it does not "relat[e] to the value of a security purchase or the consideration paid"; hence it does " not implicate [§ 10(b)'s] policy of full disclosure." Brief for Petitioners 25, 26 (emphasis deleted). But even were it the case that the Act covers only misrepresentations likely to affect the value of securities, Wharf's secret reservation was such a misrepresentation. To sell an option while secretly intending not to permit the option's exercise is misleading, because a buyer normally presumes good faith. Cf., *e.g.*, Restatement (Second) of Torts § 530, Comment *c* (1976) ("Since a promise necessarily carries with it the implied assertion of an intention to perform[,] it follows that a promise made without such an intention is fraudulent"). For similar reasons, the secret reservation misled United about the option's value. Since Wharf did not intend to honor the option, the option was, unbeknownst to United, valueless.

Finally, Wharf supports its claim for an exemption from the statute by characterizing this case as a "disput[e] over the ownership of securities." Brief for

Petitioners 24. Wharf expresses concern that interpreting the Act to allow recovery in a case like this one will permit numerous plaintiffs to bring federal securities claims that are in reality no more than ordinary state breach-of-contract claims — actions that lie outside the Act's basic objectives. United's claim, however, is not simply that Wharf failed to carry out a promise to sell it securities. It is a claim that Wharf sold it a security (the option) while secretly intending from the very beginning not to honor the option. And United proved that secret intent with documentary evidence that went well beyond evidence of a simple failure to perform. . . . .

For these reasons, the judgment of the Court of Appeals is

Affirmed.

NOTES AND QUESTIONS

1.   Is there a problem in making a federal case out of such a transaction?

One might have thought that it was a garden-variety breach of contract claim. . . . [W]hat is the harm in applying Rule 10b-5 to the *Wharf (Holdings)* fact pattern? This is . . . a private arrangement between two parties, where a federal interest seems nonexistent. State law, relying on other principles, may have resolved the dispute differently. For instance, state law may have considered the statute of frauds relevant to the outcome. That is, perhaps a plaintiff's right to acquire stock would not be enforceable at all under state law or perhaps the recoverable damages differ significantly from those available under Rule 10b-5. These policy questions, resolved under state law, are now federalized under Rule 10b-5.[94]

2.   Would Rule 10b-5 cover the organizational sale of interests in a manager-managed LLC to the LLC's owners? If so, who would be liable?

3.   How do you suggest that your client avoid Rule 10b-5 liability? Avoid the use of the means of interstate commerce? Not buy or sell a "security"? What else is there? The following excerpt catalogues the important uses of disclosure in complying with the federal securities laws — both the registration and antifraud provisions.

William W. Barker, *Outside Bucks: A Practical Guide to Raising Capital for a Business*
Business Law Today 9:6, July/Aug. 2000, at 15–16*

. . . .

Your client will at some point probably need some type of offering document whether or not it is required under the securities laws. A private placement memorandum (PPM) gives investors the same general type of information that registration would provide, which would include a description of your:

---

[94] Mark J. Loewenstein, *A Perspective on Federal Corporation Law*, 2 J. Bus. & Tech. L. 425, 429–30 (2007).

* Copyright © 2000 by the American Bar Association. Reprinted with permission.

— market;

— business, products or services, properties, etc.;

— material legal proceedings;

— capitalization and securities being sold;

— management and principal shareholders;

— material risks;

— selected financial data and financial statements; and

— some type of discussion and analysis of the financial statement and operations.

Most start-ups begin by approaching investors with a business plan, which is a scaled down version of a PPM. Both a PPM and a business plan tell the story of the company and document disclosures made to investors. Both must convey credibility and accuracy, while at the same time generating excitement and enthusiasm. Both should be thorough, professional and realistic. And both must be concise.

Early-stage investors typically invest in a "concept" and do not require detail. Statements of fact should be supported as fact, and statements of opinion or belief must have a reasonable basis. When it comes to discussing risks and uncertainties, do not hide the ball from investors for to do so will impair the credibility of you and your client. For liability reasons, it is best to let your client write his or her own plan with the aid of your comments.

A PPM is not required for every offering. For reasons discussed below, a business plan would be sufficient to raise "seed capital" under Rule 504 of Regulation D but, for example, if more than $1 million is raised in a 12-month period, such that the limitations of Rule 504 are surpassed, a PPM would be required to offer securities to nonaccredited investors in reliance on Rule 505 or Rule 506 . . . . An offering to "all accredited" investors by comparison does not require a PPM. But, even if not required, delivering a PPM or at least a detailed business plan is probably advisable for liability and marketing reasons.

Remember that even exempt transactions are subject to the antifraud provisions of the federal securities laws. Advise your client that he or she and the company will be responsible for false or misleading statements . . . .

Depending on the size of the offering and the nature of the purchasers, more or less documentation may be required. Typical documents in a private financing may include:

— Term sheet — contains the essential terms of the investment and business terms of the transaction, such as type of security, valuation/price, liquidation preference, conversion rights, registration rights, pre-emptive rights/rights of first refusal, voting rights, seats on the board of directors and dividends.

— Business plan or PPM — describes the business, products/services, and risks and may provide financial information.

. . . .

— Stock purchase agreement — sets out the terms, representations and warranties of the parties, and conditions of closing. Establishes the factual basis for exemption under federal securities laws.

. . . .

Although term sheets are not always used, using one will likely save you time and money in the long run because a term sheet helps the parties focus on key issues that need to be documented.

A "term sheet" is an item your clients may draw up, but it is something you as counsel should review (and presumably correct) with Rule 10b-5 at hand before the sheet is distributed to potential lenders or investors. Similarly, Rule 10b-5 is one of the reasons why substantial disclosures — in the form of a "private placement memorandum" or PPM — are given to investors even in offerings exempt under Rule 504 or § 4(2) where such disclosures are not explicitly required as a condition of the exemption from registration.

A PPM is something in which you should be actively involved. You know the legal background of the antifraud requirements. You know when your clients have drafted information which may be materially misleading or incomplete. You know the "legal information" which needs to be provided.

There is no shortage of forms for PPMs. There is no required format, of course, since the document is prepared pursuant to an offering exempt from registration. However, one good form is the Form 1-A offering circular, which is the form provided by the SEC for offerings made pursuant to Regulation A. As noted above, this is not a registration statement, since Regulation A is an exemption from registration. However, Form 1-A can be a good disclosure checklist. It can be downloaded from www.sec.gov. Also useful is Form U-7 which is prepared by the North American Securities Administrators Association (NASAA) to implement the Uniform Limited Offering Exemption, an exemption from registration under state law[95] coordinated with Regulation D. It can be downloaded (along with an issuer's manual) from www.nasaa.org.

E.　STATE REGULATION AND FEDERAL PREEMPTION

State regulation of the offer and sale of securities actually predates the federal securities acts. State securities laws are informally dubbed "blue sky" laws, describing the first state law passed in Kansas in 1911, "aimed at promoters who 'would sell building lots in the blue sky in fee simple.' "[96] In this part, we review the general coverage of state law and how this relates to the federal law.

---

[95] For the details of state law registration and exemption, and of Form U-7 and the state limited offering in particular, see Section E.1.a below.

[96] Loss & Seligman, *supra*, at 10.

1.   An Overview of State Regulation

As state laws proliferated, unification efforts began through the National Conference of Commissioners on Uniform State Laws ("NCCUSL").[97] A 1929 effort was largely unsuccessful, but the 1956 Uniform Securities Act ("USA") enjoyed great popularity, being adopted in 38 states and the District of Columbia.[98] An updated version was approved by NCCUSL in 2002 and has been adopted in 12 states to date.[99] Regulation under the USA, and under state blue sky law generally, falls into three categories.[100]

First, state law regulates offers and sales of securities in three different ways, by "notification," "coordination," or "qualification," depending on the status of the offering under federal law. Notification, the least intrusive and also least-used option, was available to seasoned issuers in good standing and required only minimal filing with the state. Notification has largely been replaced by "notice filing" in the 2002 version of the USA to further coordinate with federal law as discussed in Section E.2 below. Coordination is used, as the name suggests, coordinating the state filing with a federal registration statement filed under the '33 Act.[101] Qualification is the residual procedure to be used when neither notification nor coordination is applicable.

Second, state law requires registration of all persons who will be selling the securities, including brokers and agents of the issuer. Brokers and their agents are usually approved in a process coordinated with federal registration under the Securities Exchange Act of 1934. The regulation of securities industry personnel is beyond the scope of a business planning course, but it is quite common for the "blue sky" work in a securities offering to include the documentation of exemptions from broker registration or qualification for your client's officers or other employees who will be doing the actual selling of the securities.

Finally, state law has general antifraud rules, similar to federal law, prohibiting fraud and misstatements in the offer or sale of securities. The state securities administrators have broad authority, and there are civil and criminal penalties as well.

a.   Securities registration

State registration (or licensing) of offers and sales of securities falls into three categories summarized above. The first two — "notice" or "coordination" — require little discussion because the additional work is minimal and because they

---

[97] We first met NCCUSL in Chapter 2, that organization being the author of the various uniform business entity acts.

[98] 1 Blue Sky Law Reporter (CCH) ¶ 5501.

[99] Visit www.uniformsecuritiesact.org and click on "enactments" for the most recent list.

[100] A cautionary note is in order. Even in USA states, there are "greater or lesser modifications that are the curse of all 'uniform' legislation." Loss & Seligman, *supra*, at 10. The summary which follows does not obviate the need for the careful reading of the text of the laws in each state in which your clients will be offering or selling securities.

[101] Whether "coordinated" review is in fact very coordinated depends largely on the offering and the states in which it is to be registered. *See generally* Bloomenthal, *supra*, § 24:13. Full discussion of a state-registered offering, as with a federally-registered offering, is beyond the scope of our coverage here. We are looking primarily at offerings which will be exempt from federal registration and thus not subject to coordinated review.

apply only to seasoned companies and registered offerings, which are not the types normally presented to the planner for a new business. This leaves "qualification" as the method which may most often apply under state law. The qualification process varies substantially from state to state. Some states impose only rudimentary "notice filing" requirements, others impose substantial "merit review," prohibiting sales even upon full disclosure if the state authority does not deem the security worthy.[102]

Just as with federal registration, finding an exemption from the state law registration requirement will facilitate the sale of securities in your clients' new business. The USA offers a limited offering exemption in § 402(b)(9) for

> any transaction pursuant to an offer directed by the offeror to not more than ten persons (other than those designated in paragraph (8)[103]) in this state during any period of twelve consecutive months, whether or not the offeror or any of the offerees is then present in this state, if (A) the seller reasonably believes that all the buyers in this state (other than those designated in paragraph (8)) are purchasing for investment, and (B) no commission or other remuneration is paid or given directly or indirectly for soliciting any prospective buyer in this state (other than those designated in paragraph (8)); but the [Administrator] may by rule or order, as to any security or transaction or any type of security or transaction, withdraw or further condition this exemption, or increase or decrease the number of offerees permitted, or waive the conditions in Clauses (A) and (B) with or without the substitution of a limitation on remuneration.

As is apparent from the above text, this exemption has many limitations, but is nonetheless useful for "under ten" offerings which may reach the start-up capitalizations of many small businesses. The exemption has been retained and expanded in the 2002 Act, with the offeror limitation increased to 25.[104]

Although this exemption is useful, most states have adopted additional exemptions either by statute or rule which conform in varying degrees to Regulation D (see Section C.1.c.ii above), which exemptions are known as the Uniform Limited Offering Exemption, or ULOE. The most widely adopted part of the ULOE is a provision based largely on Rule 504 and thus very useful (having very limited offer or information requirements), known as the Small Corporate Offerings Registration, or SCOR. This exemption is widely accepted, and the disclosure form promulgated under SCOR, known as Form U-7, is accepted in most other states.[105]

---

[102] The statutory language indicating whether a state is a "merit review" state is found in the rules for denial of registration of securities. See, *e.g.*, § 306(a)(2)(E)–(F) of the 1956 USA or § 306(a)(7) of the 2002 USA ("will work or tend to work a fraud upon the purchasers," "has been or would be made with unreasonable amounts of . . . discounts, commissions, or other compensation," or "is being made on terms that are unfair, unjust, or inequitable."). In practice, separating "merit review" states from "disclosure" states is more difficult because actual practice may depart from statutory or administrative standards. One analyst estimates that 30 jurisdictions would apply some sort of merit review. Bloomenthal, *supra*, § 24:11 at p. 1708 ("In concept, at least, an issuer could make an offering in 20 jurisdictions that are disclosure states and not be concerned about merit requirements.").

[103] Section 402(b)(8) exempts sales to banks and other financial institutions.

[104] 2002 USA § 202(14).

[105] See generally Peter M. Fass & Derek A. Wittner, Blue Sky Practice Ch. 9 (2006–07 ed.), which includes as appendices the text of ULOE, Form U-7, and a summary of each state's limited offering exemptions. The latter is particularly useful, since the "uniform" in ULOE is misleading. The concept is

EXERCISE 4-4

Find your state's "blue sky" law securities registration statute. Is it based on the 1956 or 2002 USA, or some other model? Is there a "limited offering" exemption? [Be sure to check the rules of your state securities administrator. These exemptions can be rule-based or statutory.] How do(es) your limited offering exemption(s) compare to the federal Regulation D? What are the statutory standards applicable to offers and sales which are subject to "qualification" in your state?[106]

b.   Broker and agent registration

New securities lawyers are often surprised that they must deal with the registration of (or exemption of) their clients under the state broker-dealer registration laws. The surprise stems from the fact that they have never heard of such a requirement before even though they may have carefully studied the federal securities laws. Looking to those federal laws, they may be further surprised to find that there *is indeed* a requirement for anyone in the business of selling securities to register under federal law.[107] However, nearly all the activities of your client in selling securities will be exempted from this requirement by the following rule.

Securities Exchange Act Rule 3a4-1
Associated Persons of an Issuer Deemed not to be Brokers

17 C.F.R. § 240.3a4-1

(a)   An associated person of an issuer of securities shall not be deemed to be a broker solely by reason of his participation in the sale of the securities of such issuer if the associated person:

    (1)   Is not subject to a statutory disqualification, as that term is defined in section 3(a)(39) of the Act, at the time of his participation; and

    (2)   Is not compensated in connection with his participation by the payment of commissions or other remuneration based either directly or indirectly on transactions in securities; and

    (3)   Is not at the time of his participation an associated person of a broker or dealer; and

    (4)   Meets the conditions of any one of paragraph (a)4(i), (ii), or (iii) of this section.

        (i)   The associated person restricts his participation to transactions involving offers and sales of securities:

---

endorsed by most states, but the details do not permit principled generalization See also the index of small offering exemptions in 1 Blue Sky Law Reporter & 6461.

[106] If your state's securities laws and rules are not conveniently available online or through some other source, you may want to consult the CCH Blue Sky Law Reporter.

[107] Securities Exchange Act § 15(a) requires registration of brokers and persons associated with brokers. Section 3(a)(4)(A) defines a "broker" as "any person engaged in the business of effecting transactions in securities for the account of others." This (perhaps not obviously) includes your client's employees whose job it is to distribute the stock or membership or partnership interests to the purchaser, provided those items are "securities."

(A)   To a registered broker or dealer; a registered investment company . . . ; an insurance company; a bank; a savings and loan association; a trust company or similar institution supervised by a state or federal banking authority . . . ; or

(B)   That are exempted by reason of section 3(a)(7), 3(a)(9) or 3(a)(10) of the Securities Act of 1933 from the registration provisions of that Act; or

(C)   That are made pursuant to a plan or agreement submitted for the vote or consent of the security holders who will receive securities of the issuer in connection with a reclassification of securities of the issuer, a merger or consolidation or a similar plan of acquisition involving an exchange of securities, or a transfer of assets of any other person to the issuer in exchange for securities of the issuer; or

(D)   That are made pursuant to a bonus, profit-sharing, pension, retirement, thrift, savings, incentive, stock purchase, stock ownership, stock appreciation, stock option, dividend reinvestment or similar plan for employees of an issuer or a subsidiary of the issuer;

(ii)   The associated person meets all of the following conditions:

(A)   The associated person primarily performs, or is intended primarily to perform at the end of the offering, substantial duties for or on behalf of the issuer otherwise than in connection with transactions in securities; and

(B)   The associated person was not a broker or dealer, or an associated person of a broker or dealer, within the preceding 12 months; and

(C)   The associated person does not participate in selling an offering of securities for any issuer more than once every 12 months other than in reliance on paragraph (a)4(i) or (a)4(iii) of this section . . . .

(iii)   The associated person restricts his participation to any one or more of the following activities:

(A)   Preparing any written communication or delivering such communication through the mails or other means that does not involve oral solicitation by the associated person of a potential purchaser; *Provided, however*, that the content of such communication is approved by a partner, officer or director of the issuer;

(B)   Responding to inquiries of a potential purchaser in a communication initiated by the potential purchaser; *Provided, however*, That the content of such responses are limited to information contained in a registration statement filed under the Securities Act of 1933 or other offering document; or

(C)   Performing ministerial and clerical work involved in effecting any transaction.

     . . . .

(c)   *Definitions.* When used in this section:

(1)   The term *associated person of an issuer* means any natural person who is a partner, officer, director, or employee of:

(i)   The issuer;

(ii)   A corporate general partner of a limited partnership that is the issuer; [or]

(iii)   A company or partnership that controls, is controlled by, or is under common control with, the issuer . . . .

Is it apparent that the ordinary employees of your client will not be engaged in activities which require registration as a broker under the '34 Act? If so, then you understand the classification scheme in the federal rule and will therefore be able to follow the state law. USA Section 401 defines as follows:

> (b) "Agent" means any individual other than a broker-dealer who represents a broker-dealer or issuer in effecting or attempting to effect purchases or sales of securities. "Agent" does not include an individual who represents. (1) an issuer in (A) effecting transactions in a security exempted by clause (1), (2), (3), (10), or (11) of section 402(a), (B) effecting transactions exempted by section 402(b), or (C) effecting transaction in a covered security as described in section 18(b)(3) and 18(b)(4)(D) of the Securities Act of 1933, or (D) effecting transactions with existing employees, partners or directors of the issuer if no commission or other remuneration is paid or given directly or indirectly for soliciting any person in this state . . . . A partner, officer, or director of a broker-dealer or issuer, or a person occupying a similar status or performing similar functions, is an agent only if he otherwise comes within this definition.
>
> (c) "Broker-dealer" means any person engaged in the business of effecting transactions in securities for the account of others or for his own account. "Broker-dealer" does not include (1) an agent, (2) an issuer, (3) a bank, savings institution, or trust company, or (4) a person who has no place of business in this state if (A) he effects transactions in this state exclusively with or through (i) the issuers of the securities involved in the transactions, (ii) other broker-dealers, or (iii) banks, savings institutions, trust companies, insurance companies, investment companies as defined in the Investment Company Act of 1940, pension or profit-sharing trusts, or other financial institutions or institutional buyers, whether acting for themselves or as trustees . . . .[108]

Is it apparent that the ordinary employees of your client will not be engaged in activities which require registration as a broker under the USA?

c.   Antifraud rules

Both the 1956 and 2002 versions of the USA have nearly identical antifraud provisions, patterned closely on Securities Act § 17(a) except that they cover offer, sale and purchase of a security, and there is a private right of action for sales made by means of a material misstatement or omission. In addition, there is civil liability patterned on Securities Act § 12(a)(2), although it is not limited to misstatements or omissions made in a prospectus.[109] The USA provides remedies in addition to

---

[108] There are similar definitions in § 402(b)(3)–(5) of the 2002 USA. A lawyer first approaching New York"s unique system of broker-dealer regulation will search in vain for an exemption for agents of the issuer analogous to those just discussed. In fact, registrations must be filed in New York, but the process is relatively simple. *See* Loss & Seligman, *supra*, at 25–26. That state's requirements for *securities* registration, however, are another matter. *See* Bloomenthal, *supra*, § 24:20.

[109] *See* USA § 509 (2002), cmts. 3–4, *available at* www.uniformsecuritiesact.org (clicking on "final

those otherwise available at common law, such as fraud, deceit, breach of fiduciary duty, or breach of contract, any or all of which may be involved in a securities fraud action.

In some states, regulatory agencies are given much greater powers than the uniform act provisions. New York and California are the most prominent examples. California law includes multiple antifraud statutes patterned on different federal provisions, each with investigative authority for the state securities commissioner and criminal and civil liability.[110] New York's law, known as the Martin Act, has a sweeping definition of fraudulent conduct, with liability not dependent upon any intent, damages, or even the purchase or sale of a security. The state attorney general also has broad investigative authority under the Martin Act. Although the authority is not new, it has been used by recent New York Attorneys General to investigate problems with Wall Street brokers and dealers, corporate malfeasance, and even environmental crimes.[111]

2.　Federal Preemption

One reason it took so long to get a new Uniform Securities Act was that during the 1980s and 1990s when several relatively unsuccessful proposals were made, Congress was considering overriding or preempting some state regulation. This process came ultimately to a conclusion in the National Securities Market Improvements Act of 1996 (NSMIA),[112] which made, among others, the following additions to the federal securities laws.

Securities Act § 18
Exemption from State Regulation of Securities Offerings

(a)　Scope of exemption

Except as otherwise provided in this section, no law, rule, regulation, or order, or other administrative action of any State or any political subdivision thereof—

　(1)　requiring, or with respect to, registration or qualification of securities, or registration or qualification of securities transactions, shall directly or indirectly apply to a security that —

　　(A)　is a covered security; or

　　(B)　will be a covered security upon completion of the transaction;

　(2)　shall directly or indirectly prohibit, limit, or impose any conditions upon the use of —

---

act"). Identical language is found in an article prepared by Professor Seligman, who was the reporter for the 2002 USA. Joel Seligman, *The New Uniform Securities Act*, 81 WASH. U.L.Q. 243, 288 (2003).

[110]　*See* Loss & Seligman, *supra*, at 26–27.

[111]　*See, e.g.*, Felicity Barringer & Danny Hakim, *New York Subpoenas 5 Energy Companies*, N.Y. TIMES, Sept. 16, 2007, at A31 (detailing investigation by Attorney General Andrew Cuomo into whether energy companies adequately disclosed financial risks of new coal-fired power plants); Robert G. Morvillo & Robert J. Anello, *Securities, Investigations and Prosecutions Under the Martin Act*, N.Y.L.J., Apr. 1 2003, *available at* www.magislaw.com/articles/07004030007Morvillo.pdf (background on the Act and use by former Attorney General Elliot Spitzer, noting the "awesome power" of the attorney general's criminal investigation); *see also* Frank C. Razzano, *The Martin Act: An Overview*, 1 J. BUS. & TECH. L. 125 (2006).

[112]　P.L. 104-290, 110 Stat. 3417 (1996).

(A)   with respect to a covered security described in subsection (b), any offering document that is prepared by or on the behalf of the issuer; or

(B)   any proxy statement, report to shareholders, or other disclosure document relating to a covered security or the issuer thereof that is required to be and is filed with the Commission . . . ; or

(3)   shall directly or indirectly prohibit, limit, or impose conditions, based on the merits of such offering or issuer, upon the offer or sale of any security described in paragraph (1).

(b)   Covered securities

For the purposes of this section, the following are covered securities:

(1)   Exclusive federal registration of nationally traded securities

A security is a covered security if such security is —

(A)   listed, or authorized for listing, on the New York Stock Exchange or the American Stack Exchange, or listed, or authorized for listing, on the National Market System of the Nasdaq Stock Market (or any successor to such entities);

(B)   listed, or authorized for listing, on a national securities exchange (or tier or segment thereof) that has listing standards that the Commission determines by rule (on its own initiative or on the basis of a petition) are substantially similar to the listing standards applicable to securities describe in subparagraph (A); or

(C)   is a security of the same issuer that is equal in seniority or that is a senior security to a security described in subparagraph (A) or (B).

(3)   Sales to qualified purchasers

A security is a covered security with respect to the offer or sale of the security to qualified purchasers, as defined by the Commission by rule. In prescribing such rule, the Commission may define the term "qualified purchaser" differently with respect to different categories of securities, consistent with the public interest and the protection of investors.

(4)   Exemption in connection with certain exempt offerings

A security is a covered security with respect to a transaction that is exempt from registration under this title pursuant to —

(A)   paragraph (1) . . . of section 4, and the issuer of such security files reports with the Commission pursuant to . . . the Securities Exchange Act of 1934;

(B)   section 4(4);

(C)   section 3(a), other than the offer or sale of a security that is exempt from such registration pursuant to paragraph (4), (10) or (11) of such section . . . ; or

(D)   Commission rules or regulations issued under section 4(2) . . . .

(c)   Preservation of authority

(1)   Fraud authority

Consistent with this section, the securities commission (or agency or office performing like functions) of any State shall retain jurisdiction under the laws of such State to investigate and bring enforcement actions with respect to fraud or deceit, or unlawful conduct by a broker or dealer, in connection with securities or securities transactions.

Securities Exchange Act § 15
Registration and Regulation of Brokers and Dealers

. . . .

(h)   Limitations on State law

(1)   Capital, . . . books and records, . . . and reports

No law, rule, regulation, or order, or other administrative action of any State or political subdivision thereof shall establish capital, . . . , making and keeping records, bonding, or financial or operational reporting requirements for brokers . . . that differ from, or are in addition to, the requirements in those areas established under this title. . . . .

NOTES AND QUESTIONS

Consider how these provisions of NSMIA affect your "blue sky" work.

1.   Which of the Securities Act exemptions we have studied is now the most useful in terms of avoiding work under state securities laws? As a guide, note where § 18(b)(4) provides "covered security" status. Does it reach your *Ralston Purina* § 4(2) offering? Your § 3(a)(11) or Rule 147 offering? Your Regulation D offering? Consider the following statement: "Predictably, although not generally foreseen, almost no one purports to rely on Rule 505 anymore [after NSMIA]."[113] Why would that be the case? Is the same thing true about § 4(6) offerings?

2.   Securities Act § 18(b)(4) defines as a covered security one which "is exempt" under various exemptions from registration. But who is to determine if the exemption in fact exists? "State regulators and courts are today openly testing, if not outright challenging, the existence of NSMIA preemption where there is merely claimed reliance on, and perhaps not actual compliance with, the Rule 506 exemption."[114]

3.   There is great potential in § 18(b)(3)'s invitation to the SEC to further exempt from state regulation sales to "qualified purchasers." However, this authority has not been used by the Commission to date.

4.   Exchange Act § 15(h) does *not* "preempt" any of the rules we studied requiring your clients' employees to find an exemption from (or register under) state laws governing brokers or agents. Why not?

---

[113] Bloomenthal, *supra*, § 24:18 at p. 1718.

[114] Robert N. Rapp & Fritz E. Berckmueller, *Testing the Limits of NSMIA Preemption: State Authority to Determine the Validity of Covered Transactions and to Regulate Disclosure*, 63 Bus. Law. 809, 812 (2008).

The term "blue sky" is also a verb. To "blue sky" an exempt offering is to prepare a memorandum for your client (or your client's underwriter if it is an underwritten offering) describing how the offering is exempt from registration or qualification, and how the sellers are exempt from registration as brokers or agents, in *each* state in which offers will be made. This will be the job of the attorney who is to "blue sky" the offering. It will require research of statutes, rules and perhaps cases in each of these states. It is also customary to complete your "blue sky" work by seeking informal confirmation of your work and conclusions from an official in each state securities administrator's office.[115] Counsel will also prepare and file any "Form D" notices or consents to service of process and will assure that fees have been paid to states which require fees.[116] To "blue sky" a registered offering is to complete the notice, coordination, or qualification documents required in each state, and is normally part of the work done by those preparing the federal registered offering.

COMPREHENSIVE PROBLEM: SECURITIES DOCUMENTS FOR ENTITY ORGANIZATION

This exercise focuses on the securities law aspects of the capitalization of the venture we are organizing. You represent the client(s) identified in Exercise 1-1: Ann, Bev, Carl, the entity they will form or have already formed, or some or all of the above. The entity will be formed as you have advised at the completion of the Comprehensive Problem at the end of Chapter 2, modified as appropriate to conform to the tax requirements covered in Chapter 3.

Recall that their planned capitalization is as follows: $400,000 from Ann, $800,000 from Bev, $400,000 worth of services and property from Carl, and $6.4 million from sale of interests to investors, for a total of $8 million. Bev informs you that her stockbroker, Fred Friendly, a partner at Provident Securities (a national investment banking firm), will handle the sales to investors for a fee of $600,000 (thus increasing the amount to be sold to investors to a total of $7 million). Fred is confident that he can place $7 million of investments with current customers of Provident Securities each of whom has a wealth and investment risk profile similar to Bev's. Fred's initial review of his customer list suggests that it is highly unlikely that all these investors reside in the same state. Ann, Bev, and Carl insist that these Provident Securities client funds be raised as soon as possible. Furthermore, they have no funds to pay the additional costs of federal registration.

(1) Prepare a memorandum for your "file" on how the offers and sales of these investments will be exempt from registration under the Securities Act of 1933. In addition, discuss (i) if these offers and sales (and brokers or agents) will be exempt from registration under the blue-sky law in your state and one neighboring state

---

[115] The staff in each state securities administrator's office is used to these "blue sky" calls and will ordinarily provide the informal confirmation you desire. This is *not* formal advice and is not a substitute for your own work, of course. One reason for such confirming calls is that the applicable regulations in each state may not be publicly available. For example, some states adopt NASAA Statements of Policy but do not update them as NASAA updates them, hence the actual language may not be published anywhere. *See generally* Bloomenthal, *supra*, § 24:14 & p. 1713 ("One of the many frustrations for blue sky practitioners if the failure of several Administrators to attend to elementary housekeeping details relating to their published regulations.").

[116] The authority of states to require fees for offering or selling securities was confirmed by NSMIA; see Securities Act § 18(c)(2)(B) and (C).

and (ii) if these offers and sales will *not* be exempt under either of those laws, what needs to be done to register or qualify the securities for sale. Assume that Provident is a registered broker-dealer in good standing with the SEC, the National Association of Securities Dealers, Inc. (NASD), and that Provident and its sales personnel are duly registered in each state involved. The "file" memorandum will be the basis of, and the legal liability shield for, your firm's opinion that the offers and sales will be exempt from federal registration and will comply with the state laws indicated if the issuer follows your advice. The memorandum should summarize the relevant facts and laws and indicate any additional critical assumptions made upon which your conclusion depends. You should also indicate how the offers and sales should be made or documented to make sure that your critical assumptions are satisfied.

(2) Prepare a draft disclosure document. It should include all required formatting, captions, titles, notices, etc. You should draft all the disclosures relating to legal matters, the form of the organization, the nature of the investments, and particularly the risk factors. For the business information, management and financial projections and the like, assume that Ann, Bev and Carl have completed a draft business plan and will be able to supply this information for the areas you have marked "to be supplied by client."

(3) Prepare a certificate to be signed by each person contacted and each investor. These will be received by the issuer and retained in its files to demonstrate the basis for its assertion that the offers and sales were exempt from federal registration.

(4) Prepare a specimen form of an investment certificate (*e.g.* stock, membership interest, partnership interest) to be distributed to each Provident purchaser. Assure that all informational and restrictive legends are properly placed on the form. You may leave names, dollar amounts, and signature lines blank, and clearly indicate this is a "specimen" and not an actual form to be used.

Chapter 5

FINANCING OF BUSINESS ENTITIES

A. INTRODUCTION

A primary cause of business failure is lack of adequate financing. The promoters, investors and managers of a business may have a unique and powerful idea that they work hard to implement but, without adequate resources, the business may stagnate or fail. Sometimes businesses fail because the financing obtained at the startup of the business was insufficient to meet the basic operating needs of the business during its early stages due to poor planning, delays, market changes or unforseen factors. Other times, financing may have been adequate to get the business off the ground and operating but additional funds may be needed as the business matures to propel the company into new markets, expand operations or outperform competitors. If there is insufficient cash to meet the operating or growth needs of the business, then problems will arise unless additional financing can be obtained.

An essential part of planning and implementing a new business entity is arranging for appropriate initial financing to acquire the capital necessary to meet the projected needs of the business. At the time of formation the promoters must assess how much capital the corporation will need to purchase or lease fixed assets; acquire equipment and goods; license, purchase or develop intellectual property; hire employees; and operate the business during the startup phase. It may be quite a while before the business spins off sufficient cash to meet operating expenses, so the financing plan must be based on realistic projections of future revenues and expenses. It also makes sense at the formation stage to plan for the possibility of *additional* financing if needed for survival or growth of the company.

The promoters and investors must choose the appropriate sources, amounts and timing of finance for the short and long range success of the business. The task of the *lawyers* is to draft appropriate documentation and advise clients regarding the tax and non-tax considerations that arise in connection with the financing plans being proposed for the entity. In this regard, the objective of this chapter is to provide students with a fundamental understanding of how business ventures are financed.

B. DEBT FINANCING

When forming a business there are two elemental sources of financing to fund the startup and operations of the business — equity and debt. What is the essential distinction between these two types of financing? Equity financing is the cash, property or services contributed to the venture in exchange for ownership rights. As owners, equity holders may be looking for distributions of income from profits, or they may be looking for appreciation of the value of their ownership interests as the company matures and prospers, or both.[1] Equity investment is the riskiest form of investment. In the event of a business failure leading to bankruptcy or dissolution, the equity holders will be paid last, only after all of the creditors of the entity are paid. On the other hand, if the business is successful, equity investors are entitled to all of the profits and growth in value generated by that success. As stated in the first chapter of this book, "every owner who invests in a business enterprise as an equity holder faces the prospect of unlimited 'upside' (an increase in the value of the owner's share of the business entity) and a 'downside' (the decrease in value or complete loss of the owner's share)."[2] The downside may exceed the amount of the investment in the case of general partnerships, where the mere fact of equity investment creates unlimited liability for the contractual and non-contractual debts of the entity.

Debt financing is obtained from *creditors* who loan money to the business and expect the money to be repaid, with interest, in accordance with a set payment schedule set forth in the loan documents, regardless of the ups and downs of the business. The typical debt transaction is evidenced by a promissory note setting forth a rate of interest, the timing of interest payments and the schedule for repayment of principal.[3]

1.   Examples of Promissory Notes and Types of Loans

Assume a corporation is borrowing $100,000 on January 1, 2010, for a ten year term, at an 8% interest rate. Here are some examples of what the core provisions of the promissory note might look like:

10 Year, Fixed Rate, Self-Amortizing Promissory Note

For value received, XYZ Corp., a California corporation, promises to pay ABC Bank the principal sum of $100,000.00, together with interest on the outstanding principal balance at the rate of 8% per year. *Principal and interest* shall be payable in monthly installments of *$1,213.28* on the first day of each and every calendar month, beginning February 1, 2010 and continuing until January 1, 2020, at which time all accrued interest and outstanding principal shall be paid.

This is a "self amortizing" loan, meaning that over the term of the loan, the principal balance will be repaid. The amount of the monthly payments has been calculated to pay interest on the outstanding balance, plus repayment of some portion of the principal. The interest due for the first month will be only $666.67 (8% of $100,000 divided by 12 months) but the monthly payment is $1,213.28. The excess amount of the monthly payment over the amount of principal owed will be credited towards a reduction of principal. Over the ten year course of the loan, the principal

---

[1] In addition to a financial stake in the success of the business, equity holders may have rights to manage and control the business, depending on the type of entity and the organic structure of the entity.

[2] Equity investors who are general partners may face unlimited liability for the losses of the business, in addition to the loss of their investment. *See* Chapter 1, Section B.2.

[3] Part of the financing of the entity may consist of hybrid forms of debt/equity, such as: (i) convertible debt, where the lender is given the option to convert the loan into equity participation; or (ii) convertible stock where the holder of preferred stock has the right to convert the stock into common stock. Some parties may also have contractual rights in the form of options or warrants to buy shares of stock or debt at special prices. For now, we will consider only pure, non-hybrid forms of debt financing.

balance will be progressively reduced until it reaches zero on the date of the 120th payment in this ten year loan. Below are the amortization schedules for the first and last year of the loan. Note that each month the principal decreases, resulting in less interest being collected and more principal being paid. Towards the end of ten years, the $1,213.28 monthly payments are primarily principal.

Year 1 Amortization Schedule

Month	Payment	Interest	Principal	Loan Balance
1	$1,213.28	$666.67	$546.61	$99,453.39
2	$1,213.28	$663.02	$550.25	$98,903.14
3	$1,213.28	$659.35	$553.92	$98,349.22
4	$1,213.28	$655.66	$557.61	$97,791.60
5	$1,213.28	$651.94	$561.33	$97,230.27
6	$1,213.28	$648.20	$565.07	$96,665.20
7	$1,213.28	$644.43	$568.84	$96,096.35
8	$1,213.28	$640.64	$572.63	$95,523.72
9	$1,213.28	$636.82	$576.45	$94,947.27
10	$1,213.28	$632.98	$580.29	$94,366.97
11	$1,213.28	$629.11	$584.16	$93,782.81
12	$1,213.28	$625.22	$588.06	$93,194.75

Year 10 Amortization Schedule

Month	Payment	Interest	Principal	Loan Balance
109	$1,213.28	$92.98	$1,120.29	$12,827.26
110	$1,213.28	$85.52	$1,127.76	$11,699.50
111	$1,213.28	$78.00	$1,135.28	$10,564.22
112	$1,213.28	$70.43	$1,142.85	$9,421.38
113	$1,213.28	$62.81	$1,150.47	$8,270.91
114	$1,213.28	$55.14	$1,158.14	$7,112.77
115	$1,213.28	$47.42	$1,165.86	$5,946.91
116	$1,213.28	$39.65	$1,173.63	$4,773.28
117	$1,213.28	$31.82	$1,181.45	$3,591.83
118	$1,213.28	$23.95	$1,189.33	$2,402.50
119	$1,213.28	$16.02	$1,197.26	$1,205.24
120	$1,213.28	$8.03	$1,205.24	($0.00)

The above loan is also a "fixed rate" loan, meaning that the interest rate is fixed at 8% throughout the life of the loan. Some loans have "adjustable rates" where the interest rate is keyed to some objective index (such as the 26 week Treasury Bill rate) and are subject to adjustment at periodic intervals during the life of the loan.[4]

How is the following promissory note different from the preceding promissory note?

10 Year Fixed Rate, Interest Only Promissory Note

For value received, XYZ Corp., a California corporation, promises to pay ABC Bank the principal sum of $100,000.00, together with interest on the

---

[4] See the 10 Year Adjustable Rate, Interest Only Promissory Note later in this chapter.

outstanding principal balance at the rate of 8% per year. *Interest only* shall be payable in monthly installments of *$666.67* on the first day of each and every calendar month, beginning February 1, 2010 and continuing until January 1, 2020, at which time all accrued interest and outstanding principal shall be paid.

This is an "interest only" loan. The monthly payments of $666.67 are much lower than the $1,213.28 that would have to be paid on the self-amortizing loan because *only* interest is being paid during the life of the loan. The principal will not be repaid until the maturity date in 2020. The final payment of principal is often referred to as a "balloon" payment. Note that the corporation will have to come up with a large sum of money to make the balloon payment on the maturity date. To do so, the corporation may have to "refinance" the loan at that time by borrowing another $100,000 at the end of the loan period to repay the principal of this loan. The term "refinance" means that the corporation will have to obtain a new loan from some lender in order to pay off the principal balance. The creation of the new loan will be on interest and repayment terms to be determined in arms length negotiations with lenders at that time, and will result in the charging of substantial fees and closing costs for the new loan.[5] If the corporation has not created a sinking fund for repayment of the loan when the term expires in ten years, refinancing can be a risky gamble on the part of the corporation. It is always possible that interest rates have risen, or there has been a tightening of the credit markets. If the corporation has to raise $100,000 to refinance the loan it *may* find that obtaining the loan is difficult and costly.

Consider our final sample promissory note:

10 Year Adjustable Rate, Interest Only Promissory Note

For value received, XYZ Corp., a California corporation, promises to pay ABC Bank the principal sum of $100,000.00, together with interest on the outstanding principal balance at the annual rate equal to 500 basis points[6] in excess of the London Interbank Offered Rate for ninety (90) day obligations as published in The Wall Street Journal rounded to the nearest one-eighth of one percent (the "LIBOR Rate").[7] The interest rate so determined on the date of this promissory note is 8%. The interest rate shall be adjustable every ninety (90) days based upon any change in the LIBOR Rate on the last publication day of the preceding ninety (90) day period. *Interest only* shall be payable in monthly installments on the first day of each and every calendar month, beginning February 1, 2010 and continuing until January 1, 2020, at which time all accrued interest and outstanding principal shall be paid.

---

[5] Lenders often charge up-front fees as a condition of making the loan to a borrower. These fees have many names and are often referred to as "points" or "loan origination fees." Unlike interest, which is paid over time on the outstanding principal balance of the loan, these up-front fees are paid at the time the loan is made and can be substantial. If the $100,000 loan origination fee is 3% and closing costs are 2%, the borrower will be paying $5,000 as an up front cost to obtain the loan.

[6] A basis point is one hundredth of a percentage point (0.01%). 500 basis points would be 5%.

[7] The London Interbank Offered Rate is the rate of interest which banks offer to lend money to one another in the wholesale money markets in London. It is a standard financial index used in U.S. capital markets and can be found in the Wall Street Journal.

Adjustable rate loans can be very attractive. Lenders will often offer initial interest rates that are below fixed interest rates in order to attract borrowers. However, borrowers must beware the possibility that dramatic increases in the interest rate are possible. If there is a change in market conditions that drives the variable rate significantly higher, it could have catastrophic consequences if there is insufficient cash flow to cover the increase.

2.   Lenders

Regardless of the type of loan being made (fixed rate, adjustable rate, self-amortizing, or interest only) the debt payments are not tied to the success of the business. Although all lenders *prefer* the business to be successful so as to enhance the likelihood of full payment of the loan, the lender has no direct interest in the profits of the business, nor is the lender adversely impacted by the losses of the business (unless the business lacks the cash to make the loan payments). Unlike dividend payments to equity holders, the loan payments must be made in accordance with the terms of the notes regardless of the ups and downs of business operations or changes in the value of the business.

From a risk perspective, lenders who provide debt financing take less of a risk than equity holders. As creditors of the entity, lenders stand on the shoulders of the equity holders and are entitled to be paid before distributions can be made to equity holders. The greater the degree of equity in the entity, the more of an "equity cushion" exists to support the repayment of the debt owed to lendors. Lendors are willing to accept less of a rate of return on their debt investments than equity holders since they are taking less risk. However, as the equity-to-debt ratio decreases, the risk to the lenders will increase and, accordingly, lenders will seek higher interest rates and fees.

As discussed in Chapter 1, some lenders may be *secured* creditors, with security interests in real or personal property to secure payment of their loans. Secured lenders are exposed to the least amount of risk since they are entitled to seize and sell certain property of the business to satisfy their claims for principal and interest, boosting them ahead of both equity holders *and* unsecured creditors in the right to priority of payment. The availability of secured debt will depend on the existence of stable, long term assets such as real estate and equipment to serve as collateral.

3.   Leverage

It is important to understand the concept of *leverage* and the role that it plays in investment finance. There may be a considerable advantage to an equity investor who borrows money to finance an investment in an appreciating asset. As the amount of debt climbs, and relative degree of equity lessens, the return on investment can be greatly enhanced. For instance, suppose that an investor, Arthur, wants to purchase an office building for $1 million. He anticipates that with a good marketing plan, and upward changes in real estate values, he can sell the building in one year for $1.25 million. If Arthur uses only his own cash to purchase the building and make the improvements, he will generate a return on investment of 25%. However, what if Arthur *leverages* his purchase by using only $250,000 of his own money and borrowing $750,000 from a lender? When Arthur sells the building for $1.25 million, he will pay off the principal balance of the loan, leaving him with $500,000 — twice the amount he invested. However, Arthur's profit is not quite $250,000. To accurately compute the amount of Arthur's profit, and his return on investment, we need to consider the added financing costs for obtaining the loan and paying interest over the one year period of the loan. A loan of $750,000 at 8% would generate $60,000 in annual interest expense. In addition, Arthur probably had to pay an up-front "loan origination fee" to obtain the loan. Assuming a 1% loan origination fee of $7,500, the total costs of loan financing would be $67,500, reducing Arthur's net profits to $182,500 but would still yield a 73% return on his original investment of $250,000 (compared to 25% if Arthur does not leverage his investment). By leveraging his money in this way, Arthur can invest his original $1 million in several different investments and substantially increase his overall wealth. Of course, there is an added *risk* that accompanies the enhanced earning potential of leveraged investments. Arthur is anticipating a one-year holding period and an appreciating market. If the market stays stable or declines, Arthur will be saddled with the continuing interest expense of the debt financing or face default and foreclosure. If he hangs on to the property while he waits for changes in market conditions, the interest payments will, eventually, eliminate his anticipated gain. In the event of a default, if Arthur is personally liable on the note (which is likely), he faces the possibility of losing the property in foreclosure *and* being personally liable for any deficiency.

The concept of leverage applies to investments in business entities as well as real property and tangible assets. The return on investment for an equity investor in a corporation, partnership or LLC can be substantially increased by either: (i) incurring debt to purchase the equity interest, just as Arthur did to purchase the office building; or, (ii) by having the *entity* borrow money to purchase assets and/or operate the business. For example, an investor like Arthur may have $1 million to invest in a newly formed business entity, together with nine other investors, each contributing the same amount, for a total capitalization of $10 million. The business plan for the entity is to purchase, renovate and sell an apartment complex over a two year period. It is anticipated that the building will be sold in two years for $12.5 million, yielding a profit of $2.5 million. Under this plan, each of the ten investors will have a gain of $250,000, which constitutes a 25% return on their original $1 million investments.

What if each investor contributed only $250,000 for a total equity capitalization of $2.5 million and the *entity* borrowed $7.5 million from a commercial lender, using the building as collateral for a mortgage loan? Reasonable loan costs over a two year period would be about $1.3 million.[8] When the property is sold for $12.5 million, and the $7.5 million loan is repaid, there will be $3.7 million left to distribute to the ten investors. Each of the ten investors will receive $370,000, which constitutes a 48% return on their original $250,000 investment, compared to only a 25% return if no debt is used to fund the venture. A chart helps to see the power of leveraging in this scenario:

---

[8] We will assume a 1⅓% loan origination fee of $100,000 and $600,000 in annual interest at the rate of 8%. After two years, the total cost of financing would be $1.3 million.

Per Investor Returns — $10 Million Real Estate Venture With 10 Investors				
	Investment Amount per Investor	Distribution per Investor After Sale	Profits	Return on Investment
Unleveraged	$1,000,000	$1,250,000	$250,000	25%
Leveraged	$250,000	$370,000	$120,000	48%

What about the *downside* risks of leverage when the entity, rather than the investors, borrows money to help finance the business? In limited liability entities the risks are reduced. However, in business entities that lack limited liability, or limited liability entities where the loans are guaranteed by the equity holders, there is a serious downside risk with regard to leveraged entities. Just like Arthur in the preceding paragraph, the risk of loss can be compounded in leveraged situations, creating personal liability for general partners or guarantors if the business fails.

When investing money in equities, the projected return on investment is an important indicator of the opportunity value of the investment. The use of debt to leverage the investment can, in many cases, substantially increase the return on investment but may also enhance the risk.

C. EQUITY FINANCING

The promoters of a business venture must, somehow, generate sufficient capital to infuse the business with the assets and cash it needs to begin operations and prosper. The *equity capitalization* of the entity will occur by selling ownership interests in exchange for cash, property or services.[9] "Capital" consists of the assets, cash and services contributed by the owners to fund the entity. The term typically refers to the sum-total of value received from the equity participants. "When used with respect to the property of a corporation or association the term [capital] has a settled meaning; it applies only to the property or means contributed by the stockholders as the fund or basis for the business or enterprise for which the corporation or association was formed."[10] Or, as another court has stated simply, capital is "the money, property or means contributed by stockholders as the fund or basis for the business or enterprise for which the corporation was formed."[11]

In many newly formed entities, commercial loans from outside lenders will be unavailable. Unsecured commercial lenders rely on the existence of two essential factors in evaluating the credit-worthiness of business entities. First, unsecured lenders look to the existence of a substantial base of equity capital that serves a foundational "cushion" in the event of a loan default. Second, unsecured lenders look to the operating history of the entity to determine whether or not there will be sufficient income to meet the entity's operating costs and repay the loan. Mere financial projections are often insufficient to obtain a commercial unsecured loan for a newly formed entity, even one with a hefty base of equity capital. The chances of obtaining debt financing from unsecured lenders may be enhanced by personal guarantees of wealthy equity investors, rather than the credit-worthiness of the

---

[9] In many cases, the equity investors may also loan money to the business entity as part of the initial capitalization.

[10] Bailey v. Clark, 88 U.S. (21 Wall.) 284, 286–287 (1874).

[11] United Grocers, Ltd. v. United States, 186 F. Supp. 724, 729 (1960).

entity, but this requires that certain promoters and/or investors put their personal wealth at risk.

If the entity will have stable fixed assets, such as real property, obtaining a *secured* commercial loan may be more readily available for a newly formed entity, if the equity contributions are sufficient to create a debt-to-equity ratio that can satisfy the risk-assessment analysis of a mortgage lender. For instance, a corporation with $2.5 million in equity capital contributions might be purchasing real property worth $7.5 million and financing the purchase with a $5 million mortgage loan from a bank. The bank will have collateral worth $7.5 million to satisfy its $5 million claim (a debt-to-equity ratio of 66%). The existence of such a large equity cushion ($2.5 million) assures the lender that in the event of a default, there will be plenty of equity in the collateral to cover the bank's principal loan, accrued interest and costs of collection. A low debt-to-equity ratio reduces the risks of default and encourages mortgage lenders to make such a loan. As the debt-to-equity ratio increases, so does the risk to the lender. In the above scenario, if the borrower provides only 5% of the cost of acquiring the land ($375,000) and borrows the remaining $7,125,000, the debt-to-equity ratio would be 95-to-5. In the event of a default by the borrower, the equity cushion would be only $375,000. If the interest rate is 8%, interest will accrue at the rate of $50,000 per month for the period following default until foreclosure is completed.[12] If it takes the lender eight months to complete the foreclosure, the total amount of the lender's claims for principle ($7,125,000) and interest ($400,000) will exceed the value of the property. Furthermore, the property is unlikely to generate its full fair market value at a foreclosure sale, further reducing the funds available to satisfy the secured lender's claims.

The realistic bottom line for many newly formed entities, particularly those that are not real property ventures, is that startup capital will be obtained from active participants and outside investors, rather than commercial lenders.

There will often be times when the initial participants in a venture are supplying all of the cash and property necessary to start up and operate the business, without seeking funds from outside sources. In small startups, the participants may use personal funds, credit cards, family loans and home-equity mortgage loans to generate the startup capital for their businesses.

However, in many business enterprises, the primary objective of promoters in the early stages of business formation is to find equity investors who are willing to take the risk, and reap the potential rewards, of equity investment. To accomplish this task, the promoters will do their homework and develop a business plan to attract potential investors. The plan will set forth the proposed business concept, market analysis, financial objectives and projections, organization and management of the proposed entity, along with marketing strategy, growth analysis, and funding needs, as well as other information.[13] Finding investors with the funds and sophistication to qualify for investment in the enterprise is an arduous task. Promoters will use their address books to contact investors they have worked with in the past, friends, family, business associates, lawyers, accountants, financial planners and brokers. The search will be engaged for so-called "angel investors" —

---

[12] ($7.5 million × 8%) ÷ 12=$50,000.

[13] The business plan is a marketing, not a disclosure document. The disclosure requirements imposed by the Securities Acts will most likely require more detailed disclosures of material information before the offer or sale of securities to investors. *See* Chapter 4, Section D.

high net-worth individuals who regularly invest in new companies at an early stage. The promoters or investors may also seek capital from venture capital firms, discussed below. Similar to venture capital firms, angel investors provide cash to startup or immature companies and take equity in return but usually take less of a control position and provide less capital and guidance. Some of these angel investors are members of angel investment groups, allowing them to pool resources, spread their risks and better evaluate investment opportunities.

In planning the capitalization strategy, questions will arise as the nature of the ownership interest that equity investors will receive, the degree of control they will have, and the distribution rights they will be granted. These considerations will affect the marketability of the equity units to investors and will have an impact on the management and financial success of the venture. The promoters may have to cede some control, as well as the potential upside value of the business, in order to attract equity investment.

When the rights of equity holders are designed during the early planning stages, the answers to these questions will depend on the types of investors being sought. In very broad terms, there are three types of equity investors for non-public business entities: (i) active investors who are key players and will be participating in the management and operations of the business; (ii) passive private investors with cash to invest and seeking only limited rights of management, who are relying primarily upon the skills of the managers; and, (iii) professional investor entities such as venture capital firms that may seek substantial rights of control and financial priorities in exchange for large amounts of cash and expertise.

All equity investors in newly formed companies have one thing in common. They are willing to take risks in order to obtain a high rate of return on their investment. Depending on the investor, they may also require a certain amount of control, a bigger slice of the ownership interests in the company, or priority of distribution. The following excerpt gives an excellent overview of the types of control and financial interest that venture capital firms (as well as other large-scale investors) may require.

The Venture Capital Industry — An Overview
National Venture Capitalist Association (2007)[14]

Venture capital is money provided by professionals who invest alongside management in young, rapidly growing companies that have the potential to develop into significant economic contributors. Venture capital is an important source of equity for start-up companies.

Professionally managed venture capital firms generally are private partnerships or closely-held corporations funded by private and public pension funds, endowment funds, foundations, corporations, wealthy individuals, foreign investors, and the venture capitalists themselves.

Venture capitalists generally:

*   Finance new and rapidly growing companies;
*   Purchase equity securities;

---

[14] Reprinted with permission, National Venture Capital Association, www.nvca.org. This excerpt is available by clicking on "Resources" and then "VC Industry Overview."

* Assist in the development of new products or services;
* Add value to the company through active participation;
* Take higher risks with the expectation of higher rewards;
* Have a long-term orientation

When considering an investment, venture capitalists carefully screen the technical and business merits of the proposed company. Venture capitalists only invest in a small percentage of the businesses they review and have a long-term perspective. Going forward, they actively work with the company's management by contributing their experience and business savvy gained from helping other companies with similar growth challenges.

Venture capitalists mitigate the risk of venture investing by developing a portfolio of young companies in a single venture fund. Many times they will co-invest with other professional venture capital firms. In addition, many venture partnership will manage multiple funds simultaneously. For decades, venture capitalists have nurtured the growth of America's high technology and entrepreneurial communities resulting in significant job creation, economic growth and international competitiveness. Companies such as Digital Equipment Corporation, Apple, Federal Express, Compaq, Sun Microsystems, Intel, Microsoft and Genentech are famous examples of companies that received venture capital early in their development.

Private Equity Investing

Venture capital investing has grown from a small investment pool in the 1960s and early 1970s to a mainstream asset class that is a viable and significant part of the institutional and corporate investment portfolio. Recently, some investors have been referring to venture investing and buyout investing as "private equity investing." This term can be confusing because some in the investment industry use the term "private equity" to refer only to buyout fund investing. In any case, an institutional investor will allocate 2% to 3% of their institutional portfolio for investment in alternative assets such as private equity or venture capital as part of their overall asset allocation. Currently, over 50% of investments in venture capital/private equity comes from institutional public and private pension funds, with the balance coming from endowments, foundations, insurance companies, banks, individuals and other entities who seek to diversify their portfolio with this investment class.

What is a Venture Capitalist?

The typical person-on-the-street depiction of a venture capitalist is that of a wealthy financier who wants to fund start-up companies. The perception is that a person who develops a brand new change-the-world invention needs capital; thus, if they can't get capital from a bank or from their own pockets, they enlist the help of a venture capitalist.

In truth, venture capital and private equity firms are pools of capital, typically organized as a limited partnership, that invests in companies that represent the opportunity for a high rate of return within five to seven years. The venture capitalist may look at several hundred investment opportunities before investing in only a few selected companies with favorable investment opportunities. Far from being simply passive financiers, venture capitalists foster growth in companies through their involvement in the management, strategic marketing and planning of their investee companies. They are entrepreneurs first and financiers second.

Even individuals may be venture capitalists. In the early days of venture capital investment, in the 1950s and 1960s, individual investors were the archetypal venture investor. While this type of individual investment did not totally disappear, the modern venture firm emerged as the dominant venture investment vehicle. However, in the last few years, individuals have again become a potent and increasingly larger part of the early stage start-up venture life cycle. These "angel investors" will mentor a company and provide needed capital and expertise to help develop companies. Angel investors may either be wealthy people with management expertise or retired business men and women who seek the opportunity for first-hand business development.

Investment Focus

Venture capitalists may be generalist or specialist investors depending on their investment strategy. Venture capitalists can be generalists, investing in various industry sectors, or various geographic locations, or various stages of a company's life. Alternatively, they may be specialists in one or two industry sectors, or may seek to invest in only a localized geographic area.

Not all venture capitalists invest in "start-ups." While venture firms will invest in companies that are in their initial start-up modes, venture capitalists will also invest in companies at various stages of the business life cycle. A venture capitalist may invest before there is a real product or company organized (so called "seed investing"), or may provide capital to start up a company in its first or second stages of development known as "early stage investing." Also, the venture capitalist may provide needed financing to help a company grow beyond a critical mass to become more successful ("expansion stage financing").

The venture capitalist may invest in a company throughout the company's life cycle and therefore some funds focus on later stage investing by providing financing to help the company grow to a critical mass to attract public financing through a stock offering. Alternatively, the venture capitalist may help the company attract a merger or acquisition with another company by providing liquidity and exit for the company's founders.

At the other end of the spectrum, some venture funds specialize in the acquisition, turnaround or recapitalization of public and private companies that represent favorable investment opportunities.

There are venture funds that will be broadly diversified and will invest in companies in various industry sectors as diverse as semiconductors, software, retailing and restaurants and others that may be specialists in only one technology.

While high technology investment makes up most of the venture investing in the U.S., and the venture industry gets a lot of attention for its high technology investments, venture capitalists also invest in companies such as construction, industrial products, business services, etc. There are several firms that have specialized in retail company investment and others that have a focus in investing only in "socially responsible" start-up endeavors.

Venture firms come in various sizes from small seed specialist firms of only a few million dollars under management to firms with over a billion dollars in invested capital around the world. The common denominator in all of these types of venture investing is that the venture capitalist is not a passive investor, but has an active and vested interest in guiding, leading and growing the companies they have invested in. They seek to add value through their experience in investing in tens and hundreds of companies.

Some venture firms are successful by creating synergies between the various companies they have invested in; for example one company that has a great software product, but does not have adequate distribution technology may be paired with another company or its management in the venture portfolio that has better distribution technology.

Length of Investment

Venture capitalists will help companies grow, but they eventually seek to exit the investment in three to seven years. An early stage investment make take seven to ten years to mature, while a later stage investment many only take a few years, so the appetite for the investment life cycle must be congruent with the limited partnerships' appetite for liquidity. The venture investment is neither a short term nor a liquid investment, but an investment that must be made with careful diligence and expertise.

Types of Firms

There are several types of venture capital firms, but most mainstream firms invest their capital through funds organized as limited partnerships in which the venture capital firm serves as the general partner. The most common type of venture firm is an independent venture firm that has no affiliations with any other financial institution. These are called "private independent firms". Venture firms may also be affiliates or subsidiaries of a commercial bank, investment bank or insurance company and make investments on behalf of outside investors or the parent firm's clients. Still other firms may be subsidiaries of non-financial, industrial corporations making investments on behalf of the parent itself. These latter firms are typically called "direct investors" or "corporate venture investors."

*   *   *

Corporate Venturing

One form of investing that was popular in the 1980s and is again very popular is corporate venturing. This is usually called "direct investing" in portfolio companies by venture capital programs or subsidiaries of nonfinancial corporations. These investment vehicles seek to find qualified investment opportunities that are congruent with the parent company's strategic technology or that provide synergy or cost savings.

These corporate venturing programs may be loosely organized programs affiliated with existing business development programs or may be self-contained entities with a strategic charter and mission to make investments congruent with the parent's strategic mission. There are some venture firms that specialize in advising, consulting and managing a corporation's venturing program.

The typical distinction between corporate venturing and other types of venture investment vehicles is that corporate venturing is usually performed with corporate strategic objectives in mind while other venture investment vehicles typically have investment return or financial objectives as their primary goal. This may be a generalization as corporate venture programs are not immune to financial considerations, but the distinction can be made.

The other distinction of corporate venture programs is that they usually invest their parent's capital while other venture investment vehicles invest outside investors' capital.

*   *   *

Exits

Depending on the investment focus and strategy of the venture firm, it will seek to exit the investment in the portfolio company within three to five years of the initial investment. While the initial public offering may be the most glamourous and heralded type of exit for the venture capitalist and owners of the company, most successful exits of venture investments occur through a merger or acquisition of the company by either the original founders or another company. Again, the expertise of the venture firm in successfully exiting its investment will dictate the success of the exit for themselves and the owner of the company.

IPO

The initial public offering is the most glamourous and visible type of exit for a venture investment. In recent years technology IPOs have been in the limelight during the IPO boom of the last six years. At public offering, the venture firm is considered an insider and will receive stock in the company, but the firm is regulated and restricted in how that stock can be sold or liquidated for several years. Once this stock is freely tradable, usually after about two years, the venture fund will distribute this stock or cash to its limited partner investor who may then manage the public stock as a regular stock holding or may liquidate it upon receipt. Over the last twenty-five years, almost 3000 companies financed by venture funds have gone public.

Mergers and Acquisitions

Mergers and acquisitions represent the most common type of successful exit for venture investments. In the case of a merger or acquisition, the venture firm will receive stock or cash from the acquiring company and the venture investor will distribute the proceeds from the sale to its limited partners.

*   *   *

Management Fees

As an investment manager, the general partner will typically charge a management fee to cover the costs of managing the committed capital. The management fee will usually be paid quarterly for the life of the fund or it may be tapered or curtailed in the later stages of a fund's life. This is most often negotiated with investors upon formation of the fund in the terms and conditions of the investment.

Carried Interest

"Carried interest" is the term used to denote the profit split of proceeds to the general partner. This is the general partners' fee for carrying the management responsibility plus all the liability and for providing the needed expertise to successfully manage the investment. There are as many variations of this profit split both in the size and how it is calculated and accrued as there are firms.

As the excerpt reveals, venture capital firms can provide large amounts of cash but expect high returns, substantial control over the management of the business and a priority of distribution with respect to profits and/or liquidating distributions. The cost is high but the benefits can be substantial. Venture capital firms often have valuable expertise that can be tapped to grow the business and position it for a lucrative merger, acquisition or public offering.

D. STRUCTURING THE FINANCING OF BUSINESS ENTITIES

Many factors will contribute to the equity structure of a newly formed business entity. While the type of participation interests issued to equity holders will vary depending on whether the entity is a corporation (shares of stock), general or limited partnership (partnership interest), or limited liability company (member ship interests), there are certain common issues that will arise:

(i) *How will rights of control and management be allocated among the equity holders?* The equity holders are the owners of the business and by statute and/or documentation will be granted control over the management of the entity. The allocation of control among the equity holders is a core issue in designing the entity. To the degree that a small number of promoters are the primary equity participants, they will have to use some mechanism that assures an appropriate level of control among themselves. If the promoters intend to manage the business and use outside passive investors to provide substantial equity funding, the promoters will typically structure the equity interests to allow for centralization of management and limiting the rights of outside investors. On the other hand, as the excerpt from the National Venture Capital Association emphasizes, some deep-pocket investors, such as venture capital firms, may demand a significant degree of control as a condition to investing in the company.

The mechanisms to accomplish the allocation of *control* among equity holders are discussed in detail in Chapter 7. The remaining common issues in paragraphs 2–4 below will be focused on in this Chapter as we explore the equity structures for each type of business entity.

(ii)   *How will economic rights to distributions of profits, losses and dispositions of assets be allocated among equity holders?* Regardless of their level of control, the equity participants will enter the transaction with expectations about their percentage share of the overall ownership of the company, and their allocations of economic value that will be distributed by the company. Distribution schemes can be very simple, such as a general partnership where all of the general partners share equally in profits and losses. They can also be exceedingly complex, such as a corporation with several classes of preferred stock and convertible debt.

(iii)   *What type of consideration will be paid by equity holders and how will non-cash contributions be valued?* The amount, type and timing of equity contributions can vary widely and may not be proportional to the economic and control rights being granted to each equity holder. We will look at various mechanisms for structuring the consideration to be contributed in exchange for equity shares.

(iv)   *How will additional equity financing be obtained in the future if the company needs more money?* When forming a business entity, it is common for the promoters and investors to agree upon a scheme for infusing additional capital in the future, if the need arises. Will the early equity contributors be obligated, or given the option, to contribute additional amounts if certain triggering circumstances occur? Will additional investors be allowed to purchase equity interests in the future in exchange for new cash contributions? Interesting and complex issues arise regarding these mechanisms for future capital contributions.

1.   Financing of Corporations

At the heart of corporate finance is the authorization and issuance of shares of stock. Shares of common or preferred stock will be sold to shareholders in exchange for some consideration. Although the organizers might be contemplating a high debt-to-equity ratio, they must be careful to go through the essential formal steps of holding an organizational meeting of the board of directors and the issuance of at least some common voting stock. While the corporation is technically formed upon the filing of the articles of incorporation,[15] if operations are commenced without issuing stock, the owners of the business are risking the loss of the liability shield, as well as endangering the corporate tax status of the entity. The failure to issue stock, although not conclusive evidence, constitutes a fundamental failure to maintain the formal separation between the owners and the corporate entity, which can be a strong (but not determinative) factor in establishing alter ego liability.[16] To reduce this risk, after the articles of incorporation are filed, competent corporate lawyers assist in completing the formation of the corporation by ushering the directors through the steps of a

---

[15]   See, for instance, California Corporations Code § 200(c): "The corporate existence begins upon the filing of the articles and continues perpetually, unless otherwise expressly provided by law or in the articles." *See also* 8 Del. C. § 106, MBCA § 2.03.

[16]   Automotriz del Golfo de California S. A. de C. V. v. Resnick, 47 Cal. 2d 792, 798 (Cal. 1957) ("It has been stated that the two requirements for application of this doctrine are (1) that there be such unity of interest and ownership that the separate personalities of the corporation and the individual no longer exist and (2) that, if the acts are treated as those of the corporation alone, an inequitable result will follow. . . The failure to issue stock . . . although not conclusive evidence, is an indication that defendants were doing business as individuals . . . see Marr v. Postal Union Life Ins. Co., 40 Cal.App.2d 673"). In the *Marr* case the court stated: "While the fact standing alone that a corporation remains inchoate without stockholders or stock is not of itself determinative of an alter ego relationship upon its part, nevertheless it does indicate that such corporation may exist merely to serve the interests of another . . . " For an excellent summary of the factors, see Eric Fox, *Piercing the Veil of Limited Liability Companies*, 62 Geo. Wash. L. Rev. 1143 (1994).

formal organizational meeting at which assets are contributed by stockholders and shares of stock are issued in exchange.

Of course, the fact that some stock is issued is not sufficient to eliminate the problem of alter ego liability. The *combined* amount of debt and equity capitalization by the shareholders participants must be sufficient to give independent substance to the corporation. To the extent that the investing shareholders of a corporation are allocating their contributions between equity and debt, it is common for courts to hold that the portion allocated as "debt" is to be treated as equity *vis-a-vis* independent creditors of the entity. Particularly where the equity capitalization is thin (there is a high debt-to-equity ratio), or there is proportionality between the ratio of equity holdings to debt holdings of the shareholders, courts will apply the doctrine of equitable subordination to re-classify the debt contribution as equity.[17] Equitable subordination is a doctrine where the courts reclassify the debt obligations owed to insiders as equity when those insiders are competing with true outside creditors, such as: (i) trade creditors, without knowledge of the insider's claims; or (ii) tort claimants, who were relying on the capitalization of the corporation as a cushion for their claims. In the absence of an equitable subordination doctrine, the shareholders could bootstrap the inherent riskiness of an equity investment into a less risky debt investment. "The ability to recharacterize a purported loan emanates from the bankruptcy court's power to ignore the form of a transaction and give effect to its substance."[18] The same thinness may result in the IRS re-classifying interest payments as dividends for tax purposes in the case of C corporations, as discussed in Chapter 3, Section C.3.

Assuming that all of the early capital for the formation of the corporation will be coming from investors, rather than commercial lenders, the exact mix of debt and equity will depend on the needs of the business and the ability to attract investors. If the business is going to generate disposable cash in a fairly short period, it might make sense from a tax perspective to structure some of the investors' contributions as debt. Payments of interest will move money out of the corporation without double taxation and repayments of principal will not be taxed as capital gains to the investors. On the other hand, there may not be sufficient funds available from operations during early years to make the debt payments required by promissory notes. The planners have to be realistic about the ability of the corporation to actually fund the note payments that are being proposed if there a substantial portion of the contributions of the investors is going to be allocated to debt. In addition, if there is a plan to *eventually* obtain loans from commercial lenders, it is important to provide a solid base of equity capital to provide the equity cushion that commercial lenders may require as a condition to making a loan to the entity. A corporation with too thin a level of equity financing will have difficulty obtaining commercial loans.

---

[17] See In re Cold Harbor Assocs., L.P., 204 B.R. 904, 915 (Bankr. E.D. Va. 1997), in Section D.1.d.iv of this chapter.

[18] In re Fabricators, Inc., 926 F.2d 1458, 1469 (5th Cir. 1991); In re Autostyle Plastics, Inc., 269 F.3d 726, 748 (6th Cir. 2001); *see also* Clark, *The Duties of the Corporate Debtor to Its Creditors*, 90 Harv. L. Rev. 505 (1977).

a.   The TouchSearch, Inc. scenario

Perhaps the most sensible way to approach the issue of the mix of equity and debt is with a hypothetical scenario. Suppose that two promoters, Alice and Andy, have designed a new and powerful algorithm for searching internet web sites, which they have named TouchSearch. They intend to form a corporation ("TouchSearch, Inc.") to profit from the advanced capabilities of the technology. Under their business plan, they need $10 million in seed money to start up and sustain the business for the first two years. The plan contemplates that, after two years, the business will be generating a strong positive cash flow and will and have an attractive balance sheet, as well as a stable operating history. Alice and Andy are anticipating that, after two years, they will sell the business, or seek a growth-oriented second round of financing.

Alice and Andy will each be contributing $250,000 in cash. The remainder of their contributions will be in the form of intellectual property and pre-formation services, valued at an additional $750,000 ($375,000 each). Following formation, Alice and Andy will be employed by the corporation and receive appropriate compensation packages for the work they will perform. Alice and Andy need to retain substantial control over the management of the entity.

Alice and Andy have located eight investors (the "outside investors"). Each investor is wealthy, sophisticated and willing to contribute $1 million in cash. The plan is that Alice, Andy and the eight investors will each own one-tenth of the equity of the corporation but the outside investors will receive priority rights to payment with regard to both distributions of profits and proceeds from the sales of assets. The investors will have voting rights with respect to mergers, acquisitions or other major corporate decisions but Andy and Alice will have the rights to manage the general affairs of the corporation. What are some possible ways to structure the equity financing of this entity?[19]

b.   Common stock

Common stock is the traditional name given to the ordinary shares that represent the basic ownership and control rights of the shareholders of the corporation, as distinguished from preferred stock. In the absence of other types of stock being authorized in the articles, the proportional issuance of common stock will determine the relative voting and financial rights of shareholders. As owners of the corporation, the holders of common stock are last in priority of distribution, following the claims of creditors, and any priority rights granted to preferred stockholders. Once the rights and claims of creditors and preferred shareholders are satisfied, the owners of common stock are entitled to all of the value remaining in the corporate entity.

Before shares of any type of stock may be issued, the articles of incorporation must authorize the type and number of shares of stock to be issued. Once the shares authorized in the articles have been issued, no new stock can be issued by the corporation without an amendment to the articles. The actual issuance of the

---

[19] Keep in mind that this corporation will not be able to elect Subchapter S status regardless of the mechanism used to allocate economic rights to the participants. The plan to provide some investors with a preferred rate of return on their investments will constitute a second class of stock for purposes of Subchapter S, making a Subchapter S election improper.

stock is accomplished through formal action of the board of directors by adoption of a resolution identifying the purchasers of the shares, setting forth the number of shares to be sold and the consideration to be received for the shares. Traditionally, and still true today in approximately 20 states, statutory limits exist on the *types* of lawful consideration for which a corporation can issue shares. For instance, in California, shares may only be issued for: " . . . money paid; labor done; services actually rendered to the corporation or for its benefit or in its formation or reorganization; debts or securities canceled; and tangible or intangible property actually received . . .[20] The statute specifically excludes the issuance of shares in exchange for *unsecured* promissory notes of the shareholder and promises of future performance.[21] Quite recently, in 2004, Delaware veered away from these traditional constraints on lawful consideration when changes were made to both its constitution and statutory provisions, allowing the issuance of shares of stock for *any benefit to the corporation.*[22] Despite the recent changes in Delaware, many states still limit the types of consideration that may be exchanged for lawful issuance of corporate shares of stock. However, it is universally true that when the consideration is of a lawful *type*, such as tangible or intangible property, the *valuation* of the consideration by the board of directors is conclusive in the absence of actual fraud.[23] When shares are issued in exchange for *property* rather than cash or services, it is up to the board of directors to adopt a resolution determining the cash value to the corporation in exchange for the shares being issued.

The limits on types of consideration in states such as California do not present insurmountable problems for knowledgeable corporate planners. Even if there is a prohibition on the issuance of shares for *future* services, so long as the service-shareholder can provide some cash, property or *pre*-formation services, it is up to the board of directors to determine the amount of shares to be issued in exchange for the *lawful* consideration that the service-shareholder has to offer. With regard to issuance of shares in exchange for unsecured promissory notes, statutes such as California's prohibit only unsecured promissory notes of the *purchaser*. Unsecured promissory notes executed in favor of the stock purchaser by a family member or family trust would technically satisfy the lawful consideration requirement.

---

[20] California Corporations Code § 409(a)(1). The 2008 version of the MBCA Annotated lists 31 states which no longer have such limitations on lawful consideration.

[21] *Id.* ("but neither promissory notes of the purchaser (unless adequately secured by collateral other than the shares acquired or unless permitted by Section 408) nor future services shall constitute payment or part payment for shares of the corporation . . ."). Section 408 allows for the issuance of stock options to employees in exchange for the employee's unsecured notes if a stock option plan has been adopted by the board of directors.

[22] Prior to 2004, § 152 of the Delaware General Corporations Law implemented the requirement of Section 3 of Article IX of the Delaware Constitution that "No corporation shall issue stock, except for money paid, labor done or personal property, or real estate or leases thereof actually acquired by such corporation." Following amendment to the Delaware Constitution in 2004, § 152 was amended in to eliminate the requirement that a particular type of consideration be paid. Section 152 now states in relevant part: "The board of directors may authorize capital stock to be issued for consideration consisting of cash, any tangible or intangible property or *any benefit to the corporation*, or any combination thereof. In the absence of actual fraud in the transaction, the judgment of the directors as to the value of such consideration shall be conclusive." (Emphasis added.)

[23] *See* Del. Gen. Corp. L. § 152; *see also* Cal. Corp. Code § 409 ("In the absence of fraud in the transaction, the judgment of the directors as to the value of the consideration for shares shall be conclusive.").

Similarly, whether a secured note of the stock purchaser is "adequately secured" is a board determination, with the judgment of the board conclusive in the absence of some actual fraud.

Regardless of the technical requirements for lawful consideration, common stock is an inflexible device in situations such as our hypothetical, where the participants want to vary the relationship between the amounts and nature of their contributions and their rights to economic distributions or control of corporate affairs. In our scenario, the business deal is that all ten of the investors will have a one-tenth ownership interest but the outside investors will have preferential rights to payment, while the promoters, Alice and Andy, will have superior rights of management and control. Although the board of directors will have discretion in determining the consideration which will be accepted in exchange for common shares, once the shares are issued the allocation of control and entitlement to financial distributions is entirely dependent on the number of shares possessed by shareholders. How could common stock be used to attain the goals regarding financial priorities *and* management objectives? A possible solution would be for all ten shareholders to purchase one-tenth of the common stock in exchange for $250,000, and for the eight outside investors to each loan the corporation $750,000, to achieve the total equity and loan capitalization of $10 million. This plan would assure the outside investors a priority of payment with respect to interest and principal on their loans, as well as avoid the double taxation issue. However, there are two serious problems with this allocation of common stock and debt.

First, the corporation would be liable to the outside investors in the aggregate amount of $6 million. Even at moderate commercial rates of 7%, the monthly interest on the $10 million debt load would be $40,000 from the time that the loans are made to the corporation. The monthly cost of a ten-year, self-amortizing loan would be $118,807 in principal and interest. It's unlikely that the corporation would have the kind of cash flow during the early years to handle loan payments of this size. One creative way to deal with this problem is to "stage" the loan disbursements by the outside investors so that money is loaned to the corporation as the need for more funds arises. For instance, each of the investors might agree to loan a total of $750,000 to the corporation, to be disbursed in $50,000 segments on particular future dates, or events, or upon demand by the corporation. This would reduce the debt obligations of the corporation until later in its development when the funds are actually needed, and cash flows are improving. However, this kind of staged-lending scheme brings its own set of problems. What happens if some of the outside investors are unable or unwilling to make additional loan payments? Although the corporation would have a right to sue the investors for the additional loan funds, the last thing the corporation would need at that point is a law suit.[24]

Another creative solution that reduces the burden of interest payments, while assuring the availability of funds, is to have the $750,000 in loan funds from each investor placed in highly secure investments, such as certificates of deposit, with

---

[24] Typically, where future contributions of this kind are anticipated, the promoters will have the investors sign promissory notes for the future amounts, naming the corporation as the payee, and making the note payable upon the circumstances intended to trigger the additional loans. This simplifies collection efforts by the corporation if the investor fails to honor the note. Nevertheless, if the investor is insolvent, has filed bankruptcy, or has no non-exempt assets, it will be nearly impossible to collect on the notes.

the corporation drawing funds as needed for asset acquisition and operational costs. As the funds are withdrawn from the investment source, the debt of the corporation to the investors increases. This approach has the advantages of protecting the principal of the investors, providing the investors with interest, and reducing the costs of financing to the corporation until the money is actually utilized by the corporation. The bottom line is that when a mix of debt and equity is utilized in this way, the promoters, accountants and lawyers will carefully draft the documents to make sure that the funding intentions can be realized with the least likelihood of problems or litigation.

There is a second problem with the plan to use a mix of common stock and debt in the TouchSearch, Inc. scenario. If each of the ten equity holders receives one-tenth of the shares of common stock, then each will have equal rights to vote for the board of directors and, ultimately, exercise control over the affairs of the corporation. The right of shareholders of common stock to vote in board elections is jealously guarded by corporations statutes and it may be extremely difficult to alter the traditional statutory rules regarding shareholder voting rights.[25] Unless some mechanism for control can be worked out, Alice and Andy will not be able to rely on maintaining control of the corporation's affairs.[26] This is an extremely difficult problem that mitigates against the use of common stock as a method for distributing equity interests in the corporation. It makes far more sense, in the TouchSearch, Inc. scenario, to use a mix of common and preferred stock.

c.   Preferred stock

Preferred stock is a class of stock other than the common stock of the corporation, with specific rights to distributions of money and, sometimes, control of the corporation, authorized and spelled out in the articles of incorporation.[27] In many ways, preferred stock is similar to debt. Creditors and preferred stockholders are favored over common stockholders as to distributions and liquidations. However, the rights of preferred stockholders to participate in voting is limited to those rights specifically granted to them in the articles. If the articles are silent, the control of the corporation is vested solely in the common stockholders. Preferred stock may also have a fixed redemption date and a fixed redemption price per share, which increases the similarity to debt.

The preferences or limits placed upon preferred stock are subject to many combinations of economic and voting rights. Usually, the preferred shareholders are vested with a right to be paid dividends, or distributions from sales or liquidations, that is superior to the financial entitlements of common shareholders.

---

[25] The right of common stockholders to elect directors is "the ideological underpinning upon which the legitimacy of directorial power rests." Blasius Indus., Inc. v. Atlas Corp., 564 A.2d 651, 660 (Del. Ch. 1988). The corporations codes of most states make it difficult to alter the mechanics of shareholder voting to interfere with the essential right of shareholders to vote for board members. See Chapter 7 for a discussion of methods for altering the control structure of corporations where there is only one class of common stock.

[26] Some states, such as California, allow for the use of "shareholder agreements" to vary the control and financial rights of the shareholders, notwithstanding the allocations of common stock. To have a valid shareholder agreement, California law requires creation of a special "statutory close corporation." See Cal. Corp. Code §§ 158, 186, 300(b), 300(e), 418(c)–(d), 421.

[27] Under some circumstances, the articles may provide for authorizing the issuance of preferred stock and provide that the terms and conditions may be determined by the board of directors.

In the case of dividends, a preference may be granted requiring the payment of a dividend to preferred shareholders in a set amount before dividends can be paid to holders of common shares. For example, "Holders of preferred shares shall receive preferred dividends of $20 per share per year, payable annually . . . The dividend shall be paid before any dividend is declared or distributed to holders of common stock." Assuming that there are lawful funds available to make a distribution, the dividend preference may be *mandatory* (the board must declare a dividend to preferred shareholders in the amounts and at the times stated in the articles) or *optional* (the board has the authority but not the obligation to declare a dividend). The payment of the dividend may be *cumulative* (if the dividend is not paid during any period, it carries over to the future) or *non-cumulative* (the dividend is lost if not paid out during the applicable time period).[28] Whatever preferential rights are granted to dividend distribution, the preferred shareholders must be paid before a dividend can be declared in favor of shareholders of common or other junior classes of stock. The amount of the preferred dividends, the timing of payments, the cumulative or non-cumulative nature of the dividends and the mandatory or discretionary nature of payments must be carefully dictated in the articles. Below are some examples to consider:

(i) Non-mandatory, cumulative dividend preference:

The Series A Preferred will carry an annual 7% cumulative dividend, compounded annually, payable: (i) in such amounts and at such times as the board of directors may determine in its sole discretion, so long as such distribution is lawful; or (ii) upon a liquidation of the corporation or redemption of the preferred stock.

(ii) Non-mandatory, non-cumulative dividend preference:

Non-cumulative dividends will be paid on the Series A Preferred in an amount equal to $20 per share when and if declared by the Board, so long as such distribution is lawful (the "preferred dividend"). During any fiscal year, no dividend shall be declared or paid on the Common Stock until the preferred dividend has been paid to holders of Series A Preferred or funds have been set aside for that purpose.

(iii) Mandatory, cumulative dividend preference:

The Series A Preferred will carry an annual 7% cumulative dividend, compounded annually, payable in annual installments on the first day of April, upon declaration by the board of directors, so long as such distribution is lawful. Unpaid dividends have preference over the Common Stock and no dividend, distribution or liquidation amount shall be paid to holders of common stock until all of the cumulative dividends have been paid.

Once the preferred dividends have been paid, the preferred stockholders may have the right to participate together with the common stockholders in *additional*

---

[28] If the preference is cumulative, the preferred shareholders are entitled to be paid the full amount of the dividend for each and every dividend period before junior equity holders are entitled to receive any dividends. The preferred stock provisions may fix the amount or percentage of the dividend, or make the dividend cumulative only if earned. If not cumulative and they are not declared in the specified dividend period, the right does not carry forward. If, in the unlikely event that the articles are silent, it is normally held that dividends on preferred shares are cumulative.

dividends being declared by the board, or they may be nonparticipating, with their dividends limited to the preferred amounts.

Liquidation preferences are usually granted along with dividend preferences. Upon a sale or liquidation of the corporate assets, and following the claims of creditors, the preferred stock may have a claim on the liquidation proceeds that must be satisfied before distributions can be made to junior classes of stock. This could be the amount of capital (or some portion thereof) that was contributed at the time of purchase. Following the satisfaction of the liquidation preference, in the absence of some provision to the contrary, the holders of preferred stock have the right to share the remaining liquidation proceeds with holders of common stock.[29] On the other hand, it is sometimes the case that the rights of the preferred shareholders to liquidation proceeds will be restricted to the preferential amounts they are entitled to receive, with no right to share with the common stock shareholders in additional value received upon liquidation. When these types of restrictive caps are placed on the return of capital to preferred shareholders, the nature of the participation interest starts to look more like debt than equity.

As far as liquidation preferences, consider the following possible provisions defining the liquidation preferences of preferred stockholders:

"Upon liquidation of the corporation's assets, the net proceeds shall be distributed as follows:"

(i) Non-participating preferred stock: First pay [one[30]] times the original purchase price of the preferred stock plus any accrued and unpaid dividends on each share of Series A Preferred Stock. The balance of any proceeds shall be distributed to holders of Common Stock.

or,

(ii) Fully participating preferred stock: First pay [one] times the original purchase price of the preferred stock plus any accrued and unpaid dividends on each share of Series A Preferred Stock. Thereafter, the Series A Preferred participates with the Common Stock on an equal per-share basis, in the same proportion that each share of Series A Preferred Stock bears to the total number of Common Stock and Preferred Shares.

or

(iii) Cap on preferred stock participation rights: First pay [one] times the original purchase price of the preferred stock [plus any accrued and unpaid dividends] on each share of Series A Preferred Stock. Thereafter, Series A Preferred participates with Common Stock on an equal per-share basis, in the same proportion that each share of Series A Preferred Stock bears to the total number of Common Stock and Preferred Shares, until the holders of Series A Preferred receive an aggregate of 1.5 times the original purchase price.

---

[29] Some formula will have to be devised for this post-liquidation-preference sharing of the remaining liquidation proceeds with the holders of common shares.

[30] A different fraction or multiple can be included here. For example, "three-quarters" or "one and one-half."

Preferred stock is often authorized with limited voting rights, although corporations statutes will provide some minimal protection, giving statutory voting rights to preferred stockholders with regard to amendments of the articles or other organic changes that have an affect on the value or rights of the preferred shares. It is also common for *contingent* voting rights to be granted in the articles, to become effective if there is some substantial and continuing failure of the corporation to meet the preferred dividend obligations. There is inherent flexibility in designing control rights for holders of preferred stock and rights may be granted to vote on a long list of corporate activities. Depending on the negotiating power of the proposed preferred shareholders, some classes of preferred stock may be given voting rights that assure the class that they can elect one or more members of the board of directors. Some examples of possible voting provisions in the articles might include:

> (i) *No voting rights except as provided by law or if default:* Unless otherwise provided by law, the preferred shareholders shall have no right to vote nor notice of shareholders meetings. In the event of a default[31] in the payment of preferred dividends as required by these Articles, the holders of preferred stock, as a class, shall have the right to elect such additional directors to the board as to constitute a majority of the members of the board . . .[32]

or

> (ii) *Enhanced rights to elect board member(s):* The Series A Preferred Stock shall as a class be entitled to elect four members of the Board (the "Series A Directors").

Preferred stock provisions will also often contain "protective provisions" that limit the ability of the common stockholders to alter the structure of the corporation in a way that adversely affects the preferred stockholders:

> So long as any shares of Series A Preferred are outstanding, the Corporation will not, without the written consent of the holders of at least 75% of the Corporation's Series A Preferred, either directly or by amendment, merger, consolidation, or otherwise: (i) liquidate, dissolve or wind up the affairs of the Corporation; (ii) amend, alter, or repeal any provision of the Certificate of Incorporation or Bylaws [in a manner adverse to the Series A Preferred]; (iii) create or authorize the creation of or issue any other security convertible into or exercisable for any equity security, having rights, preferences or privileges senior to or on parity with the Series A Preferred, or increase the authorized number of shares of Series A Preferred; (iv) purchase or redeem or pay any dividend on any capital stock prior to the Series A Preferred; (v) create or authorize the creation of any debt security if the Corporation's aggregate indebtedness would exceed $[_____], other than equipment leases or bank lines of credit; or (vi) increase or decrease the size of the Board of Directors.

---

[31] To constitute a default, the dividend distributions must be mandatory or, if permissive, the board has declared a dividend to common stockholders without first making the preferred dividend distribution to preferred shareholders.

[32] There will follow extensive provisions regarding the procedures to be followed.

Moneyed investors who are putting up large amounts of cash and are receiving preferred stock might want some strategy in place to extract some of their cash investment when the profits of the corporation are sufficient to sustain a redemption of their preferred shares by the corporation. If this type of mandatory redemption is contemplated, a "sinking fund" provision will be set up to facilitate redemption when the fiscal situation of corporate operations allows. Redemption may be keyed to particular dates, or other triggering events, and the redemption price may be fixed or set to some formula. With the addition of mandatory redemption provisions to the dividend and liquidation preferences, preferred stock takes on many of the characteristics of debt. Here's an example of a redemption provision:

> The Series A Preferred shall be redeemable from funds legally available for distribution at the option of holders of at least [_____]% of the Series A Preferred commencing any time after the fifth anniversary of the issuance of the shares, at a price equal to the original purchase price plus all accrued but unpaid dividends. Redemption shall occur in three equal annual portions. Upon a redemption request from the holders of the required percentage of the Series A Preferred, all Series A Preferred shares shall be redeemed.

EXERCISE 5-1

Could some mix of common and preferred stock be used to effectively meet the planning objectives of both the inside promoters and outside investors in our TouchSearch, Inc. scenario? The promoters, Alice and Andy, want to retain control over the affairs of the entity, while the investors are seeking some priority of return for the greater amounts of capital they are providing, as well as a one-tenth share in the value of the corporation. The eight outside investors are each contributing $1 million in cash, compared to only $250,000 in cash contributed by Alice and Andy. Perhaps common stock could be issued to Alice and Andy, and preferred shares issued to the outside investors, granting them optional (rather than mandatory) cumulative *dividend* rights to compensate them for the additional cash they are making available to the venture. By making the dividend payments discretionary, but cumulative, the board of the corporation is not forced make payments until such time as there is sufficient cash being generated to pay the accumulating dividends. The outside investors could also be granted *liquidation* rights that preserve the priority of the $750,000 of extra cash that they are each providing towards the business. The liquidation preference could be capped at $750,000 (after payment of accrued dividends). Following the preferential payments, the common stock holders (Alice and Andy) and the holders of preferred stock (the eight outside investors) could all participate equally in the distribution of the remaining liquidation proceeds. Will such a financing plan be successful in achieving the objectives of the promoters and investors?

There are a few considerations that inhibit the use of preferred stock and make the use of debt more attractive:

— With two classes of stock, there is no opportunity to make an S Corporation election and the corporation will be limited to C Corporation taxation status. The benefits of partnership-type pass through taxation will not be available.

— Unlike interest paid on loans, dividend payments are not deductible to the corporation and will be subject to double taxation. [33]
— Redemption of preferred stock may be treated as a dividend for tax purposes (rather than a return of capital) under certain circumstances if the taxpayer retains an interest in the corporation.[34]
— All of the rights and privileges of the preferred shareholders must be carefully spelled out in the articles of incorporation at the time of incorporation. We have discussed some of the primary considerations that would require drafting attention but there are more, such as the convertibility of the shares, the rights of the corporation to redeem the shares, or the right of preferred shareholders to compel redemption.
— Preferred stock is a security separate and apart from the common stock being issued by the corporation. This means that separate exemptions from registration must be found for both the common stock and the preferred stock.
— Under some circumstances, shareholders of a small business corporation under IRC § 1244 can take advantage of certain beneficial provisions allowing treatment of capital losses as ordinary losses in the event the business fails. However, § 1244 benefits are not available to holders of preferred shares.

d.   Debt financing from outsiders and investors

It is possible that some portion of the early financing of the corporation may be in the form of secured or unsecured debt. The most likely source of debt financing is from moneyed investors who will be purchasing some equity participation interest as well. As discussed previously, it may make sense for some moneyed investors to be issued a *mix* of debt and equity to give them an ownership interest, establish priority of repayment and avoid double taxation on dividends, as well as provide a mechanism for the return of a portion of their principal.

There are strong advantages to funding the corporation with debt from true, outside lenders, rather than loans from equity holders. Lenders are entitled only to the payment of interest and the return of principal. Although they have priority over stockholders, and must be paid on a fixed schedule, they are *not* normally entitled to participate in the upside gain in value of the corporation. This allows the stockholders to leverage their equity contribution and, often, significantly increase their return on investment.

Also, control of corporate affairs rests with the stockholders, not the lenders, so that debt is a way of raising capital without ceding direct control over the corporation. Nevertheless, sophisticated lenders who are making large, long-term loans, are going to carefully monitor the operations of the corporation during the life of the loan. These lenders may exercise *indirect* control over the affairs of the entity by conditioning the loan on a long list of operating and reporting requirements. In large loan transactions, the loan documents will undoubtedly

---

[33] There is also some possibility that redemption payments by the corporation might be treated as an ordinary dividend, taxable to the preferred stockholder, unless the redemption completely terminates the interests of the preferred stockholders in the corporation. *See* IRC §§ 301(c), 316(a). Compare this to the repayment of principal on true debt, which is treated as a non-taxable return of capital.
[34] IRC § 302.

impose requirements that, among other things: restrict the incurring of additional debt; restrict dividend distributions unless there is sufficient capital reserves to assure repayment of the loan; impose minimum sales requirements; prohibit asset transfers; prohibit adverse changes in the financial condition of the company; or prohibit changes in ownership or management of the corporation. A failure to comply with any of these requirements will likely result in an event of default under the loan documents, giving the lender the option to accelerate payment of the loan. Indeed, well-drafted default provisions in the loan documents may allow the lender to declare a default and accelerate the balance due in the event that the lender "deems itself to be insecure." The premature acceleration of the loan under any of these default provisions could devastate the operations of the business, particularly if the credit market is has changed and it is difficult to obtain new financing.

In other words, the lender may impose many conditions upon the operations of the corporation that, in a very real sense, gives the lender substantial rights of control over the affairs of the corporation.

i.   Availability of secured debt from outsiders

If there is valuable and unencumbered property that is available to serve as collateral for a secured loan, it may be possible to find an institutional lender willing to make a long-term commitment of debt. What property can serve as collateral for a secured loan? Most forms of tangible and intangible personal property, from equipment (such as machinery and vehicles) and goods (such as inventory) to intangibles such as accounts receivable, as well as intellectual property such as trademarks, patents and copyrights can all serve as collateral. However, there is a general unwillingness among commercial lenders to rely on intellectual property as a form of collateral until such time as the intellectual property has gained some independent value in the marketplace. Of course, real property and the improvements built on real property can serve as the basis for a mortgage lien to secure debt payment.

In reality, commercial secured lenders are risk averse and are relying on the collateral to satisfy their claims in the event that the entity is unable to make the loan payments when they are due. The availability of secured debt is going to be directly related to the proven economic value of the collateral and the existence of an equity cushion to protect the secured lender. The larger the equity cushion, the more likely the secured lender will loan funds to the entity. A bank loaning $8 million to a corporation that is purchasing a parcel of land worth $9 million *may* be willing to complete the loan since it will have an 90% loan-to-value ratio resulting in an equity cushion of $1 million in the event of a default. Assuming that the property has been properly appraised, in the event of a foreclosure, the property could be sold for a value close to $9 million, which would then be used to pay principal ($8 million), plus unpaid interest, plus the costs of foreclosure.[35] However, even such a seemingly large equity cushion might not justify a commercial loan for several reasons. No lender loans money with the expectation of foreclosing. The loan will only be made if the financial forecasts are sufficient to satisfy the lender

---

[35] The accruing interest may be extensive. At an interest rate of 8%, monthly interest would accrue on this loan at a rate of $53,333 per month. The typical real property foreclosure action takes six to nine months. If the borrower was already two or three months in default at the time that the bank begins the foreclosure process, the total arrearage over ten months would be more than one half million dollars.

that there will be adequate funds available to make the loan payments when due. In the case of a real estate venture, the financial forecasts must show rental income sufficient to meet operating expenses and spin off enough to make the mortgage payments as they come due. A 90% loan-to-value loan, with a $1 million equity cushion may be insufficient to cover all of the lender's costs in the event of a foreclosure. If we add the principal balance ($8 million) and nine months of unpaid interest ($480,000), plus the costs of foreclosure (let's say $20,000) then the property must be sold for at least $8.5 million. Foreclosures are forced sales and sometimes bring less than fair market value. It is also possible that the market may have depreciated during the time since the loan was made. For this reason, many risk-averse commercial lenders will require an 80% loan-to-value ratio in real estate transactions with young corporate entities.

Except for real estate investment ventures, secured loans may be difficult to obtain for the initial funding required to startup the corporation, these types of loans will be readily available on a piecemeal basis for acquisitions of specific items of equipment. Consider a newly formed corporation that is purchasing a photocopier or automobile for $35,000. For these types of equipment, sellers universally arrange for secured financing to enable purchasers to obtain title to the equipment. The ease and speed of repossession of such items, the ubiquitous availability of secured financing and the relatively low costs of these items, will normally facilitate the purchase of equipment and inventory. However, in the overall context of financing a multi-million startup business, this type of debt plays a minor role.

ii.   Availability of unsecured debt from outsiders

Unsecured lenders are relying on two factors in determining whether to make long-term loans to business entities: the reliable and repeated availability of cash flow from business operations sufficient to meet the underlying operating needs of the business *and* make the loan payments; and, the credit worthiness of the borrower.[36] Convincing a long term commercial lender that both of these factors can be satisfied is extremely difficult for a new business entity. A newly formed entity lacks an operating history that proves the reliability of the financial forecasts for net operating revenue that will be available to fund the loan payments. Equally problematical, the entity has no inherent credit worthiness since, by definition, the shareholders and employees of the corporation are not legally liable for the debts of the entity. For this reason, even if a long-term unsecured lender can be found and convinced of the *economic* viability of the financial forecasts, it is unlikely that the lender will make the loan without the execution of personal guarantees by shareholders who have established highly rated credit histories. This can create serious concerns for stockholders who are risk-averse and unwilling to put their personal wealth at risk by guaranteeing the loan to the corporation.

Keep in mind that no rational, commercial lender will be willing to make loans to the entity without a strong cushion of equity invested by the owners. A large contribution of equity by the investors insures that, when combined manageable

---

[36] Once the business is operating and has regular cash flow, it may be possible to obtain short term lines of credit to handle acquisition of inventory or short term operations. Even so, the lender may require some collateral or guarantees before making short term, smaller loans to newly formed corporations.

debt levels, the business can operate on a sound basis and has the financial resiliency to weather periods of adversity. Large equity contributions also provides motivation for the owners to remain committed to the business. The greater the potential loss to the owners, the more motivated they will be to make the business successful.

iii.   Availability of unsecured debt from insiders

Unfortunately for many newly formed corporations, it is unlikely that *long-term* debt financing will be available from commercial lenders, such as banks, to supply the capital necessary to implement, operate and grow the business. Until the entity has been in business for a few years, it lacks the kind of financial records and operating history that a prudent commercial lender relies on to assure that there is a stream of income sufficient to make the loan payments.

On the other hand, it is quite common for *capital investors* in the corporation to also loan the corporation funds as part of the financing plan. As discussed earlier, by loaning money to the corporation, rather than contributing capital in exchange for equity shares, the lender-investors can assure a priority of payment on the portion of the cash that they contribute as debt. In addition, there may be tax advantages in the case of a C corporation since interest payments will escape double taxation and repayments of principal won't usually be taxed as capital gains — if the debt is structured as true commercial debt and paid by the corporation according to the terms of the notes.

EXERCISE 5-2

Refer to the TouchSearch, Inc. scenario above. Could some mix of common stock and loans from investors be used to effectively meet the planning objectives of both the inside promoters and outside investors in the TouchSearch, Inc. scenario? The promoters, Alice and Andy want to retain control over the affairs of the entity, while the investors are seeking some priority of return for the greater amounts of capital they are providing, as well as a one-tenth share in the value of the corporation. The eight outside investors are each contributing $1 million in cash, compared to only $250,000 in cash contributed by Alice and Andy but want some control over major decisions that might affect the value of their interests. Can you design a financing plan that would achieve the objectives of the promoters and investors?

iv.   Recharacterization of debt as equity

There are times that the contributors to the capitalization of a business entity may seek to divide their contributions between "equity" and "debt" for purposes of achieving control and financial objectives. However, this division may be ignored by the courts with respect to the relationship of the entity to outside creditors. The classic doctrine of "equitable subordination" may be used to recharacterize the debt as equity.[37]

---

[37] Pepper v. Litton, 308 U.S. 295 (1939).

IN RE COLD HARBOR ASSOCS., L.P.
United States Bankruptcy Court, Eastern District of Virginia
204 B.R. 904 (1997)

[Authors' Note: This bankruptcy case involved a limited partnership debtor. The bankruptcy court was faced with the question of counting the number of unsecured creditors of the limited partnership in order to make a determination whether an involuntary petition under Bankruptcy Code § 303(b) was properly filed. Under that section, if there are more than twelve unsecured creditors of the debtor, there must be at least three creditors who sign the involuntary petition. If there are less than twelve unsecured creditors, only one creditor need join in the petition. The single creditor that filed the involuntary petition was ALI, Inc. ("ALI"). The bankruptcy petition filed by ALI would be valid *if* there were fewer than twelve other unsecured creditors of the debtor. In fact, there were only a few other unsecured creditors — unless the court included the limited partners themselves, who had each made part of their capital contributions in the form of loans to the entity. Technically, the limited partners were unsecured creditors and, if included in the count, the total number of unsecured creditors would exceed twelve, invalidating the petition filed by ALI. The bankruptcy court was squarely faced with determining whether or not loans made by limited partners were debt or equity. The relevant portion of the bankruptcy court's opinion follows.]

The Promissory Notes

Cold Harbor introduced evidence which it argued demonstrated the existence of several claims against itself in the form of promissory notes held by its own limited partners. At the outset, the Court notes that none of the parties holding these purported promissory notes would be considered insiders under 11 U.S.C. § 101(C), so whether this proffered obligation actually does represent a claim against the debtor will depend upon whether the noted created a debt or equity relationship. . . .

Each note is virtually identical in form with the only variations being the identity of the note holder and the amount owed on each note. The terms of the notes are as follows:

FOR VALUE RECEIVED the undersigned promises to pay to the order of Matilda J. Smithers [the note holder], ON DEMAND, the sum of Three Thousand Five Hundred Eighty & 08/100 Dollars ($3,580.08) plus interest at the rate of Six Percent (6%) per annum, beginning August 1, 1992, said interest to compound annually if not paid.

If any default be made in the performance of any provision of this contract between the parties, the entire unpaid principal sum and accrued interest shall at once become due and payable without notice at the option of the holder thereof. Failure to exercise this option upon any default shall not constitute or be construed as a waiver of the right to exercise the said option in the event of any subsequent default.

This note is given without offset, for value received, and the maker or makers, endorser or endorsers, hereby waive protest, presentation, demand and notice of extension as to this obligation, and in the event of default the maker further agrees to pay all expenses incurred in collection and/or reducing to judgement the above obligation, including a reasonable attorney's fee.

The notes are dated August 12th, 1992, but were not actually drawn up and delivered to the note holders until March 30th, 1993 or later. Cold Harbor borrowed a total of approximately $63,000 from its partners, who each contributed an amount directly in proportion to his ownership interest in the partnership. The money collected was used to pay off an outstanding mortgage held by Crestar Bank which was secured by the unimproved properties of Cold Harbor.

ALI argues that this Court should recharacterize this group of transactions, evidenced by the promissory notes and hold the purported loans to have been contributions to equity. ALI claims that the nature of these notes and the circumstances surrounding their issuance more properly display the earmarks of an equity exchange between a partner and partnership rather than a debt exchange between a creditor and debtor. This Court agrees with ALI and as explained hereafter holds that none of the alleged debts purportedly evidenced by the promissory notes qualify as holders of claims for the purposes of § 303(b).

In connection with this issue, ALI has raised the doctrine of equitable subordination to buttress its claim that the alleged loans evidenced by the promissory notes are in fact equity. Under 11 U.S.C. § 510(c)(1) the Bankruptcy Court may "subordinate for purposes of distribution all or part of an allowed claim to all or part of another allowed claim or all or part of an allowed interest to all or part of another allowed interest. . . . " As part of this argument, ALI has pointed to cases in which this doctrine has been used to treat debts as equity and subordinate the claims to those of other creditors. Herzog v. Leighton Holdings, Ltd. (In re Kids Creek Partners, L.P.), 200 Bankr. 996 (Bankr. N.D. Ill. 1996); Tennessee Valley Steel Corp. v. B.T. Commercial Corp. (In re Tennessee Valley Steel Corp.), 186 Bankr. 919 (Bankr. E.D. Tenn. 1995). Cold Harbor has vigorously argued that the circumstances of the instant case does not justify equitable subordination, a remedy which they assert is to be reserved only for unusual and extraordinary circumstances. Ford v. Feldman M.D., P.A. (In re Florida Trading Co.), 177 Bankr. 374 (Bankr. M.D. Fla. 1994). Specifically, the debtor claims that equitable subordination requires some form of inequitable conduct on the part of the claim holder to justify recasting their valid debt as equity. *See e.g.* In re Fett Roofing and Sheet Metal Co., Inc., 438 F. Supp. 726 (E.D. Va. 1977)(corporation mere instrumentality or alter ego of lender), In re ASI Reactivation Inc., 934 F.2d 1315 (4th Cir. 1991)(equitable subordination inappropriate when no evidence of misconduct by principal of debtor). However, the Supreme Court has not reached a conclusion as to whether creditor misconduct is or is not required to support equitable subordination. United States v. Noland, 116 S. Ct. 1524, 134 L. Ed. 2d 748 (1996). In addition, the debtor argues that equitably subordinating the claims of the promissory note holders would be an empty act in the present circumstances. Cold Harbor claims that even if the debts were equitably subordinated, the note holders would still hold valid claims, because all equitable subordination does is reorder creditor priority. *Tennessee Valley Steel*, 186 Bankr. at 923; 80 Nassau Associates v. Crossland Federal Savings Bank (In re 80 Nassau Associates), 169 Bankr. 832 (Bankr. S.D.N.Y. 1994); Ford v. Feldman, M.D., P.A. (In re Florida Trading Co.), 177 Bankr. 374 (Bankr. M.D. Fla. 1994). Although the debtor is correct that equitable subordination would not eliminate the claims from consideration, this Court believes the debtor has misconceived ALI's assertion. ALI is not claiming that the debts at issue should be equitably subordinated, instead ALI asserts that the claims of the note holders were actually equity contributions *ab initio*. Rather than recharacterizing the exchange from debt to equity, or subordinating the claim for some reason, the question before this Court is whether the transaction created a debt or equity relationship from the outset.

This Court is not required to accept the label of "debt" or "equity" placed by the debtor upon a particular transaction, but must inquire into the actual nature of a transaction to determine how best to characterize it. Celotex Corporation v. Hillsborough Holdings Corporation (In re Hillsborough Holdings Corporation), 176 Bankr. 223 (M.D. Fla. 1994). In determining from the evidence available to it that a transaction called a loan by the debtor is actually more properly called a contribution to equity, this Court may recharacterize the alleged loan to reflect the true nature of the transaction. Matter of Herby's Foods, Inc., 2 F.3d 128 (5th Cir. 1993); Herzog v. Leighton Holdings, Ltd., 200 Bankr. 996 (Bkrtcy. E.D. Ill. 1996); Tennessee Valley Steel Corporation v. B.T. Commercial Corporation (In re Tennessee Valley Steel Corporation), 186 Bankr. 919 (Bkrtcy. E.D. Tenn. 1995). This power stems from the authority vested in the Bankruptcy Court to use its equitable powers to test the validity of debts. Pepper v. Litton, 308 U.S. 295, 60 S. Ct. 238, 84 L. Ed. 281 (1939).

The primary factor this Court is to consider when evaluating whether funds advanced by a shareholder are the result of an equity contribution or a loan is whether the transaction bears the earmarks of an arm's length negotiation. Pepper v. Litton, 308 U.S. 295, 60 S. Ct. 238, 84 L. Ed. 281 (1939); Roth Steel Tube Co. v. Commissioner of Internal Revenue, 800 F.2d 625 (6th Cir. 1986). The more such an exchange appears to reflect the characteristics of such an arm's length negotiation, the more likely such a transaction is to be treated as debt. To aid in analyzing such transactions, Courts have identified several factors which help identify the distinctions between a loan and an equity contribution. The list of factors is not exclusive, and no one factor is predominant, nor are the factors to be given rigidly equal weight. Instead, this Court is to apply these factors to the particular case at hand keeping in mind the specific circumstances surrounding the present factual situation. One Court listed the factors to be considered as including:

(1) the names given to the certificates evidencing the indebtedness;
(2) the presence or absence of a fixed maturity date;
(3) the source of payments;
(4) the right to enforce payment of principal and interest;
(5) participation in management flowing as a result;
(6) the status of the contribution in relation to regular corporate creditors;
(7) the intent of the parties;
(8) 'thin' or inadequate capitalization;
(9) identity of interest between creditor and stockholder;
(10) source of interest payments;
(11) the ability of the corporation to obtain loans from outside lending institutions;
(12) the extent to which the advance was used to acquire capital assets; and
(13) the failure of the debtor to repay on the due date or to seek postponement.

Celotex Corporation v. Hillsborough Holdings Corporation (In re Hillsborough Holdings Corporation), 176 Bankr. 223, 248 (M.D. Fla. 1994); *See also* In re Lane,

742 F.2d 1311 (11th Cir. 1984); Estate of Mixon v. United States, 464 F.2d 394 (5th Cir. 1972). The Sixth Circuit has listed a slightly different, but in many respects very similar catalogue of factors to consider when evaluating whether the transaction was made at arm's length. Just as the *Celotex* Court did, the Sixth Circuit highlighted factors including identity of interest between creditor and stockholder, adequacy or inadequacy of capitalization, the source of repayments, the name given instruments evidencing indebtedness, presence or absence of fixed maturity date and schedule of payments, presence or absence of a fixed rate of interest and interest payments, inability to obtain outside financing, subordination of advances, presence or absence of a sinking fund, and the extent to which the advances were used to acquire capital assets. Additionally, the Sixth Circuit found the presence or absence of security for the purported loan to be an important factor which should be considered. Roth Steel Tube Company v. Commissioner of Internal Revenue, 800 F.2d 625, 630–32 (6th Cir. 1986). A reading of the two lists of factors together highlights a few main themes that demarcate the distinction between loans and equity contributions in these situations. A critical group of factors concern the formality of the alleged loan agreement. The more specific and complete the parties are in identifying and codifying the terms of the alleged loan agreement, the more like a loan the transaction appears. By contrast, if the terms of such an agreement are vague and non-specific, such a transaction appears more like a shareholder contributing capital to keep his investment afloat. A second important group of factors relate to the financial situation of the corporation at the time the purported loan is made. If investing in the corporation appears to have been especially risky (e.g. it was thinly capitalized), or the source of funds to repay the loan is not made clear, then the transaction has more of the earmarks of an equity contribution. An additional group of factor in this category is the relationship between the limited partners equity ownership and the parties' participating in the making of the loan, reflected by the concern over whether there is identity between the equity holders and the alleged lenders, and whether control of the corporation is dependent upon the loan in question.

Applying these factors to Cold Harbor's shareholders/promissory note holders, this Court finds that the notes in question most properly reflect an equity contribution rather than a loan. One of these factors is clearly inapplicable to the present case: the failure of the debtor to repay on the due date or seek postponement. Simply put, because the notes are demand notes with no defined due date, and no demand appears to have been made, there is simply no evidence one way or another that would aid this Court in determining the nature of the transactions. The Court will now identify and analyze those factors which led to this determination, beginning with those factors which weigh in favor of finding the transaction in question to have been a loan.

1. *The names given to the certificates evidencing the indebtedness, and the intent of the parties.* The analysis for these two factors is generally similar, and the Court will deal with them together. First, the notes given by Cold Harbor to their shareholders are quite clearly marked as "Promissory Notes". Labeling the documents in this way is some evidence that the transaction was in fact a loan. Labeling the documents in this manner also sheds light on the intent of the parties, demonstrating that they believed that they were lending money to the partnership. The debtor also introduced deposition evidence that the note holders thought they had made a loan. These pieces of evidence cannot be regarded as conclusive, or even particularly strong evidence, as placing significant weight on the label given to the

transaction by the parties would have the effect of rendering moot much of the inquiry into the nature of the transaction. This Court is also very concerned with the approximately seven month delay between the transfers and the drawing and delivery of the notes, which raises doubts in this Court's mind as to whether the parties determined what they wanted to call the transaction until well after the actual exchange. The lack of a promissory note, in conjunction with a lack of other formalities, may indicate that advances are equities. Estate of Mixon v. United States, 464 F.2d 394, 403 (5th Cir. 1972). Although there are promissory notes in the present case, the extreme delay in delivery indicates a troubling lack of formalities. The delay also casts doubt upon the actual intent of the parties at the time of the transaction, and whether the deposition testimony given nearly four years after the transactions took place accurately represents the parties' intent when the transactions took place. Therefore, while the name given to the documents by the parties does weigh in favor of holding the transactions to be loans, and there is some evidence that the parties' intended the advances to be loans, the extended delay between the transactions and the delivery of the notes creates doubt in the Court's mind as to whether the notes do in fact reflect the parties' understanding. Given this doubt, the Court finds that the weight which should be given to this factor is limited due to this delay and other factors that follow.

2. *The right to enforce payment of principal or interest.* Unlike equity holders, debt holders have the right to enforce repayment under the terms of their note. The notes in question are styled as demand notes, payable to the holder upon his request. In addition, the note holders are entitled to attorney's fees in the event of a default on Cold Harbor's part. The note holders' right to enforce payment, and extract a penalty from Cold Harbor in the event of a failure on its part constitutes evidence weighing in favor of considering the advances to be loans rather than equity.

3. *Participation in management flowing as a result.* One characteristic of equity is the right to participate in ownership decision making. If the shareholder obtains additional rights to control the actions of the corporation as a result of lending it money, then the transaction will be viewed as having the characteristics of equity. In this case, however, there has been no evidence that the shareholders gained additional ownership rights based upon the loan, or that their degree of control was dependent upon their advancing these funds. On the other hand, this state of affairs stems primarily from the fact that the loan was made pursuant to a *pro rata* contribution arrangement based upon the lenders' original equity ownership. Given that all of the original equity holders contributed in amounts relatively equal to their original capital investment, it is not surprising that the nature of the parties' ownership interests did not change. For this reason, this Court attaches little weight to this factor.

4. *"Thin" or inadequate capitalization.* There was no evidence presented that would relate to this factor. Generally this factor is relevant when a corporation is started by the shareholders with a minimal amount of capital who then make a large loan of money to the newly formed corporation, and thus the relevant time for determining whether capitalization was adequate is generally at the corporation's creation. *See e.g. Hillsborough* 176 Bankr. at 249. However, given the long duration between the inception of the partnership and the loan made in this case, this factor is not particularly relevant to the issue at hand. In the absence of contrary proof, this Court assumes that Cold Harbor was adequately capitalized when it was

formed, and therefore, to the extent that it might be relevant, this factor would weigh in favor of holding the transactions more likely to have been loans.

These four factors tend to show that the advances from the limited partners to Cold Harbor exhibited some of the formalities associated with a loan. The purpose of the inquiry into the nature of the transaction is to determine if it is one which could have been made at arm's length. This Court finds that the following factors establish that the advances made by Cold Harbor's shareholders should be considered equity contributions, and not loans. For these reasons, the promissory notes in question do not count for § 303(b) purposes.

1. *The presence or absence of a fixed maturity date, a schedule of interest payments, a sinking fund.* Although Court's have treated these as separate factors in their analysis, they are significantly related. The basic question asked when addressing these factors is: how definite were the plans for repayment. If the terms are vague and nonspecific, then the advance takes on the appearance of equity as it is assumed that a non-shareholder bargaining at arm's length would demand specifics and formalities to protect their investment. First, the absence of a fixed maturity date, indicates that advances are capital contributions and not loans. *Roth Steel Tube*, 800 F.2d at 631; Lane v. United States, 742 F.2d 1311 (11th Cir. 1984). The notes given by Cold Harbor have no maturity date, simply being termed demand notes, and absence of scheduled periodic interest payments also demonstrates that an advance is capital and not a loan. *Roth Steel Tube*, 800 F.2d at 631; Stinnett's Pontiac Service, Inc. v. Commissioner, 730 F.2d 634 (11th Cir. 1984). Although there is a defined rate of interest on the face of the notes, no provisions have been made for the payment of interest payments prior to a demand for repayment in full by a shareholder. An open ended repayment term such as this tends to demonstrate that the advances in question bear the earmarks of an equity contribution. By the terms of the notes, they were to pay 6% interest per annum until they were redeemed by the note holders. This Court takes judicial notice that the Prime Rate on August 12, 1992 when the notes were originated, was also 6%. *Money Rates*, The Wall St. J., August 12, 1992 at C19. This Court finds implausible that a lender engaging in an arm's length negotiation would advance money at the Prime Rate on an unsecured demand note to an entity that had defaulted on an obligation of approximately $1,475,000 just four months before. Finally, there is no evidence that the debtor ever even considered establishing a sinking fund to provide for the repayment of the advances. Failure to establish a sinking fund for repayment is evidence that advances are capital contributions rather than loans. *Roth Steel Tube*, 800 F.2d at 632. This Court finds that formalities evidencing a method of repayment to either be nonexistent, or so vague as to be virtually nonexistent. An advance made for such little return on a risky investment with so little regard for the method of repayment strongly suggests that the transaction was not made on an arm's length basis, and does not bear the earmarks of a loan.

2. *The extent to which the advance was used to acquire capital assets.* Use of advances to meet the daily needs of an organization is indicative of a loan and not an equity contribution. *Roth Steel Tube*, 800 F.2d at 632. Conversely, the use of advances to acquire capital assets may indicate that the advances had the nature of a capital contribution. *In re Hillsborough*, 176 Bankr. at 249. The testimony at the factual hearing established that the funds advanced in this case were used to pay off a loan from Crestar bank which had been secured by the unimproved properties adjacent to the shopping center building. Therefore, the funds were used to

purchase a capital asset by eliminating a lien on real estate, and this factor further convinces this Court that the advances were in fact equity contributions.

3. *Presence or absence of security.* Although security was available in the form of the unimproved parking lot properties, the notes purport to be a wholly unsecured loan from the limited partners. Lack of security for a transaction is considered to be a significant indicator that an advance is not a loan. *Roth Steel Tube*, 800 F.2d at 631. This Court considers the complete lack of security to be strong evidence that the transaction was not made at arm's length, and that the advances were capital contributions instead of loans.

4. *Inability to obtain outside financing.* The question to be asked here is whether a reasonable outside creditor would have made a loan to the debtor on similar terms. *Roth Steel Tube*, 800 F.2d at 631. This Court does not hesitate to hold that the answer to this question is an unequivocal "no". There was no security given, the loan repayment schedule was nonexistent, and the notes were not delivered for many months after the transaction, just to name a few of the circumstances that would dissuade an outsider from doing business in the same manner as the partners have done. In addition, the sloppiness of drafting the notes, such as the presence of an acceleration clause on a demand note, demonstrates a lack of formality that no outside creditor would accept. These provisions, or lack thereof, in the transaction convince this Court that the advances were not made as a result of arm's length bargaining, and hence cannot be considered loans.

5. *Identity of interest between creditor and stockholder.* The final factor to be considered is the relationship between those owning equity and making the advance. This Court considers this to be the most critical factor in its determination due to the exact identity between the two groups. The purported loan was made on a *pro rata* basis, with each partner contributing a percentage of the entire advance exactly equal to his or her equity interest in the partnership. "If advances are made by stockholders in proportion to their respective stock ownership, an equity contribution is indicated . . . . A sharply disproportionate ratio between a stockholder's percentage interest in stock and debt is, however, strongly indicative that the debt is bona fide." *Roth Steel Tube*, 800 F.2d at 630 (quoting Estate of Mixon, 464 F.2d at 409). Where there is an exact correlation between the ownership interest of the equity holders and their proportionate share of the alleged loan, this Court believes this evidence standing alone is almost so overwhelming that the advance was in fact a capital contribution to equity and not a loan that coupling this with the complete lack of formality evidenced by the records of the transaction this Court is convinced that holding the advances to be equity is correct.

Weighing the various factors, this Court finds that the evidence is predominantly in favor of treating the advances as equity. Although the transactions did have some of the characteristics of a debt transaction, the factors that would favor that conclusion are generally weak. On the other hand, the factors that point to the conclusion that the notes represent an equity investment by the limited partners are quite strong. In light of these determinations, this Court holds that the promissory notes held by the limited partners do not represent a claim against Cold Harbor for the purposes of § 303(b).

Conclusion

This Court holds that Cold Harbor had six creditors for § 303(b) purposes . . .

NOTES AND QUESTIONS

1. Equitable Subordination: There were two distinct issues referred to in *Cold Harbor*. First, was the issue of equitable subordination. Equitable subordination is a doctrine where the courts reclassify the debt obligations owed to insiders as equity when those insiders are competing with true outside creditors who were relying on the capitalization of the corporation as a cushion for their claims.

In other words, investors like those in our TouchSearch, Inc. scenario can't "bootstrap" themselves into a position that diminishes the priority of the outside creditors of the corporation. Where the loans from equity holders are essentially in the nature of a capital investment, the courts will inevitably require that the investor-debt be subordinated so that the natural order of risk in limited liability entities is preserved. The true creditors of the entity should stand on the shoulders of the equity investors and be fully repaid before the owners of the entity receive payment, regardless of the technical classification of their contributions as "debt" or "equity."

2. Recharacterization of Debt as Equity: The court in *Cold Harbor* stated: "ALI is not claiming that the debts at issue should be equitably subordinated, instead ALI asserts that the claims of the note holders were actually equity contributions *ab initio*. Rather than recharacterizing the exchange from debt to equity, or subordinating the claim for some reason, the question before this Court is whether the transaction created a debt or equity relationship from the outset. This Court is not required to accept the label of "debt" or "equity" placed by the debtor upon a particular transaction, but must inquire into the actual nature of a transaction to determine how best to characterize it."

The court found that the notes in *Cold Harbor* were clearly "equity" and not debt. Therefore, there was no need to apply the equitable subordination doctrine. Can you see what convinced the court that the scheme in *Cold Harbor* was merely a mechanism for creating a priority of distribution for the "lenders" rather than any realistic resemblance to debt? To make such a determination, the court set forth a nonexclusive list of factors. Can you see the relevance of each of the factors?

(1)   the names given to the certificates evidencing the indebtedness;
(2)   the presence or absence of a fixed maturity date;
(3)   the source of payments;
(4)   the right to enforce payment of principal and interest;
(5)   participation in management flowing as a result;
(6)   the status of the contribution in relation to regular corporate creditors;
(7)   the intent of the parties;
(8)   'thin' or inadequate capitalization;
(9)   identity of interest between creditor and stockholder;
(10) source of interest payments;
(11) the ability of the corporation to obtain loans from outside lending institutions;
(12) the extent to which the advance was used to acquire capital assets; and
(13) the failure of the debtor to repay on the due date or to seek postponement.

e.   The Problem of Future Capital Contributions

Regardless of the initial mix of equity and debt that is raised to fund the initial operations of a newly formed corporation, the early promoters and investors must deal with the possible need to raise additional capital in the future. There may come a time in the life of the corporation where additional funds are needed to keep the business afloat during difficult periods. Many business startups underestimate the amount of funds necessary to nurture the business to the point of self sustenance and profit. At the earliest stages of drafting the formation documents, the parties must decide whether or not early investors will have the *obligation* or *option* to contribute additional capital if certain triggering events occur. From the perspective of early investors, this raises two primary concerns.

First, in the case of *obligations* to contribute additional capital, many investors may be concerned about "throwing good money after bad" and want to minimize any obligation to dig into their pockets to make future contributions. In addition, when the time arrives for additional mandatory contributions, some investors may lack the kind of deep-pocket financial assets to fund additional contributions. If there *is* going to be some kind of mandatory obligation to make future capital contributions, all investors will be concerned about the events that trigger the call for additional capital, the limits on the timing and amounts of any capital call, and the procedural mechanisms for dealing with failures by some investors to make the mandatory capital call.

Second, in the case of either (i) *options* granted to early investors to purchase additional equity interests; or, (ii) the ability of the corporation to sell stock to new owners, investors will be concerned with the problems of dilution of voting control and economic interests. This is a special problem in the case of corporations since the rights to participate in control, and economic distributions, are based purely on the proportions of stock ownership.

i.   Preemptive rights

In the context of corporations, option rights are granted in the form of preemptive rights in the articles, that confer upon shareholders the right, but not the obligation, to share *pro rata* in future issuances of stock by the corporation. In this way, each existing shareholder is given the opportunity to participate in future capital calls — and increase the proportional degree of stock ownership if not all existing shareholders elect to purchase additional stock. For some shareholders, this may create a specter of dilution if they don't have the resources, or feel the purchase is ill-advised. If the preemptive rights are exercised by some but not all of the shareholders, the balance of voting power may change dramatically and the proportional share of dividends and liquidation proceeds may be altered as well.

This can be a particularly difficult problem where the new shares are being issued for less than the value of existing shares. Imagine a corporation with three shareholders, Art, Barb and Clem, each holding 100 shares of stock worth $1,000 per share (assume the value of the corporation is $300,000). All three shareholders are board members. The corporation is in need of $30,000 in additional capital to fund the purchase of some essential materials for the business and, on October 1st, by a two-to-one vote (Art and Barb v. Clem), the board authorizes the issuance of an additional 300 shares at a price of $100 per share. Clem declines to purchase the 100 shares he is entitled to purchase under the preemptive provisions in the articles.[38] Art and Barb each purchase 150 shares at a cost of $15,000 each. Following the issuance, Art and Barb will each own 250 shares, while Clem continues to hold 100 shares. This has created a serious control and financial dilution for Clem, with Art and Bev together owning 5/6ths of the outstanding shares of stock of the corporation. In addition to a shift in voting control, a significant wealth transfer has occurred with respect to dividend and liquidations distributions. It's easy to see if we consider the following table (pay close attention to the impact on Clem's interest in Column D):

Dilution & Wealth Transfer of Clem's Interest

	Art	Barb	Clem	Total
1. Prior to issuance of 300 shares on October 1: Value of Corporation is $300,000				
Number of Shares	100	100	100	
% Distribution if Liquidation	33.33 %	33.33 %	33.33 %	
Cash on Liquidation	$100,000	$100,000	$100,000	$300,000
2. 300 shares sold @ $100 per share ($30,000). Value of corporation rises to $330,000				
Number of Shares	250	250	100	
% Distribution if Liquidation	42%	42%	16%	
Cash on Liquidation	$138,600	$138,600	$52,800	$330,000
Value transfer from Clem to Art and Bev	$23,600[39]	$23,600	($47,200)	

Note that Clem has lost $47,200 as a result of the issuance of additional shares to Art and Barb. The wealth transfer is primarily a result of the fixing of the price for the shares at a value less than outstanding shares. Nevertheless, in the absence of some kind of fraudulent scheme, the decision of the board of directors as to the value to place on the shares is conclusive. Clem was equally entitled to exercise his preemptive rights and participate on a pro rata basis with Art and Barb in the sale of the shares at the price set by the board. A wealth transfer like this will *always* occur in the case of preemptive rights any time that two conditions occur: (i) the stock is issued for a value less than the per-share value of outstanding shares; and (ii) not all of the existing shareholders exercise their rights to purchase all of the shares they are entitled to purchase.

Where the new shares are being issued for a value close to that of the outstanding shares, the problem of dilution of *financial rights* is reduced but not eliminated. The number of outstanding shares will double from 300 to 600 shares in our hypothetical, regardless of the price. To the extent that Clem does not participate in the purchase of the newly issued shares and holds only 100 shares, his percentage of the corporation's wealth will diminish from one-third to one-sixth. Even if the overall value of the corporation is initially enhanced, Clem's right to *future* distributions has been seriously diluted. Of course, regardless of economic rearrangements of rights caused by the issuance of new shares to Art and Barb, the

---

[38] Clem may lack the funds to make the purchase or decide it is unwise. If Clem lacks the funds, he could, theoretically, sell or pledge the shares to raise the money to make the purchase. However, in reality, the illiquidity of shares of closely held corporations makes this extremely difficult.

[39] Don't forget that Art and Barb laid out $15,000 each for their additional shares. So the total amount of wealth transfer to each excludes the additional cost of acquiring their additional shares.

problem of dilution of *voting rights* remains a serious issue.

It is the role of the lawyers in drafting the preemptive rights provisions to make sure that these concerns are accommodated. What types of provisions might you insert to assure the least possible potential for adverse consequences to stockholders who elect not to exercise their preemptive rights?

Keep in mind the fact that the more protections that are built in to the preemptive rights provisions, the greater the problems that arise for issuing shares to *new* investors. Before the shares can be issued to a new investor, they must first be offered to all shareholders holding preemptive rights on the terms and conditions that have been drafted. This will require that the procedures and time periods for responses set forth in the preemptive rights provisions must be complied with. This might take months depending on the time periods involved, creating a disincentive for new investors to provide an infusion of funds. In addition, the new investor(s) might not be willing to accept less than all of the newly issued shares, so that if some existing shareholders exercise their preemptive rights, the deal might fall though. Finally, if there are some type of restrictions for *pricing* of the shares, the board may be at a loss to comply with those pricing provisions in making the offer to a new investor under then current market conditions and based on the actual capital needs of the corporation.

ii.   New equity participants

The same voting and financial dilution issues exist with regard to issuing shares of stock to *new* investors. Once again, the value received in exchange for the stock will have an impact on whether or not a wealth transfer occurs at the time of the sale of the stock — in either direction. A lower value for the stock will result in an immediate wealth transfer from the existing stockholders to the new investor(s), while a higher value will result in the reverse, enhancing the value of the stock held by existing shareholders. Regardless of the presence of an initial wealth transfer, the issuance of substantial amounts of voting stock will: (i) alter the balance of control, and (ii) the issuance of any type of stock, common or preferred, will dilute the future dividend and liquidation distribution rights of the existing shareholders. One "solution" to this problem we've already discussed — give preemptive rights to the existing shareholders, which comes with its own set of concerns.

This is a difficult issue that should be carefully evaluated by the early participants in the venture. When the parties are initially planning the number of shares to be authorized in the articles, are they contemplating that some will remain unissued and held in reserve to raise capital in the future? Unless this is the case, the articles will have to be altered at some time in the future to authorize the issuance of additional shares of common or preferred stock, requiring action by the board of directors and the shareholders. If during that future crunch period, there is a substantial minority of shareholders in opposition to amending the articles, it may be impossible to do so. However, if the shares have previously been authorized in the original articles, they can be issued upon normal board resolution, unless the articles or bylaws provide otherwise. Keep in mind that in non-public corporations, the board of directors will consist of shareholders with substantial existing ownership interests. It's unlikely that a board acting in good faith would issue previously authorized shares to a *new* investor unless the cash was needed for the maintenance or growth of the corporation.

iii.   Loans from current equity holders

When substantial additional funds are needed in the future, a possible course of action is to borrow the money from one or more existing, deep-pocket equity holders. As lenders, they will be entitled to priority over existing equity holders. If substantial funds are needed, the equity holders who are loaning the money may insist on collateral to secure the loans, particularly if the money is being used to sustain a company that has run out of money or is having cash flow problems. Few equity holders are willing to throw extra money at a struggling business without assurances that the funds they contribute are likely to be repaid. Unless *all* equity holders are willing to loan money to the enterprise in proportion to their ownership interests, an equity holder who loans money is taking a substantially greater risk. Why would an equity holder do that? Perhaps the equity holder might be trying to keep the business alive, believing that a continuation of the business will, eventually, result in profitability, so that he or she won't lose the underlying equity investment. If this is true, a savvy lender would insist on some type of increased *equity* interest as well. After all, the "white knight" lender is taking a greater risk and deserves some greater reward beyond the mere repayment of the loan principal, plus interest.

2.   The Financing of General Partnerships, Limited Partnerships and LLCs

As discussed above, the rights to participate in corporate control, distributions, and the ownership value of a corporation is tied to ownership of stock. To allocate financial and control rights in a corporate entity in a manner that is not *pro rata* tied to the amount of common stock owned by any particular shareholder, requires a manipulation of the issuance of common stock, preferred stock and debt to accomplish the objectives of the clients. This can require complicated machinations, particularly where some participants are contributing services, others are contributing property and still others are contributing large amounts of cash.

Dealing with allocations of the economic and control rights in the context of partnerships and limited liability companies is far more straightforward, given the flexible nature of these non-corporation entities. All of the rights of the equity holders to participate in control, distributions of profits, allocation of liquidation proceeds or the proportional share of ownership will be dictated in the partnership or operating agreements. Or, in the absence of provisions in the governing documents, the rights of the partners or members will be dictated by the default provisions set forth in the state's partnership, limited partnership and limited liability company acts. We will use the Revised Uniform Partnership Act (RUPA), the Uniform Limited Partnership Act (ULPA) and the Uniform Limited Liability Company Act (ULLCA) as our primary guides to understand the relative rights of partners and members with regard to the financing of general partnerships, limited partnerships and limited liability companies.

a.   General Partnerships

In general partnerships, regardless of the amount or type of their contributions, the partners share equally in all profits and losses,[40] and each remains personally liable for the debts of the partnership, unless the partnership agreement states otherwise.[41] This can have interesting consequences where the contributions of the partners are unequal. Imagine that Al, Bet and Claire contribute, respectively, $100,000, $400,000 and $400,000 in capital to their general partnership. They will, of course, share equally in profits and losses, unless the agreement specifies otherwise. Despite the differences in the amounts of their capital contributions, this is probably their intended plan with respect to profits, particularly if Al is the "workhorse" providing much of the manpower for operations of the partnership, with Bet and Claire providing the lion's share of the capital. If the partnership is successful and generating profits, the partners will each receive one-third of those profits. If there are losses, they will share them equally. However, the obligation to share losses equally may lead to unintended results if the default rules of RUPA are followed. To fully understand the economic consequences, let's look at what happens upon winding up of the general partnership under RUPA, by focusing on RUPA sections 306, 401 and 807:

Section 306.   Partner's Liability

(a)   [A]ll partners are liable jointly and severally for all obligations of the partnership unless otherwise agreed by the claimant or provided by law.

Section 401.   Partner's Rights and Duties

(a)   Each partner is deemed to have an account that is:

(1)   credited with an amount equal to the money plus the value of any other property, net of the amount of any liabilities, the partner contributes to the partnership and the partner's share of the partnership profits; and

(2)   charged with an amount equal to the money plus the value of any other property, net of the amount of any liabilities, distributed by the partnership to the partner and the partner's share of the partnership losses.

(b)   Each partner is entitled to an equal share of the partnership profits and is chargeable with a share of the partnership losses in proportion to the partner's share of the profits.

(c)   A partnership shall reimburse a partner for payments made and indemnify a partner for liabilities incurred by the partner in the ordinary course of the business of the partnership or for the preservation of its business or property. * * *

Section 807.   Settlement of Accounts and Contributions among Partners

(a)   In winding up a partnership's business, the assets of the partnership, including the contributions of the partners required by this section, must be applied to discharge its obligations to creditors, including, to the extent permitted by law,

---

[40]   RUPA § 401(b).

[41]   RUPA § 306.

partners who are creditors. Any surplus must be applied to pay in cash the net amount distributable to partners in accordance with their right to distributions under subsection (b).

(b)   Each partner is entitled to a settlement of all partnership accounts upon winding up the partnership business. In settling accounts among the partners, profits and losses that result from the liquidation of the partnership assets must be credited and charged to the partners' accounts. The partnership shall make a distribution to a partner in an amount equal to any excess of the credits over the charges in the partner's account. A partner shall contribute to the partnership an amount equal to any excess of the charges over the credits in the partner's account under Section 306.

(c)   If a partner fails to contribute the full amount required under subsection (b), all of the other partners shall contribute, in the proportions in which those partners share partnership losses, the additional amount necessary to satisfy the partnership obligations for which they are personally liable under Section 306. A partner or partner's legal representative may recover from the other partners any contributions the partner makes to the extent the amount contributed exceeds that partner's share of the partnership obligations for which the partner is personally liable under Section 306.

What will the outcome be if the partnership is *successful* and sold for a sizable profit? Suppose that Al, Bet and Claire sell the partnership as a going concern for $2.1 million and there are no unpaid debts. This will result in a gain of $1.2 million gain over the aggregate capital contributions of $900,000. How will the proceeds be distributed under RUPA § 807(b)? RUPA provides that each partner has a capital account that will be *credited* with (i) the amount of their capital contribution, plus (ii) their share of the additional profits generated by the sale ($400,000 each):

Capital Accounts — Partnership Sold for $2.1 Million ($1.2 Million Profit)		
	Credit Capital Contributions	Credit Share of Profits on Sale	Distributed after Sale
Al	$100,000	$400,000	$500,000
Bet	$400,000	$400,000	$800,000
Claire	$400,000	$400,000	$800,000
Totals	$900,000	$1,200,000	$2,100,000

The formula in RUPA § 807(b) results in sensible and fair distribution of the net sales proceeds. From the sales proceeds of $2.1 million, Al will only get $500,000 while Bet and Claire each get $800,000. Each of the partners receives an amount that *first* returns their capital contribution, and then they each share *equally* in the profits from the sale of the partnership. Each of the three partners will share equally in the gain of $1.2 million, receiving $400,000 in excess of their capital contributions. This is surely consistent with the likely intentions of the three partners when they formed the partnership.

What will the outcome be if the partnership is *unsuccessful* and the entire $900,000 investment is lost? Do the three partners just walk away, with Al suffering a $100,000 loss and Bet and Claire each losing $400,000? Indeed, this might have been their intentions, since Bet and Claire were putting more money at risk. However, keep in mind the fundamental concept that general partners agree to share equally the profits and losses of the business, regardless of the amount of their capital contribution.[42] Let's look at the outcome under RUPA § 807(b), which states: *"A partner shall contribute to the partnership an amount equal to any excess of the charges over the credits in the partner's account"*

Capital Accounts — Partnership Suffers Loss of $900,000			
	Credit: Capital Contributions	Charge: Share of Loss	Excess of Charges Over Credits
Al	$100,000	$300,000	($200,000)
Bet	$400,000	$300,000	$100,000
Claire	$400,000	$300,000	$100,000
Totals	$900,000	$900,000	$0

RUPA 807(c) states: *"A partner [such as Bet or Claire] . . .may recover from the other partners [such as Al] any contributions the partner makes to the extent the amount contributed exceeds that partner's share of the partnership obligations for which the partner is personally liable . . . "* In other words, Al owes Bet and Claire $100,000 each.

This makes sense since, under RUPA § 401(b), the partners "agreed" to share losses equally, regardless of the amounts of their initial contributions — and this partnership suffered a $900,000 loss for which each partner is liable in the amount of $300,000. At the time of dissolution, Al would only have contributed $100,000 towards the loss, while Bet and Claire over-contributed $400,000 each. This would probably be a surprise to Al, if he had not been properly informed by his lawyer about the impact of RUPA § 807. Al might have been expecting to share losses equally in *excess* of the $900,000 of original capital but, perhaps, did not intend to undertake an obligation to compensate Bet and Claire for their proportionally greater capital contributions in the event that the business was a failure. In many business ventures, the moneyed contributors, such as Bet and Claire, fully understand that they are putting their money at risk without an expectation of compensation from the service partner, Al. If those are the parties expectations, it is essential that the partnership agreement be drafted to reflect that understanding.

The examples of Al, Bet and Claire help to drive home the point that, in a general partnership, the financial interests and obligations of the partners are independent of the amount of their capital contributions. There is a fundamental chasm between capital contributions and financial participation rights. Unlike corporations, where the rights to financial participation of equity holders are ordinarily determined by the amount of stock ownership, in general partnerships, as well as limited partnerships and LLC's, different rules may apply.

Before we continue to look at the nature of debt and equity financing for general partnerships, a few more provisions of RUPA should be reviewed:

---

[42] RUPA § 401(b). Each partner is entitled to an equal share of the partnership profits and is chargeable with a share of the partnership losses in proportion to the partner's share of the profits.

Section 401. Partner's Rights and Duties

(c) A partnership shall reimburse a partner for payments made and indemnify a partner for liabilities incurred by the partner in the ordinary course of the business of the partnership or for the preservation of its business or property.

(d) A partnership shall reimburse a partner for an advance to the partnership beyond the amount of capital the partner agreed to contribute.

(e) A payment or advance made by a partner which gives rise to a partnership obligation under subsection (c) or (d) constitutes a loan to the partnership which accrues interest from the date of the payment or advance.

We see in this part of RUPA § 401(c)–(e) a fundamental distinction between value contributed to the partnership as *equity* [43] and amounts contributed as *debt*. RUPA treats non-capital contributions or advances by individual partners as loans, making those partners creditors of the partnership. This means that the partners must be very careful about designating their contributions of money to the partnership (or advances on behalf of the partnership) as either equity or debt. To the extent that the contribution is treated as a loan, RUPA § 401(e) requires the payment of interest and § 807(a) requires that this debt be repaid fully, *before* distributions of profits to general partners. Just like debts owed to non-partner creditors, to the extent that the assets of the partnership are insufficient to satisfy the debt to a lending partner, all of the general partners are personally liable for their share of the cost of repaying the debt and, upon winding up, must make the necessary contribution to satisfy the debt, if partnership assets are insufficient to do so. Distributions of capital can be made to partners only after *all* debt has been repaid, including debt to *partners*.[44] For these reasons, it is not unusual to find a clause in well-drafted partnership agreements disempowering RUPA § 401(c)–(e). Can you think of how to draft a provision that removes the possibility of unwanted loans to the partnership caused by partners advancing funds without the general consent of the other partners? How about a provision like this:

> No Partner shall lend or advance money to, or for the Partnership's benefit, without the approval of _____[all/a majority] of the Partners. If any Partner, with the consent of the other Partners under this paragraph, lends money to the Partnership in addition to his or her contribution to its capital, the loan shall be a debt of the Partnership to that Partner and shall bear interest at the rate of [_____] percent per year. This liability shall not be regarded as an increase in the Partner's capital and shall not entitle the Partner to an increased share of the Partnership's profits. Any loan under this paragraph shall be evidenced by a promissory note delivered to the lending Partner and executed in the name of the Partnership.

---

[43] *See* RUPA § 401(a), *supra*.

[44] RUPA § 807(a) states: "[I]n winding up a partnership's business, the assets of the partnership, including the contributions of the partners required by this section, must be applied to discharge its obligations to creditors, including, to the extent permitted by law, partners who are creditors."

i.   Debt or equity contributions

When we discussed the financing of corporations, we devoted significant effort to thinking about a *mix* of debt and equity being contributed by investors in the corporation. We also discussed the related concept of issuing preferred stock. Both devices serve as mechanisms to assure that some investors are entitled to a priority of return with respect to cash payments during the life of the corporation, as well as a priority of repayment with respect to the principal (in the case of debt) or equity (in the case of preferred stock). Coming up with the right mix was important in attempting to achieve the objectives of isolating control in the hands of some equity participants, while granting big-money investors a priority position and, possibly, speedier return of all or some of their cash. Do we need to pay as much attention to a mix of debt and equity, in the financing of general partnerships? Let's reconsider the case of Al, Bet and Claire forming a general partnership in which they will all be actively engaged in a business. Al is the "rain maker" of the three and brings a large client base, as well as years of experience, to the enterprise. Al will be contributing $100,000 in cash, while Bet and Claire will be contributing $400,000 each. They all agree to share equally in profits and losses, except: (i) Bet and Claire will be entitled to a priority of distribution in the event of a sale or liquidation, so that Al receives no distribution from any proceeds until both Bet and Clare receive $300,000 each (after which, all three share equally in any remaining funds); and (ii) in the event of a business failure Al will not be liable under RUPA § 807 to compensate Bet or Claire for loss of their initial contributions of $400,000 (although he will be equally liable once losses exceed $900,000).

One way to accomplish these objectives is to follow the tactics we used in exploring the financing of corporations. Each of the three partners could make a capital contribution of $100,000, with Bet and Claire loaning the partnership an additional $300,000 each. This would furnish $900,000 to the partnership, $300,000 in the form of capital and $600,000 in the form of debt. This might work well if the partnership is profitable. Interest payments could be made to Bet and Claire to compensate them for their larger contributions of cash (although payments of interest will reduce the profits available for distribution to Al for his one-third share of the profits). In addition, the loans must be repaid before any liquidating distribution to partners, giving Bet and Claire a priority of distribution that protects their larger cash contributions. However, there are serious problems with this approach if the partnership goes bust. Under RUPA § 306, § 401 and § 807, all three partners would be personally liable for repayment of the notes. If we assume that all $900,000 has been lost, the partnership remains liable to its creditors, Bet and Claire, for the sum of $600,000. Each partner would have to contribute $200,000 towards payment of these debts. This obligation would have no impact on Bet and Claire, since they would be paying themselves, but it does mean Al would have to shell out $200,000.

Actually, there's simply no *reason* to divide up equity and debt contributions in the context of a general partnership, in view of the flexibility allowed to the partners to simply draft their economic preferences, privileges and priorities into the partnership agreement.[45] The drafting freedom given under RUPA allows the

---

[45] See RUPA § 103 which states: "Effect of Partnership Agreement; Nonwaivable Provisions. (a) Except as otherwise provided in subsection (b), relations among the partners and between the partners

parties to accomplish their financial objectives without having to rely on the traditional distinctions between debt and equity as crutches for determining the relative financial rights of the parties. Suppose, again, that the three partners make capital contributions in the amounts of $100,000 (Al) and $400,000 (Bet and Claire). Let's consider possible provisions in the partnership agreement to achieve some of their objectives regarding priorities, profits and losses:

Allocation of Profits

The Partnership's profits shall be allocated equally among the Partners.

The above provision assures that profits will be shared equally, regardless of the amounts of capital contributions. The partners are free to agree to some type of priority payment of profits to Bet and Claire to compensate them for the large amount of capital that they have invested in the business. For instance, "Bet and Claire shall each be allocated 40% of annual profits until such time as their capital accounts have been reduced to $100,000 each, at which time annual profits shall be distributed equally among the partners." An "exit" strategy for obtaining the return of their capital contributions could also be implemented by providing that, in years with sufficient profits, an additional amount be allocated towards the repayment of their capital contributions. The possibilities for allocating profits and losses are unrestricted under RUPA. As in our example, it is possible to allocate profits and losses in different proportions.

Allocation of Losses

Losses shall be allocated equally among the partners until each partner has been allocated $100,000 in losses. Thereafter, losses shall be allocated 50% to Bet and 50% to Claire until such time as an additional $300,000 has been allocated to Bet and Claire. Thereafter, losses shall be allocated equally among the partners.

Al, Bet and Claire have agreed to share losses *unequally* with regard to their initial capital contributions. The above provision assures that the unequal initial capital contributions will be charged as the parties intended.

Distributions Upon Winding Up — Surplus

If, in the event of a winding up of the partnership and after payment of all partnership debts, there is a surplus, the surplus shall be distributed as follows:

(a) Fifty percent to Bet and fifty percent to Claire until each has received the amount of $300,000, and then

(b) The remaining surplus, if any, to be shared equally by Al, Bet and Claire.

The above provision assures a priority of payment to Bet and Claire in the event that, upon liquidation, the funds received are insufficient to satisfy all of the initial capital contributions of the parties. The priority extends only to the $300,000 portion of their initial capital investment. Since Al contributed $100,000 in cash, it's

---

and the partnership are governed by the partnership agreement. To the extent the partnership agreement does not otherwise provide, this [Act] governs relations among the partners and between the partners and the partnership."

only fair that the partners share equally once the excess financial contributions of Bet and Claire have been satisfied.[46]

Distributions Upon Winding Up — Deficit

If, in the event of a winding up of the partnership, there remain outstanding debts of the partnership after all partnership assets have been exhausted, then each of the partners shall contribute equally to payment of the outstanding debts, as provided in RUPA § 807. However, notwithstanding RUPA § 807(b), Al shall be under no obligation to compensate Bet or Clair for the loss of their initial capital contributions. It is agreed that, as to the first $900,000 of losses of the partnership, Al shall be liable for $100,000 of loss, and Bet and Claire shall each be liable for $400,000 in losses. Thereafter, Al, Bet and Claire shall share losses equally.

The above provision is intended to assure that, in the event of a loss of all $900,000 in initial capital contributions, Al does not have to compensate Bet and Claire for the additional risk that they took in putting up more money than Al.

The default rules of RUPA can be changed to reflect whatever the actual intentions of the partners might be regarding profits, losses and priorities. This means that the task of the lawyers is to fully understand the financing deal being agreed to by the partners and making the appropriate changes to the statutory rules by properly drafting the provisions of the partnership agreement.

ii.   Types of consideration for partnership interests

RUPA places no limits on the types of consideration that can be exchanged for a partnership interest. A partner may contribute cash, tangible or intangible property, services, promissory notes or a mere promise. In the absence of some provision in the partnership agreement, the partners will share equally in the profits, and losses, of the partnership regardless of the form and amount of consideration that they contribute in exchange for their partnership interests. While the concept of "sharing profits and losses equally" seems simple, keep in mind the problem we discussed earlier regarding the impact of the RUPA default rules regarding distributions of surplus, or losses, upon the eventual winding up or valuation of the partnership.

Regardless of the form of consideration, under RUPA § 401(a) some value must be credited to the capital account for each partner, even if that value is zero.[47] That value is likely to have significant importance at some point in the life, or death, of the partnership. Under RUPA § 807, a low credit for the initial capital contribution will have a severe impact on the eventual entitlement to share in the profits upon winding up or, in the event of a loss, an equally severe impact on the partner's liability to his or her copartners for his or her share of the losses.[48] It is in every

---

[46] The provision assumes that there has been no earlier repayment of any portion of the initial capital contributions of the partners, prior to winding up.

[47] RUPA § 401(a) provides: "Each partner is deemed to have an account that is: (1) credited with an amount equal to the money lus the value of any other property, net of the amount of any liabilities, the partner contributes to the partnership . . . "

[48] See the charts above. RUPA § 807(b) states in pertinent part:

. . . In settling accounts among the partners, profits and losses that result from the liquidation of the partnership assets must be credited and charged to the partners' accounts.

partner's personal interest to have his or her capital account credited with the highest possible value for the contribution given in exchange for the partnership interest — or, in the alternative — to carefully alter the RUPA rules in the partnership agreement regarding the distribution of the wealth of the partnership if profitable, or the liability (if any) for the loss of the greater capital contributions of copartners. The bottom line is that, where partners are contributing unequal amounts of cash, property or services, they must confront the issues that arise under RUPA § 807 regarding the eventual allocation of profits or losses upon a winding up of the partnership, or upon some other event requiring a valuation of a partner's proportional share of the value, or obligations, of the partnership.

iii.   Contributions of services

As a reminder, don't forget that contributions of *services* raises some serious tax considerations for the partner. The interest in the partnership transferred to a partner in exchange for services is *income* and subject to taxation in the year that the partnership interest is received by the service-contributing partner.[49] The *value* of the partnership interest received will be included in the service-contributor's taxable income. What result would this have if Al contributes services for his one-third share of a partnership with Bet and Claire who, together, contribute $600,000 in cash? At the instant of the funding of the partnership what is the value of the interest received by Al? Is his share of the partnership worth $200,000 (one-third of $600,000)? If the answer is yes, Al will have to include the $200,000 in value in his gross income and pay approximately $60,000 in taxes. Could the *value* (and related tax obligation) of Al's partnership interest be reduced by provisions, like those we've previously discussed, that give a priority of distribution to Bet and Claire for the first $600,000 of cash received upon dissolution of the partnership? What would the value of Al's partnership interest be, at the time of issuance, if his share of the liquidation value of the entity is $0? See the case of *Campbell v. Commissioner*, in Chapter 3, Section H.

The bottom line, of course, is that it is essential to consult with tax professionals anytime that a partner is receiving an interest in a partnership in exchange for services to see if there is some method for reducing the impact of the tax consequences to the contributing partner.[50]

The partnership shall make a distribution to a partner in an amount equal to any excess of the credits over the charges in the partner's account. A partner shall contribute to the partnership an amount equal to any excess of the charges over the credits in the partner's account . . .

[49] See the detailed discussion in Chapter 3, Section H.2. IRC § 83 states:

(a) . . . If, in connection with the performance of services, property is transferred to any person . . .the excess of —

(1) the fair market value of such property . . . over

(2) the amount (if any) paid for such property, shall be included in the gross income of the person who performed such services in the first taxable year in which the rights of the person having the beneficial interest in such property are transferable or are not subject to a substantial risk of forfeiture, whichever is applicable . . ."

[50] See the discussion of § 83(c) in Chapter 3, Section H.2, regarding the postponement of gain realization by a service contributor such as Al where his partnership interest is contingent on some *future* event and there is a risk of forfeiture if the event does not occur.

iv.   Contributions of property

Contributions of *property* to a partnership do not ordinarily constitute a taxable event for the contributing partner, even where there is a large difference between the contributing partner's basis in the property and its fair market value at the time of contribution. This is an extremely helpful tax-postponement device for partners who have low-basis, high-value property that they will be contributing to the partnership in exchange for their partnership interest.[51]

b.   Limited Partnerships

Limited partnership acts typically provide for a broad array of types of consideration that may be exchanged for limited partnership equity interests. For instance, RULPA provides:

> A contribution of a partner may consist of tangible or intangible property or other benefit to the limited partnership, including money, services performed, promissory notes, other agreements to contribute cash or property, and contracts for services to be performed.[52]

With regard to allocation of profits and losses, unlike general partnerships, where the default statutory rules grant equal rights to share in profits and losses, the default rule for limited partnerships reflects the common practice of allocating shares of profits and losses proportionally, in the ratio that each partner's share bears to the overall capital contributions.[53] This makes sense when we consider that a limited partnership is, *vis-a-vis* the limited partners, an investment vehicle rather than a jointly managed business. Limited partnerships are inherently flexible and the statutes in all states grant broad power to the parties to alter most default statutory standards in the limited partnership agreement, including the allocations of profits and losses. RULPA § 110(a) states:

> Except as otherwise provided in subsection (b), the partnership agreement governs relations among the partners and between the partners and the partnership. To the extent the partnership agreement does not otherwise provide, this [Act] governs relations among the partners and between the partners and the partnership.[54]

---

[51] IRC §§ 721, 722. See the discussion in Chapter 3, Section H.2.

[52] RULPA § 501 (2001); *see also* Cal. Corp. Code § 15905.01 ("A contribution of a partner may consist of tangible or intangible property or other benefit to the limited partnership, including money, services performed, promissory notes, other agreements to contribute cash or property, and contracts for services to be performed.").

[53] RULPA §§ 503, 504. Section 503 provides: "Sharing of Distributions. A distribution by a limited partnership must be shared among the partners on the basis of the value, as stated in the required records when the limited partnership decides to make the distribution, of the contributions the limited partnership has received from each partner."

[54] Section 110(b) contains a list of statutory rules that cannot be altered by agreement, none of which are relevant to the financing of the partnership nor the allocation of profits and losses: "(b) A partnership agreement may not:

(1) vary a limited partnership's power under Section 105 to sue, be sued, and defend in its own name;

(2) vary the law applicable to a limited partnership under Section 106 [which state's law applies to the limited partnership]

(3) vary the requirements of Section 204; [signing of records]

The comments to RULPA § 503 recognize that the statutory default (allocation of profits and losses in relative proportion to the amount of the capital contribution) is a common practice in limited partnerships. Nevertheless, the comment contemplates that the limited partnership agreement can vary the allocational rules to fit the business and tax objectives of the constituents:

> Nearly all limited partnerships will choose to allocate profits and losses in order to comply with applicable tax, accounting and other regulatory requirements. Those requirements, rather than this Act, are the proper source of guidance for that profit and loss allocation . . . This section's rule for sharing distributions is subject to change under Section 110. A limited partnership that does vary the rule should be careful to consider not only the tax and accounting consequences but also the "ripple" effect on other provisions of this Act. See, e.g., Sections 801 and 803(c) (apportioning consent power in relation to the right to receive distributions).[55]

Most limited partnership agreements will carefully lay out the percentage interests of the parties and their entitlements to share in allocations of profits and losses in the body of the agreement or, more likely, an exhibit. For instance:

---

(4) vary the information required under Section 111 or unreasonably restrict the right to information under Sections 304 or 407, but the partnership agreement may impose reasonable restrictions on the availability and use of information obtained under those sections and may define appropriate remedies, including liquidated damages, for a breach of any reasonable restriction on use;

(5) eliminate the duty of loyalty under Section 408, but the partnership agreement may:

(A) identify specific types or categories of activities that do not violate the duty of loyalty, if not manifestly unreasonable; and

(B) specify the number or percentage of partners which may authorize or ratify, after full disclosure to all partners of all material facts, a specific act or transaction that otherwise would violate the duty of loyalty;

(6) unreasonably reduce the duty of care under Section 408(c);

(7) eliminate the obligation of good faith and fair dealing under Sections 305(b) and 408(d), but the partnership agreement may prescribe the standards by which the performance of the obligation is to be measured, if the standards are not manifestly unreasonable;

(8) vary the power of a person to dissociate as a general partner under Section 604(a) except to require that the notice under Section 603(1) be in a record;

(9) vary the power of a court to decree dissolution in the circumstances specified in Section 802;

(10) vary the requirement to wind up the partnership's business as specified in Section 803;

(11) unreasonably restrict the right to maintain an action under [Article] 10; [Actions by partners]

(12) restrict the right of a partner under Section 1110(a) to approve a conversion or merger or the right of a general partner under Section 1110(b) to consent to an amendment to the certificate of limited partnership which deletes a statement that the limited partnership is a limited liability limited partnership; or

(13) restrict rights under this [Act] of a person other than a partner or a transferee.

[55] *See* RULPA § 503 & cmt. It may occur to the constituents to allocate profits and losses disproportionally. For instance, Ann and Bob may each be allocated 40% of the profits but Ann will be allocated 80% of the losses. This is possible but the IRC requires that there be a "substantial economic effect." This is a complicated and difficult area of tax law that requires input from seasoned and knowledgeable tax professionals. See the discussion of substantial economic effect in Chapter 5, Section D.2.b.

Exhibit A — Percentage Interests & Contributions Mission Bay Enterprises, L.P. a California Limited Partnership		
General Partners	Interest	Contribution
Marion Petra	10%	$10,000 in cash & $40,000 in services (see Exhibit B)
Phillip Glass	10%	$10,000 in cash & $40,000 in services (see Exhibit B)
Limited Partners		
Andrew Toby	20%	$150,000
Shasta Collier	20%	$150,000
J.P. Humming	40%	$300,000

Note that the statutory default rule for allocations is not being followed in Exhibit A. The percentage interests of the partners in this limited partnership are not directly proportional to their capital contributions. The general partners are each contributing only $10,000 in cash and $40,000 in services (a total of $50,000 each) yet receiving a 10% allocational interest, compared to limited partners who are receiving relatively lesser interests for the cash they are contributing. If the percentage interests were allocated proportionally in accordance with the RULPA default rules, the percentage interests would be based on a total capital contribution of $700,000 and the percentage interests would be as follows:

General Partners	Interest	Contribution
Marion Petra	7%	$50,000
Phillip Glass	7%	$50,000
Limited Partners		
Andrew Toby	22.5%	$150,000
Shasta Collier	22.5%	$150,000
J.P. Humming	43%	$300,000

In other words, the general partners are getting a premium percentage entitlement to profits and losses as part of the business deal. If we consider the fact that a substantial portion of their capital contribution is in the form of pre-formation services, the general partners premium is quite high. If the percentage interests were allocated proportionally based on the *cash* contributions of the partners, the percentage interests would be based on a total capital contribution of $620,000 and the percentage interests would be as approximately as follows:

General Partners	Interest	Contribution
Marion Petra	2%	$10,000
Phillip Glass	2%	$10,000
Limited Partners		
Andrew Toby	24%	$150,000
Shasta Collier	24%	$150,000
J.P. Humming	48%	$300,000

In our example, Exhibit A sets forth the percentage interests of the partners, which vary from the RULPA default standards and are not, in fact, proportional to the amounts of their capital contributions. Of course, it is possible for the provisions of the partnership agreement to alter the *distributional priorities* with respect to the distribution of cash from operations or upon final sale or liquidation of the entity. For instance, even though the general partners each own a 10% share of the profits and losses of the limited partnership, the limited partnership agreement might provide that the moneyed partners are entitled to a priority of distribution and any profits or proceeds from sale or liquidation must first be paid to limited partners according to a preferential distribution formula. For instance, the agreement might provide:

> *Distribution of Net Cash from Operations:* Cash distributions of profits shall be distributed according to following formula. For the first three years following commencement of operations, the limited partners shall share (in proportion to the amount that their percentage interest bears to the total percentage interest of all limited partners) 85% of the cash distributed from profits and the general partners shall share (in proportion to the amount that their percentage interest bears to the total percentage interest of all general partners) 15% of the cash distributed from profits. After five years of operations, the distribution of cash from profits shall be in proportion to the percentage interests set forth in Exhibit A.

Why would the above clause be structured this way? Do the distributional priorities seem fair? As a limited partner would you find the distributional scheme more attractive than if the distributions of cash from operations were based solely on the percentage interests of the general and limited partners?

In the next paragraph, the scheme for distribution of proceeds from sales or liquidations is discussed. Keep in mind that the original capital contributions of all partners in Exhibit A were $700,000 ($620,000 in cash and $80,000 in services), with most of the cash being provided by the limited partners. The next paragraph contemplates two possibilities. First, if the business is successful and sold for a substantial profit, how should the proceeds be distributed? In this regard, consider how proceeds would be distributed if the business was sold for $2 million. Second, if the business is sold or liquidated for a loss, how should the proceeds, if any, be distributed? In this regard, consider how proceeds would be distributed if the business was sold or liquidated for only $400,000.

> *Distribution of net cash from sale or liquidations:* The net cash from a sale or liquidation of the business shall be distributed according to the following formula.
>
> (i) If the net cash exceeds the amount of $620,000, then the first $600,000 shall be distributed first to the limited partners in proportion to the amount that their percentage interest bears to the total percentage interest of all limited partners and $20,000 shall be distributed to the general partners in proportion to the amount that their percentage interest bears to the total percentage interest of all general partners. For any amounts in excess of $620,000, the net cash shall be distributed shall be in proportion to the percentage interests set forth in Exhibit A.
>
> (ii) In the event that net cash from sale or liquidation of the business is less than $620,000, the net cash shall be distributed 96% to the limited partners in proportion to the amount that their percentage interest bears to the total percentage interest of all limited partners and 4% shall be distributed to

the general partners in proportion to the amount that their percentage interest bears to the total percentage interest of all general partners.

EXERCISE 5-3

1. Using the above formulas, determine the amount of cash distributed to the general and limited partners: (a) if the business is sold for $2 million; or (b) if the business was sold for $400,000.

2. Explain why the above formulas are fair or unfair.

3. If you represented the *limited* partners, would you accept the above formulas or would you negotiate to alter the formulas?

i.   A special note about "substantial economic effect"

There are extremely complex tax provisions governing the effectiveness of allocations of profits and losses in entities taxed as partnerships.[56] Under IRC § 704(b), allocations of income, gain, loss, deduction, or credit must be made in accordance with the partners' interests in the partnership. While it is possible to vary the distributional rights of the partners in a manner that varies from those directly proportional to their ownership interests (as in our examples above), this can only be effectively accomplished for tax purposes only if there is a "substantial economic effect" to the allocation. If the agreement about distributions lacks substantial economic effect, the allocations are subject to reallocation by the IRS.

The issue usually arises when the partners or members attempt to allocate losses to some partners or members who do not, in fact, face the additional losses being allocated to them. The issue is easiest to understand if we use an LLC as an example. Suppose that three members have each contributed $100,000 to a real estate LLC. Two of the members, Alice and Bernard, lack any passive activity income against which they can deduct passive activity losses. However, the third member, Carla, has significant income from other passive investments. The members agree in the operating agreement that 100% of the losses will be *allocated* to Carla, since she can best enjoy the tax benefits of the passive activity deduction, and the other two members lack the passive activity income against which they can deduct any losses allocated to them. This kind of allocational scheme is alluring since none of the members stands to lose more than the amounts they've contributed and are *actually* liable for only one-third of the amount of the losses in the event of a liquidation or sale. For instance, if the LLC is liquidated and only $60,000 remains is available for distribution, then either, the three members will each receive $20,000, or Alice and Bernard will each receive $30,000, depending on the terms of the operating agreement. Either way, the business suffered a $240,000 loss. All of the losses were allocated to Carla, even though Carla has only really lost $100,000. In other words, the allocation of losses to Carla did not really have a substantial economic effect. Unless special adjustments are made to the partnership agreement to actually hold Carla actually accountable for 100% of the losses, the scheme to shift the passive activity loss *deductions* to Carla has no real economic effect.[57] One court has explained:

---

[56] IRC § 704(b); Treas Reg § 1.704-1.

[57] *See* Boynton v. Commissioner, 649 F.2d 1168, 1173 (5th Cir. 1981).

Substantial economic effect" in this context is a term of art, and is meant to preclude partnerships from using agreements for gain allocation in order to evade taxes. . . . In order to determine whether an allocation has substantial economic effect, the court must determine whether the partner to whom the item is allocated bears the economic burdens and benefits of that allocated item. Allison v. United States, 701 F.2d 933, 938–39 (Fed. Cir. 1983). The test of whether an allocation has "substantial economic effect has been called a capital account analysis." Ogden v. Comm'r, 788 F.2d 252, 261 (5th Cir. 1986) (internal quotations omitted). Under the capital account analysis, the partners must maintain capital accounts, and upon liquidation, distributions must be made according to the positive or negative balances in those capital accounts.[58]

The regulations governing "substantial economic effect" are sufficiently complex that variations from allocations in direct proportion to the partner's actual economic interest in the partnership require advice and input from skilled tax attorneys.

ii.   Total failure of the limited partnership

In the case of a limited partnership, what happens if there is a total loss and there is still money owing to creditors? Upon dissolution and winding up of a limited partnership, RULPA § 812 provides:

Section 812.   Disposition of Assets; When Contributions Required.

(a)   In winding up a limited partnership's activities, the assets of the limited partnership, including the contributions required by this section, must be applied to satisfy the limited partnership's obligations to creditors, including, to the extent permitted by law, partners that are creditors.

(b)   Any surplus remaining after the limited partnership complies with subsection (a) must be paid in cash as a distribution.

(c)   If a limited partnership's assets are insufficient to satisfy all of its obligations under subsection (a), with respect to each unsatisfied obligation incurred when the limited partnership was not a limited liability limited partnership, the following rules apply:

   (1)   Each person that was a general partner when the obligation was incurred and that has not been released from the obligation under Section 607 shall contribute to the limited partnership for the purpose of enabling the limited partnership to satisfy the obligation. The contribution due from each of those persons is in proportion to the right to receive distributions in the capacity of general partner in effect for each of those persons when the obligation was incurred.

   (2)   If a person does not contribute the full amount required under paragraph (1) with respect to an unsatisfied obligation of the limited partnership, the other persons required to contribute by paragraph (1) on account of the obligation shall contribute the additional amount necessary to discharge the obligation. The additional contribution due from each of those other persons is in proportion to

---

[58]   Estate of Ballantyne v. Comm'r, 341 F.3d 802, 805 (8th Cir. 2003).

the right to receive distributions in the capacity of general partner in effect for each of those other persons when the obligation was incurred.

(3) If a person does not make the additional contribution required by paragraph (2), further additional contributions are determined and due in the same manner as provided in that paragraph.

(d) A person that makes an additional contribution under subsection (c)(2) or (3) may recover from any person whose failure to contribute under subsection (c)(1) or (2) necessitated the additional contribution. A person may not recover under this subsection more than the amount additionally contributed. A person's liability under this subsection may not exceed the amount the person failed to contribute.[59]

The *limited partners*, of course face no liability for any deficit upon winding up of the limited partnership. An important point to keep in mind is that the liability of the general partners for a deficit extends only to *creditors* of the limited partnership. There is no obligation to compensate limited partners for any imbalance in the capital accounts of the partners. The comment to RULPA § 812 aptly explains, in pertinent part:

> In no circumstances does this Act require a partner to make a payment for the purpose of equalizing or otherwise reallocating capital losses incurred by partners.
>
> Example: XYZ Limited Partnership ("XYZ") has one general partner and four limited partners. According to XYZ's required information, the value of each partner's contributions to XYZ are:
>
> General partner — $5,000
>
> Limited partner #1 — $10,000
>
> Limited partner #2 — $15,000
>
> Limited partner #3 — $20,000
>
> Limited partner #4 — $25,000

XYZ is unsuccessful and eventually dissolves without ever having made a distribution to its partners. XYZ lacks any assets with which to return to the partners the value of their respective contributions. No partner is obliged to make any payment either to the limited partnership or to fellow partners to adjust these capital losses. These losses are not part of "the limited partnership's obligations to creditors."

This lack of obligation reflects the fundamental nature of a limited partnership and how it varies from a general partnership. In a general partnership, there is an underlying assumption that all partners will share profits and losses equally regardless of their initial capital contributions. However, in a limited partnership, the assumption is that the limited partners have put their capital at risk, without further liability, while the general partner operates as a partner legally liable for the debts of the entity — but only towards entity creditors. Unlike general partnerships, there is no inherent agreement to share *losses* in either direction, from general to limited partner, or from limited to general partner.

---

[59] RULPA § 812; *see also* Cal. Corp. Code § 15684.

iii.   Contributions of debt

What impact do these rules have when considering the possibility of financing the limited partnership entity with a combination of equity and *debt* from the limited partners? Will partners who loan money to the limited partnership be in a as creditors rather than equity holders? The answer is undeniably yes. As creditors of the entity, partners who loan money to the limited partnership are entitled to be paid interest and principal in accordance with the terms of the loan documents, regardless of the cash flow position of the business and prior to any distributions of profits to partners.

In the event of a winding up of the limited partnership, partners who contributed part of their capital in the form of debt must be paid before there can be a distribution to any of the other partners. From the perspective of the *limited* partners, this means that those partners who make smaller equity contributions but larger debt contributions will be taking less risk in the event of a loss — and assured of a priority of distribution in the event that there is a profit. For instance, suppose that Ace, Bert and Clint are three limited partners in a limited partnership with each having a 25% share. Ace and Bert each contributed $250,000 in cash as their capital contributions. Clint contributed $100,000 in exchange for his capital contribution and *loaned* the limited partnership $150,000. The general partner is Gary who received a 25% share in exchange for his services.

Suppose the business fails, leaving $50,000 in cash after paying off all *outside* (non-partner) creditors. The remaining $50,000 must be distributed to Clint, since he is a creditor of the limited partnership with regard to the outstanding $150,000 loan. In addition, unless there is some kind of non-recourse agreement with the general partner, Gary will owe Clint another $100,000 (as a *creditor*, not as a *partner*). If, on the other hand, the business is successful, and eventually sold for $1 million, the $150,000 loan from Clint must be repaid first, before the remaining $850,000 will be split among the four partners, with the total distribution to Clint far in excess of the distribution to other partners.

In other words, there is danger in allowing the allocation of some portion of a limited partner's share to debt, rather than equity. From the perspective of the *limited* partners, unless *all* limited partners are making the same proportional allocation between debt and equity, then some limited partners will be receiving a priority with respect to distributions. From the perspective of the *general* partner, loans from limited partners place the general partner in a liability position. In the event that there is a default in payment of interest or principal, the general partner faces personal liability for repayment of any debt obligations, including loans from limited partners. Upon the dissolution and winding up of the limited partnership, the general partner would remain fully liable for repayment of these loans, plus unpaid interest, if partnership assets were insufficient to satisfy the loans. Few general partners are willing to personally guarantee the limited partner investors that their contributions, whether in the form of equity or debt, will be repaid by the general partner in the event of a business failure.

It is possible that some of the concerns of non-lending limited and general partners can be handled by drafting special provisions into the loan documents or partnership agreement. For instance, the promissory notes could be drafted as *non-recourse* documents that eliminate the ability of the lending partners to seek payment from the general partner. Or, the economic distributions upon liquidation could be re-adjusted to take into account any loan payments to limited partners by reducing the commensurate amount of any equity distributions to those partners, until all limited partners receive equal distributions in proportion to their percentage interests in the partnership.

However, the question arises as to why anyone would bother to engage in such a complex exercise. Is there some *reason* to divide investor contributions into equity and debt in the context of financing a limited partnership? The only reasons to do so are to give the lending partners: (i) priority with respect to cash payments during the operations of the partnership in the form of interest payments; (ii) priority with respect to liquidation distributions in the form of principal repayments to creditors; and (iii) a mechanism for an early repayment of some portion of the investment in the form of principal payments under the terms of the loan documents. As with general partnerships, the flexibility granted by the statutory scheme allows the partners to simply draft their economic preferences, privileges and priorities *directly* into the limited partnership agreement, negating any reasons for using debt and equity to *indirectly* achieve the same results.[60]

The drafting freedom given under RULPA allows the parties to accomplish their financial objectives without having to rely on the traditional distinctions between debt and equity as crutches for determining the relative financial rights of the parties. The partnership agreement can simply dictate any priorities with regard to allocations of operating profits or liquidating distributions.[61] Similarly, if there is an "exit strategy" being given to some moneyed investors to allow them to pull out part of their equity contribution at certain times, or upon the achievement of certain financial milestones, this can simply be built directly into the partnership agreement.

iv.   Contributions of services and property

There are no statutory limits on the types of consideration that may be exchanged as capital for an equity interest in a limited partnership. However, there are substantial tax implications that need to be considered anytime the consideration is anything other than cash, such as property or services. See the discussions of the tax consequences of contributing services and property to a partnership entity in Chapter 3, Section H.

c.   Limited Liability Companies

Similar to limited partnerships, limited liability company acts typically provide for a broad array of types of consideration that may be exchanged for limited partnership equity interests. For instance, the ULLCA provides:

---

[60] See RULPA § 110(a) which provides: "Except as otherwise provided in subsection (b), the partnership agreement governs relations among the partners and between the partners and the partnership. To the extent the partnership agreement does not otherwise provide, this [Act] governs relations among the partners and between the partners and the partnership."

[61] Keep in mind the need to make sure that any distributional preferences must meet the "substantial economic effect" test of IRC 704(b).

Section 401. Form of Contribution.

A contribution of a member of a limited liability company may consist of tangible or intangible property or other benefit to the company, including money, promissory notes, services performed, or other agreements to contribute cash or property, or contracts for services to be performed.[62]

With regard to allocation of profits and losses, the default rules are a bit different depending on the ULLCA and statutes adopted in many states. The ULLCA provides for a default rule similar to general partnerships, with members sharing *equally* regardless of the amount of their capital contributions:

Section 405. Sharing of and Right to Distributions

(a) Any distributions made by a limited liability company before its dissolution and winding up must be in equal shares.

*   *   *

Section 806. Distribution of Assets in Winding Up Limited Liability Company's Business

(a) In winding up a limited liability company's business, the assets of the company must be applied to discharge its obligations to creditors, including members who are creditors. Any surplus must be applied to pay in money the net amount distributable to members in accordance with their right to distributions under subsection (b).

(b) Each member is entitled to a distribution upon the winding up of the limited liability company's business consisting of a return of all contributions which have not previously been returned and a distribution of any remainder in equal shares.

The comments to ULLCA § 405 explain the reasoning behind this default rule:

> Recognizing the informality of many limited liability companies, this section creates a simple default rule regarding interim distributions. Any interim distributions made must be in equal shares and approved by all members . . . The rule assumes that: profits will be shared equally; some distributions will constitute a return of contributions that should be shared equally rather than a distribution of profits; and property contributors should have the right to veto any distribution that threatens their return of contributions on liquidation. In the simple case where the members make equal contributions of property or equal contributions of services, those assumptions avoid the necessity of maintaining a complex capital account or determining profits. Where some members contribute services and others property, the unanimous vote necessary to approve interim distributions protects against unwanted distributions of contributions to service contributors. Consistently, Section 408(a) does not require the company to

---

[62] ULLCA § 401. See also Cal. Corp. Code § 17200(a) which provides: "The articles of organization or the operating agreement may provide for capital contributions of members. The contribution of a person may be in money, property, or services, or other obligation to contribute money or property or to render services."

maintain a separate account for each member, the Act does not contain a default rule for allocating profits and losses, and Section 806(b) requires that liquidating distributions to members be made in equal shares after the return of contributions not previously returned.

The ULLCA presumes that the operating agreement will almost always alter the default rule of equal distributions to all members, regardless of the amount of their capital contributions.[63] This default rule in the ULLCA is at odds with the rule in many states, such as California and Delaware, which adopt a default rule that parallels the rule for limited partnerships:

CALIFORNIA CORPORATIONS CODE

§ 17202. Allocation of profits and losses among members

The profits and losses of a limited liability company shall be allocated among the members, and among classes of members, in the manner provided in the operating agreement. If the operating agreement does not otherwise provide, profits and losses shall be allocated in proportion to the contributions of each member.

§ 17353. Distribution of remaining assets; Preferences

(a) Except as otherwise provided in the articles of organization or the written operating agreement, after determining that all the known debts and liabilities of a limited liability company in the process of winding up, including, without limitation, debts and liabilities to members who are creditors of the limited liability company, have been paid or adequately provided for, the remaining assets shall be distributed among the members according to their respective rights and preferences as follows:

. . .

(2) To members of the limited liability company for the return of their contributions.

(3) To members in the proportions in which those members share in distributions.

DELAWARE CODE ANNOTATED
Title 6

§ 18-503. Allocation of profits and losses.

The profits and losses of a limited liability company shall be allocated among the members, and among classes or groups of members, in the manner provided in a limited liability company agreement. If the limited liability company agreement does not so provide, profits and losses shall be allocated on the basis of the agreed value (as stated in the records of the limited liability company) of the contributions made by each member to the extent they have been received by the limited liability company and have not been returned.

§ 18-804. Distribution of assets.

(a) Upon the winding up of a limited liability company, the assets shall be distributed as follows:

---

[63] As of 2007, the ULLCA has been adopted in only eight states: Alabama, Hawaii, Illinois, Montana, South Carolina, South Dakota, Vermont, and West Virginia.

(1)   To creditors, including members and managers who are creditors, to the extent otherwise permitted by law, in satisfaction of liabilities of the limited liability company . . .

(3)   Unless otherwise provided in a limited liability company agreement, to members first for the return of their contributions and second respecting their limited liability company interests, in the proportions in which the members share in distributions.

Limited liability companies have the flexibility to be designed as member-managed entities in the nature of a general partnership, with all members sharing equally in the operations, management, profits and losses. They also have the flexibility to be designed as investment vehicles, with centralized promoter-managers controlling the formation and operations of the entity, while appealing to investors to make equity contributions in the nature of passive investments, akin to limited partnership interests.

The dichotomy between the ULLCA default rules, and those of California, Delaware, and most other states, reflects this essential duality in the design of limited liability companies. There is no substantial conflict between the ULLCA and those of many states since *both* default rules contemplate that, in virtually every LLC, the operating agreement will carefully and fully set forth the allocation of profits and losses among the members. Some LLCs may opt for the general partnership model and grant an equality of distribution, regardless of the nature or amount of each member's contribution. Other's may opt for the limited partnership model and grant distribution rights based on the relative values of contributions by the members — or, simply, some agreed upon percentage allocation.

i.   Contributions of debt

What impact do these rules have when considering the possibility of financing the LLC's with a combination of equity and *debt* from members of the LLC? The situation is closely analogous to that of limited partnerships, except that there is no general partner with personal liability for the debts of the LLC. Any loans to the LLC by an equity owning member will be treated just as any other debt of the LLC and entitled to priority of payment with regard to interest and principal, as set forth in the loan documents.[64] From the perspective of the members, unless *all* members are making the same proportional allocation between debt and equity, then members making loans to the LLC will be receiving a priority with respect to distributions.

Once again, it seems cumbersome and complex to try and establish priorities and cash exit strategies using a mix of equity and loans in the financing of LLCs. The flexibility granted by the statutory scheme allows the members to simply draft their economic preferences, privileges and priorities *directly* into the operating agreement, negating any reasons for using debt and equity to *indirectly* achieve the same results.[65]

---

[64] See the detailed discussion of contributions of debt to limited partnerships in Section D.2.b.

[65] See ULLCA § 103(a), which states:

Except as otherwise provided in subsection (b), all members of a limited liability company

ii.   Contributions of services and property

There are no statutory limits on the types of consideration that may be exchanged as capital for an equity interest in an LLC. However, as with any entity taxed as a partnership, there are substantial tax implications that need to be considered anytime the consideration is anything other than cash, such as property or services. See the discussions of the tax consequences of contributing services and property to a partnership entity in Chapter 3, Section H.

d.   Future Equity Contributions to General Partnerships, Limited Partnerships and Limited Liability Companies

As discussed earlier in this chapter with regard to financing *corporations*, the early promoters and investors in any type of business entity, including general partnerships, limited partnerships and limited liability companies, must deal with the potential need to raise additional capital in the future. A failure to agree in advance as to how future capital will be raised can result in a serious meltdown in the event that the need for funds arises without some kind of planning. At the earliest stages of drafting the formation documents, the parties must decide whether or not early investors will have the *obligation* or *option* to contribute additional capital if certain triggering events occur.

Many of the same issues arise with regard to these non-corporate entities that we discussed in connection with corporations. With regard to *mandatory* additional contributions, early investors may be concerned about "throwing good money after bad" and want to minimize any obligation to dig into their pockets to make future contributions. Even if they want to make additional contributions, some investors may lack the kind of deep-pocket financial assets to fund future contributions. All investors will be concerned about the events that trigger the call for additional capital, the limits on the timing and amounts of any capital call, and the procedural mechanisms for dealing with failures by some investors to make the mandatory capital call.

With regard to *options* to make additional equity contributions interests, early investors will be concerned with the problems of dilution of economic interests, as well as voting control if control is linked to the percentage of ownership.[66]

To help illuminate the issues of additional capital contributions, let's look at some potential provisions that might be included in an LLC operating agreement regarding additional capital contributions. Read them carefully and see what concerns they would raise if you were representing a potential investor:

Additional Capital contributions

Alt. 1a. <u>No Additional Capital Contributions</u>: No member shall be required to make any additional capital contributions. No member may voluntarily make any additional capital contribution.

---

may enter into an operating agreement, which need not be in writing, to regulate the affairs of the company and the conduct of its business, and to govern relations among the members, managers, and company. To the extent the operating agreement does not otherwise provide, this [Act] governs relations among the members, managers, and company.

[66] See the in-depth discussion of dilution of economic interests in Section D.1.e.

or

Alt. 1b. <u>Mandatory Additional Capital Contributions</u>: The Manager[67] may determine, prior to July 1 of each calendar year, whether additional capital contributions are reasonably necessary for the operations of the business of the company and may, based on such determination, require each member to make an additional capital contribution for that year. The Manager shall give notice in writing to all members at least 90 days before the date on which such additional capital contribution is due. The notice shall set forth the total amount of additional capital needed, the purpose for which it is needed, and the date by which the contribution is due from each member. Each member shall be required to make a proportional additional contribution in the proportion that the member's percentage interest in the company bears to the total additional capital contribution. No Member may voluntarily make any additional capital contribution.

In the case of such a mandatory additional contribution, it might be prudent to add the following paragraph:

The maximum amount of additional capital contributions that a member may be required to make under this provision in any one year is not to exceed ___ percent of the member's initial capital contribution. The aggregate amount of additional capital contributions under this paragraph may not exceed ___ per cent of the member's initial capital contribution.

And also prudent to add the following:

The Manager may not require an additional capital contribution under this paragraph unless there is consent in writing from members holding at least [fifty] percent of the percentage interests in the company.

2. <u>Enforcement of Mandatory Additional Capital Contribution</u>: [68] If a Member fails to make all or apart of an additional Capital Contribution

---

[67] Or, if member-managed, upon a vote of the members.

[68] Note that this provision imposes a *penalty* on members who fail to make the mandatory additional capital contribution. How far can the penalty clauses go? California Corporations Code § 172301(a)(3) states:

An operating agreement may provide that the interest of a member who fails to make any contribution or other payment that the member is required to make will be subject to specific remedies for, or specific consequences of, the failure. A provision shall be enforceable in accordance with its terms unless the member seeking to invalidate the provision establishes that the provision was unreasonable under the circumstances existing at the time the agreement was made. The specific remedies or consequences may include loss of voting, approval, or other rights, loss of the member's ability to actively participate in the management and operations of the limited liability company, liquidated damages, or a reduction of the defaulting member's economic rights. The reduction of the defaulting member's economic rights may include one or more of the following provisions:

(A) Diluting, reducing, or eliminating the defaulting member's proportionate interest in the limited liability company.

(B) Subordinating the defaulting member's interest in the limited liability company to that of nondefaulting members.

(C) Permitting a forced sale of the membership interest.

(D) Permitting the lending or contribution by other members of the amount necessary to meet the defaulting member's commitment.

(E) Adjusting the interest rates or other rates of return, preferred, priority, or otherwise, with respect to contributions by or capital accounts of the other members.

required under Section 1 within 30 days of the due date, then:

(a) The defaulting member shall indemnify and hold the Company and the other members harmless from any loss, cost, or expense, including reasonable attorney fees caused by the failure to make the additional capital contribution due from the defaulting member (the "Deficiency").

(b) The Manager may use any reasonable method to provide non-defaulting members the opportunity to make additional capital contributions, until the Deficiency is as fully contributed as possible. Following the non-defaulting members' making of such additional capital contributions, each member so contributing shall have that member's percentage interest adjusted to reflect based on the following formula [---].

(c) In the event of a deficiency, a member advancing an additional Capital Contribution for a defaulting member under this section shall: (1) be paid interest by the defaulting member on the amount of such advance at an annual rate, from the date of the advance until paid, equal to the [*set formula for determining interest rate*]; and (2) receive all distributions that the defaulting member would otherwise be entitled to receive under the provisions of this Operating Agreement as though the advances by the non-defaulting member were capital contributions made by such non-defaulting member. Such distributions shall be applied first to attorneys' fees, costs, and expenses; then to accrued and unpaid interest; and, finally, in reduction of the principal amount of such advance. The defaulting member grants any non-defaulting member who make advances to the Company in accordance with this section a security interest in the defaulting member's membership interest to secure the defaulting member's obligations under this section.

(b) On the occurrence of, and for the duration of, a default by any member under this section, the defaulting member shall not have any right to vote the defaulting member's membership interest or otherwise participate in the management or control of the business and affairs of the Company and any and all provisions of this Operating Agreement with respect to management and control shall be determined without including the membership interest of the defaulting member. The foregoing provisions shall be in addition to the Company's remedies under Corporations Code section the Limited Liability Company Act. On satisfaction of a defaulting member's obligations under this section, that member shall be restored to full membership status to the extent of any remaining percentage interest.

Note that the following alternative is different than the above provisions. In the next alternative, additional contributions are *optional*, not mandatory. What problems arise?

Alt. 1c. Optional Capital Contributions

(a) The Manager may reasonably determine in good faith from time to time, that additional Capital Contributions from the Members (the "Optional

---

(F) Fixing the value of the defaulting member's interest in the limited liability company by appraisal, formula and redemption, or sale of the defaulting member's interest in the limited liability company at a percentage of that value.

See also Del. Code Ann. tit. 6, § 18-502(c).

Capital Contribution") are necessary or appropriate for the conduct of the Company's business. The Manager shall provide written notice of such request for additional Capital Contributions (a "Capital Call") to each Member not less than ninety (90) days prior to the date such Optional Capital Contributions are due (the "Capital Call Due Date"). The notice shall set forth the aggregate amount of the Capital Call, the purposes for which such Capital Contributions will be used and the date on which Optional Capital Contributions are due. No Member shall be obligated to make any such Capital Contributions. However, each Member shall have the opportunity, but not the obligation, to participate in a Capital Call on a *pro rata* basis in accordance with the Member's Percentage Interest by making an Optional Capital Contribution. Immediately following any Optional Capital Contribution by a Member, the Percentage Interests shall be adjusted to reflect the new relative proportions of the Capital Accounts of the Members.

(b) If a Member (a "Non-Contributing Member") does not make an Optional Capital Contribution equal to its *pro rata* share of the Capital Call by the Capital Call Due Date, the Company shall notify each Member that made an Optional Capital Contribution equal to its pro rata share of such Capital Call (each, a "Fully-Participating Member") that such Fully-Participating Member may, within the fourteen (14) day period from the date of such notice, increase its Optional Capital Contribution to the Company to cover amounts that the Non-Contributing Member declined to contribute on a pro rata basis, in which case the Percentage Interests of the Members shall be adjusted to reflect the new relative proportions of the Capital Accounts of the Members.

After reading these provisions regarding additional capital contributions, what are some of the concerns that promoters and investors might have? It's apparent that the promoters and early investors need to give considerable thought to any mechanism for raising additional equity from the original group of investors in the venture. Although the provisions above relate to a limited liability company, equivalent provisions could easily be drafted for general or limited partnerships. It is the role of the lawyers in drafting these types of provisions to make sure that some of the parties fully understand the issues that arise in connection with future capital contributions, and to draft the provisions to comprehensively cover all of the concerns that arise.

e.   Future Contributions from New Equity Participants

One possible way to raise additional capital as the business matures is to seek equity contributions from new investors. In the case of corporations, this is done by selling additional shares of common or preferred stock. How can we accomplish this with an existing, *non-corporate* business entity?

In the case of a general partnership, in the absence of some provision in the partnership agreement to the contrary, the consent of all of the general partners is required for the admission of a new partner.[69] Similar rules exist for the admission

---

[69] See RUPA § 401(i) which provides: "A person may become a partner only with the consent of all of the partners." *See also* Cal. Corp. Code § 16401(i); Del. Ann. Code tit. 6, § 15-401(a).

of new limited partners to an existing limited partnership.[70] Under the default statutory rules, admission of a new partner will require unanimous consent among the existing partners as to the percentage of partnership financial participation and control to be transferred to the new partner. Obtaining unanimous consent may be extremely difficult in partnerships with many existing partners. Imagine the difficulty of getting 50 partners to come to agreement on the selection of a new partner, the valuation of any non-cash contributions by that partner, and the percentage interest to be granted to that partner (with a commensurate dilution of the existing partners' interests).

If, at the commencement of the partnership, it is contemplated that new partners may be added as future financial needs arise, it is helpful to alter the default rule by including in the partnership agreement some procedural mechanism other than *unanimous* consent for determining how new partners will be admitted and the allocations of control and financial participation to be granted to them.[71] It is not uncommon to alter the rules by providing for admission of new partners by some voting standard such as a majority or super-majority approval of the existing partners. The degree of economic dilution can be controlled for through negotiations at the time of admission of the new partner, or by provisions in the partnership agreement that place limits on the number of new partners and/or the maximum levels of dilution.

In the case of a limited liability companies, there are some variations in the rules regarding the admission of new members. In some states, such as California, in the absence of some provision in the operating agreement, the default rule is that admission of new members requires only a vote of the "majority in interest" of the existing members (a majority of the percentage interests, rather than the majority of members).[72] On the other hand, in Delaware the default rule is the same as that for general and limited partnerships, requiring unanimous consent.[73] In both

---

[70] ULPA § 301 provides:

A person becomes a limited partner:

    (1) as provided in the partnership agreement;

    (2) as the result of a conversion or merger under [Article] 11; or

    (3) with the consent of all the partners.

See also California Corporations Code § 15631(a)(1)which provides: "a person may become a limited partner:

    (1) In the case of a person acquiring a limited partnership interest directly from the limited partnership, upon compliance with the partnership agreement or, if the partnership agreement does not so provide, upon the written consent of all of the partners. See also, Delaware Annotated Code Title 6 § 17-301(b) which states: After the formation of a limited partnership, a person is admitted as a limited partner of the limited partnership: (1) . . . at the time provided in and upon compliance with the partnership agreement or, if the partnership agreement does not so provide, upon the consent of all partners . . .

[71] For example, the partnership agreement might provide: "A new partner may be admitted with the written approval of a [majority] [two-thirds] of the partners."

[72] See California Corporations Code § 17100(a), which provides:

    After formation of a limited liability company, a person may become a member: (1) In the case of a person acquiring a membership interest directly from the limited liability company, at the time provided in and upon compliance with the articles of organization or the operating agreement or, if the articles of organization or operating agreement do not so provide, only upon the vote of a majority in interest of the members, excluding the vote of the person acquiring the membership interest, and only when the person becomes a party to the operating agreement." * * *

[73] See Delaware Annotated Code, tit. 6, § 18-301(b), which provides:

states, the default rules can be easily altered by provisions in the operating agreement, leading to the same issues discussed above with regard to general and limited partnerships — should admission require unanimous consent of the existing partners, or should some other procedural mechanism be drafted to provide for the addition of new members without requiring universal agreement.

f.   Debt Financing for Future Operations and Expansions

As non-corporate entities mature, there is the enticing idea of borrowing money from outside sources to finance some aspects of operations or growth of the company. There are strong advantages to funding the entity with debt from true, outside lenders. The benefits and problems associated with outside debt financing are discussed in detail earlier in this chapter in Sections B and D.2.e. It is unlikely that *long-term* debt financing will be available from commercial lenders, such as banks, to supply the capital necessary to implement, operate and grow the business until the entity has been in business for several years. Prudent outside lenders will look carefully at the financial records and operating history to assure that there is a stream of income sufficient to make the loan payments. They will also look to the thickness of the equity base of the entity. The thicker the equity cushion, the more likely an outside lender might be willing to lend money to the entity.

In the case of general and limited partnerships, the general partners will be personally liable for the loans which will make debt financing more available, since the lenders can look past the partnership assets in the event of a default and rely to some degree on the credit-worthiness and assets of the general partners.[74] On the other hand, not all general partners might be willing to put additional assets at risk to pay loans that the partnership incurs. If so, these risk-averse partners will want to assure that the partnership agreement limits the ability of the partnership to incur substantial additional debt without some type of satisfactory voting control on the part of the risk-averse general partner.

In the case of limited liability companies (or limited partnerships with corporate general partners), lenders are far less willing to loan money on an *unsecured* basis, since they are limited to the assets of the entity (plus the assets of the corporate general partner of a limited partnership) in the event of a default — unless particular members or partners are willing to sign personal guarantees. It is certainly possible that the LLC may have gained sufficient asset wealth and cash flow that outside lenders are willing to loan on an unsecured basis and rely entirely on the expectation that the LLC will repay the debt but this will not often be the case until the business of the LLC has fully matured, making this type of

---

(b) After the formation of a limited liability company, a person is admitted as a member of the limited liability company: (1) In the case of a person who is not an assignee of a limited liability company interest, including a person acquiring a limited liability company interest directly from the limited liability company and a person to be admitted as a member of the limited liability company without acquiring a limited liability company interest in the limited liability company at the time provided in and upon compliance with the limited liability company agreement or, if the limited liability company agreement does not so provide, upon the consent of all members and when the person's admission is reflected in the records of the limited liability company; . . .

[74] As discussed earlier, in some limited partnerships, the general partner is a corporation. The assets of the corporate general partner are available for satisfaction of the creditors of the limited partnership but the corporate entity operates as a shield for liability of the individuals who control the general partner. In such cases, from the lender's perspective, the general partnership is equivalent to a limited liability company where no individuals are liable for the debts of the entity.

unsecured loan unavailable in times of cash crunches or to fund the expansion of the business.

One time that debt may be readily available for a non-corporate entity is when the debt is to be secured by a lien on valuable property of the entity. The availability of secured debt is going to be related to the proven economic value of the collateral and the existence of a sufficient equity cushion to protect the secured lender.[75]

COMPREHENSIVE EXERCISE:
FINANCING THE INITIAL ENTERPRISE

You may recall the following facts from the ABC Restaurant scenario in Exercise 1-1 in Section E.2 of Chapter 1. Ann, Bev and Carl are promoters seeking to start up a restaurant venture in your city. The venture will require approximately $4.6 million in capital investment, as well as loans from local banks. The three promoters will be contributing $1.6 million ($1.2 million in cash and $400,000 in services and personal property). The remainder of the capital, $3 million, will be raised by selling investment interests to investors. The entity will also be borrowing an additional $3 million from local banks in the form of secured and unsecured loans.

Ann is retired, with significant wealth in the form of equity in her home, as well as stable and low-risk investments. Ann will be contributing $400,000 to the venture. Ann will be a passive investor and will not actively participate in the regular management of the business entity. Her proposed $400,000 investment is approximately 15% of her net worth. Ann wants to invest her money for a reasonable period but would like to be able to withdraw her original contribution as quickly as possible once the restaurant operations become profitable.

Bev has a net worth in excess of $20 million, with many investments. She will be taking an active and controlling role in the management and operation of the proposed venture. Bev will be contributing $800,000. Bev wants to be able to protect her capital investment to the fullest extent possible and assure a priority of distribution from profits of the restaurant operation.

Carl is 55 years old and a successful restaurant operator. Carl will be contributing his services, expertise, good will, recipes, designs and intellectual property.[76] In the past, Carl purchased a parcel of real estate that is a perfect location for the restaurant. At this stage, Carl is proposing to sell the real estate to the business entity or, in the alternative, lease it to the business entity.

Other Equity Investors will consist of up to 30 passive investors with no regular role in the management of the business. There will be thirty investment units, each costing $100,000.

---

[75] See Sections C and D.1.d. of this chapter.

[76] Carl owns the rights to use valuable tradenames, trademarks and good will associated with his current restaurant. He also owns copyrights on computer software that assists him in operating the restaurant. Carl will retain ownership of these items of intellectual property but will license the property to the proposed venture at a nominal cost.

Below is a summary of the initial financing plan:

Total Capital from Promoters: **$1.6 million**
<u>Ann:</u> $400,000
<u>Bev:</u> $800,000
<u>Carl:</u> Intellectual property, real property &/or services valued at $400,000
Other Equity Investors: **$3 million**
Bank Loans: **$3 million**
Total: **$7.6 million**

Exercise 5-4: Corporate Entity Financing

Is it possible to set up the financing plan for this venture in the form of a corporation? How would the objectives of the promoters and potential investors be achieved? What are the pros and cons of using a corporation to achieve the financing objectives of this venture?

Exercise 5-5: General Partnership Entity Financing

Is it possible to set up the financing plan for this venture in the form of a general partnership? How would the objectives of the promoters and potential investors be achieved? What are the pros and cons of using a general partnership to achieve the financing objectives of this venture?

Exercise 5-6: Limited Partnership Entity Financing

Is it possible to set up the financing plan for this venture in the form of a limited partnership? How would the objectives of the promoters and potential investors be achieved? What are the pros and cons of using a limited partnership to achieve the financing objectives of this venture?

Exercise 5-7: Limited Liability Company Entity Financing

Is it possible to set up the financing plan for this venture in the form of a limited liability company? How would the objectives of the promoters and potential investors be achieved? What are the pros and cons of using a limited liability company to achieve the financing objectives of this venture?

Chapter 6

PROFITS AND DISTRIBUTIONS

As we said in Chapter 2, investors go into business to make money. In this chapter we will put technical and legal substance behind that statement. There are two intermediate steps between the two actions in the first sentence — between "going into business" and "making money." The first step is that the business must make a profit. The second step is that profit must be put into the hands of the entrepreneurs.[1] In Section A we learn the introductory accounting rules for a business. In Section B, we learn how "profit" is determined and the legal implications of that determination. In Section C, we cover the rules for how corporate assets are accounted for and distributed, and in Sections D and E, we cover the same rules for partnerships and limited liability companies, respectively. Section F discusses creditor-protection rules applicable to all distributions, and Section G discusses the federal income tax consequences of these distributions..

A. AN INTRODUCTION TO FINANCIAL ACCOUNTING

This section will introduce you to financial accounting terms and concepts with which every business lawyer should be familiar. Our goal in this section is to provide the foundation that business lawyers need to have an intelligent discussion with their client's accountant and can understand the basic legal issues involved in business entity accounting. We will discuss and explore the two basic financial statements which describe any business entity: a balance sheet and an income statement. Then, we will consider the basic rules governing how these statements are prepared.

1. The Balance Sheet

The balance sheet is a financial "snapshot" of the business entity. It lists, as of the date of the balance sheet, all the assets of the entity and all the claims against those assets. The assets are listed on the left or at the top, and the claims are listed on the right or at the bottom.

The assets typically consist of cash, investments, materials, supplies, land, buildings, fixtures and intangible property. A retailing or manufacturing business will also have inventory, plant and equipment. A service business will likely have few or none of these latter types of assets. It is customary for assets to be reported in large groups such as these. You will find the assets of even a very large business will be reported in no more than a dozen different categories. The assets are usually listed in order of "liquidity." Cash and the items which can be quickly and easily sold for cash are at the beginning, and the items which would be harder (or impossible) to sell for cash are at the end.

---

[1] Remember that one basic assumption from Chapter 2 onward was that the business would be a legal entity separate from its owners.

The claims are divided into two types: claims by creditors, and claims by owners. The claims by creditors — that is, the liabilities of the business — are typically listed in order of due date, with the "current" liabilities listed first, and the most long-term debt listed last. The business will list all amounts owed to suppliers, employees, contractors, lenders, and any other liabilities.[2] The claims by owners are commonly referred to as the "equity" of the business.[3] How these claims are accounted for depends primarily on the form of the business entity.

Because of the accounting assumptions we will discuss in Section A.4 below, a balance sheet will always balance. The balance sheet reflects what is known as the **fundamental accounting equation**:

$$\text{assets = liabilities + equity.}$$

This means that no assets will go unclaimed (so that assets will never be more than liabilities plus equity), and that if liabilities should be more than assets, the equity might be a negative amount.[4]

Example. Chris has a knack for spotting bargains in used books, and wants to use this talent profitably by opening a used book store. Chris spends $1000 in cash and buys used books from local resellers and sells them online. If Chris' only expense to date is the purchase of the books, a balance sheet would appear as follows:

Chris' Used Books — Balance Sheet
[today's date][5]

Assets
Books $ 1000

Liabilities and Equity
Chris — owner's equity $ 1000

Suppose that, in addition, Chris was able to borrow $ 1000 from the bank and used $500 of this to purchase more books. A balance sheet would then appear as follows:

Chris' Used Books — Balance Sheet
[today's date]

Assets
Cash $ 500
Books   1500
Total $ 2000

---

[2] So far we have considered only contractual liabilities. Other types of liabilities might be shown on the balance sheet as well, but these are rare. *See* Section A.3, *infra*.

[3] This is not to be confused with "equity" in its legal definitions. Equity as an accounting concept simply represents the difference between the assets and the liabilities, as indicated in the following paragraph and in the "fundamental accounting equation."

[4] Or put another way, assets − liabilities = equity, which is simply an algebraic restatement of the definition of "equity" above.

[5] A balance sheet caption always includes the name of the entity and the date of the balance sheet. You should immediately reject an undated balance sheet. It is like an undated photograph.

Liabilities and Equity

Bank loan	$ 1000
Chris — owner's equity	1000
Total	**$ 2000**

EXERCISE 6-1

Suppose that Chris then purchases a computer to use in the business for $700, using the $500 in the business account and a $200 additional personal investment. Prepare a balance sheet for Chris' Used Books after these events.

2.   The Income Statement

We know that a balance sheet is a "snapshot" of a business at one point in time. If, however, we are interested in how a business has performed over a period of time, it is difficult (and tedious) to line up one balance sheet "snapshot" after another to see how things have changed. We rely instead on an income statement which presents the business' revenues and expenses and net profit (or loss) for a period, which is then added to (or subtracted from) the owner's equity account.

Example. [6] Consider the balance sheet from Chris' Used Bookstore at the end of our last example.

Chris' Used Books — Balance Sheet
[first date]

Assets

Cash	$ 500
Books	1500

Liabilities and Equity

Bank loan	$ 1000
Chris — owner's equity	1000

Now, through the miracle of free enterprise, suppose Chris convinces a customer to pay $12 for a book which Chris purchased for $10. It would be a simple matter to remove the book from the balance sheet (at its cost of $10) and add the $12 cash. Our new "balance sheet" would look like this:

Chris' Used Books — Out-of-Balance Sheet
[second date]

Assets

Cash	$ 512
Books	1490
Total	**$ 2002**

Liabilities and Equity

Bank loan	$ 1000

---

[6] Adapted from Robert W. Hamilton & Richard A. Booth, Business Basics for Law Students 120–22 (4th ed. 2006).

| Chris — owner's equity | 1000 |
| **Total** | **$ 2000** |

But this "balance sheet" does not balance. The fundamental accounting equation (and our common sense) tell us that someone has a claim to that additional $2. That someone must be Chris, since the bank loan liability is fixed in amount. So we repair the situation as follows:

Chris' Used Books — New Balance Sheet
[second date]

Assets	
Cash	$ 512
Books	1490
Total	**$ 2002**

Liabilities and Equity	
Bank loan	$ 1000
Chris — owner's equity	1002
Total	**$ 2002**

If we compare the Balance Sheet and the New Balance Sheet, we see that Chris is $2 better off, but we do not know how this came to be. The New Balance Sheet would look the same if Chris had bought $1000 *more* worth of books for the bookstore, sold them for $2000, and then withdrawn the entire $2000 out of the business. The New Balance sheet would also look the same if Chris had bought 100 books for $10 each and sold each of them for $10.02. And we would probably agree that it would be important to know how Chris got that additional $2. Financial statements are supposed to not only describe a business (as a balance sheet does), but also provide some methods for evaluation and control (which a balance sheet does not do very well).

But we can connect the Balance Sheet and the New Balance Sheet by an income statement. The income statement would show that Chris' business had $12 in revenues and $10 in expenses.[7] Thus, we would have:

Chris' Used Books — Income Statement
for the Period [first date to second date][8]

Revenues	
Book sales	$ 12
Expenses	
Cost of books sold	10
Net income	**$ 2**

---

[7] Detailed coverage of the nuances of accounting terminology is beyond our introductory discussion here. Suffice it to say that revenue is an increase in assets related to the entity's operations, and expense is a decrease in assets (or increase in liabilities) also related to the entity's operations.

[8] An income statement caption always includes the name of the entity and the period covered by the statement. You should reject an income statement without a period specification; it is an undated story.

The income statement provides the exact detail on how the owner's equity accounts increased (or decreased) and makes it unnecessary to figure a balance sheet every day to measure how well the business is doing. Unlike the balance sheet "snapshot," the income statement is always for a period of time, and typically it links a balance sheet on one date with a balance sheet on another date. The period of time between balance sheet preparation dates (and hence the period covered by an income statement) is called the "accounting cycle" and is typically one year, although it does not have to be.

EXERCISE 6-2

After Chris' Used Books New Balance Sheet was prepared, in the next month Chris sold six books for $12 each, and each of those books had cost Chris $10. Prepare a balance sheet as of the end of this month and an income statement for the month.

Now you have been introduced to the two main financial statements, and how they work together. The income statement tells the story of what happens between two balance sheet dates. Therefore, a minimally complete set of financial statements should include two balance sheets and an income statement for the period between them.

3.   Accrual and Deferral

Preparation of financial statements requires the bookkeeper to make some assumptions about when assets are acquired, liabilities are incurred or paid, revenues are received, and expenses are incurred. Most individuals and many simple businesses follow a straightforward *cash basis* accounting system: revenues and expenses are recognized when cash is received or paid.

For an entity with a sophisticated business and many owners, this cash basis system has two major drawbacks. First, it fails to reflect the facts of economic life. Cash may be spent for capital assets which may have value over more than one accounting period. Cash may be received which does not automatically result in revenue "earned" by the entity for that accounting period, because there may be further contractual duties to be performed in connection with the contract. In addition, cash receipts and payments may not be timed perfectly with the beginning and end of the accounting cycle for which financial statements are prepared. Second, payment and receipt of cash is ordinarily within the control of the business managers. If cash movements in and out of the business were to determine income and expenses, it would be possible for self-interested managers to affect the results by accelerating or withholding cash receipts or payments.

The solution to these problems is to adopt accounting rules about when to recognize revenues and expenses which are not dependent on the receipt or payment of cash. This accounting system is known as an *accrual basis* system. Although it goes by the single term "accrual," the accrual accounting system incorporates two concepts: accrual and deferral. The concepts are pretty much "mirror images" of each other.

| Accrual: | Recognizing revenue or expense even though cash was ***not*** received or paid |
| Deferral: | ***Not*** recognizing revenue or expense even though cash was received or paid |

Without digressing into bookkeeping details, suffice it to say that the accrual accounting system better meets the accounting objective of matching revenues and expenses for the same underlying event in the same accounting period.

Accrual of revenues or expenses. Revenue can be accrued even without receipt of cash. A company may make sales on credit, for which it receives a customer's promise to pay later (an "account receivable") instead of cash. Rent and interest income are typically recognized as earned by the landlord or lender by the passage of time, rather than by when cash payments are made by the tenant or borrower. Conversely, expenses can be accrued even without payment of cash. Consider the "flip side" of the transactions mentioned above. A company may purchase supplies or materials, or pay for labor or other services, with a promise to pay later (an "account payable" or debt security) instead of cash. And rent and interest expense are typically recognized by the tenant or borrower by passage of time, rather than when cash payments are made. An expense can also be incurred without payment when an entity recognizes a liability (such as legal liability in a lawsuit) or the decrease in value of an asset (due to obsolescence or other causes).

Deferral of revenues or expenses. Cash received by an entity may not be "earned" as revenue at the time of payment. Advance deposits for future services and other prepayments are the most common examples. Conversely, cash expended by an entity may not be listed as an expense at the time of the payment, because what was purchased was not "used up" (as might be the case with supplies or raw materials) but was expended to acquire a capital asset (such as buildings or machinery) expected to benefit many future accounting periods. The cost of such an asset is allocated (by "depreciation") among the future periods in which the asset is used (its "useful life").

Improper accrual of revenues and deferral of costs are two of the most common sources of error in financial statements. Management will obviously be motivated to accrue revenues (even if perhaps not entitled to them) and defer costs (even though cash or other assets were expended) in order to improve the net income "bottom line." Lawyers and other sophisticated users of financial statements should be alert for such abuses of the accrual accounting system.

Examples. One doesn't have to look very far beyond the headlines for examples. Improper revenue recognition can be as brazen as booking revenue on shipments to a friend or other accomplice, to a warehouse in a distant location, or to a customer who did not place an order. And improper cost deferral is as simple as calling it an "asset." This was the astonishingly simple method used by WorldCom, Inc. to improperly defer $3.8 *billion* of costs in a famous 2002 accounting fraud.

4. Accounting Assumptions

In preparing financial statements, accountants make certain fundamental assumptions about the work they undertake. A lawyer must know and understand these assumptions in order to appreciate the usefulness and, more importantly, the limits of financial information. These assumptions follow from statements made by accounting associations over the years in an effort by the accounting profession to provide standards and stability for their work. There is no one authoritative source of such standards, but the list that follows derives from the general statements of principles which accountants have created.[9]

In our brief discussion of the balance sheet and the income statement, we have already seen several of those assumptions at work:

→ *The fundamental accounting equation.* Accounting is based on the supremacy of the fundamental equation. The fact that assets will always equal claims (liabilities plus equity) explains the universal practice of double-entry bookkeeping. Every change which is made to a financial accounting system must be balanced with another compensating change, so that at the end of *every entry*, assets must equal claims.

→ *Accounting entity.* Financial statements are prepared for a discrete economic entity. We have presented the financial position of Chris' Used Books separate from that of Chris' personal financial statements, even though the two may not be legally distinct. The "entity" assumption also requires accountants to prepare "consolidated" financial statements for economic entities which control other entities, such as parent and subsidiary corporations.

→ *Accounts.* Ordinarily, similar types of assets, liabilities, revenues and expenses are grouped together in accounts. "Cash" typically includes not only currency, but demand and time deposits and some short- term secure investments. "Accounts receivable" (an asset) and "accounts payable" (a liability) normally include rights to receive cash, or obligations to pay cash, which are to mature within the next accounting cycle. "Cost of goods sold" reflects *all* of the costs of the goods produced by the entity: the raw materials, labor, storage, transportation, packaging, and all capital costs which can be allocated specifically to the production of that good.

→ *Periodicity.* The accounting system is based on an "accounting cycle." Ordinarily this is one year, but could be a shorter period depending on the business and its operating history. The accounting cycle is normally the time period for which an income statement is prepared, and the time period within which accounts receivable and payable are expected to be converted into cash receipts and payments.

Most of the remaining assumptions were not directly involved in our simple example of Chris' Used Books, but could perhaps be seen in operation there, and are certainly involved in the financial statements of actual business entities. We briefly summarize each assumption and the major impacts or consequences for the business lawyer:

→ *Historical cost.* Accountants state the value of assets as the cost at which they were purchased (less accumulated depreciation). There are some exceptions for liquid assets with reliable market prices. This means that the financial statements may significantly misstate (usually understate) the value of older singular assets, such as real estate.

---

[9] *See* Financial Accounting Standards Board, *Statement of Financial Accounting Concepts No. 1,* Objectives of Financial Reporting of Business Enterprises ¶¶ 18–23 (1978); *Statement of Financial Accounting Concepts No. 2,* Qualitative Characteristics of Accounting Principles (1980) ("Summary of Principal Conclusions").

→ *Realization.* Accountants normally will not recognize revenue until it has been realized. In general, this means that the entity must be entitled to receive cash (or its equivalent) and the "earnings process" is complete.[10] This admittedly fuzzy standard creates many problems for accountants and lawyers in deciding whether revenue can be properly recognized. This can be critical in the case of a start-up business which is eager to show viability and profitability to present or potential owners, lenders and investors. The concept of realization is also important in many business documents or agreements which define "profits" by reference to that term's "ordinary accounting meaning" or some similar phrase.

→ *Matching.* When revenue is recognized, that is normally the time to recognize all the costs associated with producing that revenue. The need to match revenues and costs and the resulting need to accelerate or delay recognition of revenues or costs explains the accounting practices of *accrual* and *deferral* discussed in Section A.3 above.

→ *Materiality.* There are some items in the financial life of any entity which are too small or inconsequential to be accounted for. Determining this threshold of materiality requires the professional judgment of the accountant, and sometimes the lawyer, as materiality is a legal concept as well as an accounting concept.[11] Obviously materiality is context-sensitive. Chris' Used Books is likely to have a different standard of materiality than does General Electric Co., which reports on its December 31, 2006 balance sheet nearly $700 billion in assets.[12]

→ *Conservatism.* Management is likely to refer to this as "pessimism." Accountants are quick to recognize losses and slow to recognize gains. For example, the "realization" assumption discussed above does not apply to losses. If an asset has been "impaired" so that its fair market value is less than its carrying cost, and that decline in value is not temporary, then the decline must be recognized as a loss, despite the fact that no sale has been made.

→ *Consistency.* Accounting rules often take the form of a "menu" of permissible choices. Normally, however, once a choice is made it cannot be changed unless the circumstances require such a change because the accounting rules have changed, the business assets have changed, or a different method is preferable because it more clearly reflects the entity's financial position.

B. PROFITS AND LOSSES

With this grounding in financial statements and accounting terminology, we are ready to explore the *legal* issues faced by the business planner which involve these specialized concepts. We turn first to the concept of "profit" and the related concept of "loss." The desire to make profit is the engine of entrepreneurship. It is the main

---

[10] *See* Financial Accounting Standards Board, *Statement of Financial Accounting Concepts No. 5, Recognition and Measurement in Financial Statements of Business Enterprises* ¶¶ 83–84 (1984).

[11] Recall, for example, that the concept of securities fraud discussed in Chapter 4, Section D applies only to *material* misstatements or omissions. Materiality is not just a numerical concept, however; some items can be material by their nature, such as a business' transactions with its owners or managers. These are likely considered material because they have the potential for self-interested abuse by the insiders.

[12] GE's financial statements are a good example of the assumption about accounts and account titles. All of its $800 billion of assets are grouped into just 12 accounts. *See* www.ge.com/ar2008/pdf/ge_ar_2008_financial_section.pdf.

reason your clients have embarked upon their business venture. You might expect that they have spent a great deal of effort deciding exactly what the definition of "profit" is and how profit is to be shared. That expectation is rarely borne out in practice, however. A lawyer should discuss with his or her clients exactly the character, amounts and timing of "profits" they expect and document these expectations in writing.

Definition. What is "profit"? Many agreements — such as partnership or shareholder agreements — simply use the term without definition. A common alternative is to define the term as in its "ordinary accounting sense." Using this definition will incorporate all the assumptions discussed in Section A.4 of this chapter, including the rules of recognition, accrual and deferral. This may not be appropriate or necessary for a small business which could be efficiently run on a cash basis. Another common alternative is to define profit or loss in the manner in which it is calculated for federal income tax purposes. This can actually be a circular definition, because tax rules begin by defining the accounting method as the one "[by] which the taxpayer regularly computes his income in keeping his books."[13] There are exceptions, to be sure. In many instances the federal income tax rules dictate a particular accounting method based on the taxpayer's business or legal entity.[14]

Another reason that the critical term "profit" is not well defined in most agreements is that the amount of detail might soon overwhelm any workable written definition. Deciding when and how to recognize revenues and associated costs can be a complicated fact-intensive and fact-specific inquiry. Large parts of courses in financial accounting, managerial accounting, and income tax are devoted exclusively to these subjects. It is therefore reasonable that many agreements will defer to externally-defined profit measures, such as "the term 'profits' shall mean profits as determined by generally accepted accounting principles."

Calculation. The keeping of books and financial records is one important item which should be addressed in every business. A small cash-basis business might get by with having one of the partners or employees keep the books. But if there is the slightest doubt, it is best to provide for professionals to do the work "under the direction" of one of the business' managers.[15]

It is important in new, small business to distinguish among the different types of profit or income which might be realized. Many business owners find themselves in court in later years because they didn't consider what should be done with the profits from the sale of capital assets or major lines of business. Most accounting rules do not distinguish among types of income, but tax rules may be different, and state law might suggest still different answers.

In some instances, concepts of profit or loss can and should be avoided entirely. The fact that the term "profit" requires interpretation and fact-based judgments means that it is subject to self-interested manipulation. If you represent one of the constituents in a business enterprise and not the others, your approach may be substantially more adversarial than we have considered above. It is commonly said,

---

[13] IRC § 446(a).

[14] *See generally id.* §§ 446–448; Treas. Reg. § 1.446-1. In particular, Treas. Reg. § 1.446-1(c)(2)(i) requires accrual method accounting in a business with inventories.

[15] For a fuller discussion of management functions generally, see Chapter 7, Section A.

for example, that if your party is in control of the financial accounting, you can make payments from "profits" or "net" amounts, but if your party is an outsider, you should insist on being paid from "receipts" or "gross" amounts. The ability to insist upon payment from "gross receipts," or "off the top," is often a function of the bargaining power of one party. Note that those paid "off the top" such as creditors or even employees (consider Lucy in Exercise 6-3 below), receive returns from even an unprofitable enterprise. Others who wait for the "net profits," however, may find themselves with no returns from an enterprise which "made lots of money" in the colloquial sense, but had no "profits."[16]

Example 1. An employment agreement provides: "Mr. Morris [is] to be employed as Manager of the Orange, Tex. G. & W Marine Inc. store, to be paid 40% of the net profits from that store, with a guaranteed salary of $200.00 dollars per week. Salary of $200.00 to be paid weekly, and excess based on 40% net profit of store to be paid yearly, at first of year." Does the "net profit" mean profit before or after corporate income taxes? *See* G&W Marine, Inc. v. Morris, 471 S.W.2d 644 (Tex. Civ. App. 1971). The court called net profits a "chameleon-like term," citing no less than eight differing judicial interpretations. *Id.* at 647–49.

Example 2. A departing partner in a partnership was to be paid, for the value of his interest in the partnership, an amount determined over the five-year period following his departure. The amount was the lesser of 15% of gross collections or 50% of the profit. The contract defined profit as "gross collections, less staff payroll cost, less $10 per hour for partners' time, less 30 percent of staff payroll cost as a charge for overhead. If actual overhead cost was less than 30 percent of staff payroll cost, the actual figure was to be used." This formula was applied, and plaintiff was entitled to nothing when the formula produced calculations showing a loss. *See* Powel v. Burke, 178 Conn. 384, 423 A.2d 97 (1979).

Example 3. Seller agrees to sell a business to Buyer. A condition of the closing of the sale is that, for the six months prior to the closing date, the business' "normal operating expenses" (NOE) will not exceed 32% of "gross income." Buyer contends that NOE means "all actual expenses less capital and unrelated expenditures," and by that standard the condition is not met. Seller contends that "non-recurring" but non-capital expenses should not have been included in NOE, because they were not "normal." *Held* for Buyer. *See* Van der Noord v. Katz, 481 So.2d 1228 (Fla.App. 1986).

EXERCISE 6-3

Constance and Lucy have formed a partnership to own and operate an apartment building. Constance has contributed the building, worth $750,000. Lucy has contributed $250,000 in cash to make needed repairs and upgrades to the property and to get the business started. Lucy is working as the building manager and will receive a salary, but Constance is a passive investor and is seeking return on her investment only from the profits of the rental business and the underlying appreciation of the land and buildings. They have agreed that, because Lucy's salary provides her with a minimum fixed return, that the profits or losses from the

[16] The best and most litigated example is in the motion picture industry, where the ability to negotiate payments from gross receipts depends on the bargaining power of the actors involved. For a careful analysis including the legal issues involved in litigating such contracts, see Victor Goldberg, *The Net Profits Puzzle*, 97 Columbia L. Rev. 524 (1997).

business should be divided 85% to Constance and 15% to Lucy.

(1) How should Lucy's salary be treated in computation of profits? Would special language be required or wise to indicate that result? If so, draft a definition of "profits" for use in this partnership agreement.

(2) Suppose the building is sold for $1.1 million. If you have no other language than what has been drafted so far (and ignoring depreciation), how would the profit be divided? Do you think that is the result Constance and Lucy would have intended? If not, draft additional language to reach the desired result.

(3) Suppose, instead of either (1) or (2), the profits will be split 75%-25%, except that in computing profit or loss, Constance will be allocated all of the depreciation deductions. Why would they make such an agreement? How would you draft language to reflect it?

C.   CORPORATE DIVIDENDS AND DISTRIBUTIONS

In order to understand and apply the legal rules governing corporate dividends and distributions, we need some more detail on the accounting for corporate ownership interests. In the above examples regarding Chris' Used Books, we could record the ownership interest simply as "Chris — owner's equity." This account would record the value of both Chris' original contributions and the additional profits (or the subtracted losses). Unfortunately, the accounting for corporate contributions and income is more complicated. In this section we will divide our discussion into three parts: (i) defining corporate equity accounts; (ii) accounting for and regulating dividends; and (iii) accounting for and regulating other types of distributions to stockholders.

1.   Corporate Equity Accounts

A corporation typically uses two different accounts to record the value of the stock distributed in exchange for assets contributed by the stockholder. The two accounts record amounts determined by the *par value* of the stock.

In olden times (a century ago), "par value" was a dollar value which bore some faint resemblance to the amount of money or property that shareholders contributed or agreed to contribute to the corporation in exchange for their shares. The theory was that creditors relied on a balance sheet showing how much the investors contributed to the corporation, in order to be sure that it had real assets.[17] This reliance theory had two important legal consequences, both of which endure in some fashion today. First, if a shareholder did not pay par value for the shares received, payment could be demanded from the *stockholders* upon the

---

[17] With the accounting knowledge you have acquired so far, you know that it is folly to rely on the owner's equity accounts to represent any "value" of assets. That value is, of course, reflected in the *asset* accounts, not the *owners' equity* accounts.

> Whether the concept of legal capital was ever relied on . . . by a substantial number of creditors and, if so, for how long a period of American business history, are elusive historical questions. But it is fairly clear that the original concept was understood in the way described and that it stopped being of much possible utility to creditors many decades ago.

Robert C. Clark, Corporate Law 612 (1986) (quoting Bayless Manning & James J. Hanks, Jr., Legal Capital 18 (3d ed. 1990)).

corporation's insolvency.[18] Second, the par value served as a limitation on the value of assets the corporation could distribute to its shareholders. It is this second consequence which is the subject of our inquiry here.[19] Now that you know the ancient history of par value, put it far from your mind; it will only serve to confuse you.[20] Par value is still around today only because the corporation laws of many states require that a par value be stated. It has no necessary inherent value, but is simply defined in circular fashion as the amount, expressed in dollars (or some fraction of dollars) assigned to each share of stock as its par value. As we will see in the discussion which follows, it is usually best to establish the par value as a trivial amount, but not zero.

Because par value has legal significance we keep track of it in a separate account. The par value is recorded in one owners' equity account, and the remainder of the value of the consideration is recorded in another owners' equity account. Finally, when the corporation makes profits, these profits are recorded in yet a third equity owners' equity account. Unfortunately, the names for these accounts vary, depending on whether you are speaking to an accountant or a lawyer.

How to translate the terminology for corporate owners' equity accounts	Accounting term	Term used in most state laws
The amount representing par value of the shares	Common stock (par value)	Stated capital
The remainder of the amount representing consideration paid for the shares	Contributed capital in excess of par	Capital surplus or paid-in capital
Profits	Retained earnings	Earned surplus

Example. Suppose that Chris decided to embark upon the Used Book Store adventure in the corporate form instead of as a sole proprietor. Let us set up the corporation as follows. First, Chris will use his $1000 cash investment to buy stock in the corporation, and then the corporation will use the cash to purchase used books. Let us set the par value of the shares at a low amount, say one dollar, and let us issue Chris ten shares of stock in return for the $1000 contribution. Each share will have a total value of $100. Chris' Used Books Inc.'s balance sheet would appear as follows:

[18] *See* Manning & Hanks, *supra*, at 21–26. The Manning and Hanks treatise is the authoritative guide for matters involving corporate distributions and dividends, and is an entertaining reference as well. For an example of such statutes requiring shareholder contribution up to par value, see Del. Gen. Corp. Law §§ 152, 153(a), and 162. The MBCA does not require par value nor give it any legal significance.

[19] The first issue — how to value contributions to the corporation — was covered in Chapter 5, Section B.

[20] "In large degree, . . . it is an error to attempt a precise reconstruction of the way in which the nineteenth century looked at such matters [of corporate finance]. The truth is that there simply was no coherent view of these matters in the nineteenth century." Manning & Hanks, *supra*, at 20.

Chris' Used Books Inc. — Balance Sheet
[today's date]

Assets

Cash $ 1000

Liabilities and Equity

Common stock, $ 1 par $ 10
Contributed capital in excess of par   990

The division of the ownership interest into a number of shares and the resulting price per share is mostly an arbitrary decision. Some state corporation laws assess certain fees based on the number of shares authorized or outstanding, but otherwise the decision of whether to issue Chris ten, one, or one thousand shares is not critical, so long as the par value per share is kept at a small fraction of the total value.[21]

Now let's consider how the accounts vary when the corporation makes a profit or loss. The profit (or loss) at the end of each accounting period, determined according to the income statement, is added to (or subtracted from) the "retained earnings" or "earned surplus" account.

Example. Let's continue with Chris' incorporated business as we did earlier in the chapter. Suppose Chris has bought books and borrowed money, as before. The corporation's balance sheet would appear as follows.

Chris' Used Books Inc. — Balance Sheet
[first date]

Assets

Cash $ 500
Books   1500
Total $ 2000

Liabilities and Equity

Bank loan $ 1000
Common stock, $ 1 par   10
Contributed capital in excess of par   990
Total $ 2000

And again, suppose Chris convinces a customer to pay $12 for a book which Chris purchased for $10. We would show the $2 of net income as follows.

Chris' Used Books — New Balance Sheet
[second date]

Assets

Cash $ 512
Books   1490
Total $ 2002

---

[21] So if we issued Chris 1000 shares for $1 each, they should have a par value of 1¢ or less. In a closely-held corporation, it is usually a simple matter to amend the articles of incorporation to increase or reduce the number of authorized shares so that the value per share can be adjusted as desired.

Liabilities and Equity

Bank loan	$ 1000
Common stock, $ 1 par	10
Contributed capital in excess of par	990
Retained earnings	2
Total	**$ 2002**

2.   Accounting for and Regulating Dividends

We see how these three accounts — common stock, contributed capital, and retained earnings — operate to keep track of shareholders' equity as capital is invested and as profits are realized. These accounts are referred to in corporations statutes to measure the permissible amounts of dividends and other distributions. The purpose of these statutes, as we noted above, is to protect creditors from owners who would distribute all the business assets to themselves and leave nothing for the corporation's creditors. In order to understand how corporate statutes restrict distributions and protect creditors (or don't protect creditors), we need to discuss dividend accounting.

Suppose after the activity in the above examples, Chris' corporation were to declare a dividend of 20¢ per share, or a total of $2 (with 10 shares outstanding). A dividend is a payment of cash, so cash will be reduced by $2, and the corresponding change will be to reduce retained earnings by $2.

Chris' Used Books — New Balance Sheet
[after dividend]

Assets

Cash	$ 510
Books	1490
Total	**$ 2000**

Liabilities and Equity

Bank loan	$ 1000
Common stock, $ 1 par	10
Contributed capital in excess of par	990
Retained earnings	0
Total	**$ 2000**

Notice that, because the corresponding entry is to reduce retained earnings, we could say that the retained earnings account "measures" the amount of the dividend. Indeed, some attorneys may speak (inaccurately) of paying a dividend "out of retained earnings." You know that this terminology is inaccurate — the dividend is paid out of an asset account (usually cash).

Therefore, state laws restricting distributions — which were enacted to protect creditors — measure the amount of a corporation's permitted payment by reference to these equity accounts. The three state corporation laws which follow are broadly representative of the three general approaches taken by most state laws.

CALIFORNIA CORPORATIONS CODE

§ 500. Distributions; retained earnings or assets remaining after completion

Neither a corporation nor any of its subsidiaries shall make any distribution to the corporation's shareholders except as follows:

(a)   The distribution may be made if the amount of the retained earnings of the corporation immediately prior thereto equals or exceeds the amount of the proposed distribution.

(b)   The distribution may be made if immediately after giving effect thereto:

(1)   The sum of the assets of the corporation . . . would be at least equal to 1 1/4 times its liabilities . . . and

(2)   The current assets of the corporation would be at least equal to its current liabilities . . . .

(c)   The amount of any distribution payable in property shall, for the purposes of this chapter, be determined on the basis of the value at which the property is carried on the corporation's financial statements in accordance with generally accepted accounting principles.

(d)   For the purpose of applying this section to a distribution by a corporation of cash or property in payment by the corporation in connection with the purchase of its shares, there shall be added to retained earnings all amounts that had been previously deducted therefrom with respect to obligations incurred in connection with the corporation's repurchase of its shares and reflected on the corporation's balance sheet, but not in excess of the principal of the obligations that remain unpaid immediately prior to the distribution. In addition, there shall be deducted from liabilities all amounts that had been previously added thereto with respect to the obligations incurred in connection with the corporation's repurchase of its shares and reflected on the corporation's balance sheet, but not in excess of the principal of the obligations that will remain unpaid after the distribution, provided that no addition to retained earnings or deduction from liabilities under this subdivision shall occur on account of any obligation that is a distribution to the corporation's shareholders at the time the obligation is incurred.

. . . .

§ 501. Inability to meet liabilities as they mature; prohibition of distribution

Neither a corporation nor any of its subsidiaries shall make any distribution to the corporation's shareholders (Section 166) if the corporation or the subsidiary making the distribution is, or as a result thereof would be, likely to be unable to meet its liabilities (except those whose payment is otherwise adequately provided for) as they mature.

§ 114. Financial statements and accounting items

All references in this division to financial statements, balance sheets, income statements and statements of changes in financial position of a corporation and all references to assets, liabilities, earnings, retained earnings and similar accounting items of a corporation mean such financial statements or such items prepared or determined in conformity with generally accepted accounting principles then applicable, fairly presenting in conformity with generally accepted accounting principles the matters which they purport to present, subject to any specific accounting treatment required by a particular section of this division. . . .

DELAWARE GENERAL CORPORATION LAW

§ 170.   Dividends; payment; wasting asset corporations.

(a)   The directors of every corporation . . . may declare and pay dividends upon the shares of its capital stock either (1) out of its surplus, as defined and computed in accordance with . . . § 154 of this title, or (2) in case there shall be no such surplus, out of its net profits for the fiscal year in which the dividend is declared and/or the preceding fiscal year.

. . . .

§ 154.   Determination of amount of capital; capital, surplus and net assets defined.

Any corporation may, by resolution of its board of directors, determine that only a part of the consideration which shall be received by the corporation for any of the shares of its capital stockm . . . shall be capital; [and if] all the shares issued shall be shares having a par value, . . . the amount of the part of such consideration so determined to be capital need be only equal to the aggregate par value of such shares. . . . The excess, if any, at any given time, of the net assets of the corporation over the amount so determined to be capital shall be surplus. Net assets means the amount by which total assets exceed total liabilities. Capital and surplus are not liabilities for this purpose.

MODEL BUSINESS CORPORATION ACT

§ 6.40.   Distributions to Shareholders

(a)   A board of directors may authorize and the corporation may make distributions to it shareholders subject to restriction by the articles of incorporation and the limitation in subsection (c).

(c)   No distribution may be made if, after giving it effect:

(1)   the corporation would not be able to pay its debts as they become due in the usual course of business; or

(2)   the corporation's total net assets would be less than the sum of its total liabilities plus (unless the articles of incorporation permit otherwise) the amount that would be needed, if the corporation were to be dissolved at the time of the distribution, to satisfy the preferential rights upon dissolution of shareholders whose preferential rights are superior to those receiving the distribution.

Summary of the statutory requirements

The general structure of each of these statutes is similar. The statutes place two different kinds of limits on the ability of a corporation to pay dividends.

Balance sheet test. The first limitation is known as the "balance sheet" insolvency test. This test looks at the fundamental accounting equation and requires, when cash and equity are both reduced by payment of the dividend, some equity be remaining.

- Under Cal. Corp. Code § 500(a), this test is stated by reference to paying out the corporation's "retained earnings," thereby leaving the amounts represented by common stock (par value) and contributed capital in excess of par. Additional and more sophisticated measures of solvency are included in § 500(b), looking at the total-assets-to-debt ratio in subsection (1), and net working capital (current assets less current liabilities) in subsection (2).

- Under Del. Gen. Corp. Law § 170(a)(1), "surplus" is the measure of permitted dividends. Under § 154, surplus is defined as every corporate equity account *other* than "par value," although the corporation could choose to reduce surplus (and thus its ability to pay dividends) if it so chooses.

- Under MBCA § 6.40, the corporation may pay out the *entire amount* represented by *all* the corporation's capital accounts, except for the liquidation preference on the corporation's preferred stock, if any.[22]

The above statutes are summarized graphically below. The first two columns list the accounts on the "liabilities and equity" side of the balance sheet, using first their accounting and then their state law terminology.[23] Then we summarize the results from each of the three statutes. You can see a pattern, with California being the most restrictive on distributions, the MBCA being the least restrictive, and Delaware being in-between.

Accounting terminology	State law terminology[24]	Available for distribution[25] in:		
		California	Delaware	MBCA
Liabilities	Liabilities	No	No	No
Common stock (par value)	Capital stock	No	No	Yes
Contributed capital in excess of par	Capital surplus	No	Yes	Yes
Retained earnings	Earned surplus	Yes	Yes	Yes

Equity insolvency test. The second limitation is known as the "equity insolvency test." This is yet another use of the term "equity," not in the balance sheet sense, but more in the judicial "equitable" sense.[26] In any event, this test applies, even if a distribution could be made under the balance sheet test, if it would leave the corporation unable to pay its debts. Cal. Corp. Code § 501 uses the language "as they mature," and MBCA § 6.40(c)(1) adds "in the usual course of business."

---

[22] For a discussion of preferred stock and liquidation preferences, see Chapter 5, Section D.1.c.

[23] From the chart in the text at the beginning of Section C.1 of this chapter.

[24] Except in California, which uses accounting terminology; see Cal. Corp. Code § 114 reproduced above.

[25] Note that, in referring to these amounts in the equity accounts as "available for distribution," we have used the typical lawyer's terminology, assuming that these accounts represent anything of value. They, of course, do not; rather, what they do is *measure* the amount of assets which can be distributed.

[26] *See* Manning & Hanks, *supra*, at 63 (tracing the origin of the concept to the English chancery (equity) courts).

The equity insolvency test is important as a second check on the ability of a corporation to make a distribution, and a further protection of creditors. If, for example, the corporation has been profitable but has invested the assets in machines, inventory, or real estate, it may have substantial equity in the accounting sense, but have very little cash flow, if the property does not produce income and will not or cannot be sold. The corporation is "wealthy" but it may have very little cash with which to meet its obligations, and may be driven to insolvency or bankruptcy for this reason.[27]

In order to satisfy the equity insolvency test, the business planner will need to have a candid discussion with his or her client, perhaps also with an accountant or financial advisor, to budget for the distribution if it is to be one paid over time. The payment agreement will also need to take into account what happens if the purchaser defaults on payments and the type and amount of security which may be furnished to the distributee.

Delaware uses a quite different income-based test. Del. Gen Corp. Law § 170(a)(2) is known as the "nimble dividends" test.[28] It permits a corporation to pay a dividend, if there is no surplus, "out of its net profits for the fiscal year in which the dividend is declared and/or the preceding fiscal year." This short clause raises a host of interpretive questions, as noted by one commentator:

> Given the importance of Delaware as a leading state of incorporation, it might be thought that its legal capital provisions would be elegantly sophisticated in their drafting. Regrettably, the situation is otherwise. . . . [T]he interpretational questions set out below . . . are representative of the spray of issues that spume out of Delaware's delphic provision on "nimble dividends."
>
> *Accounting questions:* What is intended by "net profits"? Same as "earnings"? Why "net"? Assuming that the imprecise term "out of surplus" means "charged against surplus," what does it mean as an accounting matter to have dividends "charged against net profits"?
>
> *Substantive questions:* The provision purports to make the "net profits" avenue available as an option if but only if there is no surplus. But suppose the corporation has a $1 surplus and net profits of $20? How much can be distributed? Is it permissible to distribute $1 first and then, since no surplus is left, pay out the $20 in a second distribution? Or $19? . . . .
>
> *Timing questions:* Is the reference to the fiscal year to be taken literally (*i.e.* as meaning a full year), so that the corporation may not, at six months into the year, pay dividends "out of" the "net profits" of the first six months? On the other hand, if the corporation has its income statement for Year N, it also has the balance sheet for Year N, so the earnings in year N are already reflected on the balance sheet; if both surplus *and* earnings for that year can be used, does that not double count? And what is the

---

[27] Inability to pay debts as they become due is one ground for a debtor to be placed in bankruptcy involuntarily; see Bankruptcy Code § 303(h)(1), discussed in Chapter 10, Section E.5.d.

[28] This means "in essence that directors must be nimble in declaring dividends before the earnings are transferred to offset deficits." James D. Cox & Thomas Lee Hazen, Corporations 563n.2 (2d ed. 2003) (citing *Recent Cases, Corporations — Dividends — Virginia Statute Construed to Allow Dividends from Current Profits Despite Capital Deficit*, 62 Harv. L. Rev. 130 (1948)).

"preceding year"? Preceding what? . . . . And what is the timing relationship implied in the reference to separate dates of declaration and payment?

Miscellaneous question: What could be intended by the inviting but puzzling "and/or" in the statutory text?[29]

Despite these interpretive problems, "nimble dividends" statutes have been adopted by states which model their corporation laws on those of Delaware.[30] Most recently, New York amended its corporation law to permit such distributions, with the following justification.

> Historically, limiting the payment to dividends to surplus was intended to protect corporate creditors against excessive distributions that would jeopardize the corporation's ability to repay its debts and other obligations. . . . However, the concept of protecting creditors with the surplus limitation is now outdated. In the era of no-par and low-par shares, it has been long-recognized that stated capital provides no protection to creditors. Since most stock issued today is either no-par or low-par value, the proposed legislation is desirable in that it does away with an antiquated principle. . . . The amendment will update New York corporate law to align with the more modern trend of no-par and low-par value shares while also harmonizing it with Delaware law.[31]

This excerpt indicates a common method of avoiding limitations on distributions based on the par value of shares: simply set the par value very low. It is, after all, an arbitrary amount. Setting it at zero may not be advisable, because there can be other statutes which "deem" a zero par value to be some higher amount.[32]

EXERCISE 6-4

In each of the following phases in a corporation's life, it has the balance sheet shown below. Determine the maximum permissible dividend in Delaware, California,[33] and an MBCA state.

(1)   The stockholders buy 100 shares of $1 par common stock for $5 each.

Cash	500	Common stock	100
		Add'l paid-in capital	400
Total	500	Total	500

(2)   During its first year, the corporation borrows money to buy land, and has net income of $100. At the end of the year, its position is as follows.

---

[29] Manning & Hanks, *supra*, at 83–84 & n.34.

[30] *See, e.g.*, Kan. Stat. Ann. § 17-6420 (cited in Cox & Hazen, *supra*, at 563n.1).

[31] http://www.nysba.org/Content/ContentFolders/Legislation/LegislativeMemoranda20072008/BLSMemorandum5.pdf (May 21, 2008).

[32] *See, e.g.*, Nev. Rev. Stat. § 78.760(3) (filing fee for articles of incorporation based on the total par value of the authorized shares, but provides that if the shares have no par value, the par value is deemed to be $1 per share).

[33] For purposes of applying Cal. Corp. Code § 500(b), assume that "Cash" and "Accounts Receivable" are current assets.

Cash	200	Current liabilities	100
Accounts receivable	500	Long-term debt	1,000
Land	1,000		
		Common stock	100
		Add' paid-in capital	400
		Retained earnings	100
Total	1,700	Total	1,700

(3)   The second year doesn't go so well; the corporation has a net loss of $500.

Cash	100	Current liabilities	200
Accounts receivable	200	Long-term debt	1,000
Land	1,000		
		Common stock	100
		Add'l paid-in capital	400
		Ret. earnings (deficit)	(400)
Total	1,300	Total	1,300

(4)   Suppose instead that the land were actually worth $1,400, based on reliable appraisals. Could the directors revalue it as follows?

Cash	100	Current liabilities	200
Accounts receivable	200	Long-term debt	1,000
Land (market value)	1,400		
		Common stock	100
		Add'l paid-in capital	400
		Ret. earnings (deficit)	-0-
Total	1,700	Total	1,700

If so, what would be the maximum dividend permitted under the following authorities?

RANDALL v. BAILEY

New York Supreme Court, Trial Term, New York County
23 N.Y.S.2d 173 (1940)

WALTER, JUSTICE.

A trustee of Bush Terminal Company, appointed in a proceeding under . . . the Bankruptcy Act, here sues former directors of that company to recover on its behalf the amount of dividends declared and paid between November 22, 1928, and May 2, 1932, aggregating $3,639,058.06. At the times of the declarations and payments, the company's books concededly showed a surplus which ranged from not less than $4,378,554.83 on December 31, 1927, down to not less than $2,199,486.77 on April 30, 1932. The plaintiff claims, however, that in fact there was no surplus, that the capital was actually impaired to an amount greater than the amount of the dividends, and that the directors consequently are personally liable to the corporation for the amount thereof under Section 58 of the Stock Corporation Law. Defendants claim that there was no impairment of capital and that the surplus was actually greater than the amount which plaintiff concedes as the amount shown by the books.

The claims of the plaintiff, although branching out to a multitude of items, are basically reducible to [two]:

1. It was improper to 'write-up' the land values above cost and thereby take unrealized appreciation into account.

2. It was improper not to 'write-down' to actual value the cost of investments in and advances to subsidiaries and thereby fail to take unrealized depreciation into account.

. . . .

Until 1915 the company's land was carried upon its books at cost. In 1915 the land was written up to 80% of the amount at which it was then assessed for taxation, and in 1918 it was written up to the exact amount at which it was then so assessed. Those two write-ups totalled $7,211,791.72, and the result was that during the period here in question the land was carried on the books at $8,737,949.02, whereas its actual cost was $1,526,157.30. Plaintiff claims that the entire $7,211,791.72 should be eliminated because it represents merely unrealized appreciation, and dividends cannot be declared or paid on the basis of mere unrealized appreciation in fixed assets irrespective of how sound the estimate thereof may be. That obviously and concededly is another way of saying that for dividend purposes fixed assets must be computed at cost, not value, and plaintiff here plants himself upon that position, even to the point of contending that evidence of value is immaterial and not admissible. If that contention be sound, the company indisputably had a deficit at all the times here involved in an amount exceeding the dividends here in question. . . .

It is to be emphasized at the outset that the question is not one of sound economics, or of what is sound business judgment or financial policy or of proper accounting practice, or even what the law ought to be. My views of the business acumen or financial sagacity of these directors, as well as my views as to what the legislature ought to permit or prohibit, are entirely immaterial. The question I have to decide is whether or not an existing statute has been violated. The problem is one of statutory construction.

The words of the statute, as it existed during the period here involved, are: 'No stock corporation shall declare or pay any dividend which shall impair its capital or capital stock, nor while its capital or capital stock is impaired, nor shall any such corporation declare or pay any dividend or make any distribution of assets to any of its stockholders, whether upon a reduction of the number of its shares or of its capital or capital stock, unless the value of its assets remaining after the payment of such dividend, or after such distribution of assets, as the case may be, shall be at least equal to the aggregate amount of its debts and liabilities including capital or capital stock as the case may be.' Stock Corporation Law, § 58, as enacted by Laws 1923, c. 787.

If the part of the statute containing the words 'unless the value of its assets' etc. is to be read as relating back to the beginning of the section, the lack of merit in plaintiff's contention is apparent, for the statute would then read: 'No stock corporation shall declare or pay any dividend * * * unless the value of its assets remaining after the payment of such dividend * * * shall be at least equal to the aggregate amount of its debts and liabilities including capital or capital stock as the case may be.' I think there is much to be said in support of the view that that is what was intended, but nevertheless the structure of the statute is such as to make that reading grammatically impossible, and I hence prefer to base my decision upon the assumption that the controlling words of the statute are merely these: 'No stock corporation shall declare or pay any dividend which shall impair its capital or capital stock, nor while its capital or capital stock is impaired.'

Before one can determine whether or not capital or capital stock has been impaired, one must determine what is capital or capital stock. The words to be construed thus are words which have varied and different meanings and express radically different concepts in different connections. Capital means one thing to an economist, or, perhaps more accurately, different things to different economists, and it has still different meanings to accountants and to business men. It even means different things in different statutes. To determine its meaning in this statute it thus is essential, I think, to consider the history of the statute and what our courts have said respecting the statute's predecessors.

. . . .

It . . . appears that after using the surplus and surplus profits terminology for practically a hundred years the legislature [in 1923] completely abandoned it, and I think that is quite significant as indicating a conscious intent to get away from the idea of profits earned as a result of completed transactions as the sole source of dividends. I do not say that the legislature thereby changed the existing law. On the contrary, I think that the terms capital and capital stock as used in the earlier statutes had been construed by the courts in such a way that the terms surplus and surplus profits as used therein necessarily meant any accretion or accumulation over and above debts and the liability to stockholders, and that the legislature of 1923 recognized and adopted that construction and omitted any reference to surplus or surplus profits for the very reason that by some persons those words were believed to convey [in defining "capital"] the idea of and to be confined to an accumulation of net earnings resulting from completed transactions and for the express purpose of so clarifying the statute as to prevent the precise claim which plaintiff now here presses. . . .

. . . .

[T]he terms capital and capital stock in these statutes mean an amount, i.e. a value, of property up to the limit of the number of dollars specified as the par value of paid-up issued shares (or as the stated value of no-par shares), and that when the amount, i.e. the value, of the company's property exceeds that number of dollars the excess, whether 'contributed by the stockholders or otherwise obtained' is surplus or surplus profits and may be distributed as dividends until the point is reached where such dividends 'deplete the assets,' i.e. the value of the assets, 'below the sum,' i.e. below the number of dollars, specified as the par or stated value of the paid-up issued shares. In other words, the capital or capital stock referred to in these statutes is the sum of the liability to stockholders, and any value which the corporation's property has in addition to that sum is surplus. And I cannot doubt that [the authority of prior cases would] include an appreciation in the value of property purchased whether realized or unrealized.

. . . .

In summary, I think that it cannot be said that there is a single case in this State which actually decides that unrealized appreciation cannot be taken into consideration, or, stated in different words, that cost and not value must be used in determining whether or not there exists a surplus out of which dividends can be paid. I think, further, that such a holding would run directly counter to the meaning of the terms capital and capital stock as fixed by decisions of the Court of Appeals construing the earlier statutes, and that such construction of those terms must be deemed to have been adopted by the legislature in enacting the statute here involved. I thus obviously cannot follow decisions to the contrary in other States or any contrary views of economists or accountants. If the policy of the law be bad it is for the legislature to change it.

Throughout the period in question the company carried upon its books as assets its investments in and advances to its subsidiaries at their face value, i.e. at the cost thereof, and despite his insistence that unrealized appreciation of one asset cannot be taken into consideration, the plaintiff yet insists that these investments and advances must be written down to the value thereof as shown by the books of the subsidiaries, even though the subsidiaries are still carrying on business, and, further, that those books shall be what he calls 'properly adjusted', so as to cause them to show the actual value of the stock of and claims against those subsidiaries. He thus, as it seems to me, takes the inconsistent position that while unrealized appreciation cannot be considered, unrealized depreciation nevertheless must be. Defendants, also, take the equally inconsistent position that while unrealized appreciation must be considered, unrealized depreciation need not be. I am of the opinion that the same reasons which show that unrealized appreciation must be considered are equally cogent in showing that unrealized depreciation likewise must be considered. In other words, the test being whether or not the value of the assets exceeds the debts and the liability to stockholders, all assets must be taken at their actual value.

I see no cause for alarm over the fact that this view requires directors to make a determination of the value of the assets at each dividend declaration. On the contrary, I think that is exactly what the law always has contemplated that directors should do. That does not mean that the books themselves necessarily must be altered by write-ups or write-downs at each dividend period, or that formal appraisals must be obtained from professional appraisers or even made by the directors themselves. That is obviously impossible in the case of corporations of any considerable size. But it is not impossible nor unfeasible for directors to consider whether the cost of assets continues over a long period of years to reflect their fair value, and the law does require that directors should really direct in the very important matter of really determining at each dividend declaration whether or not the value of the assets is such as to justify a dividend, rather than do what one director here testified that he did, viz. 'accept the company's figures.' The directors are the ones who should determine the figures by carefully considering values, and it was for the very purpose of compelling them to perform that duty that the statute imposes upon them a personal responsibility for declaring and paying dividends when the value of the assets is not sufficient to justify them. What directors must do is to exercise an informed judgment of their own, and the amount of information which they should obtain, and the sources from which they should obtain it, will of course depend upon the circumstances of each particular case. If directors have blindly or complacently accepted either cost or any other arbitrary figures as indicative of value, they have not exercised either discretion or judgment and no court is required to act as if they had. When directors have in fact exercised an informed judgment with respect to the value of the company's assets, the courts obviously will be exceedingly slow to override that judgment, and clear and convincing evidence will be required to justify a finding that such judgment was not in accordance with the facts. In the last analysis, however, the issue, in any case in which it is claimed that dividends have been paid out of capital, is the value of the assets and the amount of the liabilities to creditors and stockholders at the times the dividends were declared and paid.

Upon the evidence in this case I find that the directors here did in fact exercise an informed judgment with respect to . . . the value of the land of the company, and the value of the improvements thereon, and also with respect to the value of the land and improvements thereon which were owned by the subsidiaries, Bush Terminal Buildings Company and Bush Terminal Railroad Company, and that they believed and determined that . . . such land and improvements were worth several millions of dollars more than the amounts at which they were carried on the books. At least one of the directors was thoroughly versed in real estate values by reason of long and extensive experience in buying and selling and in recommending mortgage loans on real estate and was personally and thoroughly familiar with the properties and business of all the companies just named, and of the development thereof, from the time of the organization of the company, and no one could criticise any other director for relying upon his knowledge and judgment as to the value thereof, or for basing a judgment thereon. His knowledge and judgment probably were as safe and sound a guide as any formal appraisal that could have been obtained. At least one other of the directors likewise had a thorough familiarity with these properties and business from the inception of their developments.

I find that there was not the same exercise of informed judgment with respect to the value of the investments in and advances to subsidiaries. To a very large extent the value of the investments in and advances to Bush Terminal Buildings Company and Bush Terminal Railroad Company were affected by the value of the land and improvements owned by those companies, as to which I have just found that there was an exercise of an informed judgment; but on the whole I find that the directors accepted the cost of the investments in and advances to all the subsidiaries, as the same were recorded upon the books, without in fact considering the extent to which such recorded costs reflected their true values at the times of the declaration and payment of the dividends here in controversy.

. . . .

In summary, therefore, after considering all the evidence, I find that at the times these dividends were declared and paid the value of the assets exceeded the total liabilities to creditors and stockholders by an amount in excess of the total dividends, and that there accordingly was no impairment of capital or capital stock.

. . . .

Defendants' motions for judgment at the close of the whole case are granted, and I direct the entry of judgment for defendants, with separate bills of costs to those appearing by separate attorneys.

———————

The plaintiffs' cause of action in *Randall v. Bailey* is based on a provision of New York corporation law holding directors *personally liable* for improper distributions. This liability is apart from any duty of care, self-dealing, "veil piercing," or any other theory of director liability with which you might be familiar.[34] Consider the implications of similar Delaware statutes, set forth below, on the issue of corporate distributions. Does the specter of personal liability affect your answers to the problems we posed earlier in this chapter?

DELAWARE GENERAL CORPORATION LAW

§ 172. Liability of directors and committee members as to dividends or stock redemption

A member of the board of directors, or a member of any committee designated by the board of directors, shall be fully protected in relying in good faith upon the records of the corporation and upon such information, opinions, reports or statements presented to the corporation by any of its officers or employees, or committees of the board of directors, or by any other person as to matters the director reasonably believes are within such other person's professional or expert competence and who has been selected with reasonable care by or on behalf of the corporation, as to the value and amount of the assets, liabilities and/or net profits of the corporation or any other facts pertinent to the existence and amount of surplus or other funds from which dividends might properly be declared and paid, or with which the corporation's stock might properly be purchased or redeemed.

§ 173. Declaration and payment of dividends.

No corporation shall pay dividends except in accordance with the provisions of this chapter. . . .

§ 174. Liability of Directors . . .

(a) In case of any willful or negligent violation of the provisions of sections 160[35] or 173 of this title, the directors under whose administration the same may happen shall be jointly and severally liable, at any time within six years after paying such unlawful dividend or after such unlawful stock purchase or redemption, to the corporation, and to its creditors in the event of its dissolution or insolvency, to the full amount of the dividend unlawfully paid, or to the full amount of the purchase or redemption of the corporation's stock. . . .

(b) Any director against whom a claim is successfully asserted under this section shall be entitled to contribution from the other directors who voted for or concurred in the unlawful dividend, stock purchase or stock redemption.

(c) Any director against whom a claim is successfully asserted under this section shall be entitled, to the extent of the amount paid . . . , to be subrogated to the rights of the corporation against stockholders who received the dividend on, or assets for the sale or redemption of, their stock with knowledge of facts indicating that such dividend, stock purchase or redemption was unlawful under this chapter, in proportion to the amounts received by such stockholders respectively.

---

[34] States that impose personal liability on directors for improper distributions usually also provide statutory prohibitions on the elimination of such personal liability in the bylaws or articles of incorporation. *See* Cal. Corp. Code § 204(a)(10); Del. Gen. Corp. L § 102(b)(7); MBCA § 2.02(b)(4).

[35] Section 160, relating to distributions, is set forth and discussed below in Section C.3.—Eds.

CALIFORNIA CORPORATIONS CODE

§ 316. Corporate actions subjecting directors to joint and several liability; actions; damages

(a) Subject to the provisions of Section 309, directors of a corporation who approve any of the following corporate actions shall be jointly and severally liable to the corporation for the benefit of all of the creditors or shareholders entitled to institute an action under subdivision (c):

(1) The making of any distribution to its shareholders to the extent that it is contrary to the provisions of Sections 500 to 503, inclusive.

. . . .

(b) A director who is present at a meeting of the board, or any committee thereof, at which action specified in subdivision (a) is taken and who abstains from voting shall be considered to have approved the action.

(c) Suit may be brought in the name of the corporation to enforce the liability (1) under paragraph (1) of subdivision (a) against any or all directors liable by the persons entitled to sue under subdivision (b) of Section 506 . . . .

(e) Any director sued under this section may implead all other directors liable and may compel contribution, either in that action or in an independent action against directors not joined in that action.

(f) Directors liable under this section shall also be entitled to be subrogated to the rights of the corporation:

(1) With respect to paragraph (1) of subdivision (a), against shareholders who received the distribution.

. . . .

§ 506. Receipt of prohibited dividend; liability of shareholder; suit by creditors or other shareholders; fraudulent transfers

(a) Any shareholder who receives any distribution prohibited by this chapter with knowledge of facts indicating the impropriety thereof is liable to the corporation for the benefit of all of the creditors or shareholders entitled to institute an action under subdivision (b) for the amount so received by the shareholder with interest thereon at the legal rate on judgments until paid, but not exceeding the liabilities of the corporation owed to nonconsenting creditors at the time of the violation and the injury suffered by nonconsenting shareholders, as the case may be. For purposes of this chapter, in the event that any shareholder receives any distribution of the corporation's property that is prohibited by this chapter, the shareholder receiving that illegal distribution shall be liable to the corporation for an amount equal to the fair market value of the property at the time of the illegal distribution plus interest thereon from the date of the distribution at the legal rate on judgments until paid, together with all reasonably incurred costs of appraisal or other valuation, if any, of that property, but not exceeding the liabilities of the corporation owed to nonconsenting creditors at the time of the violation and the injury suffered by nonconsenting shareholders, as the case may be.

(b) Suit may be brought in the name of the corporation to enforce the liability (1) to creditors arising under subdivision (a) for a violation of Section 500 or 501 against any or all shareholders liable by any one or more creditors of the corporation whose debts or claims arose prior to the time of the distribution to shareholders and who have not consented thereto, whether or not they have reduced their claims to judgment, or (2) to shareholders arising under subdivision (a) for a violation of Section 502 or 503 against any or all shareholders liable by any one or more holders of preferred shares outstanding at the time of the distribution who have not consented thereto, without regard to the provisions of Section 800.[36]

(c)　Any shareholder sued under this section may implead all other shareholders liable under this section and may compel contribution, either in that action or in an independent action against shareholders not joined in that action.

(d)　Nothing contained in this section affects any liability which any shareholder may have under [the Uniform Fraudulent Transfer Act].

MODEL BUSINESS CORPORATION ACT

§ 6.40.　Distributions to Shareholders

(d)　The board of directors may base a determination that a distribution is not prohibited under subsection (c) either on financial statements prepared on the basis of accounting practices and principles that are reasonable in the circumstances or on a fair valuation or other method that is reasonable in the circumstances.

§ 8.33.　Directors' Liability for Unlawful Distributions

(a)　A director who votes for or assents to a distribution in excess of what may be authorized and made pursuant to section 6.40(a) . . . is personally liable to the corporation for the amount of the distribution that exceeds what could have been distributed without violating section 6.40(a) . . . .

(b)　A director held liable under subsection (a) for an unlawful distribution is entitled to:

　(1)　contribution from every other director who could be held liable under subsection (a) for the unlawful distribution; and

　(2)　recoupment from each shareholder of the pro-rata portion of the amount of the unlawful distribution the shareholder accepted, knowing the distribution was made in violation of section 6.40(a) . . . .

EXERCISE 6-5

Answer the questions in Exercise 6-4 according to the corporation law of your state, if you have not done so already. Does your state's statute expressly permit revaluation of assets? If not, do you believe that a fair argument could be made to apply *Randall v. Bailey*? What are the risks to your client's directors, existing shareholder or new transferees? What if the corporation becomes insolvent or files a petition in bankruptcy so that creditors can bring claims on the corporation's behalf?

3.　Accounting for and Regulating other Distributions

A dividend is a payment of cash or other assets to all holders of the same class of shares *pro rata* and does not alter the relative shareholdings of each owner. It is distinguished from a repurchase of shares from one or more shareholders which,

---

[36] Section 800 refers to requirements for shareholder derivative actions.—Eds.

although also a payment of cash or other assets to shareholders, is not *pro rata* and will change the ownership ratios. Repurchases by the corporation are most commonly used when an owner departs and the plan is to have the corporation, rather than one or more of the shareholders, purchase the shares.

Despite these differing legal constructions, most state statutes treat dividends and redemptions or repurchases similarly, despite the fact that the two are fundamentally different types of distributions to a shareholder "in respect of" his or her shares.[37] Some states, however, *do* treat a repurchase differently from a dividend. Delaware's statute is an example of treating the two types of distributions differently and has served as an example for other states.[38]

DELAWARE GENERAL CORPORATION LAW

§ 160. Corporation's powers respecting ownership, voting, etc. of its own stock; rights of stock called for redemption.

(a) Every corporation may purchase, redeem, receive, take or otherwise acquire, own and hold, sell, lend, exchange, transfer or otherwise dispose of, pledge, use, and otherwise deal in and with its own shares; provided, however, that no corporation shall:

(1) Purchase or redeem its own shares of capital stock for cash or other property when the capital of the corporation is impaired or when such purchase or redemption would cause any impairment of the capital of the corporation, except that a corporation may purchase or redeem out of capital any of its own shares which are entitled upon any distribution of its assets, whether by dividend or in liquidation, to a preference over another class or series of its stock, or, if no shares entitled to such a preference are outstanding, any of its own shares, if such shares will be retired upon their acquisition and the capital of the corporation reduced in accordance with §§ 243 and 244 of this title.

. . . .

§ 244. Reduction of capital

(a) A corporation, by resolution of its board of directors, may reduce its capital in any of the following ways:

(1) By reducing or eliminating the capital represented by shares of capital stock which have been retired;

(2) By applying to an otherwise authorized purchase or redemption of outstanding shares of its capital stock some or all of the capital represented by the shares being purchased or redeemed, or any capital that has not been allocated to any particular class of its capital stock;

(3) By applying to an otherwise authorized conversion or exchange of outstanding shares of its capital stock some or all of the capital represented by the shares being converted or exchanged, or some or all of any capital that has not been allocated to any particular class of its capital stock, or both, to the extent

---

[37] See, for example, MBCA § 1.40(6) and Cal. Corp. Code § 166, each defining "distribution" to include not only dividends, but repurchases and redemptions as well.

[38] *See, e.g.*, Kan. Stat. Ann. § 17-6410, N.Y. Bus. Corp. L. § 513.

that such capital in the aggregate exceeds the total aggregate par value or the stated capital of any previously unissued shares issuable upon such conversion or exchange; or

(4)   By transferring to surplus (i) some or all of the capital not represented by any particular class of its capital stock; (ii) some or all of the capital represented by issued shares of its par value capital stock, which capital is in excess of the aggregate par value of such shares; or (iii) some of the capital represented by issued shares of its capital stock without par value.

(b)   Notwithstanding the other provisions of this section, no reduction of capital shall be made or effected unless the assets of the corporation remaining after such reduction shall be sufficient to pay any debts of the corporation for which payment has not been otherwise provided. No reduction of capital shall release any liability of any stockholder whose shares have not been fully paid.

KLANG v. SMITH'S FOOD & DRUG CENTERS, INC.
Delaware Supreme Court
702 A.2d 150 (1997)

Before VEASEY, C.J., WALSH, HOLLAND, HARTNETT and BERGER, JJ., constituting the Court en Banc.

VEASEY, CHIEF JUSTICE:

This appeal calls into question the actions of a corporate board in carrying out a merger and self-tender offer. Plaintiff in this purported class action alleges that a corporation's repurchase of shares violated the statutory prohibition against the impairment of capital. . . .

No corporation may repurchase or redeem its own shares except out of "surplus," as statutorily defined, or except as expressly authorized by provisions of the statute not relevant here. Balance sheets are not, however, conclusive indicators of surplus or a lack thereof. Corporations may revalue assets to show surplus, but perfection in that process is not required. Directors have reasonable latitude to depart from the balance sheet to calculate surplus, so long as they evaluate assets and liabilities in good faith, on the basis of acceptable data, by methods that they reasonably believe reflect present values, and arrive at a determination of the surplus that is not so far off the mark as to constitute actual or constructive fraud.

We hold that, on this record, the Court of Chancery was correct in finding that there was no impairment of capital . . . . Accordingly, we affirm.

Facts

Smith's Food & Drug Centers, Inc. ("SFD") is a Delaware corporation that owns and operates a chain of supermarkets in the Southwestern United States. Slightly more than three years ago, Jeffrey P. Smith, SFD's Chief Executive Officer, began to entertain suitors with an interest in acquiring SFD. At the time, and until the transactions at issue, Mr. Smith and his family held common and preferred stock constituting 62.1% voting control of SFD. Plaintiff and the class he purports to represent are holders of common stock in SFD.

On January 29, 1996, SFD entered into an agreement with The Yucaipa Companies ("Yucaipa"), a California partnership also active in the supermarket industry. Under the agreement, the following would take place:

(1) Smitty's Supermarkets, Inc. ("Smitty's"), a wholly-owned subsidiary of Yucaipa that operated a supermarket chain in Arizona, was to merge into Cactus Acquisition, Inc. ("Cactus"), a subsidiary of SFD, in exchange for which SFD would deliver to Yucaipa slightly over 3 million newly-issued shares of SFD common stock;

(2) SFD was to undertake a recapitalization, in the course of which SFD would assume a sizable amount of new debt, retire old debt, and offer to repurchase up to fifty percent of its outstanding shares (other than those issued to Yucaipa) for $36 per share; and

(3) SFD was to repurchase 3 million shares of preferred stock from Jeffrey Smith and his family.

SFD hired the investment firm of Houlihan Lokey Howard & Zukin ("Houlihan") to examine the transactions and render a solvency opinion. Houlihan eventually issued a report to the SFD Board replete with assurances that the transactions would not endanger SFD's solvency, and would not impair SFD's capital in violation of 8 Del.C. § 160. On May 17, 1996, in reliance on the Houlihan opinion, SFD's Board determined that there existed sufficient surplus to consummate the transactions, and enacted a resolution proclaiming as much. On May 23, 1996, SFD's stockholders voted to approve the transactions, which closed on that day. The self-tender offer was over-subscribed, so SFD repurchased fully fifty percent of its shares at the offering price of $36 per share.

Disposition in the Court of Chancery

. . . . On May 30, 1996, plaintiff filed an amended complaint as well as a motion to have the transactions voided or rescinded. . . . [H]e contended that the stock repurchases violated 8 Del.C. § 160 by impairing SFD's capital . . . .

After defendants answered the amended complaint, plaintiff took full discovery. The Court of Chancery heard plaintiff's motion to have the transactions rescinded, and released a Memorandum Opinion dismissing plaintiff's claims in full. . . .

Plaintiff's Capital-Impairment Claim

A corporation may not repurchase its shares if, in so doing, it would cause an impairment of capital, unless expressly authorized by Section 160.[39] A repurchase impairs capital if the funds used in the repurchase exceed the amount of the corporation's "surplus," defined by 8 Del.C. § 154 to mean the excess of net assets over the par value of the corporation's issued stock.[40]

---

[39] [4] The provisions of Section 160 permitting a corporation to purchase its shares out of capital under circumstances are not implicated in this case. . . .

[40] [5] Section 154 provides, "Any corporation may, by resolution of its board of directors, determine that only a part of the consideration . . . received by the corporation for . . . its capital stock . . . shall be capital. . . . The excess . . . of the net assets of the corporation over the amount so determined to be capital shall be surplus. Net assets means the amount by which total assets exceed total liabilities. Capital and surplus are not liabilities for this purpose."

Plaintiff asked the Court of Chancery to rescind the transactions in question as violative of Section 160. As we understand it, plaintiff's position breaks down into two analytically distinct arguments. First, he contends that SFD's balance sheets constitute conclusive evidence of capital impairment. He argues that the negative net worth that appeared on SFD's books following the repurchase compels us to find a violation of Section 160. Second, he suggests that even allowing the Board to "go behind the balance sheet" to calculate surplus does not save the transactions from violating Section 160. In connection with this claim, he attacks the SFD Board's off-balance-sheet method of calculating surplus on the theory that it does not adequately take into account all of SFD's assets and liabilities. Moreover, he argues that the May 17, 1996 resolution of the SFD Board conclusively refutes the Board's claim that revaluing the corporation's assets gives rise to the required surplus. We hold that each of these claims is without merit.

SFD's balance sheets do not establish a violation of 8 Del.C. § 160

In an April 25, 1996 proxy statement, the SFD Board released a pro forma balance sheet showing that the merger and self-tender offer would result in a deficit to surplus on SFD's books of more than $100 million. A balance sheet the SFD Board issued shortly after the transactions confirmed this result. Plaintiff asks us to adopt an interpretation of 8 *Del.C.* § 160 whereby balance-sheet net worth is controlling for purposes of determining compliance with the statute. Defendants do not dispute that SFD's books showed a negative net worth in the wake of its transactions with Yucaipa, but argue that corporations should have the presumptive right to revalue assets and liabilities to comply with Section 160.

Plaintiff advances an erroneous interpretation of Section 160. We understand that the books of a corporation do not necessarily reflect the current values of its assets and liabilities. Among other factors, unrealized appreciation or depreciation can render book numbers inaccurate. It is unrealistic to hold that a corporation is bound by its balance sheets for purposes of determining compliance with Section 160. Accordingly, we adhere to the principles of *Morris v. Standard Gas & Electric Co.*[41] allowing corporations to revalue properly its assets and liabilities to show a surplus and thus conform to the statute.

It is helpful to recall the purpose behind Section 160. The General Assembly enacted the statute to prevent boards from draining corporations of assets to the detriment of creditors and the long-term health of the corporation. That a corporation has not yet realized or reflected on its balance sheet the appreciation of assets is irrelevant to this concern. Regardless of what a balance sheet that has not been updated may show, an actual, though unrealized, appreciation reflects real economic value that the corporation may borrow against or that creditors may claim or levy upon. Allowing corporations to revalue assets and liabilities to reflect current realities complies with the statute and serves well the policies behind this statute.

---

[41] [7] *Morris v. Standard Gas & Electric Co.*, Del. Ch., 63 A.2d 577 (1949).

The SFD Board appropriately revalued corporate assets to comply with 8 Del.C. § 160.

Plaintiff contends that SFD's repurchase of shares violated Section 160 even without regard to the corporation's balance sheets. Plaintiff claims that the SFD Board was not entitled to rely on the solvency opinion of Houlihan, which showed that the transactions would not impair SFD's capital given a revaluation of corporate assets. The argument is that the methods that underlay the solvency opinion were inappropriate as a matter of law because they failed to take into account all of SFD's assets and liabilities. In addition, plaintiff suggests that the SFD Board's resolution of May 17, 1996 itself shows that the transactions impaired SFD's capital, and that therefore we must find a violation of 8 *Del.C.* § 160. We disagree, and hold that the SFD Board revalued the corporate assets under appropriate methods. Therefore the self-tender offer complied with Section 160, notwithstanding errors that took place in the drafting of the resolution.

On May 17, 1996, Houlihan released its solvency opinion to the SFD Board, expressing its judgment that the merger and self-tender offer would not impair SFD's capital. Houlihan reached this conclusion by comparing SFD's "Total Invested Capital" of $1.8 billion — a figure Houlihan arrived at by valuing SFD's assets under the "market multiple" approach — with SFD's long-term debt of $1.46 billion. This comparison yielded an approximation of SFD's "concluded equity value" equal to $346 million, a figure clearly in excess of the outstanding par value of SFD's stock. Thus, Houlihan concluded, the transactions would not violate 8 *Del.C.* § 160.

Plaintiff contends that Houlihan's analysis relied on inappropriate methods to mask a violation of Section 160. Noting that 8 *Del.C.* § 154 defines "net assets" as "the amount by which total assets exceeds total liabilities," plaintiff argues that Houlihan's analysis is erroneous as a matter of law because of its failure to calculate "total assets" and "total liabilities" as separate variables. In a related argument, plaintiff claims that the analysis failed to take into account all of SFD's liabilities, *i.e.*, that Houlihan neglected to consider current liabilities in its comparison of SFD's "Total Invested Capital" and long-term debt. Plaintiff contends that the SFD Board's resolution proves that adding current liabilities into the mix shows a violation of Section 160. The resolution declared the value of SFD's assets to be $1.8 billion, and stated that its "total liabilities" would not exceed $1.46 billion after the transactions with Yucaipa. As noted, the $1.46 billion figure described only the value of SFD's long-term debt. Adding in SFD's $372 million in current liabilities, plaintiff argues, shows that the transactions impaired SFD's capital.

We believe that plaintiff reads too much into Section 154. The statute simply defines "net assets" in the course of defining "surplus." It does not mandate a "facts and figures balancing of assets and liabilities" to determine by what amount, if any, total assets exceeds total liabilities.[42] The statute is merely definitional. It does not require any particular method of calculating surplus, but simply prescribes factors that any such calculation must include. Although courts may not determine compliance with Section 160 except by methods that fully take into account the assets and liabilities of the corporation, Houlihan's methods were not erroneous as a matter of law simply because they used Total Invested Capital and long-term debt as analytical categories rather than "total assets" and "total liabilities."

---

[42] [9] *See Farland v. Wills*, Del.Ch., 1 Del.J.Corp.L. 467, 475 (1975).

We are satisfied that the Houlihan opinion adequately took into account all of SFD's assets and liabilities. Plaintiff points out that the $1.46 billion figure that approximated SFD's long-term debt failed to include $372 million in current liabilities, and argues that including the latter in the calculations dissipates the surplus. In fact, plaintiff has misunderstood Houlihan's methods. The record shows that Houlihan's calculation of SFD's Total Invested Capital is already net of current liabilities. Thus, subtracting long-term debt from Total Invested Capital does, in fact, yield an accurate measure of a corporation's net assets.

The record contains, in the form of the Houlihan opinion, substantial evidence that the transactions complied with Section 160. Plaintiff has provided no reason to distrust Houlihan's analysis. In cases alleging impairment of capital under Section 160, the trial court may defer to the board's measurement of surplus unless a plaintiff can show that the directors "failed to fulfill their duty to evaluate the assets on the basis of acceptable data and by standards which they are entitled to believe reasonably reflect present values."[43] In the absence of bad faith or fraud on the part of the board, courts will not "substitute [our] concepts of wisdom for that of the directors."[44] Here, plaintiff does not argue that the SFD Board acted in bad faith. Nor has he met his burden of showing that the methods and data that underlay the board's analysis are unreliable or that its determination of surplus is so far off the mark as to constitute actual or constructive fraud.[45] Therefore, we defer to the board's determination of surplus, and hold that SFD's self-tender offer did not violate 8 *Del.C.* § 160.

. . . .

The judgment of the Court of Chancery is affirmed.

EXERCISE 6-6

Does your state's corporation law treat repurchases or redemptions differently from dividends?

4.   Distributions Made Over Time

In some cases, a repurchase or redemption may be paid for over time. We discussed above the importance of evaluating such an obligation under the "equity insolvency test," taking the corporation's other obligations into account. But how would such an obligation affect the "balance sheet" test? If a corporation gives a shareholder a note in exchange for stock, how is that to be evaluated?

---

[43] [10] *Morris*, 63 A.2d at 582.

[44] [11] *Id.* at 583.

[45] [12] We interpret 8 *Del.C.* § 172 to entitle boards to rely on experts such as Houlihan to determine compliance with 8 *Del.C.* § 160. Plaintiff has not alleged that the SFD Board failed to exercise reasonable care in selecting Houlihan, nor that rendering a solvency opinion is outside Houlihan's realm of competence. *Compare* 8 *Del.C.* § 141(e) (providing that directors may rely in good faith on records, reports, experts, etc.).

MODEL BUSINESS CORPORATION ACT

§ 6.40. Distributions to Shareholders

(e) Except as provided in subsection (g), the effect of a distribution under subsection (c)[46] is measured:

(1) in the case of distribution by purchase, redemption, or other acquisition of the corporation's shares, as of the earlier of (i) the date money or other property is transferred or debt incurred by the corporation or (ii) the date the shareholder ceases to be a shareholder with respect to the acquired shares;

(2) in the case of any other distribution of indebtedness, as of the date the indebtedness is distributed; and

(3) in all other cases, as of (i) the date the distribution is authorized if the payment occurs within 120 days after the date of authorization or (ii) the date the payment is made if it occurs more than 120 days after the date of authorization.

(f) A corporation's indebtedness to a shareholder incurred by reason of a distribution made in accordance with this section is at parity with the corporation's indebtedness to its general, unsecured creditors except to the extent subordinated by agreement.

(g) Indebtedness of a corporation, including indebtedness issued as a distribution, is not considered a liability for purposes of determinations under subsection (c) if its terms provide that payment of principal and interest are made only if and to the extent that payment of a distribution to shareholders could then be made under this section. If the indebtedness is issued as a distribution, each payment of principal or interest is treated as a distribution, the effect of which is measured on the date the payment is actually made.

CALIFORNIA CORPORATIONS CODE

§ 166. Distribution to its shareholders

. . . . The time of any distribution by way of dividend shall be the date of declaration thereof and the time of any distribution by purchase or redemption of shares shall be the date cash or property is transferred by the corporation, whether or not pursuant to a contract of an earlier date; provided, that where a debt obligation that is a security (as defined in Section 8102 of the Commercial Code) is issued in exchange for shares the time of the distribution is the date when the corporation acquires the shares in the exchange. In the case of a sinking fund payment, cash or property is transferred within the meaning of this section at the time that it is delivered to a trustee for the holders of preferred shares to be used for the redemption of the shares or physically segregated by the corporation in trust for that purpose.

NEW YORK BUSINESS CORPORATION LAW

§ 513. Purchase, redemption and certain other transactions by a corporation with respect to its own shares

(a) Notwithstanding any authority contained in the certificate of incorporation, the shares of a corporation may not be purchased by the corporation, or, if redeemable, convertible or exchangeable shares, may not be redeemed, converted

---

[46] Subsection (c) is reprinted above in Section C.2.—Eds.

or exchanged, in each case for or into cash, other property, indebtedness or other securities of the corporation (other than shares of the corporation and rights to acquire such shares) if the corporation is then insolvent or would thereby be made insolvent. Shares may be purchased or redeemed only out of surplus.

. . . .

§ 514. Agreements for purchase by a corporation of its own shares

(a) An agreement for the purchase by a corporation of its own shares shall be enforceable by the shareholder and the corporation to the extent such purchase is permitted at the time of purchase by section 513 (Purchase or redemption by a corporation of its own shares).

(b) The possibility that a corporation may not be able to purchase its shares under section 513 shall not be a ground for denying to either party specific performance of an agreement for the purchase by a corporation of its own shares, if at the time for performance the corporation can purchase all or part of such shares under section 513.

EXERCISE 6-7

Equity Corporation has the following balance sheet, at the end of its most recent fiscal year.

Assets		Liabilities and Equity	
Cash	100	Current liabilities	500
Inventory	1,200	Long-term debt	1,000
Land and buildings	3,000	Common stock	
		(100 shs $1 par)	100
		Contrib. capital	1,000
		Retained earnings	1,700
Total	4,300	Total	4,300

The shares are owned equally by A and B. The parties agree that B's shares will be purchased by the corporation for a price of $3,000, payable over ten years, with appropriate interest. How would Equity Corporation's balance sheet look if that $3,000 liability is booked after the agreement is executed? Do any of the above statutes offer solace for the business planners who would like A and B (and Equity Corporation) to have an agreement that complies with state statutes restricting distributions or imposing director liability? What provisions need to be added to your stock purchase and redemption agreement?

D. PARTNERSHIP ALLOCATIONS AND DISTRIBUTIONS

In a partnership, the "capital account" plays a key role and must be maintained as required by federal income tax law[47] as well as state partnership law.[48] A capital account will be established for each partner. The account is increased by the value of the partner's contributions and allocated profits, and is decreased by the value of

---

[47] See Treas. Reg. § 1.704-1(b)(2)(iv).

[48] RUPA § 401(a) "deems" each partner to have a capital account which meets the requirements of the federal regulations discussed in the previous note. There is no counterpart in UPA to this provision.

the partner's withdrawals and allocated losses. The general arrangement of these capital accounts is discussed in Chapter 5, Section D.2.

Partnership capital accounts are important because they keep a running total of the partner's equity (in the accounting sense) in the partnership. When a partnership dissolves[49] or a partner dissociates,[50] state law or the partnership agreement may provide for payment based wholly or partially on the amount in the partner's capital account.

1.   Contributions and Allocations

Contributions by the partner to the partnership, such as cash or property given in exchange for the partner's equity interest, will be credited to the partner's capital account. Similarly, allocations of profits will increase a partner's capital account, while allocations of losses decrease a partner's capital account. In a corporation, we didn't have to deal with allocation of losses.[51] Capital accounts operate much like the sole proprietor's equity account which we examined at the opening of this chapter.

Example. Let's suppose that instead of going it alone, Chris has partnered with Dana in the used book business. Each partner invested $500 worth of cash to buy used books and, just as with the opening example, the partnership borrowed $1000 from the bank, spending $500 of it on books and keeping the remainder in cash. We would have the following balance sheet after this activity.

C&D Used Books — Balance Sheet
[today's date]

Assets	
Cash	$500
Books	1500
Total	**$2000**
Liabilities and Equity	
Bank loan	$ 1000
Chris — owner's equity	500
Dana — owner's equity	500
Total	**$ 2000**

Just as in a sole proprietorship, if the partnership sells a book for $12 that cost the partnership $10, the partnership would have a "profit" of $2. How this is divided between Chris and Dana depends on their partnership agreement. If they have

---

[49] See Chapter 5, Section D.2 for the basics of partnership capital account operations in liquidation; the details are discussed further in Chapter 10, Section D.6.

[50] See Chapter 8, Section E.4.a for discussion and evaluation of contractual payments based on partnership capital accounts.

[51] Losses could theoretically be "allocated" in a corporation. There would simply be no point in doing so. We can allocate expenses to corporate shareholders to reduce the impact of the corporate income tax; see the full discussion in Chapter 3, Section C.3. There is a *tax* benefit available for allocating losses in a "Subchapter S Corporation," which is a corporation taxed much like a partnership. In a Subchapter S Corporation, losses are in fact allocated, to shareholders, but they must be allocated in the same manner as profits. So once again, allocation of losses is not an issue. For full coverage of these issues, see Chapter 3, Sections C.4 and D.

agreed to an equal allocation of profits, then the new balance sheet would appear as follows.

C&D Used Books — New Balance Sheet
[second date]

Assets

Cash	$ 512
Books	1490
Total	**$ 2002**

Liabilities and Equity

Bank loan	$ 1000
Chris — owner's equity	501
Dana — owner's equity	501
Total	**$ 2002**

If the books were sold at a loss of $2, the loss would be allocated equally to the capital accounts of Chris and Dana, reducing their capital accounts to $499 each. Note that the partners' capital accounts simply keep a running total of the net amount of contributions and allocated profits over withdrawals and allocated losses. The partnership capital account does not *separately* track contributions and net profits, as do the corporation's equity accounts. Even though there is only a single capital account, the lawyers and accountants will need to track the actual cost of a partner's contributions to determine the partner's tax basis in the partnership, as discussed in Section H.3.b. of Chapter 3.[52]

2.   Distributions and Repurchases

A distribution to a partner reduces the partner's capital account by the amount of the distribution. There is no separate restriction on the amount of the distribution as is the case with a corporation.

Example. Recall how C&D Used Books appeared after its first successful sale.

C&D Used Books — New Balance Sheet
[second date]

Assets

Cash	$ 512
Books	1490
Total	**$ 2002**

Liabilities and Equity

Bank loan	$ 1000
Chris — owner's equity	501
Dana — owner's equity	501
Total	**$ 2002**

[52] See Section G later in this chapter. It is customary for partnerships to prepare accounts only on a tax basis, as these are ordinarily the only accounts which are important to the partnership and the partners. As discussed in Section G, tax regulations provide for attributes which partnership agreements must have if their allocations are to be respected for tax purposes.

If Dana were to withdraw $10 in cash, assuming such a withdrawal was permitted under the partnership agreement, the new balance sheet would appear as follows.

C&D Used Books — New Balance Sheet
[third date]

Assets	
Cash	$ 502
Books	1490
Total	**$ 1992**

Liabilities and Equity	
Bank loan	$ 1000
Chris — owner's equity	501
Dana — owner's equity	491
Total	**$ 1992**

There is no law which regulates the amount of distributions which is specific to the partnership, but general statutes prohibiting payments which make an entity "insolvent" will be relevant.[53]

E. LIMITED LIABILITY COMPANY ALLOCATIONS AND DISTRIBUTIONS

As with most other coverage of limited liability companies, once you are familiar with the basic rules for corporations and partnership, there is little additional learning required. Most LLCs will follow the partnership accounting rules discussed in Section D above, because they are treated as partnerships for tax purposes. It is possible (but surely rare) that an LLC will choose to be taxed as a corporation and structure its membership interests so that they are fungible and easily transferable, as with corporate stock. However, even should the LLC do so, it is unlikely that it would inherit the corporate law equity accounting rules related to "par value" and "retained earnings" discussed in Section C above.

1. Contributions and Allocations

Contributions to an LLC are normally not restricted in type, but they must be valued since the return of contributions is ordinarily a priority, unless the operating agreement states otherwise.[54] Therefore the capital account must keep track of the value of the contributions made by each member. Unlike partnerships, where profits and losses are allocated equally (unless the partnership agreement provides otherwise), the default rules for LLC allocations are not as clear. Some state laws are silent on the topic of profit and loss allocations,[55] while others make

---

[53] These laws are discussed in Section F below.

[54] *See* ULLCA § 806(a); Re-ULLCA § 708(b)(1); Cal. Corp. Code § 17353(a)(2); Del. LLC Act § 18-804(a)(3). For a fuller discussion of the impact of this priority for return of capital, see Chapter 2, Section C.1.c).

[55] Neither ULLCA nor Re-ULLCA mention profit shares, but speak only of distributions, discussed in Section E.2 of this chapter.

reasonable default rules subject to modification by the members.[56] There are few specific cases regarding LLC allocations. Most state LLC statutes grant extensive flexibility to members to structure the management, financing and distribution schemes for the LLC. Thus, allocations are often determined according to the specific provisions in the operating agreement, rather than relying on court interpretation of statutory provisions.

2.   Distributions and Repurchases

As with contributions and allocations, the law of LLC distributions is sparse — and for the same reasons. Most statutes simply provide that an LLC may make distributions to its members or provide simple default rules,[57] and specify that a member is a creditor of the LLC to the extent of the promised distribution.[58]

In addition, because LLC statutes appeared on the scene *after* state corporation laws, every state follows the creditor protection rules of corporation law dividend and distribution statutes. The statutory restrictions typically impose the "balance sheet" test, but without regard to any notions of "par value," as well as the "equity insolvency test" relating to ability of the LLC to pay debts as they become due. Delaware, as before, has its own rules. Compare the following Delaware and California statutes.

REVISED UNIFORM LIMITED LIABILITY COMPANY ACT (2006)

§ 405.   Limitations on distribution

(a) A limited liability company may not make a distribution if after the distribution:

(1)   the company would not be able to pay its debts as they become due in the ordinary course of the company's activities; or

(2)   the company's total assets would be less than the sum of its total liabilities plus the amount that would be needed, if the company were to be dissolved, wound up, and terminated at the time of the distribution, to satisfy the preferential rights upon dissolution, winding up, and termination of members whose preferential rights are superior to those of persons receiving the distribution.

(b)   A limited liability company may base a determination that a distribution is not prohibited under subsection (a) on financial statements prepared on the basis of accounting practices and principles that are reasonable in the circumstances or on a fair valuation or other method that is reasonable under the circumstances.

(c)   Except as otherwise provided in subsection (f), the effect of a distribution under subsection (a) is measured:

---

[56] *See, e.g.*, Del. LLC Act § 18-503; Cal. Corp. Code § 17202 (providing that profits are to be allocated as provided in the LLC agreement, and providing a default rule of allocation on the basis of the value of contributions).

[57] *See* ULLCA § 405(a); Re-ULLCA § 404(a) (default rule that distributions be in equal shares); Cal. Corp. Code § 17250 (default rules for return of capital contributions based on proportionate values of members' contributions, and other distributions based on share of profits); Del. LLC Act § 18-504 (default rule that distributions be proportionate to member contributions).

[58] ULLCA § 405(c); Re-ULLCA § 404(d); Cal. Corp. Code § 17250; Del. LLC Act § 18-606. This reflects the similar rule relating to declared but unpaid dividends. *See, e.g.*, MBCA § 6.40(f).

(1) in the case of a distribution by purchase, redemption, or other acquisition of a transferable interest in the company, as of the date money or other property is transferred or debt incurred by the company; and

(2) in all other cases, as of the date:

(A) the distribution is authorized, if the payment occurs within 120 days after that date; or

(B) the payment is made, if the payment occurs more than 120 days after the distribution is authorized.

(d) A limited liability company's indebtedness to a member incurred by reason of a distribution made in accordance with this section is at parity with the company's indebtedness to its general, unsecured creditors.

(e) A limited liability company's indebtedness, including indebtedness issued in connection with or as part of a distribution, is not a liability for purposes of subsection (a) if the terms of the indebtedness provide that payment of principal and interest are made only to the extent that a distribution could be made to members under this section.

(f) If indebtedness is issued as a distribution, each payment of principal or interest on the indebtedness is treated as a distribution, the effect of which is measured on the date the payment is made.

. . . .

CALIFORNIA CORPORATIONS CODE
Title 2.5— Limited Liability Companies

§ 17254. Prohibited distributions; exceptions; return of distribution; limitations period

(a) No distribution shall be made if, after giving effect to the distribution, either of the following occurs:

(1) The limited liability company would not be able to pay its debts as they become due in the usual course of business.

(2) The limited liability company's total assets would be less than the sum of its total liabilities plus, unless the operating agreement provides otherwise, the amount that would be needed, if the limited liability company were to be dissolved at the time of the distribution, to satisfy the preferential rights of other members upon dissolution that are superior to the rights of the member receiving the distribution.

(b) The limited liability company may base a determination that a distribution is not prohibited under subdivision (a) on any of the following:

(1) Financial statements prepared on the basis of accounting practices and principles that are reasonable in the circumstances.

(2) A fair valuation.

(3) Any other method that is reasonable in the circumstances.

(c) Except as provided in subdivision (e), the effect of a distribution under subdivision (a) is measured as of (1) the date the distribution is authorized if the payment occurs within 120 days after the date of authorization, or (2) the date payment is made if it occurs more than 120 days after the date of authorization.

(d) (1)   If terms of the indebtedness provide that payment of principal and interest is to be made only if, and to the extent that, payment of a distribution to members could then be made under this section, indebtedness of a limited liability company, including indebtedness issued as a distribution, is not a liability for purposes of determinations made under subdivision (b).

(2)   If the indebtedness is issued as a distribution, each payment of principal or interest on the indebtedness is treated as a distribution, the effect of which is measured on the date the payment is actually made.

DELAWARE LIMITED LIABILITY COMPANY ACT

§ 18-607.   Limitations on distribution

(a)   A limited liability company shall not make a distribution to a member to the extent that at the time of the distribution, after giving effect to the distribution, all liabilities of the limited liability company, other than liabilities to members on account of their limited liability company interests and liabilities for which the recourse of creditors is limited to specified property of the limited liability company, exceed the fair value of the assets of the limited liability company, except that the fair value of property that is subject to a liability for which the recourse of creditors is limited shall be included in the assets of the limited liability company only to the extent that the fair value of that property exceeds that liability. For purposes of this subsection (a), the term "distribution" shall not include amounts constituting reasonable compensation for present or past services or reasonable payments made in the ordinary course of business pursuant to a bona fide retirement plan or other benefits program.

Any distribution which violates these statutes creates liability for the LLC and its managers; this liability is explicit under Re-ULLCA § 406(a). In addition, liability is imposed on a distributee who knows the distribution is improper.[59] Such liability runs only to the LLC, which may at first glance seem comforting, since it was, after all, the LLC which authorized the distribution. However, as with the corporate distribution statutes discussed above, a new plaintiff could appear abruptly. Should bankruptcy or insolvency intervene, the liability owed to the LLC could be enforced by creditors much less sympathetic to the cozy arrangements of the earlier distribution.

Repurchases would be covered under the same rules as other distributions under LLC statutes which — like the MBCA — define distributions as inclusive of redemptions.[60] Even Delaware, whose corporation law provides for different rules for dividends and redemptions, treats both events similarly under its LLC Act, referring to "interim distributions" and "distribution upon resignation."[61]

---

[59] Re-ULLCA § 406(c); Cal. Corp. Code § 17254(e); Del. LLC Act § 18-607(b).

[60] See ULLCA § 101(5); Re-ULLCA § 102(5).

[61] See Del. LLC Act §§ 18-601, 18-604. Under California law, a withdrawing LLC member simply becomes entitled to distributions as if the interest had been transferred. Cal. Corp. Code § 17252.

F.   RESTRICTIONS ON PAYMENTS UNDER FRAUDULENT TRANSFER LAWS

The final overarching concern when making distributions to owners is a statute applicable in nearly every state which generally protects creditors from extravagant distributions by debtors. This statute is known as the Uniform Fraudulent Transfer Act (UFTA).[62] The UFTA protects creditors generally by limiting the ability of any debtor — individual, partnership, corporation, or LLC — to distribute assets to owners or others when the entity would be left unable to pay its debts. Identical language can be found in § 548(a) of the Bankruptcy Code.[63] The statutes forbid transfers made with the intent to delay, hinder, or defraud creditors; most likely your clients will not be involved in such conduct (at least with *your* knowledge). More importantly, the statutes reach other transfers made without such intent.

UNIFORM FRAUDULENT TRANSFER ACT

§ 4   Transfers Fraudulent as to Present and Future Creditors

(a)   A transfer made or obligation incurred by a debtor is fraudulent as to a creditor, whether the creditor's claim arose before or after the transfer was made or the obligation was incurred, if the debtor made the transfer or incurred the obligation:

. . .

(2)   without receiving a reasonably equivalent value in exchange for the transfer or obligation, and the debtor:

(i)   was engaged or was about to engage in a business or a transaction for which the remaining assets of the debtor were unreasonably small in relation to the business or transaction; or

(ii)   intended to incur, or believed or reasonably should have believed that he [or she] would incur, debts beyond his [or her] ability to pay as they became due.

. . . .

§ 5   Transfers Fraudulent as to Present Creditors

(a)   A transfer made or obligation incurred by a debtor is fraudulent as to a creditor whose claim arose before the transfer was made or the obligation was incurred if the debtor made the transfer or incurred the obligation without receiving a reasonably equivalent value in exchange for the transfer or obligation and the debtor was insolvent at that time or the debtor became insolvent as a result of the transfer or obligation.

. . . .

---

[62] In some states, the law is still in its much older version known as the Uniform Fraudulent Conveyance Act (UFCA). We will refer to the modern version — the UFTA — which is the law in most states. Only a handful of states operate with neither the UFTA or the UFCA, but have similar principles in nonuniform or common law. For the much more ancient history of these statutes, as well as how they might apply in the context of the purchase of an interest from a departing owner, see Chapter 8, Section H.

[63] 11 U.S.C. § 548. As indicated in Chapter 8, Section H, the UFTA provisions were patterned after the Bankruptcy Code provisions.

§ 7   Remedies of Creditors

(a)   In an action for relief against a transfer or obligation under this [Act], a creditor . . . may obtain:

(1)   avoidance of the transfer or obligation to the extent necessary to satisfy the creditor's claim;

[(2)   an attachment or other provisional remedy against the asset transferred or other property of the transferee in accordance with the procedure prescribed by [ ];]

(3)   subject to applicable principles of equity and in accordance with applicable rules of civil procedure,

(i)   an injunction against further disposition by the debtor or a transferee, or both, of the asset transferred or of other property;

(ii)   appointment of a receiver to take charge of the asset transferred or of other property of the transferee; or

(iii)   any other relief the circumstances may require.

(b)   If a creditor has obtained a judgment on a claim against the debtor, the creditor, if the court so orders, may levy execution on the asset transferred or its proceeds.

*   *   *

NOTES AND QUESTIONS

1.   As indicated above, the same results obtain under the Bankruptcy Code. Section 548(a)(1)(B) reaches the same transfers as set forth in UFTA §§ 4(a)(2) and 5(a). Section 550(a) allows recovery of the transferred property from the initial transferee and any subsequent transferee the property in good faith and for value.

2.   How do these statutes apply to your dividends, repurchases and distributions to partners or LLC members? Could the company or partnership be rendered "insolvent" by such a transfer, or become unable to pay its debts? More importantly, does the company or partnership receive "reasonably equivalent value" in the exchange?

3.   The difference between the state and federal fraudulent transfer provisions is largely a matter of the proper plaintiff. A fraudulent transfer under state law can be set aside by a present creditor under UFTA § 5(a) and even by a person who becomes a creditor after the transfer under § 4(a)(2). An action under the Bankruptcy Code is taken by the trustee or debtor on behalf of the bankruptcy estate, for the benefit of all creditors.

4.   Compare these statutes with the dividend and repurchase regulation statutes in Section C of this chapter. Is the relief available under UFTA § 4(a)(2) (and the equivalent language of Bankruptcy Code § 548(a)(1)(B)(ii)(II) and (III)) broader than the "balance sheet insolvency" and "equity insolvency" tests of those statutes? Comment 3 to MBCA § 6.40 states:

> The revised Model Business Corporation Act establishes the validity of distributions from the corporate law standpoint under section 6.40 and determines the potential liability of directors for improper distributions

under sections 8.30 and 8.33. The federal Bankruptcy [Code] and state fraudulent conveyance statutes, on the other hand, are designed to enable the trustee or other representative to recapture for the benefit of creditors funds distributed to others in some circumstances. In light of these diverse purposes, it was not thought necessary to make the tests of section 6.40 identical to the tests for insolvency under these various statutes.

5.   A fraudulent transfer can be pursued under Bankruptcy Code § 548(a) if it was made within two years before filing of the bankruptcy petition. And Section 544 allows the use in the bankruptcy proceeding of any powers available to a creditor under state law, to the extent they are more favorable for the trustee. In this regard, note that the applicable period under MBCA § 8.33(c) is two years for directors and an additional one year to reach stockholder transferees (and other directors); the applicable period under UFTA § 9(b) is four years; the applicable period under Delaware Gen. Corp. Law § 174(a) is *six* years.

6.   Consider C&D Used Books balance sheet presented above in Section D.2 [third date], after Dana has made a $10 withdrawal. What would prevent Chris or Dana from selling *all* the books and taking *all* the money as a distribution to themselves? Is there anything in state partnership law which prevents such conduct?

G.   FEDERAL INCOME TAXATION OF DISTRIBUTIONS

We have considered the income tax treatment of partnerships, corporations and LLCs generally in Chapter 3, and the tax issues involved in obtaining initial contributions from the owners in Chapter 5. Here, we consider the tax aspects which may affect your planning for distributions as discussed in Sections C through E of this chapter.

1.   Partnerships

Recall that when we discuss partnerships for federal income tax purposes, our discussion ordinarily includes LLCs which have made the election to be treated as partnerships for tax purposes, as well as general partnerships and limited liability partnerships (LLPs). We consider the tax aspects of each of the major events discussed in Section E above.

a.   Contributions

In Chapter 5 we considered the state law and federal income tax aspects of contributions to partnerships. There are important tax issues involved in contribution of services or property in exchange for partnership interests. For example, careful planning is required for a services-contributing partner who does not want to incur substantial income tax liability (without receiving cash to pay it) upon the organization of the partnership.[64]

In general, once those thorny issues have been settled, each partner comes away from the organization of the partnership with a capital account consisting of the value of property contributed to the partnership. If the property had a low cost (basis) to the taxpayer, generally there is no gain recognized to the partner upon

---

[64] See the general rules in Chapter 3, Section H.2 and the specifics in Chapter 5, Section D.2.a.iii.

contribution of that property,[65] but in exchange that partner carries over his or her original basis to his or her interest in the partnership,[66] and the partnership carries over that basis to the property in its hands.[67] However, because the partner's capital account has been credited with the fair market value of the property — reflecting the economic reality — complications have been introduced requiring the assistance of a tax expert.[68]

b. Allocations

i. General rules

The general rule for tax treatment of partnership allocations is deceptively simple. Each partner takes into account his or her "distributive share" of partnership income in the amounts and the character it was recognized by the partnership.[69] The basic percentage about which partners struck an economic bargain when forming the partnership is generally respected as the "distributive share" for tax purposes. Internal Revenue Code § 704 provides in pertinent part:

(a) **Effect of partnership agreement**

A partner's distributive share of income, gain, loss, deduction, or credit shall, except as otherwise provided in this chapter, be determined by the partnership agreement.

(b) **Determination of distributive share**

A partner's distributive share of income, gain, loss, deduction, or credit (or item thereof) shall be determined in accordance with the partner's interest in the partnership (determined by taking into account all facts and circumstances), if —

(1) the partnership agreement does not provide as to the partner's distributive share of income, gain, loss, deduction, or credit (or item thereof), or

(2) the allocation to a partner under the agreement of income, gain, loss, deduction, or credit (or item thereof) does not have substantial economic effect.

Therefore, for most "garden variety" partnership profit-and-loss arrangements, the partnership agreement will dictate the tax treatment for each partner.

Example. Alpha and Beta each contribute the same amount of cash to the partnership and agree to split profits and losses equally. If the partnership recognizes $100 of ordinary income and $100 of capital gain, Alpha and Beta will each report $50 of ordinary income and $50 of capital gain on their tax returns.

---

[65] IRC § 721.

[66] IRC § 722.

[67] IRC § 723.

[68] In particular, the difference between basis and fair market value may require special allocations of tax deductions, see the following discussions of "substantial economic effect," and special treatment upon distributions of the property or distributions to the partner who contributed the property.

[69] IRC § 702(a)–(b); *see* Chapter 3, Section E.

The partnership agreement will not control, as § 704(b) indicates, if it is silent as to the particular item in question, or if the agreement does not have "substantial economic effect." In those cases, the distributive share will be determined by the partner's "interest in the partnership." We discuss each of these important concepts below.

ii. Substantial economic effect

We first met the requirement of "substantial economic effect" (SEE) in Chapter 5, Section D.2, when discussing partnership allocation of losses differently from gains. It presents very complex tax issues as well. The SEE regulations[70] are some of the most detailed in existence.[71] The business planner who is not a tax expert can best understand the SEE regulations by keeping their overall objective in mind.

> The complexity and detail of these Regulations should not obscure the overriding principle of economic substance upon which they are based. If a partner will benefit economically from an item of partnership income or gain, that item must be allocated to him so that he bears the correlative tax burden. Conversely, if a partner will suffer the economic burden of an item of partnership loss or deduction, he must be allocated the associated tax benefit. In other words, *tax must follow economics.*[72]

The SEE regulations provide specific rules for calculating distributive shares in several situations which may be common in partnerships. The presence of any of these situations should alert the business planner to have a tax expert at hand:

- property whose "book value" differs from its tax basis,
- property subject to nonrecourse debt, and
- allocation of tax items which have no obvious economic effect.[73]

In addition, the SEE regulations provide for a "safe harbor" within which an allocation will be presumed to have economic effect.[74] However, this safe harbor may not be particularly useful to many business planners, because one of its requirements is that upon liquidation, partners with deficit capital accounts must generally be unconditionally obligated to restore the amounts of their deficits to the partnership.[75] This requirement, known as a "deficit restoration obligation" or DRO, makes good economic sense, but is often untenable in the modern limited liability environment. Consider the example of a partnership which includes a partner to whom losses are valuable, but other partners to whom they are not valuable. If one partner receives loss deductions in excess of her basis, those

---

[70] Treas. Reg. § 1.704-1(b).

[71] There is another promising candidate for this distinction, that is, the regulations under IRC § 338. *See* Chapter 9, Section C.2.b.ii. You can compare the section 704(b) and section 338 regulations and make your own decision.

[72] McKee, Nelson & Whitmire, *supra*, ¶ 10.02[1] at p. 10-9 (emphasis supplied).

[73] Examples (apart from the above two categories) include "certain tax credits" and "percentage depletion in excess of the book value of depletable property." *Id.*

[74] That is to say, it will have economic effect if the tax follows the economics. Whether it is "substantial" is a separate and less specific analysis. The SEE safe harbor requirements are set forth in Treas. Reg. § 1.704-1(b)(2)(ii)(b).

[75] *Id.* § 1.704-1(b)(2)(ii)(b)(3).

deductions would be allowed only if that partner were unconditionally obligated to restore those losses (reflected by a deficit in her capital account) upon liquidation.[76] The conventional legal advice is that such a DRO is not worth the risk.

> A fear exists . . . that liability to creditors could arise to the extent a member of an [LLP or] LLC has an obligation to restore a deficit capital account. Creditors could be seen as third party beneficiaries of the deficit restoration obligation, giving them the power to enforce it. That there is no case on point only adds to the anxiety level.[77]

The SEE regulations permit avoidance of the DRO in some situations. These can add to the complexity of the documents in ways which can provide both costs and benefits.

Simon Friedman, *Partnership Capital Accounts and Their Discontents*
2 N.Y.U. Journal of Law & Business 791, 791-92 (2006)[78]

Over the last twenty years or so, business persons investing through entities such as limited liability companies that are taxed as partnerships have undoubtedly become used to agreements that include elaborate provisions designed to comply with Treasury Regulations governing the allocation of partnership income and loss. The provisions are almost comical in their intricacy. In their full glory, they include long definitions of profits and loss, book income and tax income, capital accounts and adjusted capital accounts; paraphrases of the relevant regulations highlighting technical terms such as qualified income offsets, two varieties of minimum gain chargebacks, two varieties of allocation of deductions attributable to nonrecourse debt, loss limitations and gross income allocations; precatory statements that the paraphrases be interpreted consistently with the regulations they are paraphrasing; curative allocations that provide that all preceding allocations, having been carefully made, be unmade as quickly as possible; and a final provision stating that in the year of liquidation, to the extent possible, all errors in the preceding making and unmaking of allocations be undone so that the business deal is respected. All of these provisions tend to be "boilerplate," unchanged from document to document, and taken for granted, barely skimmed by the average business person or, truth be told, even by the average tax lawyer. Often, the boilerplate provisions are preceded by transaction-specific provisions which do tend to be considered carefully, at least by tax lawyers. There is a growing trend, however, to avoid the difficulties and potential for error of devising allocations to reflect specific transactions. Instead, agreements include "targeting" or "tracking" allocations. These allocations use technical vocabulary to instruct the accountants to allocate income and loss at the end of every taxable year so that each partner's capital account balance equals the amount that would be distributed to the partner if the partnership sold its assets for their book value and liquidated. Such allocations automatically comply with the Treasury Regulations and can be identical in each document. The result is a three to four page, single spaced tax

---

[76] Review the example on these facts in Chapter 5, Section D.2.b.i, "A Special Note About 'Substantial Economic Effect."

[77] Walter D. Schwidetzky, *The Partnership Allocation Rules of Section 704(B): To Be or Not To Be,* 17 Va. Tax Rev. 707, 713 (1998).

[78] Copyright © 2006. Reprinted with permission of Mr. Friedman.

section that is impressive, impenetrable and which generally need not be read.

The development of standardized tax allocations is not all evil. The capital account system was designed with the worthy goal of relating tax allocations to the underlying risks and benefits of business transactions. The boilerplate usually causes the system to work properly. Standard forms are efficient; it is neither cost nor time-effective to reinvent the system each time a document is drafted. The danger, however, is that the system and its impressive boilerplate may be accepted as immutable, with two opposite but equally unfortunate consequences. Business persons may give primacy to the dictates of the system, modifying their transactions to fit the system and the boilerplate. This is not necessarily the most rational way to maximize profits or to allocate capital in the economy. Alternatively, business people may decide to go ahead with their predetermined business plans and ignore the system, which may result in unexpected and unpleasant tax consequences. . . .

Even if partners do not want to or cannot take advantage of the SEE "safe harbor," partnerships will normally comply with the Regulations' provisions for maintenance of capital accounts.[79] Although we cautioned above that ordinary accounting rules will not *necessarily* govern,[80] there is general harmony between the two systems.

Fortunately, because the capital account maintenance rules mandated by the Regulations are based on sound economic concepts and are generally consistent with the applicable financial accounting rules, partners will find that the required tax treatment of most, if not all, items corresponds to their economic agreement. Conversely, partners who desire tax consequences that differ from their economic agreement are likely to be frustrated by these rules.[81]

Thus, we see general congruence between the Regulations' general provisions and the rules we discussed in Section D above. Capital accounts are increased by contributions and allocated gains and are decreased by distributions and allocated losses.[82]

iii. Determining the "interest in the partnership"

If the partnership agreement does not govern a particular allocation, or cannot be respected because it does not have substantial economic effect, the allocation will be made "in accordance with the partner's interest in the partnership," a term defined with remarkable brevity in the regulations. Treas. Reg. § 1.704-1(b)(3) states in pertinent part:

Partner's interest in the partnership —

(i) In general. References in section 704(b) and this paragraph to a partner's interest in the partnership, or to the partners' interests in the partnership, signify the manner in which the partners have agreed to share

---

[79] *See* Treas. Reg. § 1.704-1(b)(2)(iv)(b).

[80] *See supra* Section D.

[81] McKee, Nelson & Whitmire, *supra*, ¶ 10.01[2][c] at p. 10-40.

[82] *See* Treas. Reg. § 1.704-1(b)(2)(iv)(b).

the economic benefit or burden (if any) corresponding to the income, gain, loss, deduction, or credit (or item thereof) that is allocated. . . .

(ii) Factors considered. In determining a partner's interest in the partnership, the following factors are among those that will be considered:

(a) The partners' relative contributions to the partnership,

(b) The interests of the partners in economic profits and losses (if different than that in taxable income or loss),

(c) The interests of the partners in cash flow and other non-liquidating distributions, and

(d) The rights of the partners to distributions of capital upon liquidation.

Example. Using the Alpha-Beta partnership in the above example, if the question were allocation of some other item (depreciation or charitable contribution deductions, for example) the allocation would be based on each partner's "interest in the partnership." According to Alpha's and Beta's agreement to make equal contributions and to share profits and losses equally, that "interest" is likely 50%. Under the above regulations, their relative shares under (ii)(a) and (b) are 50% according to their agreement, and under state law default rules, their relative shares under (d) are also 50%.[83]

The important features of the "interest in the partnership" rules are two. First, they require consideration of the interest on an item-by-item basis, as indicated by the four parts of the regulation. Second, they will, in most cases, result in allocations with substantial economic effect apart from the SEE regulations.[84]

c.   Distributions

Assuming that the business planner, with the aid of expert tax advice, has successfully negotiated the challenge of allocations which will be respected for tax purposes, the treatment of distributions is relatively simple. Here we discuss only distributions from an ongoing partnership to an ongoing partner, not distributions in redemption[85] or liquidation.[86]

The partner's "distributive share" of partnership items will have been taken into account in calculating the partner's taxable income[87] and the partner's capital account,[88] and basis in the partnership interest.[89] The distribution of property generally is a nontaxable event, but the distribution will reduce both the partner's

---

[83] Recall that both UPA and RUPA dictate that liquidating distributions will be made first according to a partner's contributions and then to each partner according to profit shares. See UPA §§ 18 and 40, RUPA § 807, and the discussion *supra* Chapter 2, Section C.2.c.

[84] "Thus, application of the partners' interests in the partnership test should, in most cases, yield results identical to those that would have been obtained if the substantial economic effect test had been satisfied in the first instance." McKee, Nelson & Whitmire, *supra*, ¶ 10.01[1] at p. 10-10.

[85] *See* Chapter 9, Section C.1.b.

[86] *See* Chapter 3, Section H.3.b, Chapter 10, Section A.2.

[87] IRC § 702.

[88] Treas. Reg. § 1.704-1(b)(2)(iv)(b)(3) (gains), (b)(7) (losses).

[89] IRC § 705(a).

capital account[90] and his or her basis in his or her partnership interest.[91]

Apart from this general rule, the business planner must be alert for specific types of property which are exceptions to these rules. This will be important in planning initial contributions or if the planner is involved at a later stage when distributions are being considered. The special kinds of property for which special advice is needed generally are:

- property with built-in gain or loss (difference between cost and fair market value when contributed to the partnership) which has not been already accounted for;[92]
- property subject to a liability;[93]
- "unrealized receivables" or inventory;[94] and
- securities;[95] and
- payments made to redeem a partner's interest.[96]

2.   C Corporations

a.   Contributions and allocations

The tax issues regarding contributions to a corporation have been covered earlier in Chapter 3. Contributions of low-basis property in exchange for stock may create a taxable income "disaster" under IRC § 83.[97] However, sophisticated lawyers may be able to structure the contribution of property in exchange for stock as a tax free exchange under IRC § 351, if certain requirements are satisfied.[98]

Allocation of income is, refreshingly, a non-issue in a C corporation. Because there is no "pass-through" of income, the corporation pays tax on its income without worry about allocation to shareholders. The corporation's income is an important tax issue because it creates "earnings and profits" which are used to measure distributions, to which we turn next.

---

[90] Treas. Reg. § 1.704-1(b)(2)(iv)(b)(4)–(5).

[91] IRC § 733.

[92] This property may produce gain or loss when distributed under IRC §§ 704(c) and 737, and may permit reallocation of basis of undistributed property under §§ 734 and 755.

[93] This property may produce deemed contributions or distributions under § 752.

[94] This property may produce gain when distributed under IRC § 751(b).

[95] To the extent securities meet the definition of "marketable securities," they are considered the equivalent of money distributed according to § 731(c).

[96] These are known as payments made in liquidation of a retiring or deceased partner's interest. In addition to the above rules applicable to specific types of property, there are timing rules applicable to such payments and other tax issues to be resolved regarding payments made over time in redemption of a partner's interest. IRC §§ 707, 708, 736.

[97] See the detailed discussion in Chapter 3, Section H.1.

[98] Compare IRC §§ 351 (contributions to corporations) and 721 (contributions to partnerships). See the fuller discussion in Chapter 3, Section H.3.a.

b.   Distributions

We deal here only with distributions to corporate shareholders in respect of their shares leaving the corporation as an ongoing entity. Other chapters discuss distributions in a corporate reorganization[99] or liquidation.[100]

The tax effects on the corporation of a distribution to its shareholders are limited. IRC § 311 generally precludes recognition of gain or loss by a corporation, except gain must be recognized if the corporation distributes appreciated property.

More complicated is the treatment of the shareholders. In general, IRC § 301(c) establishes the order of tax treatment of cash or the fair value of property received by a shareholder.

- First, it is considered a dividend to the extent of the corporation's "earnings and profits."[101] The dividend is taxable income to the shareholder recipient.[102]

- Second, if there is no remaining amount to be considered a dividend, it is a nontaxable return of capital. A return of a capital is a distribution that is not from the corporation's earnings and profits. The distribution is not taxable, but reduces the basis of the stock.

- Finally, if the taxpayer's basis has been reduced to zero, any remaining distribution in to the stockholder is treated as gain from the sale or exchange of the stock, presumably at capital gains rates (rather than dividend rates), as the shares are likely a capital asset in the hands of the taxpayer.

It is fair to say, therefore, that the "earnings and profits" of a corporation measure its dividend-paying capacity. For the business planner who is not a tax expert, it will do to note that "earnings and profits" is a concept similar to "retained earnings" or "earned surplus" discussed in Section C of this chapter. However, caution is in order, as "earnings and profits" is *not synonymous* with any similar financial accounting term. If particular issues arise in calculation of "earnings and profits" for tax purposes, the business planner should consult a tax and accounting expert.

Example. A corporation is organized with $1 million in cash contributions from four shareholders in the amounts of $250,000 each. If the corporation has $100,000 in "earnings and profits" during the year, payments of $25,000 to each of its four shareholders will be taxed as dividends. Any additional distribution in excess of $100,000 will be a return of capital and not taxed to the shareholder as a dividend. For instance, if $120,000 is distributed to the four shareholders with each receiving $30,000, then each would be taxed on $25,000 worth of dividend income, with $5,000 considered a return of capital. The $5,000 would not be taxed but would reduce each stockholder's basis to $245,000.

---

[99] *See* Chapter 9, Section C.2.

[100] *See* Chapter 10, Section A.2.

[101] This is courtesy of the cross-reference in IRC §§ 301(c)(3) to 316's definition of "dividend" as a distribution made "out of its earnings and profits."

[102] IRC § 61(a)(7) specifically including dividends in gross income. Lower tax rates may apply to dividend income. *See* Chapter 3, Section C.2. An important exception to this rule is inter-corporate dividends, which are mostly or completely tax-deferred under IRC § 243.

c. Repurchases

The only remaining tax problem is to consider how a dividend differs from a redemption. This is primarily a tax planning problem, because as we noted above, most states consider dividends and repurchases as similar events for state law.[103] A *purchase* by a corporation of a stockholder's shares by the corporation is treated as a distribution in redemption under IRC § 302(b).[104]

Example. Suppose we have the same corporation organized as above with a total of $1 million in capital received in cash from four shareholders in the amounts of $250,000 each. If, instead of paying a dividend, the corporation distributes $275,000 to one of the shareholders in exchange for her shares, the shareholder would owe tax on $25,000 as gain from the sale of a capital asset, assuming the shares were a capital asset in her hands. There would be no dividend treatment of any of the distribution.

We see that these two transactions — dividends and redemptions — have very different tax consequences.[105] IRC §§ 302, 303 and 305 dictate that everything which does not fit within their terms as a redemption of stock is taxed under the dividend rules of § 301. It is important, therefore, to know the categories of transactions subject to redemption treatment. Those categories are:

- a distribution "not essentially equivalent to a dividend,"

- a substantially disproportionate redemption, measured according to the quantitative requirements of § 302(b)(2),

- a termination of the shareholder's interest, defined in § 302(b)(3) as a "complete redemption of all the stock of the corporation owned by the shareholder,"

- a partial liquidation of the distributing corporation, as defined in § 302(e), relating to a corporation which carries on two or more businesses, and

- a redemption to pay death taxes under § 303 or a stock dividend qualifying under § 305.

All of these categories provide guidance for the business and tax planner, with the exception of the first, which is a holdover from earlier tax laws, and admittedly circular in its logic. By contrast to the other provisions which provide a modicum of certainty, the "not essentially equivalent to a dividend" test is a "facts and circumstances" inquiry, providing little planning value. "Taxpayers who cannot bring transactions within [the requirements of § 302(b)(2) or § 302(b)(3), the most commonly used provisions] can try to avail themselves of § 302(b)(1) by establishing that the redemption is not essentially equivalent to a dividend; this, however, is a treacherous route, to be employed only as a last resort."[106]

---

[103] Delaware being the notable exception. *See supra* Section C.3.

[104] IRC § 302(b) refers only to the tax treatment of the shareholder. The tax treatment of the corporation continues to be governed by IRC § 311 as discussed above.

[105] Even if the rate for dividends has been reduced to more closely resemble that from capital gains, the reduction is not precisely the same and it is likely only temporary. *See* Chapter 3, Section C.2. And the transactions are not equivalents anyway. Both have produced $25,000 gain, but in one the shareholder still owns her shares (complete with cost basis therein).

[106] Bittker & Eustice, *supra*, ¶ 9.01[3][a], at p. 9-8.

All of the rules in § 302 must be measured against attribution-of-ownership rules if there is family or entity (corporation, partnership, estate or trust) interrelationship among any of the stockholders. These rules are set forth in § 318 and must be carefully read to apply the attribution rules to the planned transaction. While complete coverage of the section is beyond our scope here, a couple of its most charming features should be noted: first, various attributions will be "chained" together but others will not;[107] and second, the family (but not entity) attribution rules can be waived in the case of a § 302(b)(3) complete liquidation.[108]

The lesson for the business planner is fairly straightforward. If a distribution from a corporation is planned, consider:

(1) to whom the distribution is to be made;

(2) what is to be distributed (e.g., proceeds from sale of a business or assets otherwise subject to the partial liquidation rules);

(2) the extent of the corporation's earnings and profits;

(3) the relative bases of each shareholder;

(4) whether shareholders are corporations (the § 243 deduction for inter-corporate dividends tends to shift the tax motivations 180 degrees); and

(5) how the § 318 attribution rules would apply.

EXERCISE 6-8

A, B and C are equal holders of all the shares of ABC Corp., which has $150 of "earnings and profits." The corporation holds the following assets: $50 in each of businesses W, X, Y and Z, and $100 in cash. Each shareholder paid $50 for his or her shares, and each shareholding has a fair market value of $100. Our planning goal is to redeem one-half of A's shares for $50 in property of ABC Corp. distributed to A, and to legitimately minimize the tax owed in so doing.

(1)   What are your best options for structuring the transaction and, importantly, what questions do you need to ask in order to have a complete answer?

(2)   How would your options change if:

(a) A were a corporation?

(b) A, B and C were all related individuals subject to § 318(a) attribution?

(c) A also owned $100 worth of ABC Corp. nonvoting preferred stock?

3.   S Corporations

a.   Background

We have discussed S corporations only generally so far.[109] Recall that an S corporation is a state law corporation like any other, but which makes an election to be treated for federal income tax purposes of allocation and distribution much

---

[107]   IRC § 318(a)(5).

[108]   IRC § 302(c)(2).

[109]   *See* Chapter 3, Section D.

like a partnership. This makes the S corporation a platypus of sorts — it is *always* a state-law corporation subject to the general state laws in Section C of this chapter. For most, but not all, federal income tax purposes, it is treated as a partnership.[110]

In Chapter 3, the business planner was cautioned that S corporation limits on the number and types of shareholders as well as types of permitted capitalization make it an inflexible and thus likely inferior entity choice when compared to an LLC. A further disadvantage exists in an S corporation which incurs debt, because the shareholders cannot increase their basis in their ownership interests, as can partners in a partnership which incurs debt.[111] One advantage which an S corporation maintains over a partnership is the ability to engage in a tax-deferred corporate reorganization.[112] On balance, however, the S corporation remains a poor choice to make from the outset when choosing an entity form for a new business.[113]

Having said that, you may be presented with the rare exception for which an S corporation is the better choice or, more likely, an existing S corporation formed by someone else from which it is now difficult or simply too costly to be converted to an LLC. So long as Subchapter S remains on the books, the business planner will need to be familiar with the basics of S corporation treatment.

b.   Contributions and allocations

There are no special rules for S corporation contributions and allocations, and therefore the general rules for C corporations apply.[114] Contributions are subject to tax-deferral under § 351 provided the control requirements are met.

An S corporation pays no tax,[115] unless it had a prior life as a C corporation.[116] It does, however, calculate taxable income and then passes through each item to its stockholders, in a fashion similar to a partnership.[117] Allocations are made *pro rata* according to each shareholder's proportion of ownership. Since an S corporation is permitted to have only one class of stock,[118] the computation of proportionate ownership is straightforward.

---

[110] For good general short guidance on S corporations, see Bittker & Eustice, *supra*, Ch. 6; Abrams & Doernberg, *supra*, Ch. 13; and Jerald David August, *Benefits and Burdens of Subchapter S in a Check-the-Box World*, 4 Fla. Tax Rev. 287 (1999).

[111] This advantage is provided to partnerships by IRC § 752(a), which has no counterpart in either C corporations or S corporations. This section is discussed in the context of sale of an interest in the partnership in Chapter 9, Section C.1.b.

[112] *See* Chapter 9, Section C.1 (partnership reorganizations generally) & Section C.2.c (tax-deferred corporate reorganizations).

[113] See August, *supra*, 4 Fla. Tax Rev. 287 at 331 (reviewing the above overall disadvantages, and concluding that "[i]deally, Subchapter K [partnership taxation] should be the paradigm passthrough model for all private business firms.").

[114] IRC § 1371(a) (generally providing that Subchapter C rules apply if nothing in Subchapter S says otherwise).

[115] IRC § 1363(a).

[116] An S corporation must pay tax on realized gain which was "built in" when it converted from C to S status, according toIRC § 1374.

[117] IRC § 1366(a) & (b).

[118] *See* Chapter 3, Section D.1.b. The rules are set forth in IRC § 1361(b)(1)(D) and (c)(4).

The proportionate income or loss is reported by each shareholder. It's worth noting that, just like partners, S shareholders will have to pay taxes on allocations of income, even if there is no actual cash distribution. In addition, just as a partner adjusts his or her basis in the partnership interest, an S corporation shareholder adjusts his or her basis in the shares owned. The basis will be increased in the amount of gain recognized and decreased in the amount of loss recognized.[119]

c.   Distributions and repurchases

S corporation shareholders receive pass-through allocations of profits and losses, as do partners in a partnership. Therefore, distributions of income to S corporation shareholders are a non-taxable event, as are income distributions to partners, since the taxes will be paid based on the allocations of income, regardless of whether or not there is an actual distribution.[120] The distribution does, however, reduce the taxpayer's basis in the S corporation stock, since the taxable income had increased it, just as is done with a partner's basis in his or her partnership interest.[121]

The above paragraph describes theoretically what happens in an S corporation to make it work much like a partnership. However, because it is a corporation, the IRC distribution rules are phrased in corporate terminology. Section 1368 provides rules for distributions from an S corporation using the same terminology as § 301, rules for distributions from a C corporation. However, where the C corporation must account for distributions "out of earnings and profits," in the S corporation there are no earnings and profits for which to provide dividend tax treatment.[122] Therefore, § 1368 provides simply that the S corporation's distribution will be treated first as nontaxable return of basis, and then as gain from sale or exchange of property, presumably a capital asset.[123] We would have the same result even if the distribution is a repurchase of the shareholder's stock, because this is what the statute commanded under § 302(b) as discussed above. Note, however, that an S corporation shareholder would *prefer* distribution treatment, because it allows the shareholder's *entire* basis in all of the shareholder's stock to be used up first, whereas redemption treatment makes available only the basis of the shares redeemed.[124]

---

[119] IRC § 1367(a); there are special rules for losses which exceed basis in IRC § 1367(b)(2).

[120] IRC § 731(a).

[121] IRC § 733(a).

[122] Unless, of course, your S corporation was previously a C corporation. In that instance, the distribution comes first out of the S corporation (nontaxable) retained earnings — known as an "accumulated adjustments account" (AAA) — and then from C corporation earnings and profits, and then the two-part rule in the next sentence of the text. *See* IRC § 1368(c)(1). The AAA is not an issue in a corporation which has always been an S corporation.

[123] Compare the three-part priority under IRC § 301(c), which assigned the distribution first to dividend treatment to the extent of earnings and profits, and then proceeded with these same two rules. *See supra* Section C.2.b. There is still, of course, no tax on the corporation (putting aside distributions of appreciated property) since § 311 applies to S corporations as well as C corporations.

[124] The trade-off is not free money, however. If it is a dividend, the taxpayer's basis is reduced with a reduced ability to shelter any later distributions from capital gain treatment. And in any event, the decision is still made using the rules of IRC § 302 to determine whether a redemption is in fact a redemption and not a dividend. *See* Abrams & Doernberg, *supra*, at 331–32.

A further technicality awaits the business planner — or perhaps the planner's tax advisor or accountant — upon redemption of S corporation shares. If shares are redeemed during the year, the accounting must await the completion of the S corporation's year so that the ratable share of gain or loss can be taxed and added to or subtracted from the taxpayer's basis.

COMPREHENSIVE EXERCISE:
DEPARTURE OF AN OWNER

This exercise requires you to help your clients with a departure of an owner, a common development in the life of a successful business. The facts in this Exercise are based on the Comprehensive Exercise at the end of Chapter 5. Once again, your clients are Ann, Bev and Carl. The business was capitalized with $400,000 from Ann, $800,000 from Bev, $400,000 worth of property from Carl, $3 million of bank loans, and $3 million in equity investments from up to 30 other investors.

The restaurant has been operating for three years now, and has finally recorded its first year of profitability. After the champagne celebration, Ann reminded Bev and Carl that it was time to "cash her out," per her original request that she be able to withdraw her investment once the restaurant became profitable.

Alternative A: The C Corporation

Assume that the entity was formed as a corporation with the following capitalization: 400 shares of common stock each to Ann and Carl[125] and 3,000 shares to the outside investors, and 800 shares of preferred stock to Bev. The initial price per common and preferred share was $1000. The common shares were designated with a par value of one cent per share. Bev's preferred shares have a par value and liquidation preference of $1000 per share, and a noncumulative annual dividend preference of $10. No dividends have been paid since the start of the business. The bank loans are ten-year loans with interest only for the first two years. Amortizing principal payments begin after two years, so for now there has been no principal repaid on the loans. The interest payments on the bank loans total $240,000 annually (about eight percent). The corporation's articles provide (with respect to the preferred stock) and the bank loan documents provide (with respect to those loans), that

> no distribution may be made in respect of common shares, other than reasonable dividends in the ordinary course of business and in compliance with the corporation's articles and bylaws, [without the consent of the preferred shareholders] (with respect to the preferred stock provisions in the articles) [without the consent of the holders hereof] (with respect to the provisions in the loan documents).

The corporation's financial position is set forth below, based on unaudited financial statements prepared by the restaurant's accountant.

---

[125] Assume that the shares issued to Carl were in respect of the property he contributed, and the valuation of $400,000 by the directors of the corporation was made in good faith.

ABC Restaurant, Inc.
Balance Sheet
Dec. 31, Last Year

Assets		Liabilities and equity	
Cash	$ 111,000	Accounts payable	$ 200,000
Accounts receivable	265,000	Other accrued liabilities	300,000
Short-term investments	124,000	Bank loan	3,000,000
Inventory	1,600,000	**Total liabilities**	**3,500,000**
Furniture and fixtures, net of accumulated depreciation	3,000,000	Preferred stock	800,000
Land	400,000	Common stock (1¢ par value)	38
Intangible assets, net of amortization	100,000	Contrib. capital in excess of par	3,799,962
		Retained earnings (deficit)	(2,500,000)
		Total equity	**2,100,000**
Total assets	**$ 5,600,000**	**Total liabilities and equity**	**$ 5,600,000**

ABC Restaurant, Inc.
Income Statements for the year ended Dec. 31[126]

	Three years ago	Two years ago	Last year
	(first year of operation)		
Revenues	$ 2,000,000	$ 4,000,000	$ 7,500,000
Cost of sales	2,900,000	5,500,000	6,000,000
Gross margin	(900,000)	(1,500,000)	1,500,000
Administrative expenses	400,000	500,000	700,000
Net income (loss)	(1,300,000)	(2,000,000)	800,000
Retained earnings (deficit), at end of year	$ (1,300,000)	$ (3,300,000)	$ (2,500,000)

Ann has indicated that she would be willing to consider $600,000 as a fair price for repurchase of her interest.[127] Bev and Carl, as the other directors of the corporation, have tentatively agreed to the proposal. Bev, as the holder of the preferred shares, will consent to the distribution to Ann in accordance with the

---

[126] Notice that there is no provision for income taxes. The losses generated in the first two years will result in no tax expenses, and the gain in year 3 is sheltered by the carryforward of the tax losses from the first two years. The corporation still has a net operating loss (NOL) carryforward of $2.5 million (the retained deficit). At current corporate tax rates, that NOL has a value of $838,250. This amount does not appear on the corporation's balance sheet, but it is an item of value inherent in this corporation.

[127] For the details of how this value might be arrived at, see Chapter 8, Section E. For now, we will assume that this is a fair value agreed upon by all parties. Our task in this chapter is to get it legally in Ann's hands.

articles and bylaw provisions regarding her preferred stock. The bank[128] will consent to the distribution to Ann under their loan agreements, so long as any note given by the corporation to Ann is junior to the bank's loan. Bev and Carl believe that the restaurant can generate sufficient cash flow to pay Ann her $600,000 over approximately ten years (at a reasonable interest rate). Ann is fine with this so long as the deal is memorialized in a note from the corporation for the $600,000. Bev and Carl would also like to know if any dividend can be paid to the shareholders at this time. Recent reliable appraisals of the land have suggested that it is worth about $1 million.

Alternative B: The LLP or LLC

Assume that the entity was formed as an LLP or LLC with the following capitalization and profit and loss shares: a 17.4% interest to Bev, an 8.7% interest each to Ann and Carl, and the 20 outside investors each with a 3.26% interest. Bev paid $800,000 for her interest, Ann and Carl $400,000 for theirs,[129] and each of the outside investors paid $150,000 for their interests. The partnership/operating agreement provides for Ann's repayment "once the restaurant operations become profitable," and for Bev to be allocated all income from the entity until her capital account is restored to its original $800,000, and for the profit and loss shares to return to the original contribution amounts thereafter. The restaurant's income statements are identical to those presented above for the corporation, but its balance sheet appears as follows:

ABC Restaurant, LLP/LLC
Balance Sheet
Dec. 31, Last Year

Assets		Liabilities and equity	
Cash	$ 111,000	Accounts payable	$ 200,000
Accounts receivable	265,000	Other accrued liabilities	300,000
Short-term investments	124,000	Bank loan	3,000,000
Inventory	1,600,000	**Total liabilities**	**3,500,000**
Furniture and fixtures, net of accumulated depreciation	3,000,000	Partners'/Members' capital*	2,100,000
Land	400,000	**Total equity**	**2,100,000**
Intangible assets, net of amortization	100,000		
Total assets	**$ 5,600,000**	**Total liabilities and equity**	**$ 5,600,000**

* Capital account detail

---

[128] If the loans are provided by a syndicate of different banks, one of them will normally have been designated as the "Lead Bank" responsible for negotiations and waivers. Here we will assume that you will only have to deal with one bank which can speak on behalf of all the lending banks.

[129] Ann's payment was cash; Carl's payment was property valued by the partners or members at $400,000.

Gain (loss) for year		Year 1	Year 2	Last year
		$ (1,300,000)	$ (2,000,000)	$ 800,000.00
Capital accounts:	Initial	End of Year 1	End of Year 2	End of last year
Ann	$ 400,000	286,900	112,900	132,545
Bev	800,000	573,800	225,800	839,289
Carl	400,000	286,900	112,900	132,545
Other investors, total	3,000,000	2,152,400	848,400	995,621
Total	$ 4,600,000	$ 3,300,000	$ 1,300,000	$ 2,100,000

Again, the value of the land is about $1 million, and Ann, as well as the other partners/members have tentatively agreed to a buyout price of around $600,000, to be paid out over approximately ten years. As above, the bank will agree so long as any note Ann receives is subordinate to the bank's loan. What would be the best way to structure the transaction?

Alternative C: The S Corporation with additional debt

Assume that the entity was formed as an S corporation, with the capitalization for Ann, Carl, and the other common shareholders as in Alternative A above. Here we meet the main disadvantage of the S corporation. We are unable to give Bev her desired preference without creating an impermissible second class of stock. This alternative assumes that Bev's desire for protection and priority was resolved by having her lend $800,000 to the corporation in a manner which qualifies under the "straight debt" safe harbor.[130] Further, this alternative assumes that the corporation was required to pay (in addition to the interest on the bank loan) 10% interest on Bev's loan, for an additional total expense of $80,000 per year. Bev's loan is interest only for a ten year term, with no principal payments until the end of the ten year term, when all of the principal must be repaid. Bev's loan is subordinated to the bank's loan. Under these assumptions, the corporation's financial statements would appear as follows.

ABC Restaurant, Inc.
Balance Sheet
Dec. 31, Last Year

Assets		**Liabilities and equity**	
Cash	$ 111,000	Accounts payable	$ 200,000
Accounts receivable	225,000	Other accrued liabilities	300,000
Short-term investments	124,000	Loan from Bev	800,000
Inventory	1,400,000	Bank loan	3,000,000

---

[130] *See* IRC § 1361(c)(5); Treas. Reg. § 1.1361-1(*l*)(5). An infinite variety of options are available; if Bev desires to have some of the pass-through losses and is willing to give up her priority to this extent, she could be *both* a shareholder and a creditor. So long as this arrangement is respected for non-tax law (the interest payments on the debt are timely made, for example), it will be given the expected tax treatment. Moreover, if the corporation generates losses in excess of Bev's basis in her stock, she would be permitted to use those losses to reduce the basis in her debt; *see* IRC § 1367(b)(2).

Assets		Liabilities and equity	
Furniture and fixtures, net of accumulated depreciation	3,000,000	**Total liabilities**	4,300,000
Land	400,000	Common stock (1¢ par value)	38
Intangible assets, net of amortization	100,000	Contrib. capital in excess of par	3,799,962
		Retained earnings (deficit)	(2,740,000)
		Total equity	1,060,000*
Total assets	**$ 5,360,000**	**Total liabilities and equity**	**$ 5,360,000**

* Analysis of adjusted basis reconciliation with equity follows the income statements.

ABC Restaurant, Inc.
Income Statements for the year ended Dec. 31

	Three years ago	**Two years ago**	**Last year**
	(first yr of operation)		
Revenues	$ 2,000,000	$ 4,000,000	$ 7,500,000
Cost of sales	2,980,000	5,580,000	6,080,000
Gross margin	(980,000)	(1,580,000)	1,420,000
Administrative expenses	400,000	500,000	700,000
Net income (loss)	(1,380,000)	(2,080,000)	720,000
Retained earnings (deficit), at end of year	$ (1,380,000)	$ (3,460,000)	$ (2,740,000)

The S corporation would have operated as follows with respect to the shareholders, who own a total of 3800 shares with an original cost basis of $1000 each.

Share-holder's basis	Initial investment	First year's loss	Second year's loss	Third year's gain	Adjusted basis, end of third year
Ann & Carl (each)	$ 400,000	$ (145,263)	$ (218,947)	$ 75,789	$ 111,579
Other investors (per $100,000 investment unit)	$ 100,000	$ (36,316)	$ (54,737)	$ 18,947	$ 27,894
Total for all share-holders†	$ 3,800,000	$ (1,380,000)	$ (2,080,000)	$ 720,000	$ 1,060,000
† Totals may not add due to rounding.					

Notice how Ann and Carl have fared as S corporation shareholders compared to Alternative B, where they were partners in a partnership. They have borne a larger proportionate share of the losses, because they own a larger proportion of the business (since Bev is not an owner in this Alternative C). Assume, as with Alternative A, that the price for Ann's stock is $600,000 payable over ten years at a reasonable interest rate, that the bank is agreeable to the buyout so long as Ann's note is subordinate to their loan, and Bev agrees with a similar condition regarding her debt as applies to the bank.

Would you want to make any other arrangement with regard to Bev's interest? Is there something other than 100% debt-financing which would be better for Bev, not worse for Ann or Carl, and still meet the S corporation requirements?

Chapter 7

MANAGEMENT AND CONTROL

Your clients wear many hats. They ay be any or all of the following: active owners, passive investors, managers, employers/employees, lessors/lessees, lenders/borrowers, or vendors/vendees. This can quickly become an unmanageable morass if you do not carefully determine, map out, and document your clients' roles in their business.

This chapter begins in Section A with an overview of the basic conceptual management and control issues that arise in any new business. We look at the common control and management issues your clients may have considered, as well as many more which they probably have *not* considered. Sections B through D consider these issues specifically as they relate to the different types of business entities: partnerships, corporations, and limited liability companies. In Section E, we consider overarching concepts of fiduciary duty which may apply to your client regardless of his or her role in the business.

A. CONCEPTUAL OVERVIEW

In most cases, clients who come to you with a business opportunity envision some type of active role in its operations. The roles may vary from day-to-day work in some or all of the business' operations to a more distanced supervisory or consulting role. Even the absentee financier or venture capitalist will want some say in business decisions.

Because this is one area in which your clients will probably have done some serious work before consulting with a lawyer, you will have some information upon which to build. Here is an excellent opportunity for you as counselor and business planner to add value to your clients' business plans. We begin with a discussion of the plans your clients may have brought to you, and then suggest other responsibilities or issues they have not considered.

1. The Clients' Initial Division of Responsibility

Your clients will have some idea about which of them will run the business and what that entails. If they do not divide all the anticipated responsibilities among them, they will likely have thought about who should hire and supervise employees to complete the rest of the tasks. This mapping out of jobs is the function of a good business plan, which you should encourage your clients to have prepared before going any further with the business organization.[1] It is also possible that they will have decided to delegate all the authority to one person, although this is much less

---

[1] *See* Damon Lim, *Preparing a Business Plan, in* Emerging Companies Guide: A Resource for Professionals and Entrepreneurs 51–52 (2005).

likely.[2] In reviewing your clients' business plan, you should help them assure that they have accounted for all major phases of manufacturing, production, sales, distribution, advertising, and service(s) that apply to their business. Although your role is not that of a business consultant, these arrangements will help ensure that you have avoided legal trouble by planning for control and management of all anticipated outcomes of the business venture.

Example. A business might include the following provisions in its partnership agreement (if a partnership), bylaws or shareholder agreement (if a corporation), or operating agreement (if a limited liability company). This example is general, and would be modified according to the particulars of your clients' business and their planned division of responsibilities.

The [partners / members / shareholders] agree that:

(1) Smith will be responsible for all matters relating to production, including hiring and supervision of employees engaged in the manufacture or preparation of goods to be sold or services to be offered, hours and locations of production, and the purchase and sale in the ordinary course of all goods and machinery necessary for these functions;

(2) Jones will be responsible for sales and administrative matters, including the keeping of books and records, filing of all necessary forms, applications, licenses and returns, hiring and supervision of office and sales employees, hours and location of sales of products or offering of services, and advertising and marketing;

(3) Williams will have no direct responsibility for any of the matters mentioned in parts (1) and (2) above, but will only provide capital to the business and share in the profits and losses as indicated in Article __ of this Agreement.

2. Other Responsibilities

There are important responsibilities in addition to business operations. Many times clients have not considered these important administrative details.

Financial. Every business entity must have someone in charge of the finances and financial management of the business. Many businesses will hire an accountant for this purpose, especially if the business is treated as a partnership for income tax purposes, since complex forms and schedules must be prepared for the business and for each owner. As a business grows beyond an elementary stage, however, oversight over financial matters must be brought into the formal management structure. We have seen in Chapters 3, 5 and 6 that there are important tax, financial and accounting issues which will affect the operation of the business, the financial allocations and distributions to equity holders, and the legal rights and obligations of all of the constituents of the entity. This does not mean

---

[2] *See* Terence Floyd Cuff, *A Personal Perspective on Drafting Partnership and LLC Agreements, in* Tax Strategies for Corporate Acquisitions, Dispositions, Spin-Offs, Joint Ventures, Financings, Reorganizations & Restructurings 2004 at 339 (PLI Tax Law & Estate Planning Course Handbook Series No. 2995) (describing two types of management arrangements: "strong manager with all power," and a manager with day-to-day control of business subject to oversight of major decisions).

that every business ownership structure must include a financial expert,[3] but it must include someone whose *responsibility* is to see that these functions are carried out. Hence we have the oft-seen language that the financial matters of a business will be carried out "by *or under the direction of*" a treasurer (or chief financial officer), managing partner, or some other designated person.

Custodial. Your clients will need someone to attend to the basic tasks of keeping the business' records complete, updated, and accessible. Every business entity other than a sole proprietorship is a nonhuman legal "person," and therefore must employ agents to conduct its business.[4] It is important for a business to keep track of these agents and the scope of their authority. It would be a sad circumstance indeed if your client was unable to enforce a beneficial contract because the individual who signed "on behalf of" the client had no authority to do so. We have seen that the law may penalize those who do not carefully respect the formalities of their business organization, as in the case of "piercing the veil" of a corporation or other limited liability entity.[5] It is highly unlikely that failure to maintain formalities, standing alone, will result in loss of limited liability, but it would be foolish to provide *any* ammunition to a plaintiff seeking to hold owners or controlling individuals personally liable. As with the financial matters, nonfinancial records and reports should be at least supervised by a responsible member of management.[6]

Administrative. Every business must tend to the administrative details, as distinct from the operational details. These can be as trivial as office supplies and as vital as employment decisions, policies, manuals, and compliance with statutory, regulatory and contractual requirements. For example, partners may agree that one of them should be in charge of "hiring," but what about compensation, performance review, promotion, and the like?

These additional duties can easily be overlooked by new entrepreneurs, but they must be attended to for that business to succeed. It makes sense then that the traditional offices for a business, club, or other organization are a president, vice president, secretary and treasurer. If we envision the president in charge of operations, the vice president in charge of administration, the secretary in charge of custodial details, and the treasurer in charge of financial details, then we will have made sure that each of these important duties is properly assigned. Although your clients might attach importance to the actual titles given to the officers in the business, it is the actual assignment of duties which is important.[7]

---

[3] However, in the case of public companies (those filing periodic reports under the Securities Exchange Act of 1934), Sarbanes-Oxley Act § 407(a) requires them to disclose whether the audit committee of the board of directors includes a person classified as a "financial expert," and if not, why not. A "financial expert" is defined by the SEC (as required by the Sarbanes-Oxley Act) in Item 407(d)(5) of Regulation S-K and Regulation S-B.

[4] *See generally* Chapter 2, Section C.2.

[5] *See generally* Chapter 2, Section C.3.b.

[6] We will see in Section C below that such a person is required by law in a corporation, due to its unique agency arrangements.

[7] Two qualifications are in order to the rule that duties are more important than titles. First, some type of "inherent" authority might attach to someone who has an office called "president," by virtue of the commonly-understood meaning of that word. "Inherent" authority is a type of authority disfavored by modern agency rules including the Restatement (Third) of Agency, but the concept has shown some tenacity among courts. Second, it is not good drafting practice to invent titles which do not intuitively

Example. In the above Smith-Jones-Williams business, we might add to clause (2) that Jones

> will: (i) keep or cause to be kept accurate books and records; (ii) file or cause to be filed all required reports, returns, licenses and filings to assure compliance with applicable laws and regulations; (iii) assure compliance by all employees and supervisors with all such laws and regulations, and review at least annually the compensation and performance of all employees [except for the partners / shareholders / members].

3. Resolution of Disagreements

The foregoing list of responsibilities will help you and your clients anticipate and assign to appropriate officers, the important functions in the business. However, even the most complete listing of tasks and responsibilities will be imperfect because the future always brings unanticipated problems. Therefore, the business management structure should include provisions to deal with these unanticipated problems.

No responsibility assigned. Despite your excellent drafting, at some point in the life of the business something will have to be done which no one wants to do, and which was not assigned to anyone. The individual who recognizes that X must be done — whether an employee, owner, or someone else — must have a way to bring this to the attention of the management so that the task can be assigned and someone must have the authority to undertake the task, or delegate authority for the task.

Overlapping claims of responsibility. Despite your excellent drafting, a business can face the opposite problem from that of the previous paragraph. Rather than a job that no one wants to do, there is a job that *more than one person* wants to do. You may have been careful to avoid explicitly assigning the same responsibility to two different persons or positions, but imprecise language can create problems. Suppose, for example, one officer is in charge of production and another in charge of marketing. Who would make decisions about packaging design or product delivery? Either officer might have a legitimate understanding that "this is my job," and discord can result.

Example. If we have made specific assignments of authority as above, it would still be prudent to add language which fills in all the "gaps" similar to the following:

> (a) In the case of any disagreement among the [partners / shareholders / members] regarding responsibility for any matter related to the conduct of the business, the matter will be decided by a majority vote of the [partners / shareholders / members] at a meeting, which may be called by any [partner / member / shareholder] for this purpose.

> (b) In the case of any responsibility which is not assigned by this agreement, any [partner / shareholder / member] may take that responsibility or see that it is properly assigned, subject to the procedure for resolution of disagreements in (a) above.

---

compare to duties. Thus, a "secretary" shouldn't be vested with solely financial duties, or a "president" or "chairman" with unimportant ministerial tasks.

An alternative "architecture" for such an agreement, rather than listing specific responsibilities and providing for resolution of disputes, would be to give managers general authority but provide a list of "basic decisions" which require consent of the owners.[8]

Removal. Even if all jobs are perfectly assigned, one of the managers may not be performing in a manner which meets everyone's expectations. The business planner should anticipate this problem and determine how the clients would agree *now* to solve this problem should it occur *later*. The main questions to be resolved are: (1) who decides whether a manager should be removed, (2) whether removal must be justified according to certain standards or whether it may be "without cause," and (3) whether removal as a manager affects the manager's ownership interests, if any. There are no "right" answers to these questions,[9] but having your clients think about them now will reduce discord and perhaps even avoid litigation when these events occur.

Examples. If the clients want to provide for removal without cause and with no other consequences, they might provide:

A [manager / officer] is subject to removal without cause upon the affirmative vote of a majority of the [partners / members / shareholders] at a meeting called for that purpose.

If the removal is to be with cause, the causes should be specified:

A [manager / officer] is subject to removal only upon the affirmative vote at a meeting called for that purpose of the [partners / members / shareholders] that the [manager / officer]:

(i)   willfully and consistently failed to perform assigned duties;
(ii) has committed a material breach of this agreement;
(iii) was [accused / found guilty] of [list applicable crimes];
(iv) had a personal representative appointed for [him / her] by a court.

At the meeting, the [manager / officer] subject to removal will be provided with a statement of the causes alleged against [him / her] and an opportunity to respond to the allegations.

Regardless of whether removal is with or without cause, if the removal is to result in the termination of the individual's ownership interests, the agreement should so indicate. You will find some sample clauses regarding buyouts of the ownership interests of terminated employees in Section D.5 of Chapter 8. In the case of a corporation, the agreement should also deal specifically with removal of the individual as a director or as an officer. There may be specific legal provisions

[8] For an example of such a partnership agreement requiring approval by a majority of the partners for certain defined "Major Decisions," see *Whitney v. Citibank, N.A.*, 782 F.2d 1106 (2d Cir. 1986), reproduced below.

[9] There are some *legally* correct answers; for example, removal of directors by the shareholders under MBCA § 8.08(a) may be "without cause" unless the articles of incorporation specify that removal may be "for cause" only. There are also some *strategically* correct answers; for example, whether a manager believes removal should be "for cause" may depend on whether he or she believes the power is likely to be exercised *by* that manager (presumably fewer restrictions would be bargained for) or *against* that manager by the others (presumably more restrictions would be bargained for).

concerning removal of directors which would apply.[10]

Replacement. Even if not removed, managers may leave or die. The business planner should also anticipate this problem and determine how clients will decide upon a replacement.[11] If a manager's position is tied to an ownership interest, the manager's departure will cause problems regarding the buy-out of the departing manager's equity interest, and the buy-in of any replacement manager. The problems of buy-ins and buy-outs are discussed in Chapter 8.

Examples. Regardless of how a manager is removed, or if a manager dies or becomes incapacitated, the agreement can provide for "filling a vacancy" as follows:

> If any [office / managerial position] becomes vacant, it may be filled by a majority vote of the [partners / members / shareholders *or* directors].

If the manager must also be a partner, member, or shareholder, this would be covered by provisions relating to new owners as follows:

> New [partners / members / shareholders], including the amount(s) to be contributed to the business and the [number of shares/units *or* profit/loss shares] must be approved by a majority vote of the existing [partners / members / shareholders]. In addition, any new member must agree to be bound by the [partnership / stockholders' / operating] agreement in effect at the time of admission.

4.   Decision-Making Process

In the above situations, your clients may have dictated something similar to "if *X* occurs, we'll decide the appropriate course of action at that time." This has the advantage of optimum flexibility, but it only provides any advantage of certainty if you, as the business planner, have provided a means by which "they" can make such a decision.

A good management agreement does not have to replicate *Robert's Rules of Order*, but your clients must realize that some degree of formality is required for them to make a decision. Otherwise the result of the decision may not be respected or even recognized by all the owners and/or managers, and discord, strife, and perhaps even litigation might be the result. To avoid this problem, any time that a decision must or should be made by any group, the entity documentation should provide for the following procedures.

- *Should a "meeting" be required?* Is this a problem which requires all the owners or managers to get together so that they might have the benefit of each others' input, suggestions, and debate? Might the problem be solved by one or more of them subject to ratification by the others?

- *Basic meeting rules.* If a meeting is required — of the partners, shareholders, directors, members, managers — there are three basic provisions which must be addressed in order to make the outcome of any meeting practically and legally effective.

---

[10] *See id.*

[11] Another possibility is that the owners or managers might decide to terminate the business. This is discussed in Chapter 8.

→ *Call and notice.* Who may invoke this "meeting" process? Typically a meeting may be called by one or more of the participants. But the passive voice in the preceding sentence hides a number of practical problems. How is a meeting "called"? An agreement should specify to whom the "call" is delivered, and should make that person (or someone else) responsible for providing notice of the meeting. The notice should provide the time, place, and subject-matter of the meeting. The purpose of the notice is equivalent to service of process in a lawsuit; proper notice followed by lack of response or reply will affect the recipient's legal rights. Therefore it is important that call and notice provisions be adequately drafted so that no one later claims the process was unfair.

→ *Quorum.* What if we held a meeting and no one showed up? You must have rules specifying what makes a "meeting," or one individual who could not or chose not to attend may claim that the action was not binding. Choosing the size of the quorum for a meeting may have strategic implications. A small quorum will increase flexibility but may increase the potential for a majority (or even minority) to take action without the presence of the others. A large quorum will ensure that most or all of those who are to meet will have a say in the decision, but it presents the potential for some individuals to prevent the meeting from happening by staying away.[12]

→ *Attendance.* Physical attendance is *passé* today. Your agreement may provide for virtual attendance of various means, be they the relatively low-tech conference call or higher-tech versions such as a chat room or instant messaging.[13] Failing any such provision, however, attendance in person is likely the default rule. This may prove difficult if the owners or managers are widely dispersed. And the perceived harshness of a high quorum may be mitigated if attendance by these alternative means is permitted. Another variation on attendance is whether proxies should be permitted. A small group of closely-associated and familiar owners or managers might well decide not to permit attendance by proxy, but a larger impersonal group could reach a different conclusion. The lawyer must be sure to determine the clients' wishes and know the default rules[14] to determine if modification is necessary.

Example. The following is a standard version of meeting rules.

> *Annual meeting.* The annual meeting of the [partners / members / shareholders] will take place on the second Tuesday of January at the Principal Office.[15]

---

[12] Whether such an absence will be effective depends on a corporate analogy. Ordinarily, shareholders may freely stay away to prevent a quorum or meeting, but directors may be held to a higher standard. *See* Gearing v. Kelly, 11 N.Y.2d 201, 182 N.E.2d 391 (1962); M. Thomas Arnold, *Shareholder Duties Under State Law*, 28 Tulsa L.J. 213, 221–23 (1992).

[13] What is important as a practical matter (and many legal rules so state) is that all the participants be aware of who is attending, and that everyone can "hear" everyone else. "Side conversations" by instant message or cell phone text messages are inevitable, and probably acceptable, just as two individuals could whisper or step outside of the presence of a physical meeting for a private discussion.

[14] For example, MBCA § 7.22(a) permits shareholder voting by proxy, similarly for members or managers in a limited liability company under ULLCA § 4.04(e), and limited partners under Re-RULPA § 118.

[15] The location of the "Principal Office" or "Business Office" is usually defined elsewhere in the agreement.

Special meeting. A special meeting[16] of the [partners / members / shareholders] will be held upon the submission to [manager / officer] of a written request stating the purpose of the meeting and signed by [_____% of the number of partners / members *or* owners of _____% of the outstanding shares / units of interest], or at any time when a meeting is required under this Agreement[17]. The [manager / officer] will thereupon call a meeting at the Principal Office on a date between _____ and _____ days following receipt of the request.

Quorum. At any meeting, [_____% of the [partners / members *or* holders of _____% units of interest / shares] shall constitute a quorum. An individual attends a meeting for purposes of this rule if physically present or connected by electronic or other device permitting the individual to hear and be heard by all others attending.

Proxies. [Here you should either permit or forbid voting by proxy.]

B. IN A PARTNERSHIP

We face a different problem with respect to the management of general partnerships. Because a general partner has presumptive wide-ranging authority,[18] the issue may more often be *limiting* that authority rather than *providing* any authority.

How authority is limited in partnership can be a difficult problem. If his or her authority is not otherwise limited by the partnership agreement, each partner has authority to act in the "ordinary course" of the partnership's business.[19] A majority of the partners can change the "ordinary course,"[20] but unanimity is required otherwise.[21] This can create irreducible uncertainty for third parties as to whether an action is in the "ordinary course."[22]

In addition, if the partnership agreement does limit a partner's authority, any limitation on an agent's authority is normally only effective to a third party who knows of that limitation.[23] We can, however, provide some relief for a partnership from an errant partner's actions. The following language may be typical:

If any partner, although acting outside the scope of his authority, none-theless binds the partnership to any obligation to or with any third party,

---

[16] A meeting is referred to as a "special" meeting if is not a "regular" or "annual" meeting which need not be called, but happens as stated in the bylaws or agreement each year or other period.

[17] This latter clause takes into account all the times above which the agreement has specified "votes" of owners; it makes clear that these votes will be taken at a properly called meeting.

[18] *See* Chapter 2, Section C.2.b.

[19] One difference here between UPA and RUPA is that RUPA "clarifies that a partner's apparent authority includes acts for carrying on in the ordinary course 'business of the kind carried on by the partnership,' not just the business of the particular partnership in question." RUPA § 301 cmt. 2.

[20] UPA § 9(1); RUPA § 301(1).

[21] UPA §§ 9(2), 18(h); RUPA §§ 301(2), 401(j).

[22] See the classic cases of *Covalt v. High,* 100 N.M. 700, 675 P.2d 999 (1983); *Summers v. Dooley,* 94 Idaho 87, 481 P.2d 318 (1971); and *National Biscuit Co. v. Stroud,* 249 N.C. 467, 106 S.E.2d 692 (1959).

[23] Under RUPA, "[a] notification [of limitation of a partner's authority] may be effective upon delivery, whether or not it actually comes to the other person's attention. To that extent, the risk of lack of authority is shifted to those dealing with partners." RUPA § 301 cmt. 2.

he shall hold the partnership harmless and indemnify it for any damage caused to it by his actions.

A prudent planner might wish instead to prevent the transaction in the first place. How is a limitation on a partner's authority communicated to the world of third parties? And what if the third party is also in on the scheme?

WHITNEY v. CITIBANK, N.A.
United States Court of Appeals, Second Circuit
782 F.2d 1106 (1986)

Before FRIENDLY, MANSFIELD and PRATT, CIRCUIT JUDGES.

MANSFIELD, CIRCUIT JUDGE:

Citibank, N.A. appeals from a judgment of the Southern District of New York, entered after a bench trial before Chief Judge Constance Baker Motley, awarding compensatory and punitive damages against it in this diversity action based on its inducement of and knowing participation in a breach of fiduciary duty on the part of co-defendants Carl Berger and Richard Timpone. The amended complaint also asserted claims of fraud, civil conspiracy, commercial bribery and negligent misrepresentation against Citibank, based on the same core of facts as that forming the basis of the breach of fiduciary duty claim. Having found in plaintiff's favor on the breach of fiduciary duty claim and that the defendants had acted pursuant to a common understanding between them, Judge Motley declined to consider the other claims, from which holding plaintiff cross-appeals. We affirm.

The material facts are either undisputed or embodied in findings of the district court supported by substantial record evidence. On October 20, 1977, plaintiff Robert B. Whitney, a real estate entrepreneur residing in California, formed a New York general partnership known as Urban Recycle One Associates (URO) with Carl Berger, an architect, and Richard Timpone, a carpenter, both of whom are residents of New Jersey. The purpose of the partnership was to purchase and develop for residential apartment use approximately 11 acres of land with an abandoned factory, located in Edgewater, New Jersey, and known as the Alcoa property. The three partners initially made the following capital contributions to the partnership:

(1) *Whitney*: $183,700, in the form of an option to purchase the property from its then owner, Tri-Terminal Corporation (Tri-Terminal), and investments made by him in a site analysis, architectural drawings, work product of legal counsel and consultants, zoning applications and a land survey.

(2) *Berger*: $5,000 in architectural-services.

(3) *Timpone*: $50,000 in the form of part ownership of the option to purchase the property from Tri-Terminal and $11,871 in legal work product.

Under the partnership agreement Whitney and Timpone committed themselves to make additional capital contributions of $11,300 and $13,128 respectively. Profits and distributions of assets of the partnership other than return of capital contributions were to be allocated 40% to Whitney, 40% to Berger and 20% to Timpone. The parties' written partnership agreement (§ 2.01) provided that all

"Major Decisions" of the partnership (which are defined[24]) should be made by a majority vote of the partners. The agreement also established the position of Manager of the Venture, whose function would be to implement those decisions and to conduct the ordinary and usual business of the partnership. Whitney was designated as Manager. By letter dated April 11, 1979, the partners agreed that each would inform the others of "matters relating to URO action pursuant to the URO partnership agreement."

In December 1977, URO's option to acquire the Alcoa property expired. In June 1978 Tri-Terminal, having defaulted on its mortgage of the property to Citibank, conveyed the property by deed in lieu of foreclosure to [Citibank]. . . . A limited partnership, Edgewater Associates (Edgewater), was then formed for the purpose of acquiring the Alcoa property. It consisted of URO as the sole Limited Partner with a 25% interest and Kenneth Gladstone as the General Partner. Edgewater purchased the property on October 4, 1978, from [Citibank] for $2,090,000, $25,000 in cash and $2,065,000 by notes from Edgewater to Citibank, secured by two mortgages to Citibank. Pursuant to extensions the notes became due on April 1, 1980.

On April 1, 1980, Edgewater defaulted on the mortgage loan, which by that date had been reduced to $2 million. Citibank thereupon began foreclosure proceedings against Edgewater and URO. However, Citibank preferred to obtain from Edgewater a deed in lieu of foreclosure, which would enable the bank, upon sale of the Alcoa property to a third party, to avoid lengthy foreclosure proceedings and to pocket for itself any proceeds over the mortgage debt. Gladstone was willing to give such a deed and toward that end sought URO's written consent as a limited partner because Citibank was concerned that without URO's consent Gladstone might not be able to convey clear title. Art. X, Par. 10.2 of the Edgewater limited partnership agreement provided that, although the General Partner (Gladstone) had broad powers with respect to the management of the Edgewater partnership, including sale of Partnership property, the limited partner (URO) could object in writing to a proposed sale on the ground that it was not fair and equitable. . . . Since the consent of URO partners to a sale of the Alcoa property in lieu of foreclosure would amount to a "Major Decision" as defined in § 2.01 of the URO partnership agreement, for which a majority vote of the three partners was required, each partner was entitled, after being informed of the essential facts, to cast his vote on the question of whether the URO consent should be given.

Whitney, still the manager of URO in June 1980, believed that its residual 25% interest in the Alcoa property after satisfaction of the mortgage debt was worth as much as $900,000. However, rather than refuse to give URO's consent, a course which would probably have led to a foreclosure sale, he was agreeable to a sale by Citibank in lieu of foreclosure provided he could obtain from Citibank a commit-

---

[24] [2] The definition of "Major Decisions" included:

"(3) sale or other transfer (except sales or transfers pursuant to Article V), or leasing (except for certain space leases as permitted to be made without approval as specified in subsection (4) below) or mortgaging or the placing or suffering the placing of any encumbrance on the Property or the Improvements or any parts thereof;

"(12) the adjustment, settlement, or the compromise of any claim, obligation, debt demand, suit or judgment against the Venture, or Manager;

"(14) any other decision or action which by the provisions of this Agreement is required to be Approved by the Venturers or which materially affects the Venture or the assets or operations thereof."

ment that would enable him to refinance the $2 million debt to it or, in the event of a sale in lieu of foreclosure to a third party, to share in the proceeds over and above the $2 million debt. Accordingly, he and his URO partner Berger negotiated with Randall G. Frisk, Vice-President in Citibank's Real Estate Industries Division, for such a "proceeds-sharing" arrangement.

In August 1980 Frisk told Whitney that Citibank . . . would offer the property for sale at $5 million in lieu of foreclosure, which Frisk characterized as a "cheap" price, and distribute to Edgewater any proceeds in excess of the mortgage debt.[25] Relying on this oral representation, Whitney had URO's attorney . . . prepare a URO consent, which Whitney executed. . . . However, Berger and Timpone were unwilling to [execute the consent]. . . . Gladstone of Edgewater then threatened suit against URO because of its refusal to give a deed in lieu of foreclosure, which he wanted in order to avoid having Edgewater's record include a foreclosure based on its failure to pay its debt to Citibank.

In view of the disagreement that thus developed between Whitney and his two URO partners regarding the best method of dealing with Gladstone and Citibank, Whitney on September 9, 1980, resigned as URO Manager. That role then passed to Berger. In his resignation letter Whitney advised Berger and Timpone, among other things, "the two of you are on your own." As his letter made clear, however, this statement referred to preparation of "a defense to Gladstone's court action," not to the management of URO's business generally, as Whitney emphasized in a September 16, 1980, letter to them stating, "I am also holding you responsible for upholding the URO partnership agreement with respect to my rights." . . . .

. . . .

Within a few weeks after Whitney's resignation as Manager of URO, Frisk, who was aware of the schism between Whitney and his URO partners, initiated negotiations with Berger and Timpone for their individual consents. As a result, on September 30, 1980, they executed such consents, which were drafted by the bank and placed in escrow with Berger's attorney, . . . pending the conclusion of a satisfactory agreement between the two partners and Citibank. On November 7, 1980, [Citibank offered to] Berger and Timpone . . . , in return for their consents, . . . 50% of all proceeds over $2.5 million up to $3.5 million realized from the sale of the Alcoa property and 25% of all proceeds received in excess of $3.5 million. Berger and Timpone [agreed] . . . . Neither the executed consents nor the draft agreement with Citibank made any mention of Whitney's rights individually or as a partner of URO. The agreement did not mention URO's consent, but referred only to the consents of Berger and Timpone. The consents themselves were signed "individually, and as a partner of [URO]." On November 21, 1980, Citibank obtained a final foreclosure judgment against Edgewater in the sum of $2,264,994.21 with interest, counsel fees and costs. [The consideration paid by Citibank for Berger's and Timpone's consents was later modified by mutual agreement in January 1981 to a total of $200,000.]

. . . .

Despite the fact that Whitney was in frequent communication with Berger, Timpone, Frisk and Citibank's real estate broker, Palin, during the period of

---

[25] [4] Under the Edgewater limited partnership agreement URO, as a 25% limited partner, would be entitled to 25% of the proceeds in excess of the mortgage debt paid by Citibank to Edgewater.

Citibank's negotiations with Berger and Timpone, and was keeping them advised as to his own efforts to obtain a refinancing or "proceeds of the sale" agreement, they kept Whitney in the dark as to their activities. He was completely unaware of Citibank's negotiations for the Berger, Timpone and URO consents. . . .

Upon learning from Palin in early 1981 that Citibank was about to sell the Alcoa property . . . , Whitney [inquired of Citibank] about URO's rights in the matter. [H]e was falsely advised by [Citibank] that the bank had all of the necessary documents for transfer of title. On March 17, 1981, [Citibank] falsely advised Whitney . . . that Citibank was relying solely on the deed in lieu of foreclosure received from Gladstone as sufficient to convey complete title and that Citibank had no obligation to pay to URO or Whitney any part of such amount as might be received over the defaulted mortgage debt. In fact, of course, Citibank had by the January 1981 agreement agreed to pay $200,000 to Berger and Timpone for their consents and that of URO.

. . . .

Having . . . tried unsuccessfully over a period of several months to obtain from Citibank and its counsel the facts with respect to their dealings with Berger and Timpone regarding consents to sale of the Alcoa property in lieu of foreclosure, Whitney in September 1981 commenced the present lawsuit. After a lengthy trial Judge Motley on November 13, 1984, filed a 32-page opinion detailing her findings of fact and conclusions of law. She concluded that Berger and Timpone had breached their fiduciary duty to URO and Whitney, entitling Whitney to an accounting; that Citibank had induced their breach, entitling Whitney to $236,677.25 compensatory damages and $250,000 punitive damages against Citibank, plus pre-judgment interest on the compensatory damages and costs. . . .

Citibank appeals from the final judgment against it. . . .

DISCUSSION

Citibank does not question the well settled elements of a claim for inducing or participating in a breach of fiduciary duty. The claimant must prove (1) a breach by a fiduciary of obligations to another, (2) that the defendant knowingly induced or participated in the breach, and (3) that the plaintiff suffered damages as a result of the breach. . . .

Citibank concedes that Berger and Timpone as URO partners had a fiduciary duty to disclose to Whitney the terms on which URO's consent was to be given to Citibank and to account to him for proceeds received for that consent. However, it contends that the evidence was insufficient to permit a finding that it *knowingly* or *intentionally* participated in their misconduct. It emphasizes that it was entitled under § 2.01(b)(3) of the URO Partnership Agreement, which requires only a majority vote of the partners to approve a major decision, to rely on the consent of Berger and Timpone. It further argues that it reasonably relied upon the authority of Berger as Managing Partner, a position he assumed in September 1980 upon Whitney's resignation. The bank points to the absence of any evidence that it was aware of the April 11, 1979 letter agreement between the partners, holding each to a duty of full disclosure to the others with respect to his actions on behalf of URO, or of Whitney's September 16, 1980, letter to his partners asking them to protect his rights under the URO Partnership Agreement. Citibank argues that, on the contrary, once the differences between Whitney and his partners regarding the Alcoa property arose in September 1980, it believed that Whitney had abandoned his partners, and was trying to promote a deal for himself with respect to the property, and accordingly wanted to terminate the partnership, leaving Berger and Timpone free to negotiate the January 13, 1981 consents on their own.

If the evidence were limited to that relied upon by Citibank, it probably could not be held responsible for the misconduct of Berger and Timpone in breach of their fiduciary duty to Whitney. Ordinarily, absent awareness of facts indicating that a partner is acting beyond his real or apparent authority, a third party is not obligated to investigate the matter further or search for some limitation on that partner's authority. *Restatement (Second) of Agency* §§ 159, 161, 166 (1958). But here there *was* additional evidence, which is sufficient to support the district court's finding that Citibank knowingly participated in the misconduct of Berger and Timpone.

In the first place, Citibank and its counsel knew that URO's interest in the Alcoa property was the partnership's sole remaining asset. It is questionable whether the final disposition of that asset for the sum of $200,000 amounted to "carrying on in the usual way the business of the partnership" within the meaning of §§ 20(1) and (3) of the New York Partnership Law,[26] which delineates a partner's authority. It is more likely that transfer of URO's consent required the acquiescence of all three partners as specified by § 20(3)(c) of the New York law. Indeed, the prospective dissolution of the URO partnership was known to all, including Citibank. . . . [T]here were red flags flying all over the place. Once Citibank was put on notice of questions concerning the authority of Berger and Timpone to bind URO without Whitney's consent, it owed a duty to reveal the facts to Whitney and determine whether his partners were authorized to act on URO's behalf in giving its consent . . . .

. . . .

The judgment of the district court is affirmed.

NOTES AND QUESTIONS

1. Although litigation is an anathema to business planners, we can learn a lot from studying litigation. Note that all parties in this story had lawyers from large well-respected firms. Was anyone badly advised?

---

[26] [6] Section 20 of the New York Partnership Law (McKinney's 1948) provides in pertinent part:

"§ 20 *Partner agent of partnership as to partnership business*

"1. Every partner is an agent of the partnership for the purpose of its business, and the act of every partner, including the execution in the partnership name of any instrument, for apparently carrying on in the usual way the business of the partnership of which he is a member binds the partnership, unless the partner so acting has in fact no authority to act for the partnership in the particular matter, and the person with whom he is dealing has knowledge of the fact that he has no such authority.

"2. An act of a partner which is not apparently for the carrying on of the business of the partnership in the usual way does not bind the partnership unless authorized by the other partners.

"3. Unless authorized by the other partners or unless they have abandoned the business, one or more but less than all the partners have no authority to:

"(c) Do any other act which would make it impossible to carry on the ordinary business of the partnership."

2. Planning helps provide certainty which can add value to business deals. Here, Citibank was taking a risk by dealing with Berger and Timpone, two of the three partners in the URO partnership, and shunning Whitney. If you were Citibank's lawyer here, what could you have done to provide certainty? Would it have been in your client's best interests?

3. If you were URO's lawyer, or Whitney's lawyer, what could be done to ensure that the Citibanks of the world come to all the partners when dealing with certain matters?

4. Conversely, if you wish to assure that the rest of the world knows that *one* of the partners is authorized to deal on behalf of the firm, how can you do so?

REVISED UNIFORM PARTNERSHIP ACT (1997)

§ 303. Statement of Partnership Authority.

(a) A partnership may file a statement of partnership authority, which:

(1) must include:

(i) the name of the partnership;

(ii) the street address of its chief executive office and of one office in this State, if there is one;

(iii) the names and mailing addresses of all of the partners or of an agent appointed and maintained by the partnership . . . ; and

(iv) the names of the partners authorized to execute an instrument transferring real property held in the name of the partnership; and

(2) may state the authority, or limitations on the authority, of some or all of the partners to enter into other transactions on behalf of the partnership and any other matter.

. . .

(d) Except as otherwise provided in subsection (g), a filed statement of partnership authority supplements the authority of a partner to enter into transactions on behalf of the partnership as follows:

(1) Except for transfers of real property, a grant of authority contained in a filed statement of partnership authority is conclusive in favor of a person who gives value without knowledge to the contrary, so long as and to the extent that a limitation on that authority is not then contained in another filed statement. A filed cancellation of a limitation on authority revives the previous grant of authority.

(2) A grant of authority to transfer real property held in the name of the partnership contained in a certified copy of a filed statement of partnership authority recorded in the office for recording transfers of that real property is conclusive in favor of a person who gives value without knowledge to the contrary, so long as and to the extent that a certified copy of a filed statement containing a limitation on that authority is not then of record in the office for recording transfers of that real property. The recording in the office for recording transfers of that real property of a certified copy of a filed cancellation of a limitation on authority revives the previous grant of authority.

(e) A person not a partner is deemed to know of a limitation on the authority of a partner to transfer real property held in the name of the partnership if a certified copy of the filed statement containing the limitation on authority is of record in the office for recording transfers of that real property.

(f)   Except as otherwise provided in subsections (d) and (e) . . . , a person not a partner is not deemed to know of a limitation on the authority of a partner merely because the limitation is contained in a filed statement.

(g)   Unless earlier canceled, a filed statement of partnership authority is canceled by operation of law five years after the date on which the statement, or the most recent amendment, was filed with the [Secretary of State].

QUESTIONS

The ABC partnership is comprised of partners A, B and C. Assume that all filings mentioned below meet the requirements in § 303(a)(1).

1.   If C is given authority to contract on all matters involving the partnership, is the rest of the world "put on notice" by a statement of authority filed with the Secretary of State stating that "C is authorized to conduct any business on behalf of the ABC Partnership"?

2.   Conversely, if A and B want to assure that C has no authority to bind the partnership at all, is the rest of the world "put on notice" by a statement of limitation on authority filed with the Secretary of State stating that "C is not authorized to conduct any business on behalf of the ABC Partnership"?

3.   If your answer to either of the above questions is "no," is the value of a statement of partnership authority or limitation of authority very useful? If so, how?

General and limited partnership laws do not require meeting of the partners.[27] Statutes are sparse regarding the details about how partners should go about commencing or conducting a meeting. The main default rule, as noted above, is simply that each partner is entitled to equal rights of management and control, regardless of the amount of capital contributed or profit shares held by each. Informality of management may be workable in a small partnership, but larger partnerships will need to impose some standards for the notice, commencement and conduct of formal meetings.[28] One commentator notes that "[t]ypically, partnership agreements provide for partner meetings when, as and if called by the managing general partner, and borrow heavily from the corresponding corporate law for concepts of record dates, notice, quorums and other voting matters."[29] Some examples of this type of language were given and discussed in Section A.4 of this chapter.

---

[27] The closest to a meeting requirement is the "non-requirement" of Re-RULPA § 118: "Action requiring the consent of partners . . . may be taken without a meeting, and a partner may appoint a proxy to consent or otherwise act for the partner." The comment to § 118 states simply that "This Act imposes no meeting requirement and does not distinguish among oral, record, express and tacit consent. The partnership agreement may establish such requirements and make such distinctions."

[28] J. William Callison & Maureen A. Sullivan, Partnership Law and Practice § 9:1 (2004).

[29] Gregory C. Smith & Susan Cooper Philpot, Start-up and Emerging Companies § 3.03[13] (2006).

C. IN A CORPORATION

In contrast to partnerships, corporations have detailed default rules regarding distribution of authority among the three major constituencies: shareholders, directors, and officers. Recall from Chapter 2 the basic structure of the corporation. The shareholders are the owners, but they have very limited powers. The directors have plenary power to manage the corporation (indeed, the duty to do so) but they need not be owners. The officers are the human agents of the corporation, vested with authority to act on behalf of the corporation.[30]

The formal structures imposed by general corporations statutes work well in the case of large corporations where there are meaningful distinctions between these constituencies. However, in small business ventures, the highly-formal default rules for control and management are often ill-suited for the realties of managing the affairs of the corporation. Below we consider some common statutory rules that allow for alteration of the traditional corporate structures for control and management.

1.   Common Law Rules on Shareholder Agreements

The traditional corporation's central feature is "director primacy."

> Director primacy includes the following principal elements. First, directors have broad power both to make all management-type decisions, including the day-to-day operation of the company, managerial compensation, and distributions to shareholders, and to initiate major decisions, including amendment of the charter, or sale, dissolution or merger of the firm.
>
> Second, shareholders lack the power to make management-type decisions or to initiate major decisions. Shareholder power is essentially limited to voting on major decisions and electing and removing directors. Thus, the directors are not really the shareholders' agents in the traditional sense of being under the shareholders' direct supervision and control.
>
> Third, and perhaps most importantly, the balance of power between directors and shareholders described in the preceding two paragraphs is not effectively subject to contrary agreement. A basic principle of corporate law has long been that the firm cannot "sterilize" the board — that is, seriously impair its basic functions. Though corporate statutes provide that management by the board can be qualified to some extent by contrary provisions in the articles of incorporation, these provisions do not clarify how far such restrictions may go. The existence of some limitation is supported by the fact that corporate statutes explicitly permit reduction or elimination of board functions only in special provisions applying to closely held corporations.[31]

In the following famous case, the Illinois Supreme Court provided an enduring statement of the extent to which "sterilization" is permitted at common law.

---

[30] *See* Chapter 2, Section C.2.b.

[31] Larry E. Ribstein, *Why Corporations?*, 1 BERKELEY BUS. L.J. 183, 197 (2004).

GALLER v. GALLER
Supreme Court of Illinois
203 N.E.2d 577 (1964)

UNDERWOOD, JUSTICE.

Plaintiff, Emma Galler, sued in equity for an accounting for specific performance of an agreement made in July, 1955, between plaintiff and her husband, of one part, and defendants, Isadore A. Galler and his wife, Rose, of the other. Defendants appealed from a decree of the superior court of Cook County granting the relief prayed. The First District Appellate Court reversed the decree and denied specific performance . . . . That decision is appealed here on a certificate of importance.

There is no substantial dispute as to the facts in this case. From 1919 to 1924, Benjamin and Isadore Galler, brothers, were equal partners in the Galler Drug Company, a wholesale drug concern. In 1924 the business was incorporated under the Illinois Business Corporation Act, each owning one half of the outstanding 220 shares of stock. . . .

In March, 1954, Benjamin and Isadore, on the advice of their accountant, decided to enter into an agreement for the financial protection of their immediate families and to assure their families, after death of either brother, equal control of the corporation. . . .

    . . . .

The . . . agreement in question here, entered into between Benjamin, Emma, Isadore and Rose, recites that Benjamin and Isadore . . . desired to provide income for the support and maintenance of their immediate families. . . . The essential features of the contested portions of the agreement are substantially as set forth in the opinion of the Appellate Court: that the bylaws of the corporation will be amended to provide for a board of four directors; that the necessary quorum shall be three directors; and that no directors' meeting shall be held without giving ten days notice to all directors. The shareholders will cast their votes for the above named persons (Isadore, Rose, Benjamin and Emma) as directors at said special meeting and at any other meeting held for the purpose of electing directors. In the event of the death of either brother his wife shall have the right to nominate a director in place of the decedent. Certain annual dividends will be declared by the corporation. The dividend shall be $50,000 payable out of the accumulated earned surplus in excess of $500,000. If 50% of the annual net profits after taxes exceeds the minimum $50,000, then the directors shall have discretion to declare a dividend up to 50% of the annual net profits. If the net profits are less than $50,000, nevertheless the minimum $50,000 annual dividend shall be declared, providing the $500,000 surplus is maintained. Earned surplus is defined. The certificates evidencing the said shares of Benjamin Galler and Isadore Galler shall be a legend that the shares are subject to the terms of this agreement. A salary continuation agreement shall be entered into by the corporation which shall authorize the corporation upon the death of Benjamin Galler or Isadore Galler, or both, to pay a sum equal to twice the salary of such officer, payable monthly over a five-year period. Said sum shall be paid to the widow during her widowhood, but should be paid to such widow's children if the widow remarries within the five-year period. . . . In the event either Benjamin or Isadore decides to sell his shares he is required to offer them first to the remaining shareholders and then to the corporation at book value, according each six months to accept the offer.

The Appellate Court found the . . . agreement void because 'the undue duration, stated purpose and substantial disregard of the provisions of the Corporation Act outweigh any considerations which might call for divisibility' and held that 'the public policy of this state demands voiding this entire agreement'.

. . . .

The power to invalidate the agreements on the grounds of public policy is so far reaching and so easily abused that it should be called into action to set aside or annul the solemn engagement of parties dealing on equal terms only in cases where the corrupt or dangerous tendency clearly and unequivocally appears upon the face of the agreement itself or is the necessary inference from the matters which are expressed, and the only apparent exception to this general rule is to be found in those cases where the agreement, though fair and unobjectionable on its face, is a part of a corrupt scheme and is made to disguise the real nature of the transaction.

. . . .

At this juncture it should be emphasized that we deal here with a so-called close corporation. . . . For our purposes, a close corporation is one in which the stock is held in a few hands, or in a few families, and wherein it is not at all, or only rarely, dealt in by buying or selling. Moreover, it should be recognized that shareholder agreements similar to that in question here are often, as a practical consideration, quite necessary for the protection of those financially interested in the close corporation. While the shareholder of a public-issue corporation may readily sell his shares on the open market should management fail to use, in his opinion, sound business judgment, his counterpart of the close corporation often has a large total of his entire capital invested in the business and his no ready market for his shares should he desire to sell. He feels, understandably, that he is more than a mere investor and that his voice should be heard concerning all corporate activity. Without a shareholder agreement, specifically enforceable by the courts, insuring him a modicum of control, a large minority shareholder might find himself at the mercy of an oppressive or unknowledgeable majority. Moreover, as in the case at bar, the shareholders of a close corporation are often also the directors and officers thereof. With substantial shareholding interests abiding in each member of the board of directors, it is often quite impossible to secure, as in the large public-issue corporation, independent board judgment free from personal motivations concerning corporate policy. For these and other reasons too voluminous to enumerate here, often the only sound basis for protection is afforded by a lengthy, detailed shareholder agreement securing the rights and obligations of all concerned.

[T]here has been a definite, albeit inarticulate, trend toward eventual judicial treatment of the close corporation as sui generis. Several shareholder-director agreements that have technically 'violate' the letter of the Business Corporation Act have nevertheless been upheld in the light of the existing practical circumstances, i.e., no apparent public injury, the absence of a complaining minority interest, and no apparent prejudice to creditors. However, we have thus far not attempted to limit these decisions as applicable only to close corporations and have seemingly implied that general considerations regarding judicial supervision of all corporate behavior apply.

The practical result of this series of cases, while liberally giving legal efficacy to particular agreements in special circumstances notwithstanding literal 'violations' of statutory corporate law, has been to inject much doubt and uncertainty into the thinking of the bench and corporate bar of Illinois concerning shareholder agreements.

It is therefore necessary, we feel, to discuss the instant case with the problems peculiar to the close corporation particularly in mind.

It would admittedly facilitate judicial supervision of corporate behavior if a strict adherence to the provisions of the Business Corporation Act were required in all cases without regard to the practical exigencies peculiar to the close corporation. However, courts have long ago quite realistically, we feel, relaxed their attitudes concerning statutory compliance when dealing with close corporate behavior, permitting 'slight deviations' from corporate 'norms' in order to give legal efficacy to common business practice. *See e. g.,* Clark v. Dodge, 269 N.Y. 410, 199 N.E. 641; Benintendi v. Kenton Hotel, 294 N.Y. 112, 60 N.E.2d 829, 159 A.L.R. 280 (dissenting opinion subsequently legislatively approved.) This attitude is illustrated by the following language in *Clark v. Dodge*:

> Public policy, the intention of the Legislature, detriment to the corporation, are phrases which in this connection [the court was discussing a shareholder-director agreement whereby the directors pledged themselves to vote for certain people as officers of the corporation] mean little. Possible harm to bona fide purchasers of stock or to creditors or to stockholding minorities have more substance; but such harms are absent in many instances. If the enforcement of a particular contract damages nobody — not even, in any perceptible degree, the public — one sees no reason for holding it illegal, even though it impinges slightly upon the broad provisions of (the relevant statute providing that the business of a corporation shall be managed by its board of directors.). Damage suffered or threatened is a logical and practical test, and has come to be the one generally adopted by the courts.

Clark v. Dodge, 199 N.E. 641, 642.

. . . .

Perhaps, as has been vociferously advanced, a separate comprehensive statutory scheme governing the close corporation would best serve here. See Note 'A Plea for Separate Statutory Treatment of the Close Corporation', 33 N.Y.U.L.Rev. 700. Some states have enacted legislation dealing specifically with the close corporation.

At any rate, however, the courts can no longer fail to expressly distinguish between the close and public-issue corporation when confronted with problems relating to either. What we do here is to illuminate this problem-before the bench, corporate bar, and the legislature, in the context of a particular fact situation. To do less would be to shirk our responsibility, to do more would, perhaps be to invade the province of the legislative branch.

We now, in the light of the foregoing, turn to specific provisions of the 1955 agreement.

The Appellate Court correctly found many of the contractual provisions free from serious objection, and we need not prolong this opinion with a discussion of them here. That court did, however, find difficulties in the stated purpose of the agreement as it relates to its duration, the election of certain persons to specific offices for a number of years, the requirement for the mandatory declaration of stated dividends (which the Appellate Court held invalid), and the salary continuation agreement.

Since the question as to the duration of the agreement is a principal source of controversy, we shall consider it first. The parties provided no specific termination date, and while the agreement concludes with a paragraph that its terms 'shall be binding upon and shall inure to the benefits of' the legal representatives, heirs and assigns of the parties, this clause is, we believe, intended to be operative only as long as one of the parties is living. It further provides that it shall be so construed as to carry out its purposes, and we believe these must be determined from a consideration of the agreement as a whole. Thus viewed, a fair construction is that its purposes were accomplished at the death of the survivor of the parties. While these life spans are not precisely ascertainable, and the Appellate Court noted Emma Galler's life expectancy at her husband's death was 26.9 years, we are aware of no statutory or public policy provision against stockholder's agreements which would invalidate this agreement on that ground. . . .

The clause th[at] provides for the election of certain persons to specified offices for a period of years likewise does not require invalidation. . . .

We turn next to a consideration of the effect of the stated purpose of the agreement upon its validity. The pertinent provision is: 'The said Benjamin A. Galler and Isadore A. Galler desire to provide income for the support and maintenance of their immediate families.' Obviously, there is no evil inherent in a contract entered into for the reason that the persons originating the terms desired to so arrange their property as to provide post-death support for those dependent upon them. Nor does the fact that the subject property is corporate stock alter the situation so long as there exists no detriment to minority stock interests, creditors or other public injury. It is however, contended by defendants that the methods provided by the agreement for implementation of the stated purpose are, as a whole, violative of the Business Corporation Act to such an extent as to render it void *in toto*.

The terms of the dividend agreement require a minimum annual dividend of $50,000, but this duty is limited by the subsequent provision that it shall be operative only so long as an earned surplus of $500,000 is maintained. . . . The minimum earned surplus requirement is designed for the protection of the corporation and its creditors, and we take no exception to the contractual dividend requirements as thus restricted.

The salary continuation agreement is a common feature, in one form or another, of corporate executive employment. It requires that the widow should receive a total benefit, payable monthly over a five-year period, aggregating twice the amount paid her deceased husband in one year. This requirement was likewise limited for the protection of the corporation by being contingent upon the payments being income tax-deductible by the corporation. The charge made in those cases which have considered the validity of payments to the widow of an officer and shareholder in a corporation is that a gift of its property by a noncharitable corporation is in violation of the rights of its shareholders and *ultra vires*. Since there are no shareholders here other than the parties to the contract, this objection is not here applicable, and its effect, as limited, upon the corporation is not so prejudicial as so require its invalidation.

. . . .

Accordingly, the judgment of the Appellate Court is reversed except insofar as it relates to fees, and is, as to them affirmed. The cause is remanded to the circuit court of Cook County with directions to proceed in accordance herewith.

Affirmed in part and reversed in part, and remanded with directions.

2.   Statutory Modifications

The common law rules summarized above in *Galler* are imprecise. Legislatures have stepped in to provide more certainty. These statutes take two different forms. First, eighteen states have comprehensive statutes regulating close corporations. Second, twenty-one states have a shorter provision authorizing the use of shareholder agreements to modify traditional corporate norms.[32] We consider each in turn.

ZION v. KURTZ
Court of Appeals of New York
405 N.E.2d 681 (1980)

MEYER, JUDGE.

On these appeals we conclude that when all of the stockholders of a Delaware corporation agree that, except as specified in their agreement, no "business or activities" of the corporation shall be conducted without the consent of a minority stockholder, the agreement is, as between the original parties to it, enforceable even though all formal steps required by the statute have not been taken. We hold further that the agreement made by the parties to this action was violated when the corporation entered into two agreements without the minority stockholder's consent . . . .

Defendant Lombard-Wall Incorporated ("Lombard") was owned by Equimark Corporation. Wishing to acquire Lombard, defendant Kurtz, a dealer in unregistered securities, caused a corporation originally known as H-K Enterprises, Inc., the name of which was later changed to Lombard-Wall Group, Inc. ("Group"), to be formed under Delaware law. Kurtz was the sole stockholder of Group, but neither Kurtz nor Group could provide the $4,000,000 needed to acquire Lombard from Equimark. It was in fact acquired with a short-term loan from a Swiss bank, shortly thereafter repaid from Lombard's cash, loaned by Lombard to Group on Group's noninterest bearing note.

Since Lombard's business required book assets at the full value of $4,000,000 and Group had no assets other than Lombard's stock, Group's note to Lombard was secured by a nonrecourse guarantee from Half Moon Land Corporation, of which plaintiff Zion is the principal shareholder, collateralized by California lands owned by Half Moon. . . .

At the time the note, loan agreement and guarantee were entered into Zion, Kurtz and Group entered into a stockholders' agreement. Zion and Kurtz were the

---

[32] *See* Chapter 2, Section A.4.

sole stockholders of Group at that time, Zion holding class A stock and Kurtz, class B. Section 3.01(a) of the agreement expressly provided that without the consent of the holders of class A stock:

> "Anything in its Certificate of Incorporation or By-Laws to the contrary notwithstanding, [Group] shall not:

> "(a) Engage in any business or activities of any kind, directly or indirectly, whether through any Subsidiary or by way of a loan, guarantee or otherwise, other than the acquisition and ownership of the stock of [Lombard] as contemplated by this Agreement . . . ."

Notwithstanding that provision, Group and Lombard some eight months thereafter, at the suggestion of Group's accountants, entered into an agreement which made the previously noninterest bearing loan from Lombard to Group bear interest provided interest could be paid out of earnings, and an escrow agreement with Chase Manhattan Bank pursuant to which Group deposited $580,000 in bonds to secure payment of the note. The two agreements were authorized by Group's board over Zion's objection.

. . . .

Plaintiffs thereafter began this action for declaratory and injunctive relief, asking in their first cause of action that the interest and escrow agreements executed without Zion's consent be declared in violation of the stockholders' agreement and annulled . . . .

. . . .

For the reasons hereafter stated we conclude (1) that under Delaware law, which governs, the provision proscribing corporate action without the consent of a minority stockholder is not against the public policy of that State and under the circumstances of this case is enforceable even though not incorporated in the corporation's charter, (2) that plaintiffs are entitled to summary judgment declaring that execution of the interest and escrow agreements violated the shareholders' agreement . . . .

The stockholders' agreement expressly provided that it should be "governed by and construed and enforced in accordance with the laws of the State of Delaware as to matters governed by the General Corporation Law of that State", and that is the generally accepted choice-of-law rule with respect to such "internal affairs" as the relationship between shareholders and directors (cf. Greenspun v. Lindley, 36 N.Y.2d 473, 478, 369 N.Y.S.2d 123, 330 N.E.2d 79; see Restatement, Conflict of Laws 2d, § 302, Comment g). Subdivision (a) of section 141 of the General Corporation Law of Delaware provides that the business and affairs of a corporation organized under that law "shall be managed by a board of directors, except as may be otherwise provided in this chapter or in its certificate of incorporation." Included in the chapter referred to are provisions relating to close corporations, which explicitly state that a written agreement between the holders of a majority of such a corporation's stock "is not invalid, as between the parties to the agreement, on the ground that it so relates to the conduct of the business and affairs of the corporation as to restrict or interfere with the discretion or powers of the board of directors" (§ 350) . . . or "on the ground that it is an attempt by the parties to the agreement or by the stockholders of the corporation to treat the corporation as if it were a partnership" (§ 354), and further provides that "The certificate of incorporation of a close corporation may provide that the business of the corporation shall be managed by the stockholders of the corporation rather than the board of directors" and that such a provision may be inserted in the certificate by amendment if "all holders of record of all of the outstanding stock" so authorize (§ 351).

Clear from those provisions is the fact that the public policy of Delaware does not proscribe a provision such as that contained in the shareholders' agreement here in issue even though it takes all management functions away from the directors. Folk, in his work on the Delaware Corporation Law, states concerning section 350 that "Although some decisions outside Delaware have sustained 'reasonable' restrictions upon director discretion contained in stockholder agreements, the theory of § 350 is to declare unequivocally, as a matter of public policy, that stockholder agreements of this character are not invalid" (at p. 518), that section 351 "recognizes a special subclass of close corporations which operate by direct stockholder management" (at p. 520), and with respect to section 354 that it "should be liberally construed to authorize all sorts of internal agreements and arrangements which are not affirmatively improper or, more particularly, injurious to third parties" (at p. 526).

Defendants argue, however, that Group was not incorporated as a close corporation and the stockholders' agreement provision was never incorporated in its certificate. The answer is that any Delaware corporation can elect to become a close corporation by filing an appropriate certificate of amendment (Del. General Corporation Law, § 344) and by such amendment approved by the holders of all of its outstanding stock may include in its certificate provisions restricting directors' authority (ibid., § 351). Here, not only did defendant Kurtz agree in paragraph 8.05(b) of the stockholders' agreement to "without further consideration, do, execute and deliver, or cause to be done, executed and delivered, all such further acts, things and instruments as may be reasonably required more effectively to evidence and give effect to the provisions and the intent and purposes of this Agreement", but also as part of the transaction by which the Half Moon guarantee was made and Zion became a Group stockholder, defendant Kurtz, while he was still the sole stockholder and sole director of Group, executed a consent to the various parts of the transaction under which he was "authorized and empowered to execute and deliver, or cause to be executed and delivered, all such other and further instruments and documents and take, or cause to be taken, all such other and further action as he may deem necessary, appropriate or desirable to implement and give effect to the Stockholders Agreement and the transactions provided for therein." Since there are no intervening rights of third persons, the agreement requires nothing that is not permitted by statute, and all of the stockholders of the corporation assented to it, the certificate of incorporation may be ordered reformed, by requiring Kurtz to file the appropriate amendments, or more directly he may be held estopped to rely upon the absence of those amendments from the corporate charter . . . .[33]

---

[33] [3] The fallacy of the dissent is that it converts a shield into a sword. The notice devices on which the concept of the dissent turns are wholly unnecessary to protect the original parties, who may be presumed to have known what they agreed to. To protect an original party who has not been hurt (indeed, has expressly agreed to the limitation he is being protected against and affirmatively covenanted to see to it that all necessary steps to validate the agreement were taken) because a third party without notice could have been hurt had he been involved can only be characterized as a perversion of the liberal legislative purpose demonstrated by the Delaware statutes quoted in the text above.

The result thus reached accords with the weight of authority which textwriter F. Hodge O'Neal tells us sustains agreements made by all shareholders dealing with matters normally within the province of the directors (1 Close Corporations § 5.24, p. 83), even though the shareholders could have, but had not, provided similarly by charter or by-law provision sanctioned by statute (ibid., § 5.19, pp. 73–74). . . .

. . . .

GABRIELLI, JUDGE (dissenting in part).

. . . .

It is beyond dispute that shareholder agreements such as the one relied upon by plaintiff in this case are, as a general rule, void as against public policy. Section 3.01 of the agreement, as interpreted both by plaintiff and by a majority of this court, would have precluded the board of directors of Group from taking any action on behalf of the corporation without first obtaining plaintiff's consent. This contractual provision, if enforced, would effectively shift the authority to manage every aspect of corporate affairs from the board to plaintiff, a minority shareholder who has no fiduciary obligations with respect to either the corporation or its other shareholders. As such, the provision represents a blatant effort to "sterilize" the board of directors in contravention of the statutory and decisional law of both Delaware and New York.

Under the statutes of Delaware, the State in which Group was incorporated, the authority to manage the affairs of a corporation is vested solely in its board of directors (Del.General Corporation Law, s 141, subd. (a)). The same is true under the applicable New York statutes (Business Corporation Law, s 701). Significantly, in both States, the courts have declined to give effect to agreements which purport to vary the statutory rule by transferring effective control of the corporation to a third party other than the board of directors . . . . The common-law rule in Delaware was aptly stated in Abercrombie v. Davies, 35 Del.Ch. 599, 611, 123 A.2d 893, 899, rev'd on other grounds 36 Del.Ch. 371, 130 A.2d 338: "So long as the corporate form is used as presently provided by our statutes this Court cannot give legal sanction to agreements which have the effect of removing from directors in a very substantial way their duty to use their own best judgment on management matters."

True, the common-law rule has been modified somewhat in recent years to account for the business needs of the so-called "close corporation". The courts of our State, for example, have been willing to enforce shareholder agreements where the incursion on the board's authority was insubstantial (Clark v. Dodge, 269 N.Y. 410, 199 N.E. 641) or where the illegal provisions were severable from the otherwise legal provisions which the shareholder sought to enforce. Neither the courts of our State nor the courts of Delaware, however, have gone so far as to hold that an agreement among shareholders such as the agreement in this case, which purported to "sterilize" the board of directors by completely depriving it of its discretionary authority, can be regarded as legal and enforceable. To the contrary, the common-law rule applicable to both closely and publicly held corporations continues to treat agreements to deprive the board of directors of substantial authority as contrary to public policy.

Indeed, there heretofore has been little need for the courts to modify the general common-law rule against "sterilizing" boards of directors to accommodate the needs of closely held corporations. This is because the Legislatures of many States, including New York and Delaware, have enacted laws which enable the shareholders of closely held corporations to restrict the powers of the board of directors if they comply with certain statutory prerequisites (Del.General Corporation Law, §§ 350, 351; Business Corporation Law, § 620, subd. (b)). The majority apparently construes these statutes as indications that the public policies of the enacting States no longer proscribe the type of agreement at issue here in cases involving closely held corporations. Hence, the majority concludes that there is no bar to the enforcement of the shareholder agreement in this case, even though the statutory requirements for close corporations were not fulfilled. I cannot agree.

Under Delaware law, as the majority notes, the shareholders of a close corporation are free to enter into private, binding agreements among themselves to restrict the powers of their board of directors (Del.General Corporation Law, § 350). The same appears to be true under the present New York statutes (Business Corporation Law, § 620, subd. (b)). Both the Delaware and the New York statutory schemes, however, contemplate that such variations from the corporate norm will be recorded on the face of the certificate of incorporation (Del.General Corporation Law, § 351; Business Corporation Law, § 620, subd. (b)). New York additionally requires that the existence of a substantial restriction on the powers of the board "shall be noted conspicuously on the face or back of every certificate for shares issued by (the) corporation" (Business Corporation Law, § 620, subd. (g)). Significantly, in both Delaware and New York, a provision in the certificate of incorporation restricting the discretion of the board has the effect of shifting liability for any mismanagement from the directors to the managing shareholders (Del.General Corporation Law, § 351, subds. (2)–(3); Business Corporation Law, § 620, subd. (f)).

In my view, these statutory provisions are not merely directory, but rather are evidence of a clear legislative intention to permit deviations from the statutory norms for corporations only under controlled conditions. In enacting these statutes, which are tailored for "close corporations", the Legislatures of Delaware and New York were apparently attempting to accommodate the needs of those who wished to take advantage of the limited liability inherent in the corporate format, but who also wished to retain the internal management structure of a partnership. At the same time, however, the Legislatures were obviously mindful of the danger to the public that exists whenever shareholders privately agree among themselves to shift control of corporate management from independent directors to the shareholders, who are not necessarily bound by the fiduciary obligations imposed upon the board. In order to protect potential purchasers of shares and perhaps even potential creditors of the corporation, the Legislatures of Delaware and New York imposed specific strictures upon incorporated businesses managed by shareholders, the most significant of which is the requirement that restrictions on the statutory powers of the board of directors be evidenced in the certificate of incorporation. This requirement is an essential component of the statutory scheme because it ensures that potential purchasers of an interest in the corporation will have at least record notice that the corporation is being managed in an unorthodox fashion. Absent an appropriate notice provision in the certificate, there can be no assurance that an unsuspecting purchaser, not privy to the private shareholder agreement, will not be drawn into an investment that he might otherwise choose to avoid.

Since I regard the statutory requirements discussed above as essentially prophylactic in nature, I cannot subscribe to the notion that the agreement in this case should be enforced merely because there has been no showing that the interests of innocent third parties have actually been impaired. As is apparent from the design of the relevant statutes, the public policies of our own State as well as those of the State of Delaware remain opposed to shareholder agreements to "sterilize" the board of directors unless notice of the agreement is provided in the certificate of incorporation. . . . [W]here, as here, the shareholders have entered into a private agreement to "sterilize" the board of directors and have failed to comply with the simple statutory prerequisites for "close corporations", the agreement must be deemed void and unenforceable in light of the inherent potential for fraud against the public. Indeed, since it is this very potential for public harm which renders these agreements unlawful, the mere fortuity that no one was actually harmed, if that be the case, cannot be the controlling factor in determining whether the agreement is legally enforceable. . . .

By its holding today, the majority has, in effect, rendered inoperative both the language and the underlying purpose of the relevant Delaware and New York statutes governing "close corporations". According to the majority's reasoning, the only requirements for upholding an otherwise unlawful shareholder agreement which concededly deprives the directors of all discretionary authority are that all of the shareholders concur in the agreement and that no "intervening rights of third persons" exist at the time enforcement of the agreement is sought. . . . If, as the majority's holding suggests, th[e] requirement of notice to the public through the certificate of incorporation is without legal effect unless and until a third party's interests have actually been impaired, then the prophylactic purposes of the statutes governing "close corporations" would effectively be defeated. It is this aspect of the majority's ruling that I find most difficult to accept.

For all of the foregoing reasons, I must respectfully dissent . . . .

JASEN, JONES and FUCHSBERG, JJ., concur with MEYER, J.

GABRIELLI, J., dissents in part and votes to modify in a separate opinion in which COOKE, C. J., and WACHTLER, J., concur.

NOTES AND QUESTIONS

1. Should the election under the state's close corporation statutes be the exclusive method of obtaining special treatment? Is that appropriate deference to the legislature (as the dissent suggests) or "converting a shield into a sword" (as the majority states)? Consider the following analysis by Professor Edwin Bradley. He does not specifically refer to *Zion*, but he obviously has the case (or one like it) in mind.

[I]t is left to the courts to deal with agreements in close corporations that do not make the statutory election. Hopes for sensible treatment by the courts of those agreements if unanimously approved may seem justified[,] but the very existence of the close corporation elective status may influence courts negatively when they are asked to sustain agreements in nonelecting companies. The election process has no countervailing regulatory purpose. The fact that is simple and merely cost free is no answer because of the well known high incidence of close corporations that are formed eschewing formal statutory close corporation status, perhaps because of their fearsome complexity . . . .[34]

2.   Examine the close corporation statutes of your state, or, if your state does not have comprehensive statutes regulating close corporations, the Delaware statute discussed in *Zion*. (We will consider other statutory alternatives in the next section.) Of what value is the close corporation election? Apart from the blessing of shareholder agreements which might otherwise be held to "sterilize" board action, many commentators have concluded that the statutes offer very little substantive assistance to close corporations which cannot be provided by careful planning and research.[35] Do you agree?

At the same time as Prof. Bradley's article referenced above, a survey of 209 corporate attorneys revealed that 46% favored comprehensive elective "close corporation" statutes, 24% favored "scattered" special statutory provisions allowing use of shareholder agreements to alter some corporate norms, and 29% favored no special rule, but preferred flexible provisions generally applicable to all corporations.[36] Despite this purported popularity of the special comprehensive statutes, actual use of such statutes tends to be quite limited.[37] In addition, when the American Bar Association Committee on Corporate Laws considered the question of statutory alternatives, it recognized that most states which adopted the MBCA were not adopting the "Model Close Corporation Supplement," and even in those states which did adopt the statute, it would protect only those corporations which "opt into" its coverage.[38] The Committee instead proposed a stand-alone statute which eventually was adopted in the following form.

MODEL BUSINESS CORPORATION ACT

§ 7.32   Shareholder Agreements

(a)   An agreement among the shareholders of a corporation that complies with this section is effective among the shareholders and the corporation even though it is inconsistent with one or more other provisions of this Act in that it:

(1)   eliminates the board of directors or restricts the discretion or powers of the board of directors;

(2)   governs the authorization or making of distributions whether or not in proportion to ownership of shares, subject to the limitations in section 6.40;

---

[34] Edwin J. Bradley, *An Analysis of the Model Close Corporation Act and a Proposed Legislative Strategy*, 10 J. Corp. L. 817, 826 (1985).

[35] Some good analyses of these statutes can be found at 1 Robert B. Thompson, O'Neal & Thompson's Close Corporations and LLCs § 1:19, pp. 1-113 to 1-121 (2004); Franklin Gevurtz, Corporation Law § 5.2 at pp. 505–509 (2000); Dennis S. Karjala, *An Analysis of Close Corporation Legislation in the United States*, 21 Ariz. St. L.J. 663 (1989).

[36] William S. Hochstetler & Mark D. Svedja (student authors), *Statutory Needs of Close Corporations — An Empirical Study: Special Close Corporation Legislation or Flexible General Corporation Law?*, 10 J. Corp. L. 849, 980 n.1165 (noting 209 responses from attorneys) & 1020n.1336 (percentage results) (1985).

[37] *See* O'Neal & Thompson's Close Corporations and LLCs, *supra*, at § 1:20 at pp. 1-121 to 1-124 (2004); Gevurtz, *supra*, at § 5.2 at p. 507 (2000); Bradley, *supra*.

[38] *Changes in the Revised Model Business Corporation Act — Amendments Pertaining to Closely Held Corporations*, 46 Bus. Law. 297, 297 (1990). This conclusion was reached despite the willingness of courts such as *Zion* to entertain common-law protection outside of the statute's reach.

(3)   establishes who shall be directors or officers of the corporation, or their terms of office or manner of selection or removal;

(4)   governs, in general or in regard to specific matters, the exercise or division of voting power by or between the shareholders and directors or by or among any of them, including use of weighted voting rights or director proxies;

(5)   establishes the terms and conditions of any agreement for the transfer or use of property or the provision of services between the corporation and any shareholder, director, officer or employee of the corporation or among any of them;

(6)   transfers to one or more shareholders or other persons all or part of the authority to exercise the corporate powers or to manage the business and affairs of the corporation, including the resolution of any issue about which there exists a deadlock among directors or shareholders;

(7)   requires dissolution of the corporation at the request of one or more of the shareholders or upon the occurrence of a specified event or contingency; or

(8)   otherwise governs the exercise of the corporate powers or the management of the business and affairs of the corporation or the relationship among the shareholders, the directors and the corporation, or among any of them, and is not contrary to public policy.

(b)   An agreement authorized by this section shall be:

(1)   set forth

(A)   in the articles of incorporation or bylaws and approved by all persons who are shareholders at the time of the agreement or

(B)   in a written agreement that is signed by all persons who are shareholders at the time of the agreement and is made known to the corporation;

(2)   subject to amendment only by all persons who are shareholders at the time of the amendment, unless the agreement provides otherwise; and

(3)   valid for 10 years, unless the agreement provides otherwise.

(c)   The existence of an agreement authorized by this section shall be noted conspicuously on the front or back of each certificate for outstanding shares or on the information statement required by section 6.26(b). If at the time of the agreement the corporation has shares outstanding represented by certificates, the corporation shall recall the outstanding certificates and issue substitute certificates that comply with this subsection. The failure to note the existence of the agreement on the certificate or information statement shall not affect the validity of the agreement or any action taken pursuant to it. Any purchaser of shares who, at the time of purchase, did not have knowledge of the existence of the agreement shall be entitled to rescission of the purchase. A purchaser shall be deemed to have knowledge of the existence of the agreement if its existence is noted on the certificate or information statement for the shares in compliance with this subsection and, if the shares are not represented by a certificate, the information statement is delivered to the purchaser at or prior to the time of purchase of the shares. An action to enforce the right of rescission authorized by this subsection must be commenced within the earlier of 90 days after discovery of the existence of the agreement or two years after the time of purchase of the shares.

(d)   An agreement authorized by this section shall cease to be effective when shares of the corporation are listed on a national securities exchange or regularly traded in a market maintained by one or more members of a national or affiliated securities association. If the agreement ceases to be effective for any reason, the board of directors may, if the agreement is contained or referred to in the corporation's articles of incorporation or bylaws, adopt an amendment to the articles of incorporation or bylaws, without shareholder action, to delete the agreement and any references to it.

(e)   An agreement authorized by this section that limits the discretion or powers of the board of directors shall relieve the directors of, and impose upon the person or persons in whom such discretion or powers are vested, liability for acts or omissions imposed by law on directors to the extent that the discretion or powers of the directors are limited by the agreement.

(f)   The existence or performance of an agreement authorized by this section shall not be a ground for imposing personal liability on any shareholder for the acts or debts of the corporation even if the agreement or its performance treats the corporation as if it were a partnership or results in failure to observe the corporate formalities otherwise applicable to the matters governed by the agreement.

(g)   Incorporators or subscribers for shares may act as shareholders with respect to an agreement authorized by this section if no shares have been issued when the agreement is made.

NOTES AND QUESTIONS

1.   Suppose you are in a jurisdiction with a special statute such as the close-corporation statute at issue in *Zion* or MBCA § 7.32 or a similar statute. Which of the following provisions would likely be valid in your state in a shareholder agreement?

(a)   specification of individuals to be directors
(b)   specification of individuals to be officers
(c)   salary payments to officers
(d)   dividends to shareholders
(e)   right of first refusal by original shareholders before shares can be sold
(f)   mandatory repurchase by corporation at specified price.

2.   Suppose your jurisdiction has adopted a statute similar or identical to MBCA § 7.32. Your clients have come to you with an agreement which does not meet the notice requirements of § 7.32(c), but is in a writing signed by all the shareholders. Would you apply the reasoning of *Zion* (or *Galler*) to hold that the agreement is nonetheless valid? Suppose it were signed by all the shareholders except one shareholder who refused to sign. Would the agreement be enforceable among the signatories?

3.   Contracts often include "severability" clauses, usually in the section at the end of "miscellaneous" terms. Such clauses provide that, in the event part of the contract is held to be invalid or unenforceable, the remaining parts of the contract will remain in force. If you drafted a shareholder agreement, would you include such a severability clause in it? Or would you prefer to have the whole agreement nullified (and presumably, renegotiated) if any of it were found invalid or unenforceable?

4. Transfer restrictions and required repurchases, including buy-sell agreements, are discussed in summary in Chapter 2, Section C.4, and in detail in Chapter 8.

3.   Documenting the Arrangement

The business planner must be careful in documenting the control arrangements made by his clients when they choose the corporate form. This is because these arrangements are typically placed in two different documents. The first is the corporation's bylaws, which traditionally contain the arrangements governing the distribution of control and power among the shareholders, directors, and officers, and rules governing meetings of the shareholders and directors. The second is an agreement among shareholders, which provides for distribution of powers among the shareholders *as* shareholders, such as voting for directors, restrictions on transfer of shares, repurchase requirements, and the like. However, as the preceding section discussed, modern state law permits a wide variety of subjects to be addressed in a shareholder agreement. Therefore, in many respects, the division of rules between the bylaws and a shareholder agreement is dictated largely by custom. State laws usually require that a corporation *have* bylaws,[39] so it may not be an option to rely solely on a shareholder agreement for all of the corporation's control arrangements. Consider the following typical distributions of subjects among bylaws and shareholder agreements.

---

[39] *See, e.g.*, MBCA § 2.06(a).

Bylaws [40]	Shareholder Agreement [41]

I. Shareholders
  A. Annual meeting
  B. Special meeting
  C. Action without a meeting
II. Directors
  A. Number, election, and terms
  B. Meetings
  C. Action without a meeting
  D. Vacancies
III. Officers
  A. Offices
  B. Appointment and term of officers
  C. Removal of officers
IV. Shares
  A. Certificates
  B. Transfer of shares[42]
V. Amendment[43]
	I. Selection of Directors and Officers
	  A. Voting agreement for directors
	  B. Selection and appointment of
	officers
	II. Extraordinary Corporate Actions
	  Requiring Shareholder Approval
	  A. Shareholder approval required
	  B. Actions requiring shareholder
	approval
	III. Transfer of Shares
	  A. Restriction on Sale
	  B. Buy-Sell Agreement
	    1. Right of First Refusal
	    2. Mandatory Repurchase
	IV. Miscellaneous provisions
	  [Amendment, integration, choice
	of law, binding on successors]

Care is required when distributing rules among the corporation's bylaws and a shareholder agreement, because the forms of those documents will normally be respected by the courts. For example, a shareholders' agreement may be binding only on those individuals who were shareholders at the time of the agreement, while bylaws are binding on all shareholders. In addition, shareholder agreements can be amended only by unanimous consent of the parties to the agreement, while bylaws can ordinarily be amended by a majority of the directors or shareholders. These may seem like trivial distinctions, but they can create trouble if they are not scrupulously followed.

BLOUNT v. TAFT
North Carolina Supreme Court
246 S.E.2d 763 (1978)

Action by minority stockholders to specifically enforce an alleged stockholders' agreement.

Plaintiffs and defendants are the owners of all of the outstanding 578.5 shares of the capital stock of Eastern Lumber and Supply Company (Eastern), a closely held North Carolina corporation having its principal office in Winterville, North Carolina. Plaintiffs are all members of the Blount family. Together they are the direct or beneficial owners of 41% Of the outstanding shares of Eastern. The

---

[40] From James R. Burkhard, *Model Bylaws To Be Used With The Revised Model Business Corporation Act (1984)*, 46 Bus. Law. 189 (1990).

[41] This list of subjects is distilled from Robert L. Brown & Alan S. Gutterman, Emerging Companies Guide § 3.04 (2005). For more details on most of the subjects involved in a shareholder agreement relating to departure of an owner and purchase or sales of shares and restrictions, see Chapter 8.

[42] Note that this subject is typically dealt with in both documents. The bylaw provisions usually relate to the mechanics of transfer (certification, endorsement and the like). The shareholder agreement provisions usually relate to the substantive requirement (when is purchase or sale required or forbidden).

[43] Note that this subject is also dealt with in both documents. If this seems like a technicality to you, consider the *Blount v. Taft* case below.

defendant, E. Hoover Taft, Jr., and the three members of his family named in the caption as defendants also own 41% Of Eastern's capital stock, and defendant McGowan owns the remaining 18%. At the time this action was instituted McGowan held the post of Treasurer and as such was the "chief operating officer" of Eastern. The parties stipulated that shares of Eastern's capital stock are not traded in the markets maintained by securities dealers and brokers.

In brief summary, plaintiffs' evidence, summarized except when quoted, tended to show:

[In 1971,] Eastern was negotiating a $250,000 business expansion loan and the directors deemed it necessary to revise and update the old bylaws, to have more frequent meetings, and to conduct the corporation's business on a more orderly and formal basis. Accordingly, E. H. Taft, Jr., and Mrs. Nelson Blount Crisp, both of whom are attorneys, drafted new bylaws to be presented to the shareholders and directors for their approval at a special joint meeting held on 20 August 1971. This meeting was called primarily to gain director and stockholder approval for the $250,000 loan. A transcript of that meeting, introduced in evidence by plaintiffs, shows that the proposed bylaws were read, article by article; that discussion frequently followed the reading of an article; and that thereafter various changes were made in the proposals.

Article III, Section 7 of the bylaws (hereinafter referred to as Section 7), which is the subject of this action, as originally drafted and presented to the stockholders, read:

"Executive Committee. The Board of Directors may, by the vote of a majority of the entire board, designate three or more directors to constitute and serve as an Executive Committee, which committee to the extent provided in such resolution, shall have and may exercise all of the authority of the Board of Directors in the management of the corporation."

. . . .

Additional bylaws were read and discussed, including Article VIII, Section 4, which provided:

"Amendments. Except as otherwise provided, these bylaws may be amended or repealed and new bylaws may be adopted by the affirmative vote of a majority of the directors then holding office at any regular or special meeting of the Board of Directors." (Here it is noted that no provisions for amendments were "otherwise provided" in the bylaws adopted 20 August 1971.)

Finally, McGowan moved that the proposed bylaws be adopted as modified. Mrs. Crisp seconded the motion, but before a vote could be taken, the following exchange took place:

"M. K. BLOUNT, SR.:   You haven't brought in some amendment — don't you know?

"NELSON CRISP: This was as to full-time employees, the approval of full-time employees.

"MARVIN BLOUNT, JR.:   Why don't you put where you have 'executive committee represented by members of each family, and Ford,' that all employees be unanimously approved. Is there any objection?

"E. H. TAFT, JR.:   I have no objection.

"NELSON CRISP: He just brought out something, and this was my feeling from the beginning, that probably we do not need that in the by-laws, but rather in the meeting and in the minutes of a meeting.

"MARVIN BLOUNT, JR.:   Would it hurt to put it in the by-laws?

"JOHN CAMPBELL: No."

After further discussion and an addition suggested by Mr. McGowan, Section 7 was unanimously adopted in the following words:

"Executive Committee. The Board of Directors may, by the vote of a majority of the entire board, designate three or more directors to constitute and serve as an Executive Committee, which committee to the extent provided in such resolution, shall have and may exercise all of the authority of the Board of Directors in the management of the corporation. Such committee shall consist of one member from the family of M. K. Blount, Sr., one member from the family of E. H. Taft, Jr., and one member from the family of Ford McGowan. Minutes of all such meetings shall be kept and a copy mailed to each member of the Board of Directors and action of the committee shall be submitted to the Board of Directors at its next meeting for ratification.

"The Executive Committee shall have the exclusive authority to employ all persons who shall work for the corporation and that the employment of each individual shall be only after the unanimous consent of the committee and after interview."

Following this last amendment to Article III, Section 7, a motion that the bylaws be adopted as changed and read was seconded and unanimously approved by all the stockholders and directors.

At trial the testimony of plaintiffs' witnesses related mainly to their recollections of what took place at the 20 August 1971 meeting. All conceded that neither before or after the stockholders had achieved unanimity as to the terms of Section 7 did any stockholder refer to their final concurrence as "a stockholders' agreement"; that Section 7 was voted on as a part of the bylaws; and that no one had mentioned or suggested that Section 7 was not a bylaw or that it was not subject to amendment. However, Mr. Marvin K. Blount, Jr., testified that it was his "understanding" at the time that this section could not be amended except by the unanimous consent of the stockholders.

    . . . . Thereafter the minutes of subsequent stockholders' and directors' meetings reveal continuous controversy between the Blounts and the Taft-McGowan group over McGowan's management of the company and the authority of the executive committee. In all controversial matters before the board of directors the Blounts were outvoted by the Tafts and McGowans.

    . . . .

[New bylaws were adopted by the directors on 20 June 1974.] [F]rom the statement of facts contained in the briefs of both plaintiffs and defendants we learn that "the amended bylaws did not contain the provisions of Art. III, Sec. 7 as adopted on August 20, 1971." Deleted were "the provisions of an Executive Committee composed of a representative of each of the three families, and the provision for approval of full-time employees by the Executive Committee." In lieu of the deleted provisions, "the defendants adopted over the objections of those plaintiffs who were present, a new Article III, Section 9, . . . " providing as follows:

"9. Executive Committee: The Board of Directors may, by resolution adopted by a majority of the number of directors fixed by resolution under these bylaws, designate two or more directors to constitute an Executive Committee, which Committee, to the extent provided in such resolution, shall have and may exercise all of the authority of the Board of Directors in the management of the corporation."

. . . .

Defendants' evidence consisted of the testimony of Ford McGowan, E. H. Taft, Jr., E. H. Taft III, and another. In essence their testimony tended to show that there had never been any discussion between them or anyone else as to whether Article III, Section 7 of the bylaws adopted on 20 August 1971 was an irrevocable shareholders' agreement.

At the close of all the evidence the judge announced that he would hold Section 7 to be a valid stockholders' agreement which could be amended only by a majority vote of the directors. Thereafter, he entered judgment in which he found facts consistent with the evidence summarized herein and adjudged, Inter alia, (1) that Section 7 constituted "a valid and binding stockholders' agreement within the intent and meaning of N.C.Gen.Stats. § 55-73(b); (2) that the terms of Section 7 were clear and unambiguous and, "having been unanimously assented to, it was not and is not subject to amendment or repeal in any manner for a period not to exceed ten (10) years from August 20, 1971, except upon and by the unanimous assent of all the shareholders of Eastern Lumber and Supply Company"; (3) that Section 7 was not repealed or amended by the bylaws enacted by the board of directors on 20 June 1974; and (4) that with the exception of Section 7 the bylaws adopted August 20, 1971 were subject to amendment and were in fact, amended on June 20, 1974. (Enumeration ours.)

The court then ordered that plaintiffs have specific enforcement of Article III, Section 7. Defendants appealed and the Court of Appeals reversed, holding that there was no evidence in the record to support the conclusion of the trial court that Section 7 was a shareholders' agreement "which could not be amended as provided by Article VIII, Section 4, of the said bylaws or the conclusion that said Section 7 was not validly amended, as were other bylaws, at the meeting of the board of directors on 20 June 1974." Plaintiffs' petition for discretionary review was allowed.

SHARP, CHIEF JUSTICE.

This appeal presents a two-part question: Was Section 7 of Eastern's bylaws, adopted 20 August 1971, a valid shareholders' agreement; and, if so, was it subject to amendment under Section 4, which authorized amendment, repeal, or re-write of the bylaws by the affirmative vote of a majority of the stockholders?

The trial judge found as a fact that on 20 August 1971 all the shareholders of Eastern, by unanimous vote, adopted a set of bylaws. Among these was Section 7, which authorized the board of directors, by a majority vote, to designate an executive committee composed of three of its members one from each of the three families who owned the stock of Eastern. This committee was given exclusive authority to select the company's employees but the unanimous consent of its members was required for the employment of any individual. . . .

. . . .

By means of a shareholders' agreement a small group of investors who seek gain from direct participation in their business and not from trading its stock or securities in the open market can adopt the decision-making procedures of a partnership, avoid the consequences of majority rule (the standard operating procedure for corporations), and still enjoy the tax advantages and limited liability of a corporation. Such businesses are, with reason, often called "incorporated partnerships."

. . . .

To protect their investment minority shareholders frequently resort to agreements (usually, and wisely, made at the time of incorporation) between themselves and the other shareholders which guarantee to the minority such things as restrictions on the transfer of stock; a veto power over hiring and decisions concerning salaries, corporate policies or distribution of earnings; or procedures for resolving disputes or making fundamental changes in the corporate charter. . . . It has been said that "a well-drawn stockholders' agreement entered into contemporaneously with the formation of a corporation is the most effective means of protecting the minority shareholder." Elson, Shareholders Agreements, a Shield for Minority Shareholders of Close Corporations, 22 Bus. Lawyer 449, 457 (1967).

. . . . G.S. 55-73(a) validates and makes enforceable against its signatories for a limited period, a written "agreement between two or more shareholders" regarding the voting of their stock. Stein v. Capital Outdoor Adv. Inc., 273 N.C. 77, 159 S.E.2d 351 (1968). Section (c) of the statute provides that "an agreement between all or less than all of the shareholders" will not be invalidated as between the parties to it on the ground that it interferes with the discretion of the board of directors, but imposes upon the shareholder-parties liability for managerial acts similar to that which is imposed on directors. However, it is Section (b) of G.S. 55-73 which shareholders in a close corporation, whose stock is not generally traded in the markets maintained by securities dealers or brokers, regard as the most significant.

G.S. 55-73(b) provides, *inter alia*, that "no written agreement to which all of the shareholders have actually assented . . . which relates to any phase of the affairs of the corporation, . . . shall be invalid . . . on the ground that it is an attempt by the parties thereto to treat the corporation as if it were a partnership or to arrange their relationships in a manner that would be appropriate only between partners." Such an agreement may be "embodied in the charter or bylaws or in any side agreement in writing and signed by all the parties thereto." This language has been widely borrowed for the close corporations statutes of several other jurisdictions. However, no decision from any of these jurisdictions involving the questions we consider here has been called to our attention.

Counsel have debated at length the question whether Section 7 of Eastern's bylaws is a bylaw or a shareholders' agreement within the meaning of G.S. 55-73(b). In our view this debate is sterile, for these terms are not mutually exclusive. Bylaws which are unanimously enacted by all the shareholders of a corporation are also shareholders' agreements. Consensual agreements coming within G.S. 55-73(b) are shareholders' agreements whether they are embodied in the bylaws or in a duly executed side agreement. No particular title, phrasing or content is necessary for a consensual arrangement among all shareholders to constitute a "shareholders' agreement." Consequently, we hold that Section 7 of the bylaws adopted on 20 August 1971 is a shareholders' agreement within the meaning of G.S. 55-73(b). The decision of the Court of Appeals to the contrary is disapproved.

. . . .

The trial judge ruled that Section 7, as a shareholders' agreement, was incapable of amendment or repeal for ten years except by unanimous assent of all the stockholders. Section 7, however, was only one of a complete set of bylaws, all of which after a section-by-section consideration which involved several revisions of Section 7 — were unanimously adopted as a whole by a vote of all of Eastern's shareholders. Thus, the entire bylaws constituted an agreement among the shareholders. Article VIII, Section 4 of those bylaws (hereinafter "Section 4") authorized the repeal of "these bylaws" by a majority vote of the directors, except as otherwise provided therein. As we noted in the preliminary statement of facts, neither in Section 7 nor elsewhere in the bylaws was there any other provision regarding amendment or repeal of "these bylaws." Nothing else appearing, therefore, the presumption is that the parties intended Section 4 to apply to every section of the bylaws.

Plaintiffs argue, however, that because Section 7 is the only bylaw which "arranges (the shareholders') relationships in a manner that would be appropriate only between partners," it alone should be treated as a shareholders' agreement and thus be the only bylaw not subject to amendment or repeal under Section 4. This contention misunderstands the significance of G.S. 55-73(b).

That section creates no distinctions between a shareholders' agreement in which the parties seek to deal with the corporation as a partnership and any other stockholders' agreement "which relates to any phase of the affairs of the corporation." It adds nothing, either expressly or impliedly, to the words of the agreement; nor does it suspend the rules of contract law relating to its construction, modification or rescission . . . .

. . . .

"All contemporaneously executed written instruments between the parties, relating to the subject matter of the contract, are to be construed together in determining what was undertaken." Yates v. Brown, 275 N.C. 634, 640, 170 S.E.2d 477, 482 (1969). Here Section 7 and Section 4 were unanimously incorporated into the bylaws at the same time. There being no internal provision in Section 7 or elsewhere in the bylaws prohibiting its amendment except by unanimous consent of the shareholders, we conclude that the parties intended Section 7 to be subject to amendment by the directors or shareholders according to the procedures applicable to the other bylaws. In any event, that is the agreement they made. We hold, therefore, that if a shareholders' agreement is made a part of the charter of bylaws it will be subject to amendment as provided therein or, in the absence of an internal provision governing amendments, as provided by the statutory norms.

Ordinarily the function of a shareholders' agreement is to avoid the consequences of majority rule or other statutory norms imposed by the corporate form. Since the purpose of these arrangements is to deviate from the structures which are generally regarded as the incidents of a corporation, it is not unreasonable to require that the degree of deviation intended be explicitly set out. Most commentators advise the draftsman of a shareholders' agreement to include a specific provision governing amendments. Requiring the insertion of such an amendment provision works no undue hardship on the parties if all are agreed upon its inclusion.

. . . .

For the reasons stated in this opinion the action of the Court of Appeals in reversing the judgment of the trial court is

Affirmed.

NOTES AND QUESTIONS

1. The court held that fact that Section 7 was a "shareholders' agreement" did not prevent it from being amended as any other part of the bylaws. How could the Blount family have protected their rights from later change by a majority? Consider the following language in a corporation's bylaws:

> **Article __. Amendment.** These bylaws are subject to amendment only upon the unanimous written consent of the shareholders existing at the time of the amendment.

Would this provision protect the Blounts to the same extent as would a shareholder agreement? Would such an article be subject to challenge in a state which did not have the benefit of a statute such as North Carolina Gen. Stats. § 55-73(b) — or a modern version such as MBCA § 7.32? Could such an article be read to "interfere" with the ability of the directors to run the company? Consider in this regard MBCA § 10.20:

AMENDMENT BY BOARD OF DIRECTORS
OR SHAREHOLDERS

(a) A corporation's shareholders may amend or repeal the corporation's bylaws.

(b) A corporation's board of directors may amend or repeal the corporation's bylaws, unless:

(1) the articles of incorporation or section 10.21 reserve that power exclusively to the shareholders in whole or part; or

(2) the shareholders in amending, repealing, or adopting a bylaw expressly provide that the board of directors may not amend, repeal, or reinstate that bylaw.

Can the problem be solved by dealing with amendment of bylaws in the articles of incorporation?

2. Many close corporations adopt a single document called "Bylaws and Shareholder Agreement." The purpose of such a designation is, presumably, to

fulfill the statutory requirement for bylaws,[44] as well as to provide the contractual protections for all signatories to a shareholders agreement (typically, that shareholders agreement can be amended only by consent of all the parties, as noted by the court in *Blount*). Would the Article in Note 1 above (requiring unanimous consent of shareholders to alter the bylaws) be more likely to be valid if it were included in a hybrid "Bylaws and Shareholder Agreement"?

3. To be enforceable as a contract, as well as bylaws, the hybrid "Bylaws and Shareholder Agreement" should meet the requisite contractual formalities: consideration (usually supplied by the mutual promises of the shareholders), provisions at the end governing binding effect on successors, integration, choice of law, and amendment. It should be signed by all the parties intended to be bound thereunder. If the corporation has obligations under this agreement (for example, to repurchase shares of a departing officer or director or selling shareholder, discussed in detail in Chapter 8), the corporation (through a duly designated officer) should also sign the agreement.

4. If the hybrid document is *not* signed by all the shareholders, is it binding on the non-signatories, who either chose not to sign it (or forgot to sign it), or upon later purchasers of stock? MBCA § 6.27(b) requires that transfer restrictions must be "noted conspicuously" on the stock certificate in order to be enforceable against a transferee.[45] In regard to other provisions in a shareholder agreement (not specifically involving transfer restrictions), MBCA § 7.32(b) provides default rules:

(b) An agreement authorized by this section shall be:

(1) set forth (A) in the articles of incorporation or bylaws and approved by all persons who are shareholders at the time of the agreement or (B) in a written agreement that is signed by all persons who are shareholders at the time of the agreement and is made known to the corporation;

(2) subject to amendment only by all persons who are shareholders at the time of the amendment, unless the agreement provides otherwise; and

(3) valid for 10 years, unless the agreement provides otherwise.

Under these rules, can a shareholder agreement respecting governance, such as the executive committee in *Blount*, be made binding on subsequent purchasers?

D. IN A LIMITED LIABILITY COMPANY

As in many other areas, once you understand the workings of partnerships and corporations, limited liability companies can be best understood as a combination of, or choices between, the two. Your task as a business planner is to skillfully manage these combinations to your clients' legal and operational advantage.

Most states require that a limited liability company be designated as "member-managed" or "manager-managed." Under most LLC statutes, the management choice must be noted in the company's articles of organization (the document filed with the Secretary of State to create the company). There are important exceptions

---

[44] *See, e.g.*, MBCA § 2.06(a).

[45] If the stock is "uncertificated," MBCA § 6.27(b) requires that written notice of the restriction be provided to the shareholder on an "information statement." Similar rules apply under Uniform Commercial Code provisions applicable to investment securities. *See* UCC § 8-204.

to this rule and the distinctions between "member-managed" and "manager-managed" LLCs may sometimes be blurry.[46] They are, however, exceptions, and there are substantial consequences which flow from this choice between management of an LLC by its members or managers.

1.   The Member-Managed LLC

A member-managed LLC follows what has been termed the "partnership model."[47] Here is the relevant language of the partnership statute:

> Each partner is an agent of the partnership for the purpose of its business. An act of a partner, including the execution of an instrument in the partnership name, for apparently carrying on in the ordinary course the partnership business or business of the kind carried on by the partnership binds the partnership, unless the partner had no authority to act for the partnership in the particular matter and the person with whom the partner was dealing knew or had received a notification that the partner lacked authority.[48]

Now compare a typical LLC statute:

> Each member is an agent of the limited liability company for the purpose of its business, and an act of a member, including the signing of an instrument in the company's name, for apparently carrying on in the ordinary course the company's business or business of the kind carried on by the company binds the company, unless the member had no authority to act for the company in the particular matter and the person with whom the member was dealing knew or had notice that the member lacked authority.[49]

The differences are mostly cosmetic. It is apparent that the scope of authority of members in a member-managed LLC is comparable to that of a partner in a general partnership. The problems are comparable as well. We saw earlier in *Whitney v. Citibank N.A.* (Section B of this chapter) that unintended consequences follow from the general agency authority which partners possess. Although RUPA has created some mechanisms to put the world on notice of partners who lack specific authority,[50] "it is unclear whether the LLC can limit the apparent authority of a person within the class of those holding statutory apparent authority."[51]

Not only is it uncertain whether the authority granted to a member in a member-managed partnership can be reclaimed or otherwise limited, the precise

---

[46] *See* Thomas E. Rutledge, *The Lost Distinction Between Agency and Decisional Authority: Unfortunate Consequences of the Member-Managed versus Manager-Managed Distinction in the Limited Liability Company*, 93 Ky. L. J. 737, 744 n.22 (2005) (noting that neither Virginia nor Delaware require any such designation in the company's organizational filing). The Revised Uniform Limited Liability Company Act (Re-ULLCA) has dispensed with this categorical management type of distinction among LLCs. *See* Re-ULLCA § 301 and comments thereto. Re-ULLCA is discussed in detail in Section D.3 below.

[47] *Id.* at 741.

[48] RUPA § 301(1).

[49] ULLCA § 301(a)(1).

[50] See RUPA § 303, "Statement of Authority," set forth and discussed in Section B above.

[51] Rutledge, *supra*, at 745.

scope of this authority — "for the purpose of its business" and "apparently carrying on in the ordinary course the company's business" — default rules vary among jurisdictions as to the voting power required to be exercised to approve other actions outside these fuzzy boundaries.[52]

EXERCISE 7-1

One problem which is legion in the reported cases is the attempt to restrict authority granted to a partner in a general partnership once it has been exercised. Consider D, E and F, who are members in a member-managed LLC which engages in the business of owning and operating a local hotel. Would each of them have authority to bind the LLC in matters of purchasing supplies? Hiring or firing employees? Buying additional land adjacent to the hotel property for expansion? If the three of them agreed that the authority of any one of them would be limited, how would you as their counsel communicate this limitation to the rest of the world, so that the unfortunate events of *Whitney v. Citibank* would not be replicated? Answer these questions under a model statute such as the ULLCA and under the LLC law of your state. Which is better?

2.   The Manager-Managed LLC

A manager-managed LLC follows what has been termed the "corporate model."[53] In a corporation, the owners (shareholders) have no management rights by virtue of that designation alone. Rather, it is the directors who manage the corporation,[54] and they typically appoint several agents (officers) to undertake the day-to-day management.[55] As with Section D.2 above, now consider the typical LLC statute's provisions regarding a member-managed LLC.

> [I]n a manager-managed company . . . [a] member is not an agent of the company for the purpose of its business solely by reason of being a member. Each manager is an agent of the company for the purpose of its business, and an act of a manager, including the signing of an instrument in the company's name, for apparently carrying on in the ordinary course the company's business or business of the kind carried on by the company binds the company, unless the manager had no authority to act for the company in the particular matter and the person with whom the manager was dealing knew or had notice that the manager lacked authority.[56]

In this way, the managers of an LLC resemble a combined director-officer in a corporation, rather than a shareholder. They do not have ownership interests, and they possess the ability to bind the LLC.

---

[52] *Id.* at 747.

[53] Rutledge, *supra*, at 742. Actually, the analogy is closer to limited partners in a limited partnership, but because that form is becoming obsolete except for a few "niche" businesses, *see* Chapter 2, Section A.3, we will stick to the more familiar corporate analogy.

[54] See, for example, MBCA § 8.01(b), which provides that "[a]ll corporate powers shall be exercised by or under the authority of, and the business and affairs of the corporation managed by or under the direction of, its board of directors . . . ."

[55] Recall the general description of this arrangement at the beginning of Section C above, and the more detailed discussion in Chapter 2, Section C.2.b.

[56] ULLCA § 301(b)(1).

Example. An LLC operating agreement may provide for selection of managers in a fashion similar to how a closely-held corporation might provide for selection of officers, similar to the apportionment of authority in the first example in Section A of this chapter.

Article __. Managers

A. Duties

The managers of the Company shall consist of the following, with the duties and responsibilities of each as indicated.

1. Operations Manager: will be responsible for all matters relating to production, including hiring and supervision of employees engaged in the manufacture or preparation of goods to be sold or services to be offered, hours and locations of production, and the purchase and sale in the ordinary course of all goods and machinery necessary for these functions.

2. Business Manager: will be responsible for sales and administrative matters, including the keeping of books and records including filing of all necessary forms, applications, licenses and returns, hiring and supervision of office and sales employees, hours and location of sales of products or offering of services, and advertising and marketing.

B. Appointment and term

Smith is appointed as Operations Manager, and Jones is appointed as Business Manager. [Each will serve a one-year term and each may be reappointed for an indefinite number of terms / Their terms shall be indefinite];[57] but any manager may be removed without cause by a majority vote of the members at a special meeting called for that purpose. A vacancy in either office may be filled by an individual appointed by a majority vote of the members for such term as they may specify.

At this point, the corporate analogy becomes remote and is no longer helpful. Because the LLC has its historical roots in partnership and limited partnership law rather than corporate law, the managers in a manager-managed LLC typically appear more like general partners or general agents. Each manager may bind the LLC by his or her actions in the ordinary course of business,[58] and the members need be consulted to approve only few types of actions.[59] Ordinarily, directors or officers in a corporation do not have such wide-ranging authority.[60]

---

[57] The term of office is problematic for a planner. Annual terms are traditional; however, small business may fail to abide by these elections, leaving unelected management with dubious claims of authority. On the other hand, providing an indefinite term may give rise to the inference of contractual rights in the office or a promise of lifetime employment.

[58] ULLCA § 404(b)(1).

[59] *Id.* § 404(b)(3). The actions which require member approval in a manager-managed LLC include most importantly amendment of the operating agreement or the articles of organization, and approval of organic changes such as merger, liquidation, or sale of substantially all the company's assets.

[60] Recall that we discussed in Section C above how these general rules can be varied in the case of a closely-held corporation to allow its management structure to more closely resemble that of a partnership.

EXERCISE 7-2

Consider G, H and J, who are members in a manager-managed LLC. They have agreed that K will be the manager. Under the ULLCA (or the limited liability company law of your state) is K's authority absolute? Could G, H and J somehow limit K's authority, or do we have the *Whitney v. Citibank* problem all over again? For some guidance from more established rules in this area, consider what the answer might be if G, H and J were shareholders and directors of a corporation with K as the sole officer.

3.   The Changing LLC Landscape

The distinctions between member-managed and manager-managed LLCs have been fundamental since the invention of this business entity in 1988. However, as the use of LLCs has grown and matured, lawyers have recognized the artificiality of tying down the LLC to any kind of "default" management and control arrangement. The changes in this area — and the ability of the LLC to abide any management and control structure your clients desire — will likely be one of the next revolutions in business planning.

The Revised Uniform Limited Liability Company Act (Re-ULLCA), adopted in 2006, represents the first of what may be termed "next generation" LLC statutes. The Act dispenses with the requirement that LLCs be designated as member- or manager-managed, and eliminates any default rules about authority of members or managers. In this regard, the new LLCs will look less like partnerships and more like corporations or other entities with ordinary agents. Re-ULLCA also embraces the concept of one-member LLCs and the idea that an "operating agreement" can be enforceable with only one member. Note how Re-ULLCA again treats LLCs less like a partnership and more like a corporation, which has allowed one owner for many years. Recognizing the informal nature of the modern LLC, Re-ULLCA also gives near total primacy to the operating agreement over the articles or the statute.[61]

E.   FIDUCIARY DUTIES AND THE BUSINESS PLANNER

In your study of partnerships or corporations, you have probably been introduced to the concept of fiduciary duties owed by the constituents of these entities. The familiar case of *Meinhard v. Salmon* [62] described in glowing and oft-cited language the duty owed by a partner in a general partnership as "the punctilio of an honor the most sensitive" and "the duty of the finest loyalty" among other quotable excerpts.[63] The equally familiar and somewhat surprising case of *Donahue v. Rodd Electrotype* [64] established that shareholders in a corporation can, in some cases, owe similar duties.

---

[61] For an excellent summary and commentary, see Daniel S. Kleinberger & Carter G. Bishop, *The Next Generation: The Revised Uniform Limited Liability Company Act*, 62 Bus. Law. 515 (2007). Professors Kleinberger and Bishop were the co-Reporters for the Re-ULLCA project. Also helpful are the act itself and commentary, *available at* www.law.upenn.edu/bll/archives/ulc/ullca/2006act_final.htm.

[62] 249 N.Y. 458, 164 N.E. 545 (1928).

[63] *Id.* at 463–64, 164 N.E. at 546.

[64] Donahue v. Rodd Electrotype Co. of New England, Inc., 367 Mass. 578, 328 N.E.2d 505 (1975).

Just as in a partnership, the relationship among the stockholders must be one of trust, confidence and absolute loyalty if the enterprise is to succeed. Close corporations with substantial assets and with more numerous stockholders are no different from smaller close corporations in this regard. All participants rely on the fidelity and abilities of those stockholders who hold office. Disloyalty and self-seeking conduct on the part of any stockholder will engender bickering, corporate stalemates, and, perhaps, efforts to achieve dissolution.[65]

Fiduciary duties in the partnership are well recognized. Those same duties among participants in a close corporation are commonplace but not universal.[66]

In addition, statutes provide fiduciary duties. RUPA provides a detailed comprehensive statement of partners' fiduciary duties, paralleling the familiar duties of care and loyalty of corporation law.[67] Similar duties are provided under ULLCA for LLCs,[68] although this comprehensive approach was jettisoned in Re-ULLCA, permitting and inviting courts to continue to fashion common-law fiduciary duties.[69]

Why are litigation-based fiduciary duties or hortatory legislative statements relevant for a drafter or planner? They will be the ultimate "gap fillers" in an arrangement among the owners in which you are trying (imperfectly) to protect all of them from opportunistic conduct by the others. As a drafter, when you invoke notions of "reasonableness" or "good faith," you are incorporating by reference some judicial notions of fiduciary duty.

Example 1. Rather than provide detailed and formalistic notice provisions for a meeting of partners, members, or shareholders, an agreement might simply provide that:

> **Notice.** Whenever notice is required in this agreement, it shall be given in a manner reasonably calculated to timely reach each party to this agreement.

Such a provision may be more than adequate for a business in which the owners see each other every day. By incorporating "reasonableness," the business planner deals indirectly with conduct by which some of the owners might want to act without the consent of the others.[70]

---

[65] *Id.* at 587, 328 N.E.2d at 512.

[66] For example, the duties mentioned in *Donahue* were limited one year later by the same court in *Wilkes v. Springside Nursing Home, Inc.*, 370 Mass. 842, 353 N.E.2d 657 (1976). Other jurisdictions, most notably Delaware, have refused to create any special duties for close corporations. *See* Nixon v. Blackwell, 626 A.2d 1366, 1379–80 (Del. 1993) (holding that the Delaware close-corporation statute and general legal principles governing directors' duties are sufficient).

[67] RUPA § 404(a)–(c).

[68] ULLCA § 409(a)–(c). The uniformity of standards of care in the uniform acts has been criticized as not reflecting the reality of the different relationships in each entity. *See* William J. Callison, *"The Law Does Not Perfectly Comprehend. . . ": The Inadequacy of the Gross Negligence Duty of Care Standard in Unincorporated Business Organizations*, 94 Ky. L.J. 451 (2005).

[69] *See* Re-ULLCA § 409 & cmt. to subsections (a) and (b) ("[T]his Act: (i) eschews 'only' and 'limited to' — the words RUPA used in an effort to exhaustively codify fiduciary duty; (ii) codifies the core of the fiduciary duty of loyalty; but (iii) does not purport to discern every possible category of overreaching.") One important consequence is to allow courts to continue to use fiduciary duty concepts to police disclosure obligations in member-to-member and member-LLC transactions.

[70] *See, e.g.*, Whitney v. Citibank N.A., *supra*.

Example 2. A transfer restriction might require the approval of one or more of the other owners. In order to invoke mutable notions of fair conduct, the restriction might provide:

> **Consent required.** No shareholder may transfer his or her shares without the written consent of a majority of the other shareholders. Such consent shall not be unreasonably withheld.[71]

COMPREHENSIVE EXERCISE: DRAFTING MANAGEMENT PROVISIONS

In the Comprehensive Exercise at the end of Chapter 2, you were asked to sketch out the management responsibilities of Ann, Bev and Carl. Recall their management arrangements from Chapter 1: Ann intends to be a "passive investor," Bev wants involvement "to be able to protect her capital investment to the fullest extent possible," and Carl "will be contributing his services." Draft the portion of the applicable partnership agreement, LLC operating agreement, or corporate bylaws and/or shareholder agreement to effectuate their desired management arrangement. Despite Ann's role as a "passive" investor, you should give both Ann and Bev some sort of power to approve (or disapprove) major business decisions. Be sure to specify the delineation of duties, appointment and removal, and how to deal with disagreements.

---

[71] This parallels the requirement of MBCA § 6.27(d)(3) that consent to a transfer may be required "if the requirement is not manifestly unreasonable."

Chapter 8

DEPARTURE OF AN OWNER AND BUY-SELL AGREEMENTS

A. DEPARTURES OF AN OWNER AND THE NEED FOR A BUY-SELL AGREEMENT

1. Positive Departures

All equity owners anticipate the day that they will exit the business and reap the rewards of their investment. Active owners will want to retire or withdraw from management, and/or business operations, at some time in the future. Passive investors will eventually want to sell their interests in the business and reinvest their original capital, plus any capital gains, in some new business venture. It is the hope of every equity owner, active or passive, that over time the value of their equity interest will have appreciated in value and created a substantial gain. This is particularly true for moneyed investors who are not interested in keeping their equity in any one investment for an unlimited period of time. Moneyed investors will be seeking an "exit strategy" for the return of their capital contribution and gains as soon as it is financially wise to do so.

Exit strategies to realize the positive consequences of investing in a business may be numerous and complex. From the perspective of a self-maximizing investor, one ideal exit strategy might be:

(i)   assure the earliest possible repayment of the *original* capital contribution;
(ii) continue to retain the ownership interest in the company while the company grows and the interest appreciates in value;
(iii) eventually sell the ownership interest for a significant profit.

Such a strategy would be ideal in the sense that, once the capital contribution is returned to the investor, the return on the retained investment interest is unlimited. Suppose a moneyed investor, Mandy, contributes $1 million to a startup business and receives a thirty percent ownership interest. There are two other investors who will be operating the business, Olive and Orson. Olive and Orson can gather about $600,000 of their own cash and property to finance the startup of the business. They have a need for someone like Mandy who can provide them with a large amount of capital to get the business on its feet and profitable. Mandy is willing to make this risky investment but only if she can assure a quick exit strategy for her money. Mandy wants to receive *preferential* distributions over the course of the first five years of the venture, in the aggregate amount of $1 million.[1] After that, Mandy will continue to own her thirty percent equity interest but will

---

[1] For example, if there is net cash from operations in the first five years, Mandy might be entitled to receive some fixed percentage (30%, 60%, 80%, 100%) of the cash available for distribution until she has been paid $1 million.

share proportionally with Olive and Orson in the profit distributions from the business (30%-35%-35%). After five years, Mandy will have her full $1 million returned to her, which she can use to reinvest in other ventures, while still participating as an equity holder in the original venture. This is the aim of many venture capital firms. They will negotiate preferential payment provisions that assure them a priority return of their cash infusion into the business, while still retaining an ownership interest that, as the company expands and grows, becomes more and more valuable.

Another exit strategy, available for any investor, is to simply wait for the value of the equity interest to appreciate with the success of the business and then sell the equity interest. Purchasers of Google stock paid $110 per share when the stock was first issued in an initial public offering on August 23, 2004. In October of 2007, the stock price hit well over $700. Obviously, a good exit strategy would be to sell the stock when the price hit $700.

2.   Negative Departures

Exit strategies are not just about reaping the enhanced value brought about by the growth and success of the business. Sometimes active participants in the venture are *forced* to withdraw by events such as death,[2] disability, retirement, incapacity, expulsion, bankruptcy[3] or creditor lien execution.[4] Other times, the business may not be as profitable as an owner anticipated and the owner wants to "cut his/her losses" by exiting the business before further losses are incurred. If a business continues for any significant amount of time, there will inevitably be negative, as well as positive, changes in the owners of the business.

Sometimes the owners of the business become alienated from each other, or experience irreconcilable differences regarding the operations of the business. In such cases, one or more owners may wish to exit the business while others desire to continue operations of the business.

3.   All Departures

Regardless of the reasons for an owner's departure, positive or negative, important issues will arise regarding the continuation of the business. For the business to continue successfully, it's important to have a pre-existing agreement to assure that the objectives of all of the parties, departing or non-departing, can be achieved, Typically, the agreement will provide that the non-departing owners

---

[2] Or dissolution in the case of an *entity* equity holder.

[3] An owner may be indebted to creditors and unable or unwilling to pay debts as they come due. When an individual or entity suffers financial reverses, a voluntary or involuntary bankruptcy petition may be filed, leading to the liquidation or reorganization of the debtor's financial assets, including the debtor's ownership interest in business entities. Upon the filing of a bankruptcy petition, the debtor's interests in business entities will automatically pass into the hands of the bankruptcy trustee (or the debtor-in-possession in chapter 11 cases), who has the legal right under federal bankruptcy law to dispose of the assets in accordance with the liquidation of the debtor's assets under chapter 7, or the reorganization plan under chapter 11.

[4] In the absence of bankruptcy, state law allows creditors with judgments against a debtor to obtain a lien interest in non-exempt assets of the debtor, including the debtor's equity interests in business entities. The lien will be enforced by selling the equity interest at a foreclosure sale.

get to continue operating the business, while paying the departing owner (or the estate of the departing owner) a fair price.

Without a plan to buyout the interest of the departing owner that is satisfactory to all parties, the departure may cause the failure of an otherwise successful business. For instance, if the company is heavily dependent on the skills of a particular owner, the death, retirement or withdrawal of that owner from the operations of he business may cause insurmountable barriers to the continuation of the business. Or, if a departing owner holds a very large share of the equity of the company, the remaining owners will not be in a position to buyout the large-owner's interest, unless they have carefully planned for the financing of the purchase of the large-owner's interest.

It is always possible that the objectives of the non-departing owners may *not* include continuation of the business if certain owners depart, or if the business is not operating successfully. In such cases, the non-departing owners will *not* want to be saddled with the burden of buying out a departing owner. Whether the non-departing owners are obligated to buyout the departing owner's share, or have the *option* to do so if they deem it worthwhile, is an important negotiating point.

4.   Concerns of Non-Departing Owners

From the perspective of the non-departing owners, there are some serious considerations when one of the owners departs: (i) how can the exit be accomplished in a way that cause the least disruption or, in a worst-case scenario, the dissolution of the business; (ii) will any proposed successors to the ownership interest of a departing owner be acceptable to the remaining owners; (iii) will the remaining owners have a "right of first refusal" to purchase the interest of the departing owner if there is a proposed sale of that interest (whether the sale is voluntary or involuntary); (iii) will there be an *obligation*, either statutory or contractual, to buy out the interest of the departing owner in order to avoid a dissolution of the business;[5] and, (iv) if dissolution is desired by the non-departing owners, how will an orderly and financially optimizing dissolution be accomplished?

5.   Concerns of Departing Owners

From the perspective of the departing owner (or his/her successors in the case of death, bankruptcy or lien enforcement), there are equally serious considerations: (i) there may not be a public market for a sale of the investment interest and finding a private investor to purchase the interest of an exiting owner may be very difficult; (ii) the formation documents, and/or applicable statutes, may limit the ability to sell an ownership interest without the approval of the other owners with regard to the admission of the transferee into the business, diminishing the ability of the departing owner to find a purchaser at a fair, full price.; (iii) the formation documents may grant a right of first refusal to non-departing owners which will make it difficult to find a purchaser at a fair, full price since any proposed purchaser will have to wait (perhaps for months) while the non-departing owners decide whether or not to exercise their right of first refusal; (iv) under some circumstances, the formation documents may *obligate* the departing

---

[5] If such an obligation exists, difficult issues of funding the buyout will arise. See Section E later in this chapter.

owner to sell to the non-departing owners at a price and pursuant to terms agreed to in the documents, rather than dispose of the interest on the open market.

These types of considerations can be even more complicated for owners who are retiring, and were counting on the equity in the company to fund their retirement, or owners who die and intended their equity interest to provide for loved ones following death. Unless there is some practical mechanism for assuring a sale of the ownership interest at a fair price upon death or retirement, the owner's objectives may end up being frustrated.

6.   Preparing for Departures at the Formation or Joinder Stages

There is little doubt that the time to negotiate the departures of owners is at the *formation* stage (or the *joinder* stage for later investors), rather than the time of departure. By planning ahead, the parties can assure that their objectives are well-planned for and they can avoid the discord and litigation that often takes place when departures occur without pre-planning. This is usually accomplished by including appropriate "buy-sell" provisions in the formation documents or the execution of a separate buy-sell agreement among the owners.

Planning for departures at the formation stage can cause some discomfort and discord at the time that these provisions are being negotiated. The uneasiness will arise from the naturally different objectives that the owners have for their investments in the business, and their plans for the future. Depending on the age of the owners, the relative wealth and liquidity of the owners, the level of risk averseness of the owners and many other factors, they may find themselves on different sides of the negotiating table as the provisions of the buy-sell agreement are worked out. However, despite the discomfort this may entail during the otherwise "honeymoon" phase of formation, it is best to work out these matters on the front end, when tempers are cool, rather than at the time of departure, when disagreements may lead to expensive litigation and/or dissolution of the business. Indeed, it is a helpful and essential exercise for any investor to contemplate the mechanisms for the eventual departure of owners, *before* investing large sums of money in a business venture. This will help to flush out, and deal with, any unspoken expectations regarding eventual departures from the business.

7.   Summary — Purposes of Buy Sell Agreements

Buy-sell agreements serve many functions, including the following:

- Allows non-departing owners to determine whether they will share control and ownership with proposed successors and precludes outsider purchasers or successors from obtaining an ownership interest without the consent of non-departing owners.
- Guarantees continuity of management and control in the hands of original owners and only those new owners admitted with consent of the remaining owners.
- Provides a marketplace for the sale and purchase of the departing owner's interest in the event of death, disability, retirement, or other forced or voluntary departure.
- Generates cash for the family of a deceased owner to pay taxes, provide cash for loved ones and settle estate obligations.

- Allows some owners to terminate the involvement of certain active participants (such as managers) who discontinue employment with the entity through discharge, withdrawal or retirement.
- Fixes the value of the departing owner's interest for estate and gift tax purposes.
- Allows for the ouster of one or more owners, without dissolving the business, by paying them an agreed-upon fair value for their ownership interest.
- Forces the owners, early in the venture, to think about mechanisms for funding the departure of owners.
- Gives the owners of *corporations* the ability to prevent a statutory right of dissolution by creating an agreement-based method for buying out any shareholders seeking to exercise a statutory right to dissolve the corporation.[6]

B. THE COMPONENTS OF A BUY-SELL AGREEMENT

A buy-sell agreement can be broken down into several major components:

- Permitted Transfers
- Events Triggering a Buyout
  - Optional Buyouts
  - Compulsory Buyouts
- Setting the Price
- Planning for and Paying the Price
- Procedures to be Followed

1.   Permitted Transfers

Before discussing the events that *trigger* an optional or mandatory buyout, it is important to recognize that not all transfers by equity owners will serve as triggers. There is a substantial difference in the approach that will be taken in planning buy-sell agreements depending on whether the departing owner is an active or passive investor. The voluntary or involuntary transfer by a *passive* investor without substantial control will have little impact on the business and is rarely the subject of a buy-sell agreement. For instance, suppose that a limited liability company has three active and controlling owners: Ann, Bob and Carol, who own 30% of the business. There are also ten passive moneyed investors who share equally the remaining 70% of the business (each passive investor has a 7% share of the ownership). Ann, Bob and Carol are the managers of the LLC and also employed by the LLC to run its daily operations. The participation of the ten passive members is limited to major changes laid out in the local LLC statute.[7] The

---

[6] In some circumstances, if one or more shareholders seeks an involuntary dissolution of the corporation, the corporation (or 50% of its shareholders) can prevent the dissolution by paying, in cash, the "fair market value" of the interests of the shareholders seeking dissolution. While the buy-sell agreement can't alter the statutory rights to seek dissolution, it can be used to accumulate the necessary funds or otherwise arrange for the financing of a buyout under such circumstances. See, e.g., Cal. Corp. Code § 2000, discussed in Section F.2.b of this chapter.

[7] In a manager managed LLC, the voting rights of the non-manager members can be severely limited. With the exception of matters such as dissolution and merger, the rights of non-manager members can be virtually eliminated. See Calif. Corp. Code § 17103, Uniform Limited Liability Company

identity of the passive investors is irrelevant, since their primary participation is economic. Indeed, in planning the initial investment structure of the business, the promoters will want to make these passive investment units as freely transferable as is legally possible, to encourage potential passive investors to purchase the units. The more transferable the units, the more appealing they will be to potential investors. This would be true regardless of the form of the business entity. Whether an LLC, corporation or limited partnership, the transfer of units by passive investors without controlling interests in the business has little impact on any of the justifications for the drafting of a buy-sell agreement. Unless the passive investor is a large, moneyed investor with substantial bargaining power, it is unlikely that a passive investor with a small interest in the entity will be included in the scope of the buy-sell agreement.

As we begin to look at the events that trigger the application of buy-sell obligations, we will see that the triggers will be applicable only to investors who have substantial rights of voting control, or are active in the day-to-day affairs of the business as employees or managers. Under some of the following circumstances, there is no need to limit the transfer of ownership interests:

- If the owner is a mere *passive* investor with a less-than-controlling interest.
- If an individual owner is transferring *all* of his/her interest to a revocable trust created for the benefit of the member and his/her family, so long as the member retains a beneficial economic interest in the trust and also retains *all* of the non-economic rights of ownership, until the owner's death or disability.[8]
- If an individual owner is directly transferring his/her *economic* interest to family members but retaining the management, voting and other non-economic rights. Depending on the tax advantages, family needs and estate-planning objectives of an owner, there may be some advantages to transferring some of the economic rights of ownership (such as the rights to distributions) to family members while the owner retains all of the remaining non-economic rights to voting, management and access to information. So long as the recipients of the *economic* interests have no rights to engage in non-economic components of ownership, there is little advantage in preventing owners from making such transfers — although it is common to limit the economic transfers to spouses and lineal descendants.
- If the transfer is from one owner to another existing owner — unless the transfer might upset the balance of power with regard to control of the entity.

The voluntary transfers described above may frequently be permitted in the formation and buy-sell documents. However, in other situations, such as a

---

Act § 404(b)–(c), and generally Chapter 7, Section D.2.

[8] It is common for estate-planning purposes to make an inter-vivos transfer of property to a family trust, with the individual-transferor acting as trustee and retaining rights of ownership and control during his or her lifetime. Upon death or disability, a successor trustee will take over and distribute the beneficial interests in property as directed in the trust document. The use of such inter-vivos trusts to transfer property prior to death avoids the necessity of having the property pass via will (and the accompanying lengthy and expensive probate process) and may have tax advantages as well.

proposed sale of all of part[9] of an ownership interest to an *outsider*, the remaining equity holders may be deeply concerned and want to restrict or limit the voluntary transfer. If the transfer is of only the economic interest, the transferring owner's motivation regarding control and management will be significantly diminished. If the transfer is of all of the rights of the owner, the remaining owners will be faced with the possibility of dealing with an unknown and potentially disruptive co-owner.

2. Integration With Organic Documents

It is essential that the terms of any buy-sell agreement comply and coexist with the fundamental organic documents that govern the formation and operation of the entity. In the case of corporations, the articles of incorporation and bylaws must be reviewed (and modified if necessary) to assure that the terms of the buy-sell agreement are consistent with the articles and bylaws. The same is true for partnership agreements, and LLC articles and operating agreements.

C. INTRODUCTION TO TAX ASPECTS OF BUY-SELL AGREEMENTS

There are many tax considerations that need to be reviewed in constructing a buy-sell agreement. One serious tax concern arises when a buyout is triggered by the death of an owner. If the decedent has a high-value interest in the business, the transfer at death may be subject to federal estate taxation. The IRC requires that a fair market value be fixed for the ownership interest being transferred at death.[10] This valuation serves two important functions. First, it sets the amount of the wealth transfer subject to estate taxation. Second, it sets the new basis for the property in the hands of the recipients of the transfer. For instance, if the fair market value of the ownership interest at the time of death is $11 million and the shares are left by will to the decedent's children, the amount generally subject to estate taxation is $11 million (certain deductions and exclusions may apply) and the basis of the shares in the hands of the children will be $11 million. While a low value might help to reduce the estate taxes, it will also result in a low basis for the children, resulting in significant capital gains if the shares are then sold. An arms-length buy-sell agreement can be used to set the value of the ownership interest and will be accepted by the I.R.S., even if that value is less than "fair market value" if certain conditions are satisfied. Those conditions require that the buy-sell agreement:

> (1) . . . is a bona fide business arrangement.

---

[9] The transferring owner may be transferring only part of the ownership rights, such as the *economic* interest, while retaining others.

[10] IRC § 2701 provides:

> The fair market value is the price at which the property would change hands between a willing buyer and a willing seller, neither being under any compulsion to buy or to sell and both having reasonable knowledge of relevant facts. The fair market value of a particular item of property includible in the decedent's gross estate is not to be determined by a forced sale price. Nor is the fair market value of an item of property to be determined by the sale price of the item in a market other than that in which such item is most commonly sold to the public, taking into account the location of the item wherever appropriate.

See also Treas. Reg. § 20.2031-1

(2) . . . is not a device to transfer such property to members of the decedent's family for less than full and adequate consideration in money or money's worth.

(3) . . . terms are comparable to similar arrangements entered into by persons in an arms' length transaction.[11]

In transactions where the owners are not the natural objects of each other's wills, the buy-sell agreement can serve the important tax function of setting the value at death. However, using a buy-sell agreement to arrange for the transfer of a decedent's interest to the surviving owners probably makes little sense when the remaining owners are family members, such as the decedent's spouse. Because of the marital and other deductions,[12] it will often make more sense to allow the interest to pass via the decedent's will, rather than a purchase pursuant to a buy-sell agreement.

1. Partnership Tax Considerations

For entities that are taxed as partnerships, there are some potentially important tax consequences that need to be considered in preparing the buy-sell agreement. Depending on whether the buyout is structured as an entity purchase or a cross-purchase, the tax consequences can vary considerably. If the entity buys the ownership interest from the partner, the purchase may be considered a liquidation of the partner's interest. If the other partners buy the interest in a cross-purchase deal, it is considered a sale. The results are that in some buyouts, the purchase may be deductible to the entity allowing the use of *pre-tax* dollars to fund the purchase — but resulting in ordinary income to the departing partner (or the successor(s) to a deceased partner). In other buyouts, the purchase may be considered as a nondeductible repurchase of the departing owner's interest, resulting in capital gain treatment for the excess of the payment(s) over the adjusted basis of the owner's capital account.[13] The difference between these two tax classifications can have dramatic consequences for the departing owner (or the estate of the departing owner). For instance, suppose a buyout price of $300,000 to a partner who has an adjusted basis of $75,000 in his or her capital account:

---

[11] See IRC § 2703, which states in its entirety:

Certain rights and restrictions disregarded

(a) General rule: For purposes of this subtitle, the value of any property shall be determined without regard to —

(1) any option, agreement, or other right to acquire or use the property at a price less than the fair market value of the property (without regard to such option, agreement, or right), or

(2) any restriction on the right to sell or use such property.

(b) Exceptions: Subsection (a) shall not apply to any option, agreement, right, or restriction which meets each of the following requirements:

(1) It is a bona fide business arrangement.

(2) It is not a device to transfer such property to members of the decedent's family for less than full and adequate consideration in money or money's worth.

(3) Its terms are comparable to similar arrangements entered into by persons in an arms' length transaction.

[12] If the decedent owned an interest in a qualifying family owned business, a deduction from the gross estate in the amount of up to $1,100,000 may be available under IRC § 2057.

[13] *See* 2 Willis, Pennell & Postlewaite, Partnership Taxation ¶¶ 15.06[3]–15.06[4] (6th ed. 1997). See also the discussion of "capital accounts" and "adjusted basis" in Section D of Chapter 6.

— If taxed as a sale: The partner will pay capital gains taxes on the excess of the price received over the adjusted basis which will be $225,000.[14] At the 2008 capital gains rate of 15%, the departing partner will pay $33,750 in taxes.[15]

— If taxed as a liquidation: The entire $300,000 will be considered ordinary income. Taxed at about the 30% rate applicable to high income tax payers, the departing partner will pay approximately $100,000 in taxes.[16]

The above example is extremely general and meant only to dramatize the extreme difference in tax consequences for the departing partner. The primary rules governing these tax consequences, IRC §§ 736, 741, 751 and 1014 are extremely complex and require input from a tax specialist.

2.   Tax Considerations for Corporations and Stockholders

For tax purposes, the purchase by a C corporation of its shares is considered a redemption.[17] Regardless of the treatment of the *stockholder's* receipt of funds as capital gains, dividends, or the non-taxable return of capital, the impact on the C corporation is the same. The payments are not deductible to the corporation and there is no gain or loss recognized by the corporation in a cash buyout.[18]

With regard to the selling stockholder, a cross-purchase sale to other shareholders, or a *redemption* sale to the corporation, is usually treated as the sale of a capital asset, with the stockholder having to pay capital gains taxes only on the increase in value received over the basis in the shares of stock.[19] However, if a portion of the payment for the shares constitutes payment for services rather than stock redemption, that amount will be taxed as ordinary income.

There might be circumstances where a repurchase by a corporation may be classified as a dividend payment.[20] As of 2008, the tax rate for dividends and capital gains was the same (15%). However, if classified as a dividend, the *entire* amount of the buyout payment would be taxed rather than the difference between the price paid and the taxpayer's basis in the stock. Those circumstances where the buyout might be considered a dividend involve situations where the redemption is of less than all of the outstanding shares of stock of the departing stockholder. The purchase will still be treated as a stock redemption, rather than a dividend, even if the corporation uses an installment plan to repurchase the stock, or (ii) the corporation buys only some of the shares but the remainder of the shares are purchased by a subsequent cross-purchase by other stockholders, so long as there is a "firm and fixed plan" to buyout all of the shares of the departing stockholder.[21]

---

[14] $300,000 (buyout price) − $75,000 (adjusted basis) = $225,000.

[15] IRC §§ 741, 751.

[16] IRC § 736.

[17] IRC §§ 162, 302(a).

[18] IRC § 311. The outcome might be different if the buyout is funded by a distribution of appreciated property. *See* IRC § 311(a).

[19] IRC § 301(c)(2)-(3). If there is a loss, the taxpayer may deduct the loss, subject to the usual passive activity loss limits discussed in Chapter 3.

[20] IRC §§ 301(c)(1), 316.

[21] IRC § 302(b); *see also* Merrill Lynch & Co. v. Comm'r, 386 F.3d 464, 470 (2d Cir. 2004).

3. Other Tax Considerations

There are other tax aspects that should be considered when drafting buy-sell agreements, such as:

- The use of appreciated property by a corporation to purchase stock will cause income to be recognized by the corporation at the time of the purchase.[22]
- If life insurance proceeds are being used to fund the purchase, and the proceeds are payable directly to a corporation, the alternative minimum tax might apply.[23]
- In S corporations, if the purchase is set up as an installment sale,[24] the deduction of interest paid on behalf of the departing member's successors might not be fully deductible by the partners, members or S shareholders.[25]
- The ability of the decedent's estate to defer inheritance taxes by paying the purchase price in installments might be impacted by the structure of the buy-sell agreement.[26]

The bottom line is that input from a tax specialist is important in planning for transfers at death.

D. EVENTS TRIGGERING A BUYOUT

1. Death

In a closely held business, the death of an owner may create problems for the decedent's successors, as well as the surviving owners, particularly if the deceased owner: (i) owned a large share of the business; (ii) was participating in control or management of the business; or (iii) was employed by the business. In the absence of some mechanism for buying out the ownership interest, it will pass by will, family trust or intestacy to the decedent's successors. This raises some serious concerns:

- Continuity and Control: Unless the decedent's successor is acceptable to the surviving owners as an active owner or participant in the business, the surviving owners will want the opportunity to buy out the shares of the deceased owner in order to maintain control over the affairs of the business.
- Providing a Market for the Liquidation of the Decedent's Shares: It is often the case that the successors to the decedent have low or no interest in

---

[22] IRC § 311.

[23] IRC § 56(g)(4)(B).

[24] Rather than a one-time payment, the decedent's successors will receive the value of the ownership shares spread out over time, together with interest. For instance, suppose the shares of the decedent are worth $200,000 at the time of the decedent's death. Rather than a one-time payment, the buy-sell agreement provides for monthly installment payments over a five year period, together with interest at 6%. The amount of the monthly payments would be $5,799.86 and the total paid over five years would be $200,000 in principal and $31,993.62 in interest.

[25] IRC § 163(a), (d)(1).

[26] IRC § 6166.

actively participating in the affairs of the business but have a keen interest in liquidating the ownership shares. In the absence of some pre-arranged mechanism for selling the shares to the surviving owners at a fair price, there is unlikely to be a marketplace for the sale of the deceased owner's shares. Liquidity might be extremely important to the decedent's successors who may need the funds to pay debts, administrative expenses and inheritance taxes, as well as for general living expenses. Because shares of privately held businesses are difficult to sell (particularly if the decedent has a less-than-controlling share), a buy-sell agreement is essential to establish a value, and financing scheme, for the transfer of the shares from the successors to the non-departing owners. In the absence of such an agreement, the decedent's successors are at the mercy of the surviving owners in negotiating a fair price following the death of the former owner.[27]

- <u>Legal Requirements:</u> The buy-sell agreement can be used to insure that there are no transfers by the decedent via will/intestacy/trust that would violate the requirements for maintaining a corporation's S election (such as a will that divides the interest of the decedent amount several beneficiaries, causing the total number of shareholders to exceed the 75 allowed by the IRC).

In other words, it is often in the best interests of both the departing and non-departing owners to *impose* an obligation on the surviving owners to buy-out the decedent's shares. Keep in mind the distinction between an *option* versus the *obligation* to purchase the shares if the triggering event is death. While an *option* to purchase might make sense in other circumstances (such as an *inter-vivos* sale of an ownership interest), when the trigger is death, the potential decedent will always want to impose an obligation to purchase the shares of a closely held corporation, since there may be no other market mechanism to convert the value of the shares into cash equivalents for his or her successors.[28]

Provisions containing possible mandatory and optional death "triggers" might be structured as follows:

Mandatory Purchase Upon Death

Within 90 days after the death of a partner,[29] the officer(s) of his or her estate shall sell, and the Partnership shall purchase, the decedent's interest in the Partnership, at the price and on the terms provided in this Buy-Sell Agreement. In the event that the appointment of an executor or adminis trator is delayed beyond the 90 day period, or there are procedural probate

---

[27] This would be equally true in a family-held business. The existence of the buy-sell may help to reduce family tensions by fixing the price for the transfer of the shares.

[28] This may not be true if the business is family owned. If the primary owners are related (or the natural objects of each other's estate plans), then an obligation to purchase at death may, or may not, be an appropriate since the successors may be the very people who already own interests in the business. We will assume for purposes of our discussion that all owners are unrelated and not the natural recipients of dispositions upon the death of co-owners.

[29] This provision is drafted for a general partnership interest. However, it could serve equally well for an LLC or corporation with changes in terminology.

requirements that prevent completion of the sale within the 90 day period, the sale shall be completed as soon as is reasonably possible following the death of the partner.

During the period following the partner's death and until the purchase is completed, the rights of management and voting of such partner shall be suspended.

Optional Purchase Upon Death

Within 30 days after the death of a partner, the Partnership shall have the option of purchasing all of the decedent's interest in the Partnership at the price and on the terms provided in this Buy-Sell Agreement.

Upon notification of the option by the Partnership to purchase the interest of the decedent, the officer(s) of his or her estate shall sell, and the Partnership shall purchase, the decedent's interest in the Partnership within 60 days following delivery of the notice. In the event that the appointment of an executor or administrator is delayed beyond the 60 day period, or there are procedural probate requirements that prevent completion of the sale within the 60 day period, the sale shall be completed as soon as is reasonably possible following the death of the partner.

During the period following the partner's death and until the purchase is completed, the rights of management and voting of such partner shall be suspended.

Note that these provisions *disable* the voting and management rights of the deceased partner during the option and purchasing periods. Although often left out of buy-sell agreements, such a provision seems essential to prevent the deceased owner's executor or administrator from exercising rights of management and control while the business entity is engaging its rights to purchase the ownership interest.

In some business entities, it might also make sense to extend to the remaining equity holders the additional right to purchase the interest of a departing owner (a "cross-purchase" agreement), in the event that the business entity is unwilling or unable to make the purchase.[30] The business entity may lack the funds to complete the purchase or there may be statutory constraints restricting the purchase by the entity. There may also be tax advantages to a cross-purchase, rather than entity-purchase, particularly when the entity is a C corporation. It might make sense to add the following to the death buyout provisions:

In the event that the partnership does not exercise the option within the 60 day period, any individual partner or group of partners shall have the option, for an additional 15 days, to purchase the ownership interest of the partner whose employment is terminated for the price and in accordance with the procedural requirements set forth in Paragraph ___ of this Buy-Sell Agreement.

The parties to the buy-sell agreement face two additional and serious concerns when drafting provisions related to death. They must come up with a method for

---

[30] See the discussion of cross-purchase agreements in Section F.1. of this chapter.

valuing the shares of the decedent and arrange a financial plan for the purchase of those shares by the surviving owners. Both of these concerns can be extremely difficult to negotiate and plan for, since the interests of the decedent and the surviving owners will be in opposition. The decedent will want to assure the highest possible price with the most favorable payment terms — while the surviving owners will be motivated to set a lower price, with financing terms that impose the least cost to them. It's the task of the drafters of the buy-sell agreement to negotiate a fair mechanism for valuing the shares and, in addition, help all of the owners come up with a way of financing the purchase that is reasonable and feasible. Both of these issues, valuation and financing, will be discussed later in this chapter.[31]

2.   Voluntary Transfers

In privately held businesses, it is possible to limit the ability of shareholders, partners or members to voluntarily transfer their interests without the consent of the non-departing owners. While this might make sense in a closely held business where all of the owners work as part of a team to manage the business, the ability to transfer ownership interests is often an essential characteristic that attracts passive investors, and assures active investors that they can dispose of their interests if they desire to do so. Without the ability to voluntarily transfer ownership interests (or force a buyout by the remaining owners), equity holders are at a severe disadvantage when it comes to realizing the potential for capital gains, avoiding potential losses, and planning for the wealth maximization for themselves and their families.

Most buy-sell agreements take a two-pronged approach to voluntary transfers to outsiders. First, the agreement will often give the remaining owners the *option to purchase* the ownership interest of the selling owner on the same conditions and for the same price set forth in the proposed contract of sale (sometimes called a "right of first refusal"). This requires procedural mechanisms obligating the proposed seller to provide a copy of the contract of sale to the other owners (and/or the entity) and giving the holders of the right of first refusal sufficient time to decide whether to exercise the right, arrange financing, and consummate the purchase. Option periods may run from a few weeks to several months. Care must be taken when burdening potential sales with the condition that a right of refusal must be observed. Any sale to an outsider will be delayed while the same deal is offered to existing owners, or the business entity, or both. Realistically, the longer the option period, the greater the downward pressure on the price that a proposed seller can obtain for the sale of a partial interest in a closely held business. There is no ready marketplace for ownership interests in closely held business entities and it is the rare and lucky owner who can find a potential purchaser. The fact that the sale cannot be consummated during a one, two or three month delay while the same deal is first offered to other owners, will further restrict the marketability of the equity interest.

Second, if the option to purchase is not available, or is not exercised, the *admission* of the new owner as a partner, member or shareholder may be limited to approval by the non-transferring owners.[32] This will assure that, if a sale to an

---

[31] See Section E for the discussion of valuation and Section F for the discussion of financing the purchase.

[32] In a partnership or LLC, the statutes and/or documents may restrict the transfer of an owner's

outsider occurs, that the transfer of non-economic rights cannot be consummated without the non-departing owners having the opportunity to approve the admission of the new owner.

3.   Encumbrances

Ownership interests in business entities can be a valuable source of equity for borrowing money or guaranteeing obligations of the *equity holders*. Just like tangible property such as residences, office buildings and automobiles, the intangible property rights of the equity owner can serve as collateral for borrowing money or securing the performance of other obligations. Suppose an equity owner, Ann, has a 10% interest in a business venture, with the entire business valued at approximately $20 million. Ann might use her ownership interest (worth approximately $2 million) as collateral for a $1.8 loan from her bank. The bank will insist on a security interest in Ann's equity interest that gives the bank the right to resort to the collateral to help satisfy it's claim against Ann in the event that she defaults on the loan from the bank. The security interest will be an "encumbrance" on Ann's ownership interest and will give the bank the right to exercise the remedies available under Part 5 of Article 9 of the Uniform Commercial Code. In the event of a default under the note or security agreement, the ownership interest will either: (i) be sold to the highest bidder at a foreclosure sale,[33] or (ii) retained by the lender in strict foreclosure.[34] Either way, there may be a transfer of Ann's interest in the entity to some new partner, member or shareholder.

The ability to use equity interests in business entities as a source of collateral can be an important source of financing for owners who want to borrow money for other business or personal purposes. Indeed, as the business entity becomes more valuable, many investors will want to retain their rights of ownership (rather than selling their interests) and "pull out" cash from their equity holdings by using their ownership interest as collateral for loans.

However, the existence of a voluntary encumbrance creates the possibility that, in the event of default, there will be a transfer of the interest to some outsider. For this reason, buy-sell provisions may sometimes limit or condition the ability of owners to pledge their ownership interests as collateral for loans.

Some buy-sell provisions may simply prohibit the creation of voluntary encumbrances. This might make sense in some circumstances but such

---

interest to only the economic portion until the transferee is admitted as a partner or member, in accordance with the voting or other approval mechanisms set forth in the statutes and/or documents. Until admitted as a partner or member, the new "owner" merely acquires the economic rights of the transferor. While this is more difficult to accomplish in corporate entities, similar restraints can be provided for in the documentation of closely held corporations.

[33] UCC § 9-504 gives the secured party the right to dispose of the debtor's interest in the property at a public or private foreclosure sale, extinguishing the debtor's rights in the collateral and transferring the debtor's interest in the collateral to the purchaser at the sale. Any surplus (amount received by the secured party in excess of the debt, interest and expenses) must be returned to the debtor. If the sale price is insufficient to satisfy the entire obligation to the secured party, the debtor will remain liable and the creditor may pursue a deficiency judgment against the debtor.

[34] UCC § 9-505(2) gives the secured party the right the right to accept the collateral in discharge of the obligation. Under § 9-505(2), the acceptance of the collateral in strict foreclosure results in a satisfaction of the entire obligation owed to the secured party and denies to the secured party the right to a deficiency judgment against the debtor.

prohibitions deny to the owners the ability to pull out equity in the form of collateralized loans. Perhaps a wiser solution is to allow encumbrance of ownership interests but condition the validity of the encumbrance on an agreement by the secured party that, in essence, gives the other owners the equivalent of a right of first refusal in the event of a default by the debtor-owner. For instance:

> A partner (the "Pledgor") may voluntarily pledge, hypothecate or encumber his or her interest in the business entity as collateral for a debt, provided that the Pledgor first obtains an agreement from the secured party, in form and substance acceptable to the partnership, that the secured party agrees:
>
>> To provide the partnership with a copy of the executed note, security agreement and any other related documents (the "Loan Documents").
>>
>> Not to make any changes to the terms of the Loan Documents without first complying with the terms of this section as though a new loan was being made.
>>
>> In the event of a default under Loan Documents, the secured party shall give written notice of the default to the partnership by registered mail at the address set forth below. The notice shall set forth:
>>
>>> The name, address, telephone number, loan number and other essential contact information for the secured party, including the names and direct telephone numbers for the employees with authority to comply with the terms of the agreement.
>>>
>>> The basis for the default.[35] If the default is monetary, the amount of the outstanding principal balance, accrued interest and other charges and fees due under the Loan Documents.
>
> Upon receipt of the notice of default, the partnership shall have 30 days to exercise one of the following options. In the event that the partnership does not exercise one of the following options within the 30 day period, any individual partner or group of partners shall have an additional 15 days to exercise one of the following options:
>
> 1. Cure any monetary defaults by paying any past due amounts and fees.
> 2. Cure any non-monetary defaults, if possible to do so.
> 3. Redeem the partnership interest of the debtor by paying the outstanding amount of the balance of the debt and any fees or charges provided for in the Loan Documents.
>
> In voting by the partnership on whether or not to exercise one of the above options, the defaulting partner's vote shall be deemed to be in favor of the majority of votes cast on the matter by other partners. In the event that a default occurs and the partnership, or any individual partner or group of partners exercises any of the above options (the "Curing Party"), the

---

[35] The default may not always be the failure to make a payment when due. Non-monetary defaults may be included in the loan documents. Such non-monetary defaults may include changes in the debtor's financial condition, additional loans incurred by the debtor, changes in the value of the collateral, changes in market conditions, or even the good faith decision by the secured party that it simply deems the loan to be "insecure."

defaulting partner's ownership interest shall be subject to a lien in favor of the Curing Party for amounts paid by the Curing Party, together with interest thereon at the annual rate of 10%. The Curing Party shall also have the option to purchase the ownership interest of the defaulting partner and apply all amounts paid by the Curing Party, as well as interest owed to the curing party, towards the purchase price. The purchase price and the procedural requirements for the purchase shall be determined as set forth in Paragraph ___ of this Buy-Sell Agreement.[36]

4. Involuntary Transfers and Bankruptcy

There are times when creditors may obtain a non-consensual lien and, eventually, enforce the lien by having the debtor's ownership interest in a business entity sold at a foreclosure sale. Liens in intangible property have traditionally been created by "garnishment" liens but some states, such as California, may allow the lien to be established by writ of execution. Garnishment and execution liens require that the creditor first obtain a judgment against the owner, establishing a right to payment. The creditor can then obtain a garnishment or execution lien by following the procedures established under the statutory provisions of the state where the entity is formed.

Typically, all that is required is that a copy of the judgment, along with appropriate papers and fees, be delivered to the clerk of the court in the county where the business entity is located, and the clerk will issue a writ of garnishment (or a writ of execution in some states). The sheriff will then serve the writ on the business entity.[37] Upon delivery of the writ, a lien will be established in the debtor's ownership interest. The writ will direct the entity to withhold any distributions to the partner, member or shareholder until the debt is paid or the lien is foreclosed. If the judgment is not paid, the creditor will have the right, after following notice and other procedures, to sell the ownership interest at a foreclosure sale. The foreclosure will transfer the partner's, member's or shareholder's economic rights to the purchaser at the sale. Whether or not the purchaser will be admitted as a fully entitled owner, with non-economic rights, will depend on the formation documents of the business.

Whether admitted or not, the sale pursuant to a writ of garnishment or execution raises all of the usual concerns of the non-departing owners with regard to the transfer of an existing owner's interest to an outsider — and there should be some protections built into the formation documents, or buy-sell agreement, to give the non-departing owners an *option* to purchase the shares at a fair, or even favorable, price.

A buy-sell provision that is triggered by involuntary liens might mimic the provisions used for voluntary liens. Perhaps something like the following:

---

[36] The purchase price and procedures will probably be the same as those for an involuntary transfer, bankruptcy or termination of employment. See Section E.2 for some approaches to setting the price.

[37] Have you ever noticed a sheriff's or marshall's car parked outside a bank in the early morning hours? The officer is most likely delivering garnishment/execution writs to create liens on the bank accounts of judgment debtor's.

In the event of the creation of a garnishment or execution lien in a partner's[38] ownership interest, the partnership shall have the option for 30 days to satisfy the writ by paying the amounts and fees required by the writ. In the event that the partnership does not exercise the option within the 30 day period, any individual partner or group of partners shall have the option, for an additional 15 days, to satisfy the writ by paying the amounts and fees required by the writ.

In voting by the partnership on whether or not to exercise one of the above options, the defaulting partner's vote shall be deemed to be in favor of the majority of votes cast on the matter by other partners. In the event that the partnership, or any individual partner or group of partners exercises any of the above options, the defaulting partner's ownership interest shall be subject to a lien in favor of the Curing Party for amounts paid by the Curing Party, together with interest thereon at the annual rate of 10%. The Curing Party shall also have the option to purchase the ownership interest of the defaulting partner and apply all amounts paid by the Curing Party, as well as interest owed to the curing party, towards the purchase price. The purchase price and the procedural requirements for the purchase shall be determined as set forth in Paragraph ____ of this Buy-Sell Agreement.[39]

A similar problem may occur if an owner voluntarily files a liquidating bankruptcy under chapter 7 of the United States Bankruptcy Code — or if an involuntary petition is filed against an owner. In a liquidating bankruptcy, all of the debtor's non-exempt assets will be sold by the bankruptcy trustee and the proceeds will be used to pay the debtor's creditors.[40] In a chapter 7 liquidation case, the bankruptcy trustee is given broad powers under § 363 of the Bankruptcy Code to sell the debtor's assets, notwithstanding any contractual or state law limitations on transfer, including the debtor's ownership interests in business entities.

It is important to recognize that the outcome might be different in a chapter 11 or chapter 13 reorganization bankruptcy case. If the debtor files a chapter 11 or 13, the debtor will be allowed to retain ownership of his or her assets while coming up with a "plan" to pay creditors from sources other than liquidation of assets. Plans under these chapters will often provide that the debtor retain ownership of business entities (although in chapter 11 the plan may provide for the sale of the ownership interest). So long as the plan is confirmed and the debtor is retaining the ownership interest, there is no impact on the other partners, members or shareholders.

Many buy-sell agreements provide for action in the event of the filing of a bankruptcy petition by, or against, an owner. Can you see that such a broad based triggering event may not be appropriate if the debtor is filing a chapter 11 or 13 and there is no provision in the plan for the sale of the ownership interest? Indeed, the bankruptcy trigger found in many buy-sell agreements is unrefined. The trigger should only be activated if the bankruptcy is a liquidating bankruptcy (or is converted to a liquidating bankruptcy). A sensible buy-sell provision might provide:

---

[38] This provision is drafted for a general partnership interest. However, it could serve equally well for an LLC or corporation.

[39] The purchase price and procedures will probably be the same as those for an involuntary transfer, bankruptcy or termination of employment. See Section E.2 for some approaches to setting the price.

[40] Bankruptcy is discussed in detail in Chapter 10.

In the event that a partner:[41] (i) voluntarily files a chapter 7 bankruptcy petition under the U.S. Bankruptcy Code; (ii) has an involuntary chapter 7 petition filed against him/her and the order for relief is granted;[42] or (iii) voluntarily files a chapter 11 petition and proposes a plan of reorganization that provides for the sale or transfer of the partner's ownership interest, then the partnership shall have the option for 60 days after such event to purchase the ownership interest of the debtor-partner for the price and in accordance with the procedural requirements set forth in Paragraph ____ of this Buy-Sell Agreement. In voting by the partnership on whether or not to exercise one of the above options, the defaulting partner's vote shall be deemed to be in favor of the majority of votes cast on the matter by other partners.

In the event that the partnership does not exercise the option within the 30 day period, any individual partner or group of partners shall have the option, for an additional 15 days, to purchase the ownership interest of the debtor-partner for the price and in accordance with the procedural requirements set forth in Paragraph ____ of this Buy-Sell Agreement.

The enforcement of such provisions might be restricted by the provisions of the U.S. Bankruptcy Code, which pre-empt state law and contract-based agreements in many circumstances. However, if the price to be paid for the bankrupt-owner's interest is a fair price, the bankruptcy trustee is likely to cooperate in completing the transfer — since the alternative is for the trustee to find a buyer in the open marketplace. The sale of partial ownership interests under the forced-sale conditions of a bankruptcy case is unlikely to bring a high price for the ownership interest.

5.   Termination of Employment

The option to purchase upon termination of an owner who is an employee may be extremely important. Whether the termination is voluntary or involuntary, the continued employment might be an essential condition of ownership. This might be true because *all* of the equity holders are also employees, or because the ownership rights of a particular owner were conditioned on long-term employment. When an equity holder is fired from employment, or leaves employment under unfavorable circumstances, the remaining owners will often want to have the *option* to buyout the terminated employee's interest, to assure that continued control and management is not adversely affected.

On the other hand, depending on the size of the entity and the importance of the employee-owner's participation in the day-to-day operations of the business, some owners might want to assure that the trigger is only available for specific types of terminations or only for certain periods of time. For instance, the trigger for

---

[41] This provision is drafted for a general partnership interest. However, it could serve equally well for an LLC or corporation.

[42] Under Bankruptcy Code § 303, the filing of an involuntary petition does not necessarily result in the conclusion that the debtor should be subjected to adjudication in bankruptcy. The debtor can contest the involuntary petition and, if the creditors don't meet certain requirements, have the petition dismissed. However, if the debtor does not take timely action, or is unsuccessful in contesting the involuntary petition, an "order for relief" will be granted, causing the debtor's property to be subject to the trustee's powers of sale.

voluntary terminations might be available only during the first five years of employment. After that period, the voluntary termination will not result in triggering an option to purchase in the other owners. Similarly, *involuntary* terminations might be limited to only those which meet certain specific, written causes, such as embezzlement, poor performance, conviction of a felony, intentional misconduct, etc. It may also be the case that a particular owner's employment is minor in nature and termination of that employment is not important to the operation of the business. In such cases, that owner will be excluded from the termination of employment trigger in the buy-sell agreement.

An example of a termination of a *broad* employment trigger might be:

> If a partner is employed by the Partnership and his or her employment is terminated for any reason, the Partnership shall have the option, for 60 days following the effective date of such termination, to purchase all of the interest owned by the partner. If the Partnership elects to purchase the interest, the price and procedural requirements shall be as set forth in Paragraph _____ of this Buy-Sell Agreement. In voting by the Partnership on whether or not to exercise this option, the vote of the partner whose employment is terminated shall be deemed to be in favor of the majority of votes cast on the matter by other partners.

> In the event that the Partnership does not exercise the option within the 60 day period, any individual partner or group of partners shall have the option, for an additional 15 days, to purchase the ownership interest of the partner whose employment is terminated for the price and in accordance with the procedural requirements set forth in Paragraph _____ of this Buy-Sell Agreement.

The above provisions give the entity, or non-departing owners, the *option* to purchase the interest of an owner whose employment is terminated. Depending on the bargaining power of a particular employee-owner, there are times when the entity and it's non-departing owners may be saddled with the *mandatory* obligation to buy out the interest of an employee-owner whose employment is terminated. If such a mandatory obligation is imposed, the other owners must take care to make sure that there is some mechanism for financing the purchase.[43] An example of a mandatory provision might be:

> If a partner is employed by the Partnership and his or her employment is terminated for any reason, the Partnership shall have the obligation, to purchase all of the interest owned by the partner. The price and procedural requirements shall be as set forth in Paragraph _____ of this Buy-Sell Agreement.

The sample termination of employment provisions above are extremely broad in scope and create an option or obligation to purchase for *any* termination, voluntary or involuntary. The employment termination trigger might be *narrowed* to only some types of terminations. Some examples:

> If the employment of any of the following partners is terminated voluntarily or involuntarily during the first five years of employment, commencing with the date of this Buy-Sell Agreement, then the Partnership shall have

---

[43] See the discussion on financing in Section F of this chapter.

the option [or obligation] to purchase all of the interest owned by the partner. The price and procedural requirements shall be as set forth in Paragraph _____ of this Buy-Sell Agreement. The partners subject to this provision are: James Jones and Jessica Jones.

Or:

If a partner is employed by the Partnership and his or her employment is terminated by the Partnership for cause,[44] then the Partnership shall have the option, for 60 days following the effective date of such termination, to purchase all of the interest owned by the partner. If the Partnership elects to purchase the interest, the price and procedural requirements shall be as set forth in Paragraph _____ of this Buy-Sell Agreement. In voting by the Partnership on whether or not to exercise this option, the vote of the partner whose employment is terminated shall be deemed to be in favor of the majority of votes cast on the matter by other partners.

6.   Disability

For the same reasons that termination of employment might give rise to an option to purchase, the disability of a key employee or manager might serve as a trigger. In a closely held entity, the fact that an individual owner is disabled can cause severe consequences with respect to the operations and control of the business, if his or her participation in the business is essential. Unlike triggers related to *employment*, triggers for disability might apply to owners who are not employees but participate directly in the control and management of the business. It is only such key persons who should be subject to such disability triggers. During the negotiation of the buy-sell agreement, key employees or managers who are subject to the disability trigger should not object, so long as the value paid for the ownership interest of the disabled individual is fair. After all, the business needs these key persons to operate effectively.

The tough parts of drafting triggers for disability are defining what constitutes a long-term disability and how the determination of disability will be made. Consider the following possible provisions:

Option to Purchase on Disability of Partner

Definition of "Disability": In the event that the Partnership owns or pays for a disability insurance policy for a Partner, or a key-person insurance policy for a partner, the term "disability" shall be the same as the definition of disability in the policy. In the event that there is no such a policy, "disability" shall mean that the partner is unable to perform the material and substantial regular duties required of him or her, even if the partner is able to do other types of duties unrelated to the business. Disability may be the result of physical illness, injury or mental condition".

Determination of Disability: The Partnership and the Partner (or the Partner's legal representative) may agree in writing that the Partner is:

(i) disabled as that term is used in this section;

---

[44] "Cause" will have to be carefully defined.

(ii) that the disability is likely to continue for more than 12 continuous months from the onset of the disability; and,

(iii) the date that the disability began.

In the event that the Partnership and the Partner (or the Partner's legal representative) cannot agree on all or any of the above determinations, then the parties agree that the determinations shall be made as follows . . .[45]

Exercise of Option

If it has been determined that a Partner is disabled for more than two months, and that the disability is likely to continue for more than 12 continuous months from the onset of the disability the Partnership shall have the option[46] for 90 days following such determination to purchase all of the ownership interest of the disabled Partner at the price and on the terms set forth in Section ____.

If the disabled Partner is also a paid employee, the Partnership shall continue to pay the salary of the Partner for the 12 month period of disability, less any amounts received by the partner under any policy of disability, or key employee insurance policy, or received under any federal or state disability compensation program.

If the disable Partner should die after becoming disabled, but before the actual purchase of his or her partnership interest, then the purchase and sale will be treated as the purchase and sale of a deceased Partner's interest under Section ____.

If the parties can't agree upon whether or not the owner is disabled, likely to remain disabled, and the date the disability began, it may prove difficult to agree on a satisfactory procedure for making the determinations. Some buy-sell agreements revert to arbitration clauses. However, as discussed later in this chapter, arbitration clauses can result in expensive and frustrating litigation-type proceedings. For example an arbitration clause might provide:

In the event the Partnership and the Partner (or the Partner's legal representative) cannot agree on all or any of the above determinations, then the parties agree that the determinations shall be made as follows: The Partner (or the Partner's legal representative) and the Partnership shall each designate an arbitrator, and the two arbitrators shall make the determinations. If the arbitrators cannot agree, they shall designate a third arbitrator to make the determinations.

Can you imagine the cost and uncertainty of such a provision. How long will the proceedings last? What type of *standards* will be used to determine value? What

---

[45] See the discussion immediately following this sample "Option to Purchase on Disability of Partner."

[46] It's also possible that the purchase on disability is *mandatory*, not *optional*. In the event that purchase is mandatory, the non-departing owners need to make sure that they plan some time of financing mechanism for making the purchase.

types of evidence will be presented? What types of witnesses and experts will be allowed?[47]

There has to be a better way of setting standards for making the determinations regarding disability, projected length of disability and the date of onset of the disability. Might it make sense to agree on some *medical* standards and procedures, instead of arbitration? Perhaps pre-selecting a hospital or medical facility to make the determinations? What ideas can you come up with to resolve this problem?

7.   Other Triggers

There are many other events that the parties might include in the buy-sell agreement, giving one or more owners the option or obligation to buyout the interest or another owner, including but not limited to:

- Divorce settlements where an owner's ex-spouse may be granted some part (or all) of the owner's interest
- Criminal Conviction
- Intentional Misconduct
- Breach of the Formation Documents or Buy-Sell Agreements

Depending on the importance of such triggers, the parties may, or may not want to include provisions in the buy-sell agreement creating an option or obligation to purchase an ownership interest upon the occurrence of such triggering events.

E.   BUYOUT PROCEDURES AND VALUATION

After the option or obligation to buyout has been triggered, the buy-sell agreement must contain appropriate provisions regarding how the buyout will procedurally be accomplished and the price to be paid for the ownership interest. Realistically, at the time the buy-sell agreement is negotiated, the parties must also deal with the issue of financing the buyout — especially if the buyout is mandatory. How will the entity or its non-departing owners pay for what could be a costly purchase of the departing owner's interest? The procedure to be followed and, perhaps, the price to be paid, might vary depending on the nature of the trigger. In this section we will look first at procedures and then at valuation. In Section F we will focus on how to finance the buyout.

1.   Rights of First Refusal

If a partner, member or shareholder proposes a voluntary sale of an ownership interest, the buy-sell agreement may trigger a right of first refusal in the entity and/or other owners. The right of first refusal typically requires that the proposed seller first offer the ownership interest to the business entity (an entity-purchase agreement), or to the existing owners of the business (a cross-purchase agreement), or some combination of both types of purchase opportunities.[48] The entity and/or owners, will then have an option period during which a decision can be made whether or not to meet the terms of the offer. Often, the provisions will

---

[47] See the discussion in Section E.4. of this chapter for a more in-depth discussion of this issue.

[48] The distinctions between these two types of rights of first refusal are discussed in Section F.1 later in this chapter.

require that the option must be exercised as to *all* of the interest of the proposed seller, not just part. Can you see why a purchase of the entire interest of the proposed seller is important from the perspective of the seller?[49]

Right of First Refusal

Except for permitted transfers described in Section ____, no partner (the "Selling Partner") shall voluntarily sell, transfer or dispose of his or her interest in the Partnership (or any part of the interest) without obtaining prior written consent of the Partnership and of all other Partners or, in the alternative, first giving the Partnership and Other Partners the option to purchase the Selling Partner's interest in accordance with the provisions of this Section. Any attempted voluntary transfer in violation of this Section shall be void.

Within 5 days after entering into an enforceable agreement for the sale of the Selling Partner's interest (the "Offer"), the Selling Partner shall give written notice to the Managing Partner in accordance with the notice provisions of Section ____. The notice shall include a full and complete copy of any written Offer together with any other documents related to the proposed transfer, the name and address of the proposed transferee, the price to be paid and the terms of payment.

Upon receipt of the notice, the Managing Partner shall promptly send a copy to each of the Partners in accordance with the notice provisions in Section ____.

The Partnership shall have 30 days following receipt of the notice to exercise the option to purchase all of the interest described in the Offer at the price and on the terms stated in the Offer. In voting by the partnership on whether or not to exercise the option, the Selling Partner's vote shall be deemed to be in favor of the majority of votes cast on the matter by other partners. If the Partnership timely exercises the option to purchase, the Partnership shall promptly give written notice to the Selling Partner. The Partnership shall pay the purchase price in accordance with the terms set forth in the Offer and the Selling Partner shall execute the transfer documents deemed necessary by the Partnership to complete the transfer.

If the option is not exercised by the Partnership within the 30 day period, the Other Partners shall have 30 days to exercise the option to purchase all of the interest described in the Offer at the price and on the terms stated in the Offer (the "Partner's Option Period"). In the event that more than one of the Other Partners wants to purchase all or some portion of the of the interest described in the Offer, the following rules shall apply with regard to apportionment of the Selling Partner's interest among the Other Partners seeking to acquire the interest:

Any Partner seeking to acquire any part, or all of the interest, shall deliver to the Managing Partner, in writing within the first 10 days of the Partner's Option Period, a notice of election to purchase the interest or

---

[49] A purchase of just part of the ownership interest will most likely torpedo the outstanding offer. The price being offered for the equity interest is likely to be dependent on the transfer of all of the interest, since this will affect the control and financial rights of the proposed seller.

a proportion of the interest. If the total elections exceed 100% of the interest, then the following formula shall be used to apportion the Selling Party's interest among the Partners electing to take advantage of the offer: . . .[50]

If neither the Partnership nor the Other Partners agree to purchase all of the interest set forth in the Offer within the periods set forth above, the Selling Partner may complete the transfer as set forth in the Offer. The purchaser will hold the interest subject to the provisions of this Buy-Sell Agreement. Until the purchaser is admitted as a Partner in accordance with the provisions of Section ____, the purchaser shall be entitled only to the economic rights of the Selling Partner.

Note that if the entity declines to make the purchase and a secondary option is given to the non-departing owners, some formula will need to be agreed upon in the event that the proportional elections to purchase made by the non-departing owners exceeds 100% of the interest identified in the offer. There are many ways of fairly apportioning the interest of the selling owner among the other owners seeking to take advantage of the right of first refusal. Does the following make sense:

Each Partner shall have priority, up to the proportion of interest specified the notice of election, to purchase the proportional interest, in the same proportion that the proportion of the Partner's interest in the Partnership bears to the total proportion of Partnership interests held by all Other Partners electing to purchase.

The above provisions require that the option to purchase be on the same terms as the bona-fide offer and for *all* of the interest in the proposed sale. Any other agreement would allow the entity (or owners if there's a secondary right of first refusal given to them) to purchase a mere fraction of the seller's interest, resulting in a likely termination of the sale to the outsider — and leaving the selling owner in a difficult position.

The existence of the right of first refusal is important in closely held entities where the control and management of the business might be adversely affected by the sale to an outsider. However, the existence of the right of first refusal will place a significant impediment in the way of owners who are seeking to sell to outsiders. Depending on the option periods in the buy-sell agreement, any proposed contract between an equity owner and a potential buyer will have to incorporate a delay for the total time of the option periods — and allow for the potential preemption of the buyer's deal by the entity and/or its owners. Given the difficulty in finding buyers for closely held business interests, the existence of the right of first refusal will further suppress the price and shrink the market of potential buyers. To reduce this negative impact of the right of first refusal, it's important to make sure that the option periods are not too long. Image how difficult it would be to find an outside buyer if the options periods are 90 days each for the entity and its owners (a total of 180 days). Such a six month delay is likely to make a sale to an outsider extremely difficult.

---

[50] See the text following this provision.

2.   Valuation of Ownership Interests

Depending on the trigger in the buy-sell agreement, the non-departing owners may have the option, or obligation, to buy out a departing owner's interest at a price to be determined by some formula in the Agreement. This can be an intense area of negotiation for the parties. An older owner who is anticipating retiring, or facing the possibility of a not-too-distant death, will want to assure the highest possible price for his or her ownership interest. On the other hand, the younger owners, anticipating a long-term involvement with the entity, will want to assure that the price paid at death or retirement is not excessive and the terms of payment do not disrupt the business at the time that death triggers a buyout.

This is an area of negotiation and drafting that is problematic, since it requires that the parties commit to a formula for the buyout early in the lifespan of the entity. As we will see, parties often have a rough time reaching agreement on a valuation formula. Rather than face the difficult task of choosing standards for setting the price, the end result in many buy-sell agreements is the parties will fall back to a default provision that: (i) requires them to use "good faith" to determine a price at the time of the buyout and, if they can't agree; or (ii) refers the determination to an arbitrator or group of arbitrators. For reasons we discuss below, this common type of valuation mechanism can be expensive, frustrating and unfair.

The ultimate objective of a well-drafted valuation provisions is to create an efficient, inexpensive mechanism for determining a fair price for the ownership interest of the departing owner.

The valuation formula may vary depending on the type of trigger that causes the buyout. For instance, a trigger based upon the early *termination* of an employee-owner may require valuation based on asset value or book value, while a trigger based upon the *death* of an owner may require valuation based on capitalization of earnings.

3.   The Problems With "Fair Market Value"

Virtually everyone is familiar with the term "fair market value." The term supposes the existence of some objective marketplace where willing buyers and sellers would agree on a price for the property being sold. The most obvious and useful example is the residential real estate market. Appraisers are often hired by mortgage lenders to assess the "fair market value" of a house before the lender is willing to make a mortgage loan to the homeowner. The purpose of the appraisal is to assure the lender that the fair market value of the property will be sufficient to cover the repayment of principal and interest on the proposed loan in the event of a default by the borrower.[51] The appraiser will use "comparables" in the same or

---

[51] Prudent mortgage lenders will require that the fair market value be 10–20% higher than the amount of the loan. This means the borrower will have to have savings sufficient to cover the other 10–20% of the value of the property in the form of cash (for a purchase) or equity (for a refinance). For instance, if the fair market value of the property is $200,000, a prudent lender requiring a 20% down payment from the debtor (or equity in the case of a refinance) won't loan more than $160,000. The purpose of the equity cushion is to assure that, in the event of the default by the borrower, there will be sufficient value in the collateral to cover: (i) unpaid principal, (ii) accrued interest, and (iii) the costs of collection. The typical foreclosure takes six to nine months in many states. Interest at 6% on a loan of $160,000 would accrue monthly in the amount of $800 ($7,200 over a nine month period). The equity

similar neighborhoods in the vicinity to determine the price at which similar houses[52] have been sold in the last six to twelve months. In this way, the appraisers can determine a "fair market value" for the residence being appraised. It's important to notice that it takes the existence of a *marketplace* with frequent sales of similar properties to be able to easily determine a "fair *market* value."

Other examples of marketplaces for the determination of "fair market value" are the public securities and commodities exchanges. The exchanges serve as central marketplaces for the sale of property. The centrality and large volume of transactions yields a ready determination of "fair market value" for ownership interests in business entities (in the case of stock exchanges) and contracts for goods (in the case of commodities exchanges). The total value of the shares of stock of a listed corporation gives us the *market capitalization value* — the current amount of equity in the corporation. Simply multiple the current stock price by the number of shares.[53]

Notwithstanding that such marketplaces give us a fair market value for the market capitalization and the concomitant *fractional ownership* interests traded on the exchanges, they don't *necessarily* give us a fair market value for the sale of the *entire* business. The value of stocks traded on the public exchanges may change radically when there is a takeover bid for a listed company. This is sometimes caused by the fact that the company was "undervalued" by the stock market price and, indeed, is worth far more. Takeover specialists will attempt to buy the company at a price near to the current stock price, or pay a premium over the existing stock price, because the takeover purchaser anticipates that there is more value in the company than reflected on the stock exchange. The opposite may also be true. Companies may be "overvalued" with the stock price far in excess of the actual value of the company if the entire company was to be put up for bid to knowledgeable and informed buyers.

The types of business entities discussed in this book are closely held entities that are *not* traded on public exchanges. Valuing such closely held business entities, and the proportional value of the fractional ownership interests, can be extremely difficult. Parties to buy-sell agreements may sometimes refer to "fair market value." However, there is rarely a "marketplace" for the sale of investment interests in closely held businesses — nor is there a ready marketplace for the sale of the *entire* business (which would allow determination of the value of ownership interests by dividing the total market worth of the company among the owners in the same proportions as the ownership interests). One of the great errors made by drafters is the use of the phrase "fair market value" as a *standard* for determining value in connection with a buyout.

In addition to the absence of a marketplace for determining fair market value, the term can have different meanings depending upon whether the business is being sold as a going concern, of if its assets are being liquidated. A company that

---

cushion also helps to cover the possibility of a decline in value of the property.

[52] The appraiser will do an inspection of the property being appraised to determine its size, the number of bedrooms, the quality of construction, the history of renovations, etc. He or she will then comb through the real estate records to find similar houses that have sold in the vicinity or in similarly situated residential communities.

[53] Note that the term used is *market* capitalization and the price of shares *publicly* traded. There may be privately held shares of stock in the corporation as well.

is operating with a strong financial history of profits, a skilled workforce, talented managers and financing will have a value as a going concern that is usually far higher than the aggregate value of its assets.[54] On the other hand, a company that has ceased business operations will be worth only the liquidation value that can be obtained by selling it's property. Both "going concern" and "liquidation" values are fair market values, depending upon the circumstances. As you can see, the term "fair market value" is fraught with ambiguity.

4.   The Problems With Arbitrators and Appraisers

In the absence of some additional standards based on some type of *objective criteria*, it's highly unlikely that the parties will be able to agree on fair market value at the time the buyout is to occur. Often, the parties to a buy-sell agreement may simply refer the matter to arbitration, or to appraisers, in the event that they cannot agree on a price at the time of the buyout. If the matter is referred to arbitrators or appraisers, without some objective standards for determining "fair market value," the arbitrators or appraisers are in no better a position than the parties to make the determination of "fair market value." Once again, in the absence of a ready market for the sale of an ownership interest (or the entire business), the arbitrators or appraisers may disagree on the standards to be used to determine fair market value. We will see that, depending on the standards chosen by these third parties, the valuation price can vary widely.

A common arbitration provision often looks something like this:

> The purchase price shall be determined by good faith negotiation between the entity, and/or the continuing owners if entitled to purchase the interest under this Agreement, and the selling owner or his or her personal representative. If the parties are unable to agree on a price within 90 days after commencement of negotiations, either party may terminate the negotiations and require that the question of the purchase price be submitted to arbitration.

> The party seeking arbitration shall deliver written notice to the other party(ies) naming an arbitrator. The other party(ies) shall have the right to name an second arbitrator by serving notice on the first party within 30 days after delivery of the first notice. The two arbitrators shall select a third arbitrator. If the responding party(ies) do not elect a second arbitrator, then the first arbitrator shall solely conduct the arbitration. If only one arbitrator is selected, the parties shall share the fees and expenses of arbitration equally. If two or three arbitrators are named, each party shall pay the fees and expenses of his or her selected arbitrator and share equally the fees and expenses of the third arbitrator.

> The arbitrators shall determine the fair market value of the interest to be sold under this Buy-Sell Agreement and set forth the determination in writing, together with their opinions and factual considerations used by them to reach their decision. A signed copy shall be delivered to each party, within 75 days after commencing the arbitration hearings. Except as to procedures specifically set forth in this Buy-Sell Agreement, the form and

---

[54] This additional value is the company's "goodwill" and is discussed in greater detail later in this chapter.

substance of the arbitration proceeding shall be governed by the then-current rules of arbitration of the American Arbitration Association. The determination of the arbitrators shall be final and binding on the parties.

There are many flaws with the concept of using third parties such as arbitrators or appraisers to determine the value of the interest to be purchased. Can you identify some concerns after having read the above arbitration provision? Consider the following problems:

- Selection of Arbitrators & Procedures: The arbitrators derive their authority solely from the parties. Arbitration clauses typically require that the parties submit to a litigation-type proceeding where one or more arbitrators will decide what the appropriate value should be. To be "fair," many arbitration clauses allow each party to select an arbitrator and then to have the two arbitrators select a third arbitrator for the initial proceeding (or for a subsequent proceeding if the two arbitrators can't agree). The parties must agree on the procedures to be followed, the types of evidence that may be presented, the witnesses and experts that will testify. If these matters are not set forth in the buy-sell agreement, then the parties will have to select some standard procedures, such as the rules of the American Arbitration Association.

- The Nature of the Proceedings: Arbitration is one short step away from full-fledged litigation. It is an extra-judicial, adversarial process. The proceedings will move faster than court proceedings since there is no jury and no need to deal with the overloaded court calendars. However, the arbitration proceedings will require preparation, evidence, declarations, witness and expert testimony. If requested, the parties will have to prepare legal memoranda as well.

- Costs: Arbitrators typically earn $300 per hour. Lawyers' fees run in the same neighborhood. Imagine the cost to the parties if the arbitration proceeding is in front of three arbitrators, with each party represented by a capable law firm. If the proceedings last even a few days, the costs will run into *tens* of thousands of dollars for each party. In the absence of any standards for making the determinations, there might be days of testimony by expert witnesses (who will also need to be paid). This procedure will need to be repeated each time the valuation clause is triggered by the departure of an owner. In a business entity with 10 or 15 owners, over the course of several years the aggregate cost of valuing ownership interests could run into the hundreds of thousands of dollars.

- Absence of Standards: The problems of arbitration are exacerbated by the absence of standards for determining value. Without any standards, part of the adversarial process will be to convince the arbitrators to choose among several competing formulas to apply in making a determination of value. Do the arbitrators use a "book value" formula? An income capitalization formula?[55] A market comparison formula?

- Potential for Unfairness: Arbitrators may be retired judges, or lawyers who have moved away from practice and developed a business as an arbitrator. Just like judges, arbitrators will have hidden biases, preferences and quirks. In the absence of some clear, objective standards, the parties are at the whim of the arbitrator in determining a price for the interest.

---

[55] A detailed discussion of objective standards is set forth below.

In some buy-sell agreements, the parties may provide for referral to *appraisers* rather than arbitrators. Appraisers are specialists in the art of valuing property. The referral to appraisers, rather than arbitrators, means that the proceedings will be less litigation-based than arbitration. Nevertheless, at the time of the buyout of an owner's interest, the fundamentally opposed positions of the parties means that both the seller and the buyer(s) will be seeking to convince the appraisers to use a particular standard, and factual arguments, that favors each of them. Although the cost will probably be less than arbitration, in the end, many of the same problems remain. Consider this typical appraisal provision:

> The purchase price shall be determined by good faith negotiation between the entity, and/or the continuing owners if entitled to purchase the interest under this Buy-Sell Agreement, and the selling owner or his or her personal representative. If the parties are unable to agree on a price within 90 days after commencement of negotiations, either party may terminate the negotiations and require that the question of the purchase price shall be determined by an independent appraiser.

> If the parties are unable to agree on the selection of an appraiser within 30 days after the event triggering the purchase and sale, each party shall select an independent appraiser within 10 days after the 30 day period. The two appraisers shall independently appraise the interest. If the difference in the two appraisals does not exceed 5%, the fair market value shall be deemed to be the average of the two appraisals. If the difference between the two appraisals exceeds 5%, the two appraisers shall select a third appraiser who shall also independently appraise the interest and that appraisal shall conclusively be the fair market value of the interest.

> The appraiser(s) shall determine the fair market value of the interest to be sold under this Buy-Sell Agreement after considering all memoranda, evidence and declarations submitted to them by the parties, or otherwise obtained by the appraiser(s). The determination shall be put in writing, along with opinions and factual considerations used by the appraiser(s) to reach the determination. A signed copy shall be delivered to each party, within 75 days after referral of the appraisal to the appraiser(s).

> The fees and expenses of the appraisers shall be paid . . .

Do the same problems arise with regard to: (i) selection of appraisers and procedures to be followed; (ii) the costs of valuing the ownership interest; (iii) the absence of standards for the appraisers to use; and (iv) the potential for unfairness?

5.   The Problems With Valuation by Agreement

One approach to valuation is for the parties to agree on the pro-rata worth of each of the shares or interests in a company. This may be a simple approach at the startup of the business but it becomes difficult over the long term as the business grows (or shrinks). The owners might agree at the time of formation on an initial value and then agree to update that value from time to time, such as every two years. Can you anticipate the flaws of such a valuation scheme?

Revaluations almost never occur when the time comes. It's quite common for the owners to simply forget. Unless the lawyers have continued to represent one or more of the parties to the buy-sell agreement, the parties are unlikely to program the necessity of a revaluation into their calendars. Even if they properly program reminders into their calendars, the task of revaluation can be difficult, acrimonious and expensive. Rather than face the hard task of revaluation, the owners often let it slip by without taking action. Why is it so hard to revalue the ownership interests?

The owners may have great difficulty reaching agreed-upon values as their personal circumstances change and the business evolves. At the time of revaluation, what criteria will the owners use? For the revaluation to occur, the buy-sell agreement will often require a near-unanimous or super-majority vote of the ownership interests. Depending on each owner's personal and business objectives, some will want a high valuation while others will want a low valuation. In a company with five, ten, twenty or more owners they will certainly have different ideas about the worth of the company and be motivated by factors such as age, liquidity needs, anticipated departures, etc. Any owner who foresees an upcoming departure in his or her near future will push for a high value, while those owners who anticipate remaining (but recognizing that other owners may depart) will hold out for a low value.

As a result of inadvertence, aversion to the process, or failure to agree, many years may go by without the owners updating the values. This could lead to a wide variance between the "value" stated in the agreement and the actual market value of the interests. Even if the owners are assiduous in observing the revaluation process, values can change radically *during* the gap between valuations. Even over a one or two-year term, the actual value of the business may be far higher, or lower, than the value agreed to in the buy-sell agreement. This could have a severe impact in the case of an involuntary departure (such as death) if the price in the buy-sell agreement is below market price. Moreover, the mere existence of a variance between market and agreement prices might: (i) prompt an owner to accelerate his or her departure to take advantage of an artificially high price in the agreement; (ii) cause an owner to delay a voluntary departure in the case of an artifically low price; (iii) influence other owners to force the departure of an owner when the price is artificially low.

A sample valuation by agreement provision follows:

Valuation by Agreement

The initial purchase price for each partnership interest is set forth following this paragraph (the "Initial Price"). The Initial Price shall remain unchanged unless the partners agree to a revaluation, in writing, in accordance with the terms of this section:

Interest of Jane Doe:	$_____
Interest of John James:	$_____

[. . . .]

Periodic Revaluations: The Initial Price shall be subject to periodic revaluations by agreement of the partners. In the event of a revaluation, the price shall be adjusted (the "Adjusted Price") in accordance with the agreement. Within 60 days after the beginning of each calendar year, the partners shall agree that: (i) there will be no change in the Initial Price or then-current Adjusted Price; or (ii) agree upon a new Adjusted Price. The price may be adjusted only upon the agreement of the partners holding 80% of the partnership interests.

6. Objective Valuation Standards

Well-drafted buy-sell agreements will seek to propose a fair and objective formula for determining the value of the departing owner's interest in the business. The parties can be creative in this regard. Some of the more common formulas are considered below.

a. Book Value

Book value has the allure of a purely objective valuation device. Unfortunately, book value is often a poor indicator of actual market worth of an ownership interest in a business. Consider the following common partnership provision:

Book Value of Partnership Interest

The price of a partner's interest shall be the total of all of the following amounts, calculated as of the end of the last calendar quarter prior to the event triggering the purchase. The amounts shall be determined by the partnership's regularly employed certified public accountant or an unaffiliated and independent certified public accountant.

— The positive balance, if any, in the partner's capital account. If there is a deficit in the capital account, it shall be deducted from any other positive amounts below;
— Plus the amount of any debt owed to the partner by the partnership;
— Plus the partner's share of net profit or loss for the period from the last allocation of profits or losses to partners capital accounts and the date of the end of the calendar quarter (unless already allocated to the partner's capital account)
— Plus any other sums due the partner from the partnership;
— Less any debt(s) owed by the partner to the partnership.

The amount of the partner's capital account shall not include any goodwill or other intangible assets such as trade names, patents, and copyrights or any other intangibles.

Capital accounts are required to be maintained by Treasury Regulation § 1.704-1(b)(iv)[56] and keep track of the partner's equity in the entity, based upon the actual amounts of capital contributed (additions to the capital account) or distributed to

---

[56] Treasury Regulation § 1.704-1(b)(iv) provides that the capital account shall be:

[I]ncreased by (1) the amount of money contributed by him to the partnership, (2) the fair market value of property contributed by him to the partnership (net of liabilities secured by such contributed property that the partnership is considered to assume or take subject to under section 752), and (3) allocations to him of partnership income and gain (or items thereof), . . . ; and is decreased by (4) the amount of money distributed to him by the partnership, (5) the fair market value of property distributed to him by the partnership (net of liabilities secured by such distributed property that such partner is considered to assume or take subject to under section 752), (6) allocations to him of expenditures of the partnership . . . and (7) allocations of partnership loss and deduction . . .

the partner (deductions from the capital account). The capital account is adjusted on a regular basis to reflect allocations of profits (additions) and losses (subtractions) to each of the partners, in accordance with their relative shares of profits and losses. To the extent that there were profits or losses since the last formal adjustment to the capital account, those amounts are added or subtracted. The formula in the sample provision also allows the addition of loans by the partner to the partnership or subtraction of loans by the partnership to the partner. Together these provisions use a book value based solely upon the amount of cash and property that the partner has invested in the partnership.

This type of "book value" ignores any additional value of the entity based on "goodwill" or earning power of the partnership and may *severely* undervalue the partner's interest in the entity. Goodwill is a common accounting term used to identify the fraction of the market value of a business entity that is *not* attributable to its assets and liabilities. It is the value the business might be sold for in excess of a piecemeal sale of its personal and real property. Matters that affect goodwill will include the value of the trademarks and tradenames associated with the company's goods and services, the strength of the company's management team and key employees, the financial history of profits and other intangible factors.

By definition, "book value" excludes goodwill and other indicators of goodwill, such as the value of the company's tradename or trademark. As we will see below, there are other formulas that measure the company's earning power beyond its mere book value. Such formulas indirectly take into account the goodwill value of the company.

There is little doubt that there is often no meaningful relationship between the "book value" and *market value* of an entity. Imagine a partnership with three partners who have started an explosively successful Internet social networking website. They each contributed only $40,000 in cash and property to start up the business and agreed to share equally the profits and losses of the business. After three years, the business has grown rapidly. There is a pending sale of the business to Microsoft for $1 billion, when one of the partners dies, with only $40,000 in his or her capital account and no outstanding loans to or from the business. The other partner's are "obligated" to buy out the interest of the deceased partner using the book value of $40,000. As you can see, the book value might be completely unrelated to the market value of the business.

The book value may also severely *overstate* the value of the partner's interest in the partnership, since it does not take into account the debts of the partnership. Imagine, once again, that three partners started up an Internet social networking website with initial capital contributions of $40,000 each. The partnership borrowed $300,000 from a lender to start up the business and all of the funds have been expended in the initial phase of the business. Since each of the partner's is liable for one-third of the debt of the business, the actual market value each partner's interest in the business is well below zero. Unfortunately, one of the partner's died before the business started to generate income or establish goodwill. If the two surviving partners are obligated to buy out the deceased partner's share based on a book value formula, they will have to pay $40,000 to the estate of the deceased partner notwithstanding the fact that the market value of the deceased partner's share was worthless.

Similar book value formulas could be used for a corporate entity. Consider the following:

> The purchase price per share shall be its book value calculated as of the end of the last calendar quarter prior to the event triggering the purchase. The corporation's book value shall mean the difference between the total assets and the total liabilities of the corporation as determined by the normal practices of the corporation and according to generally accepted accounting principles but shall not include goodwill. The per share book value shall be determined by dividing the book value by the shares outstanding as of the end of the last calendar quarter prior to the event triggering the purchase.

Book value of a corporation is based on the balance sheet account balance — the value of the assets of the corporation minus the liabilities of the corporation. It's important to understand that the corporation's bookkeeping or accounting records do not generally reflect the *market value* of assets and liabilities. The initial book value is usually the acquisition cost (or its actual cash value at the time of acquisition). Assets such as buildings, land and equipment may be further reduced in value on the books of the corporation based on depreciation formulas that may, or may not, accurately reflect the current market value of the assets. If the property was acquired several years in the past, the "book value" will not reflect upward (or downward) changes in the value of the property. This is particularly true when assets such as land or commodities have appreciated in value due to market forces. An office building shown on the corporation's books as worth $100,000 (it's acquisition cost less depreciation), it may actually have a market value of over a million dollars.

With regard to intangibles such as the corporation's goodwill, tradenames and trademarks, the value shown on the books of the corporation may show these amounts as "$0," unless they were *purchased* rather than *created* by the corporation.[57] Either way, the cost reflected on the books may be unrelated to the true value of these intangible assets.

As you can see, book value is a poor method for valuing the actual market worth of a departing owner's interest in a business. Some buy-sell agreements attempt to adjust for the difference between book value and market value by providing for percentage adjustments or adjustments keyed to market indexes. Such adjustments may, by pure chance, result in a value that is closer to true market value but that would be a serendipitous event.

b.   Capitalized Earnings

One objective method of computing the value to be paid for a departing owner's interest is to use capitalized earnings. This type of valuation mechanism is sensible where the business is one with few capital assets, such as most service-based businesses. In asset-rich business ventures, such as real estate, the capitalized earnings approach may also be fair and objective, although there may be alternative valuation procedures that are equally objective and fair.[58] By looking at

---

[57] Intellectual property that has been *purchased* will be listed at the purchase price. For instance, patents purchased by the company will be shown on the books. However, the going concern or goodwill value will not.

[58] See the Asset Valuation discussion below.

the earnings record of the business over a certain period, a capitalized earnings formula can be used to figure the return on investment that an owner can expect to receive.

For example, suppose that the business has net profits of $100,000 in each of the last five years and is expected to continue earning profits at that rate, without much risk of market changes. A buyer who purchased this business for $1 million would expect to receive a 10% return on investment every year. If the investment is low risk, this is far better return on investment than placing the $1 million in certificates of deposit, or government treasury bills, that return only 2–5% interest every year. If most similar businesses in the same industry are returning about 10% profit on capital invested, then an accurate price for ownership of this business would be $1 million. To value the entity, we would use a capitalization formula of "10 x earnings," which produces a value for the entity that will yield a 10% annual return on investment.

If an owner owns 25% of the business, then that ownership interest would be worth about $250,000, which is 25% of the overall capitalized earning value of $1 million. The computation for purchasing the interest of an owner would look something like this:

(5 years' earning × $100,000 per year) / 5 = annual net profit of $100,000

Capitalization multiplier of 10 = Value of business is $1 million

$1 million / 25% ownership interest = Value of the owner's interest of $250,000

Stated more simply, the formula is: Projected Annual Earnings times Capitalization Rate = Price

As the risk associated with the type of business increases, buyers will want a larger return on investment to accommodate the greater risk of ownership they are taking by purchasing interests in a risk-prone company. Rates of return on investment of 20% or above might be common for small businesses in volatile markets or in early phases of operations. If a 20% rate of return is expected, the capitalization multiplier would be 5 (100% / 20%). The value of the *entire* business would only be $500,000 (5 x $100,000 earnings per year). Therefore, an owner's 25% share would only be worth $125,000. The computation would change as follows:

(5 years' earnings × $100,000 per year) / 5 = annual net profit of $100,000

Capitalization multiplier of 5 = Value of business is $500,000

$500,000 / 25% ownership interest = Value of the owner's interest of $125,000

Capitalized earnings formulas can be effective and fair mechanisms for determining value of ownership interests but there are a couple of problems with using this type of formula. First, until the business has an established earnings history, the formula won't be very helpful, so the participants will want to include an alternative formula for valuing ownership interests if a purchase occurs prior to the earnings period (such as 3 or 5 years) chosen for the capitalized earnings formula. Second, it may be difficult to predict a capitalization multiplier. The parties to the buy-sell can look to similar businesses and industries and attempt to come up with a fair multiplier for the capitalization formula. Keep in mind that the higher the multiplier, the more the valuation will be for ownership interests and, conversely, the lower the multiplier, the less the valuation will be. Here's a sample valuation provision:

Capitalized Earnings

The purchase price to be paid for the partner's interest shall be computed as follows:

— The net profits (prior to state and federal income taxes) of the partnership for each of the last five fiscal years shall be added together and divided by five to determine the annual average net profits (the "ANP").
— The ANP shall be multiplied by a factor of eight.
— The resulting amount shall be multiplied by the partner's percentage ownership interest in the profits of the partnership.

c.   Rental Income

Capitalized earnings formulas are not limited to companies with income from the sale of goods or the delivery of services as the sources of average annual income. In the case of a business that consists entirely of commercial real property, the income from leases serves as an excellent source of objective criteria to set a price for the interest of a departing owner. If a twenty story office building is generating a net annual profit of $1 million, then we can use a capitalization multiplier factor to set a value for the business. In a stable marketplace, office building rentals may be a low-risk investment, with investors happily accepting a 10% or 15% return on investment, yielding respective multiplier factors of 10 and 6.66, and producing overall respective values of $10 million and $6,666,666.

Nevertheless, capitalizing the income flow from a real estate business is not necessarily the *best* objective formula for assessing the value of the primary asset. Oftentimes, asset valuation can be done by direct reference to appraisals based on established market conditions, as discussed in the next section.

d.   Asset Valuation

Real estate operation is not the only type of asset-rich business. The value of transportation companies, such as airlines and trucking firms, may be primarily based on the assets they own. The same is often true of commodities companies such as grain wholesalers and oil companies. It may also be true for manufacturing businesses such as auto or computer manufacturers.[59] For these types of asset-rich companies, there are often ready markets available to determine the value of their assets.

A common example is commercial real estate in urban and suburban locations, where appraisers can easily find recent comparable sales of similar properties, thereby determining exactly what buyer's are willing to pay for the commercial real estate. Although the price will often reflect the capitalized net rentals, other factors may influence, positively or negatively, the amount that buyers in that region are willing to pay for that type of property. Therefore, a market-based

---

[59] A manufacturing business will have tangible assets such as real estate, equipment and fixtures. There will also be inventory consisting of unassembled parts and completed items ready for delivery. The total value of these assets may be quite high, even when earnings have been low.

analysis by appraisers based on asset-by-asset valuation can be fair and objective.[60] This is particularly true when the business has not yet begun to generate annual income in a reliable and predictable manner — or is operating at a loss. Despite the lack of an earning history, or a negative earnings history, the value of an asset-rich business may still be quite high. Of course, the aggregate value of all of the assets must be reduced by any liabilities owed by the company to accurately compute the value of the company based on asset valuation. Consider the following valuation formula for a company that operates a manufacturing business:

Value Based on Asset Appraisal

> The appraisers shall value real estate, including improvements and fixtures, at fair market value based upon common practices for appraising real estate in the market where the property is located. Machinery and equipment shall be valued at the lower of replacement cost or fair market value, whichever is lower. Completed inventory shall be valued at the lower of cost of completion or market value. Unassembled goods shall be valued at cost, using the normal and ordinary cost accounting methods used by the company in preparing its financial statements. Accounts receivable shall be valued at face value, reduced for uncollectible amounts based upon the history and age of the accounts. Notes payable, accounts payable and other non-contingent liabilities shall be deducted in the amount stated. A reserve for reasonably foreseeable contingent liabilities shall also be deducted.

Other assets might be important to include in the list of property to be valued, depending on the company. Real estate and tangible goods, such as equipment and inventory, are the tip of the iceberg.[61] Other assets might include cash and cash equivalents (notes and checks), patents, trade secrets, customer lists, contracts, accounts receivable, etc.

e.   Combinations of Valuation Formulas

Depending on the form of the wealth and earnings of the business enterprise, there may be combinations of some of the above formulas. For instance, a business with *both* large asset and proven annual profits might employ a buy-out valuation formula that combines both: (i) an asset valuation formula; and (ii) a capitalization formula. Or, a business with lots of investment capital, as well as proven annual profits might employ a combination of book value and capitalization formulas.

7.   Conclusion — Valuation Formulas

The negotiation of the valuation formula for buying the ownership interest of a departing owner is an essential part of planning a buy-sell agreement. Without some objective mechanism for determining a fair price at the time of the buyout,

---

[60] Note that using appraisers to value hard *assets* is quite different than using appraisers to value the *business*. Valuing the business may be done by any of the methods being discussed in this chapter. Appraisers can often be relied upon to value assets such as real estate, commodities, equipment, inventory and similar property.

[61] The Uniform Commercial Code includes some examples of the many types of personal property that might be included in the valuation: goods (including consumer goods, inventory, farm products and equipment), fixtures, accounts, instruments, chattel paper and general intangibles. *See* U.C.C. § 9-105.

the buy-sell agreement will be of limited use. Despite the central importance of the valuation formula, many drafters default to a hazy, unclear formula that often transfers the task of determining the price to arbitrators or appraisers but without objective guidance as to how these third-parties are supposed to evaluate the worth of the interest being purchased. In the absence of objective formulas of some kind, the task of valuing the interest can become extremely expensive, time-consuming and possibly unfair.

The time to negotiate the formula for determining the price of a departing owner's interest is at the *formation* or *joinder* stage, when the parties can make their objectives clear and assure that they agree on a fair formula before investing large sums of money and commitments of time. The negotiations will be impacted by many considerations. Some owners will own larger percentages than others. The interest of some owners may be large enough that a buyout is not realistic and might, instead, cause a liquidation of the company. To help the other owners survive the departure of a large-interest holder, it's essential that realistic financing be arranged for the buyout. Some owners may be older or closer to retirement and will want favorable terms for exiting the business in the forseeable future and may have special estate tax considerations. Others may perceive their involvement as much greater in terms of time. Still others will be employed by he company and, in the event of the termination of their employment, might want to be able to dispose of their interests quickly and for the greatest possible amounts — while the other owners will want exactly the opposite in the event of a termination of employment.

If the parties have a rough time agreeing on a formula, it's the job of the lawyers to act as problem solvers and negotiation experts. They must assist the parties in identifying objectives, accommodating needs of other parties and reaching an accord that can be written into the buy-sell agreement without leaving the eventual valuation to some future agreement or protracted adversarial proceeding.

F.   FINANCING THE PURCHASE

An important factor influencing the drafting of the buy-sell agreement will be the mechanism for financing the purchase of a departing owner's interest. In a closely held business, the departure of an owner may leave the remaining owners with the obligation of buying out the interest or the option to do so if they want to continue the business and are unwilling to allow the departing owner to sell or transfer his/her ownership interest to a new owner. Planning for a way to finance the buyout is essential to the effectiveness of any buy-sell agreement.

1.   Introduction to Cross-Purchase vs. Entity Purchase Agreements

The method for financing the purchase will vary depending on the form of the entity and whether the buyout is a cross-purchase agreement or a purchase by the entity. In a cross-purchase agreement, each of the owners is obligated (or in some cases, given the option) to buy a proportional share of the departing owners interest. Cross-purchase agreements can become complex and difficult to structure depending on the number of owners and the willingness and financial ability of each of the non-departing owners to fund the purchase. Imagine the difficulties that arise when there are ten owners of a partnership, each with a ten-percent interest. One of the owners dies, triggering a mandatory buyout and the value of his/her interest is $225,000. This means each of the nine surviving owners must pay $25,000 within the time period required in the buy-sell agreement. What happens if two of the surviving owners cannot comply? Must the other seven owners now purchase the entire $225,000 interest, costing each of them $32,142? If so, will the relative percentage ownership interests of the surviving partners be adjusted to account for the greater capital contributions of the seven owners who laid out the money for the purchase of the departing owner's share? As you can see, cross-purchase agreements can become complex to draft and difficult to implement. One solution to the problem is to assure that there is an adequate plan for financing the purchase (such as life insurance policies discussed below), to assure that all non-departing owners can fulfill their obligations to buy their proportional shares.

In an entity purchase, the business *entity* agrees to purchase the interest of the departing owner. In a corporate setting, the corporation has the obligation or option to redeem the shares of a stockholder upon the triggering event and the redeemed shares become treasury stock. The impact of a stock redemption is the same as a cross-purchase, since the proportional ownership interests of the non-departing owners' interests are increased by the same proportion in either case.[62] An entity purchase agreement tends to be simpler to structure and execute, as well as easier to finance, particularly if: (i) the entity is a corporation; and/or (ii) the number of owners is high.

For an example of a provision that grants an option to purchase first to the business entity, and then a cross purchase option to the individual owners, see Section E.1. of this chapter. Reread those provisions now.

Below is an example of a *mandatory* obligation to buyout the interest of an owner who has died. The provisions have been drafted from the perspective of a corporate entity:

Purchase Upon Death of a Stockholder

Subject to the exceptions below, within 90 days after the death of a stockholder, the officer(s) of his or her estate shall sell, and the Corporation shall purchase, the decedent's shares at the price and on the terms provided in this Buy-Sell Agreement. In the event that the appointment of an executor or administrator is delayed beyond the 90 day period, or there are procedural probate requirements that prevent completion of the sale within the 90 day period, the sale shall be completed as soon as is reasonably possible following the death of the stockholder.

During the period following the stockholder's death and until the purchase is completed, the voting rights the deceased stockholder shall be suspended.

---

[62] For example, suppose there are five owners, each holding 20% of the stock of a corporation. In a cross-purchase agreement, each of the four non-departing owners would buy one-fourth of the departing owner's interest, leaving each of the four remaining owners with 25% of the ownership interests. On the other hand, in a stock redemption agreement, the departing owner's shares would be purchased by the corporation, leaving 100% of the outstanding shares in the hands of the four remaining owners — each holding 25% of the ownership interests in the corporation.

In the event that the corporation is legally restricted from making the purchase,[63] or lacks sufficient funds to make the purchase, then the President or Secretary of the corporation shall immediately notify the remaining stockholders. Within 60 days of receiving the notice, the remaining shareholders shall purchase that portion of the decedent's shares that the corporation is unable to purchase due to legal restrictions or insufficient funds. Each of the remaining stockholders shall provide sufficient funds to purchase the deceased stockholder's shares in proportions determined by the ratio that the number of shares owned by each remaining stockholder bears to the total number of shares owned by all the remaining stockholders (the "Proportional Shares").

In the event that a remaining stockholder fails to provide the required funds within the 60 day period (the "Defaulting Stockholder"), then the other remaining stockholders shall be obligated to provide proportional additional funds to cover the amounts that the Defaulting Stockholder fails to contribute. The percentage additional amount shall be determined by dividing the total shares all of the remaining, non-defaulting members by each members shares. The non-defaulting stockholders shall have a lien on the shares of the Defaulting Stockholder (in the same proportion as the additional contribution of non-defaulting stockholders).

There is a possibility of severe financial consequences if there is an obligation to purchase the shares of a departing owner. If, in the above example, the corporation cannot repurchase the shares of the deceased owner, what would the outcome be if the shares are worth $500,000 and there are ten remaining owners? What if four or five of those owners simply don't have the $50,000 required to purchase their proportion of the shares — or are unwilling to make such a large additional investment in the corporation? It is quite likely that, under such circumstances, the death of the stockholder will lead to a dissolution of the corporation. It is essential to the success of any buyout scheme that, somehow, the parties have pre-planned for the financing of any *obligatory* buyout as well as to the realistic success of any *optional* buyout.

A common form of financing a buyout triggered by death, or disability, is to pay for life insurance, and/or disability insurance, policies covering the parties to the buy-sell agreement. We will discuss this and other forms of financing the buyout starting at Section F.2. later in this chapter. Prior to looking at some of the common forms of financing a buyout, read the two cases that follow and respond to the questions and comments following each case.

---

[63] There are often statutory restrictions on the payment of dividends or distributions to stockholders. See the discussion in Chapter 6, Section C on dividend distributions. If the corporation lacks the balance sheet equity or cash flow sufficient to meet dividend distribution statutes, the purchase of the deceased shares of stock will have to be by cross-purchase agreement.

LUBIN MEYER, P.C. v. LUBIN
Massachusetts Supreme Judicial Court
693 N.E.2d 136 (1998)

LYNCH, J.

This appeal involves a stock redemption agreement between the plaintiff professional corporation Lubin & Meyer, P.C. (corporation), and its three principal stockholders, Donald M. Lubin, Philip J. Crowe, Jr., and Andrew C. Meyer. When Donald N. Lubin (Lubin) died, a dispute concerning the rights under the agreement arose among the corporation, its two remaining stockholders, and the defendant, Nancy N. Lubin, administratrix of the estate of Donald M. Lubin (estate).[64] The corporation sought a declaratory judgment in the Superior Court

---

[64] [3] The "Stock Purchase Agreement," dated August 26, 1988, provided the following:

"AGREEMENT . . . by and between Lubin & Meyer, P.C., a professional corporation organized under the laws of the Commonwealth of Massachusetts (hereinafter called the "Corporation") and Donald M. Lubin, Philip J. Crowe, Jr. and Andrew C. Meyer, Jr. (hereinafter each called the "Stockholder" or "Stockholders" collectively).

"WHEREAS, the Corporation has issued outstanding shares of its common capital stock standing in the names of the Stockholders; and

"WHEREAS, the parties believe that it is in the best interests of the Corporation and the Stockholders to make provision for the future disposition of the shares of common capital stock of the Corporation owned by each Stockholder upon the death of a Stockholder (such shares being hereinafter called "Stock").

"NOW, THEREFORE, in consideration of the mutual [covenants] and agreements herein contained and for other good and valuable consideration, the parties hereto hereby covenant and agree as follows:

"1. Purchase Price

"The corporation presently owns and will continue to own life insurance insuring the lives of each of the three Stockholders. It is agreed between and among the three Stockholders that if one of the Stockholders is to die, that the purchase price for any and all interest that Stockholder has in the corporation by way of shares and any and other interest including that of decedents, heirs and assigns, shall be satisfied by the payment of the death benefit paid pursuant to said life insurance, which death benefit shall be maintained as a minimum of Two Million Dollars for each Stockholder unless otherwise agreed by Stockholders.

"2. Modification

"No change or modification of this Agreement shall be valid unless made in writing and signed by each of the parties hereto.

"3. Binding Effect

"This Agreement shall be binding upon and shall inure to the benefit of the successors, assigns, personal representatives, heirs and legatees of the respective parties hereto.

"4. Integration

"This agreement constitutes the entire agreement of the parties in relation to the subject matter hereof and there are no promises, representations, conditions, provisions or terms related to the subject hereof other than those set forth in this Agreement. This Agreement supersedes all previous understandings, agreements, and representations between the parties regarding the subject matter hereof.

"5. Applicable Law

"This Agreement is drawn to be effective and shall be construed in accordance with the law of the Commonwealth of Massachusetts.

"IN WITNESS WHEREOF, the corporation has caused this Agreement to be signed by its duly authorized officer and its corporate seal to be affixed hereto, and the Stockholders have hereunto set their hands and seals, all as of [August 26, 1988].

"LUBIN AND MEYER, A PROFESSIONAL CORPORATION

"By: /s/ Philip J. Crowe, Jr., "President

"/s/ Donald M. Lubin

and the estate, in turn, counterclaimed against the corporation and added the remaining stockholders as third-party defendants. A trial was held before a Superior Court judge sitting without a jury and the corporation and third-party defendants appealed from the judgment. The estate filed a cross appeal. We granted the application of the corporation and third-party defendants for direct appellate review.

The corporation and the surviving shareholders assert that the agreement was intended to operate as a liquidation and final release of any future claims by Lubin's estate. The estate argues that the agreement only provided for the amount to be paid for the redemption of Lubin's shares. The estate also asserts the following claims: (I) breach of the stock purchase agreement; (II) breach of an employment agreement; (III) quantum meruit for services rendered by Lubin; (IV) breach of fiduciary duty; and (V) breach of contract.

The judge ruled that the agreement extinguished all claims of Lubin's estate on payment by the corporation to the estate of two million dollars. With respect to the estate's claims, the judge ruled the corporation violated the stock purchase agreement (count I) because it failed to deliver the insurance proceeds until nearly one year after Lubin's death.[65] The judge further ruled that, because of the corporation's breach, the estate retained rights as a shareholder and awarded damages on count IV in the amount of one-third of the dividends earned while the estate remained a stockholder.[66] In addition, the judge awarded interest on the insurance proceeds for the period that they remained unpaid to the estate.

1. We briefly summarize the relevant facts found by the judge. The corporation was formed in 1988 as a professional corporation engaged in the practice of law in Massachusetts. The corporation had previously operated as a general partnership specializing in personal injury litigation. The partnership had been created in 1974 by Lubin and Meyer, who maintained at all times an informal, oral agreement to share equally the net income generated from the firm.[67] When Crowe later joined the partnership in 1981, Lubin, Meyer, and Crowe agreed to share profits in three equal shares.[68] There had never been a written partnership agreement.[69] For the most part the corporation maintained the informal equal income sharing

---

"/s/ Philip J. Crowe, Jr.

"/s/ Andrew C. Meyer, Jr."

[65] [4] After the corporation determined that the issues in the case would not be resolved until after June, 1991, over one year after Lubin's death, it tendered the proceeds to the estate on June 18, 1991, before the judgment entered in this case.

[66] [5] After ruling that the corporation was entitled to declaratory judgment on its interpretation of the agreement, the judge dismissed the estate's claims based on quantum meruit (count III) and breach of an employment contract (count II). The judge also dismissed the estate's claim of breach of contract (count V) based on alleged statements by Meyer to Lubin's spouse. The estate has not sought appellate review of this determination.

[67] [6] The partners agreed orally that distributions would be made when both agreed that the corporation's available funds exceeded foreseeable expenses.

[68] [7] The partners decided to share equally with Crowe all profits attributable to cases opened by the partnership *after* January 15, 1981, the date Crowe joined the partnership. The partners agreed that profits generated from cases opened before that date would continue to be distributed equally between Lubin and Meyer.

[69] [8] In addition to the partners' equal-sharing arrangement, the partners maintained other informal agreements to distribute profits among various salaried employees from time to time.

arrangement established while it had been a partnership.[70]

Before the partners incorporated the law firm, the partnership acquired "key man" life insurance policies on Lubin, Meyer, and Crowe in 1982. After incorporation, the corporation replaced the partnership as the owner and designated beneficiary of the policies and deducted the premiums as a business expense.

In 1988, the corporation and Meyer, Crowe, and Lubin entered in the stock purchase agreement.[71] The following provision is central to the resolution of the question whether payment of the insurance proceeds constituted a complete satisfaction of all claims held by the estate:

> "It is agreed between and among the three Stockholders that if one of the Stockholders is to die, that the purchase price for *any and all interest that Stockholder has in the corporation by way of shares and any other interest including that of descendants, heirs and assigns, shall be satisfied by the payment of the death benefit paid pursuant to said life insurance*, which death benefit shall be maintained as a minimum of Two Million Dollars for each Stockholder unless otherwise agreed by Stockholders" (emphasis added).

The judge concluded that the agreement obligated the corporation to pay to the deceased shareholder's estate the insurance proceeds, and that such payment would serve as total compensation to the estate for its entire interest in the corporation.

2. *The estate's appeal.* The estate argues that the judge's ruling that the agreement barred all claims was error. The judge made comprehensive written findings of fact, which will not be set aside unless clearly erroneous. See Mass. R. Civ. P. 52 (a), 365 Mass. 816 (1974).

The judge found that the agreement was intended to resolve fairly and finally all interests of Lubin's estate. Specifically, the judge credited Meyer's testimony that the inclusion of the clause "and any other interest" was added further to clarify the parties' mutual intention that the agreement operate as a final release. The judge, having heard the testimony, was in the best position to evaluate the witnesses' credibility . . . The judge was correct that, on receipt of the insurance proceeds, the agreement barred the estate from asserting any additional claims against the corporation.[72]

The estate asserts that the agreement was nothing more than a redemption agreement, designating a purchase price for the deceased shareholder's stock,

---

[70] [9] The judge specifically found, "Over the years Lubin and Meyer and later Lubin, Meyer and Crowe acted as though they were partners in the operation of a law firm and that their total compensation would consist of a sharing in the distribution of the net profits of that partnership." The judge continued, "There was no separate understanding or agreement regarding any additional rights that they might have as officers, directors, stockholders or employees of the Corporation or the law firm."

[71] [10] General Laws c. 156A, § 12 (a), provides in pertinent part: "It shall be provided in the articles of organization or by-laws of a professional corporation, or in agreement binding upon all of its shareholders, that the corporation shall redeem all of the shares of a shareholder upon the occurrence of . . . such shareholder['s] death . . . "

[72] [11] Based on our conclusion that the judge's ruling that the agreement precluded any additional claim by the estate was not erroneous, we must similarly uphold his dismissal of the estate's claims based on quantum meruit (count III) and breach of employment agreement (count II).

pursuant to G. L. c.156A, 12(2(a), because G. L. c. 156A, § 12(d), preserves its claims against the corporation based on other theories of recovery. We do not agree.

The estate emphasizes that G. L. c. 156A, § 12(d), provides: "Nothing herein shall affect the obligations of a professional corporation to a shareholder whose interest in the corporation is terminated hereunder *with respect to compensation, benefits or other matters accrued prior to his termination or disqualification*" (emphasis supplied). Section 12(d) says nothing about precluding a redemption agreement from operating additionally as a release, while providing a value for redemption of a deceased shareholder's stock.

3. *The corporation's appeals.* The corporation challenges the judge's conclusion that the agreement required it to pay the insurance proceeds to the estate as soon as it was reasonably able to do so after Lubin's death. Therefore, it asserts, judgment for the estate on its breach of contract claim was error. The corporation argues that (1) pursuant to G. L. c. 156A, § 12(b), it was allowed to tender payment any time within a twelve-month period, and (2) it was relieved of paying the estate, or otherwise excused from immediate payment, because the estate had an obligation to execute a release before its right to the proceeds arose.

The agreement did not state when the estate was required to tender the deceased shareholder's stock, nor did it specify when after a shareholder's death the corporation was required to pay the insurance proceeds to the estate. However, the articles of organization required that the redemption take place as soon as reasonably possible. The judge properly concluded that, in the absence of a designated time for performance specified in the agreement, the corporation was obligated to tender payment to the estate as soon as was reasonably possible. See *Mishara Constr. Co. v. Transit — Mixed Concrete Corp.*, 365 Mass. 122, 125, 310 N.E.2d 363 (1974) (inferring reasonable time for performance absent specific agreement).

The corporation was not entitled to withhold the insurance proceeds for nearly one year after Lubin's death on the basis of the language in G. L. c. 156A, § 12(b), requiring that redemption take place within twelve months of the shareholder's death. According to § 12(b), the corporation was required to redeem the stock "within twelve months after [the shareholder's death], *unless a shorter time is specified in the articles of organization, by-laws or said shareholder agreement*" (emphasis added). Thus, the twelve-month period was not applicable here where, as noted above, the articles of organization of the corporation required redemption "as soon as reasonably possible."[73]

The corporation received the proceeds of the policy on July 28, 1990.[74] Once received, the corporation had a duty to tender payment to the estate as soon as it was reasonably able to do so. The judge found that the corporation was "reasonably able" to make payment on August 10, 1990. We see no basis to quarrel with the judge's conclusion that fourteen days after the corporation received the proceeds on July 28, 1990, was a reasonable time within which payment should have been made.

---

[73] [12] The articles stated that, in the event that a shareholder becomes ineligible or deceased, "the administrator or other legal representative . . . shall dispose of [the deceased's] shares as soon as reasonably possible."

[74] [13] Neither the parties' briefs nor the record contains a precise date on which the corporation filed the insurance claim.

We reject, as did the judge, the corporation's argument that the agreement imposed on the estate, as a precondition for payment, an obligation to execute a release or to assure the corporation that it would do so prior to receiving payment of the insurance proceeds.

The agreement contained no requirement that the estate execute a release as a precondition to its right to receive the insurance proceeds. The corporation was not entitled to withhold its performance for one year on the basis of the fact that the estate challenged, in good faith, the effect of the agreement.

4. *Remedy for breach.* Although the judge was correct in ruling the corporation in breach of the agreement, his conclusion that the consequence of this action placed the estate in the "position of a stockholder until June, 1991," was error. General Laws c.156A, § 12(e), does not confer such status on a deceased shareholder's estate. That § 12(e) allows a shareholder's estate to vote the decedent's shares does not compel the conclusion that, during that temporary period, the estate is entitled to receive dividends. Such a conclusion would be contrary to the provisions of S.J.C. Rule 3:06(2)(a), as appearing in 382 Mass. 765 (1981), which requires all shareholders of such a corporation to be licensed to practice law in the Commonwealth.

Furthermore, for the estate to receive dividends from the corporation would contravene the prohibition against fee sharing among nonlawyers. See S.J.C. Rule 3:07, Canon 3, as appearing in 382 Mass. 777 (1981) (Code of Professional Responsibility incorporating the Canons of Ethics and Disciplinary Rules). Moreover, the requirement under S.J.C. Rule 3:06 (2)(b), as appearing in 382 Mass. 766 (1981), that the estate turn over the deceased's stockholder's shares *as soon as is reasonably possible*, underscores the impropriety of the estate retaining participatory shareholder status. The estate had only a limited ability to vote the shares until redemption under G. L. c.156A, § 12(e), and a right to receive value for the stock under G. L. c. 156A, § 12(c).

5. *Conclusion.* Because the estate did not receive the payment due within a reasonable time, it is entitled to interest calculated from the date on which the corporation was reasonably able to make payment. We affirm the declaratory judgment in behalf of the corporation and the judgment against the corporation for breach of the stock purchase agreement with interest from August 10, 1990, to June 18, 1991. We vacate the judgment against the corporation for breach of fiduciary duty (count IV) and the case is remanded to the Superior Court for the entry of an order dismissing that claim.

So ordered.

NOTES AND QUESTIONS

1. The buy-sell agreement is a contract, pure and simple. Its terms control: (i) the relationship of the shareholders to each other and the corporation regarding the procedures and price to be paid; and (ii) the rights of the departing owner (or his/her estate) until the purchase is actually completed.

2. Financing. Note the ease of funding the buyout in the *Lubin Meyer, P.C.* case. By taking out life insurance policies on each of the "key" owners, there was no problem funding the $2 million buyout of the deceased stockholder. In addition, the valuation problem was solved by fixing the price for the shares of the deceased owner was fixed by the agreement as the amount of the insurance proceeds.

3. Breach of agreement. The remaining stockholder, Phillip Crowe, delayed paying the $2 million life insurance benefits to the estate of the Donald Lubin for one year. The court held that, in the absence of a provision in the buy-sell agreement governing the timing of the payment, the remaining stockholder, Phillip Crowe, had a "reasonable" amount of time to make the payment and complete the buyout. The court held that a one-year delay was a breach of the buy-sell agreement and required Crowe to pay $2 million *plus interest*. How would you have drafted the agreement to avoid litigation over the issue of timing of the payout? Would you include specific time frames? Would you include penalty clauses for an unjustified delay?

4. Release of other claims. A buy-sell agreement is simply a contractual mechanism to buy the *ownership* interest of a departing owner. That owner may have rights against the business entity for recovery of loans made to the entity, breach of employment agreements, sexual harassment or many other claims that are unrelated to the value of the ownership interest and the obligation or option of the entity, or other owners, to buy out the departing owner's interest. In *Lubin Meyer, P.C.*, the administratrix of the estate wanted to pursue claims the deceased had against the corporation, in addition to recovering the $2 million for the shares of the deceased.

How should the buy-sell agreement have been drafted to cover such matters as: (i) loans owed to the deceased; (ii) claims of the deceased based on breach of employment contract; and (iii) claims of the deceased as a minority shareholder for breach of fiduciary duty by the majority shareholder?

It would seem that, in the absence of some provision in the buy-sell agreement limiting these other claims against the corporation, they would be unaffected by the buyout agreement. If so, why did the court in *Lubin Meyer, P.C.* hold that these other claims were released? The court relied on the following language, and testimony at the trial about its meaning, to conclude that the buy-sell agreement *did* include a general release by the estate of all claims against the corporation:

> It is agreed between and among the three Stockholders that if one of the Stockholders is to die, that the purchase price for *any and all interest that Stockholder has in the corporation by way of shares and any other interest including that of descendants, heirs and assigns, shall be satisfied by the payment of the death benefit paid pursuant to said life insurance*, which death benefit shall be maintained as a minimum of Two Million Dollars for each Stockholder unless otherwise agreed by Stockholders.

Was the court correct? As a prudent drafter who *did* intend a release of *all* claims upon payment of the $2 million, how would you re-draft this provision?

5. Completion of the buyout. What is the status of the estate of Donald Lubin as a stockholder during the period following his death until the actual completion of the buyout? Should Donald Lubin's estate be entitled to his share of distributions prior to the completion of the buyout. Normally, prior to completion of the buyout, the estate is the stockholder and is entitled to all of the rights that Donald Lubin had, including rights to distributions, examination of books and records, and voting. The court reached the opposite conclusion in *Lubin Meyer, P.C.* based on the fact that the corporation was a *professional* corporation and applicable state statutes and regulations prohibited participation by non-lawyers. Would the outcome be different in a regular business corporation? See the next case.

Keep in mind that the buy-sell agreement is a contract and can alter the rights of the estate as a stockholder pending the completion of the buyout.

STEPHENSON v. DREVER
California Supreme Court
947 P.2d 1301 (1997)

Mosk, J.

In this case a "buy-sell agreement" gives a closely held corporation the right and obligation to repurchase the shares of a minority shareholder-employee on termination of his employment, but is silent as to his shareholder rights during the post-employment period necessary to determine the value of his shares pursuant to the agreement. The narrow issue before us is whether the agreement nevertheless implies on its face an intention by the parties to deny the minority shareholder those rights during that period. As will appear, we conclude that it does not, and therefore reverse the judgment of the Court of Appeal affirming the judgment of dismissal in this action brought by the minority shareholder. Because the Court of Appeal did not reach an alternate ground on which the judgment was challenged, we will direct the court to address that ground.

FACTS[75]

1. * * * Plaintiff Allen W. Stephenson was employed by Drever Partners, Inc. (hereafter Drever Partners), a closely held corporation, in 1980, and became its chief financial officer in 1983. On December 15, 1990, a contract entitled "Stock Purchase Agreement" (hereafter the contract) was signed by Drever Partners, by its majority shareholder, Maxwell Bruce Drever (hereafter Drever), and by plaintiff. The contract recited that in recognition of the value of plaintiff's services and as an incentive for him to remain in its employ, Drever Partners agreed to sell plaintiff 500 shares of its common stock at par value. It provided that "In the event of the termination of Stephenson's employment for any reason whatsoever, including his retirement or death, then, on or before ninety (90) days after the date of such termination, Drever Partners shall have the right and obligation to repurchase all of the Shares" that it agreed to sell to plaintiff. It further provided that after September 15, 1991, the repurchase price of the shares would be "the fair market value thereof"; that if the parties could not agree on the fair market value, it would be fixed by an independent appraiser; and if the parties could not agree on the selection of such an appraiser, each party would appoint one appraiser and those two would appoint a third whose appraisal would be binding.

Drever Partners sold the 500 shares to plaintiff pursuant to the contract. The shares amounted to 11 percent of the outstanding common stock of the corporation; Drever owned the remaining 89 percent himself.

On May 16, 1994, Drever and plaintiff entered into an agreement (hereafter the 1994 agreement) providing that plaintiff's employment by Drever Partners would terminate as of July 1, 1994, and that for purposes of the stock repurchase

---

[75] [1] Plaintiff failed to pursue his creditor's remedies in the trial court, and the Court of Appeal rejected his belated request for leave to amend his complaint. Plaintiff has not challenged this aspect of the Court of Appeal's decision. [Footnote has been relocated.—Eds.]

provision of the contract plaintiff's shares would be valued as of May 1, 1994.[76]

The parties were unable to agree on the fair market value of plaintiff's shares, and a dispute over the appraisal process ensued. Because of that dispute the fair market value of plaintiff's shares has not yet been determined, Drever Partners has not yet repurchased those shares, and plaintiff remains their record owner.

On May 8, 1995, plaintiff filed the present action against Drever and two other persons (hereafter collectively defendants) in their capacities as officers and directors of Drever Partners. The complaint alleged that Drever controls Drever Partners by virtue of his position as chairman of its board of directors and his ownership of the 89 percent of its stock that plaintiff does not own. The complaint further alleged that since May 16, 1994, defendants caused Drever Partners to pay excessive compensation to Drever, used corporate assets of Drever Partners to satisfy personal judgments against Drever, and manipulated corporate accounts to falsely reflect a paydown of certain debts owed by Drever to the corporation; that the effect of the foregoing payments was to make undeclared distributions to Drever's majority shares without any corresponding distributions to plaintiff's minority shares; and that the purposes of such payments were to render Drever Partners unable to make distributions to plaintiff's minority shares, to undermine the fair market value of those shares, and to impair the corporation's power to repurchase those shares pursuant to the contract.

The complaint also alleged that Drever used his control of Drever Partners to deny plaintiff information on the financial condition of the corporation, to avoid holding the required annual shareholders' meeting, and to manipulate elections to the board of directors and reduce the size of the board so as to ensure that plaintiff did not become a director and thereby obtain the financial information he had been denied.

On the basis of these allegations the complaint charged that Drever breached the fiduciary duty that he owed as a director and as controlling shareholder to treat plaintiff, as the minority shareholder, fairly and in good faith and in a manner that benefits all shareholders proportionately. The complaint prayed for compensatory and punitive damages.

Defendants demurred on two principal grounds. First, they contended that they owed no fiduciary duty to plaintiff at any of the times alleged in the complaint because his status as a shareholder assertedly terminated as of May 1, 1994, the valuation date of the shares he had agreed to resell to Drever Partners upon leaving its employ.

---

[76] [2] Although the parties refer frequently to the 1994 agreement in their briefs, they have declined to allow us — or any court involved in this litigation — to see it. Their reason for this odd behavior may be inferred from a declaration that Drever filed in the related action cited above (fn. 1, *ante*); he there says that the 1994 agreement contains a "confidentiality provision" which, he explains in another pleading, prohibits its disclosure without prior written consent of the other party. Neither party, apparently, has consented to allow the courts to see the agreement. Instead, Drever asks the courts to take judicial notice of a declaration that plaintiff filed in the related action (in opposition to a motion for preliminary injunction) in which plaintiff either paraphrases or quotes — although for a wholly different purpose — selected provisions assertedly found in the 1994 agreement. This circuitous method of informing us of the facts of the case does not inspire confidence; the best evidence of a writing, of course, is the writing itself. (See Evid. Code, § 1500.) At oral argument counsel for Drever belatedly offered to move to augment the record on appeal to include the 1994 agreement. Because that agreement is not dispositive of any issue under the view we take of this case, we need not order such augmentation.

Second, defendants contended the action was derivative in nature and (1) plaintiff lacked standing to sue derivatively because his shareholder status terminated on May 1, 1994, (2) even if plaintiff retained his shareholder status after that date he failed to allege the conditions precedent to a derivative action, and (3) plaintiff failed to join the corporation, which is an indispensable party in a derivative action, as a defendant.

The trial court sustained the demurrer on the first ground, without leave to amend. Relying on a group of out-of-state cases that we discuss below, the court ruled as a matter of law that on the face of the contract defendants' fiduciary duty to plaintiff by reason of his status as a shareholder ceased as of May 1, 1994, and after that date plaintiff's rights were contractual only and his relationship to Drever Partners was as a creditor, not as a shareholder.

The court also recited: "As a further reason to sustain the demurrer, the Court finds Defendants' arguments relating to the issue of derivative action quite persuasive." Like the Court of Appeal, we construe this recital as a formal ruling sustaining the demurrer on defendants' second ground as well.

The court then dismissed the complaint with prejudice.

The Court of Appeal affirmed the judgment of dismissal on the first ground of the demurrer, and for that reason declared it unnecessary to reach the second ground. We granted review.

(1) The contract in issue is of the type commonly known as a buy-sell agreement.[77] A buy-sell agreement is a contract by which the stockholders of a closely held corporation . . . seek to maintain control over the ownership and management of their business by restricting the transfer of its shares. The typical buy-sell agreement provides for the mandatory or optional repurchase of a stockholder's shares by the corporation or by the other stockholders upon the occurrence of a certain event; the most common of the events that can trigger the repurchase are the stockholder's death or, if he is also an employee, his retirement or the voluntary or involuntary termination of his employment . . . The typical buy-sell agreement also specifies the method to be used to determine the repurchase price of the shares, selecting from such options as an agreed price with periodic revisions, a formula price based on book value or capitalization of earnings, or third party appraisal or arbitration . . . Although the agreement often serves multiple purposes, its principal objective is to permit the original owners of the corporation to retain control over the identity of their business associates; a secondary purpose is to protect the investment of the departing (or the estate of the departed) shareholder by facilitating the valuation and sale of an interest that might otherwise have no ready market . . .

Despite its specialized nature and purposes a buy-sell agreement remains a contract, and is therefore subject to the rules governing the validity, interpretation, and enforcement of contracts laid down by statute and case law. When we inquire what kind of contract a buy-sell agreement is, we see that in essence it is an executory contract to buy and sell personal property — specifically, shares of corporate stock owned by an employee — if and when a particular event occurs, i.e., the termination of his employment.

---

[77] [3] Such a contract is also known by such names as a buy-back agreement, a buy-out agreement, a stock repurchase agreement, a stock redemption agreement, or a first option agreement.

Plaintiff invokes the general rule that "Upon an executory agreement to buy and sell personal property, title does not pass to the buyer until delivery is made to him or is due to him and is offered to be made, unless there is something in the contract specifying or implying a different intention . . . ." (*Gilfallan v. Gilfallan* (1914) 168 Cal. 23, 31, 141 P. 623.) The cited case applied this rule to an executory contract for the sale of stock, concluding that until title thus passes the legal owner of the shares remains entitled to the dividends paid on the shares. (*Ibid.*; accord, *Richards v. Pacific S. W. Discount Corp.* (1941) 44 Cal. App. 2d 551, 555, 112 P.2d 698.)

Defendants seek to distinguish *Gilfallan v. Gilfallan, supra*, 168 Cal. 23, and *Richards v. Pacific S. W. Discount Corp., supra*, 44 Cal. App. 2d 551, on the ground they involved disputes between buyers and sellers of stock (*Gilfallan*) or of a corporation (*Richards*) over the rights to dividends, rather than a corporation's mandatory stock repurchase triggered by termination of the shareholder's employment; in the latter context, defendants argue, the question is not who has the rights to dividends but whether such rights exist at all. But this is a distinction without a difference. Even in the context of a corporation's repurchase of its stock from an employee, the question of when title passes from the employee to the corporation must still be answered, and that question is governed by the general rule of *Gilfallan*.[78]

Plaintiff has not delivered his shares to Drever Partners because their fair market value has not been determined and tendered to him. Under the foregoing general rule, therefore, legal title to plaintiff's shares has not passed to Drever Partners and plaintiff remains a shareholder of record of the corporation with all the rights appurtenant to that status, "unless there is something in the contract specifying or implying a different intention . . . ." (*Gilfallan v. Gilfallan, supra*, 168 Cal. at p. 31.) As the Court of Appeal correctly observed, "the parties have the power to agree that a shareholder loses his status as a shareholder upon some event other than actual transfer of shares to another." But the court went on to hold that in all mandatory repurchase agreements "the parties agree to end the shareholder's participation in the corporation upon the occurrence of the event triggering the right and obligation to repurchase," and hence that under the contract in the case at bar plaintiff lost his status as a shareholder immediately upon termination of his employment by Drever Partners. Plaintiff contends the contract before us does not so provide, either expressly or impliedly. The contention is meritorious.

First, the contract does not *expressly* provide that when plaintiff's employment terminates he immediately loses his status as a shareholder and is, in the Court of Appeal's words, "entitled to the value of his shares, but no longer . . . entitled to participation in the corporation." Defendants correctly concede in their brief that the contract "is silent on the issue of shareholder rights during consummation of the repurchase . . . ."[79]

---

[78] [4] Defendants also contended at oral argument that we deal here with an executed rather than an executory contract. We disagree. Although the contract is executed with respect to plaintiff's original purchase of his shares from Drever Partners, it remains executory with respect to Drever Partners' repurchase of those shares from plaintiff because the price of that repurchase has not yet been agreed upon or determined pursuant to the contract.

[79] [5] To avoid misunderstanding we emphasize that although the contract is silent on this matter it could have expressly provided that plaintiff's rights and status as a shareholder terminate immediately

(3) Defendants contend the contract nevertheless *implies* on its face an intention by the parties to cut off plaintiff's shareholder rights immediately upon termination of his employment. The contention is unpersuasive for several reasons.

First, the claimed implication is inconsistent with express provisions of the contract. To begin with, the contract is *not* silent on the legal consequence of the termination of plaintiff's employment: Rather than leaving that consequence to inference, the contract declares that in such event Drever Partners "shall have the right and obligation to repurchase all of the Shares" held by plaintiff. The fact that the contract expressly so provides tends to negate any inference that the parties also intended another consequence to flow from the same event. *Expressio unius est exclusio alterius.* (*Grupe Development Co. v. Superior Court* (1993) 4 Cal. 4th 911, 921, 16 Cal. Rptr. 2d 226, 844 P.2d 545.)

More important, the same provision of the contract plainly contemplates some delay in consummating the repurchase of plaintiff's shares after the termination of his employment. Thus the contract first provides that the repurchase may take place at any time "on or before ninety (90) days after the date" of plaintiff's termination. Second, the contract provides that if the parties cannot agree on the fair market value of the shares, that value will be established not by the immediate application of a predetermined formula (e.g., book value) but by a *process* — i.e., appraisal — that involves several steps and hence will necessarily take time to complete. On this subject the contract provides that (1) the parties must find and appoint an appraiser agreeable to both; (2) that appraiser must make his own appraisal of the fair market value of the shares;[80] (3) if the parties cannot agree on an appraiser, each must appoint an appraiser of his own choosing; (4) the two appraisers thus appointed must find and appoint a third appraiser agreeable to both; and (5) the third appraiser must then make his own appraisal of the fair market value of the shares (see fn. 6, *ante*). The fact that the contract expressly provides for this process tends to negate any inference that the parties intended that the repurchase of the shares be consummated — and a fortiori that plaintiff's status as a shareholder be terminated — immediately upon plaintiff's termination as an employee.

Next, the claimed implication must be viewed in light of the statutory scheme in which the contract operates. This is not a case of a contract for the sale of ordinary commercial goods; in such a case recognition of an implied termination provision in the contract affects only rights created by the contract itself, i.e., rights of private

upon termination of his employment. There is no statutory bar to such a provision. Compare the case of shareholders who compel the corporation to repurchase their shares at fair market value because they dissent to a proposed reorganization or merger. (Corp. Code, § 1300 et seq.) Although any cash dividends paid after the merger is approved but before the shares are paid for will be credited against their eventual repurchase price (*id.*, § 1307), "holders of dissenting shares continue to have all the rights and privileges incident to their shares, until the fair market value of their shares is agreed upon or determined." (*Id.*, § 1308.) A provision one way or the other on this question in a buy-sell agreement would advance the purposes of the agreement.

[80] [6] Such an appraisal is itself a time-consuming process: "Before using any particular valuation method, an appraiser is required to make a study of the economics of the particular industry of which the company is a part, the company's competitive market position, the economic environment of the market served, the experience and capability of management and the assembled work force, the company's financial position and earnings record, and other pertinent factors." . . . Each of the most common valuation methods — i.e., asset valuation, earning power, or market comparisons . . . — requires careful analysis of the data. And the ensuing report will ordinarily contain the appraiser's premises, methods, facts, reasoning, and conclusions . . .

origin. . . . Here the contract is for the sale of shares of corporate stock, and recognition of the implied termination provision urged by defendants would affect plaintiff's statutory rights as a shareholder under California law.[81]

A shareholder has a wide range of statutory rights to participate in corporate affairs. For example, annual shareholders' meetings must be held for the election of directors and the transaction of other corporate business, and each shareholder is entitled to attend in person or by proxy. (See § 600, subds. (a) and (b).) Any shareholder may obtain an order compelling the corporation to hold the annual meeting if it fails to do so, and the shares represented at that meeting ipso facto constitute a quorum. (Id., subd. (c).)[82] A special meeting of the shareholders may be called at any time by the holders of 10 percent of the shares entitled to vote at the meeting. (§ 600, subd. (d).) At shareholders' meetings each shareholder is entitled to offer proposals to be voted on and to vote on proposals presented by management, and to nominate directors and to vote on the slate of directors nominated by management. Unless otherwise provided in the articles of incorporation, on each matter submitted to a vote every shareholder of record is entitled to cast one vote for each share owned. (§ 700, subd. (a).) Upon notice given by any one shareholder, all shareholders are entitled to engage in cumulative voting for all nominated candidates for directors. (§ 708, subds. (a) and (b).) A shareholder has the right to vote by proxy (§ 705), or to join with other shareholders in a voting trust (§ 706, subd. (b)) or, in the case of a statutory "close corporation," in a voting agreement (id., subd. (a)).

A shareholder also has valuable property rights. Foremost among these is the right to receive dividends. (See § 166.) When a dividend is lawfully declared by the board of directors it vests in the owner of record of the shares and creates a debt in his favor against the corporation . . . The shareholder's vested right to such dividend "cannot be defeated by later revocation of the dividend without his consent." (Meyers v. El Tejon Oil & Refining Co. (1946) 29 Cal. 2d 184, 188, 174 P.2d 1.) In addition, unless otherwise provided in the articles of incorporation or in the stock certificate, a shareholder has the right to transfer or hypothecate his shares. (See § 204, subd. (b).) And only a shareholder, of course, has the right to bring derivative suits on behalf of the corporation. (§ 800.)

Finally, the foregoing rights are protected by a number of further rights to receive information concerning the corporation. Thus a shareholder has the right to written notice of any shareholders' meeting, stating its time and place and the business to be transacted (§ 601), and to be informed upon request of the results of any shareholders' vote taken at the meeting (§ 1509). A shareholder is entitled to receive an annual report or an equivalent financial statement. (§ 1501, subds. (a) and (c).) For any purpose reasonably related to his interests as a shareholder, a shareholder has the right to inspect and copy all shareholder lists and records (§ 1600, subd. (c)), the accounting books and records of the corporation and its subsidiaries (§ 1601, subd. (a)), and the minutes of meetings of the board of directors and its committees (ibid.). These statutory rights, moreover, cannot be limited by the articles or bylaws. (§ 1600, subd. (d), 1601, subd. (b).)

---

[81] [7] All statutory references hereafter are to the Corporations Code unless otherwise specified.

[82] [8] This quorum provision is "a powerful tool in forcing management to call the regular annual meeting." (Counseling Cal. Corporations (Cont.Ed.Bar 1990) § 3.22, p. 202.)

Defendants do not contend the foregoing statutory provisions are inapplicable to closely held corporations. Yet the implied contractual provision urged by defendants would have the effect of stripping plaintiff of all these statutory shareholder's rights even though he remains the legal owner of record of shares representing 11 percent of Drever Partners' equity. A shareholder without a shareholder's rights is at best an anomaly, and at worst a shadowy figure in corporate limbo who would be voiceless in the conduct of the business of which he is part owner and largely defenseless against neglect or overreaching by management. We will not interpret the contract to produce this result without a compelling reason to draw the inference proposed by defendants. Defendants fail to provide such a reason. We are not persuaded that their proposed inference is, as they urge, a "plain meaning" of the contract.

Plaintiff, moreover, is not just a shareholder of Drever Partners; he is its sole *minority* shareholder. For this reason defendants' claimed implication must also be viewed in light of the case law governing the relationship between directors and majority shareholders on the one hand and minority shareholders on the other.

*   *   *

Again defendants do not contend the foregoing rule of fiduciary duty of majority shareholders is inapplicable to closely held corporations.[83] Yet the implied contractual provision urged by defendants would have the effect of relieving them of this fiduciary duty even though plaintiff remains the owner of the minority shares. During the period in which the parties are attempting to determine the fair market value of plaintiff's shares, the claimed implied provision would allow defendants to disregard this fiduciary duty and "use their power to control corporate activities to benefit themselves alone or in a manner detrimental to the minority." (*Jones, supra,* 1 Cal. 3d at p. 108.) As noted in our statement of facts, the complaint alleges instances of just such conduct by defendants. *Jones* forcefully affirmed "the strong public interest in assuring that corporate officers, directors, majority shareholders and others are faithful to their fiduciary obligations to minority shareholders." (*Steinberg v. Amplica, Inc.* (1986) 42 Cal. 3d 1198, 1210 [233 Cal. Rptr. 249, 729 P.2d 683].) We will not interpret the contract to defeat that strong public interest without a compelling reason to draw the inference urged by defendants. Once more, they fail to provide such a reason.

*   *   *

[A]n employee-shareholder *may* bargain away his right to remain a shareholder after termination of his employment, and with it the benefits of the fiduciary duty owed by majority to minority shareholders.

But that proposition is not in question in this case; here the issue is whether the particular buy-sell agreement before us should be interpreted to imply an intention of the parties to terminate the plaintiff's status as a shareholder immediately upon the termination of his employment and before his shares are valued and their purchase price tendered . . .

*   *   *

---

83 [9] *Jones* was itself a case involving a closely held corporation. (See 1 Cal. 3d at p. 102 & fn. 3.)

Defendants next contend that the rule adopted by the Court of Appeal is supported by "public policy considerations." The point is without merit.

First, defendants cite no authority for the proposition that "public policy considerations" can trump the rule of substantive law that a shareholder under an executory contract to sell his stock is entitled to the benefits of ownership until delivery is made or tendered to the buyer, "unless there is something in the contract specifying or implying a different intention . . . ." (*Gilfallan v. Gilfallan, supra,* 168 Cal. 23, 31.) As we have seen, defendants show no such "different intention" on the face of the contract before us.

Second, defendants present no compelling "public policy considerations" in any event. They stress the beneficent purposes of buy-sell agreements in general, but plaintiff does not deny the purposes of such agreements or their value. Defendants also refer to the agreement assertedly entered into by the parties on May 16, 1994; they characterize this agreement as a "settlement" and invoke the broad policy in favor of settlements, citing *Neary v. Regents of University of California* (1992) 3 Cal. 4th 273, 277 [10 Cal. Rptr. 2d 859, 834 P.2d 119]. But even if this document were before us and even if it amounted to a true "settlement" within the meaning of the cited policy, the rule we apply herein would not be inconsistent with that policy. On the contrary, the rule we apply supports that policy by giving corporations and their majority shareholders incentive to expedite the process of repurchasing the shares of former employees pursuant to such settlements.

That same incentive also counterbalances a policy proposed by the Court of Appeal, i.e., that to hold as we do "would encourage employee-shareholders to initiate frivolous litigation in order to delay the repurchase of their shares." It could equally well be argued that to hold as the Court of Appeal did would encourage corporations and their majority shareholders to delay consummating the repurchase of the shares of a former employee after terminating his employment, thereby extending the period during which the latter remains, as we have said, a shareholder without a shareholder's rights, voiceless in the conduct of the business and defenseless against neglect or overreaching by management. Indeed, during this same period management could impair or defeat even the former employee's basic contractual right to be *paid* for his canceled shares, e.g., by making excess distributions to the majority shareholders.[84]

Finally, defendants contend that if plaintiff were allowed to claim, as an element of damages in this action, his proportionate share of distributions from corporate profits earned after his separation from employment, it would result in an impermissible "double recovery" because those earnings will also be included in the calculation of the fair market value of his shares under the buy-sell agreement. Defendants rely on the general rule that "the current market value of a business as a going concern includes the discounted present value of its estimated flow of future earnings." (*California Shoppers, Inc. v. Royal Globe Ins.* (1985) 175 Cal. App. 3d 1, 61 [221 Cal. Rptr. 171].)

The contention is unpersuasive. The quoted rule is appropriate when the valuation is wholly prospective, in which case all the earnings accruing after the

---

[84] [10] A corporation's repurchase of its stock is deemed a distribution (§ 166), and a corporation is barred from making any distribution unless it can meet the retained earnings or net worth tests imposed by law (§ 500). If a corporation becomes unable to meet those tests for any reason, a buy-sell agreement to which it is a party ipso facto becomes unenforceable. (1 Ballantine, *supra,* § 63.03, p. 4–76.)

valuation date will be "future" earnings that can only be "estimated." But when, as in the case at bar, the valuation will be partly retrospective because it will refer back to an earlier valuation date (here, May 1, 1994), earnings that accrued in the interim will be actual earnings that will not need to be "estimated." To the extent that any such actual earnings are distributed to the shareholder (or, as here, recovered by the shareholder as damages) before the appraiser determines the fair market value of the shares, it is true that double recovery could result from a mechanical application of the foregoing general rule. But it is also true that the appraiser can avoid such double recovery by the simple expedient of crediting any actual distributions received against the fair market value otherwise determined. Plaintiff asserts that such a credit is standard appraisal practice in valuing shares under a buy-sell agreement, and defendants do not contend the contrary.[85]

We conclude that the trial court erred in sustaining the demurrer on the first ground, and hence the judgment of the Court of Appeal upholding that ruling should be reversed.

In the Court of Appeal plaintiff also challenged the second ground on which the trial court sustained the demurrer — i.e., that the action was derivative in nature — and defendants likewise defended the ruling on that ground. The Court of Appeal did not resolve that contention, and we will now direct it to do so.[86]

The judgment of the Court of Appeal is reversed and that court is directed to resolve the issues relating to the second ground on which the trial court sustained the demurrer herein.

GEORGE, C. J., KENNARD, J., BAXTER, J., WERDEGAR, J., and CHIN, J., concurred. BROWN, J., Dissenting.

*   *   *

NOTES AND QUESTIONS

1. Valuation. Note the difficulty the parties faced regarding a valuation of their shares. The contract stated that the parties were to exercise good faith in agreeing to a fair market value and, if that failed, they would refer the matter to an appraiser. They failed to indicate any formula for the appraiser to follow in reaching a conclusion about the value of the shares. What will happen following the decision of the California Supreme Court?

2. Stockholder Rights. The plaintiff, Allen Stephenson, owned 11% of the shares of the corporation, while the defendant, Maxwell Drever, owned the

---

[85] [11] Again it is instructive to compare the case of shareholders who compel the corporation to repurchase their shares at fair market value because they dissent to a proposed reorganization or merger. (§ 1300 et seq.) As noted above (fn. 5, *ante*), any dividends distributed to the dissenting shares after approval of the reorganization but before payment for the shares by the corporation "shall be credited against the total amount to be paid by the corporation therefor." (§ 1307.)

[86] [12] If the Court of Appeal affirms the judgment of dismissal on the second ground of the demurrer, the case will be at an end; if it does not, the judgment will be reversed and the case will proceed. If the case reaches the trial stage, and if extrinsic evidence is introduced on the issue of the meaning of the contract with regard to plaintiff's shareholder rights during the repurchase process, nothing we say here is meant to limit the power of the trial court to determine the credibility and weight of that evidence and to interpret the contract in its light. (See *Parsons v. Bristol Development Co.* (1965) 62 Cal. 2d 861, 865–866 [44 Cal. Rptr. 767, 402 P.2d 839].)

remaining 89%. Stephenson sought more than just payment for his shares in the corporation. His complaint included causes of action for non-payment of dividends and breach of the fiduciary duty that Drever owed as a director and controlling shareholder to treat plaintiff, as a minority shareholder, fairly, in good faith and in a manner that benefits all shareholders proportionately. Stephenson sought both compensatory and punitive damages based on the theory that he remained a shareholder, notwithstanding that the termination of his employment. He asserted that, until *completion* of the repurchase by the corporation, or a cross-purchase by Drever, Stephenson retained all the rights of a shareholder. The California Supreme Court agreed with Stephenson. Why?

What rights does the shareholder retain? The court lists many of the rights of stockholders under California law, including:

— Participation in person or proxy in the annual shareholders' meetings for the election of directors and the transaction of other corporate business,
— The calling of a special meeting of shareholders by the holders of 10 percent of the shares entitled to vote at the meeting.
— The right to receive dividends.
— The right to bring derivative suits on behalf of the corporation.
— The right to receive information concerning the corporation and inspect the books and records of the corporation.

Was it in the best interests of Drever to act quickly to accomplish the buyout of Stephenson's shares? Considering that the buyout was triggered by the termination of Stephenson's employment, what should Drever have insisted upon including in the buy-sell agreement? Pay close attention to the court's statements in footnote 5:

> To avoid misunderstanding we emphasize that although the contract is silent on this matter it could have expressly provided that plaintiff's rights and status as a shareholder terminate immediately upon termination of his employment . . .

2.   Financing Schemes

No buyout can be successful unless the entity (in the case of an entity buyout) or the non-departing owners (in the case of a cross-purchase buyout) have the funds necessary to accomplish the purchase. When the trigger occurs, the company and its owners may not be in a position to lay out the funds to purchase the interest of the departing owner. Even if there is cash in the company sufficient to fund the buyout, that cash may be needed for operating needs or expansion of the business. For the business to continue, there has to be a pre-planned source for funding the buyout.

There are several common schemes for financing a buyout: (i) life and disability insurance; (ii) installment payment plans; or (iii) establishing a fund for this purpose and using operating profits to build up a substantial reserve. All three have advantages and disadvantages — but it will be very hard to fund a buyout without choosing one of these types of financing schemes.

a.   Life Insurance Plans

When the trigger for a buyout is death, the existence of a life insurance policy can simplify the buyout process and assure the continuation of the business without economic disruption. As we saw in *Lubin Meyer, P.C.* the life insurance policy can be used to set the value of the deceased owner's interest in the company, without having to resort to some external measurements. The $2 million life insurance proceeds adequately covered (and probably exceeded) the market value of the deceased's interest in the law firm and solved three common problems. First, the value of the deceased's ownership interest was fixed at $2 million, thereby avoiding a potentially lengthy and expensive battle over the value of the deceased's interest. Second, the insurance policy provided the necessary financial resources to execute the buyout without the corporation, or its remaining stockholder, having to borrow money or dig deep into his pocket to fund the buyout. Third, it fulfilled the estate objectives of the deceased stockholder by assuring his successors that his interest in the law firm would be highly valued and there would be resources available to the firm to fund the buyout.

If the parties to a buy-sell elect to use life insurance as a financing mechanism, they will have to choose between varying types of life insurance policies. The primary choice is between "term" and "whole life" insurance. Term insurance has a fixed term, such as ten years, and must be renewed at the end of each term. Premiums for term life insurance are subject to increases over time as the policy is renewed at the end of the term. Term insurance is also subject to non-renewal (except at exorbitant premium costs) as the insured ages. Whole life insurance is continuous for the life of the insured and premiums are fixed at the outset of the policy, based on actuarial tables and the health of the insured. The cost of term insurance may be less than whole life in the early years if the owners are young and healthy but, in later years, or as owners become unhealthy, term insurance may become extremely expensive to renew, while the cost of whole life insurance is predictable. Whole life insurance also has the added benefit of building up "loan value" over time. The policy's loan value is a liquid asset that can make borrowing easier. There are many different options for life insurance products and the owners will have to consult with insurance specialists to obtain the right one for their objectives.

Of course, life insurance is not free and the cost of carrying the insurance must be considered and weighed against the cost of other forms of financing, such as borrowing. The cost of life insurance policies may be quite reasonable if the owners are relatively young and healthy — and there aren't too many of them. As the number of owners rises, the cost of maintaining policies on many owners can become prohibitively expensive. Imagine the difficulty of acquiring and maintaining life insurance policies on twenty or thirty owners.

The costs of maintaining the policies in amounts sufficient to fund the buyout, will be affected by the insurability of each of the owners. Factors such as age and health will result in different costs for insuring different owners. For instance, in *Lubin Meyer, P.C.* it appears that all three of the insured owners were approximately the same age and of equivalent health when the $2 million policies were purchased and the premiums were established. What if two of the owners were young and healthy, while the third owner (whom we will call Andy) was in his late 50s and had heart problems? There would be a *dramatic* difference in the cost of the policies, with Andy's policy costing many times more. Two questions arise under such circumstances. First, does it make sense to purchase a life insurance policy for Andy if the cost is driven to extremely high rates by his age and health? Second, is it fair to the other owners for the company to pay premiums for all three policies, or should there be some adjustment in distribution of profits to allocate the higher costs of one policy to the owner who's age and health status caused the higher premiums?

Some owners may, simply, be uninsurable due to their age or health status. If that's true, then some alternative funding mechanism will have to be planned for that owner, such as a reserve fund or installment plan, discussed below.

It's important to note that the policies might become valuable property of the business entity as the loan-value of the policies increases. Creditors of the entity may resort to seizure of the loan value to satisfy their claims against the entity. The increase in the value of the life insurance policies will increase the overall value of the entity, increasing the valuation of the departing owner's interest. While this might increase the objective value of the departing owner's interest, it will not usually result in an increase in the cost of purchasing that interest since the *price* of the buyout is usually fixed at the amount of the policy payout, rather than the actual value of the departing owner's share. However, if the value is going to be determined by resorting to book value or asset value of the entity, the presence of all of the policies will increase the overall value of the entity, increasing the cost of the buyout.

Serious questions will arise about the *ownership* of the policies and related tax issues, especially in corporate settings. If the owner of the policies is a C corporation, the corporation usually pays the premiums and is often named as the beneficiary of the policies. The premiums are *not* deductible to the corporation if the entity is the direct, or indirect, beneficiary of the policy, which would be true if the policy proceeds are going to be used to fund the buyout of the insured's ownership interest.[87] Generally, the *proceeds* of the life insurance policy are not taxable to the corporation.[88]

Cross-purchase life insurance policies have the benefit of removing the value of the policies from the entity, thereby eliminating the ability of creditors of the *entity* to seize the policy loan values and also removing the policy values from valuation of the ownership interests in the entity. On the other hand, the ownership and loan value of the policies is now subject to the creditors of each of the individual owners, creating a very similar problem.

Financing buyouts through insurance policies becomes less feasible in cross-purchase agreements, especially as the number of owners increases. Each of the owners will obtain a life insurance policy for each of the other owner's. Each owner will pay the premiums on each of the policies for each of the other owners, so that funds will be available to fund the buyout of each of the other parties to the buy-sell agreement in the event of death. This can become expensive and complex. If there are ten owners of the entity, each would have to acquire policies on the other nine owners, resulting in *ninety* policies being issued. Realistically, there needs to

---

[87] Treas. Reg. § 1.264-1.

[88] There are some very circumstances when the insurance proceeds might be taxed to the corporation. *See* IRC § 101(a)(1), (j). It may make sense under those circumstances to make the proceeds of the policies payable directly to the estate — so it is important to consult with a tax specialist before setting up the policies to make them payable to the corporation.

be a better solution if policies are going to be used to fund cross purchase buyouts. Perhaps an effective solution is to form a trust which will own and pay for the policies, with each of the owners contributing to the trust his or her proportional share of the premiums. In our example of ten owners, this would reduce the number of policies from ninety to ten — a far more manageable and less expensive alternative. In the event of death, the proceeds can be made payable to the trustee, who then pays out the proceeds to the deceased's estate, receiving in return a transfer of the ownership interest which can be divided among the remaining owners in accordance with the parameters of the cross-purchase agreement.

In addition, if the trust is properly setup, the trust assets (the insurance policies and their loan values) will be held free of any claims of creditors of *either* the entity or the owners, assuring that the policies will be available to fund death-triggered buyouts.

There are some potential tax advantages to setting up the policies as part of a cross-purchase agreement. The insurance proceeds received by the surviving owners are not subject to income taxation. The new shares or interests they are purchasing will be entitled to a tax basis equal to the purchase price. The stepped-up basis will reduce future income taxes if the surviving owners sell their interests in the future. Compare this to the result in an C corporation stock redemption, where the remaining stockholders do not get the benefit of a step-up in basis when the corporation purchases the deceased's shares. Each of the remaining stockholders retains his or her original basis in the corporation. Therefore, if a remaining stockholder sells his or her stock before death, there will be significantly higher capital gains. This will occur because the corporation's value will remain unchanged but each remaining stockholder will own a larger proportion of the company, causing their shares to escalate in value.[89] There could be a dramatic difference in the ultimate capital gains attributable to a subsequent sale of the shares of remaining owners. For instance, suppose there are four owners of a corporation worth $4 million with each stockholder owning 25% of the shares and having a basis of $1 million. As a result of either a corporate redemption, or a cross-purchase agreement, each of the remaining three stockholders will have a 33 1/3% interest in the corporation worth $1.33 million. Compare the results below regarding the basis of each of the remaining stockholders:

1. Cross-Purchase Agreement:

    a. Value of shares following buyout: $1.33 million
    b. Basis of shares following buyout: $1.33 million

2. Corporate Redemption:

    a. Value of shares following buyout: $1.33 million
    b. Basis of shares following buyout: $1 million

If the shares of a remaining stockholder are sold in the future for $1.33 million, there will be *no* capital gains to be taxed in the case of a cross-purchase agreement but $333,333 of capital gains in the case of a corporate buyout.

---

[89] This is generally true if the buyout is a cross-purchase agreement and the policies are owned by the remaining owners since no corporate assets will be used to fund the buyout. If the corporate entity owns the policies, there may be some decrease in the value of the corporation's assets since the policies themselves have value. For purposes of this example, we are assuming that either: (i) the buyout is funded through a cross-purchase agreement; or (ii) if the corporation owns the policy, its value when compared to overall corporate assets is minor.

The tax consequences to the decedent's *estate* also bear consideration. In a cross-purchase plan, the proceeds from the life insurance are not included in the deceased shareholder's estate since the deceased is not the owner of the policy. The same is true of entity buyouts where the entity owns the life insurance policies and receives the proceeds. However, in a corporate setting, if a stockholder with more than a 50% interest (directly or indirectly) is deemed to control a corporation, under IRC § 267 the stockholder is considered to have an ownership interest in the life insurance policy for tax purposes. This can cause the proceeds of the policy to be included in the decedent's estate. In the event that the decedent has a large enough estate to be subject to estate taxes, this could result in the payment of significant taxes on the life insurance proceeds in the form of estate taxes.

However, in the absence of a corporate stockholder with a controlling interest, the tax outcome to the estate is the same regardless of whether the owner of the policies is the entity or the other stockholders. The life insurance proceeds will not be included in the estate and the testate or intestate successors of the deceased owner's shares will have a tax basis equal to the fair market value of the stock at the date of death, avoiding any income tax capital gains as a result of the redemption of the shares by the corporation or a purchase of the shares through a cross-purchase agreement.

b.   Installment Payments

The most obvious, and common, mechanism for financing a buyout is an agreement to pay the departing owner the purchase price, with interest, over a period of time that allows the non-departing owners to finance the purchase from future operations of the business. For instance, if the valuation of the departing owner's share is $300,000, a buy-sell agreement might provide that the entity (or other owners in the case of a cross-purchase agreement) will pay this amount over a five year period with six percent interest. That would result in monthly loan payments of principal and interest in the amount of $5,799.84.[90] Over a ten year period at the same interest rate, the payments of principal and interest would be only $3,330.62. When drafting the buy-sell agreement, parties who expect to have a long-term ownership in the entity will almost always seek to stretch out the length of the installment payment plan to reduce the amount of the monthly payments. Undoubtedly, owners who are forsee an early departure will apply negotiating pressure for a shorter period, resulting in larger monthly payments.

The departing owner is at substantial risk under this arrangement. If the owner transfers his or her ownership interest to the entity or other owners in exchange for the *promise* of future payments, what happens if the business subsequently suffers a financial reversal or dissolution? Or, what if the entity (or non-departing owners) simply fail to honor the installment plan and miss many of the payments? What recourse does the departing owner have? After all, the departed owner has transferred his or her interests and no longer retains control over the affairs of the entity.

Even a business that is valuable at the time the owner departs may fall apart at some time in the future. An obvious example is a lawyer, Linda Lever, who leaves a 25-person law firm that was a successful limited liability partnership or a

---

[90] The amount owed would be amortized over the period of the loan. See Section B, Chapter 5 for a discussion of loan amortization.

professional corporation. At the time of Lever's departure, her ownership interest was valued at $1 million. Under the terms of the buy-sell agreement, the law firm *entity* repurchased Linda's ownership interest and signed a promissory note, obligating the entity to make monthly payments of $11,102.05 over a ten year period.[91] Linda was given a promissory note to evidence the debt and she transferred her ownership interest back to the firm. Linda did not obtain any collateral to secure payment of the debt. Less than one year later, in an unexpected move, some key partners in the firm resigned and opened their own boutique law firm, causing a cascade of lawyer departures and a devaluation of the firm. There is insufficient income to pay the normal operating expenses of the firm and, consequently, the firm stopped making the installment payments. What are Linda's remedies? She is a mere unsecured creditor who must compete with all of the other creditors of the firm for payment. If the firm has few assets and/or large amounts of debt, there is little likelihood that Linda will be paid. Even if there are assets available to pay some portion of the debt to Linda, the cost of collecting will be high. She will have to commence a law suit, obtain a judgment, find unencumbered assets of the entity and establish liens in that property, *before* any of the other creditors seize the assets to satisfy their claims.

Whether the entity is a law firm, a software business, a manufacturing company or a real estate venture, the issues are the same. The departing owner who accepts an installment payment plan needs some type of collateral to enhance the chances that departing owner will actually be paid the amounts promised to him or her.

The most obvious collateral is the ownership interest itself. A self-protective departing owner might have the right under the buy-sell agreement to retain (or give his estate the right to retain) the ownership interest as collateral for performance of the installment plan. In such an arrangement the parties will most likely agree that the retention of the ownership interest is solely for the purposes of creating a security interest, without any rights to distributions, control, voting or any other rights, unless a default occurs.[92] Once a default occurs, at least the departed owner (or his/her estate) has the right to step back into the position of an owner and exercise rights to vote, obtain information and manage the entity. The value of the ownership interest at the time (which may be diminished or enhanced, depending on the circumstances) is restored to the departed owner (or his/her estate).

There are many other types of collateral. If the entity has unencumbered assets with sufficient equity,[93] a security interest in the assets can be created to assure that the departing owner has a priority right to use those assets in the event of a default in the installment plan.

---

[91] The amount necessary to pay the principal of $1,000,000 plus 6% interest over the ten year term of the installment plan.

[92] An alternative is to allow the repurchase of the ownership interest but execute the necessary documents to create a security interest in the ownership interest that entitles the departing owner (or his/her estate) to a full reassignment of the ownership interest in the event of a default. Both methods of using the ownership interest as collateral for performance of the installment plan create a security interest under Article 9 of the U.C.C. It will be necessary for the departing owner to satisfy the requirements for attaching and perfecting the security interest.

[93] A security interest in an asset already encumbered with a prior lien may have little value to the departing owner. If the entity owns a semi-trailer truck worth $200,000 but subject to a valid first lien of $190,000, there is only $10,000 worth of equity available as collateral.

Realistically, there may not be much equity in collateral available to serve as security for performance of the installment plan. Even if there is equity, the entity may need that equity to serve as collateral for secured loans to support expansion plans, obtain operating funds. Some property, such as inventory or equipment, may need to be sold free and clear of liens and won't be available as collateral for performance of the installment buyout plan.

In the absence of equity in property is there some other source of securing payment of the installment plan buyout? Another source of protection is personal *liability* (in the case of a cross-purchase buyout) or personal *guarantees* (in the case of an entity purchase) executed by the non-departing owners. In a cross-purchase buyout, each of the purchasing owners could sign a contract or promissory note for his or her proportional share of the future installment payments. Regardless of the future success of the business entity, each of the non-departing owners will be personally liable for the payments, enhancing the likelihood of payment. The same result can be accomplished in an *entity* buyout, by requiring the execution of guarantees by the non-departing owners, giving rise to personal liability in the event that the entity fails to make the installment plan payments.

Of course, some risk remains for the selling owner, since the financial positions of each of the non-departing owners may change adversely over time. In addition, without collateral, the only way to collect from a defaulting owner (whether based on direct or contractual or guarantor liability) is to pursue unsecured collection procedures, which can be expensive, time consuming and, ultimately, fruitless if the defendant(s) have few or no unencumbered and non-exempt[94] assets.

It makes sense that the non-departing owners agree to guarantee the departing owner that any installment payment plan will be performed. After all, at the time of the departure, the departing owner has a valuable interest that he or she is entitled to be paid *at that time*. This payment is in exchange for allowing the non-departing owners to continue to operate the business, notwithstanding the departure which, in the absence of agreement, might result in liquidation of the company. If the non-departing owners want to reserve the right to spread out the payment over an installment time period, it is reasonable to provide assurances of payment.

Indeed, this is the result reached under some statutory schemes in the absence of express buyout provisions. For instance, in general partnerships, RUPA § 701 provides that a partner who dissociates is entitled to payment *at the time of dissociation* if the business is not dissolved and wound up. If a partner *wrongfully* dissociates,[95] the remaining partners must still buy out the interest of the partner (using the statutory formula for valuation) for cash but have the *option* to buy out

---

[94] The problem of recovering an unsecured debt against an *individual* is compounded by the existence of exemption laws. Even if a guarantor has equity in some assets, exemption laws may place that equity out of the reach of judgment creditors. For instance, in California, $50,000 to $100,000 worth of equity in the personal residence of a debtor is exempt from creditor attachment. The Texas and Florida constitutions provide no limit to the value of the exemption for most types of real property homesteads — *all* of the equity in an individual debtor's residence is exempt. *See* Vernon's Ann. Texas Const. Art. 16, § 51, Fla. Const. Art. X, § 4.

[95] A partner wrongfully dissociates when he or she dissociates in contravention of the partnership agreement if the partnership is for a definite term or a particular undertaking.

the partner using an *delayed or installment* plan. Regarding an installment plan, § 701(h) provides:

> (h) A partner who wrongfully dissociates before the expiration of a definite term or the completion of a particular undertaking is not entitled to payment of any portion of the buyout price until the expiration of the term or completion of the undertaking, unless the partner establishes to the satisfaction of the court that earlier payment will not cause undue hardship to the business of the partnership. A deferred payment must be adequately secured and bear interest.

In a corporation setting, departing stockholders may be able to force a liquidation or buyout in a voluntary or involuntary dissolution. In states such as California, a suit for voluntary dissolution may be brought by 50% or more of the stockholders, or an involuntary dissolution may be commenced by minority stockholders under some circumstances.[96] In either type of dissolution proceeding, voluntary or involuntary, the other stockholders are given the statutory right to buy out the interests of the stockholders moving for dissolution, based on the liquidation of the corporation. California Corporations Code § 2000 states:

> (a) Subject to any contrary provision in the articles, in any suit for involuntary dissolution, or in any proceeding for voluntary dissolution initiated by the vote of shareholders representing only 50 percent of the voting power, the corporation or, if it does not elect to purchase, the holders of 50 percent or more of the voting power of the corporation (the "purchasing parties") may avoid the dissolution of the corporation and the appointment of any receiver by purchasing for cash the shares owned by the plaintiffs or by the shareholders so initiating the proceeding (the "moving parties") at their fair value . . .

> *   *   *

> (d) If the purchasing parties desire to prevent the winding up and dissolution, they shall pay to the moving parties the value of their shares ascertained and decreed within the time specified pursuant to this section . . . On receiving such payment or the tender thereof, the moving parties shall transfer their shares to the purchasing parties. * * *

Note that stockholders wanting to continue operating the corporation must pay the funds soon after the value of the shares of the stockholders seeking dissolution, in cash. There is no provision for an installment plan. This is consistent with the idea that the departing shareholders are entitled to payment *at the time of departure*, and that a proposal to pay in installments will have to be negotiated with the

---

[96] Cal. Corp. Code § 1800 provides:

> (a) A verified complaint for involuntary dissolution of a corporation on any one or more of the grounds specified in subdivision (b) may be filed in the superior court of the proper county by any of the following persons:

> *   *   *

> (2) A shareholder or shareholders who hold shares representing not less than 331/3 percent of [the shares of the corporation]

> (3) Any shareholder if the ground for dissolution is that the period for which the corporation was formed has terminated without extension thereof.

> (4) Any other person expressly authorized to do so in the articles.

departing stockholders who, of course, will demand some type of collateral or guarantee that the obligation to make the installment payments will actually be fulfilled. It is possible that your state, unlike California, may follow MBCA ¶ 14.34(e), which gives courts the discretionary authority to provide that the buyout payments be made in installments.

This concept of protecting the rights of minority shareholders to force a liquidation or buyout has, over the years, morphed into statutory and judicial doctrines in many states that provide "oppressed" minority shareholders with a judicially created buyout remedy:

> Over the years, state legislatures and courts have developed two significant avenues of relief for the "oppressed" close corporation shareholder. First, many state legislatures have amended their corporate dissolution statutes to include "oppression" by the controlling shareholder as a ground for involuntary dissolution of the corporation. Moreover, when oppressive conduct has occurred, actual dissolution is not the only remedy at the court's disposal. Both state statutes and judicial precedents have authorized alternative remedies that are less drastic than dissolution. As the alternative forms of relief have broadened over the years, orders of actual dissolution have become less frequent. *The most prevalent alternative remedy today is a buyout of the oppressed investor's holdings.* Thus, oppression has evolved from a statutory ground for involuntary dissolution to a statutory ground for a wide variety of relief.[97]

The Revised Uniform Limited Liability Company Act (2006) adopts a similar position for LLCs:

§ 701   Events Causing Dissolution

(a)   A limited liability company is dissolved, and its activities must be wound up, upon the occurrence of any of the following:
* * *

(5)   on application by a member, the entry by [appropriate court] of an order dissolving the company on the grounds that the managers or those members in control of the company:

(A)   have acted, are acting, or will act in a manner that is illegal or fraudulent; or

(B)   have acted or are *acting in a manner that is oppressive* and was, is, or will be directly harmful to the applicant. *(emphasis added)*

(b)   In a proceeding brought under subsection (a)(5), *the court may order a remedy other than dissolution. (emphasis added)*

Comment

* * *

Subsection (a)(5) — ULLCA § 801(4)(v) contains a comparable provision, although that provision also gives standing to dissociated members. Even in non-ULLCA states, courts have begun to apply close corporation

---

[97] Douglas K. Moll, *Shareholder Oppression & Dividend Policy in the Close Corporation*, 60 Wash & Lee L. Rev. 841, 851 (2003) (emphasis added).

"oppression" doctrine to LLCs. This provision's reference to "those members in control of the company" implies that such members have a duty to avoid acting oppressively toward fellow members. Subsection (a)(5) is non-waivable. See Section 110(c)(7).

Subsection (b) — In the close corporation context, many courts have reached this position without express statutory authority, most often with regard to court-ordered buyouts of oppressed shareholders. This subsection saves courts and litigants the trouble of re-inventing that wheel in the LLC context. However, unlike, subsection (a)(4) and (5), subsection (b) can be overridden by the operating agreement. Thus, the members may agree to a restrict or eliminate a court's power to craft a lesser remedy, even to the extent of confining the court (and themselves) to the all-or-nothing remedy of dissolution

---

It is clear that when an owner departs and is entitled by agreement, statute or judicial doctrines to payment to prevent liquidation of the company, that payment is expected to be in cash. Keep in mind that, regardless of the departing owners rights to force a liquidation or buyout, the non-departing owners often *want* to buyout the departing owner to maintain continuity and avoid dealing with the departing owner and his/her successors. The common foundation of all buyouts is that, in the absence of some agreement, the departing owner is entitled to cash payment for his or her ownership interest. A negotiated installment plan should assure, through a collateralized security interest or personal guarantees, that the installment plan will be completed. As discussed above, this outcome is codified in cases of general partnerships under RUPA § 701.

c.   Reserve Plans

Another way of funding buyouts is to regularly sink money from operating profits into a reserve fund. This approach to financing requires sufficient cash flow to both operate the business, fund expansion *and* build a reserve that is sufficient to fund any buyouts. This may be difficult to accomplish during the early years of the business and may remain true for mature businesses as well. There is always a need for cash to operate and expand a successful business. On the other hand, if the business is regularly generating sufficient cash to meet the needs of the business and producing regular profits, a sinking fund can be a viable mechanism for funding buyouts, especially when the cause for the buyout is unrelated to death or disability and can't be funded with insurance.

There is one problem that should be addressed if a reserve fund is successfully established for buyouts. The existence of the fund as an asset of the entity will increase the overall value of the company — possibly affecting the valuation of the departing owner's shares. If the valuation mechanism relies to some degree on the book or market value of assets of the company, then a large cash reserve will enhance the value of the company, raising the cost of the buyout. In addition, the cash reserve is subject to creditor attachment in the event the *company* incurs large debts.

d.   Borrowing Money

One additional financing mechanism is to borrow the funds necessary to accomplish the buyout. However, the ability of the company to borrow money may be affected by the operating profitability and available asset equity of the business. To the extent that there *is* borrowing capacity based on operating history and asset equity, the company and its remaining owners may be unwilling or unable to lock up the borrowing capacity of the company by borrowing funds for a buyout. That borrowing capacity may be essential to future operations, expansion of the business, or possible reorganizations of the business. Keep in mind that the loan will have to be repaid with interest, which will reduce future operating profits. In addition, depending on the loan documentation, there may be many events of default that may cause the loan to be accelerated and repayment demanded before the due date of the note, putting the entire business at risk if there are insufficient funds to repay the loan. For instance, the loan documents may contain provisions that allow the lender to declare a default if there are material adverse changes in the financial status of the business, or changes in the ratio of accounts receivable to accounts payable, or reductions in inventory, or further changes in the owners or managers of the business. Some loan documents simply allow the lender to declare a default and demand that the entire loan be repaid if the lender, in good faith, deems itself to be insecure about the ability of the company to repay the loan according to its terms. In other words, borrowing to pay off a buyout obligations creates some serious burdens and risks for the company and its remaining owners.

3.   Summary — Financing The Buyout

We have looked at four mechanisms for funding possible buyouts of departing members: insurance, installment plans, reserve funds and borrowing. It's common that various combinations of all of these types of financing schemes may be used to accomplish the task of raising sufficient funds to fund a buyout. While each type of financing method has benefits, there are negative factors for each of them that must be considered and explained to clients during the process of negotiating the buy-sell agreement.

There is one last source of funding a buyout that is worth discussing. If each of the owners is sufficiently wealthy, or has personal borrowing capacity, then a cross-purchase buyout may be a viable mechanism for funding the buyout. This success of this type of funding method improves as the number of owners increases, thereby decreasing the proportional amount that each owner must shell out to accomplish the buyout. In a company with thirty owners, the obligation to pay a departing owner $300,000 for his or her interest places upon each non-departing owner only a $10,000 burden. Even if there are some of the remaining twenty-nine owners who can't manage to come up with $10,000 in funds, there will be other, wealthier owners who can absorb the non-purchasing owners' obligatory share of the buyout and, consequently, obtain a greater percentage interest in the ownership of the company. If the company is successful and has good prospects for future growth, there should be enough remaining owners who will be willing to take up the proportional shares of other owners who can't afford the $10,000 cost of the buyout.

G. ENTITY-SPECIFIC CONSIDERATIONS

1. Statutory Limitations on Corporate Buyouts

The advantages of an entity buyout, compared to cross-purchase agreements, are the simplicity involved[98] and the use of the entity's funds to fund the purchased. However, at least in the case of *corporations*, there may statutory limits on the ability of the corporation to fund a stock redemption. These restrictions take the form of dividend limitations, stock repurchase limitations and fraudulent conveyancing statutes.

In all corporate structures, the rights of stockholders to be paid from the assets of the corporation are subordinate to the rights of creditors. This makes sense since the corporation is a separate legal entity that must pay its debts before it can distribute profits to its owners whether those payments are in the form of dividends, or a repurchase of the shares of a stockholder. Dividend payment and redemption statutes often limit the ability of corporations to pay dividends or repurchase shares unless there are sufficient assets remaining to assure that *creditors* of the corporation can be paid when due, and that in the event of liquidation, creditors can be fully repaid. For instance, consider the following excerpts from the California Corporations Code:

Chapter 5   Dividends & Reacquisition of Shares

§ 500. Distributions; retained earnings or assets remaining after completion; exemption of broker-dealer licensee meeting certain net capital requirements

Neither a corporation nor any of its subsidiaries shall make any distribution to the corporation's shareholders . . . except as follows:

(a) The distribution may be made if the amount of the retained earnings[99] of the corporation immediately prior thereto equals or exceeds the amount of the proposed distribution.

Generally accepted accounting principles ("GAAP"), are accounting rules used to prepare and report financial statements business and government entities. Under GAAP guidelines, "retained earnings" are the accumulation of earnings over

---

[98] If life insurance is being used to fund the purchase, only one policy needs to be purchased for each stockholder, compared to multiple policies in the case of cross-purchase agreements. The redemption also accomplishes with ease a proportional distribution of the ownership interest of the departing stockholder, since the departing owner's interest is extinguished and the remaining owners increase their ownership interest in direct proportion to their remaining percentage interests.

[99] Cal. Corp. Code § 114 defines "retained earnings" and similar terms as follows:

All references in this division to financial statements, balance sheets, income statements, and statements of cashflows, and all references to assets, liabilities, earnings, retained earnings, and similar accounting items of a corporation mean those financial statements or comparable statements or items prepared or determined in conformity with generally accepted accounting principles then applicable, fairly presenting in conformity with generally accepted accounting principles the matters that they purport to present, subject to any specific accounting treatment required by a particular section of this division . . .

time.[100] This is the amount that remains over time after income from operations has been added and losses subtracted — and further reduced by the payment of any dividend. By requiring that dividend payments be made from retained earnings, the statute is assuring that distributions cannot be made to stockholders from assets unless the company has profits left over from which to declare a dividend.

Alternatively, the California statute allows dividend distributions to stockholders, or stock redemptions, out of assets that are not retained earnings (such as a sale of assets by the corporation) if the remaining assets of the corporation are sufficient to assure that there the creditors of the corporation can be fully paid, even in the case of a subsequent liquidation. Section 500(b) provides:

> (b) The distribution may be made if immediately after giving effect thereto:
>
> (1) The sum of the assets of the corporation (exclusive of goodwill, capitalized research and development expenses and deferred charges) would be at least equal to 1¼ times its liabilities (not including deferred taxes, deferred income and other deferred credits); and
>
> (2) The current assets of the corporation would be at least equal to its current liabilities . . .

Note that § 500(b)(1) requires that balance sheet assets exceed liabilities by at least 25% — and *disallows* the use of certain intangible assets such as goodwill. In other words, the statute requires a liquidation analysis to assure that the corporation is solvent *and* imposes 25% equity cushion if distributions are made from non-retained earnings. The California statute (which is followed in most other states) goes even further and requires under § 500(b)(2) that *current* assets be sufficient to satisfy *current* liabilities as they come due. In other words, the statute requires that even if the liquidation value of the company exceeds assets by 25%, the projected *cash flow* from operations in the future must be sufficient to cover debts that are scheduled to be paid. This point is reinforced in § 501 which applys to any distribution to stockholders, whether made under the retained earnings test or the asset solvency test.

§ 501. Inability to meet liabilities as they mature; prohibition of distribution

Neither a corporation nor any of its subsidiaries shall make any distribution to the corporation's shareholders . . . if the corporation . . . is, or as a result thereof would be, likely to be unable to meet its liabilities (except those whose payment is otherwise adequately provided for) as they mature.

This test is commonly referred to as "equity insolvency." The term refers to whether or not the entity will have sufficient cash flow to pay debts as they come due, regardless of a balance sheet analysis of assets and liabilities.

As discussed in Sections C.1 and C.2 of Chapter 6, some states, such as Delaware, provide a slightly more lenient test if the corporation is proposing to

---

[100] A similar phrase, used synonymously in statutes and cases, is "earned surplus." See the table in Chapter 6, Section C.1.

make a distribution to a stockholder in exchange for shares of stock. Under § 160(a)(1) of the Delaware General Corporations Law, a redemption or purchase of shares is not allowed when the corporation's capital is already impaired or would become impaired by acquisition of shares. This means that the payment for the acquisition of shares must come from surplus, which is computed in accordance with §§ 154 and 244 as the excess of a corporation's net assets over the amount determined to be capital. However, unlike the some other states, Delaware makes no distinction between earned surplus and "paid in" or "capital" surplus. Delaware law allows money paid in exchange for the shares to be allocated to surplus and then used to pay dividends or redeem shares from a shareholder. In addition, as discussed in the case of *Klang v. Smith's Food & Drug Centers, Inc.* and the accompanying notes in Chapter 6, there is no fixed method for computing "net assets." The directors are given reasonable leeway when ascertaining the value of assets. Taken together, these rules give the directors some "wiggle room" when using assets to purchase or redeem shares under Delaware law. Finally, there is an exception to the rule that the purchase or redemption of shares must be charged only to surplus if the re-purchased shares are retired and the capital of the corporation is reduced. This would be helpful to a corporation seeking to buy out a retiring shareholder.

The point to keep in mind is that, to protect creditors, all states provide *some* restrictions on the sources of corporate assets used to redeem or repurchase of shares from existing stockholders.[101] To the extent that the corporation has insufficient assets to meet the required statutory restrictions, an entity-purchase may not be available as a source of the buyout of a departing stockholder.[102] Thus, it's essential to draft an alternative to a corporate entity buyout, such as a cross-purchase option, in the event that the corporation is restricted by statute from purchasing all or a portion of the departing stockholder's shares.

One last point about corporate buyouts. What is the impact of funding a corporate entity buyout with life insurance or disability insurance with regard to the statutory restraints on dividends and stock repurchases? Although the policies are owned by the corporation and constitute a corporate asset, the payment of benefits to repurchase stock upon death or disability should be outside of the statutory restrictions, since the proceeds cannot be used by the corporation for other purposes (such as paying creditors) and have no impact on the balance sheet solvency or equity solvency of the corporation.[103]

---

[101] In addition to dividend and repurchase restrictions contained in corporations codes, state and federal law also prohibits transfers to owners if the transfer would constitute a "fraudulent conveyance." See the discussion in Section H of this chapter.

[102] Additional restrictions may apply if there is more than one class of stock. If there are preferred classes, then junior classes may not be entitled to receive distributions in the nature of dividends or stock redemptions if it would reduce the ability to repay *both* creditors and senior stockholders. *See, e.g.,* Cal. Corp. Code § 503; Del. Corp. Code §§ 151(c), 160(a)(1), 170(a).

[103] *See, e.g.,* Cal. Corp. Code § 503.1:

"The provisions of Sections 500, 501, 502 and 503 shall not apply to a purchase or redemption of shares of a deceased shareholder from the proceeds of insurance on the life of such shareholder in excess of the total amount of all premiums paid by the corporation for such insurance, in order to carry out the provisions of an agreement between the corporation and such shareholder to purchase or redeem such shares upon the death of the shareholder."

2.   Non-Statutory Considerations & Limitations for Partnership and LLC Buy-Sell Agreements

Unlike corporations, partnerships and LLCs will have extensive formation documents governing the relationships between the owners. The statutory constraints on ownership, formation, financing, operations and distributions for these entities are far less restrictive than for corporations. Many, if not most, of the statutory rules are subject to modification in the partnership and operating agreements. Because of the inherent flexibility of these entities and variations in the partnership and operating agreements, it is important to make sure that the buy-sell agreement is consistent with the provisions of the basic partnership or operating agreement. Indeed, it is not uncommon to incorporate the contents of the buy-sell agreement directly into the original partnership or operating agreement rather than as a separate document.

3.   Statutory Considerations for General Partnerships

As discussed earlier, § 701 of the Revised Uniform Partnership Act contains default provisions regarding the buy out of departing general partners if the remaining partners wish to avoid dissolution and continue operating the partnership. A general partner who dissociates is entitled to payment *at the time of dissociation* if the business is not dissolved and wound up. RUPA contains time periods for accomplishing the buyout and a statutory formula for valuation in the event that the parties can't agree on the price:

§ 701.   Purchase of Dissociated Partner's Interest.

(a)   If a partner is dissociated from a partnership without resulting in a dissolution and winding up of the partnership business . . . , the partnership shall cause the dissociated partner's interest in the partnership to be purchased for a buyout price determined pursuant to subsection (b).

(b)   The buyout price of a dissociated partner's interest is the amount that would have been distributable to the dissociating partner under Section 807(b)[104] if, on the date of dissociation, the assets of the partnership were sold at a price equal to the *greater of* the liquidation value or the value based on a sale of the entire business as a going concern without the dissociated partner and the partnership were wound up as of that date. Interest must be paid from the date of dissociation to the date of payment. (*emphasis added*)

(c)   Damages for wrongful dissociation under Section 602(b), and all other amounts owing, whether or not presently due, from the dissociated partner to the partnership, must be offset against the buyout price. Interest must be paid from the date the amount owed becomes due to the date of payment.

---

[104] RUPA § 807 covers the distribution of assets in a partnership dissolution. It requires first that all debts be paid. The assets of the partnership must be applied first to discharge its obligations to creditors. The surplus, if any, will then be applied to pay the net amount distributable to partners. That net amount is determined by charging the profits, if any, that result from the liquidation of the partnership assets to each of the partners' capital accounts in accordance with the partner's share of profits and losses. The partnership must then make a distribution to a partner in an amount equal to any total excess of credits over charges in the partner's account. In the case of a negative capital account, the partner must contribute that amount to the partnership.

(d) A partnership shall indemnify a dissociated partner whose interest is being purchased against all partnership liabilities, whether incurred before or after the dissociation, except liabilities incurred by an act of the dissociated partner under Section 702.

(e) If no agreement for the purchase of a dissociated partner's interest is reached within 120 days after a written demand for payment, the partnership shall pay, or cause to be paid, in cash to the dissociated partner the amount the partnership estimates to be the buyout price and accrued interest, reduced by any offsets and accrued interest under subsection (c).

(f) If a deferred payment is authorized under subsection (h), the partnership may tender a written offer to pay the amount it estimates to be the buyout price and accrued interest, reduced by any offsets under subsection (c), stating the time of payment, the amount and type of security for payment, and the other terms and conditions of the obligation.

* * *

(h) A partner who wrongfully dissociates before the expiration of a definite term or the completion of a particular undertaking is not entitled to payment of any portion of the buyout price until the expiration of the term or completion of the undertaking, unless the partner establishes to the satisfaction of the court that earlier payment will not cause undue hardship to the business of the partnership. A deferred payment must be adequately secured and bear interest.

(i) A dissociated partner may maintain an action against the partnership, pursuant to Section 405(b)(2)(ii), to determine the buyout price of that partner's interest, any offsets under subsection (c), or other terms of the obligation to purchase. The action must be commenced within 120 days after the partnership has tendered payment or an offer to pay or within one year after written demand for payment if no payment or offer to pay is tendered. The court shall determine the buyout price of the dissociated partner's interest, any offset due under subsection (c), and accrued interest, and enter judgment for any additional payment or refund. If deferred payment is authorized under subsection (h), the court shall also determine the security for payment and other terms of the obligation to purchase. The court may assess reasonable attorney's fees and the fees and expenses of appraisers or other experts for a party to the action, in amounts the court finds equitable, against a party that the court finds acted arbitrarily, vexatiously, or not in good faith . . .

———————

Note that unless there is a wrongful dissociation,[105] the remaining partners must buyout the interest of the partner (using the statutory formula for valuation) for *cash*, unless some other agreement is reached. As discussed earlier, if the dissociation is wrongful, § 701(h) gives the remaining partners the option to buyout the partner using an delayed or installment plan but the installment plan must be secured by adequate collateral or guarantees.

The bottom line in a RUPA-style buyout is that litigation is likely unless the parties agree on all of the following matters:

———————

[105] A partner wrongfully dissociates when he or she dissociates in contravention of the partnership agreement, if the partnership is for a definite term or a particular undertaking.

— the *greater of* the liquidation value or the value based on a sale of the entire business as a going concern
— the amount of any damages caused by a wrongful dissociation
— the form and content of the indemnification required under § 701(d)
— the terms of any installment plan authorized by § 701(h) and the security for performance of the plan
— payment of costs for appraisers, experts and possibly attorneys' fees

The RUPA buyout provisions are fair but the general nature of the provisions leads to many problems, limiting the utility of the buyout provisions. A departing partner is entitled to his or her share of the profits at the time of departure. RUPA properly asks the parties to consider what would happen if the business was liquidated on the date of the partner's departure. The business would be sold or liquidated, debts would be fully paid and profits, if any, would be distributed. If the remaining partners wish to remain in business, then they should pay the departing partner exactly that amount *and* indemnify him or her for the unpaid debts of the partnership.[106] The problem with the RUPA buyout requirements is that they don't contain sufficiently specific standards for making the required determinations listed above, which will almost always lead to litigation unless the partners are unusually cooperative and able to reach agreement at the time the partner departs.

In view of these RUPA buyout rules, it is essential that a *superceding* written buy-sell agreement be reached to avoid the costly litigation that the RUPA default rules are likely to cause. As we have seen, a well drafted agreement can reduce the costs of accomplishing a buyout by imposing clear standards for valuing the interest of the departing owner, imposing clear payment terms (including installment plans for non-wrongful dissociations) and, if necessary, dictate the form and content of any indemnifications.

4. Statutory Considerations for LLCs

The 1996 version of the Uniform Limited Liability Company Act (the "ULLCA"),[107] mimics to a substantial degree the default buyout rules of RUPA. A member's dissociation from an LLC can potentially result in a *mandatory* buyout of that member's interest or, alternatively, the *dissolution* of the LLC. Dissociation can be caused by all the usual departure events, including: (i) express will to withdraw, (ii) events specified in the operating agreement, (iii) a transfer of the member's distributional interest, (iv) expulsion pursuant to the operating agreement, (v) expulsion by unanimous vote of the other members if certain conditions have been satisfied, (vi) expulsion by judicial determination if certain conditions have been satisfied, (vii) becoming a debtor in bankruptcy,[108] (viii) death of an individual member, and (ix) appointment of a guardian or conservator for a member, or judicial determination that the member has otherwise become incapable of performing the member's duties under the operating agreement.

---

[106] Can you see why an indemnification is fair if the partners continue the business without dissolving?

[107] The ULLCA was not widely adopted but serves as a good example of default statutory rules regarding the impact when a member departs from an LLC.

[108] ULLCA also provides for dissociation upon state law insolvency proceedings such as an assignment for the benefit of creditors or the appointment of a trustee or receiver for all, or substantially all, of the debtor's property.

Regardless of whether or not the member's dissociation is wrongful,[109] ULLCA provides:

Section 603.   Effect of Member's Dissociation.

(a)   Upon a member's dissociation:

(1)   in an at-will company, the company must cause the dissociated member's distributional interest to be purchased under [Article] 7; and

(2)   in a term company:

(i)   if the company dissolves and winds up its business on or before the expiration of its specified term, [Article] 8 applies to determine the dissociated member's rights to distributions; and

(ii)   if the company does not dissolve and wind up its business on or before the expiration of its specified term, the company must cause the dissociated member's distributional interest to be purchased under [Article] 7 on the date of the expiration of the term specified at the time of the member's dissociation.

Note that dissociation does not dissolve the company but does place a burden on the remaining members to buy out the dissociated member. If the LLC is "at-will" the buyout must be done immediately but if the LLC is a "term" LLC, the buyout does not have to occur until the scheduled end of the term.[110] Article 7 of the ULLCA provides the mechanism for valuation and the procedures to be followed:

Article 7.   Member's Dissociation When Business Not Wound up

Section 701.   Company Purchase of Distributional Interest.

(a)   A limited liability company shall purchase a distributional interest of a:

(1)   member of an at-will company for its *fair value determined as of the date of the member's dissociation* if the member's dissociation does not result in a dissolution and winding up of the company's business under Section 801; or *(emphasis added)*

(2)   member of a term company for its *fair value determined as of the date of the expiration of the specified term* that existed on the date of the member's dissociation if the expiration of the specified term does not result in a dissolution and winding up of the company's business under Section 801.

(b)   A limited liability company must deliver a purchase offer to the dissociated member whose distributional interest is entitled to be purchased not later than 30 days after the date determined under subsection (a). The purchase offer must be accompanied by:

---

[109]   Under ULLCA § 602, a dissociation is "wrongful" if: (1) it is in breach of an express provision of the agreement; (2) it is before the expiration of the specified term of a term company and either (i) the member withdraws by express will, (ii) the member is expelled by judicial determination, (iii) the dissociated is caused by the member becoming a debtor in bankruptcy; or (iv) in the case of a member who is not an individual, trust or estate, the member is expelled or otherwise dissociated because it willfully dissolved or terminated its existence.

[110]   The remaining LLC members may extend the term at some future time but the payout must occur on the scheduled end of term as it existed on the date of the member's dissociation.

(1)   a statement of the company's assets and liabilities as of the date determined under subsection (a);

(2)   the latest available balance sheet and income statement, if any; and

(3)   an explanation of how the estimated amount of the payment was calculated.

(c)   If the price and other terms of a purchase of a distributional interest are fixed or are to be determined by the operating agreement, the price and terms so fixed or determined govern the purchase unless the purchaser defaults. If a default occurs, the dissociated member is entitled to commence a proceeding to have the company dissolved . . .

(d)   If an agreement to purchase the distributional interest is not made within 120 days after the date determined under subsection (a), the dissociated member, within another 120 days, may commence a proceeding against the limited liability company to enforce the purchase . . .

(e)   The court shall determine the fair value of the distributional interest in accordance with the standards set forth in Section 702 together with the terms for the purchase. Upon making these determinations, the court shall order the limited liability company to purchase or cause the purchase of the interest.

(f)   Damages for wrongful dissociation under Section 602(b), and all other amounts owing, whether or not currently due, from the dissociated member to a limited liability company, must be offset against the purchase price.

Pay careful attention to the above provisions and answer these two questions: (i) when is the date of valuation of the interest of the dissociated member; and, (ii) how is the value of the interest to be determined? Note that valuation dates differ between subsections 701(a)(1) and (a)(2). In an at-will LLC, the valuation date is the date of dissociation. In a term LLC the valuation date is the date of the expiration of the term specified in the operating agreement at the date of dissociation. This places some risk on a term LLC dissociated member between the date of dissociation and valuation date.

Section 701(a) uses the phrase "fair value" not "fair market value." If the operating agreement is silent on the matter, what formula or standard is the court (or court appointed appraisers) supposed to use? Does the following section of the ULLCA, and accompanying Comment, help to clarify what is meant by "fair value"?

Section 702.   Court Action to Determine Fair Value of Distributional Interest.

(a)   In an action brought to determine the fair value of a distributional interest in a limited liability company, the court shall:

(1)   determine the fair value of the interest, considering among other relevant evidence the going concern value of the company, any agreement among some or all of the members fixing the price or specifying a formula for determining value of distributional interests for any other purpose, the recommendations of any appraiser appointed by the court, and any legal constraints on the company's ability to purchase the interest;

(2)   specify the terms of the purchase, including, if appropriate, terms for installment payments, subordination of the purchase obligation to the rights of the company's other creditors, security for a deferred purchase price, and a covenant not to compete or other restriction on a dissociated member; * * *

(c)   If the purchase is not completed in accordance with the specified terms, the company is to be dissolved upon application under Section 801(b)(5)(iv). If a limited liability company is so dissolved, the dissociated member has the same rights and priorities in the company's assets as if the sale had not been ordered. * * *

Comment

The default valuation standard is fair value. Under this broad standard, a court is free to determine the fair value of a distributional interest on a fair market, liquidation, or any other method deemed appropriate under the circumstances. A fair market value standard is not used because it is too narrow, often inappropriate, and assumes a fact not contemplated by this section — a willing buyer and a willing seller.

The court has discretion under subsection (a)(2) to include in its order any conditions the court deems necessary to safeguard the interests of the company and the dissociated member or transferee. The discretion may be based on the financial and other needs of the parties.

Once again we can see that this statutory scheme imposes some potentially expensive, unpredictable and undesirable obligations on business owners to buy out the interest of a departing owner. The 1996 ULLCA was not widely adopted and the 2006 version of the ULLCA alters the outcome in the event of the dissociation of a member. Under the 2006 version, there is no direct statutory obligation to buy out a dissociated member in the absence of a buyout agreement: [111]

Section 404.   Sharing of and Right to Distributions Before Dissolution.

. . .

(b)   A person has a right to a distribution before the dissolution and winding up of a limited liability company only if the company decides to make an interim distribution. *A person's dissociation does not entitle the person to a distribution.*

Under the 2006 version of the ULLCA, there is no statutory obligation to buy out a dissociated member. Dissociated members are merely given the right to approach the courts to seek a buyout when circumstances might justify such an outcome. However, even that right can be stripped away if the operating agreement or a

---

[111] The Summary preceding the 2006 Act states in paragraph 9: "In the 1996 Act dissociation (resigning from membership) of a member by express will triggers an obligation to buy the interest of that member in an at-will or term company. Failure to buy may subject the company to a judicial dissolution and winding up of the business. The 2006 Act provides no obligation to buy out a dissociating member, nor a ground based upon failure of a buyout for judicial dissolution. The company has greater stability under the 2006 Act, notwithstanding any dissociation of a member."

related buy-sell agreement expressly dictates the circumstances of when a buyout may be compelled.[112]

California has adopted a provision similar to the 2006 ULLCA. The California Limited Liability Company Act states: " . . . unless the articles of organization or written operating agreement provide otherwise, the withdrawn member shall not be entitled to payment for the member's interest in the limited liability company." On the other hand, Delaware has adopted provisions more in line with the 1996 version of the ULLCA: " . . . if not otherwise provided in a limited liability company agreement, such member is entitled to receive, within a reasonable time after resignation, the fair value of such member's limited liability company interest as of the date of resignation based upon such member's right to share in distributions from the limited liability company.[113]

The lesson to be learned is that in the absence of clear buyout (or anti-buyout) provisions in the operating agreement of an LLC, or related buy-sell agreement, the LLC statute in that state or the courts may compel a buyout, at a value, and in accordance with procedures, that may be undesirable from the perspective of some (and perhaps all) of the members of an LLC. It is critically important that during the drafting of the operating agreement, the LLC statute for the state be consulted and express provisions included in the operating agreement regarding the obligation (or non-obligation) to buy out departing members.

5.   Regulatory and Licensing Rules

For some professional entities, regardless of the format of the entity, participation as an owner may be restricted to individuals who are properly licensed. For instance, all owners of a law firm must be licensed to practice law whether the firm is organized as a professional corporation, general partnership, limited liability company or limited liability partnership.[114] Or if the entity owns a liquor license, changes in the ownership structure caused by a departure or admission of a new owner may require approval of the liquor licensing agency or the liquor license may be suspended. The buy-sell agreement must contain appropriate provisions to reflect the practical realty that regulatory requirements might restrict the buy out or require compliance with regulatory formalities. The need for a buyout agreement of some kind is magnified in professional corporations, such as law firms. When an owner dies, becomes disabled, withdraws from practice or is suspended or disbarred, it is essential to make sure that the interest of a departing owner is promptly acquired by the entity or the remaining owners.

H.   FRAUDULENT TRANSFERS AND ENTITY REPURCHASES

In addition to any statutory restrictions in the corporations codes on the payment of dividends or repurchase of corporate shares, there are state and federal restrictions on transfers by *any* entity to owners with the actual intent, or the

---

[112] See the discussion of § 701(a)(5) and (b) in Section F.2.b. of this chapter.

[113] 6 Del. C. § 18–604.

[114] This is often true for accountants, lawyers, architects, and physicians.

"presumptive" intent, to hinder, delay or defraud creditors. The federal Bankruptcy Code provides in § 548 that a transfer by any entity can be avoided and recovered by a bankruptcy trustee under circumstances that include the buyout of owners.

§ 548. Fraudulent transfers and obligations

(a) (1)   The trustee may avoid any transfer . . . of an interest of the debtor in property, . . . that was made or incurred on or within two years before the date of the filing of the petition, if the debtor voluntarily or involuntarily —

(A)   made such transfer or incurred such obligation with *actual intent*[115] to hinder, delay, or defraud any entity to which the debtor was or became, on or after the date that such transfer was made or such obligation was incurred, indebted; or

(B) (i)   received less than a reasonably equivalent value in exchange for such transfer or obligation; and

(ii) (I)   was insolvent on the date that such transfer was made or such obligation was incurred, or became insolvent as a result of such transfer or obligation;

(II)   was engaged in business or a transaction, or was about to engage in business or a transaction, for which any property remaining with the debtor was an unreasonably small capital;

(III)   intended to incur, or believed that the debtor would incur, debts that would be beyond the debtor's ability to pay as such debts matured; or

* * *

(b)   The trustee of a partnership debtor may avoid any transfer of an interest of the debtor in property, or any obligation incurred by the debtor, that was made or incurred on or within two years before the date of the filing of the petition, to a general partner in the debtor, if the debtor was insolvent on the date such transfer was made or such obligation was incurred, or became insolvent as a result of such transfer or obligation.

The first fraudulent conveyancing statute was enacted in 1571 in England.[116] The statute only applied to the conveyance of personal property but a similar statute prohibiting the fraudulent conveyance of real property was enacted in 1584.[117] Both statutes prohibited transfers with the intent to delay, hinder or defraud creditors. Because the statute relied on *actual* intent, it was difficult to show the subjective intent of the transferor to actually hinder, delay or defraud creditors. Nevertheless, courts quickly developed "badges of fraud" — factual circumstances that indirectly indicate the presence of an intention to hinder, delay or defraud creditors.[118] Transfers under the following circumstances often result in a finding of actual

---

[115] Emphasis added.—Eds.

[116] Stat. 13 Eliz. c. 5 (1571)

[117] Stat. 27 Eliz. c. 4 (1584)

[118] *Twyne's Case*, Star Chamber, 3 Coke, 80b, 76 Eng. Rep.809 (1601). In *Twyne's Case*, the debtor,

intent to hinder, delay or defraud creditors:

— Transfers in close proximity to recent or threatened law suits
— Retention of possession or control by the transferor
— Transfers made in secret
— Transfers of substantially all property
— Transfers to insiders or relatives
— Gifts or transfers atwithout commensurate compensation in exchange
— Transfers in close proximity to bankruptcy or receiverships

In 1918 the National Conference of Commissioners on Uniform State Laws adopted the Uniform Fraudulent Conveyance Act (the "UFCA"), which was eventually enacted in 26 states. The UFCA divided fraudulent conveyance into two types: transfers with the *actual intent* to hinder, delay or defraud creditors; and, transfers while insolvent for less than a "fair equivalent value." Note that the second type of fraudulent conveyance does not require an inquiry into the transferor's *actual* intentions but, instead, focuses on the impact of the transfer on creditors. Regardless of intent by the transferor, certain types of transfers by debtors will have the same negative impact on creditors as a transfer with actual intent. Suppose that Denise Debtor owes Calvin $20,000. She has a single non-exempt asset (her computer) worth $10,000. On January 1st she transferred title to the computer to her best friend, Ann, with the *intention* of making sure that Calvin would not be able to seize it by writ of execution. Obviously, this is a fraudulent conveyance. Now suppose that she gave it to her friend Ann as a *gift* with no intention to hinder, delay or defraud Calvin. From Calvin's perspective, is one transfer less harmful than the other? Does it matter to him whether Denise transfers away her only non-exempt asset with, or without, an intention to defraud him? The impact on Calvin is the same either way.

Section 548 was based upon, but not identical to, the UFCA. It allows the trustee to avoid transfers under § 548(a)(1)(A) that are made with the intention to hinder, delay or defraud creditors. This includes transfers to stockholders, partners or members in the form of distributions, repurchases or asset transfers that are part of a scheme of transferring wealth from the entity to its owners, while depleting the assets of the entity available to satisfy the creditors of the entity. Section 548 also follows the 1918 UFCA and adopts the concept of "presumptively fraudulent conveyances" under § 548(a)(1)(B). Regardless of the intent of the transferor, transfers that are made while the debtor was insolvent for less than "reasonably equivalent value" can be avoided. This includes distributions to equity holders while the entity is insolvent or unable to pay creditor debts as they come due.[119]

Pierce, owed money to a creditor. Pierce transferred all of his assets to his friend, Twyne but retained possession of the property, continued to care for and shear the sheep and sell other chattels. The Star Chamber held that "intent" was shown, even without direct proof of subjective intent because of some obvious badges of fraud: (i) the transfer was made in secret, (ii) Pierce retained possession of the assets, (ii) the consideration given by Twyne (a small debt) was far less than the value of the goods conveyed, (iii) the transfer was made in contemplation of, or close in time to, pending litigation by a creditor, (iv) the transfer was of all of the debtor's assets, even his clothes.

[119] For more insight into fraudulent transfers, see *Granfinanciera v. Nordberg*, 492 U.S. 33, 47 (1989). In that case the trustee sought to recover $1.7 million in payments to stockholders made by the debtor-corporation prior to filing bankruptcy. The case focuses primarily on the issue of whether a jury trial is required in a bankruptcy-based fraudulent conveyance action but contains an in-depth summary and analysis of fraudulent conveyancing law.

In 1984, the Uniform Fraudulent Transfer Act (the "UFTA"), was adopted by the National Conference of Commissioners on Uniform State Laws, to make the UFCA more consistent with the provisions of § 548 of the Bankruptcy Code.

What do the federal Bankruptcy Code, the UFCA and UFTA add to the task of designing buy-sell agreements? It's important to keep in mind that *entity-based* buyouts cannot be undertaken if there are anti-dividend statutes or fraudulent transfer statutes that prohibit the use of entity assets in a manner that injuriously depletes the assets available to creditors. The best laid plans of the parties in the buy-sell agreement will by futile if the purchase by the entity runs afoul of state or federal fraudulent transfer laws. When drafting buy-sell agreements, it is essential to make sure that if the *entity* cannot complete the purchase of an owner's interest because of statutory limitations, that an alternative method for the buyout (such as a cross-purchase agreement) is in place to assure that the buyout can be completed.

Chapter 9

SALE OR RESTRUCTURING OF THE BUSINESS ENTITY

As a business matures, it faces growing pains. The organization you created as a start-up may have become obsolete. The owners may have changed their plans, opportunities may have arisen, or the business may have developed in ways which make the current entity obsolete in a major way. It may be time for a fundamental reorganization of the entity and that is the subject of this chapter. Any reorganization can be thought of as either a combination with another business or entity, or a division of the existing entity.[1] In Section A, we discuss the three main methods by which these changes are accomplished: a purchase and sale of assets, a purchase and sale of ownership interests in the entity, or a "combination" under state law which could be either a "sale of assets" or a "sale of interests" arrangement. In Section B, we discuss each of these methods in the entity-specific contexts of partnerships, corporations, and limited liability companies, dealing with the organic law issues regarding each type of entity. In Section C, we deal with the federal income tax issues which may, in some instances, drive the choice of sale or reorganization and other strategic issues.

A. METHODS OF RESTRUCTURING

If our business, such as the ABC Restaurant, desires to expand, perhaps to acquire another existing restaurant in town, it can do so in two different ways. It can buy the assets of the restaurant, or it can buy the ownership interests of the business entity which owns the assets. If the restaurant is a sole proprietorship — not legally distinct from the individual — the ABC Restaurant will have only one choice: to buy the assets. But if the "target"[2] is organized in any other form, we will have the second option of acquiring the ownership of the business, which itself owns the assets.

1. Sale of Assets

General structure of the transaction. Sale and purchase of assets is normally handled by a purchase and sale agreement. These agreements commonly include the following provisions:

- Introduction and recitals

- Agreement of seller to sell and agreement of buyer to buy, with specific description of the subject property

- Price, payment terms, closing date

---

[1] Some reorganizations are pursued in the federal bankruptcy courts, rather than by contractual agreements between the parties. Reorganizations in bankruptcy are discussed in Chapter 10.

[2] We use "target" to generically refer to the business or assets to be acquired. This does not necessarily mean that this is a "hostile" takeover or any other such sophisticated corporate acquisition.

- Representations and warranties of buyer and seller

- Conditions

- Miscellaneous provisions (amendment, merger, choice of law and consent to jurisdiction, notice, alternative dispute resolution procedures).

The price and payment provisions will likely be "business terms" determined by your client and the other party. The description of the property may be the most tedious drafting challenge for the lawyer in a business of any size, because there will likely be many assets that need to be identified and included in the agreement. Often the body of the agreement will include only general references to types of assets ("land and improvements," "inventory," "equipment," etc.), while the complete lists of assets will be attached to the purchase and sale agreement as schedules or exhibits. The creation of these schedules or exhibits will take enormous work by the lawyers, accountants, officers and employees of the entities to make sure that no assets are excluded. This can be quite tedious in a transaction involving a multi-million or multi-billion dollar purchase and sale. Representations and warranties are normally standard terms, though they may vary if the assets are unusual. The conditions to closing and the extent to which representations and warranties survive closing are also essential "business terms" but the extent and severity will depend in large part upon the parties' relative negotiating strength.

Other issues raised by the transaction. There are many other issues raised in a sale of assets transaction apart from the entity-specific rules which are taken up in Section B of this chapter. The following is a list of some important issues typically raised in purchase and sale transactions.

- *Recording of transfer.* Property which is titled, such as real property, motor vehicles, and aircraft, will have formal deed requirements, or documents of title, which must be transferred to the new owner(s) and recorded in the appropriate locations. This involves local filing for real property, usually state filing for motor vehicles, and federal filing for aircraft.

- *Taxes other than income taxes.* If a portion of the business to be sold consists of inventory or other items to be sold in the regular course of business, sales tax may be an issue. The following California regulations sketch out the typical issues.

CALIFORNIA CODE OF REGULATIONS
TITLE 18. PUBLIC REVENUES

§ 1595.   Occasional Sales — Sale of a Business — Business Reorganization.

(a)   Activities Requiring Seller's Permit.

(1)   General. Tax applies to all retail sales of tangible personal property including capital assets whether sold in one transaction or in a series of sales, held or used by the seller in the course of an activity or activities for which a seller's permit or permits is required or would be required if the activity or activities were conducted in this state. . . .

(2)   Property Held or Used in an Activity, or Activities Requiring the Holding of a Seller's Permit. A seller's permit is required of a person engaged in the business of selling tangible personal property. An activity requiring the holding of that permit includes, but is not limited to, the acquisition and sale of tangible personal property, whether the person's sales are all at retail, all for resale, or include both sales at retail and sales for resale.

. . . .

(b) Sale or Reorganization of All or Part of a Business.

(1) General. In general, when a person sells a business which is required to hold a seller's permit, tax applies to the gross receipts from the retail sale of tangible personal property held or used by that business in the course of its activities requiring the holding of the seller's permit. The gross receipts from the sale of the business include all consideration received by the transferor, including cash, notes, and any other property as well as any indebtedness assumed by the transferee. It is irrelevant that the indebtedness assumed may have arisen solely in connection with the transferor's acquisition of the tangible personal property transferred, the other property transferred, or some combination thereof. That is, the transferor is selling a business, and all consideration received is for that business. The measure of tax is the price agreed to by the parties. In the absence of an agreement as to the price of the tangible personal property, the gross receipts from that sale is allocated among the taxable portion and the nontaxable portion by dividing the selling price of the tangible personal property acquired by the purchaser for use rather than resale by the selling price of the entire business sold, and then multiplying that amount by the total gross receipts (i.e., all consideration) received for the business. Book value will be regarded as establishing the price of properties sold. . . .

• *Mortgages and Security interests.* Property, whether real or personal, may be subject to security interests or liens. The mortgages or deeds of trust (in the case of real property), or security agreements (in the case of personal property) may contain contractual restrictions on the transfer of the property without the express consent of the creditors.[3] In many cases, a substantial part — if not a majority — of the purchase and sale negotiation consists of a three-cornered deal among the transferor, the transferee, and the transferor's creditors. Sales or transfer of assets may result in default under leases, loans, shareholder agreements, buy-sell agreements, or other agreements. There is no substitute for a thorough and comprehensive review of all existing documents of the selling entity and its equity holders to determine whether there are any contractual restrictions that must be satisfied to accomplish the transfer.

• *Restrictions on transferability.* These may be imposed by the terms of the transferor's title to property (whether real or personal and if personal whether tangible or intangible property). There may also be regulatory approvals required for transfer of the assets of a licensed business.

• *Fraudulent transfers.* Any transfer of property which is not for adequate consideration and which leaves the transferor "insolvent" under fraudulent transfer law may be recoverable by the creditors of the transferor. Fraudulent transfer law is discussed in detail in Chapters 6 and 8.

---

[3] Alternatively, the mortgage, lien or security interest might simply remain attached to the property in the hands of the purchaser; *see, e.g.,* UCC §§ 9-203 (attachment) and 9-309 (perfection). Under UCC § 9-320(a) a buyer in the ordinary course may take free of a security interest of "the buyer's seller," but the types of sales we are discussing here are rarely "in the ordinary course," *see* UCC § 1-201(b)(9). Moreover, the continuation of a mortgage or security interest may not be an important consideration where the sale itself (without the consent of the lender) is a breach of the mortgage or security agreement, as is often the case.

- *Restrictions on sales of inventory.* The source of restrictions on sales of inventory was historically Article 6 of the Uniform Commercial Code (UCC) on "bulk sales." The rationale is described in the "Prefatory Note" to UCC Article 6.

> Bulk sale legislation originally was enacted in response to a fraud perpetrated around the turn of the century: a merchant would acquire his stock in trade on credit, then sell his entire inventory ("in bulk") and abscond with the proceeds. The creditors had the right to sue the merchant on the unpaid debts, but this right was of little practical value.

The UCC drafters have recognized that Article 6 provides no significant protection to modern diligent creditors, and is primarily an expensive pointless formality for buyers and a trap for the unwary. They have recommended repeal of Article 6, which, dutifully, most states have done. We can therefore relegate discussion of bulk sales to the history books except in the four jurisdictions which still retain Article 6: California, The District of Columbia, Indiana, and Virginia.[4] Practitioners who worry about bulk sales law are thus either working with clients in one of these jurisdictions or out of date.

In keeping with the limited scope of Article 6, we offer only a brief summary of how Article 6 works. The statute requires a buyer of "bulk"[5] inventory to notify the creditors of the seller of the sale. There are many sales exempt from this requirement. The most widely applicable exemption is likely § 6-103(3)(j) for a sale to a U.S. buyer who assumes the debts of the seller[6] — a common practice.

> This exemption is applicable in numerous cases, for there are significant business advantages to a transferee who buys a business in this way. The transferee in effect steps into the shoes of the transferor with respect to any ongoing business relationships developed with suppliers. And a transferee who assumes such debts does not have to dig up as much cash . . . .[7]

If the sale is not exempt, the notice requirements of § 6-104 must be followed. These are the buyer's obligations, and although noncompliance risks liability under § 6-107, "in general, the plaintiff is likely to leave a[n] Article 6 lawsuit empty handed unless the buyer has colluded with the seller to stiff the seller's creditors."[8] Furthermore, any noncompliance will not affect the buyer's title to the goods or the validity of the sale.[9]

2. Sale of Ownership Interests

By contrast to the complexity of asset-by-asset transfer and recording, the sale of ownership interests will seem relatively simple. Although the client does not have to transfer each individual asset, there may still be some detailed inquiry

---

[4] *See* 2C Uniform Laws Annotated 14 (2005); 3 James J. White & Robert S. Summers, Uniform Commercial Code 228 (5th ed. 2008). Ordinarily, accessible "student editions" of treatises are cited in this book, but Profs. White and Summers have omitted any discussion of Article 6 from the student edition of their treatise, so the citation here is to the Practitioner Edition.

[5] That is, a sale not in the ordinary course of more than half the seller's inventory as measured by value. UCC § 6-102(1)(c).

[6] The buyer must also not be insolvent and must file a notice of the sale. UCC § 6-103(3)(j)(ii) to (iii).

[7] 3 White & Summers, *supra*, at 235–36.

[8] *Id.* at 244.

[9] UCC § 6-107(8).

required. Some assets may be affected by a change in control of the owner of the asset. Every license, contract, loan, lease, or other agreement by the transferor must be reviewed to determine those which will be breached by the sale (there probably will be some) and whether the breach can be cured or waived by the other party to the agreement. This is particularly true if the transferors have an agreement among themselves (such as a shareholders' agreement or operating agreement) which may limit the transferability of these interests. The proposed sale to an outsider should be carefully reviewed and planned in the context of these buy-sell and control agreements which we studied in Chapters 7 and 8.

In addition, the sale of the ownership interests may involve sales of securities subject to federal or state securities laws.[10] Chapter 4 covers the rules regarding which types of ownership interests would likely be considered "securities" under these laws, and the standards governing resale of those securities.[11] If securities are indeed involved, exemptions must be found from registration requirements which might otherwise apply to these offers and sales.[12] Violation of the registration requirements, you may recall, ordinarily gives the purchaser a right to rescind the transaction. In addition, the business lawyer needs to remember that the broad antifraud proscriptions of these laws apply to even a one-time sale of securities between unsophisticated parties.[13] Other securities law rules governing "tender offers" or "going private" transactions could govern a sale of controlling interests as well, but these statutes apply only to entities with substantial assets and widely-dispersed ownership.[14] In most cases, small closely-held business will not be subject to these special rules.

Finally, the sale of ownership interests in a regulated entity will be subject to restrictions distinct from those applicable to a sale of the entity's assets. The licensing authority may require the business' owners to be members of the profession or group, or may impose other restrictions on the sale of the interests generally.[15]

3.   Combinations

In addition to an ordinary sale of assets, or sale of ownership interests, state laws governing partnerships, corporations or LLCs may provide a statutory method for combining two or more of these entities together. Such a transaction is

---

[10] The same securities law issues would be involved in a "sale of assets" transaction discussed in Section A.1 above if the assets of the transferor included securities. In many cases, the transferor may hold back cash and other liquid assets such as securities, but if not, the rules governing resale of those securities must be addressed.

[11] In particular, at least under federal securities law, the "sale of business" doctrine has been rejected. This doctrine provided that sale of *all* the ownership interests in an entity was not a sale of securities but rather a constructive sale of the underlying assets. This position was rejected by the Supreme Court in *Landreth Timber Co. v. Landreth*, 471 U.S. 681 (1985), discussed in Chapter 4, Section B.

[12] *See* Chapter 4, Section A.1.

[13] See *Wharf Holdings Ltd. v. United International Holdings, Inc.* in Chapter 4, Section D.

[14] These requirements apply to companies with more than $10 million in assets and more than 500 shareholders of record, or to companies whose securities are listed for trading on a national securities exchange, and to companies which, although they do not meet these requirement, voluntarily register their shares under the Securities Exchange Act of 1934. *See* Securities Exchange Act § 12(a), (g).

[15] *See* Chapter 8, Section G.5.

ordinarily known as a "merger," although this can be an inaccurate term in some cases.

The oldest and most familiar of these types of laws provide for corporate mergers, consolidations or share exchanges. A **merger** is ordinarily a transaction in which two corporations combine and one is the surviving corporation. A **consolidation** (less common) is a transaction in which two corporations combine and form a completely new corporation. A **share exchange** is a transaction in which shareholders of one corporation exchange their shares for shares in another corporation, usually leaving the two corporations in a parent-subsidiary relationship. The corporate combination rules are discussed in Section B.2.c below.

More recently, these traditional types of corporate statutes have been copied for use in combinations of partnerships and limited liability companies. We discuss partnership and LLC combination rules in Sections B.1.c and B.3.c below. In addition, the newest varieties of combination statutes permit combinations *among* different types of entities, for example, a corporation and an LLC combining to form either a corporation or an LLC. Re-ULLCA (adopted in 2006) contains some new cross-entity combination provisions.[16] There is also a recently proposed "Model Entity Transactions Act" (META), proposed in 2005, that is a joint effort of the National Conference of Commissioners on Uniform State Laws and the American Bar Association. META is a comprehensive approach to cross-entity combinations made necessary by the proliferation of entities since the advent of the LLCs. The cross-entity combination rules in both of these model acts are relatively new and will, undoubtedly, be the subject of future development as states consider adopting the model provisions. We can offer only a basic analysis of these rules at this time. The Prefatory Note to META describes the current state of the law.

> Prior to the development of this Act, state business organization statutes (both incorporated and unincorporated) varied in their approach to same-type and cross-type mergers, consolidations, divisions, conversions, share/interest exchanges, and domestications by or among domestic and foreign for-profit and nonprofit entities. The dissimilarities in state statutes included: (1) which transactions were authorized; (2) whether entities of more than one type could be parties to the same transaction; (3) inclusion of for-profit and nonprofit entities; (4) inclusion of incorporated and unincorporated organizations; and (5) single or dual status for converting, domesticating, or transferring entities. For example, The Uniform Partnership Act (1997) ("RUPA") authorized the conversion or merger of partnerships or limited partnerships. RUPA did not, however, anticipate the conversion or merger of types of business entities other than partnerships or limited partnerships nor did it address divisions, interest exchanges, or domestications. The Uniform Limited Partnership Act (1976 with 1985 amendments) ("RULPA") is silent regarding mergers and any form of cross-type transaction. A RULPA limited partnership could, however, effect a conversion or merger by "linking back" to the limited RUPA merger or conversion provisions. The Uniform Limited Partnership Act (2001) ("Re-RULPA") anticipated for-profit and nonprofit cross-type conversions and mergers, but not cross or same-type interest exchanges,

---

[16] Re-ULLCA §§ 1002–05.

divisions, or domestications. The Uniform Limited Liability Company Act (1996) ("ULLCA") authorized cross-type mergers and conversions but was silent regarding for-profit and nonprofit cross or same-type interest exchanges, divisions, and domestications.

New Chapter 9 of the Revised Model Business Corporation Act ("MBCA"), approved in 2003, authorized a domestic business corporation to become a different type of entity and permitted a non-domestic business entity to become a domestic business corporation. The transactions addressed in Chapter 9 of the MBCA include: (1) domestication (a procedure in which a corporation may change its state of incorporation, either domestic to foreign, or foreign to domestic); (2) nonprofit conversion (a procedure that permits a domestic business corporation to become either a domestic nonprofit corporation or a foreign nonprofit corporation); (3) foreign nonprofit domestication and conversion (a procedure that permits a foreign nonprofit corporation to become a domestic business corporation); and (4) entity conversion (procedures that authorize a domestic business corporation to become a domestic or foreign other entity or that permit a foreign other entity to become a domestic business corporation). Chapter 9 of the MBCA authorized only those transactions that involve a domestic business corporation either at the outset or at the termination of the transaction.[17]

Entity consolidation statues will surely be an important development for business lawyers over the coming years.[18]

In addition, there can be important non-acquisitive reorganizations, such as a recapitalization to make way for new owners or a change of state reorganization. Alternatively, a business entity may undertake a unilateral change of form apart from the combination discussed in the preceding paragraph. These are beyond the scope of our introductory coverage.[19]

B. ORGANIC LAW ISSUES

To fully understand the sale or restructuring of business entities, we must consider the entity-specific issues which may arise in each case: sale of assets, sale of ownership interests, and consolidations. We will review these issues first with partnerships, second with corporations, and third with LLCs.

---

[17] Model Entity Transactions Act, Prefatory Note, available at: www.law.upenn.edu/bll/archives/ulc/ueta/2005OctMETAfinal.htm#TOC2_1.

[18] *See generally*, Robert C. Art, *Conversion and Merger of Disparate Business Entities*, 76 WASH. L. REV. 349 (2001).

[19] For a thorough discussion, see the recent Symposium on "Entity Rationalization" at 58 BUS. LAW. 1003-72 (2003) (Part 1) and 58 BUS. LAW. 1385-1448 (2003) (Part 2).

1.   Partnerships

a.   Sale of Assets

If a partnership chooses to sell all, or substantially all, of its assets, it can be presumed that such a sale is not in the "ordinary course" of the partnership's business. Partnership law therefore requires that the sale be authorized by all the partners.[20] There may be times when it's not quite clear whether or not the sale is of all (or substantially all) of the partnership's assets. Also, depending on the partnership agreement it may be unclear whether unanimous consent is required or whether only a majority or super-majority vote is sufficient to authorize the sale. For these reasons, prudent buyers will insist on one of the following, to eliminate any possibility that the sale is not valid under the partnership agreement or applicable partnership statutes: (i) a unanimous vote of the partners authorizing the sale; or (ii) requiring that all of the partners sign the sale and purchase in their individual capacity as a partner.

If one of the partnership assets to be sold is real estate, there are additional details which require attention, depending on the record ownership. Recall from partnership law that property can become "partnership property" even without a transfer of title from a partner to the partnership. This may create complications in later transfer where the actual and record ownership differ.

REVISED UNIFORM PARTNERSHIP ACT (1997)

§ 302.   Transfer of Partnership Property.

(a)   Partnership property may be transferred as follows:

(1)   Subject to the effect of a statement of partnership authority under Section 303, partnership property held in the name of the partnership may be transferred by an instrument of transfer executed by a partner in the partnership name.

(2)   Partnership property held in the name of one or more partners with an indication in the instrument transferring the property to them of their capacity as partners or of the existence of a partnership, but without an indication of the name of the partnership, may be transferred by an instrument of transfer executed by the persons in whose name the property is held.

(3)   Partnership property held in the name of one or more persons other than the partnership, without an indication in the instrument transferring the property to them of their capacity as partners or of the existence of a partnership, may be transferred by an instrument of transfer executed by the persons in whose name the property is held.

(b)   A partnership may recover partnership property from a transferee only if it proves that execution of the instrument of initial transfer did not bind the partnership under Section 301 and:

---

[20]   RUPA § 301(2) actually says "authorized by the other partners," but § 401(j) requires "consent of all of the partners." Although § 401 is meant to be binding only among the partners, and § 301 is meant to apply to third parties, see § 401(k), it would nonetheless be prudent to obtain unanimous consent to a sale of partnership property outside the ordinary course of business.

(1)   as to a subsequent transferee who gave value for property transferred under subsection (a)(1) and (2), proves that the subsequent transferee knew or had received a notification that the person who executed the instrument of initial transfer lacked authority to bind the partnership; or

(2)   as to a transferee who gave value for property transferred under subsection (a)(3), proves that the transferee knew or had received a notification that the property was partnership property and that the person who executed the instrument of initial transfer lacked authority to bind the partnership.

(c)   A partnership may not recover partnership property from a subsequent transferee if the partnership would not have been entitled to recover the property, under subsection (b), from any earlier transferee of the property.

Unlike its predecessor, RUPA § 302 governs real and titled personal property.[21] As to the reference to § 303, that section provides for filed "statements of partnership authority," and can provide authority for transfer of real property if the statement is certified and filed with the land records.[22]

Ordinarily a sale of partnership assets is not an event of dissociation or liquidation of the partnership. Although partnership statutes provide that a partnership may be liquidated upon termination[23] or completion[24] of a "particular undertaking," it is not necessarily the case that sale of all or substantially all of the partnership assets will render the undertaking complete. It is possible that a partnership originally formed to purchase, construct, own, lease, or operate particular assets may be "terminated" or "completed" when those assets are sold.[25] However, the business lawyer who has carefully read the partnership agreement specifying such an undertaking would be alert to that possibility and would either have the partners agree to end the partnership or amend the partnership agreement to avoid any uncertainty.

b.   Sale of Partnership Interests

If a partnership chooses instead to sell "the business" by selling partnership interests rather than partnership assets, different issues arise.[26] Although the parties would consider departure of one partner and replacement by another to be all part of the same transaction, the law will have different rules for each.

A partner cannot simply leave a partnership and transfer his or her interest, "lock, stock and barrel" to a new purchaser. Ordinarily a purchaser of a partner's interest is an "assignee of a partnership interest." Such a person is entitled only to that partner's share of profits and other distributions, but is not entitled to participate in management, and does not succeed to the transferring partner's

---

[21] *See* RUPA § 302, cmt. 2. UPA § 10 governed only real property in this regard.

[22] *See* RUPA § 303(d)(2) (covered in Chapter 7, Section B).

[23] UPA § 31(1)(a).

[24] RUPA § 801(2)(iii).

[25] *See, e.g.*, II Alan R. Bromberg & Larry E. Ribstein, Bromberg & Ribstein on Partnership § 7.02(b), pp. 7:24 to 7:25 (collecting cases).

[26] For the purposes of our discussion here, it makes no difference if we are considering a general partnership or an LLP; the basic governance issues are the same.

liability for losses.[27] If the seller wants to no longer be a partner, he or she must dissociate from the partnership (to use the RUPA terminology). At that point, unless the partners have provided otherwise, the dissociating partner is to be paid the value of his or her interest.[28] In addition (and more disruptively) *each other partner* has the right to demand *liquidation* of the partnership.[29]

State law provides as a default rule that new partners can be admitted only with the consent of all the partners.[30] When planning the new partnership, it is unlikely that the partners had taken into account the possibility that one partner would leave and be replaced by another. This is not because of lack of good planning, but rather because the facts and circumstances would be difficult to anticipate. Admitting a new partner will require renegotiation of the value of capital contributions, profit and loss shares, and management responsibilities — in short virtually every facet of the partnership arrangement. It is therefore likely that the default rule would still be in place, and consent of all the partners would be required.

It is therefore very unlikely that your partnership agreement (for a small business) can provide for the replacement of a partner's controlling interest in the business. If such a transaction becomes possible, it is likely all the parties (current partners, departing partner, and new partner) will need to come back to the bargaining table (and the lawyer's office) to write a new partnership agreement.

c.   Combinations

Instead of selling assets of a partnership to new owners, or selling interests from one partnership to another, two partnerships may agree to combine into one. For the reasons discussed under Section B.1.b above, this event is unlikely to be covered in the original partnership agreement of either partnership. Absent any further agreement, the transaction would likely be viewed as a liquidation of at least one of the partnerships, if not both. If both are liquidated, a new partnership will be formed.

All of this can be handled with a carefully drawn agreement among the partners of the combining partnerships. However, a sale of interests — however styled — may be considered to be a sale of the underlying assets, or it may trigger other unintended consequences under agreements or state partnership laws. To remedy this situation, RUPA has adopted a nonexclusive "safe harbor" for partnership mergers, patterned after the long-existing more familiar structure of corporation mergers and consolidations.

---

[27] UPA § 27; RUPA § 503.

[28] RUPA § 601(1). The dissolution provisions of the old and new partnership acts differ substantially in order and terminology. We will stick to the RUPA scheme here.

[29] RUPA § 801(1). This disruption is normally avoided in partnership agreements by providing that, upon dissociation of a partner, "the business of the partnership (or the partnership) shall be continued by the remaining partners." See the discussion of these rules in Chapter 10, Section D.3.a.

[30] UPA § 18(g); RUPA § 401(i).

REVISED UNIFORM PARTNERSHIP ACT (1997)

Article 9. Conversions and Mergers

. . . .

Comment [to § 901]

1. Article 9 is new. The UPA is silent with respect to the conversion or merger of partnerships, and thus it is necessary under the UPA to structure those types of transactions as asset transfers. RUPA provides specific statutory authority for conversions and mergers. It provides for continuation of the partnership entity, thereby simplifying those transactions and adding certainty to the legal consequences. A number of States currently authorize the merger of limited partnerships, and some authorize them to merge with other business entities such as corporations and limited liability companies. A few States currently authorize the merger of a general and a limited partnership or the conversion of a general to a limited partnership.

2. As Section 908 makes clear, the requirements of Article 9 are not mandatory, and a partnership may convert or merge in any other manner provided by law. Article 9 is merely a "safe harbor." If the requirements of the article are followed, the conversion or merger is legally valid. Since most States have no other established procedure for the conversion or merger of partnerships, it is likely that the Article 9 procedures will be used in virtually all cases.

. . . .

§ 905. Merger of Partnerships.

(a) Pursuant to a plan of merger approved as provided in subsection (c), a partnership may be merged with one or more partnerships or limited partnerships.

(b) The plan of merger must set forth:

(1) the name of each partnership or limited partnership that is a party to the merger;

(2) the name of the surviving entity into which the other partnerships or limited partnerships will merge;

(3) whether the surviving entity is a partnership or a limited partnership and the status of each partner;

(4) the terms and conditions of the merger;

(5) the manner and basis of converting the interests of each party to the merger into interests or obligations of the surviving entity, or into money or other property in whole or part; and

(6) the street address of the surviving entity's chief executive office.

(c) The plan of merger must be approved:

(1) in the case of a partnership that is a party to the merger, by all of the partners, or a number or percentage specified for merger in the partnership agreement; and

(2) in the case of a limited partnership that is a party to the merger, by the vote required for approval of a merger by the law of the State or foreign

jurisdiction in which the limited partnership is organized and, in the absence of such a specifically applicable law, by all of the partners, notwithstanding a provision to the contrary in the partnership agreement.

. . . .

§ 906.   Effect of Merger.

(a)   When a merger takes effect:

(1)   the separate existence of every partnership or limited partnership that is a party to the merger, other than the surviving entity, ceases;

(2)   all property owned by each of the merged partnerships or limited partnerships vests in the surviving entity;

(3)   all obligations of every partnership or limited partnership that is a party to the merger become the obligations of the surviving entity; and

(4)   an action or proceeding pending against a partnership or limited partnership that is a party to the merger may be continued as if the merger had not occurred, or the surviving entity may be substituted as a party to the action or proceeding.

. . . .

(c)   A partner of the surviving partnership or limited partnership is liable for:

(1)   all obligations of a party to the merger for which the partner was personally liable before the merger;

(2)   all other obligations of the surviving entity incurred before the merger by a party to the merger, but those obligations may be satisfied only out of property of the entity; and

(3)   except as otherwise provided in Section 306, all obligations of the surviving entity incurred after the merger takes effect, but those obligations may be satisfied only out of property of the entity if the partner is a limited partner.

(d)   If the obligations incurred before the merger by a party to the merger are not satisfied out of the property of the surviving partnership or limited partnership, the general partners of that party immediately before the effective date of the merger shall contribute the amount necessary to satisfy that party's obligations to the surviving entity, in the manner provided in Section 807 or in the [Limited Partnership Act] of the jurisdiction in which the party was formed, as the case may be, as if the merged party were dissolved.

(e)   A partner of a party to a merger who does not become a partner of the surviving partnership or limited partnership is dissociated from the entity, of which that partner was a partner, as of the date the merger takes effect. The surviving entity shall cause the partner's interest in the entity to be purchased under Section 701 or another statute specifically applicable to that partner's interest with respect to a merger. The surviving entity is bound under Section 702 by an act of a general partner dissociated under this subsection, and the partner is liable under Section 703 for transactions entered into by the surviving entity after the merger takes effect.

Comment

. . . .

This scheme of liability is similar to that of an incoming partner under Section 306(b). Only the surviving partnership itself is liable for all obligations, including obligations incurred by every constituent party before the merger. A general partner of the surviving entity is personally liable for obligations of the surviving entity incurred before the merger by the partnership of which he was a partner and those incurred by the surviving entity after the merger. Thus, a general partner of the surviving entity is liable only to the extent of his partnership interest for obligations incurred before the merger by a constituent party of which he was not a general partner.

. . . .

Although subsection (e) does not expressly provide that a partner's withdrawal upon the merger of a term partnership is rightful, it was assumed that the unanimity requirement for the approval of a merger would afford a withdrawing partner adequate opportunity to protect his interest as a condition of approval. This question is left to the partnership agreement if it provides for merger without the approval of all the partners.

Under subsection (e), a dissociating general partner's lingering agency power is wound down, pursuant to Section 702, the same as in any other dissociation. Moreover, a dissociating general partner may be liable, under Section 703, for obligations incurred by the surviving entity for up to two years after the merger. A dissociating general partner can, however, limit to 90 days his exposure to liability by filing a statement of dissociation under Section 704.

§ 907. Statement of Merger.

(a)   After a merger, the surviving partnership or limited partnership may file a statement that one or more partnerships or limited partnerships have merged into the surviving entity.

. . . .

(c)   Except as otherwise provided in subsection (d), for the purposes of Section 302, property of the surviving partnership or limited partnership which before the merger was held in the name of another party to the merger is property held in the name of the surviving entity upon filing a statement of merger.

(d)   For the purposes of Section 302, real property of the surviving partnership or limited partnership which before the merger was held in the name of another party to the merger is property held in the name of the surviving entity upon recording a certified copy of the statement of merger in the office for recording transfers of that real property.

§ 908. Nonexclusive.

This [article] is not exclusive. Partnerships or limited partnerships may be converted or merged in any other manner provided by law.

NOTES

1. This language is similar to the corporation statutes which provide for merger of those types of entities. The corporate statutes are discussed in Section B.2.c below.

2. Review the powerful language of RUPA § 906(a) and the awesome events which happen by operation of law when the merger becomes effective. This can be a powerful aide to business attorneys combining businesses of any size with far-flung and varied assets and interests. MBCA § 11.07(a) provides for similar transformations upon the effective date of a corporate merger.

3. Section 906(e) provides for partners who do not assent to the merger to have their interests purchased as if they were rightfully dissociating. The comments note that the partnership agreement might otherwise provide. This is in distinction to state corporation law which, upon a corporate merger, more carefully proscribes the ability of a shareholder to avoid the consequences of a merger.

4. Section 907 provides for notice of the transfer of property, and refers to the rules in § 302 governing recording of transfer of real property. Section 302 is set forth and discussed *supra* in Section (B)(1)(a).

2.   Corporations

a.   Sale of Assets

If a corporation chooses to sell its assets, the sale must be properly authorized by resolution of the board of directors and carried out by officers with the agency authority to negotiate the sale and execute the requisite documents. Of course, the board must act in accordance with their duties of care and loyalty. It is also probable that state corporation law will require that shareholder in some circumstances.

The Model Business Corporation Act provides in § 12.01 that "No approval of the shareholders of a corporation is required, unless the articles of incorporation otherwise provide: (1) to sell, lease, exchange or otherwise dispose of any or all of the corporation's assets in the usual and regular course of business." In Section 12.02(a), the Act provides that shareholder approval of a disposition of assets is required if it is not described in § 12.01 and "if the disposition would leave the corporation without a significant continuing business activity." The section goes on to provide a "safe harbor" if the corporation retains an activity amounting to at least 25% of total assets and 25% of revenues or income before taxes from continuing operations. This language is different from the Act's prior language and from the similar provisions in most states which require shareholder approval for sale of "all or substantially all" of the corporation's assets.[31]

The "all or substantially all" language exists in the current version of § 271 of Delaware's corporation law, and was interpreted in the leading case of *Gimbel v. Signal Companies, Inc.*[32] as follows.

---

[31] MBCA § 12.02 Comment 1.

[32] 316 A.2d 599 (Del. Ch.), *aff'd* 316 A.2d 619 (Del. 1974).

The key language in the Court of Chancery opinion in *Philadelphia National Bank* [v. B.S.F. Co., 41 Del. Ch. 509, 199 A.2d 557 (Ch. 1964), *rev'd on other grounds*, 42 Del. Ch. 106, 204 A.2d 746 (Supr. Ct. 1964)] is the suggestion that "the critical factor in determining the character of a sale of assets is generally considered not the amount of property sold but whether the sale is in fact an unusual transaction or one made in the regular course of business of the seller." 41 Del.Ch. at 515, 199 A.2d at 561. Professor Folk suggests from the opinion that "the statute would be inapplicable if the assets sale is 'one made in furtherance of express corporate objects in the ordinary and regular course of the business.'" . . . Folk [The Delaware General Corporation Law] Section 271, p. 401.

But any "ordinary and regular course of the business" test in this context obviously is not intended to limit the directors to customary daily business activities. Indeed, a question concerning the statute would not arise unless the transaction was somewhat out of the ordinary. While it is true that a transaction in the ordinary course of business does not require shareholder approval, the converse is not true. Every transaction out of normal routine does not necessarily require shareholder approval. The unusual nature of the transaction must strike at the heart of the corporate existence and purpose. As it is written at 6A Fletcher, Cyclopedia Corporations (Perm. Ed. 1968) § 2949.2, p. 648:

> "The purpose of the consent statutes is to protect the shareholders from fundamental change, or more specifically to protect the shareholder from the destruction of the means to accomplish the purposes or objects for which the corporation was incorporated and actually performs."

It is in this sense that the 'unusual transaction' judgment is to be made and the statute's applicability determined. If the sale is of assets quantitatively vital to the operation of the corporation and is out of the ordinary and substantially affects the existence and purpose of the corporation, then it is beyond the power of the Board of Directors. . . .[33]

Thus, we have a qualitative as well as a quantitative test. A recent Delaware Chancery Court opinion provided the following helpful summary of relevant cases in that state.[34]

[T]ransactions involving various asset percentages have been found to constitute or not constitute a sale of substantially all of a company's assets.

Case	% of assets	Vote required?
Thorpe v. CERBCO, Inc., 676 A.2d 436, 444 (Del. 1996)	68%	Yes
Oberly v. Kirby, 592 A.2d 445, 464 (Del. 1991)	80%	No
Winston v. Mandor, 710 A.2d 835, 843 (Del. Ch. 1997)	60%	Possibly (survived motion to dismiss)

[33] *Id.* at 606.

[34] The court's discussion of cases has been rearranged in tabular form for ease of reference.

Case	% of assets	Vote required?
Katz v. Bregman, 431 A.2d 1274, 1275–76 (Del. Ch. 1981)	51% 45% of sales 52% of pre-tax net operating income	Yes
Gimbel v. Signal Cos., 316 A.2d 599, 607-08 (Del. Ch. 1974)	26% total assets 41% net assets	No
Bacine v. Scharffenberger, 1984 Del. Ch. LEXIS 501, *7–8 (Dec. 10, 1984)	53% of 9-mo. income	No

Any wise counselor would therefore approach the question of whether a disposition of a particular division or subsidiary would involve a sale of "substantially all" of a company with extreme caution.[35]

With this background, you can appreciate the unsettled nature of an "all or substantially all" inquiry, and perhaps you will be glad of a "safe harbor" such as that provided in the recent amendments to MBCA § 12.02(a) discussed above.

This may seem like a lot of worry over a minor issue. A shareholder vote should be a mere formality, after all, since we are likely dealing with a closely-held corporation whose shareholders have already informally agreed to the sale. However, it is important to ascertain if a shareholder vote is necessary for at least two reasons. First, if a vote is required and it is *not* taken, the buyer may be free to walk away from the sale on the ground that it was not validly authorized by the seller. Second, if the selling shareholders are not unanimous in their desire, the requirement of a vote may trigger dissenter's appraisal rights on the part of the objecting shareholder.[36] This may create additional procedural complications, as well as a potentially significant cash drain, as the requesting shareholder is ordinarily entitled to payment of the fair value of his or her shares in cash.

b.   Sale of Stock

The transaction we discuss here is a sale of shares by existing shareholder(s) to outside purchasers. We have already covered other variations of this transaction: a purchase by existing shareholders was covered in Chapter 8, and a purchase by the corporation (a variety of a "distribution") was covered in Chapter 6.

Ordinarily such a transaction will involve the sale of a controlling interest in the corporation. Whenever a sale of control is involved, the business planner should consider whether or not and to what degree the noncontrolling shareholders can or should be involved.

The commercial reality is that parties to such transactions are reluctant to transfer corporate control without first having involved minority sharehold-

---

[35] *In re* General Motors Class H Shareholders Litigation, 734 A.2d 611, 623 & n.10 (Del. Ch. 1999).

[36] See, e.g., MBCA § 13.02(a), which provides that "[a] shareholder is entitled to appraisal rights, and to obtain payment of the fair value of that shareholder's shares, in the event of any of the following corporate actions: . . . (3) consummation of a disposition of assets pursuant to section 12.02 if the shareholder is entitled to vote on the disposition . . . ." There is an exception to this right in § 13.02(b)(1) if the shares are publicly-traded, but this exception will likely not apply to the ordinary closely-held corporation.

ers. The parties and their legal advisors have traditionally structured transactions in a manner that enables minority shareholders to participate (directly) or benefit (indirectly) from the transaction's results. . . . [C]onsideration of the minority is not the result of a positive norm, but rather is voluntary. . . .

Current law goes beyond regulation of the exercise of control. It intervenes in control transactions by imposing a fiduciary duty on the controller to preempt any attempt by a potential looter to acquire control. It also prohibits the controller from selling her office in the corporation or selling commercial opportunities which are corporate property, in the guise of a transaction for the sale of corporate control. Where the private sale of control is tainted with any such element of breach of fiduciary duty, the minority would receive the remedy appropriate to the facts of the case (annulment, damages, etc.).[37]

Liability for "Sale of Control." A seller of controlling shares owes a duty to the corporation and the remaining shareholders to be on the alert for "looters." A good statement of the general rule comes from *De Baun v. First Western Bank & Trust Co.*[38]

Early case law held that a controlling shareholder owed no duty to minority shareholders or to the controlled corporation in the sale of his stock. Decisional law, however, has since recognized the fact of financial life that corporate control by ownership of a majority of shares may be misused. Thus the applicable proposition now is that "In any transaction where the control of the corporation is material," the controlling majority shareholder must exercise good faith and fairness "from the viewpoint of the corporation and those interested therein." (*Remillard Brick Co. v. Remillard-Dandini*, 109 Cal.App.2d 405, 420 [241 P.2d 66] quoted in *Jones v. H.F. Ahmanson & Co.*, 1 Cal.3d 93, 110 [81 Cal.Rptr. 592, 460 P.2d 464]. That duty of good faith and fairness encompasses an obligation of the controlling shareholder in possession of facts "[s]uch as to awaken suspicion and put a prudent man on his guard [that a potential buyer of his shares may loot the corporation of its assets to pay for the shares purchased . . . to conduct a reasonable and adequate investigation [of the buyer]." *Insuranshares Corporation v. Northern Fiscal Corp.* (E.D.Pa. 1940) 35 F.Supp. 22, 25. . . .[39]

These so called "looting" cases are very fact-dependent. Different purchasers will present very different facts which may "awaken suspicion" alone or with other facts which the seller knew or — a more difficult situation — "should have known." The result may also depend on whether the seller alone holds controlling shares, or whether the seller assists other shareholder in their sales which in the aggregate transfer control to the buyer.

The business lawyer should always be on the lookout for fact concerning the purchasing shareholder which might, in the language of the *Remillard Brick* court,

---

[37] Yedidia Z. Stern, *The Private Sale of Corporate Control: A Myth Dethroned*, 25 J. Corp. L. 511, 513, 540 (2000).

[38] 46 Cal. App. 3d 686, 120 Cal. Rptr. 354 (1975).

[39] *Id.* at 696, 120 Cal. Rptr. at 359–60 (citations omitted).

"awaken suspicion." Prudence dictates at least a rudimentary inquiry into the purchaser's source of funds and plans for the business after control is obtained. Any concern which is substantiated should be the subject of careful further negotiations and, if necessary, representations and warranties in the contract of sale.

"Equal opportunity" doctrine. We discussed *Donahue v. Rodd Electrotype*[40] at the end of Chapter 7, in a general discussion of fiduciary duties owed in close corporations. However, the precise holding of *Donahue* is important in this context, as it required a corporation repurchasing shares from a founding shareholder to make the same offer to *all* shareholders of the corporation.[41] However, the court in *Donahue* noted that it was *not* extending its holding to transactions *not* involving the corporation.[42] Nonetheless, because the scope of *Donahue* continues to be uncertain and evolving, it is a common-law doctrine which may concern a business lawyer if the corporation is involved, even indirectly, in facilitating the sale of control by one or more shareholders.

"Corporate opportunity" doctrine. There are many different formulations of this common law rule, but in general they require that a corporate "insider" cannot take for himself or herself an opportunity which belongs to the corporation. Most of the variations in these rules concern whether the opportunity is one which belongs to the corporation. If an opportunity was improperly taken, normally it is the individual who did the taking who is liable to the corporation.

The corporate opportunity doctrine can be relevant in a sale-of-control context if it is determined that the offer to buy control was intended for the corporation, but it was taken instead by a controlling shareholder. How could an offer to sell control be "intended for" the corporation, since the corporation itself cannot sell its ownership interests? In the closely-held corporation, often times courts are not especially careful with the doctrinal niceties, and can hold officers, directors, and even selling shareholder who have no other role liable for refusing to extend to other shareholders an opportunity to participate in the sale of a controlling interest in the corporation. Furthermore, this liability can be held to extend not to the corporation but to the minority shareholders. The rationale for this modification of a duty normally owed *to the corporation* is that, since the defendant holds a controlling interest in the corporation, most of the liability would be paid by the defendant to his or her own pocket. Therefore, because the "corporate opportunity" doctrine might actually hold one *shareholder* liable to another, it doctrine appears to do what the *Donahue* court said it would not do: extend fiduciary duties to the selling shareholder(s) in transactions not involving the corporation at all.

[40] Donahue v. Rodd Electrotype Co. of New England, Inc., 367 Mass. 578, 328 N.E.2d 505 (1975).

[41] *See id.* at 598, 328 N.E.2d at 518.

[42] *See id.* at 593 n.18, 328 N.E.2d at 515 n.18 ("We express no opinion as to the standard of duty applicable to transactions in the shares of the close corporation when the corporation is not a party to the transaction.")

HARRIS v. CARTER
Delaware Court of Chancery
582 A.2d 222 (1990)

ALLEN, CHANCELLOR.

Two distinct groups of defendants have moved to dismiss the Amended and Supplemental Complaint in this action, ("amended complaint"). They assert . . . that the amended complaint does not state a claim upon which relief may be granted . . . .

Certain of the legal issues presented are novel questions under our law and they arise in a case of some factual and procedural complexity.

The litigation arises from the negotiation and sale by one group of defendants (the Carter group) of a control block of Atlas stock to Frederic Mascolo; the resignation of the Carter group as directors and the appointment of the Mascolo defendants as directors of Atlas, and, finally, the alleged looting of Atlas by Mascolo and persons associated with him. Insofar as the Carter defendants are concerned it is alleged that they were negligent and that their negligence breached a duty that, in the circumstances, they owed to the corporation. It is not claimed that they stand as an insurer of the corporation generally, but that the specific circumstances of their sale of control should have raised a warning that Mascolo was dishonest. . . .

Procedural History

Plaintiff is a minority shareholder of Atlas. He brought this action after the change in control from the Carter group to the Mascolo group had occurred. . . .

. . . .

[I]t is alleged that the Carter group, *qua* shareholders, owed a duty of care to Atlas to take the steps that a reasonable person would take in the circumstances to investigate the *bona fides* of the person to whom they sold control.[43] It is said that the duty was breached here, and that if it had been met the corporation would have been spared the losses that are alleged to have resulted from the transactions effected by the board under the domination of Mascolo. There is no allegation that the Carter group conspired with Mascolo. Indeed the Carter group did not sell for cash but for shares of common stock of a corporation that plaintiff claims was a worthless shell and which was later employed in the transactions that are said to constitute a looting of Atlas. Thus, accepting the allegations of the complaint, they suggest that the Carter group was misled to its own injury as well as the injury of Atlas and its other shareholders. . . .

. . . .

The amended complaint seeks appointment of a receiver, rescission, and damages.

---

[43] [3] Carter owned 46% of Atlas' stock and the Carter group as a whole owned 52% of the Atlas stock. Several individuals designated in the amended complaint as members of the Carter group are not named as defendants.

I.

The facts as alleged are involved. As alleged they appear as follows.

The Company

Atlas Energy Corporation is a Delaware corporation which, before Mascolo acquired control of it, engaged in oil and gas exploration and production. It conducted its business primarily through the acquisition of oil and gas properties which were resold to drilling programs. It then acted as sponsor and general partner of the drilling programs.

The Stock Exchange Agreement

The Carter group, which collectively owned 52% of the stock of Atlas, and Mascolo entered into a Stock Exchange Agreement dated as of March 28, 1986. That agreement provided that the Carter group would exchange its Atlas stock for shares of stock held by Mascolo in a company called Insuranshares of America ("ISA") and contemplated a later merger between ISA and Atlas. ISA was described in the preamble to the Stock Exchange Agreement as "a company engaged in the insurance field by and through wholly-owned subsidiaries." The Stock Exchange Agreement contained representations and warranties by Mascolo to the effect that ISA owned all of the issued and outstanding capital stock of Pioneer National Life Insurance Company and Western National Life Insurance Company. It is alleged that those representations were false. ISA did not own stock in either company and had no insurance subsidiaries.

In the course of negotiations, the Mascolo group furnished the Carter group with a draft financial statement of ISA that reflected an investment in Life Insurance Company of America, a Washington corporation ("LICA"). No representation concerning LICA was made in the Stock Exchange Agreement, however. The existence of a purported investment by ISA in LICA was fictitious. It is alleged that the draft ISA financial statement was sufficiently suspicious to put any reasonably prudent business person on notice that further investigation should be made. Indeed Atlas' chief financial officer analyzed the financial statement and raised several questions concerning its accuracy, none of which were pursued by the Carter group.

The Stock Exchange Agreement further provided that Mascolo would place in escrow 50,000 shares of Louisiana Bankshares Inc. 8% cumulative preferred stock, $10 par value. It was agreed that if Atlas consummated an exchange merger for all of the outstanding common stock of ISA on agreed upon terms within 365 days of the date of the Stock Exchange Agreement, the bank stock would be returned to Mascolo. If no merger took place within the specified time, then that stock was to be distributed *pro rata* to the Carter group members.

It was agreed, finally, that as part of the stock exchange transaction, the members of the Carter group would resign their positions as Atlas directors in a procedure that assured that Mascolo and his designees would be appointed as replacements.

The gist of plaintiff's claim against the Carter defendants is the allegation that those defendants had reason to suspect the integrity of the Mascolo group, but failed to conduct even a cursory investigation into any of several suspicious aspects of the transaction: the unaudited financial statement, the mention of LICA in negotiations but not in the representations concerning ISA's subsidiaries, and the ownership of the subsidiaries themselves. Such an investigation, argues plaintiff, would have revealed the structure of ISA to be fragile indeed, with minimal capitalization and no productive assets.

. . . .

The ISA Transaction

Plaintiff asserts that ISA is nothing more than a corporate shell. Pursuant to the Stock Exchange Agreement Mascolo acquired a controlling (52%) stock interest in Atlas in exchange for 518,335 ISA shares. Atlas then acquired all the outstanding ISA shares in exchange for 3,000,000 newly issued shares of Atlas common stock. As a result of that transaction, the Mascolo group as a whole came to own 75% of Atlas' shares. The minority shareholders of Atlas saw their proportionate ownership of Atlas reduced from 48% before the ISA transaction to 12% upon its consummation. For Atlas to exchange 3,000,000 of its shares for the stock of this "corporate shell" was, argues plaintiff, equivalent to issuing Atlas stock to the Mascolo group (the holders of the ISA stock) without consideration.

. . . .

V.

. . . I turn to the Carter defendants motion to dismiss for failure to state a claim upon which relief may be granted. This motion raises novel questions of Delaware law. Stated generally the most basic of these questions is whether a controlling shareholder or group may under any circumstances owe a duty of care to the corporation in connection with the sale of a control block of stock. If such a duty may be said to exist under certain circumstances the questions in this case then become whether the facts alleged in the amended complaint would permit the finding that such a duty arose in connection with the sale to the Mascolo group and was breached. In this inquiry one applies the permissive standard appropriate for motions to dismiss: if on any state of facts that may reasonably be inferred from the pleaded facts plaintiff would be entitled to a judgment, a claim that will survive a Rule 12(b) motion has been stated.

A.

A number of cases may be cited in support of the proposition that when transferring control of a corporation to another, a controlling shareholder may, in some circumstances, have a duty to investigate the *bona fides* of the buyer — that is, in those circumstances, to take such steps as a reasonable person would take to ascertain that the buyer does not intend or is unlikely to plan any depredations of the corporation.[44] The circumstance to which these cases refer is the existence of facts that would give rise to suspicion by a reasonably prudent person. The leading

---

[44] [15] *See Insuranshares Corporation v. Northern Fiscal Corporation*, 35 F. Supp. 22 (E.D.Pa. 1940); *Clagett v. Hutchison*, 4th Cir., 583 F.2d 1259, 1262 (1978); *Swinney v. Keebler Company*, 4th Cir., 480 F.2d 573, 577 (1973) . . . .

case is *Insuranshares Corporation*, 35 F.Supp. 22 (E.D.Pa. 1940).

In that case defendants, who comprised the entire board of directors of the corporation involved, sold their 27% stock interest in the corporation and resigned as directors. The resignations were done seriatim, in a way that permitted the designation of the buyers as successor directors. The buyers proceeded to loot the corporation.

As here, the sellers contended that they could have no liability for the wrongs that followed their sale. They merely sold their stock and resigned. These were acts that they were privileged to do, they claimed. Judge Kirkpatrick rejected this position:

> Those who control a corporation, either through majority stock ownership, ownership of large blocks of stock less than a majority, officeholding, management contracts, or otherwise, owe some duty to the corporation in respect of the transfer of the control to outsiders. The law has long ago reached the point where it is recognized that such persons may not be wholly oblivious of the interest of everyone but themselves, even in the act of parting with control, and that, under certain circumstances, they may be held liable for whatever injury to the corporation made possible by the transfer. Without attempting any general definition, and stating the duty in minimum terms as applicable to the facts of this case, it may be said that the owners of control are under a duty not to transfer it to outsiders if the circumstances surrounding the proposed transfer are such as to awaken suspicion and put a prudent man on his guard-unless a reasonably adequate investigation discloses such facts as would convince a reasonable person that no fraud is intended or likely to result.

*	*	*

> If, after such investigation, the sellers are deceived by false representations, there might not be liability, but if the circumstances put the seller on notice and if no adequate investigation is made and harm follows, then liability also follows.

35 F.Supp. at 25.

This statement represents the majority view on the subject. . . .

Although there are few cases applying the principle of the *Insuranshares* case that do fix liability on a seller, it is the principle of *Insuranshares* and not the actual notice rule of *Levy* that has commanded the respect of later courts. In *Swinney v. Keebler Company*, 480 F.2d 573, 577 (1973), the [Fourth] Circuit Court of Appeals acknowledged *Insuranshares* as "the leading case." It aptly summarized the principle of that case:

> Liability was predicated upon breach of a duty not to transfer control since the circumstances surrounding the transfer were "such as to awaken suspicion and put a prudent man on his guard-unless a reasonably adequate investigation discloses such facts as would convince a reasonable person that no fraud is intended or likely to result." 35 F.Supp. at 25.

Swinney v. Keebler Company, 480 F.2d at 577.

B.

While Delaware law has not addressed this specific question, one is not left without guidance from our decided cases. Several principles deducible from that law are pertinent. First, is the principle that a shareholder has a right to sell his or her stock and in the ordinary case owes no duty in that connection to other shareholders when acting in good faith. *Frantz Manufacturing Co. v. EAC Industries*, Del.Supr., 501 A.2d 401, 408 (1985).

Equally well established is the principle that when a shareholder presumes to exercise control over a corporation, to direct its actions, that shareholder assumes a fiduciary duty of the same kind as that owed by a director to the corporation. *Sterling v. Mayflower Hotel Corp.*, Del. Supr., 93 A.2d 107, 109–10 (1952). A sale of controlling interest in a corporation, at least where, as is alleged here, that sale is coupled with an agreement for the sellers to resign from the board of directors in such a way as to assure that the buyer's designees assume that corporate office, does, in my opinion, involve or implicate the corporate mechanisms so as to call this principle into operation.

More generally, it does not follow from the proposition that ordinarily a shareholder has a right to sell her stock to whom and on such terms as she deems expedient, that no duty may arise from the particular circumstances to take care in the exercise of that right. It is established American legal doctrine that, unless privileged, each person owes a duty to those who may foreseeably be harmed by her action to take such steps as a reasonably prudent person would take in similar circumstances to avoid such harm to others.[45] While this principle arises from the law of torts and not the law of corporations or of fiduciary duties, that distinction is not, I think, significant unless the law of corporations or of fiduciary duties somehow privileges a selling shareholder by exempting her from the reach of this principle. The principle itself is one of great generality and, if not negated by privilege, would apply to a controlling shareholder who negligently places others foreseeably in the path of injury.

That a shareholder may sell her stock (or that a director may resign his office) is a right that, with respect to the principle involved, is no different, for example, than the right that a licensed driver has to operate a motor vehicle upon a highway. The right exists, but it is not without conditions and limitations, some established by positive regulation, some by common-law. Thus, to continue the parallel, the driver owes a duty of care to her passengers because it is foreseeable that they may be injured if, through inattention or otherwise, the driver involves the car she is operating in a collision. In the typical instance a seller of corporate stock can be expected to have no similar apprehension of risks to others from her own inattention. But, in some circumstances, the seller of a control block of stock may or should reasonably foresee danger to other shareholders; with her sale of stock will also go control over the corporation and with it the opportunity to misuse that power to the injury of such other shareholders. Thus, the reason that a duty of care is recognized in any situation is fully present in this situation. I can find no universal privilege arising from the corporate form that exempts a controlling shareholder who sells corporate control from the wholesome reach of this common-law duty.[46]

---

[45] [16] *See Restatement of Torts Second* § 281; Prosser & Keeton on Torts p. 284-90 (5th Ed. 1984); *Palsgraf v. Long Island Railroad Co.*, 248 N.Y. 339, 162 N.E. 99 (1928) . . . .

[46] [17] A privilege arguably does exist with respect to foreseeable risk of financial injury to share

Certainly I cannot read the Supreme Court's opinion in *Frantz, supra*, as intending to lay down a rule applicable to the question here posed.

Thus, I conclude that while a person who transfers corporate control to another is surely not a surety for his buyer, when the circumstances would alert a reasonably prudent person to a risk that his buyer is dishonest or in some material respect not truthful, a duty devolves upon the seller to make such inquiry as a reasonably prudent person would make, and generally to exercise care so that others who will be affected by his actions should not be injured by wrongful conduct.

The cases that have announced this principle have laid some stress on the fact that they involved not merely a sale of stock, but a sale of control over the corporation. Thus, in *Insuranshares*, the agreement that the sellers would resign from the board in a way that would facilitate the buyers immediately assuming office (*see* 35 F.Supp. at 24) was given importance. That circumstance is pleaded here as well.

One cannot determine (and may not on this type of motion determine) whether Mr. Carter and those who acted with him were in fact negligent in a way that proximately caused injury to the corporation. Indeed one cannot determine now whether the circumstances that surrounded the negotiations with Mascolo were such as to have awakened suspicion in a person of ordinary prudence. The test of a Rule 12(b)(6) motion is, as noted above, permissive. It is sufficient to require denial of this motion to dismiss that I cannot now say as a matter of law that under no state of facts that might be proven could it be held that a duty arose, to the corporation and its other shareholders, to make further inquiry and was breached. . . .

That Mr. Carter may well have been misled to his own detriment may be a factor affecting the question whether a duty to inquire arose, as Carter might be assumed to be a prudent man when dealing with his own property. But that assumption is essentially evidentiary and can be given no weight on this motion.

For the foregoing reasons the pending motions will be denied.

NOTES AND QUESTIONS

1. What about the escrow of Louisiana Bankshares stock (third paragraph under *The Stock Exchange Agreement* in the court's opinion). This is "earnest money" in common parlance. Did this not establish Mascolo's *bona fides*?

2. From what status do these duties derive? Would it matter if the seller was not a director or officer in the selling company? And to whose benefit does this duty run — the minority shareholders, the purchasers? How can it run to the purchasers?

3. How do these rules differ from those of the California court announced in *DeBaun*?

A business lawyer should be alert to the application of duties under state corporation law to the selling shareholder in a sale-of-interests transaction. The

---

values that might arise from a risky though honest future business plan that the buyer may have in mind. Such a privilege would not be involved here when the thrust of the complaint is that Mascolo engaged in — and Carter defendants should have foreseen or at least investigated — dishonest transactions.

buy-sell agreement should recite that the offer is made only to the selling shareholder(s),[47] and the selling shareholder(s) should represent and warrant that they have not communicated the offer or agreed to extend the offer to the other shareholders, and to indemnify the purchaser against any such liability.[48] If this representation and warranty cannot be made, the purchaser should consider (1) whether to extend the offer to the other shareholders, which could substantially affect the price of the deal, or (2) whether the deal can be completed at all.

c.   Combinations

In addition to the sale of assets or sale of stock, state laws provide for binding mergers and share exchanges. In short, two corporations are permitted to merge (with one of them surviving or with a new corporation surviving) or one corporation may exchange its shares for those of the other (leaving the two in a parent-subsidiary relationship). In general, a merger or share exchange is done pursuant to a plan of merger adopted by the boards of directors of both corporations and, in most cases, by some of the shareholders of both corporations. Once the plan is approved by the requisite constituencies, what it directs takes place by operation of law. Section 11.07 of the MBCA is representative of the power of a merger.

§ 11.07.   Effect of Merger or Share Exchange

(a)   When a merger becomes effective:

(1)   the corporation or eligible entity that is designated in the plan of merger as the survivor continues or comes into existence, as the case may be;

(2)   the separate existence of every corporation or eligible entity that is merged into the survivor ceases;

(3)   all property owned by, and every contract right possessed by, each corporation or eligible entity that merges into the survivor is vested in the survivor without reversion or impairment;

(4)   all liabilities of each corporation or eligible entity that is merged into the survivor are vested in the survivor;

(5)   the name of the survivor may, but need not be, substituted in any pending proceeding for the name of any party to the merger whose separate existence ceased in the merger;

(6)   the articles of incorporation or organic documents of the survivor are amended to the extent provided in the plan of merger;

(7)   the articles of incorporation or organic documents of a survivor that is created by the merger become effective; and

(8)   the shares of each corporation that is a party to the merger, and the interests in an eligible entity that is a party to a merger, that are to be converted under the plan of merger into shares, eligible interests, obligations, rights to acquire securities, other securities, or eligible interests, cash, other property, or

---

[47] This conclusion assumes, of course, you have read and resolved the above cases and doctrines and have determined that the non-selling shareholders can be safely excluded.

[48] Admittedly, whether this indemnity runs in favor of buyers or sellers would depend in large part on the bargaining positions of each.

any combination of the foregoing, are converted, and the former holders of such shares or eligible interests are entitled only to the rights provided to them . . . .

A merger may result in a "cash out" of the selling corporation's shareholders, or they may receive stock in the surviving corporation, debt securities, other property, or some combination of the above. You can see, therefore, that a merger can be used to pursue both a "sale of assets" and a "sale of interests."

It is difficult to meaningfully generalize further. Each state's merger laws will differ in many of the following ways.

• *Board approval:* the standard of approval required by the board of directors, and the effect (if any) of conflict of interest on the board's recommendation to the shareholders, or whether the merger may be submitted to the shareholders without the board's recommendation;

• *Shareholder approval:* which of the "target" or "disappearing" or "subsidiary" corporation's shareholders get to vote (regular voting stock, preferred stock also, even *nonvoting* stock), under what circumstances, in what proportion (one vote per share, approval required by each class voting separately) and what overall approval is required (majority, two-thirds); whether the "purchasing" or "surviving" share-holders get to vote;

• *Triangular mergers:* if the merger can be conducted between two corporations but using the stock of some other corporation (usually the parent of one of the merging corporations) as consideration;

• *Dissenters' rights:* whether stockholders who vote against the merger are entitled to institute a proceeding, ordinarily a judicial proceeding, for cash payment of the appraised fair value of their shares; and

• *Anti-takeover laws:* whether a combination is prohibited with an "interested person," usually defined as an entity which has purchased a certain percentage of the target corporation's voting shares, or whether it is subject to supermajority or other special voting requirements.

EXERCISE 9-1

Review your state's merger and/or share exchange laws against the above standards. Make sure you know the basics: who approves; who votes; who has dissenters' rights; and how your state's anti-takeover laws work.

Another important issue to be resolved under your state's laws is the application of a rule known alternatively as the "*de facto* merger rule" or the "doctrine of independent legal significance" or "independent statutory significance" as it is called in the following excerpt.

> For example, assume Corporation A sells its assets to Corporation B and as part of the deal B assumes A's obligations and A dissolves. Thereafter, Corporation A distributes the proceeds of the sale (the B securities) to its shareholders under its plan of dissolution. In reviewing these transactions some courts may determine that there has been a de facto merger . . . . Two significant effects of so treating transactions . . . are: The sharehold-

ers of the "purchasing" corporation will be entitled to vote on the transaction, and an appraisal remedy is available to all shareholders entitled to vote.[49]

A far greater number of jurisdictions, including Delaware,[50] refuse to embrace the de facto merger doctrine. This refusal is based on the doctrine of "independent statutory significance" or equal dignity. This doctrine holds that each authorizing provision of the state's corporation statute is entitled to its own independent significance such that the substantive effects and procedural requirements of one provision are not to be harmonized with another provision under which the same objective could have also been accomplished . . . . Thus, under the doctrine of independent statutory significance, if the formal requirements of the sale-of-assets statute are complied with, the transaction [might] be considered a sale rather than a merger . . . .[51]

This is an important topic for the business lawyer for two reasons. First, it emphasizes the need to read the statute and plan with the legal requirements in mind. But second and perhaps more importantly, it provides a good vehicle to consider strategic legal planning generally. There are usually multiple ways of achieving all or most of a client's objectives. Sometimes a lawyer will find another way which seems to work but is cheaper, easier, and/or more certain. Is this brilliant work and value creation by transactional lawyers, or will it be swept away as some kind of subterfuge?

ELLIOTT ASSOCIATES, L.P. v. AVATEX CORPORATION
Delaware Supreme Court
715 A.2d 843 (1998)

VEASEY, CHIEF JUSTICE:

In this case of first impression, we hold that certain preferred stockholders have the right to a class vote in a merger where: (1) the certificate of incorporation expressly provides such a right in the event of any "amendment, alteration or repeal, whether by merger, consolidation or otherwise" of any of the provisions of the certificate of incorporation; (2) the certificate of incorporation that provides protections for the preferred stock is nullified and thereby repealed by the merger; and (3) the result of the transaction would materially and adversely affect the rights, preferences, privileges or voting power of those preferred stockholders. In so holding, we distinguish prior Delaware precedent narrowly because of the inclusion by the drafters of the phrase, "whether by merger, consolidation or otherwise."

---

[49] [See the leading *de facto* merger case, *Faris v. Glen Alden Corp.*, 143 A.2d 25 (Pa. 1958).—Eds.]

[50] [6] *See* Hariton v. Arco Elec., Inc. 188 A.2d 123 (Del. 1963), *aff'g* 182 A.2d 22 (Del. Ch. 1962); . . . Graeser v. Phoenix Fin. Co., 254 N.W. 859 (Iowa 1934); Good v. Lackawanna leather Co., 233 A.2d 201 (N.J. Super. Ct. Ch. Div. 1967).

[51] James D. Cox & Thomas Lee Hazen, Corporations 598–99 (2d ed. 2003). The hypothetical used by Professors Cox and Hazen is not hypothetical at all, but the basic facts of *Faris* (adopting the *de facto* merger rule) and *Hariton* (applying the opposite "independent statutory significance" doctrine).

Facts

Defendant Avatex Corporation ("Avatex") is a Delaware corporation that has outstanding both common and [First Series] preferred stock. Plaintiffs in these consolidated cases are all preferred stockholders of defendant Avatex. The individual defendants are all members of the Avatex board of directors.

Avatex created and incorporated Xetava Corporation ("Xetava") as its wholly-owned subsidiary on April 13, 1998, and the following day announced its intention to merge with and into Xetava. Under the terms of the proposed merger, Xetava is to be the surviving corporation. Once the transaction is consummated, Xetava will immediately change its name to Avatex Corporation. The proposed merger would cause a conversion of the preferred stock of Avatex into common stock of Xetava. The merger will effectively eliminate Avatex' certificate of incorporation, which includes the certificate of designations creating the Avatex preferred stock and setting forth its rights and preferences. The terms of the merger do not call for a class vote of these preferred stockholders. Herein lies the heart of the legal issue presented in this case.

Plaintiffs filed suit in the Court of Chancery to enjoin the proposed merger, arguing, among other things, that the transaction required the consent of two-thirds of the holders of the First Series Preferred stock. Defendants responded with a motion for judgment on the pleadings, which the Court of Chancery granted, finding that the provisions governing the rights of the First Series Preferred stockholders do not require such consent.

The plaintiffs allege that, because of Avatex' anemic financial state, "all the value of Avatex is [currently] in the preferred stock." By forcing the conversion of the preferred shares into common stock of the surviving corporation, however, the merger would place current preferred stockholders of Avatex on an even footing with its common stockholders. In fact, the Avatex preferred stockholders will receive in exchange for their preferred stock approximately 73 % of Xetava common stock, and the common stockholders of Avatex will receive approximately 27% of the common stock of Xetava.

Under the terms of the Avatex certificate of incorporation, First Series stockholders have no right to vote except on:

(a) any "amendment, alteration or repeal" of the certificate of incorporation "whether by merger, consolidation or otherwise," that

(b) "materially and adversely" affects the rights of the First Series stockholders.

The text of the terms governing the voting rights of the First Series Preferred Stock is set forth in the certificate of designations as follows:

Except as expressly provided hereinafter in this Section (6) or as otherwise . . . required by law, the First Series Preferred Stock shall have no voting rights.

. . .

So long as any shares of First Series Preferred Stock remain outstanding, the *consent* of the holders of at least two-thirds of the shares of the *First*

Series Preferred Stock outstanding at the time (voting separately as a class . . .) . . . *shall be necessary to permit, effect or validate* any one or more of the following:

. . .

(b) *The amendment, alteration or repeal, whether by merger, consolidation or otherwise, of any of the provisions of the* Restated *Certificate* of Incorporation or of [the certificate of designations] which would *materially and adversely affect any right, preference, privilege or voting power of the First Series Preferred Stock* or of the holders thereof. . . .[52]

These are the operative terms of Section 6 of the certificate of designations (with emphasis supplied) setting forth the rights and preferences of the First Series Preferred stock . . . .

Analysis

Delaware law permits corporations to create and issue stock that carries no voting power.[53] Professor Buxbaum, in his seminal article on preferred stock nearly 45 years ago, noted, among many other cogent observations, that: (a) statutes often permit alteration of preferred stock rights and preferences by merger;[54] (b) the merger may be with a "paper subsidiary created for that purpose with no independent business validity";[55] (c) "corporate articles [often] require consent of two-thirds (or a majority) of the preferred shareholders as a class for the consummation of any merger. . . . ";[56] and (d) courts have struggled with "controls in the name . . . of 'fairness' and generally abandoned them [, which] is as it should be [since the] issue is one of corporate power."[57]

---

[52] [6] In addition, Section 4 of the Avatex certificate of incorporation provides, in relevant part:

So long as any of the preferred stock remains outstanding, the consent of the holders of at least a majority of all outstanding shares of preferred stock . . . shall be necessary for effecting or validating any amendment, alteration or repeal of any of the provisions of this Article [including certain board resolutions] which increase or decrease the par value of the preferred stock or would adversely affect the rights or preferences of the preferred stock, or of the holders thereof. . . .

See also 8 Del.C. § 242(b)(2)(providing by statute a class vote in certain circumstances). When an amendment to a certificate of incorporation is sought to be effected *under that section*:

The holders of the outstanding shares of a class shall be entitled to vote as a class upon a proposed amendment, whether or not entitled to vote thereon by the certificate of incorporation, if the amendment would increase or decrease the aggregate number of authorized shares of such class, increase or decrease the par value of the shares of such class, or alter or change the powers, preferences, or special rights of the shares of such class so as to affect them adversely.

Id. Because the merger here implicates a different statute (8 Del.C. § 251, which does not itself require a class vote), the provisions of Section 242 are not implicated, the two statutes being of independent legal significance. *See Warner Communications Inc. v. Chris-Craft Indus., Inc.*, Del.Ch., 583 A.2d 962, 970, aff'd, Del.Supr., 567 A.2d 419 (1989). Likewise, Section 4 of the Avatex certificate is not applicable. . . .

[53] [10] *See* 8 Del.C. § 151(a).

[54] [11] Richard M. Buxbaum, *Preferred Stock-Law and Draftsmanship*, 42 Cal. L. Rev. 243, 303 (1954).

[55] [12] *Id.* at 300 n.295.

[56] [13] *Id.* at 307.

[57] [14] *Id.* at 309.

The Avatex certificate of incorporation provides that Avatex preferred shares have no right to vote except on matters set forth therein or required by law.[58] This denial of the right to vote is subject to an exception carved out for any "amendment, alteration or repeal" of the certificate "whether by merger, consolidation or otherwise" that "materially and adversely" affects the rights of the preferred stockholders. Such an event requires the consent of two-thirds of the First Series Preferred stockholders voting as a class.

This appeal, then, reduces to a narrow legal question: whether the "amendment, alteration or repeal" of the certificate of incorporation is caused "by merger, consolidation or otherwise" thereby requiring a two-thirds class vote of the First Series Preferred stockholders, it being assumed for purposes of this appeal that their rights would be "materially and adversely" affected. The Court of Chancery answered this question in the negative. Although we respect that Court's craftsmanlike analysis, we are constrained to disagree with its conclusion.

Relying primarily on *Warner Communications Inc. v. Chris-Craft Industries Inc.*[59], the Court of Chancery held that it was only the *conversion* of the stock as a result of the merger, and not the *amendment, alteration or repeal* of the certificate, that would adversely affect the preferred stockholders. It is important to keep in mind, however, that the terms of the preferred stock in *Warner* were significantly different from those present here, because in *Warner* the phrase "whether by merger, consolidation or otherwise" was not included. The issue here, therefore, is whether the presence of this additional phrase in the Avatex certificate is an outcome-determinative distinction from *Warner*.

In *Warner*, the question was whether the Series B preferred stock of Warner Communications, Inc. had the right to a class vote on a proposed merger of Warner with Time, Inc. (renamed Time Warner Inc.) and TW Sub, its wholly-owned subsidiary. As the first step in a two-step transaction, Time had acquired approximately 50% of Warner's common stock in a tender offer. The second step was the "back-end" merger in which TW Sub was merged into Warner, which survived as a wholly-owned subsidiary of Time. The Warner common stock not held by Time was converted into cash, securities and other property. In the merger, the Warner Series B preferred would be converted into Time Series BB preferred stock. The parties stipulated that the Warner Series B stockholders would thereby be adversely affected.

The Chancellor held that the drafters of the Warner Series B certificate of designations did not intend for two-thirds of the Series B stockholders to have a veto over every merger in which their interest would be adversely affected because the right to vote was conferred expressly (as it must [be] under Delaware law), and "only in narrowly defined circumstances . . . not present here."[60] The two

---

[58]   [15] This last qualification is irrelevant to this case since, as the Court of Chancery correctly noted, there is no requirement in the Delaware General Corporation Law that preferred stockholders vote to approve a proposed merger. *See* R. Franklin Balotti & Jesse A. Finkelstein, The Delaware Law of Corporations and Business Organizations § 9.15, at 9–26 (3d ed. 1998) ("Whether or not the holders of shares are entitled to vote on a merger is governed by the provisions of the certificate of incorporation setting forth the voting rights of the shares of stock.").

[59]   [16] 583 A.2d 962.

[60]   [20] *Warner*, 583 A.2d at 964.

provisions in the certificate of designations involved in *Warner* were as follows. Section 3.3 provided:

> So long as any shares of Series B Stock shall be outstanding and unless the consent or approval of a greater number of shares shall then be required by law, . . . the affirmative vote or written *consent* of the holders of at least two-thirds of the total number of the then outstanding shares of *Series B Stock* . . . voting a class, *shall be necessary to alter or change any rights, preferences or limitations of the Preferred Stock so as to affect the holders of all such shares adversely* . . . . [61]

Section 3.4 provided:

> So long as any shares of Series B Stock shall be outstanding and unless the consent or approval of a greater number of shares shall then be required by law, *without* first obtaining the *consent* or approval of the holders of at least two-thirds of the number of shares *of the Series B Stock* . . . the *Corporation shall not (i) amend, alter or repeal any of the provisions of the Certificate of Incorporation or By-laws of the Corporation so as to affect adversely* any of the preferences, rights, powers or privileges of the Series B Stock or the holders thereof. . . .[62]

We note again that nowhere in the Series B certificate of designations was found the phrase "by merger, consolidation or otherwise," which is the key phrase in the present case. Nevertheless, the heart of the *Warner* rationale, which we must address here, is that it was not the amendment, alteration or repeal of the Warner certificate that adversely affected the Warner Series B stock. The Chancellor held that it was only the conversion of the Warner Series B Preferred to Time Series BB Preferred that caused the adverse effect, and, moreover, that the conversion was permissible under 8 Del.C. § 251,which (unlike 8 Del.C. § 242) does not require a class vote on a merger. Further, the Chancellor held that no contractual protection of the Warner Series B stock provided for a class vote on a merger. . . .

. . . .

Plaintiffs here [validly] argue that *Warner* is distinguishable [because] the words "whether by merger, consolidation or otherwise" were not present in the Warner Series B certificate . . . .

. . . . The operative events here are that the proposed downstream merger of Avatex into Xetava results in the conversion of Avatex stock to Xetava stock and the elimination "by merger" of the certificate protections granted to the Avatex First Series Preferred. Thus, it is *both* the stock conversion *and* the repeal of the Avatex certificate that causes the adverse effect to the First Series Preferred. In *Warner*, it was only the stock conversion that caused the adverse effect because the phrase, "whether by merger, consolidation or otherwise" was not present.

The relevant statutory provisions are found in Sections 251(b) and 251(e) of the Delaware General Corporation Law ("DGCL"), which provide, in pertinent part:

> § 251. Merger or consolidation of domestic corporations.

---

61 [21] *Id.* at 964–65 (emphasis supplied).

62 [22] *Id.* at 965 (emphasis supplied).

* * *

(b) The board of directors of each corporation which desires to merge or consolidate shall adopt a resolution approving an agreement of merger or consolidation. The agreement shall state: (1) The terms and conditions of the merger or consolidation; (2) the mode of carrying the same into effect; (3) in the case of a merger, such amendments or changes in the certificate of incorporation of the surviving corporation as are desired to be effected by the merger, or, if no such amendments or changes are desired, a statement that the certificate of incorporation of the surviving corporation shall be its certificate of incorporation; (4) in the case of a consolidation, that the certificate of incorporation of the resulting corporation shall be as is set forth in an attachment to the agreement; (5) the manner of converting the shares of each of the constituent corporations into shares or other securities of the corporation surviving or resulting from the merger or consolidation and, if any shares of any of the constituent corporations are not to be converted solely into shares or other securities of the surviving or resulting corporation, the cash, property, rights or securities of any other corporation or entity which the holders of such shares are to receive in exchange . . . ; and (6) such other details or provisions as are deemed desirable. . . .

* * *

(e) In the case of a merger, the certificate of incorporation of the surviving corporation shall automatically be amended to the extent, if any, that changes in the certificate of incorporation are set forth in the agreement of merger.

In short, Section 251 of the DGCL describes three ways that a merger or consolidation can affect the certificate of a constituent corporation:

(1) *Section 251(b)(3) Amendments.* First, the merger agreement may call for amendments to the pre-existing certificate of the surviving corporation.

(2) *Displacement and Substitution by Merger.* Second, the merger can designate the certificate of one of the constituent corporations as the certificate of the surviving entity, and thereby render the certificate of every other constituent corporation a legal nullity.

(3) *Displacement and Substitution via Consolidation.* Finally, in the case of a consolidation, the certificate of the resulting corporation displaces and renders a legal nullity the certificate of every disappearing constituent corporation.

In speaking of the "amendment, alteration or repeal" of the Avatex certificate by "merger, consolidation or otherwise," the drafters must have been referring to some or all of the events permitted by Section 251. Therefore, Section 251 provides the relevant backdrop for the interpretation of the First Series Preferred voting rights.

. . . .

In our view, the merger does cause the adverse effect because the merger is the corporate act that renders the Avatex certificate that protects the preferred stockholders a "legal nullity," in defendants' words. That elimination certainly fits within the ambit of one or more of the three terms in the certificate: *amendment* or *alteration* or *repeal*. The word *repeal* is especially fitting in this context because it contemplates a nullification, which is what defendants concede happens to the Avatex certificate.

Articulation of the rights of preferred stockholders is fundamentally the function of corporate drafters. Construction of the terms of preferred stock is the function of courts. This Court's function is essentially one of contract interpretation against the background of Delaware precedent. These precedential parameters are simply stated: Any rights, preferences and limitations of preferred stock that distinguish that stock from common stock must be expressly and clearly stated, as provided by statute Therefore, these rights, preferences and limitations will not be presumed or implied. . . .

In our view, the rights of the First Series Preferred are expressly and clearly stated in the Avatex certificate. The drafters of this instrument could not reasonably have intended any consequence other than granting to the First Series Preferred stock the right to consent by a two-thirds class vote to any merger that would result in the elimination of the protections in the Avatex certificate if the rights of the holders of that stock would thereby be adversely affected. The First Series Preferred stock rights granted by the corporate drafters here are the functional equivalent of a provision that would expressly require such consent if a merger were to eliminate any provision of the Avatex certificate resulting in materially adverse consequences to the holders of that security.

The drafters were navigating around several alternatives. First, all parties agree that pure amendment protection available to the First Series Preferred stockholders as granted by Section 242(b)(2) of the DGCL and Section 4 of the certificate does not — absent the very phrase at issue here — apply to this merger. Although *Warner* was decided after the Avatex certificate of designations became effective, *Warner* clearly supports this view and it continues to be valid precedent for that proposition.[63] Second, all parties agree that if Avatex would have been the survivor, and its certificate were amended in the merger as contemplated by 8 Del.C. § 251(c)(3).

If Section 6 of the certificate does not guarantee a class vote to the First Series Preferred in this merger, what could it conceivably be interpreted to mean? Defendants argue that the certificate can be construed to apply *only* in the second instance noted above-namely, in the case where Avatex is the survivor and its certificate is amended, altered or repealed, as contemplated by Section 251(b)(3). But, as plaintiffs point out, this cannot be the *only* outcome the drafters intended because the certificate grants the First Series Preferred this protection in a consolidation where Section 251(b)(3) does not apply. Because the word *consolidation* is included, it cannot reasonably be argued that the protections of Section 6 of the certificate applicable to the First Series Preferred are confined to a Section 251(b)(3) amendment. Therefore, the term *consolidation* cannot be ignored or wished away as surplusage, as defendants argue. It is well established that a court interpreting any contractual provision, including preferred stock provisions, must give effect to all terms of the instrument, must read the instrument as a whole, and,

---

[63] [48] 583 A.2d at 970 (relying on *Orzeck v. Englehart*, Del.Supr., 195 A.2d 375 (1063), for the "bedrock doctrine of independent legal significance," which establishes that class voting rights granted under 8 Del.C. § 242(b)(2) and parallel contractual provisions in a certificate do not apply in a merger and that only the provisions of 8 Del.C. § 251 and any express certificate provisions need be satisfied).

if possible, reconcile all the provisions of the instrument.

Conclusion

The Court of Chancery held, and defendants contend on appeal, that *Warner* compels a different result from that which we reach because *Warner* held that there it was only the stock conversion, not the amendment that adversely affected the preferred. But the short answer here is that the language of the First Series Preferred stock is materially different from the language in *Warner* because here we have the phrase, "whether by merger, consolidation or otherwise." This provision entirely changes the analysis and compels the result we hold today. Here, the repeal of the certificate and the stock conversion cause the adverse effect.

. . . .

The path for future drafters to follow in articulating class vote provisions is clear. When a certificate (like the Warner certificate or the Series A provisions here) grants only the right to vote on an amendment, alteration or repeal, the preferred have no class vote in a merger. When a certificate (like the First Series Preferred certificate here) adds the terms "whether by merger, consolidation or otherwise" and a merger results in an amendment, alteration or repeal that causes an adverse effect on the preferred, there would be a class vote. When a certificate grants the preferred a class vote in any merger or in any merger where the preferred stockholders receive a junior security, such provisions are broader than those involved in the First Series Preferred certificate. We agree with plaintiffs' argument that these results are uniform, predictable and consistent with existing law relating to the unique attributes of preferred stock.

The judgment of the Court of Chancery is reversed and the matter is remanded for further proceedings consistent with this Opinion.

NOTES AND QUESTIONS

1.   The issue in *Avatex* was whether the protection normally given to preferred stock to be able to vote before their preferred rights are taken away must be respected over the provisions of the merger statute which apparently did not give those same protections. The *de facto* merger / independent legal significance issue also commonly arises in "sale of assets" cases where the state merger statute provides for dissenters' appraisal (and cash payment) rights but the sale-of-assets statute does not. Delaware and California are the main examples of such laws.[64] Delaware has adopted the "independent legal significance" rule, whereas California has embraced the *de facto* merger rule by statute. Cal. Corp. Code §§ 1200–1201 and § 1300 apply the director approval, shareholder vote, and dissenters' appraisal rights to any "reorganization." Section 181, in turn, defines a "reorganization" as any one of the following:

(a) A merger pursuant to Chapter 11 (commencing with Section 1100) other than a short-form merger (a "merger reorganization").

(b) The acquisition by one domestic corporation, foreign corporation, or other business entity in exchange, in whole or in part, for its equity

---

[64] *See* Cox & Hazen, *supra*, at 598.

securities (or the equity securities of a domestic corporation, a foreign corporation, or another business entity which is in control of the acquiring entity) of equity securities of another domestic corporation, foreign corporation, or other business entity if, immediately after the acquisition, the acquiring entity has control of the other entity (an "exchange reorganization").

(c) The acquisition by one domestic corporation, foreign corporation, or other business entity in exchange in whole or in part for its equity securities (or the equity securities of a domestic corporation, a foreign corporation, or another business entity which is in control of the acquiring entity) or for its debt securities (or debt securities of a domestic corporation, foreign corporation, or other business entity which is in control of the acquiring entity) which are not adequately secured and which have a maturity date in excess of five years after the consummation of the reorganization, or both, of all or substantially all of the assets of another domestic corporation, foreign corporation, or other business entity (a "sale-of-assets reorganization").

The legislative history of this statute describes the motivation. "The new law treats various methods of corporate fusion as different means to the same end. This approach is intended to adopt and codify the so-called "de facto merger" doctrine so that the rights of shareholders in a corporate combination do not depend upon the form in which the transaction is cast. As a basis for this approach, the term "reorganization" is defined to encompass the three principal methods of corporate fusion . . . " West's Ann. Cal. Corp. Code § 181, Legislative History (Assembly Committee Comments, 1975).

2.   Do you see the significance of independent legal significance (ILS)? Does it lean too much on "technicalities" in permitting an easy way around the merger statutes? Or does it respect the legislature's judgment in providing a different route to the same destination?

3.   The ILS doctrine is important in so-called "preference stripping cases." In these cases, preferred shares may have been given priorities in distribution or dividends, as well as the ability to vote on certain transactions, such as the issuance of other series of preferred stock. However, a corporation might structure a transaction as a merger and avoid the preferred vote, where such a vote is not otherwise required under state law.[65] This is an important result — as well as an important drafting lesson — because of the prominence of preferred stock as a financing vehicle for venture capital investors. For a discussion of the use of preferred stock, including an example of voting protection which avoids the result in *Avetex*, see Chapter 5, Section D.1.c.

4.   How does the *de facto* merger doctrine (the "flip side" of ILS) relate to the securities law rule of "integration" or the tax law "step transaction" rule? These doctrines were first discussed in Chapter 4, Section C.1.d.

---

[65] See, *e.g.*, *Benchmark Capital Partners IV, L.P. v. Vague*, 2002 Del. Ch. LEXIS 90 (Jul. 15, 2002), an unreported case holding that "independent legal significance" applied and permitting the transaction over the objection of the preferred shareholders. For a good discussion of *Benchmark* in this context as well as a doctrinal overview, see D. Gordon Smith, *Independent Legal Significance, Good Faith, and the Interpretation of Venture Capital Contracts*, 40 WILLAMETTE L. REV. 825 (2004).

ILS will not be a defense where there is no statutory alternative expressly permitting or forbidding the result achieved by the challenged transaction or where the issue is whether the corporation simply complied with a single statute. . . . ILS will only apply when a statutory alternative exists . . . . The courts do not view it as applying when the issue is whether the corporation complied with a single statute or a provision in a contract. Nonetheless, equity is available in both circumstances, and the courts can apply the equitable substance-over-form doctrine (or its tax-law equivalent, the step-transaction doctrine) to override the transactional form desired by the corporation, regardless of whether the transaction is statutorily valid.[66]

5.   The above excerpt indicates how courts employing a broad brush may cover discussions about equitable doctrines with ILS paint. A similar argument is made by D. Gordon Smith criticizing cases in which the courts use ILS language when they are actually using the contract doctrine of implied good faith, discussing the *Benchmark* case referred to in note 3 above.

When faced with a conflict like *Benchmark*, the Delaware courts have chosen the path of abstention through the doctrine of independent legal significance, rather than the path of intervention through the doctrine of good faith. In doing so, they express a preference for the outcome of *ex ante* bargaining over *ex post* judicial intervention. The elephant in this room is the fact that all contracts are incomplete. If the Delaware courts expect their "tough love" to induce complete contracting, they are simply delusional. *Benchmark* is a case in point: After decades of experience with rights stripping of preferred stock, the courts still regularly hear cases in which "sophisticated" parties leave themselves open to opportunistic behavior. The decision by the Delaware courts to do nothing, therefore, is a decision to ignore the reality of incomplete contracts.[67]

EXERCISE 9-2

A Corp. and B Corp., both Delaware corporations, have agreed to merge, with B Corp. shareholders receiving publicly-traded A Corp. stock in exchange for their B Corp. stock. When the dust settles, therefore, B Corp. will be a wholly-owned subsidiary of A Corp. Under relevant state law, B Corp. shareholders do not have dissenters' appraisal rights if they receive only publicly-traded stock, but they would have such rights if they are required to accept anything other than such stock. When B Corp. becomes the subject of an outside unsolicited hostile bid by another suitor, B Corp. sweetens the deal by agreeing to declare a substantial dividend to its stockholders, conditioned on the effectiveness of the planned merger. The issue is whether adding the dividend effectively changes the merger into a partial cash-out providing appraisal rights to B Corp. shareholders. Is the question properly analyzed under the ILS doctrine or the "substance-over-form" equitable rule?[68]

[66] C. Stephon Bigler & Blake Rohrbacher, *Form or Substance? The Past, Present, and Future of the Doctrine of Independent Legal Significance*, 63 Bus. Law. 1, 20, 23 (2007).

[67] Smith, *supra*, 40 WILLAMETTE L. REV. at 850.

[68] *See* Bigler & Rohrbacher, *supra*, 63 Bus. Law. at 14–15 (discussing Louisiana Municipal Police Employees' Retirement System (LAMPERS) v. Crawford, 918 A.2d 1172 (Del. Ch.), *review refused sub nom.*, Express Scripts, Inc. v. Crawford, 931 A.2d 1006 (table decision) (Del. 2007)).

In addition to these state law rules, federal tender offer and "going private" laws under the Securities Exchange Act of 1934 govern the substantive terms and disclosures required in an offer to purchase shares of stock of another corporation, or repurchases by an issuer which would result in its shares being no longer publicly traded.[69] Each of these rules applies only to large corporations — those with more than $10 million in assets and 500 shareholders of record or with stock listed on stock exchanges[70] — or those which voluntarily opt into the application of these laws.[71] The small business company with which we deal primarily in these materials would likely not be subject to these 1934 Act requirements, so they are not covered in detail here.

The Securities Act of 1933 may also apply to the transaction. That Act requires the registration of any non-exempt offer or sale of securities.[72] Securities Act Rule 145 provides that an "offer" or "sale" subject to the Act's requirements is made if a reclassification, merger, or sale of assets in exchange for securities is submitted for a shareholder vote under applicable state law.[73] The requirements of the 1933 Act, unlike those of the 1934 Act discussed in the prior paragraph, apply regardless of the size of the corporation(s) involved.

3.   Limited Liability Companies

As we have seen many times before, the state laws governing limited liability companies (LLCs) have two attributes important for the business lawyer. First, there is substantial variety among them, which makes generalizations difficult. Second, the statutes borrow freely from both partnership and corporation law concepts, which makes learning the new rules somewhat easier.

a.   Sale of Assets

A sale of assets by an LLC is — as with both partnerships and corporations — a question initially of authority. If the LLC is member managed, the partnership analogy provides authority for a member to sell the assets if it is in the ordinary course of business, but requires consent of all the members if the action is outside the ordinary course of business.[74] There are also specific rules governing proof of authority and filing of statements of authority of members or managers to transfer assets, particularly real property.[75]

---

[69] *See* Securities Exchange Act §§ 14(d) & (e) (tender offers), 13(e) ("going private" transactions). These sections together are usually known as the "Williams Act," after Sen. Harrison Williams, primary sponsor of the legislation passed in 1968 which added these provisions to the federal securities laws.

[70] *See id.* § 12(b).

[71] By registering the issuer's stock under Securities Exchange Act § 12(g).

[72] *See generally* Chapter 4, Section A.1.

[73] *See* Rule 145(a). If an "offer" or "sale" exists as so defined, exemptions from the registration requirement may nonetheless be used if available. *See id.* Preliminary Note 1. Exemptions from registration are discussed in Chapter 4, Section C.

[74] *See* ULLCA § 301; Re-ULLCA § 407(b); *supra* Section B.1.a. *But see* Del. LLC Act § 18-402 (in manager-managed company, majority of interests can make decision). Cal. Corp. Code § 17150 provides that members may allocate authority as the articles or operating agreement provide, and § 17154 provides for selection of officers and a statement of apparent authority in subsection (c).

[75] ULLCA § 301(c) provides, as a default rule, that each member or manager has this authority;

In addition to requirements of authority, many LLC statutes provide — borrowing from the corporate law — that special approval is required in order to sell "all or substantially all" the LLC's assets. Under the ULLCA the default rule is unanimous consent (much like the usual partnership law rule),[76] but other statutes relax this number to a majority in interest (much like the usual corporation law rule).[77]

b.   Sale of Membership Interests

Recall that a partnership interest which is freely transferrable does not include with it the power to participate in management or become a partner without the consent of all the existing partners.[78] Generally the same rules apply to the transfer of LLC interests, although the articles of organization and operating agreement can provide for transfer in full of an interest much as if it were a share of stock.[79] ULLCA is relatively clear in this regard,[80] but Re-ULLCA is less so, providing that a transferable interest may be "certificated" and thereby fully transferrable.[81]

One trap for the unwary is a default rule in both acts that a transfer of all or substantially all of a member's interest is an event of dissociation, ordinarily requiring the payment to the transferee member of the value of that interest. ULLCA § 601(3) provides that transfer of entire interest is a dissociation, and § 601(5)(ii) provides for expulsion by unanimous vote of the other members upon transfer of "substantially all" of the interest. Re-ULLCA § 602(4)(B) revises this rule, providing for expulsion by unanimous vote upon transfer of *all* of the interest.[82]

Re-ULLCA § 302 provides for filing of a statement of authority similar to RUPA § 302 discussed *supra* Section B.1.a.

[76] ULLCA § 404(c)(12); Re-ULLCA § 407(b)(4) (member-managed LLC), (c)(4)(A) (manager-managed LLC).

[77] *See, e.g.*, New York Lim. Liab. Co. Law § 402(d)(2) (a majority in interest).

[78] *See supra* Section B.1.b.

[79] The state's law must be read carefully to ascertain the exact nature of the default rule. When in doubt, the operating agreement should "detail the members' right, if intended, to transfer all or part of their membership interests." J. William Callison & Maureen A, Sullivan, Limited Liability Companies: A State-By-State Guide to Law and Practice § 4:4, p. 62 (2007).

[80] ULLCA § 503(a) provides: "A transferee of a distributional interest may become a member . . . if and to the extent that the transferor gives the transferee the right in accordance with authority described in the operating agreement or all the other members consent." *Accord* Del. LLC Act § 18-704(a). Cal. Corp. Code § 17303(a) has a similar rule but the consent required is only of "a majority in interest" of the other members.

[81] *See* Re-ULLCA § 502(d). Section 502(h) refers to liability rules in the case of a transfer "to a person that becomes a member with respect to the transferred interest," providing authority for such a transfer by implication.

[82] The rationale of the drafters is that "a member's transferee can protect itself from the vulnerability of 'bare transferee' status by obligating the member/transferor to retain a 1% interest and then to exercise its governance rights (including the right to bring a derivative suit) to protect the transferee's interests." Re-ULLCA § 602(4)(B), cmt.

c.   Combinations

Most states permit LLCs to combine in a fashion similar to mergers of corporations. In general, a plan of merger must be adopted by each LLC and approved by the members.[83] As in a corporate merger, the plan of merger may specify that some members receive cash or other property in exchange for their interests, so the merger may be a vehicle for either a "sale of assets" or "sale of interests" transaction. In addition, because LLCs are one of the most recent types of entities authorized by statute, many LLC statutes recognize the modern trend in "cross-entity" combinations.[84]

C.   FEDERAL INCOME TAX ISSUES

As discussed in Chapter 3, every business attorney must be conversant in tax law, at least insofar as being able to recognize tax issues and competently rely on tax experts. In the case of the sale or restructuring of a business, tax considerations may become paramount. In many cases, requirements for favorable tax treatment may drive the very structure of the deal from the beginning. A lawyer who waits to consult the tax expert — or consider the tax consequences — until the deal is arranged may be put in an embarrassing and impossible situation. In order to avoid placing you in such a situation, we discuss here the broad outlines of the tax issues involved and why they must be one of your first concerns in restructuring a business.

1.   Taxation of Partnership Reorganizations

Recall that when we discuss entity-specific tax treatment, a "partnership" generally includes a multi-member limited liability company or any other entity other than a corporation which has elected to be taxed as a partnership. Therefore we do not need separate discussion of limited liability companies or other non-corporate entities.[85]

a.   Sale of Assets

If a partnership decides to sell its productive assets to another business, we can begin with familiar principles of federal income tax law. The difference between the amount realized on the sale and the basis of the property will be gain (or loss) to the partnership, characterized as "ordinary" or "capital" depending upon the characterization of the assets to the partnership.[86] Each partner will then "take

---

[83] ULLCA § 904(c)(1) (unanimous consent or the consent required by the operating agreement); Re-ULLCA § 1003(a) (unanimous consent required). Section 1014(a)(1) purports to authorize consent by less than all the members, but that provision relates specifically to the case in which a remaining member will have personal liability with respect to any one of the surviving entities. Cal. Corp. Code § 17551(a) requires approval by a majority in interest or a greater percentage specified in the articles or operating agreement. Del. LLC Act § 18-209(b) requires majority-in-interest approval "unless otherwise provided in the [LLC] agreement."

[84] *See supra* Section A.3.

[85] *See* Chapter 3, Taxation of Limited Liability Companies.

[86] As to characterization as used by the partnership, see IRC § 702(b). If assets which are capital assets in the hands of the partner become "non-capital" assets to the partnership, special rules prevent the conversion of a capital loss into an ordinary loss by this contribution.

into account" his or her distributive share of this gain or loss.[87] Although these general rules should be familiar, there are certain special situations relating to partnerships and partners which need to be considered by the business lawyer.

Property with "built-in" gain or loss. Special rules apply in the case of property contributed by a partner when that property is later sold by the partnership. These rules are intended to prevent shifting of tax liability between a partner and the partnership with respect to assets which have so-called "built in" gains or losses.[88] Recall that contribution of property to a partnership in exchange for a partnership interest is generally a non-event for tax purposes. This means that neither the partner or the partnership recognizes gain or loss on the contribution,[89] and the partnership generally takes the partner's basis in the assets contributed.[90] The basic rule of Section 704(c) is that this built-in gain or loss is to be allocated to the contributing partner upon sale of the asset by the partnership. The dizzying complexity of the rest of Section 704(c) and the implementing regulations[91] deals with allocations with respect to property with a basis which differs from its fair market value. Conceptually, the goal is straightforward.

> [I]n general, the economic consequences to the partners should be unaffected by the fact that the tax basis of contributed property differs from its market value, provided the capital account maintenance rules are complied with, while the tax consequences attendant upon such difference should be visited (to the extent possible) on the contributing partner under § 704(c)(1)(A).[92]

This is important for the business lawyer to understand, since it will affect the after-tax amounts realized by their clients, but the details can be left to the tax attorneys and accountants. It is likely sufficient for the adviser on the sale or purchase of assets to inquire into and therefore be aware of the fact that there could be "low basis" (or "high basis") assets in the partnership, whose sale may have disparate consequences to different partners.

Characterization of gain or loss. Congress appears ever mindful of the potential of a partnership to transmute the character of "ordinary" and "capital" property to the benefit of taxpayers and loss to the Treasury. Section 724 prohibits any such recharacterization in three situations. In the case of contributed property which constituted unrealized receivables or inventory in the hands of the contributing partner,[93] the sale of such property by the partnership results in ordinary gain or loss even if the property is a capital asset to the partnership.[94] Similarly, in the case

---

[87] IRC § 702(a). The gain or loss is calculated on an asset-by-asset basis, even if the agreement does not allocate values but simply provides for a bulk sales price. If the assets sold constitute a "trade or business," IRC § 1060 provides for a method to allocate the purchase price to tangible assets with clear market-based fair values, then to other tangible assets, and finally to intangible assets.

[88] *See* Chapter 3, Section H.3.b.

[89] IRC § 721(a).

[90] IRC § 723.

[91] *See generally* Treas. Reg. § 1.704-3.

[92] William S. McKee, William F. Nelson & Robert L. Whitmire, Federal Income Taxation of Partnerships and Partners § 10.04[1], p. 10-137 (3d ed. 2006).

[93] We will see these two suspect classes again in Section C.1.b below, dealing with sale of partnership interests.

[94] IRC § 724(a), (b). The rule with respect to inventory has a five-year limit; the rule with respect to

of capital assets contributed with a "built-in" loss, any loss realized by the partnership on the sale of that property within five years its contribution must be characterized as a capital loss.[95]

Example. In the ABC Restaurant, Ann contributes $400,000, Bev contributes $800,000, and Carl contributes "expertise, good will, recipes, designs and intellectual property" worth $400,000.[96] Ann and Bev would have a 100% basis in the cash contributed, but Carl would likely have a low (probably zero) basis in the assets contributed by him. The partnership would therefore have combined assets of $1.6 million with a basis of $1.2 million.[97] Carl has "built-in gain" of $400,000 in the assets he contributed. If there were no adjustments to the values of those assets,[98] and a buyer later purchases the assets of the partnership for $2 million, the partnership would have an $800,000 gain to account for. Of this $800,000 gain, $400,000 is allocated to Carl, and the remaining $400,000 is allocated among the partners according to their profit shares: $200,000 to Bev and $100,000 each to Ann and Carl. If the assets contributed by Ann, Bev or Carl had included inventory or unrealized accounts, the gain from sale is not a capital gain to the partnership, even if the assets are sold "in bulk" and not in the ordinary course of business.

Treatment of sale of assets and a liquidation of the partnership. Often a partnership will choose to combine with another by selling its assets, as in the above example. The tax treatment of the transaction may drive the structure of the deal, so it is important for the business lawyer to consult tax experts at the outset. The following general discussion is meant to guide the business lawyer in understanding the tax terminology and issues involved in such a transaction.

If a partnership sells its assets to another entity, this is generally known as an ***"assets over" transaction***. The partnership (and the partners) will realize gain or loss as discussed in the above paragraphs. If the partnership then liquidates,[99] § 731 generally provides that the distribution of partnership property to the partners is not a taxable event to either the partners or the liquidating partnership.[100] And § 732 provides for a carryover basis of the partner's interest in the partnership to the assets received in liquidation. One would expect §§ 731 and 732 to operate in similar fashion if the assets are distributed *first* to the partners in liquidation and *then* transferred to the purchaser, generally known as an ***"assets up" transaction***. And in general, this expectation is borne out. However, the details of calculations can differ, and sometimes considerably, depending upon the exact nature of the assets contributed by each partner and each partner's individual income tax

---

unrealized receivables has no such limit, perhaps because such property is unlikely to remain unrealized for so long.

[95] IRC § 724(c).

[96] To keep the tax treatment simple, let's assume that there is no value assigned to Carl's contribution of services.

[97] This is because IRC § 721 provides that Carl's gain is not recognized when he contributes these assets to the partnership, and § 722 provides for carryover basis to the partnership. We are also at this point ignoring the other passive investors, who would have tax treatment similar to Ann and Bev.

[98] This is where the complication of IRC § 704(c) comes in if the assets contributed by Carl are subject to deductions in the hands of the partnership for depreciation or amortization, or other credits or deductions.

[99] This happens either when the partnership actually liquidates under state law, or when it ceases to conduct any other business and is deemed to have liquidated under IRC § 708(b)(1)(A).

[100] But IRC § 731(a) requires gain to be recognized if cash distributed exceeds the partner's basis.

situation. The business lawyer should always be alert to transaction alternatives which appear similar from a logical or "result" perspective, and be aware that they may have quite different tax consequences.

If the purchaser is a corporation, there is obviously no "continuing partnership, but the combination of

— nonrecognition on incorporation under § 351 (if the selling partners receive a controlling interest in the corporation),

— recognition of gain or loss by a partnership (and partners) in the sale of assets as described above,

— recognition of gain or loss by a partner transferring an interest under § 741, and

— nonrecognition on liquidation of a partnership under § 731, will likely produce tax-deferred treatment of either the "assets over" or "assets up" form, just as if the partnership "incorporated" alone.[101] There may be some different consequences pertaining primarily to adjustments to basis and the calculation of holding periods.

Conclusion. The overall lesson for the business lawyer when structuring a combination done by a sale of partnership assets is in two parts. First, the form of the transaction will likely be respected for tax purposes. Second, notwithstanding that general rule, the tax consequences *can* be significant and *may* drive the transaction, and can be understood according to the above principles upon consultation with your tax expert.

b.   Sale of Partnership Interests

If a partner determines to sell his or her interest in the partnership to another person, who presumably then becomes a partner the partnership agreement, see Section B.1.b of this chapter, we can apply familiar rules of federal income tax law. Gain or loss is calculated by comparing basis with the amount received. As above, these general rules have some technical qualifications which must be considered by the business lawyer.

Sale of interests as a liquidation of the partnership. A partnership may continue under state law if a controlling partner sells his or her interest to another person subsequently admitted as a partner.[102] A similar result occurs under tax law, but instead through the following rather amazing events "deemed to occur" on the date of the transfer of an interest which tips the balance to more than 50 percent of interests transferred in the preceding year. The partnership is terminated,[103] and

> The partnership contributes all of its assets and liabilities to a new partnership in exchange for an interest in the new partnership; and, immediately thereafter, the terminated partnership distributes interests in the new partnership to the purchasing partner and the other remaining

---

[101] *See* Rev. Rul. 84-111, 1984-2 C.B. 88 (situations 1 and 2). If the partners do not control the corporation after the sale, § 351 will not operate to defer gain on the exchange.

[102] *See* RUPA § 701(a); *supra* Section B.1.b.

[103] IRC § 708(b)(1)(B).

partners in proportion to their respective interests in the terminated partnership in liquidation of the terminated partnership . . . . [104]

When the dust settles, there is a new partnership consisting of the old partners and the new partner who purchased the outgoing partner's interest. Because such transfers normally are tax-deferred under § 731 (in liquidation) and § 721 (on contribution to the new partnership) few tax consequences attach to this transformation. If this event is combined with payments to the departed partner from the partnership, that person remains a partner until such time as the payments are completed.[105]

Characterization of gain. The general rule of computing gain or loss (difference between basis and amount realized) discussed above does not tell us whether the gain or loss is "ordinary" or "capital." A moment's reflection would suggest that a partnership interest is a capital asset, and indeed, section 741 confirms that conclusion, with an exception for certain types of assets.[106] These assets: "unrealized receivables" and "inventory" will produce ordinary income to the selling partner *when the partnership interest is sold* even though the assets themselves have not been sold, courtesy of section 751(a).[107]

Treatment of partnership liabilities. In general, if a taxpayer borrows money to purchase an asset, the amount borrowed is included in the taxpayer's cost, or basis.[108] The consequence of this rule is that relief from that indebtedness is included in income when the property is sold.[109] These are basic rules of income taxation, and they apply to sales of partnership interests through the explicit language of Section 752(d):

> In the case of a sale or exchange of an interest in a partnership, liabilities shall be treated in the same manner as liabilities in connection with the sale or exchange of property not associated with partnerships.

There are, however, special questions due to the application to *partners* of basis for *partnership* liabilities. If a partnership asset sold was subject to a liability, the relief

---

[104] Treas. Reg. § 1.708-1(b)(4).

[105] Treas. Reg. § 1.736-1(a)(ii). Payments by the partnership to a partner are discussed in Chapter 8, Section C.1.

[106] IRC § 742 provides: "In the case of a sale or exchange of an interest in a partnership, gain or loss shall be recognized to the transferor partner. Such gain or loss shall be considered as gain or loss from the sale or exchange of a capital asset, except as otherwise provided in section 751 (relating to unrealized receivables and inventory items)."

[107] IRC § 751(a) provides:

The amount of any money, or the fair market value of any property, received by a transferor partner in exchange for all or a part of his interest in the partnership attributable to —

(1) unrealized receivables of the partnership, or

(2) inventory items of the partnership,

shall be considered as an amount realized from the sale or exchange of property other than a capital asset.

[108] *See* Boris I. Bittker, Martin J. McMahon, Jr. & Lawrence A. Zelenak, Federal Income Taxation of Individuals 29-6 n.12 (2002) ("For nearly as long as anyone can remember, the notion that a cash method taxpayer acquired basis by paying for property with a promissory note has been beyond question.").

[109] *See id.* at 29-54 to 29-56 (discussing *Crane v. Commissioner*, 331 U.S. 1 (1947)). The result is now "codified" in the regulations. *See* Treas. Reg. § 1.1001-2(a); Bittker, McMahon & Zelenak, *supra*, at 29-56 & nn.200-01.

of that liability is included in the amount realized from the sale of the asset.

Example. Donna is a one-third partner in the DEF partnership. The partnership owns Splendid Towers which the partnership purchased in part with debt of $900,000, all of which is still outstanding. When Donna sells her interest in the partnership to George for $500,000, she is treated as receiving not only the cash, but relief from her one-third (assuming the liability was equally allocated to each partner) of the partnership debt. Her "amount realized" would be the $500,000 cash plus $300,000 of "debt relief."[110] This will reflect the economic realities of the transaction, because when the partnership borrowed the money to purchase Splendid Towers, Donna's basis in her partnership interest was increased by her share of the partnership debt, or $300,000, at that time. If George becomes a partner in the (now EFG) partnership, the basis of his partnership interest would be his $500,000 cash cost,[111] plus $300,000 if he assumes his proportionate share of that partnership liability.[112]

Adjustments to basis of partnership property. The purchaser of a partner's interest normally takes as his or her basis the value of the property transferred to the selling partner, just as basis is calculated for any other purchase.[113] However, because the partnership's basis in its assets has not changed (even though a new partnership is deemed to have been created), the transferee partner would not ordinarily receive a tax benefit in the form of allocated deductions based on this higher cost.

Example. Suppose the ABC Restaurant has been in business for a few years, and Carl sells his interest in the partnership to Daniel, who pays $500,000 cash to Carl. Carl recognizes gain based on the basis of his interest in the partnership (which, recall, was low or zero, but may have been increased by allocated gain in the meantime). But because the partnership's basis of the assets contributed by Carl was low or zero, there are no depreciation or amortization deductions available to Daniel. He could have received such benefits if he had purchased the assets from Carl and then contributed them to the partnership.

Section 743 attempts to remedy this unfairness (with respect only to the new partner) by allowing a revaluation of the *partnership's basis* in its assets ("inside basis") to reflect the new higher basis of the transferee partner in his partnership interest ("outside basis"). This adjustment only affects the new transferee partner, and not the other continuing partners.[114]

---

[110] IRC § 752(b).

[111] IRC § 722.

[112] IRC § 752(a). If he doesn't assume a share of the partnership debt, the debt would be reallocated to E and F and would increase their bases in their partnership interests according to § 752(a).

[113] IRC § 742, referring to the general "basis as cost" rule of § 1012.

[114] In order to take advantage of this treatment, the partnership must so elect under IRC § 754. A similar basis adjustment can be made under § 734 if a distribution is made to a partner by the partnership which requires the distributee partner to recognize gain under § 731.

c.   Combinations

Two partnerships may combine, or "merge," either under specific state law authorizing such an arrangement,[115] or by an agreement among the partnerships and partners. Generally, tax law considers the partnership whose members own more than half of the capital and profits interests to be the "continuing" partnership.[116] The "assets over" or "assets up" form of the transaction will be respected for tax purposes,[117] and the tax consequences to the resulting partnership will follow accordingly.[118]

Alternatively, one partner might be considered to be selling his or her interest in the partnership to the resulting partnership, rather than receiving an interest in the resulting partnership. If this is the case, the results which follow are similar to those from any other sale of interests, despite the fact that the remaining partnership interests may be exchanged in a merger or similar reorganization. In order to qualify for this treatment, the merger agreement must specify that treatment. The language might be like this:

> ABC [the resulting or continuing partnership] is purchasing from D his/her interest in the DEF [terminating partnership] in consideration of [list assets and payment terms]. D consents to treatment of this transaction as a sale of the partnership interest under the Internal Revenue Code of 1986 and applicable regulations.[119]

In general, there is no "interests over" form of partnership reorganization, a result which might obtain if the partners were transferring their interests to a corporation. This is because, even if the transaction were styled as a sale of interests by all (or most) of the partners, the transaction is treated as a liquidation of the transferring partnership,[120] and the sale-and-liquidation rules discussed above would apply.[121]

2.   Taxation of Corporate Reorganizations

When a business to be purchased or sold is held by a corporation, the business planning is complicated by the interposition of another taxpayer — the corporation — into the deal. Congress has provided that such purchases and sales can be accomplished without current payment of tax in many situations. The first decision to be made by the business lawyer, therefore, is whether the transaction can or should be arranged into one of the types which permits such tax-deferred treatment. This is the subject of Subsection a, in which we discuss generally the tax rules applicable to taxable and non-taxable transactions. Subsection b then

---

[115] *See supra* Section B.1.c.

[116] IRC § 708(b)(2)(A).

[117] *See* T.D. 8925, 2001-1 C.B. 496; 66 Fed. Reg. 715 (2001). Note that these effects do not relate to broad principles of gain or loss recognition which are similar regardless of which form is used. See the above paragraph.

[118] Treas. Reg. § 1.708-1(c). See *supra* Section C.1.a for discussion of "assets up" and "assets over" transactions and their respective tax treatment.

[119] For authority for this treatment as well as the language from which this example was drawn, see Treas. Reg. § 1.708-1(c)(4).

[120] IRC § 708(b)(1)(B).

[121] *See* Treas. Reg. § 1.708-1(c)(1); *supra* Section C.1.a.

discusses the basic rules applicable to taxable transactions. Subsection c discusses the categories of transactions treated as tax-deferred "reorganizations" — a term of tax law art, but critical for the business lawyer to understand. The general rules discussed here are applicable both to C corporations and S corporations, although the business lawyer should consult an S corporation expert when merging an S corporation and a C corporation, regardless of which type is intended to survive the merger.

a. The Basic Decision: Taxable or Tax-deferred?

General principles of income tax provide a good starting point. A taxable transaction results in taxable gain or loss to the seller, based on the difference between the basis and amount received. The purchaser then receives a basis in the assets equal to the purchaser's cost. These should be familiar rules from Subchapter O.[122] Conversely, a tax-deferred transaction ordinarily results in no tax liability but an accompanying carryover of the seller's tax basis in the assets sold to the purchaser.[123]

A transaction can be deliberately designed to fit within either of the above tax regimes. For example, if the parties desire a taxable transaction, so that losses can be recognized, the transaction can be designed so that it fails to meet one or more of the requirements for tax-free reorganization. Alternatively, the transaction may be such that tax-free treatment is impossible because of events which predate the planned transaction. The role of the business lawyer is defined at the outset by these tax rules which, unavoidably, become part of the "business terms" of the deal and the tax planning required of the lawyers.

Study of the Overall State of the Federal Tax System and Recommendations for Simplification
Vol. II, pp. 239, 245[124]

Tax-free corporate transactions in general

A number of special provisions enable corporations to combine or separate their businesses, and permit the corporate shareholders to shift their investment interests to the combined or separated enterprises, without the tax impact that would otherwise generally occur on an exchange of appreciated corporate assets for other assets, or of shareholder investment interests for other interests.

Some rules are directed at "acquisitive" transactions, in which one corporation acquires the stock or assets of another. Other rules are directed at "divisive" transactions, in which one corporation divides its business or subsidiaries into

---

[122] IRC § 1001 *et seq.*

[123] *See generally* IRC §§ 362(a)–(b) (basis), 381 (operating losses, earnings and profits, and other tax credits, deductions and benefits).

[124] Prepared by the Staff of the Joint Committee on Taxation (2001), available at www.jct.gov/s-3-01vol2.pdf. *See* www.jct.gov/about-us/overview.html ("The Joint Committee on Taxation is a nonpartisan committee of the United States Congress, originally established under the Revenue Act of 1926. The Joint Committee operates with an experienced professional staff of Ph.D economists, attorneys, and accountants, who assist Members of the majority and minority parties in both houses of Congress on tax legislation.").

entities separately owned by the corporate shareholders. In practice, an acquiror may wish to acquire less than all the assets of a "target" corporation, so that there may be preliminary divisions of assets, or separations of subsidiaries, to accommodate the needs of a particular transaction. The ease with which such changes can occur as part of a transaction and still retain tax-free treatment varies among the different provisions.

. . .

The different rules permitting particular corporate transactions to receive tax-free treatment are varied and frequently inconsistent. In some cases, more than one rule could apply to the form of a particular corporate transaction. The statute and the administrative pronouncements of the IRS over the years have attempted to resolve overlap situations and to provide guidance regarding other interpretive issues.

The structure of present law is in part a result of the historical development and aggregation of provisions. The structure also reflects reactions to judicial decisions interpreting particular provisions, and reflects legislative developments establishing new rules and accompanying concern that existing provisions, if not limited, might conflict with or undermine the new rules.

The different, and often overlapping, variations within the merger and acquisition rules can be viewed as a significant source of complexity. On the other hand, these rules, as they have been interpreted and clarified over the years through administrative pronouncements, provide a large amount of taxpayer selectivity and certainty. Taxpayers are relatively assured of obtaining a specific tax result so long as the transaction satisfies the formalistic requirements of the chosen merger and acquisition provision. Moreover, comprehensive reform of these rules and the imposition of consistency could not generally be accomplished without recommending fundamental changes in the tax policy reflected by one or another of the provisions.

NOTES AND QUESTIONS

1. The Joint Committee indicates that you, as a business planner, can be assured of desired tax treatment if you design your transaction to fit within parameters which are sure as to their outline, although they may be unclear in their origin, policy, or rationale. "The legal form or business bargain is often adjusted to eliminate questions that will be decided adversely by the [IRS]. . . . Rarely do the participants deliberately invite a test of strength in the courts."[125] Although reforms have been suggested to make the tax treatment of a planned reorganization optional or determinable by the taxpayer,[126] such is not presently the case and is not likely to be. Thus, the tax consequences are not optional or elective and may drive the transaction from the beginning.

2. Suppose the ABC Restaurant Inc. has been in operation for several years.

---

[125] Boris I. Bittker & James S. Eustice, Federal Income Taxation of Corporations and Shareholders ¶ 12.01[4], at p. 12-14 (7th ed. 2000).

[126] *See, e.g.,* American Law Institute, Federal Income Tax Project: Subchapter C at 43 (1982) (Proposal A1, providing in part that "whether a particular transaction is a carryover-basis or a cost-basis acquisition should be made explicitly elective").

Recall that A's and B's investments, as well as those of the outside investors, were cash (high basis assets), but C's investment was recipes, services, and intangible assets (low- or no-basis assets). If the corporation has operated at a loss and is being touted to an outside buyer, which of these individuals is likely to want a taxable transaction? A tax-deferred transaction? Will you be able to represent all the owners simultaneously?

b.   The Taxable Transaction

i.   Sale of assets

When a corporation sells its assets, it realizes gain or loss based on the amount realized from the sale in excess of the corporation's basis in the assets. The purchaser obtains a basis in the assets equal to the cost to the purchaser.[127] Because there is presently no capital-gains preference with regard to corporate income taxes,[128] characterization of any gain as income or capital gains is not an important planning issue.

Following a sale of all of the assets of a corporation, issues arise regarding the actions that should be taken regarding the continuation of the corporation, since the only assets will be cash or promissory notes (secured or unsecured) received in exchange for the sale of the assets. The corporation may also have continuing obligations under the purchase and sale contract with regard to warranties regarding the assets or other matters. Perhaps more importantly, there may be significant tax consequences regarding how the proceeds from the sale are distributed. If the corporation chooses to liquidate, the shareholders will recognize capital gain or loss, but not ordinary income.[129] If, instead, the corporation makes nonliquidating distributions to its shareholders, those distributions will be considered ordinary income to the extent of the corporation's earnings and profits.[130] Congress has provided guidance in § 302(e) regarding a distribution which is a "partial liquidation" of the corporation, providing liquidation treatment to the extent of the partial liquidation.[131] A liquidation will produce gain to the corporation in any event under § 336 unless the distribution is by a subsidiary corporation to its parent.[132] Prior to 1986, there was a tax benefit to distributions by a corporation of appreciated property, which created an incentive to structure the liquidation of appreciated property carefully in relation to its sale. Although those rules no longer apply,[133] they generated two brief cases which retain their

---

[127] As with the sale of assets by a partnership, there is the issue of allocation of the sales price. The gain or loss is calculated on an asset-by-asset basis, even if the agreement does not allocate values but simply provides for a bulk sales price. If the assets sold constitute a "trade or business," IRC § 1060 provides for a method to allocate the purchase price to tangible assets with clear market-based fair values, then to other tangible assets, and finally to intangible assets.

[128] *See* IRC §§ 11, 1201.

[129] IRC § 332.

[130] IRC §§ 301, 316.

[131] The definition of a "partial liquidation" in § 302(e)(1)(A) is somewhat circular. The liquidation must be "not essentially equivalent to a dividend" (determined at the corporate level) and pursuant to a plan which is adopted and carried out within the current or the current and the next taxable year(s).

[132] This last exception is courtesy of IRC § 337, discussed below under taxable sale of interests transactions.

[133] Section 336 was amended in 1986 to repeal the *General Utilities* doctrine, which refers to an old

validity to this day as general statements about what constitutes good tax planning and what constitutes a "sham transaction."

COMMISSIONER OF INTERNAL REVENUE v. COURT HOLDING CO.
United States Supreme Court
324 U.S. 331 (1945)

MR. JUSTICE BLACK delivered the opinion of the Court.

An apartment house, which was the sole asset of the respondent corporation, was transferred in the form of a liquidating dividend to the corporation's two shareholders. They in turn formally conveyed it to a purchaser who had originally negotiated for the purchase from the corporation. The question is whether the Circuit Court of Appeals properly reversed[134] the Tax Court's conclusion[135] that the corporation was taxable under . . . the Internal Revenue Code[136] for the gain which accrued from the sale. The answer depends upon whether the findings of the Tax Court that the whole transaction showed a sale by the corporation rather than by the stockholders were final and binding upon the Circuit Court of Appeals.

It is unnecessary to set out in detail the evidence introduced before the Tax Court or its findings. Despite conflicting evidence, the following findings of the Tax Court are supported by the record:

The respondent corporation was organized in 1934 solely to buy and hold the apartment building which was the only property ever owned by it. All of its outstanding stock was owned by Minnie Miller and her husband. Between October 1, 1939 and February, 1940, while the corporation still had legal title to the property, negotiations for its sale took place. These negotiations were between the corporation and the lessees of the property, together with a sister and brother-in-law. An oral agreement was reached as to the terms and conditions of sale, and on February 22, 1940, the parties met to reduce the agreement to writing. The purchaser was then advised by the corporation's attorney that the sale could not be consummated because it would result in the imposition of a large income tax on the corporation. The next day, the corporation declared a 'liquidating dividend', which involved complete liquidation of its assets, and surrender of all outstanding stock. Mrs. Miller and her husband surrendered their stock, and the building was deeded to them. A sale contract was then drawn, naming the Millers individually as vendors, and the lessees' sister as vendee, which embodied substantially the same terms and conditions previously agreed upon. One thousand dollars, which a month and a half earlier had been paid to the corporation by the lessees, was applied in part payment of the purchase price. Three days later, the property was conveyed to the lessees' sister.

---

case, *General Utilities & Operating Co. v. Helvering*, 296 U.S. 200 (1935), in which the Supreme Court held that no gain was recognized by a corporation distributing appreciated property. *See generally* Boris I. Bittker & James S. Eustice, *supra* ¶ 8.20.

[134] [1] 143 F.2d 823.

[135] [2] 2 T.C. 531.

[136] [Here the Court cites provisions of the Internal Revenue Code which provided, prior to amendment in 1986, that a corporation was taxable on gain on sale of property, but not upon any gain on distribution of appreciated property to its shareholders in liquidation.—Eds.]

The Tax Court concluded from these facts that, despite the declaration of a 'liquidating dividend' followed by the transfers of legal title, the corporation had not abandoned the sales negotiations; that these were mere formalities designed 'to make the transaction appear to be other than what it was', in order to avoid tax liability. The Circuit Court of Appeals drawing different inferences from the record, held that the corporation had 'called off' the sale, and treated the stockholders' sale as unrelated to the prior negotiations.

There was evidence to support the findings of the Tax Court, and its findings must therefore be accepted by the courts. On the basis of these findings, the Tax Court was justified in attributing the gain from the sale to respondent corporation. The incidence of taxation depends upon the substance of a transaction. The tax consequences which arise from gains from a sale of property are not finally to be determined solely by the means employed to transfer legal title. Rather, the transaction must be viewed as a whole, and each step, from the commencement of negotiations to the consummation of the sale, is relevant. A sale by one person cannot be transformed for tax purposes into a sale by another by using the latter as a conduit through which to pass title. To permit the true nature of a transaction to be disguised by mere formalisms, which exist solely to alter tax liabilities, would seriously impair the effective administration of the tax policies of Congress.

It is urged that respondent corporation never executed a written agreement, and that an oral agreement to sell land cannot be enforced in Florida because of the Statute of Frauds. But the fact that respondent corporation itself never executed a written contract is unimportant, since the Tax Court found from the facts of the entire transaction that the executed sale was in substance the sale of the corporation. The decision of the Circuit Court of Appeals is reversed, and that of the Tax Court affirmed.

It is so ordered.

UNITED STATES v. CUMBERLAND PUBLIC SERVICE CO.
United States Supreme Court
338 U.S. 451 (1950)

MR. JUSTICE BLACK delivered the opinion of the Court.

A corporation selling its physical properties is taxed on capital gains resulting from the sale. There is no corporate tax, however, on distribution of assets in kind to shareholders as part of a genuine liquidation. The respondent corporation transferred property to its shareholders as a liquidating dividend in kind. The shareholders transferred it to a purchaser. The question is whether, despite contrary findings by the Court of Claims, this record requires a holding that the transaction was in fact a sale by the corporation subjecting the corporation to a capital gains tax.

Details of the transaction are as follows. The respondent, a closely held corporation, was long engaged in the business of generating and distributing electric power in three Kentucky counties. In 1936 a local cooperative began to distribute Tennessee Valley Authority power in the area served by respondent. It soon became obvious that respondent's Diesel-generated power could not compete with TVA power, which respondent had been unable to obtain. Respondent's shareholders, realizing that the corporation must get out of the power business unless it obtained TVA power, accordingly offered to sell all the corporate stock to the cooperative, which was receiving such power. The cooperative refused to buy the stock, but countered with an offer to buy from the corporation its transmission and distribution equipment. The corporation rejected the offer because it would have been compelled to pay a heavy capital gains tax. At the same time the shareholders, desiring to save payment of the corporate capital gains tax, offered to acquire the transmission and distribution equipment and then sell to the cooperative. The cooperative accepted. The corporation transferred the transmission and distribution systems to its shareholders in partial liquidation. The remaining assets were sold and the corporation dissolved. The shareholders then executed the previously contemplated sale to the cooperative.

Upon this sale by the shareholders, the Commissioner assessed and collected a $17,000 tax from the corporation on the theory that the shareholders had been used as a mere conduit for effectuating what was really a corporate sale. Respondent corporation brought this action to recover the amount of the tax. The Court of Claims found that the method by which the stockholders disposed of the properties was avowedly chosen in order to reduce taxes, but that the liquidation and dissolution genuinely ended the corporation's activities and existence. The court also found that at no time did the corporation plan to make the sale itself. Accordingly it found as a fact that the sale was made by the shareholders rather than the corporation, and entered judgment for respondent. One judge dissented, believing that our opinion in *Commissioner v. Court Holding Co.*, required a finding that the sale had been made by the corporation. Certiorari was granted to clear up doubts arising out of the *Court Holding Co.* case.

Our *Court Holding Co.* decision rested on findings of fact by the Tax Court that a sale had been made and gains realized by the taxpayer corporation. There the corporation had negotiated for sale of its assets and had reached an oral agreement of sale. When the tax consequences of the corporate sale were belatedly recognized, the corporation purported to 'call off' the sale at the last minute and distributed the physical properties in kind to the stockholders. They promptly conveyed these properties to the same persons who had negotiated with the corporation. The terms of purchase were substantially those of the previous oral agreement. One thousand dollars already paid to the corporation was applied as part payment of the purchase price. The Tax Court found that the corporation never really abandoned its sales negotiations, that it never did dissolve, and that the sole purpose of the so-called liquidation was to disguise a corporate sale through use of mere formalisms in order to avoid tax liability. The Circuit Court of Appeals took a different view of the evidence. In this Court the Government contended that whether a liquidation distribution was genuine or merely a sham was traditionally a question of fact. We agreed with this contention, and reinstated the Tax Court's findings and judgment. Discussing the evidence which supported the findings of fact, we went on to say that 'the incidence of taxation depends upon the substance of a transaction' regardless of 'mere formalisms,' and that taxes on a corporate sale cannot be avoided by using the shareholders as a 'conduit through which to pass title.'

This language does not mean that a corporation can be taxed even when the sale has been made by its stockholders following a genuine liquidation and dissolution.[137] While the distinction between sales by a corporation as compared with distribution in kind followed by shareholder sales may be particularly shadowy and artificial when the corporation is closely held, Congress has chosen to recognize such a distinction for tax purposes. The corporate tax is thus aimed primarily at the profits of a going concern. This is true despite the fact that gains realized from corporate sales are taxed, perhaps to prevent tax evasions, even where the cash proceeds are at once distributed in liquidation. But Congress has imposed no tax on liquidating distributions in kind or on dissolution, whatever may be the motive for such liquidation. Consequently, a corporation may liquidate or dissolve without subjecting itself to the corporate gains tax, even though a primary motive is to avoid the burden of corporate taxation.

Here, on the basis of adequate subsidiary findings, the Court of Claims has found that the sale in question was made by the stockholders rather than the corporation. The Government's argument that the shareholders acted as a mere 'conduit' for a sale by respondent corporation must fall before this finding. The subsidiary finding that a major motive of the shareholders was to reduce taxes does not bar this conclusion. Whatever the motive and however relevant it may be in determining whether the transaction was real or a sham, sales of physical properties by shareholders following a genuine liquidation distribution cannot be attributed to the corporation for tax purposes.

The oddities in tax consequences that emerge from the tax provisions here controlling appear to be inherent in the present tax pattern. For a corporation is taxed if it sells all its physical properties and distributes the cash proceeds as liquidating dividends, yet is not taxed if that property is distributed in kind and is then sold by the shareholders. In both instances the interest of the shareholders in the business has been transferred to the purchaser. Again, if these stockholders had succeeded in their original effort to sell all their stock, their interest would have been transferred to the purchasers just as effectively. Yet on such a transaction the corporation would have realized no taxable gain.

Congress having determined that different tax consequences shall flow from different methods by which the shareholders of a closely held corporation may dispose of corporate property, we accept its mandate. It is for the trial court, upon consideration of an entire transaction, to determine the factual category in which a particular transaction belongs. Here as in the *Court Holding Co.* case we accept the ultimate findings of fact of the trial tribunal. Accordingly the judgment of the Court of Claims is

Affirmed.

MR. JUSTICE DOUGLAS took no part in the consideration or decision of this case.

---

[137] [3] What we said in the *Court Holding Co.* case was an approval of the action of the Tax Court in looking beyond the papers executed by the corporation and shareholders in order to determine whether the sale there had actually been made by the corporation. We were but emphasizing the established principle that in resolving such questions as who made a sale, fact-finding tribunals in tax cases can consider motives, intent, and conduct in addition to what appears in written instruments used by parties to control rights as among themselves.

NOTES AND QUESTIONS

1.   Although mentioned before these cases, it bears repeating that the tax law which made the order of the sale and liquidation important no longer exists, there could certainly be other instances where the order of things is important. Although the law now generally provides for recognition of gain on a liquidating distribution by a corporation, the same is not necessarily true of losses. If, for example, a corporation distributes property at a loss, and the property was acquired within two years in a nonrecognition transaction, no loss may be taken by the corporation. And if the liquidating distribution is to a related person, a five-year look-back applies.[138]

2.   If you can carefully distinguish *Court Holding* and *Cumberland Valley*, you're on your way to sophisticated tax planning. In both cases, the sale was contemplated as one by the corporation, but the form was changed once the tax consequences were discovered, the property was distributed to the shareholders and *then* sold. In these respects the cases are nearly identical. Apart from deference to lower court findings of fact, what — if anything — accounts for the difference in results?

ii.   Sale of shares

If, instead of a sale of assets, the transaction is structured as a sale of stock in the corporation constituting "control" of the corporation and, therefore control of the assets, we can apply familiar tax law rules. The selling *stockholders* (but not the corporation) recognize gain or loss (presumably capital gain or loss) on the difference between their basis in the stock and the amount realized in exchange for the stock. Because no assets have been transferred by the corporation, there is no gain or loss to be recognized by the corporation, and the assets remain as they were before the sale.

From the perspective of the acquiring person(s) or entity, an important consideration is the basis in the acquired property. If structured as a sale of assets, the basis of the acquiring person(s) or entity is adjusted upward to the amount paid for the assets. However, if the sale is structured as a sale of stock, the basis of the assets of the acquired corporation remains the same (and that basis may be low). This can create large income gain for the acquiring entity if the acquired assets are sold in the future. What is needed is a mechanism by which a corporation which purchases another corporation's stock — and thereby has a subsidiary corporation — can obtain the (presumably higher) cost-value basis in the *subsidiary corporation's assets*, just as if it had purchased the assets directly.

Liquidation of the subsidiary ordinarily will not produce that result, because, in the case of liquidation of a parent corporation by its subsidiary, the assets have not left corporate "solution," and generally the result is that no gain or loss is recognized and basis and holding periods carry over.[139] In IRC § 338, Congress provided a solution by allowing corporations the election to obtain the cost basis in the assets of the subsidiary to match the high cost basis in their stock. This is done by means of a deemed sale of the subsidiary's assets *to itself* and payment of the

---

[138]   *See* IRC § 336(d).

[139]   For the details, see IRC §§ 332 (no gain or loss to parent-stockholder), 337 (no gain or loss to liquidating subsidiary), 334(b) (carryover of basis), 381 (carryover of other attributes, such as net operating losses, capital losses, and earnings and profits), and 1223(2) (carryover of holding period).

tax due on that deemed sale.[140] Allocation of these deemed sale proceeds to the subsidiary's assets is done in the same manner as with asset sales discussed earlier.[141]

c.   The Nontaxable Transaction

i.   Background on "reorganizations"

A nontaxable transaction can be either a transfer of assets *or* a transfer of interests. What makes it nontaxable is that it fits within the definition of a "reorganization" under IRC § 368(a)(1). There is defensible tax policy behind the complex provisions which we survey here.

> The traditional theory of the reorganization provisions is that gain or loss should not be recognized on changes of form when the taxpayer's investment remains in corporate solution or when a formal distribution, directly or through exchange of securities, represents merely a new form of the previous participation in an enterprise involving no change of substance in the rights and relations of interested parties one to another or to the corporate assets."[142]

In tax jargon, a "reorganization" that qualifies under IRC § 368(a)(1) is *always* nontaxable, while the term "reorganization" in its ordinary sense might be referring to a taxable or a nontaxable transaction. It is incumbent upon the business lawyer — and any other careful lawyer — to use the term "reorganization" properly and carefully mind the contextual distinction between tax and non-tax reorganizations.

ii.   Consequences of "reorganization" treatment

Section 368(a)(1) is only a definition; it tells the reader what constitutes a "reorganization" but nothing more. One needs to read elsewhere in the Code to find the consequences, which are generally those we would expect in a nontaxable (tax-deferred) transaction.

• *No tax to stockholders*: no gain or loss is recognized to the holders of stock or securities in corporations which are party to a reorganization if they receive stock or securities of another party to the reorganization in exchange — § 354.

• *Carryover of basis to stockholders*: § 358.

• *No tax to corporation*: no gain or loss is recognized to the corporation which is party to a reorganization and exchanges its property for stock or securities of another corporation which is party to the reorganization — §§ 361 and 1032.

---

[140] IRC § 338(a).

[141] See § 1060 and the discussion of sales of assets earlier. Indeed, the proceeds-distribution rules of § 1060 are actually found in the regulations under § 338. *See* Treas. Reg. § 1.338-6. If there is a prize for the longest and most convoluted regulations, the § 338 regulations are certainly in the running for that "honor." Suffice it to say that the above paragraph in the text describes the § 338 election only in the most general terms. The details will be important to planning the transaction, but they can be left at this point to the tax specialist and the tax specialist's or the client's accountant.

[142] Bittker & Eustice, *supra*, ¶ 12.01[3] at p. 12-12 (quoting Bazley v. Commissioner of Internal Revenue, 331 U.S. 737, 740 (1947)).

- *Carryover of tax attributes to purchasing corporation:* a corporation generally succeeds to basis and other tax attributes of a corporation whose assets it purchases — § 362(b) (basis), § 381 (other attributes, including earnings and profits, net operating losses, and capital loss carryovers).

iii.   Definition of a "reorganization"

What types of transactions qualify for this special "reorganization" treatment? Section 368(a)(1) defines seven different types of reorganizations, which are always referred to by the letter of the subsection of § 368(a)(1) providing the definition. Hence, the reorganization defined in § 361(a)(1)(A) is known as a "Type A" reorganization or more simply as an "A" reorganization. Of the seven, three will not concern us at all,[143] and this leaves us with four: the "A" through "D" reorganizations.

"A" Reorganization. The Code defines this type of reorganization as "a statutory merger or consolidation." One commentator notes that this is "beguilingly simple,"[144] and there is substantial judicial and regulatory gloss on this simple phrase. The purpose thereof is to distinguish the "real" reorganizations from the "fake" ones. As the regulations state matter-of-factly, "a short-term purchase money note is not a security of a party to a reorganization, an ordinary dividend is to be treated as an ordinary dividend, and a sale is nevertheless to be treated as a sale even though the mechanics of a reorganization have been set up."[145]

"B" Reorganization. This type of reorganization is a stock-for-stock exchange which leaves one corporation as a subsidiary of another after the exchange.

"C" Reorganization. This type reorganization is a stock-for-property exchange, in which one corporation purchases the assets of another for stock.

"D" Reorganization. This type of reorganization is difficult to summarize. It is a transfer by a (transferor) corporation of its assets to another (transferee) corporation of which the transferor and/or its shareholders are in control, followed by a distribution of stock of the transferee corporation by the transferor corporation.[146] This results in a replacement of the all or part of the transferor corporation by the transferee corporation, depending on how much of the assets are transferred. If the transfer of assets is total, the transferee replaces the transferor; this is known as a "non-divisive D reorganization."[147] If only some of the assets are transferred, the result is to split up transferor into two separate corporations; this is known as a "divisive D reorganization."[148]

Example. Transferor Corp.'s stock and Transferee Corp.'s stocks are owned by A and B. Transferor Corp. transfers its assets to Transferee Corp. in exchange for

---

[143] We set aside "E" and "F" reorganizations as beyond the scope of our introductory coverage. The "G" reorganization is discussed in Chapter 10.

[144] Howard E. Abrams & Richard L. Doernberg, Federal Corporate Taxation 210 (4th ed. 1998) (quoting from the regulations as in our text accompanying the next note).

[145] Treas. Reg. § 1.368-1(b).

[146] Some of these requirements leak into § 368(a)(1)(D) by its reference to §§ 354 and 355.

[147] It is accomplished with the further help of § 354(b).

[148] It is accomplished with the further help(?) of § 355.

Transferee Corp. shares and then distributes those Transferee Corp. shares to A and B. The net result is to simply replace Transferor Corp. with Transferee Corp.

A brief reflection. If you were expecting a complete, crisp, and exhaustive catalogue of distinct tax-deferred reorganizations from which to choose, the above list is probably most unsatisfying. Although a statutory merger can be an "A" reorganization, not all statutory mergers will meet the additional "continuity" tests discussed below. A statutory merger could also be used in a "B" or "C" reorganization. All three of these reorganizations can be done through "triangular" methods, in which two corporations combine but the shares issued are those of a parent of the acquiring corporation. This is done through the use of a "parenthetical B" or "parenthetical C" reorganization — referring literally to the parenthetical language in those subsections allowing the use of parent corporation stock — and in the case of the "A" reorganization by additional permissive and restrictive language in § 368(a)(2)(D) and (E). A transfer of assets from one corporation to another could qualify either as a "C" or a "D" reorganization, depending on the particulars of who gets what in exchange.[149] A divisive "D" reorganization is given its reorganization treatment through § 355, which doesn't mention "reorganizations" at all.[150] But do not despair. We will first discuss two additional requirements common to all reorganizations, and then consider the major features of each type which will be the first ones to consider in choosing which reorganization to use for your transaction.

iv.   General requirements for all reorganizations

Substantial judicial gloss on the sparse language of § 368(a)(1) has been "codified" in the income tax regulations which require of all reorganizations a *continuity of business enterprise (COBE)* and a *continuity of interest*.

Treas. Reg. § 1.368-1. Purpose and scope of exception of reorganization exchanges

(d)   Continuity of business enterprise —

(1)   General rule. Continuity of business enterprise (COBE) requires that the issuing corporation (P), as defined in paragraph (b) of this section,[151] either continue the target corporation's (T's) historic business or use a significant portion of T's historic business assets in a business. . . . The policy underlying this general rule, which is to ensure that reorganizations are limited to readjustments of continuing interests in property under modified corporate form, provides the guidance necessary to make these facts and circumstances determinations.

(2)   Business continuity.

(i)   The continuity of business enterprise requirement is satisfied if P continues T's historic business. The fact P is in the same line of business as T tends to establish the requisite continuity, but is not alone sufficient.

(ii)   If T has more than one line of business, continuity of business enterprise requires only that P continue a significant line of business.

---

[149]   The Code anticipates this, providing that a "D" trumps a "C" reorganization if it qualifies as both. *See* § 368(a)(2)(A).

[150]   The omission is largely academic, because § 355 imposes by its own terms most of the requirements applicable to "reorganizations" generally, as we will see shortly.

[151]   [Essentially, P is the "acquiring corporation" and T is the "target corporation."—Eds.]

(iii)   In general, a corporation's historic business is the business it has conducted most recently. However, a corporation's historic business is not one the corporation enters into as part of a plan of reorganization.

(iv)   All facts and circumstances are considered in determining the time when the plan comes into existence and in determining whether a line of business is "significant."

(3)   Asset continuity.

(i)   The continuity of business enterprise requirement is satisfied if P uses a significant portion of T's historic business assets in a business.

(ii)   A corporation's historic business assets are the assets used in its historic business. Business assets may include stock and securities and intangible operating assets such as good will, patents, and trademarks, whether or not they have a tax basis.

(iii)   In general, the determination of the portion of a corporation's assets considered "significant" is based on the relative importance of the assets to operation of the business. However, all other facts and circumstances, such as the net fair market value of those assets, will be considered.

(e)   Continuity of interest —

(1)   General rule.

(i)   The purpose of the continuity of interest requirement is to prevent transactions that resemble sales from qualifying for nonrecognition of gain or loss available to corporate reorganizations. Continuity of interest requires that in substance a substantial part of the value of the proprietary interests in the target corporation be preserved in the reorganization. A proprietary interest in the target corporation is preserved if, in a potential reorganization, it is exchanged for a proprietary interest in the issuing corporation (as defined in paragraph (b) of this section), it is exchanged by the acquiring corporation for a direct interest in the target corporation enterprise, or it otherwise continues as a proprietary interest in the target corporation. However, a proprietary interest in the target corporation is not preserved if, in connection with the potential reorganization, it is acquired by the issuing corporation for consideration other than stock of the issuing corporation, or stock of the issuing corporation furnished in exchange for a proprietary interest in the target corporation in the potential reorganization is redeemed. All facts and circumstances must be considered in determining whether, in substance, a proprietary interest in the target corporation is preserved. For purposes of the continuity of interest requirement, a mere disposition of stock of the target corporation prior to a potential reorganization to persons not related . . . to the target corporation or to persons not related . . . to the issuing corporation is disregarded and a mere disposition of stock of the issuing corporation received in a potential reorganization to persons not related . . . to the issuing corporation is disregarded.

(ii)   For purposes of paragraph (e)(1)(i) of this section, a proprietary interest in the target corporation (other than one held by the acquiring corporation) is not preserved to the extent that consideration received prior to a potential reorganization, either in a redemption of the target corporation stock or in a distribution with respect to the target corporation stock, is treated as other property or money received in the exchange for purposes of section 356, or would be so treated if the target shareholder also had received stock of the issuing corporation in exchange for stock owned by the shareholder in the target corporation.

NOTES AND QUESTIONS

1.   We have included only a portion of the full regulations. We have omitted technical details and dozens of demonstrative examples provided by the IRS.

2.   If A Corp. and B Corp. merge under state law, and the merger agreement provides that each share of A Corp. becomes one share of B Corp., are the continuity tests met?

3.   Suppose instead that the merger agreement provides that B Corp. acquires the A Corp. shares from the A Corp. shareholders for cash. Are the continuity tests met?

4.   Suppose instead that the merger agreement is as provided in question 2, but then B Corp. sells the assets of A Corp. Are the continuity tests met?

5.   Although the regulations apply these requirements to all reorganizations, they are most important in "A" reorganizations. As discussed below, each of the other types of reorganizations include more specific rules regarding continuity of business enterprise and continuity of interest.

v.   Particular requirements

In order to demonstrate why the business lawyer must consult tax experts early in the planning process, we will consider some of the specific details related to each of the four types of reorganizations.

(A)   "A" reorganizations and "triangular" mergers

Because the statutory language is brief, the main requirements are the "continuity" rules excerpted above. Additional requirements are imposed upon "triangular" mergers — so called because a lawyer's diagram resembles this geometric shape of the three entities involved — when the statutory merger is between the target corporation and a *subsidiary* of the acquiring corporation.

Why do lawyers so often use triangular mergers? There are many reasons, but two reasons predominate and can serve as useful examples.

•   The acquiring corporation may want to keep the target corporation's business in a separately organized subsidiary. This result occurs if B Corp. acquires A Corp.'s assets directly and then "drops down" the A Corp. assets into B-Sub Corp., a new wholly-owned subsidiary of B Corp. This may create problems if the A Corp. assets are not transferrable or come along with known (or unknown) liabilities from which B Corp. would like to insulate its major business assets. The temporary residence of the A Corp. assets in B Corp.'s ownership will not be disregarded. The solution is to create B-Sub Corp. *first*, and *then* merge A Corp. with B-Sub Corp., with the A Corp. shareholders receiving not B-Sub Corp. shares, but rather B Corp. shares.

•   A merger between A Corp. and B Corp. will require a vote of both corporations' shareholders, even though A Corp. is realistically and economically "acquiring" B Corp. and it is not an event of sufficient size to merit consideration by B Corp. shareholders. B Corp. management may desire to avoid the cost and publicity of solicitation of votes in favor of the merger. It can do so by creating B-Sub Corp. and substituting B-Sub Corp. in its place. If a vote of B-Sub's stockholders is required, then that is a mere formality since all of the shares of B-Sub Corp. are owned by B Corp. This device does not always work. If the merger is sufficiently large to require a lot of B Corp. stock to be issued to acquire A Corp., a vote of B Corp. shareholders is required.[152]

Assume that we can deal with the non-tax issues regarding shareholder approval in such a triangular merger. The *tax* problem created is that the "parties to the reorganization" — defined in § 368(b) — are only A Corp. and B-Sub Corp. B Corp. is *not* a party according to tax law, regardless of its status under governing state law. Therefore, the transfers of its stock do not fit within the non-recognition provisions of either § 354 (tax treatment of the shareholders) or § 361 (tax treatment of the corporation). This problem is solved by § 368(a)(2)(D) and (E), allowing an "A" reorganization which uses stock of the corporate parent of one of the parties, and corresponding language in § 368(b), which makes these parent corporations "parties to the reorganization."

The difference between the two triangular provisions is difficult to read and even more difficult to justify. Section 368(a)(2)(D) governs so-called "forward" triangular mergers, where the surviving corporation is the acquisition subsidiary.[153] So if B Corp. creates B-Sub to merge with A Corp., giving B Corp. stock to former A Corp. shareholders, it is a "forward" triangular merger if B-Sub is designated as the surviving corporation. Section 368(a)(2)(E) governs so-called "reverse" triangular mergers, where the surviving corporation is the target.[154] In our example, this would be the case if A Corp. were designated as the surviving corporation in an A Corp. — B-Sub Corp. merger.

Under state law, the designation of the corporation which survives the merger is simply a matter of the merger agreement.[155] The choice of which corporation survives may be simply a matter of convenience, or it may be dictated by restricted transferability of A Corp. assets or an important A Corp. trade name or other feature which could not be easily accessed by B-Sub Corp.[156]

It may therefore seem odd that Congress has chosen to graft more requirements upon the reverse triangular merger than on the forward triangular

---

[152] This amount is usually 20% of the amount outstanding before the acquisition. *See, e.g.,* MBCA § 11.04(g)(4) (by reference to § 6.21(f)); Cal. Corp. Code § 1201(b). Under California law, the approval of the parent corporation's board of directors is explicitly required even if the subsidiary is the party to the merger. *See* Cal. Corp. Code § 1200(e).

[153] We know this because it speaks of issue of stock of a corporation which is "in control of the acquiring corporation."

[154] We know this because it speaks of issue of stock of a corporation which "before the merger was in control of the merged corporation."

[155] *See, e.g.,* MBCA § 11.02(c)(1) ("The plan of merger must include the name of each corporation or other entity that will merge and the name of the corporation or other entity that will be the survivor of the merger.").

[156] The name is often not an obstacle. If "A Corp." is a name worthy of keeping, a forward triangular merger can still be done, and often is done. The next day (or at the same time), B-Sub Corp. (which survived the merger) may change its name to "A Corp." This was the outcome in the *Avatex-Xetava* case reprinted in Section B.2.c above.

merger, since the outcomes are roughly equivalent under state law and the motivations for choosing one over the other are not tax related. Nonetheless, Congress has spoken, albeit cryptically. The reverse triangular merger is a "reorganization" only if it otherwise qualifies as an "A" reorganization, *and* if:

> (i) after the transaction, the corporation surviving the merger holds substantially all of its properties and of the properties of the merged corporation (other than stock of the controlling corporation distributed in the transaction); and

> (ii) in the transaction, former shareholders of the surviving corporation exchanged, for an amount of voting stock of the controlling corporation, an amount of stock in the surviving corporation which constitutes control of such corporation.[157]

To continue with our example, if A Corp. is to survive the A Corp. — B Sub Corp. merger, *and* the merger is to qualify as a reorganization, A Corp. must hold (after the merger) substantially all of the properties held by A Corp. and B-Sub Corp. before the merger. This is one reason why B-Sub Corp., when it is created, is usually vested with only nominal assets. Second, the former A Corp. shareholders (who received B Corp. stock in the merger) must have surrendered enough A Corp. stock to have constituted "control" of A Corp. These additional restrictions make the reverse triangular merger (but not the forward) more closely resemble a "B" reorganization, to which we next turn. One commentator thus concluded: "[f]or reasons known only to Congress (if to anyone), the reverse subsidiary merger is a strange creature, one part A, one part B, and one part like nothing else."[158]

(B)   "B" reorganizations

The statutory restrictions on a "B" reorganization are two. First, only voting stock of the acquiring corporation[159] can be used to buy stock of another corporation. Second, the acquiring corporation must control the other corporation after the transaction. "Control" is a term of art, meaning ownership of 80% of the voting power of voting stock and 80% of all the shares of all other stock.[160]

This language is powerful as far as it goes, but it goes no further. The "solely for voting stock" restriction applies only to the target corporation stock, but it applies to all the target corporation stock.[161] Nothing else may be paid for the target stock, but *anything* else may be paid for anything else purchased as part of the merger transaction.

---

[157] IRC § 368(a)(2)(E).

[158] Abrams & Doernberg, *supra*, at 228.

[159] Or stock of the parent of the acquiring corporation can be used (a "parenthetical B" reorganization) but not both.

[160] IRC § 368(c).

[161] This makes a "creeping 'B' reorganization" difficult. Some of the stock purchased before the merger may be considered by the IRS or a court to be part of the transaction and, since it was presumably bought for cash, would spoil the "B" reorganization. Other stock purchased sufficiently long ago will not be part of the transaction. *See* Abrams & Doernberg, *supra*, at 229 & nn. 27–29 (discussing *Chapman v. Commissioner*, 618 F.2d 856 (1st Cir. 1980)).

(C)   "C" reorganizations

The statutory restrictions on a "C" reorganization are principally three. First, the acquiring corporation must acquire "substantially all" the assets of the target corporation. Unlike the use of the identical phrase under state corporation law,[162] there is no definitive guidance for tax purposes. Planners often rely on a Revenue Procedure which provides a safe harbor under the "substantially all" requirement if there is a transfer of 90 percent of the target's net assets and 70 percent of the target's gross assets.[163] Second, the acquisition of substantially all of the target's assets must "solely for all or part of" its voting stock.[164] Here, however, there is a statutory relaxation of the word "solely" not available in the "B" reorganization. Section 368(a)(2)(B) permits use of other property, so long as 80% of the target's assets are acquired for voting stock. Finally, the target corporation (which received the acquiring corporation's stock) must liquidate, courtesy of § 368(a)(2)(G).

(D)   Nondivisive "D" reorganizations

The "D" reorganization which does not divide a corporation results in the substitution of the surviving corporation for the transferring corporation. This happens by a transfer of assets to the controlled corporation and a distribution which meets the additional requirements of § 354. For purposes of the "D" reorganization, however, "control" does not mean what it has meant so far, but rather only 50% control. This is accomplished by a special rule tucked in § 368(a)(2)(H) by reference to § 304(c).[165]

Section 354(b) adds two wrinkles to the nondivisive "D" reorganization. First, the acquiring corporation must purchase "substantially all" the assets of the transferor corporation.[166] Second, the property received in the exchange by the transferring corporation must be distributed as part of the plan of reorganization.

(E)   Divisive "D" reorganizations

We have saved for last the divisive "D" reorganization. It results in a corporation acquiring property for stock of a subsidiary and then distributing the subsidiary's stock to some or all of its shareholders. If the stock is distributed pro-rata to the shareholders, as a stock dividend, the transaction is known as a "spin-off." If the stock is distributed to some of the shareholders in redemption of their shares of the transferor corporation, the transaction is known as a "split-off." This is commonly used in a situation to effect a "divorce" of business owners.[167] If the transferee corporation creates two subsidiaries, distributes the shares of both and

---

[162] *See supra* Section B.2.a.

[163] *See* Rev. Proc. 77-37, 1977-2 C.B. 568 (known as the "90/70" or "70/90" test).

[164] Or stock of the parent of the acquiring corporation can be used (a "parenthetical C" reorganization) but not both.

[165] This rule is a good example of a requirement of good tax (and business) planning: read the Code, and read it again, all the way to the end.

[166] For a discussion of what constitutes "substantially all," see *supra* the discussion of "C" reorganizations. However, the phrase in § 354(b) "has been interpreted, somewhat surprisingly, more flexibly than the phrase . . . in ["C" reorganizations]." Bittker & Eustice, *supra*, at ¶ 12.26[4], p. 12-114.

[167] Recall, for example, the problem at the end of Chapter 6. If Ann were interested in taking part of the business instead of cash or other property, this may present one type of a divisive "D" reorganization.

then liquidates, the transaction is known as a "split-up."

All of the divisive "D" reorganizations work by reference to § 355. Subsection (a)(1) imposes three detailed requirements on the reorganization. In general, they can be described as follows.

• The reorganization cannot be a "device" for tax-free distribution of earnings and profits which escape dividend treatment. For example, if one of the recipients of the securities distributed under § 355 immediately resells them and pays only capital gain on the transaction, earnings and profits will disappear without ever subjecting any distribution to dividend treatment. The regulations provide examples of "devices" for distribution as well as "nondevices"[168] which may aid in planning the transaction.[169]

• Both corporations must continue an active trade or business. As specified in § 355(b)(2), such business must have been conducted for *five years* preceding the distribution which constitutes the second part of the "D" reorganization.

• All or most of the stock of the controlled corporation must be distributed.

Finally, § 355(d) and (e) impose limitations on any transfers of stock which take place before or after the reorganization. These look-back and look-forward periods extend for many years on either side of the divisive "D" reorganization, and therefore require substantial tax consultation before even beginning to consider this option for your corporate divorce.

COMPREHENSIVE PROBLEM:
SALE OF THE BUSINESS

We are now five years into the operation of what became the BC Restaurant, since Ann was bought out as she desired (see Comprehensive Problem in Chapter 6), and eight years since the inception of the business. Bev, Carl and the other investors have continued to run a profitable business. Ann's interest has been repurchased and fully paid for. The bank loans have been partially repaid, but there are still two years remaining before they are fully retired.

An interested buyer has appeared on the scene, and initial discussions have been promising. Bev, Carl, and the other investors are considering selling the business (in whatever form you recommend) in exchange for some combination of cash, short-term debt, and equity interests in, or stock of the buyer. The buyer is Interstate Restaurants, a company with about $50 million in assets and approximately 200 owners. Its interests are not subject to the "publicly-held stock" requirements of the Securities Exchange Act of 1934.

Alternative A: The Sale of an LLP or LLC to Another LLP or LLC

Assume the entity being sold was formed and continues to operate as a C corporation, renamed the BC Corporation after Ann's shares were repurchased. The profit and loss shares were readjusted on Ann's departure as follows: 25% to Bev, 15% to Carl, and 3% to each of 20 outside investors. The entity's financial condition is shown below as of the end of the most recent fiscal year. The buyer is Interstate Restaurants, which is also an LLP or LLC (the same type as the BC

---

[168] A term of art which only a tax lawyer can appreciate.

[169] Treas. Reg. § 1.355-2(d).

restaurant), and all entities are organized in your state. The banks' consent is required under terms of the loan agreement to any merger or sale of assets. The bank has given preliminary consent to the deal if the bank is either repaid in the buyout or receives debt obligations of Interstate Restaurants with similar terms to the existing loans to BC Restaurant, including a two year remaining maturity date.

BC Restaurant, LLP/LLC
Income Statements for the year ended Dec. 31

	Two years ago	Last year
Revenues	$ 10,000,000	$ 11,000,000
Cost of sales	8,000,000	8,500,000
Gross margin	2,000,000	2,500,000
Administrative expenses	800,000	900,000
Net income (loss)	1,200,000	1,600,000

BC Restaurant, LLP/LLC
Balance Sheet
Dec. 31, Last Year

Assets		Liabilities and equity	
Cash	$ 270,000	Accounts payable	$ 200,000
Accounts receivable	350,000	Other accrued liabilities	300,000
Short-term investments	200,000	Bank loan	1,200,000
Inventory	2,200,000	**Total liabilities**	**1,700,000**
Furniture and fixtures, net of accumulated depreciation	2,500,000	Partners'/Members' capital*	4,300,000
Land	400,000	**Total equity**	**4,300,000**
Intangible assets, net of amortization	80,000		
Total assets	**$ 6,000,000**	**Total liabilities and equity**	**$ 6,000,000**

* Capital account detail.

	Opening balance	Allocated gain	Distributions	Balance, end of year
Bev	$ 1,000,000	$ 400,000	$ 325,000	$ 1,075,000
Carl	700,000	240,000	195,000	745,000
Other investors, total	1,300,000	960,000	780,000	1,480,000
Total	$ 4,000,000	$ 1,600,000	$ 1,300,000	$ 4,300,000

For each of the alternatives discussed below, consider how and whether the transaction could be organized under the laws of your state. Whose approval would be required? Would any interests exchanged be subject to the registration requirements of the Securities Act of 1933? What would be the federal income tax consequences?

(1) Could the sale of the business be structured as a sale of the assets of BC Restaurant in exchange for Interstate Restaurants' cash or ownership interests?

(2) Could the sale be structured as a sale of the interests of BC Restaurant by Bev, Carl, and the others in exchange for Interstate Restaurants' cash or ownership interests?

(3) If the deal is an interests-for-interests exchange, what if some of the outside investors insist on being cashed out? Can those outside investors be accommodated? What if (for this or some other reason) some of the outside investors don't go along with the proposed sale? Can they scuttle the deal?

Alternative B: The Corporation

Assume the entity being sold was formed and continues to operate as a C corporation, renamed the BC Corporation after Ann's shares were repurchased. Bev owns 800 shares of preferred stock. Bev's preferred stock receives a distribution and liquidation preference and is entitled to vote on a per-share basis with the common stock. Bev and Carl are BC Corporation's directors and two of its senior officers. BC Corporation has never made an S election for federal income tax purposes.[170] Thus, its business has operated slightly differently than would the LLP or LLC. Its income has been subject to tax at the corporate level when earned, and again when distributed to the shareholders.[171] Although the corporate business finds itself in a similar financial position to the LLP or LLC, it arrived there by a very different path.[172]

The bank's consent is required and has been given as described in Alternative A above. The buyer is Interstate Restaurants Corporation (IRC), of the same size and status as the buyer in Alternative A. Both BC Corporation and IRC are incorporated in your state.

For each of the alternatives discussed below, consider how and whether the transaction could be organized under the laws of your state. Whose approval would be required? Would any interests exchanged be subject to the registration requirements of the Securities Act of 1933? What would be the federal income tax consequences?

(1) Could the sale of the business be structured as a sale of the assets of BC Restaurant in exchange for Interstate Restaurants' cash or stock?

(2) Could the sale be structured as a sale of BC Restaurant's stock by Bev, Carl, and the others in exchange for Interstate Restaurants' cash or stock? Are there any complications introduced by Bev's status as a preferred stockholder?

---

[170] We will put aside the complications which might arise if an S corporation were used. Assume for purposes of this problem that if it was an S corporation earlier, it has now converted to a C corporation and that all the tax carryover problems have disappeared.

[171] For purposes of this exercise, assume that the corporation's "retained earnings" for book purposes approximates its "earnings and profits" for tax purposes.

[172] This seems like a lot of money to have voluntarily contributed to the Treasury, but there could be legitimate reasons for such an operation. One reason, discussed in Chapters 3 and 6, is the inability of the S corporation to accommodate Bev's preferred stock interest. Alternatively, or in addition, the outside investors could be entities which are not eligible to be S corporation shareholders, or they could be other corporations whose dividend income mostly tax-deferred under IRC § 243, or they could be tax-exempt organizations or individuals with substantial tax losses.

(3) If the deal is a stock-for-stock deal, what if some of the outside investors insist on being cashed out? Can those outside investors be accommodated? What if (for this or some other reason) some of the outside investors don't go along with the proposed sale? Can they scuttle the deal?

(4) Assume instead that IRC wants to purchase the real estate of the BC Restaurant and its favorable "restaurant zoning" (and that transfer of the zoning rights is permitted under local law). The location will then be transformed into one of IRC's chain restaurants. Carl is amenable to the sale, but wants to be permitted to open his new-age video restaurant business again in another location in town, and perhaps attract other investors or convince his son, Carl Jr., to go into the business.[173] IRC proposes that BC Corp. will transfer its real estate, entitlements, and licenses to a subsidiary, and then distribute the assets of that subsidiary either (a) to Bev and the outside investors who would then sell the shares to IRC, or (b) have IRC purchase Bev's and the outside investors' shares before the distribution. At the end of the day, IRC would own its desired location suitable for conversion to the chain restaurant business. Carl would own the remaining BC Corporation assets (his originally contributed intellectual property, some appliances and fixtures, as well as the right to use the BC Restaurant name in another location in town), to which IRC is agreeable. How could these results be accomplished? If it would be advantageous for any of the parties involved, would it be possible to structure the deal as a tax-deferred transaction?

BC Restaurant, Inc.
Balance Sheet
Dec. 31, Last Year

Assets		Liabilities and equity	
Cash	$ 270,000	Accounts payable	$ 200,000
Accounts receivable	350,000	Other accrued liabilities	300,000
Short-term investments	200,000	Bank loan	1,200,000
Inventory	2,200,000	**Total liabilities**	**1,700,000**
Furniture and fixtures, net of accumulated depreciation	2,500,000	Preferred stock	800,000
Land	400,000	Common stock (1¢ par value)	34
Intangible assets, net of amortization	80,000	Contrib. capital in excess of par	3,399,966
		Retained earnings	100,000
		Total equity	**4,300,000**
Total assets	**$ 6,000,000**	**Total liabilities and equity**	**$ 6,000,000**

---

[173] Unfortunately, for now Carl Jr. has an inexplicable preference for hamburgers over seafood, but Carl hopes to be able to groom him to take over the business eventually.

BC Restaurant, Inc. Income Statements for the year ended Dec. 31

	Two years ago	Last year
Revenues	$ 10,000,000	$ 11,000,000
Cost of sales	8,000,000	8,500,000
Gross margin	2,000,000	2,500,000
Administrative expenses	800,000	900,000
Net income before taxes	1,200,000	1,600,000
Income taxes	400,000	530,000
Net income	800,000	1,070,000

Chapter 10

DISSOLUTION UNDER STATE AND FEDERAL LAW

A. INTRODUCTION TO DISSOLUTIONS

There comes a time in the life of many business entities when the entity will be terminated and its remaining assets, if any, disposed of. Termination may occur for many reasons:

1. The owners' agree to terminate the business, pay off its debts, and pull out their capital and profits, if any.[1]
2. The formation documents limit the life of the entity to a certain term, or completion of a particular purpose, and the term has expired or the purpose has been completed.
3. The formation documents provide for termination of the entity upon the happening of certain events (such as death, divorce, bankruptcy, disability, changes in financial structure, achievement of certain goals, the vote of a certain percentage of ownership interests, etc.).
4. Termination is forced upon the owners by financial reverses, inability to pay debts, adverse market changes, law suits or other negative factors.
5. There are irreconcilable differences among owners and the buy-sell provisions, if any, can't be fulfilled in a way that allows some owners to buy out their antagonistic co-owners.
6. The owner of a large share of the entity departs and the other owners cannot afford to buy out the departing owner.

We are going to take a look at the voluntary and involuntary dissolution of business entities under *state* law. For reasons discussed later in this chapter, many insolvent entities will end their existence in federal bankruptcy court, rather than state law dissolution proceedings. We will begin by looking at dissolutions under state law then, later in this chapter, we will focus on liquidations of business entities under federal bankruptcy law.[2]

1. Cooperation and Forums for Dissolutions

When the owners agree to dissolve an entity, or the formation documents provide for the dissolution of the entity, the path the owners take to implement the dissolution will depend on whether or not the entity has a positive or negative net worth. In a positive-net-worth company it is in the best interests of *all* of the owners to cooperate in the dissolution. To the degree that they can maximize the value received for assets and reduce administrative costs, they will increase the *pro rata* distribution to the owners.

---

[1] In the case of general and limited partnerships, dissolution may include an obligation of some or all of the partners to contribute to *losses* as well.

[2] 11 U.S.C. § 101 *et. seq.*

The voluntary dissolution of an entity with a positive net worth will require three steps: (i) selling the assets of the company for the greatest possible value in an efficient and timely manner;[3] (ii) determining and paying off the company debts (or providing for their future payment); and, (iii) distributing the remaining proceeds in accordance with the distribution scheme set forth in the formation documents or in accordance with statutory default rules for distribution, if the formation documents are unclear.

An optimizing dissolution of a positive-net-worth company may not be as simple as it appears. Some of the owners may disagree about the worth of assets and the best methods for selling the assets of the company. While one owner may believe that a sale of the entire business is best, other owners may believe that an asset-by-asset approach will yield greater returns and be easier to accomplish. There may also be disagreements about who is authorized to conduct the sale, what approvals are needed by the other owners and the adequacy of the price for the asset or assets being sold.

Hopefully, the formation and buy-sell documents provide clear procedures for conducting a voluntary dissolution to augment the statutory dissolution requirements. Otherwise, what starts as a voluntary dissolution may end up in the hands of the courts as the owners begin to disagree on the procedures to be followed or prices to be accepted for the assets of the company.

On the other hand, in the case of a company with a *negative* net worth, it may or may not be in the interests of equity holders to oversee and cooperate in the dissolution but, instead, file for bankruptcy under the federal bankruptcy code.[4] Can you see why in the case of negative net worth company, the owners of a *corporation* or *LLC* might simply walk away and leave the liquidation to the bankruptcy system, while owners of a *general partnership* might prefer to cooperate and maximize the distribution to *creditors*? Later in this chapter we will look more closely at this question with regard to the dissolution of each type of entity.

2.   Tax Considerations for Dissolutions

Other important considerations for voluntary dissolutions are the tax consequences. For instance, the dissolution of a C corporation constitutes a liquidation that will result in dual-level taxation. Generally, the corporation will have to pay taxes on the aggregate amount by which the sale or distribution of assets exceeds the corporation's basis in those assets. The subsequent distribution of after-tax proceeds to the stockholders will result in capital gains taxes assessed against the stockholders to the degree that a stockholder receives a distribution in excess of the stockholder's basis in the shares of stock,[5] or capital losses to the extent that the distribution value is less than the stockholder's basis in the stock.

---

[3] An alternative scheme is to distribute the property of the company, cash and non-cash, directly to the owners. This requires elaborate and carefully planned mechanisms for valuing any non-cash property and fairly distributing the cash and non-cash property to the owners in accordance with their investment interests. In most business dissolutions, the distribution will be in cash following a liquidation of the company's assets and that is the assumption we will be using in this book.

[4] The preference for bankruptcy over state law dissolution will be discussed later in this chapter.

[5] This is true even if the corporation liquidates by distributing the *assets* to its stockholders, rather than first liquidating the assets and then distributing the proceeds to the stockholders. *See* IRC §§ 331,

The liquidation of an entity taxed as a *partnership* or S corporation won't result in double taxation. Any gain or loss will be passed directly through to the partners, members or S-stockholders,[6] without any taxation at the entity level. Nevertheless, there are tax impacts on each of the owners (particularly those that contributed low basis but appreciated property in exchange for their ownership interest) that should be carefully considered as part of a well-structured dissolution.[7]

B. DISSOLUTION OF CORPORATIONS

At the heart of state dissolutions and federal bankruptcy liquidations is the concept of priority of distribution discussed in Chapter One of this book.[8] Particularly in the case of corporations, which insulate equity holders from the claims of creditors, this priority scheme is present throughout the lifetime of the corporation with regard to dividends and other distributions,[9] and is certainly true when the corporation is dissolved under state law, or liquidated in federal bankruptcy court. Only after creditors have been fully satisfied, or adequate provisions made for payment to them, can distributions be made to stockholders.

As an entity created by state statute, a corporation can *only* be dissolved in accordance with state statutory requirements, if not liquidated in federal bank-ruptcy court. We are going to use the California Corporations Code as a good example of how states handle the issues that arise with regard to corporate dissolutions

Title 1 of the California Corporations Code contains three primary chapters addressing the dissolution of corporations:

— Chapter 18 (§§ 1800–1809): Involuntary Dissolutions
— Chapter 19 (§§ 1800–1809): Voluntary Dissolutions
— Chapter 20 (§§ 2000–2011): General Provisions Relating to [both Voluntary and Involuntary] Dissolution

1. Voluntary Dissolutions of Corporations

The provisions of the California Corporations Code serve as a good example of state law rules governing voluntary dissolutions of corporate entities.[10] It is important to understand the statutory rules when preparing the formation

---

336. IRC § 336(a) states: "General rule. Except as otherwise provided in this section or section 337, gain or loss shall be recognized to a liquidating corporation on the distribution of property in complete liquidation as if such property were sold to the distributee at its fair market value."

[6] The consequences for S Corporation stockholders The shareholder consequences of a complete liquidation of an S corporation are governed by §§ 331 and 1001. The stockholder's adjusted basis in the stock is subtracted from the cash and fair market value of other property received from the corporation. The gain or loss recognized by the S stockholder will depend on whether the stock is a capital asset in the stockholder's hands and whether any capital gains are considered long-term or short-term gains.

[7] See the discussion of partnership taxation in Section E of Chapter 5.

[8] See the discussion of corporate priorities in Section B.4 of Chapter 1.

[9] See the discussion of dividend limitation provisions in Section G.1 of Chapter 8 and the discussion of fraudulent conveyances in Section H of Chapter 8.

[10] Pacific Scene, Inc. v. Penasquitos, Inc., 46 Cal. 3d 407, 411, 758 P.2d 1182 (1988) (reproduced below). The California Supreme Court stated: "Sections 1800 to 2011 of the Corporations Code, enacted as part of a comprehensive statutory revision in 1977, comprise a broad and detailed scheme regulating virtually every aspect of corporate dissolution." *See also* Keeler v. Schulte, 47 Cal. 2d 801, 803 (1957) ("A

documents, particularly buy-sell agreements, so as to avoid some of the pitfalls that might arise during a dissolution and, perhaps, adjust for those pitfalls in the formation documents. As you read these provisions keep in mind three important points: (i) state law *voluntary* dissolution provisions are used primarily for the winding up of positive-net-worth companies; (ii) when a business entity has a *negative* net worth, the liquidation of that entity will almost always end up in federal bankruptcy proceedings; (iii) state law *voluntary* dissolution provisions generally give the board of directors the power to complete a dissolution and winding up of a corporation without court supervision but state statutes give other parties (such as stockholders or creditors) the power to request *court* supervision of dissolutions in both voluntary and involuntary cases, under certain circumstances; and (iv) in both voluntary and involuntary dissolution proceedings, the stockholders who do not participate in initiating or consenting to the dissolution may have the statutory right to buyout the interests of the shareholders moving for dissolution, based on the *liquidation* value of the corporation — pay close attention to § 2000.[11]

The starting place for California corporate dissolutions is the right of creditors to be paid before stockholders receive any distribution from either a voluntary or involuntary dissolution:

§ 2004.   Authority for and duty to distribute corporate assets among shareholders; When distribution to be made

After determining that all the known debts and liabilities of a corporation in the process of winding up have been paid or adequately provided for, the board shall distribute all the remaining corporate assets among the shareholders according to their respective rights and preferences or, if there are no shareholders, to the persons entitled thereto. If the winding up is by court proceeding or subject to court supervision, the distribution shall not be made until after the expiration of any period for the presentation of claims which has been prescribed by order of the court.

It may not be as easy as it appears to resolve the liabilities owed to creditors. There may be *unmatured* contractual claims such as long term loans, installment purchase contracts, or employment contracts, where payments are not due under the contracts until some future time. This creates problems since the *current* value of the payments to be made over the life of the contract will be significantly less than the overall contractual amount. Current value is the amount that, if properly invested, would yield the fully matured contractual value over the period of the contract. The right to receive a fixed amount of money at some time in the *future* is worth less at the time that the obligation arises. Consider the typical state-run lottery. If you win a $20 million prize, the lottery agency will typically give you two choices: (i) pay you $1 million over each of the next twenty years; or, (ii) pay you a one-time "cash value" amount. The cash value is the amount which, if invested at a reasonable interest rate, would yield a total of $20 million over twenty years. At a

---

California corporation can only be dissolved in the manner and under the conditions prescribed in the Corporations Code . . . ").

[11] This buyout right was discussed briefly in Section F.2.b of Chapter 8.

six-percent compound interest rate, the cash value at the time of the award would be about $6.24 million. If invested in certificates of deposit at a six-percent rate, this amount would grow to $20 million over the next 20 years.

Therefore, there are two different ways to handle unmatured claims. Either: (i) a fund can be established to pay these debts as they come due; or, (ii) the total amount due under the contract can be "reduced to current value" and paid at the time of dissolution. Can you see that the amount the corporation must pay for an unmatured claim will be the same whether the corporation elects to set up a fund to pay the debt as it matures, or, alternatively, pays off the unmatured debt by paying the current value? Why would a corporation prefer to fully pay off the current value rather than set up a fund? Can the corporation *force* the creditor of an unmatured claim to accept a one-time current value payment? Answers to some of these questions are revealed below.

There may also be *contingent* claims based on breach of contract, torts or myriad forms of civil actions that need to be considered. These may be hard to predict and accommodate at the time of dissolution. There may be pending and unresolved law suits against the corporation. There may also be known and unknown civil claims, such as products liability claims, that have not yet been filed in the courts. Somehow, the corporation must provide for the payment of these claims. If not, the stockholders might face liability for the return of any distributions made to them, in the event that unpaid creditors bring post-dissolution actions to recover on these contingent claims against the corporation.[12]

We shall see, later in this chapter, that one mechanism for handling contingent (as well as unmatured) claims is to shift the dissolution to the jurisdiction of the courts. Other methods include insurance (for tort liability claims such as products liability), and two additional courses of action allowed by Cal. Corp. Code §§ 2005 and 2008:

§ 2005. Adequacy of provision for payment of debt or liability

The payment of a debt or liability, whether the whereabouts of the creditor is known or unknown, has been adequately provided for if the payment has been provided for by either of the following means:

(a)   Payment thereof has been assumed or guaranteed in good faith by one or more financially responsible corporations or other persons or by the United States government or any agency thereof, and the provision (including the financial responsibility of such corporations or other persons) was determined in good faith and with reasonable care by the board to be adequate at the time of any distribution of the assets by the board pursuant to this chapter.

(b)   The amount of the debt or liability has been deposited as provided in Section 2008. This section does not prescribe the exclusive means of making adequate provision for debts and liabilities.

---

[12] See the discussion of stockholder liability in Section B.2 later in this chapter.

§ 2008. Disposition of unclaimed distributive shares in certain cases; Payment to owner by depositary; Handling money and other property deposited in State Treasury; Recovery of such money and property

(a)   If any shareholders or creditors are unknown or fail or refuse to accept their payment, dividend, or distribution in cash or property or their whereabouts cannot be ascertained after diligent inquiry, or the existence or amount of a claim of a creditor or shareholder is contingent, contested, or not determined, or if the ownership of any shares of stock is in dispute, the corporation may deposit any such payment, dividend, distribution, or the maximum amount of the claim with the Controller[13] in trust for the benefit of those lawfully entitled to the payment, dividend, distribution, or the amount of the claim. The payment, dividend, or distribution shall be paid over by the depositary to the lawful owners, their representatives or assigns, upon satisfactory proof of title.

Keeping in mind the statutory edict that creditors must be paid or provided for, we can see that a *voluntary* dissolution will usually not be elected by a *negative-net-worth* corporation. Why would the board go through the time consuming and expensive process of a dissolution if there is no money available for distribution to stockholders? Of course, it's the "right" thing to do — the assets of the corporation should be liquidated and paid to creditors regardless of whether or not there are proceeds available for stockholders. However, a voluntary dissolution under state law is an expensive and less efficient mechanism for liquidation of a negative-net-worth company, when compared to chapter 7 of the federal bankruptcy code.[14] As we will see, the federal system for liquidation of insolvent entities is cheaper, faster and likely to increase the distribution to creditors when compared to relatively clumsy state-law dissolution proceedings. In the case of a negative-net-worth corporation, the board and equity holders are far more likely to simply file a chapter 7 liquidation petition under the U.S. Bankruptcy Code and transfer the job of liquidating the corporation, and paying creditors, to the highly-empowered bankruptcy trustee. Following the filing of the petition, the board and stockholders are relieved of further obligations and can simply walk away from the insolvent corporation. Compare this to state law dissolution proceedings which require much time and effort on the part of the board of directors, and expense on the part of the corporation. There is little economic incentive for the stockholders to utilize state law dissolution proceedings for a corporation with a negative net worth when federal bankruptcy law provides a virtually cost free liquidation process that, as a result, enhances the distribution to creditors.

From a practical perspective, the provisions for state law *voluntary* dissolution are really intended for positive-net-worth corporations, where there will be funds available for distribution to stockholders after the debts of the corporation are paid or provided for. Keep this in mind as you read about *who* can initiate a voluntary dissolution:

---

[13]   The "Controller" is the Chief Fiscal Officer of California. *See* Cal. Const. Art. V.

[14]   See the discussion of bankruptcy beginning in Section E of this chapter.

Chapter 19   Voluntary Dissolutions

§ 1900.   Elections by vote of shareholders; Election by approval of board

(a)   Any corporation may elect voluntarily to wind up and dissolve by the vote of shareholders holding shares representing 50 percent or more of the voting power.

(b)   Any corporation which comes within one of the following descriptions may elect by approval by the board to wind up and dissolve:

(1)   A corporation as to which an order for relief has been entered under Chapter 7 of the federal bankruptcy law.

(2)   A corporation which has disposed of all of its assets and has not conducted any business for a period of five years immediately preceding the adoption of the resolution electing to dissolve the corporation.

(3)   A corporation which has issued no shares.

How are subsections § 1900(a) and (b) different? Subsection (a) provides the primary statutory grounds for a voluntary dissolution of a functioning corporation upon approval of the *shareholders*. As discussed above, this is unlikely to happen unless 50% or more of the shareholders believe that liquidation is in the best interests of the *shareholders* — an event that will only occur if there is perceived positive-net-worth in the corporation.

The three grounds in subsection (b) are mere housecleaning provisions that allow the *board* to go through the technical steps of dissolving a corporation when the corporation has already been effectively terminated, or is in the process of being liquidated in federal bankruptcy court. Specific procedures and requirements for corporations that have not issued shares are set forth in § 1900.5, which authorizes the board to complete the dissolution or, if no board is named in the articles nor elected, by the incorporator or a majority of the incorporators. There is one additional, mandatory ground for dissolution of California Corporations — when the term of the corporation has expired without renewal.[15]

The remaining sections of Chapter 19 of the California Corporations Code deal some of the procedural aspects of a voluntary dissolution and answer important questions about commencement, conduct and control of the voluntary dissolution proceeding. Take care to identify the purpose of each section and subsection:

---

§ 1903.   Commencement of voluntary proceedings for winding up; Conduct of proceedings; Cessation of business on commencement of proceedings; Notice

(a)   Voluntary proceedings for winding up the corporation commence upon the adoption of the resolution of shareholders . . . of the corporation electing to wind up and dissolve, or upon the filing with the corporation of a written consent of shareholders thereto.

---

[15] See Cal. Corp. Code § 1906, which states: "Except as otherwise provided by law, if the term of existence for which any corporation was organized expires without renewal or extension thereof, the board shall terminate its business and wind up its affairs; . . . "

(b) When a voluntary proceeding for winding up has commenced, the board shall continue to act as a board and shall have full powers to wind up and settle its affairs, both before and after the filing of the certificate of dissolution.

(c) When a voluntary proceeding for winding up has commenced, the corporation shall cease to carry on business except to the extent necessary for the beneficial winding up thereof and except during such period as the board may deem necessary to preserve the corporation's goodwill or going-concern value pending a sale of its business or assets, or both, in whole or in part. The board shall cause written notice of the commencement of the proceeding for voluntary winding up to be given by mail to all shareholders (except no notice need be given to the shareholders who voted in favor of winding up and dissolving the corporation) and to all known creditors and claimants whose addresses appear on the records of the corporation.

§ 1904. Judicial supervision of winding up; Petition and notice; Order protecting shareholders and creditors

If a corporation is in the process of voluntary winding up, the superior court of the proper county, upon the petition of (a) the corporation, or (b) a shareholder or shareholders who hold shares representing 5 percent or more of the total number of any class of outstanding shares, or . . . (d) three or more creditors, and upon such notice to the corporation and to other persons interested in the corporation as shareholders and creditors as the court may order, may take jurisdiction over such voluntary winding up proceeding if that appears necessary for the protection of any parties in interest. The court, if it assumes jurisdiction, may make such orders as to any and all matters concerning the winding up of the affairs of the corporation and for the protection of its shareholders and creditors as justice and equity may require. The provisions of Chapter 18[16] . . . shall apply to such court proceedings.

————————

Does § 1904 make sense? Should certain parties be able to shift a *voluntary* dissolution from the control of the board of directors into the jurisdiction of the courts? Certainly such a shift will increase the cost of the dissolution, perhaps dramatically, and will also extend the time it takes to complete the dissolution, reducing the assets available for distribution to both creditors and stockholders.

§ 1904 has two different requirements for shifting control to the courts: (i) first, only certain shareholders, creditors or the corporation itself are entitled to file a petition with the court to remove the voluntary dissolution to the courts; and (ii) second, the courts are granted discretion to supervise the dissolution. The courts "may take jurisdiction over such voluntary winding up proceeding if that appears necessary for the protection of any parties in interest." What would satisfy such grounds for judicial oversight?

It makes sense to allow court supervision to protect the rights of minority shareholders (or shareholders of a different class) if the majority is engaging in mismanagement, overreaching or oppressive conduct. The same is true from the perspective of creditors who will be impacted by the actions of the board in conducting the dissolution.[17]

————————

[16] Chapter 18 is the chapter dealing with *involuntary* dissolutions.

[17] It's unlikely that creditors would take advantage of this opportunity to shift the dissolution to the

It is also possible that the *board* may petition, on behalf of the corporation, to shift the dissolution to the courts. This makes sense when there are outstanding claims against the corporation that are not yet matured or contingent in nature. The board can use the courts to obtain final resolution of any contingent claims and reduce any unmatured claims to a present value for purposes of distribution:

§ 1806. What jurisdiction of court to include

When an involuntary[18] proceeding for winding up has been commenced, the jurisdiction of the court includes:

(a) The requirement of the proof of all claims and demands against the corporation, whether due or not yet due, contingent, unliquidated or sounding only in damages, and the barring from participation of creditors and claimants failing to make and present claims and proof as required by any order.

(b) The determination or compromise of all claims of every nature against the corporation or any of its property, and the determination of the amount of money or assets required to be retained to pay or provide for the payment of claims.

(c) The determination of the rights of shareholders and of all classes of shareholders in and to the assets of the corporation.

By shifting the dissolution to the courts, the board can eliminate, or at least vastly reduce, the possibility that disgruntled creditors or stockholders will attack the validity of the distributions made under the voluntary dissolution chapter. Unlike voluntary proceedings conducted entirely outside of the courts, the final order of the court is free from attack regarding the lawfulness of distributions to creditors and stockholders:

§ 2009. Recovery of amounts improperly distributed; Joinder of shareholders as defendants; Ratable contribution; What "process of winding up" includes

(a) Whenever in the process of winding up a corporation any distribution of assets has been made, *otherwise than under an order of court*, without prior payment or adequate provision for payment of any of the debts and liabilities of the corporation, any amount so improperly distributed to any shareholder may be recovered by the corporation. Any of such shareholders may be joined as defendants in the same action or brought in on the motion of any other defendant. [Emphasis added.]

---

state courts. If the creditors are unhappy with the progress of the dissolution or worried about its fairness, they will be far more likely to pursue an involuntary petition in bankruptcy under § 303 of the federal Bankruptcy Code if they meet the federal requirements. See the discussion of § 303 in Section E.5.d of this chapter.

[18] Section 1806 applies to *voluntary* dissolutions as well. Note the last line of § 1904. It cross-refers to Chapter 18 (the involuntary dissolution chapter) for the powers of the court to conduct *voluntary* dissolutions under § 1904.

If for any reason, there are creditors who were not paid or adequately provided for in an non-court-supervised voluntary dissolution, and assets were distributed to shareholders, the shareholders will remain liable for their pro-rata share of any recovery against the corporation by such creditors. However, if a court order is obtained, the shareholders are protected under § 2009. This makes sense since pre-dissolution creditors will be given notice and opportunity to present their claims under court supervision.

A related provision in § 1907 allows the board to seek court *confirmation* of the board-conducted dissolution at the *end* of the process, rather than using the courts to oversee the entire dissolution:

§ 1907 Order declaring corporation duly wound up and dissolved; Petition for order; Order to show cause; Contest of petition; Entry, filing and effect of order

(a) The board, in lieu of filing the certificate of dissolution, may petition the superior court of the proper county for an order declaring the corporation duly wound up and dissolved . . .

(b) Upon the filing of the petition, the court shall make an order requiring all persons interested to show cause why an order should not be made declaring the corporation duly wound up and dissolved and shall direct that the order be served by notice to all creditors, claimants and shareholders . . .

(c) Any person claiming to be interested as shareholder, creditor or otherwise may appear in the proceeding at any time before the expiration of 30 days from the completion of publication of the order to show cause and contest the petition, and upon failure to appear such person's claim shall be barred.

(d) Thereafter an order shall be entered and filed . . .

What's the difference between §§ 1904 and 1907? Both provisions, §§ 1904 and 1907, allow the board to use the courts to obtain a final order regarding creditor claims against the corporation to assure that known claims are fully satisfied before distributions of any proceeds to stockholders. In the absence of a court order, the board will file a certificate of dissolution after following all of the procedural requirements, including the payment or provision for all of the debts of the corporation:

§ 1905. Certificate of dissolution; Contents; Filing; Cessation of existence; Prerequisite showing of satisfaction of taxes

(a) When a corporation has been completely wound up without court proceedings therefor, a majority of the directors then in office shall sign and verify a certificate of dissolution stating:

(1) That the corporation has been completely wound up.

(2) That its known debts and liabilities have been actually paid, or adequately provided for, or paid or adequately provided for as far as its assets permitted, or that it has incurred no known debts or liabilities, as the case may be. If there are known debts or liabilities for payment of which adequate

provision has been made, the certificate shall state what provision has been made, setting forth the name and address of the corporation, person or governmental agency that has assumed or guaranteed the payment, or the name and address of the depositary with which deposit has been made or any other information that may be necessary to enable the creditor or other person to whom payment is to be made to appear and claim payment of the debt or liability.

(3)   That its known assets have been distributed to the persons entitled thereto or that it acquired no known assets, as the case may be.

(4)   That the corporation is dissolved.

2.   Distributions to Stockholders

Note § 1905(a)(3) above, and also § 2004, which states: "After determining that all the known debts and liabilities of a corporation in the process of winding up have been paid or adequately provided for, the board shall distribute all the remaining corporate assets among the shareholders according to their respective rights and preferences or, if there are no shareholders, to the persons entitled thereto . . . " Section 2006 adds more information about the stockholder distributions:

§ 2006.   Distribution in money or in kind; Distribution in installments

Distribution may be made either in money or in property or securities and either in installments from time to time or as a whole, if this can be done fairly and ratably and in conformity with the provisions of the articles and the rights of the shareholders, and shall be made as soon as reasonably consistent with the beneficial liquidation of the corporate assets.

If there are assets remaining after paying or providing for creditors, the board must distribute the assets to the shareholders in proportion to their ownership interests, subject to any distribution preferences set forth in the articles, if there is more than one class of stock. While it is permitted under the statutory scheme for assets other than cash to be distributed "in-kind," it is extremely difficult to accomplish unless there are limited assets and few shareholders. A corporation with liquid assets such as securities might have an easier time with an in-kind distribution but tangible assets are difficult to allocate fairly and that difficulty increases exponentially as the number of shareholders increases and their relative percentage interests in the company varies. Imagine trying to fairly distribute the assets of a manufacturing company (equipment, inventory, vehicles, accounts receivable) to thirty different stockholders in a fair and equitable manner that satisfies all of them, particularly when some have only a small percentage interest, while others own large shares of the outstanding stock. In the vast majority of cases, the assets will be converted to cash prior to distribution to avoid the task of in-kind distribution.

What is the potential liability of stockholders for the debts of the corporation following dissolution? Keep in mind § 2009 (Section B.1. of this chapter), which insulates stockholders from creditor claims in the event of a court order approving the voluntary dissolution. However, in the absence of a court order:

§ 2011(a)   Causes of action against dissolved corporation; Service of process; Survival in quiet title action

(1)   Causes of action against a dissolved corporation, whether arising before or after the dissolution of the corporation, may be enforced against any of the following:

(A)   Against the dissolved corporation, to the extent of its undistributed assets, including, without limitation, any insurance assets held by the corporation that may be available to satisfy claims.

(B)   If any of the assets of the dissolved corporation have been distributed to shareholders, against shareholders of the dissolved corporation to the extent of their pro rata share of the claim or to the extent of the corporate assets distributed to them upon dissolution of the corporation, whichever is less. A shareholder's total liability under this section may not exceed the total amount of assets of the dissolved corporation distributed to the shareholder upon dissolution of the corporation.

(2)   Except as set forth in subdivision (c), all causes of action against a shareholder of a dissolved corporation arising under this section are extinguished unless the claimant commences a proceeding to enforce the cause of action against that shareholder of a dissolved corporation prior to the earlier of the following:

(A)   The expiration of the statute of limitations applicable to the cause of action.

(B)   Four years after the effective date of the dissolution of the corporation.

(3)   As a matter of procedure only, and not for purposes of determining liability, shareholders of the dissolved corporation may be sued in the corporate name of the corporation upon any cause of action against the corporation. This section does not affect the rights of the corporation or its creditors under Section 2009, or the rights, if any, of creditors under the Uniform Fraudulent Transfer Act,[19] which may arise against the shareholders of a corporation.

Sections 2011(a)(1) and (2) of the California Corporations Code protect creditors for a limited time (four years) after the completion of a voluntary dissolution by allowing a statutory right to recover amounts distributed to *stockholders* if the creditors bring a claim against the dissolved, no-asset corporation. Don't forget that if the board gets a court order of dissolution by shifting the voluntary dissolution to the courts under § 1904 or obtaining a confirmation of the dissolution under § 1907, there is no right to proceed against shareholders following the dissolution. In other words, § 2011(a)(1) allows recovery of distributed amounts from post-dissolution shareholders only if the voluntary dissolution was completed without resort to the courts. However, § 2011(a)(3) specifically allows creditors to bring fraudulent conveyance actions.[20] But what about *other* rights of creditors to pursue stockholders?

In the following case, the California Supreme Court interpreted § 2011(a) and the impact of the statute on the rights of creditors to pursue stockholders following

---

[19]   See the discussion of fraudulent conveyances in Section H of Chapter 8.

[20]   *Id.*

dissolution of the corporation. The case is based on a prior version of § 2011(a) which, at the time, stated:

> In all cases where a corporation has been dissolved, the shareholders may be sued in the corporate name of such corporation upon any cause of action against the corporation *arising prior to its dissolution.* [Emphasis added.]

Within a few years after the case, § 2011(a) was amended[21] to codify the holding of the California Supreme Court and changed the highlighted phrase to *"whether arising before or after the dissolution* of the corporation . . . " [Emphasis added.] Keep in mind the distinction as you read the case.

PACIFIC SCENE, INC. v. PENASQUITOS, INC.
California Supreme Court
758 P.2d 1182 (1988)

Opinion by Mosk, J., expressing the unanimous view of the court. Lucas, C. J., Broussard, J., Panelli, J., Arguelles, J., Eagleson, J., and Kaufman, J., concurred.

We are called upon in this case to determine whether an action under the equitable "trust fund" theory can be maintained against the former shareholders of a dissolved corporation, to the extent of their distribution of corporate assets, when a defective product manufactured by the corporation causes injury after dissolution. We conclude that the Legislature has barred such an action.

Pacific Scene, Inc. (hereafter Pacific) is a corporation producing tract homes. Prior to its dissolution in 1979, Penasquitos, Inc., was a California corporation in the business of developing and finishing residential lots suitable for tract home construction. Pacific purchased a number of lots from Penasquitos in 1974, and in 1975 sold tract homes constructed thereon. In 1982 nine homeowners discovered damage caused by the subsidence of lots sold by Penasquitos. They sued Pacific on various theories, including strict products liability, negligence, and breach of warranty.

Pacific cross-claimed against Penasquitos, which demurred. The court sustained the demurrer without leave to amend and dismissed the cross-complaint, concluding that Corporations Code section 2011 barred suits against dissolved corporations on claims arising after dissolution. Pacific appealed. The Court of Appeal agreed that the corporation itself could not be sued, but reversed with directions to grant Pacific leave to cross-complain against the former shareholders of Penasquitos under the equitable "trust fund" theory. We granted the shareholders' petition for review.

As will appear, we conclude that the Legislature has generally occupied the field with respect to the remedies available against the former shareholders of dissolved corporations, thus preempting antecedent common law causes of action, and that the trust fund theory furthermore conflicts with specific provisions of the Corporations Code. Pacific's postdissolution claim under the trust fund theory therefore is barred.

---

[21] CA Stats. 1992 ch. 189 § 2 (1992)

Discussion

Dissolution of a corporation under the common law "[terminated] its existence as a legal entity, and [rendered] it incapable of suing or being sued as a corporate body or in its corporate name." (*Crossman* v. *Vivienda Water Co.* (1907) 150 Cal. 575, 580 [89 P. 335].) The trust fund theory was developed to ameliorate the harsh result of this common law rule, which allowed corporations to shield their assets from the reach of creditors through distribution to shareholders pursuant to dissolution. (Wallach, *Products Liability: A Remedy in Search of a Defendant — The Effect of a Sale of Assets and Subsequent Dissolution on Product Dissatisfaction Claims* (1976) 41 Mo.L.Rev. 321, 328 (hereafter Wallach).) The doctrine traces its roots to Justice Story's opinion in *Mumma* v. *The Potomac Co.* (1834) 33 U.S. (8 Pet.) 281 [8 L.Ed. 945], in which the high court held that the assets of a dissolved corporation were subject to equitable distribution among creditors . . .

Under the equitable theory, "a creditor of the dissolved corporation may follow [the distributed assets] as in the nature of a trust fund into the hands of stockholders. The creditors have the right to subject such assets to their debts and for that purpose the stockholders hold them as though they were trustees. In other words, the assets of the dissolved corporation are a trust fund against which the corporate creditors have a claim superior to that of the stockholders. A stockholder who receives only a portion of the assets is liable to respond only for that portion. Where the assets coming into the hands of a stockholder suffer a change in value, the creditor must take the trust fund as he finds it, securing the advantage of any increase and suffering any decrease, unless the stockholder is responsible for the decrease. Where the trust property has been used by the stockholder for his own purpose, or disposed of by him, he may be held personally liable for the full value thereof." (*Koch* v. *United States* (10th Cir. 1943) 138 F.2d 850, 852.) The existence of the trust fund doctrine was first acknowledged by this court more than 80 years ago. (*Crossman* v. *Vivienda Water Co., supra,* 150 Cal. at p. 579 . . .)

I.

The shareholders first contend that the Legislature has completely occupied the field concerning the rights and remedies attending corporate dissolution, thus preempting antecedent common law remedies such as the trust fund theory. We observed in *I. E. Associates* v. *Safeco Title Insurance Co.* (1985) 39 Cal.3d 281 [216 Cal.Rptr. 438, 702 P.2d 596], that " 'general and comprehensive legislation, where course of conduct, parties, things affected, limitations and exceptions are minutely described, indicates a legislative intent that the statute should totally supersede and replace the common law dealing with the subject matter.' " (*Id.* at p. 285.) The shareholders maintain that statutory provisions now comprehensively define the remedies available with respect to assets distributed pursuant to a corporate dissolution, and therefore that the trust fund theory has been supplanted in its entirety.

Sections 1800 to 2011 of the Corporations Code, enacted as part of a comprehensive statutory revision in 1977, comprise a broad and detailed scheme regulating virtually every aspect of corporate dissolution. (See Stats. 1975, ch. 682, § 7.). Included therein are two sections specifically governing claims asserted by creditors against former shareholders for the recovery of distributed corporate assets. Section 2009 provides:

"(a) Whenever in the process of winding up a corporation any distribution of assets has been made . . . without prior payment or adequate provision for payment of any of the debts and liabilities of the corporation, any amount so improperly distributed to any shareholder may be recovered by the corporation . . .

(b) Suit may be brought in the name of the corporation to enforce the liability under subdivision (a) against any or all shareholders receiving the distribution by any one or more creditors of the corporation, whether or not they have reduced their claims to judgment." Section 2011, subdivision (a) (hereafter section 2011(a)), provides: "In all cases where a corporation has been dissolved, the shareholders may be sued in the corporate name of such corporation upon any cause of action against the corporation arising prior to its dissolution."

* * *

As enacted in 1977, section 2009 . . . restored to creditors a direct remedy against the former shareholders of dissolved corporations. (§ 2009, subd. (b).) At the same time the Legislature enacted section 2011(a), authorizing suits against former shareholders in the corporate name on claims arising prior to dissolution. (Cf. § 3305.2 added by Stats. 1969, ch. 1610, § 26, p. 3374.) Sections 2009 and 2011(a) thus created causes of action encompassing precisely the kinds of claims previously asserted under the trust fund theory. Wallach explains their potential effect on the availability of equitable relief: "Equitable remedies exist to supply relief where no legal remedy exists, or where the existing legal remedy is inadequate under the circumstances of a particular case. The 'trust fund' theory evolved to fill a void in creditor's remedies created by the common law abatement rule. Now that a statutory remedy exists, it may be argued that an adequate legal remedy is available which deprives the court of equitable jurisdiction." (Wallach, *supra*, at p. 332, fn. omitted.)

In this regard, two prominent commentators on California corporate law have concluded that . . . the 'equitable cause of action does not survive adoption of the statute." (1A Ballantine & Sterling, Cal. Corporation Laws (4th ed. 1988) ch. 15, § 317.04, p. 15–40; 2 Marsh's Cal. Corporation Law (2d ed. 1981) § 20.32, p. 650.)

* * *

Courts construing Texas and Illinois law have likewise held that the statutory remedies now available against former shareholders "completely regulate and control both the substantive and procedural rights of the parties" to the exclusion of antecedent equitable remedies, thus precluding reliance on the trust fund theory for the assertion of post-dissolution claims. (*Reconstruction Finance Corporation* v. *Teter* (7th Cir. 1941) 117 F.2d 716, 727; see *Hunter* v. *Fort Worth Capital Corp.* (Tex. 1981) 620 S.W.2d 547, 551, fn. 6 [20 A.L.R.4th 399] (hereafter *Hunter*).) As the Texas Supreme Court concluded, "The effect of these [predecessor] statutes was to supplant the equitable trust fund theory by declaring a statutory equivalent." (*Hunter, supra*, at p. 550.)

In view of the detailed statutory remedies now encompassing virtually all claims previously asserted in equity against the former shareholders of dissolved corporations, we must similarly conclude that the Legislature has occupied the field and precluded resort to dormant common law doctrines for the provision of extra-statutory relief. This conclusion is especially compelling on the facts before us, insofar as the equitable relief sought by Pacific would require us to confront a variety of intractable policy questions intimately bound up with the provisions and objectives of the existing statutory scheme.[22] Once the Legislature has evinced an intent to comprehensively define the contours of a particular field, however, such complex policy determinations must plainly remain beyond the reach of our equitable jurisdiction.

II.

The shareholders maintain that even if the Legislature did not intend to completely occupy the field with respect to the rights and remedies attending corporate dissolution, the assertion of post-dissolution claims under the trust fund theory nonetheless conflicts with the specific intent of section 2011(a).

Section 2011(a) provides: "In all cases where a corporation has been dissolved, the shareholders may be sued in the corporate name of such corporation upon any cause of action against the corporation arising *prior* to its dissolution. This section is procedural in nature and is not intended to determine liability." (Italics added) The shareholders argue that this language, by negative implication, evinces an intent to preclude actions against former shareholders for injuries arising after corporate dissolution, and thus that any corresponding equitable action must be similarly barred. "While equitable relief is flexible and expanding, its power cannot be intruded in matters that are plain and fully covered by positive statute, nor will a court of equity lend its aid to accomplish by indirection what the law or its clearly defined policy forbids to be done directly." (*Marsh* v. *Edelstein* (1970) 9 Cal.App.3d 132, 140–141 [88 Cal.Rptr. 26].)

The Court of Appeal reasoned that although section 2011(a) plainly preempts the trust fund theory with respect to pre-dissolution claims, the statute simply fails to address the post-dissolution context and therefore need not be read to bar equitable relief for claims then arising. Courts and commentators considering this argument have been troubled by its implication that legislators uselessly created a redundant statutory remedy for a subclass of claims concurrently remediable in equity. As the

---

[22] [2] Reflecting on the procedural pitfalls of an equitable remedy for post-dissolution claimants, the court in *In re Citadel Industries, Inc.* (Del.Ct.Ch. 1980) 423 A.2d 500, observed that "Once a corporation is dissolved, . . . all known debts paid, all remaining assets distributed to shareholders, books and records destroyed, and officers and directors gone on to other endeavors, how can any court be expected to get everyone reconvened and reorganized . . . ? How can a vast number of former shareholders be compelled to return any final distribution of assets . . . ? [These] factors, along with a myriad of others, would have to be considered . . . . In the case of a large, publicly-held corporation, the task would be enormous and the potential problems and considerations would be boundless." (*Id.* at p. 506.) With respect to the policy implications of the undertaking, the court in *Gonzales* v. *Progressive Tool & Die Co.* (E.D.N.Y. 1979) 463 F.Supp. 117, noted that the remedy would "inevitably entail the weighing of conflicting policies, that of corporate repose and certainty and that of compensating the injured.

A court . . . is ill equipped to strike the balance. Indeed, the matter seems to involve too many imponderables to be susceptible of any satisfactory judicial solution. The lengthy statute of limitations inherent in holdings that the claim accrues on injury may render it difficult for a seller of tangible assets to estimate the potential liability, to obtain insurance, or to keep it in force. [para.] A legislature, far more than a court, has the capability of determining the extent of the problem and of assessing accurately the overall effect of the choice of one policy over another." (Id. at p. 120, citations omitted.)

court in *Hunter* observed with respect to a similar statute, "we must assume that when the legislature enacted [the statute] it knew to what extent the equitable doctrine already provided a remedy for pre-dissolution claims. With this in mind, no real purpose would be served by the enactment of [the statute], permitting suits against officers, directors, and shareholders of a dissolved corporation [for pre-dissolution claims], unless the legislature intended for the statute to bar resort to the trust fund theory apart from the statute in order to enforce post-dissolution claims." (*Hunter, supra,* 620 S.W.2d at p. 551, citations omitted; *Wallach, supra,* at p. 331.)

In anticipation of this concern, the Court of Appeal struggled at length to invest its construction of section 2011(a) with some plausible legislative intent. The court ultimately concluded that the statute serves the purpose of expediting relief for pre-dissolution claimants by providing them with a simple and direct legal remedy, while relegating post-dissolution claimants to the more burdensome procedural requirements of equity . . . As the court asserted, "The fact that the Legislature has provided in section 2011(a) for a streamlined procedural mechanism applicable to pre-dissolution claims is not inconsistent with retention of the more cumbersome equitable 'trust fund' theory as to post-dissolution causes of action." Notably, the court declined to speculate why the Legislature would wish to draw this odd procedural distinction if it indeed desired to allow post-dissolution claims to proceed.

We find it difficult to believe that the Legislature would have labored to expressly limit the reach of section 2011(a) simply to bring forth this procedural mouse. In the unfortunate absence of legislative history to guide our construction of section 2011(a), logic suggests that language limiting its remedy to pre-dissolution claims must reflect some larger purpose than contemplated by the court below. This is particularly true in light of the fact that the predecessor statute to section 2011(a) did not similarly exclude post-dissolution claims: former section 3305.2 provided that "In *all* cases where a corporation has forfeited its charter or right to do business, or has dissolved, the trustees of the corporation and of its stockholders or members may be sued in the corporate name of such corporation." (Stats. 1969, ch. 1610, § 26, p. 3374, italics added.) Thus the Court of Appeal maintains that the Legislature, by amending the Corporations Code to expressly exclude post-dissolution claims formerly within the reach of section 3305.2, simply intended to return post-dissolution claimants to the archaic and relatively more burdensome remedy of equity. The analysis strains credulity.

The foregoing construction is even less credible in view of the general legislative objectives of certainty and finality undergirding the dissolution provisions of the Corporations Code . . . Although the finality interests of a dissolving corporation and those of its shareholders are not synonymous, insofar as post-dissolution claims against shareholders "do . . . not prevent the final termination of an entity, as does the possibility of delayed claims against the dissolved corporation" (Wallach, *supra,* at p. 333), shareholders nonetheless possess an important statutory interest in the final and certain termination of their involvement with the affairs of a dissolving corporation . . . The Court of Appeal conceded, however, that its construction of section 2011(a) would subject shareholders to the possibility of "unending liability . . . ." As the court in *Blankenship* v. *Demmler Mfg. Co.* (1980) 89 Ill.App.3d 569 [411 N.E.2d 1153], concluded, this result is at odds with the very notion of dissolution: "We agree with defendant that extension of the trust fund theory to cover plaintiff's [post-dissolution] claim would mean that the corporation could never completely dissolve but would live on indefinitely through its shareholders. We do not believe that this result would be in accordance with the spirit of the laws governing the dissolution of corporations." (*Id.* at p. 1156.)

We are aware, of course, that other interests are reflected in the dissolution provisions of the Corporations Code, not the least of which is payment to corporate creditors . . . This interest stands in inherent conflict with the final and certain conclusion of a corporation's affairs, as the comment to section 14.07 of the 1985 Model Business Corporations Act explains: "[On] the one hand, the application of a mechanical . . . limitation period to a claim for injury that occurs after the period has expired involves obvious injustice to the plaintiff. On the other hand, to permit these suits generally makes it impossible ever to complete the winding up of the corporation . . . ." (Model Bus. Corp. Act Ann. (1985) § 14.07, com. at p. 1501; see also *Gonzales* v. *Progressive Tool & Die Co., supra,* 463 F.Supp. at p. 119, and Henn & Alexander, *Effect of Corporate Dissolution on Products Liability Claims* (1971) 56 Cornell L.Rev. 865, 911 (hereafter Henn & Alexander).) The 1985 model act reconciles these conflicting interests by allowing the assertion of claims against former shareholders during a five-year period following corporate dissolution, but barring claims arising thereafter. (1985 Model Bus. Corp. Act Ann., *supra,* at § 14.07, p. 1499.) Here we are asked to infer that the Legislature has balanced the same interests entirely on the shoulders of shareholders, who assertedly are required to face such claims in perpetuity.

We recognize that the final sentence of section 2011(a), considered in isolation, could arguably support the analysis of the Court of Appeal. It reads: "This section is procedural in nature and is not intended to determine liability." The Court of Appeal concluded that the language manifests the Legislature's desire to avoid interference with substantive rights in their entirety, and thus that all potential applications of the trust fund theory have been left unimpaired. However, it is equally plausible that the language is intended to reaffirm the limited principle that shareholders are not personally liable for a corporation's debts, as once they were in California. (See, e.g., former art. XII, § 3, Cal. Const. of 1879, repealed in 1930.) Under this construction, the sentence merely forestalls the misunderstanding that might result from the statutory authorization of suits against shareholders "in the corporate name," and is therefore irrelevant to the question whether section 2011(a) precludes post-dissolution equitable remedies. Either interpretation is tenable absent evidence of legislative intent, of which there is none; the quoted language thus cannot advance our analysis.

We must choose, then, between a construction of section 2011(a) premised on a silent legislative intent to procedurally encumber post-dissolution creditors in the unending assertion of their claims, or alternatively a construction precluding post-dissolution claims in a manner consistent with the statutory objectives of certainty and finality. We accordingly determine that the statute bars the assertion of post-dissolution claims in equity . . .

Courts in several other jurisdictions construing similar statutory provisions have reached the same result. A number of states have enacted statutes substantially identical to section 105 of the 1969 Model Business Corporations Act, which allows actions against dissolved corporations and their officers, directors, and shareholders on pre-dissolution claims brought within two years of corporate dissolution. (Model Bus. Corp. Act Ann. (1969) § 105; see, e.g., Tex. Bus. Corp. Act, art. 7.12; Ill.

Ann. Stat., ch. 32, § 12.80; Iowa Code Ann., § 496A.102.).[23] Courts considering such statutes in Texas, Illinois, and Iowa have each concluded that the exclusive statutory authorization of pre-dissolution claims bars the assertion of claims arising thereafter. (*Hunter, supra*, 620 S.W.2d at p. 551 [trust fund action barred]; *Suarez v. Sherman Gin Co.* (Tex.Civ.App. 1985) 697 S.W.2d 17, 19–20 (writ ref. n.r.e.) [same]; *Reconstruction Finance Corp. v. Teeter, supra*, 117 F.2d at p. 727 [same, under predecessor statute in Illinois]; *Blankenship* v. *Demmler Manufacturing Co., supra*, 411 N.E.2d at p. 1157 [same]; *Bishop* v. *Schield Bantam Co., supra*, 293 F.Supp. at p. 95 [construing Iowa law]; see also *Bazan v. Kux Machine Co.* (1971) 52 Wis.2d 325 [190 N.W.2d 521, 525]; cf. *Chadwick* v. *Air Reduction Company* (N.D.Ohio 1965) 239 F.Supp. 247, 251 ["It is . . . quite clear that under the Model Business Corporation Act, and those state statutes patterned after it, a corporation may be sued for pre-dissolution torts only. The Ohio statute . . . does not conform to the language of the Model Act."].) Our analysis of section 2011(a) is thus consistent with the substantial body of precedent construing the parallel statutory provisions of our sister states.[24]

Conclusion

For the reasons stated, we conclude that the Legislature has precluded the assertion of post-dissolution claims against the former shareholders of a dissolved corporation under the equitable "trust fund" theory. We emphasize, however, that this determination does not insulate dissolving corporations or their shareholders from actions for the recovery of fraudulently transferred assets. Thus if a corporation were to mass produce defective products and then dissolve to avoid liability, "leaving a multitude of potential claims in its wake" (Henn & Alexander, *supra*, 56 Cornell L.Rev. 865, 909, fn. 222), grave questions would be raised under the Uniform Fraudulent Transfer Act. (See Civ. Code, §§ 3439.01, subd. (b), 3439.04.) In the case at bar, no such allegation was made.

The judgment of the Court of Appeal is reversed with directions to affirm the judgment of dismissal entered by the superior court.

---

[23] [3] Section 105 of the 1969 Model Business Corporations Act provides: "The dissolution of a corporation . . . shall not take away or impair any remedy available to or against such corporation, its officers, directors, or shareholders, for any right or claim existing, or any liability incurred, *prior to such dissolution* if action or other proceeding thereon is commenced within two years after the date of such dissolution." (Italics added.) Significantly, the drafters of the model act itself recently concluded that the emphasized language failed to adequately provide for the assertion of post-dissolution claims, and have entirely rewritten the provision to authorize the assertion of such claims during the first five years following dissolution. (See 1985 Model Bus. Corp. Act Ann., *supra*, at § 14.07.)

[24] [4] In an attempt to distinguish the weight of this authority, the Court of Appeal accorded great significance to the limited time period during which pre-dissolution claims must be brought under statutes modelled after section 105 of the 1969 Model Business Corporations Act. Looking to the decisions in *Hunter, supra*, 620 S.W.2d 547, and *Blankenship* v. *Demmler Manufacturing Co., supra*, 411 N.E.2d 1153, the court asserted that "It was difficult for [the] courts to believe that their respective state legislatures intended to create a system with a two- or three-year limitation on pre-dissolution claims but with no limitation on post-dissolution suits. . . . Unlike the Texas and Illinois statutes, California's section 2011(a) imposes no time limitation on pre-dissolution claims. It is thus not even impliedly inconsistent with the legislative intent in enacting that section to retain the broader-but-more-cumbersome 'trust fund' doctrine as to post dissolution causes of action." Neither the *Hunter* nor *Blankenship* court, however, relied solely on this argument; instead, both courts relied initially and primarily on the absence of any statutory authorization for post-dissolution claims. (See *Hunter, supra*, 620 S.W.2d at pp. 550–551; *Blankenship, supra*, 411 N.E.2d at p. 1155.)

NOTES AND QUESTIONS

1. There were two distinct issues before the court in *Pacific Scene, Inc. v. Penasquitos, Inc.* First, the court was faced with the issue of whether or not the enactment of a comprehensive corporations code dealing with dissolution was sufficient to "occupy the field" and eliminate the common law "equitable trust fund" doctrine. The equitable trust fund doctrine made sense as a device to protect creditors from improper corporate dissolutions. As pointed out in the *Pacific Scene* opinion, the doctrine arose in a U.S. Supreme Court case in 1834.[25] Under the equitable trust fund doctrine, the distributions to stockholders were held in an equitable "trust" for creditors who were, after all, entitled to priority of distribution in the dissolution (even if they were unknown at the time). The problem with the doctrine was that it left a never-ending haze over the final distribution to stockholders. In a sense, the corporation was never really wound up, since unknown creditors of the corporation might appear many years later and recover claims against the former stockholders. This was a particularly difficult problem when the corporation was a publicly traded one. The modern corporations codes of California, Illinois, Texas, Iowa and other states adopted the approach of the 1969 Model Business Corporations Act, which allows actions against shareholders on pre-dissolution claims brought within two years (as long as four years under the current version of § 2011(a) in California) of corporate dissolution.[26] In all of these states, the courts have held that adoption of provisions such as § 2011(a) displace the common law doctrine of equitable trust. As the court points out, the provisions of § 2011(a) allow unknown creditors some opportunity to recover against stockholders for wrongful distributions but puts a cap on the time period. It allows corporations and their stockholders to, eventually, completely wrap up their affairs while giving creditors some adequate time to bring their claims. Is this fair or should stockholders always have to "cough up" distributions that should not have been made in view of the outstanding debts to creditors?

2. The second issue in *Pacific Scene, Inc.* revolved around whether or not a creditor with a claim that arose *post*-dissolution was meant to be covered by the language of former § 2011(a), which stated: "In all cases where a corporation has been dissolved, the shareholders may be sued in the corporate name of such corporation upon any cause of action against the corporation *arising prior to its dissolution*." (Emphasis added.) The creditors in the case were landowners. Their claims were based on subsidence of land originally sold by the dissolved corporation, Pacific Scene, Inc., to the land developer, Penasquitos, Inc., who built structures and, in turn, sold the land to the landowners. The subsidence did not occur until after the dissolution of Pacific Scene, Inc. The landowner-creditors were asserting that the language of § 2011(a) was meant to pre-empt the equitable trust doctrine only as to *pre*-dissolution claims, not *post*-dissolution claims. The court disagreed and held that the legislature intended § 2011(a) to apply to all claims arising against a dissolved corporation. Less than three years after the case, the California legislature amended the language of § 2011(a) to specifically include *post*-dissolution claims as well. Is this a good outcome? What if the landowners didn't discover the defect until ten years after the dissolution?

3. Can you identify the exact circumstances when a creditor of a dissolved

---

[25] Mumma v. The Potomac Co. (1834), 33 U.S. (8 Pet.) 281 [8 L.Ed. 945].

[26] Model Bus. Corp. Act Ann. § 105 (1969).

corporation may recover against stockholders when distributions have been made to the stockholders in a dissolution? Review the following California Corporations Code sections to answer the question: §§ 1904, 1907, 2009, 2011.

3. Involuntary Dissolutions

a. Grounds for Involuntary Dissolution

Involuntary dissolution of a corporation is a drastic remedy. It is initiated by the filing of a petition with the courts and, if not dismissed, will put the corporation out of business and force the winding up of the company. What would serve as motivation for a *stockholder* to institute such a proceeding? If the corporation has a negative-net-worth, it's highly unlikely that a stockholder would initiate an involuntary dissolution. If there are no assets available for distribution to stockholders after creditors are paid or provided for, then no self-maximizing stockholder would have the incentive to file a *dissolution* proceeding, voluntary or involuntary. The best place to resolve the affairs of an insolvent corporation is in federal bankruptcy court.

On the other hand, if the corporation has a positive-net-worth, or is operating profitably, what would motivate a minority stockholder to commence an involuntary dissolution, particularly if the other stockholders are opposed? The only sensible reason is that the petitioning stockholder is unhappy with the management of the business. However, there are alternatives to dissolution for minority stockholders who are concerned about the management of a solvent corporation. They are entitled to bring stockholder derivative actions,[27] and petition the California courts to remove directors in cases of fraudulent acts, dishonest acts or gross abuse of authority.[28] So why commence an involuntary dissolution proceeding? To answer this question, perhaps it is best to start with the statutory *grounds* for an involuntary dissolution under California law:

§ 1800 Verified complaint; Persons filing; Grounds for proceeding; Intervention by "shareholder" or creditor; Corporations exempt from section's provision

(b) The grounds for involuntary dissolution are that:

(1) The corporation has abandoned its business for more than one year.

(2) The corporation has an even number of directors who are equally divided and cannot agree as to the management of its affairs, so that its business can no longer be conducted to advantage or so that there is danger that its property and business will be impaired or lost, and the holders of the voting shares of the corporation are so divided into factions that they cannot elect a board consisting of an uneven number.

---

[27] Cal. Corp. Code § 800.

[28] Cal. Corp. Code § 304 states:

The superior court of the proper county may, at the suit of shareholders holding at least 10 percent of the number of outstanding shares of any class, remove from office any director in case of fraudulent or dishonest acts or gross abuse of authority or discretion with reference to the corporation and may bar from reelection any director so removed for a period prescribed by the court . . .

(3)   There is internal dissension and two or more factions of shareholders in the corporation are so deadlocked that its business can no longer be conducted with advantage to its shareholders or the shareholders have failed at two consecutive annual meetings at which all voting power was exercised, to elect successors to directors whose terms have expired or would have expired upon election of their successors.

(4)   Those in control of the corporation have been guilty of or have knowingly countenanced persistent and pervasive fraud, mismanagement or abuse of authority or persistent unfairness toward any shareholders or its property is being misapplied or wasted by its directors or officers.

(5)   In the case of any corporation with 35 or fewer shareholders . . . liquidation is reasonably necessary for the protection of the rights or interests of the complaining shareholder or shareholders.

(6)   The period for which the corporation was formed has terminated without extension of such period.

Subsections (b)(1) and (b)(6) are technical in nature — the corporation has stopped doing business, or the term of the corporation has ended without the stockholders agreeing to an extension of the term. All of the other grounds focus on fundamental failures in the control and/or management of the corporation, or abusive unfairness by those in control of the corporation and seem to provide a justificatory basis for dissolving the corporation. Nevertheless, dissolution remains a drastic remedy that should be used only as a last resort. If there is some way that the discord can be resolved, or the unfairness eliminated, those possibilities pose a far less expensive and ruinous alternative to dissolution. In fact, the courts are given the power to resolve the problems *without* dissolving the corporation, by such means as appointing provisional directors, removing directors, appointing a receiver to temporarily take control of the corporation or other actions:

§ 1802.   Appointment of provisional director where directors deadlocked

If the ground for the complaint for involuntary dissolution of the corporation is a deadlock in the board as set forth in subdivision (b)(2) of Section 1800, the court may appoint a provisional director. The provisions of subdivision (c) of Section 308[29] apply to any such provisional director so appointed.

§ 1803.   Appointment of receiver; Application, hearing and notice; Security; Powers

If, at the time of the filing of a complaint for involuntary dissolution or at any time thereafter, the court has reasonable grounds to believe that unless a receiver

---

[29]   Section 308(c) states:

   A provisional director shall be an impartial person, who is neither a shareholder nor a creditor of the corporation, nor related . . . to any of the other directors of the corporation . . . A provisional director shall have all the rights and powers of a director until the deadlock in the board or among shareholders is broken or until such provisional director is removed by order of the court or by approval of the outstanding shares . . . Such person shall be entitled to such compensation as shall be fixed by the court unless otherwise agreed with the corporation.

of the corporation is appointed the interests of the corporation and its shareholders will suffer pending the hearing and determination of the complaint, upon the application of the plaintiff, and after a hearing upon such notice to the corporation as the court may direct . . . the court may appoint a receiver to take over and manage the business and affairs of the corporation and to preserve its property pending the hearing and determination of the complaint for dissolution.

§ 1804. Decree for winding up and dissolution; Further judicial relief

After hearing the court may decree a winding up and dissolution of the corporation if cause therefor is shown or, *with or without winding up and dissolution*, may make such orders and decrees and issue such injunctions in the case as justice and equity require. [Emphasis added.]

§ 1806. What jurisdiction of court to include

When an involuntary proceeding for winding up has been commenced, the jurisdiction of the court includes:

. . .

(f) The filling of any vacancies on the board which the directors or share-holders are unable to fill.

(g) The removal of any director if it appears that the director has been guilty of dishonesty, misconduct, neglect or abuse of trust in conducting the winding up or if the director is unable to act. The court may order an election to fill the vacancy so caused, and may enjoin, for such time as it considers proper, the reelection of the director so removed; or the court, in lieu of ordering an election, may appoint a director to fill the vacancy caused by such removal. Any director so appointed by the court shall serve until the next annual meeting of sharehold-ers or until a successor is elected or appointed. . . .

(j) The making of orders for the withdrawal or termination of proceedings to wind up and dissolve, subject to conditions for the protection of shareholders and creditors.

As the above excerpts indicate, the court is granted extremely broad authority to appoint directors, remove directors, appoint interim directors and issue other decrees that assist in resolving the dispute or deadlock between stockholders and/or the board without actually declaring that the corporation be wound up.

The court is also granted the authority to appoint a "receiver." The appointment of a receiver is a more dramatic remedy than appointment or removal of a director but may help to prevent the dissolution of the corporation. A receiver is a person skilled in the operation of that type of business who is appointed by the court to take over control and management of the day-to-day affairs of the corporation while the involuntary dissolution is pending and the court has not yet determined whether or not dissolution is an appropriate course of action. Receiver's can serve a valuable role in continuing the operations of a functioning corporation while the deadlock among directors and/or stockholders is resolved. A neutral receiver operates the corporation and maintains its value during the pendency of the involuntary case and, if necessary, the winding up of the corporation.

In view of the broad powers given to the court, the filing of an involuntary petition by a minority stockholder (or group of minority stockholders) may be a strategic attempt to break a deadlock or enlist the aid of the courts to deal with mismanagement or fraud, rather than the actual liquidation of the corporation — although that may be the ultimate goal of some minority stockholder(s) who want to exit the business even if it results in reduced distributions because of the expense of an involuntary dissolution.

There is one last mechanism in the statute to deal with dissident stockholders who initiate an involuntary dissolution. There is a statutory right of the non-initiating stockholders to buyout the stockholders who initiate the dissolution.[30]

b.   Parties Entitled to Initiate Involuntary Dissolutions

In *involuntary* cases, which will always be commenced in a judicial action, an operating company may be compelled to dissolve notwithstanding the lack of consent of a majority of the stockholders. *Who* has the right to initiate such an involuntary dissolution of a corporation? The answer is in § 1800(a):

§ 1800   **Verified complaint; Persons filing; Grounds for proceeding; Intervention by "shareholder" or creditor; Corporations exempt from section's provision**

(a)   A verified complaint for involuntary dissolution of a corporation on any one or more of the grounds specified in subdivision (b) may be filed . . . by any of the following persons:

(1)   One-half or more of the *directors* in office. [Emphasis added.]

(2)   A shareholder or shareholders who hold shares representing not less than 331/3 percent of (i) the total number of outstanding shares (assuming conversion of any preferred shares convertible into common shares) or (ii) the outstanding common shares or (iii) the equity of the corporation, exclusive in each case of shares owned by persons who have personally participated in any of the transactions enumerated in paragraph (4) of subdivision (b), [or any shareholder or shareholders of a close corporation.[31]]

(3)   Any shareholder if the ground for dissolution is that the period for which the corporation was formed has terminated without extension thereof.

(4)   Any other person expressly authorized to do so in the articles.[32]

---

[30] Cal. Corp. Code § 2000. See the in depth discussion later in this chapter in Section B.4.

[31] The term "close corporation" has special meaning. In California there are provisions allowing the formation of statutory close corporations that operate less formally than traditional corporations. When properly formed, all of the shareholders may agree to a shareholder's agreement that allows the corporation to operate without the traditional meetings of stockholders or appointment of a board of directors. These statutory close corporations must have special provisions in the articles and no more than 35 stockholders. *See* Cal. Corp. Code §§ 158, 300(b)–(e), 186. Because of the uniqueness of the California statutory close corporation, we will not be addressing the rights of the stockholders of these types of entities.

[32] [The Attorney General may also commence involuntary dissolution proceedings against a corporation when it is in the interests of the state to do so. *See* Cal. Corp Code §§ 1801. —Eds.]

Compare § 1800(a) above to the list of persons who may initiate *voluntary dissolutions* under § 1900.[33] In voluntary dissolution cases (which are commenced and can be completed without judicial action) only 50% or more of the *shareholders* may initiate a dissolution of an *operating* corporation.[34] The authority of directors in voluntary cases is limited to cases where the corporation has already filed a bankruptcy petition or is otherwise not operating. At first glance, it appears that the directors are given greater authority to commence an involuntary dissolution. However, this is not true as a practical matter if we review the *grounds* for dissolution. Why would the board elect to force the corporation into *involuntary* dissolution if a majority of the shareholders (or 50/50 split) are unwilling to elect a *voluntary* dissolution. The answer lies in the grounds set forth in § 1800(b). Two of the grounds are likely to be the subject of board action: § 1800(a)(1) ("The corporation has abandoned its business for more than one year") or (a)(6) ("The period for which the corporation was formed has terminated without extension of such period.").

If the corporation is still in business and its term has not expired, all of the other grounds listed in § 1800(b) focus on fundamental failures in the control and/or management of the corporation, or abusive unfairness by those in control of the corporation.[35] If that's true, there is unlikely to be a majority of directors who will agree to use the mechanism of an involuntary dissolution to force a resolution of irreconcilable differences in the control and management of the corporation. Realistically, the initiation of an involuntary dissolution in cases of an *operating* corporation whose term has not expired requires the consent of holders of one-third of the equity-holders of the corporation — a large minority.

c.   Conducting the Dissolution

Involuntary dissolutions are rare. As discussed above, minority stockholders have other less drastic mechanisms available to them when the majority stockholders, or directors who represent majority interests, are abusing their control, engaging in fraud or mismanaging the corporation. In the event that the court is unable to work out some lesser alternative (such as appointment of a provisional director or removal of directors) the court will issue an order for the winding up of the corporation. What happens following that order? Once the order is issued, the process is much like the voluntary dissolution of a corporation. Unless a receiver is appointed, the board (subject to court appointments and removals) will oversee the liquidation, payment to and provisions for creditors, and distributions to stockholders, if any. Note the following provisions of the California Corporations Code:[36]

---

[33] *See* Section B.1. of this chapter.

[34] The directors have some authority to initiate voluntary dissolutions under § 1900 but only if the corporation is effectively out of business.

[35] Cal. Corp. Code § 1800(b)(2) through (5) is set forth in full in Section 3.a above.

[36] These provisions also apply when a *voluntary* dissolution is moved to the courts under § 1904 ("The provisions of Chapter 18 . . . shall apply to such court proceedings.").

§ 1805. Commencement of involuntary proceedings for winding up; Conduct of proceedings; Cessation of business on commencement of proceedings; Notice

(a) Involuntary proceedings for winding up a corporation commence when the order for winding up is entered under Section 1804.

(b) When an involuntary proceeding for winding up has commenced, the board shall conduct the winding up of the affairs of the corporation, subject to the supervision of the court, unless other persons are appointed by the court, on good cause shown, to conduct the winding up. The directors or such other persons may, subject to any restrictions imposed by the court, exercise all their powers through the executive officers without any order of court.

(c) When an involuntary proceeding for winding up has commenced, the corporation shall cease to carry on business except to the extent necessary for the beneficial winding up thereof and except during such period as the board may deem necessary to preserve the corporation's goodwill or going-concern value pending a sale of its business or assets, or both, in whole or in part. The directors shall cause written notice of the commencement of the proceeding for involuntary winding up to be given by mail to all shareholders and to all known creditors and claimants whose addresses appear on the records of the corporation, unless the order for winding up has been stayed by appeal therefrom or otherwise or the proceeding or the execution of the order has been enjoined.

§ 1806. What jurisdiction of court to include

When an involuntary proceeding for winding up has been commenced, the jurisdiction of the court includes:

(a) The requirement of the proof of all claims and demands against the corporation, whether due or not yet due, contingent, unliquidated or sounding only in damages, and the barring from participation of creditors and claimants failing to make and present claims and proof as required by any order.

(b) The determination or compromise of all claims of every nature against the corporation or any of its property, and the determination of the amount of money or assets required to be retained to pay or provide for the payment of claims.

(c) The determination of the rights of shareholders and of all classes of shareholders in and to the assets of the corporation.

. . .

(f) The filling of any vacancies on the board which the directors or shareholders are unable to fill.

(g) The removal of any director if it appears that the director has been guilty of dishonesty, misconduct, neglect or abuse of trust in conducting the winding up or if the director is unable to act. The court may order an election to fill the vacancy so caused, and may enjoin, for such time as it considers proper, the reelection of the director so removed; or the court, in lieu of ordering an election, may appoint a director to fill the vacancy caused by such removal. Any director so appointed by the court shall serve until the next annual meeting of shareholders or until a successor is elected or appointed.

(h) Staying the prosecution of any suit, proceeding or action against the corporation and requiring the parties to present and prove their claims in the manner required of other creditors.

(i) The determination of whether adequate provision has been made for payment or satisfaction of all debts and liabilities not actually paid.

. . .

(k) The making of an order, upon the allowance or settlement of the final accounts of the directors or such other persons, that the corporation has been duly wound up and is dissolved. Upon the making of such order, the corporate existence shall cease except for purposes of further winding up if needed.

§ 1807. Claims against corporation; Time for presentation; Notice to creditors; Publication and mailing of notice; Rights of holders of secured claims; Payment; Actions on rejected claims

(a) All creditors and claimants may be barred from participation in any distribution of the general assets if they fail to make and present claims and proofs within such time as the court may direct, which shall not be less than four nor more than six months after the first publication of notice to creditors unless it appears by affidavit that there are no claims, in which case the time limit may be three months. If it is shown that a claimant did not receive notice because of absence from the state or other cause, the court may allow a claim to be filed or presented at any time before distribution is completed.

. . .

(d) Before any distribution is made the amount of any unmatured, contingent or disputed claim against the corporation which has been presented and has not been disallowed, or such part of any such claim as the holder would be entitled to if the claim were due, established or absolute, shall be paid into court and there remain to be paid over to the party when the party becomes entitled thereto or, if the party fails to establish a claim, to be paid over or distributed with the other assets of the corporation to those entitled thereto; or such other provision for the full payment of such claim, if and when established, shall be made as the court may deem adequate. A creditor whose claim has been allowed but is not yet due shall be entitled to its present value upon distribution.

4. The Statutory Buyout Right

There are times when some stockholders of a corporation desire the dissolution of the corporation, while others do not. Dissolution is a drastic remedy that, in many cases, is likely to result in a loss. It may be in the best interests of all stockholders to provide a buyout right to those stockholders who desire to continue the operations of the corporation. Hopefully, there is a buy-sell agreement that creates such rights and establishes procedures, valuation mechanisms and financing terms that allow for a smooth buyout. Even in the absence of a private buy-sell agreement, the California Corporations Code provides a *statutory* buyout right in *both* voluntary and involuntary cases. Why would the California Corporations Code create such a right?

§ 2000.   **Avoiding dissolution by purchasing plaintiffs' shares; Determination of fair value; Stay of proceedings; Appointment and award of appraisers; Appeal**

(a)   Subject to any contrary provision in the articles, in any suit for involuntary dissolution, or in any proceeding for voluntary dissolution initiated by the vote of shareholders representing only 50 percent of the voting power, the corporation or, if it does not elect to purchase, the holders of 50 percent or more of the voting power of the corporation (the "purchasing parties") may avoid the dissolution of the corporation and the appointment of any receiver by purchasing for cash the shares owned by the plaintiffs or by the shareholders so initiating the proceeding (the "moving parties") at their fair value. The fair value shall be determined on the basis of the liquidation value as of the valuation date but taking into account the possibility, if any, of sale of the entire business as a going concern in a liquidation. In fixing the value, the amount of any damages resulting if the initiation of the dissolution is a breach by any moving party or parties of an agreement with the purchasing party or parties may be deducted from the amount payable to such moving party or parties . . . The election of the corporation to purchase may be made by the approval of the outstanding shares . . . excluding shares held by the moving parties.

This section limits buyouts in *voluntary* dissolution cases only to situations where there is a 50/50 split among the stockholders regarding the decision to dissolve. In *involuntary* dissolution cases, there is no limit on the right of non-initiating stockholders to buy out the stockholders who initiated the law suit. Whether the dissolution is voluntary or involuntary, the statute grants any non-petitioning stockholders who wish to continue the operations a statutory buyout right. Non-petitioning stockholders can buy out the stockholders that initiated the voluntary or involuntary dissolution. This makes sense, since the purchasing stockholders will do so only if there is inherent value in continuing the operations of the corporation — value that might be lost in a dissolution proceeding.

Although the buyout right arises by force of statute, the same issues arise that we discussed in Chapter 8 regarding the valuation of shares. Section 2000(a) uses the term "fair value" and adds the definition: "The fair value shall be determined on the basis of the liquidation value as of the valuation date but taking into account the possibility, if any, of sale of the entire business as a going concern in a liquidation." Once this amount is determined, the purchasing stockholders must pay the funds soon thereafter — in cash. There is no provision for an installment plan or other financing mechanism. What happens if the "moving parties" (the parties initiating the dissolution) and the "purchasing parties" (the parties seeking to buyout the moving parties) can't agree on a "fair value"?

§ 1800.   **Verified complaint; Persons filing; Grounds for proceeding; Intervention by "shareholder" or creditor; Corporations exempt from section's provision**

(b)   If the purchasing parties (1) elect to purchase the shares owned by the moving parties, and (2) are unable to agree with the moving parties upon the fair value of such shares, and (3) give bond with sufficient security to pay the estimated reasonable expenses (including attorneys' fees) of the moving parties if such expenses are recoverable under subdivision (c), the court upon application of the purchasing parties, either in the pending action or in a proceeding initiated in the superior court of the proper county by the purchasing parties in the case of a voluntary election to wind up and dissolve, shall stay the winding up and dissolution proceeding and shall proceed to ascertain and fix the fair value of the shares owned by the moving parties.

(c)   The court shall appoint three disinterested appraisers to appraise the fair value of the shares owned by the moving parties, and shall make an order referring the matter to the appraisers so appointed for the purpose of ascertaining such value . . . The award of the appraisers or of a majority of them, when confirmed by the court, shall be final and conclusive upon all parties. The court shall enter a decree which shall provide in the alternative for winding up and dissolution of the corporation unless payment is made for the shares within the time specified by the decree. If the purchasing parties do not make payment for the shares within the time specified, judgment shall be entered against them and the surety or sureties on the bond for the amount of the expenses (including attorneys' fees) of the moving parties. Any shareholder aggrieved by the action of the court may appeal therefrom.

. . .

(f)   For the purposes of this section, the valuation date shall be (1) in the case of a suit for involuntary dissolution under Section 1800, the date upon which that action was commenced, or (2) in the case of a proceeding for voluntary dissolution initiated by the vote of shareholders representing only 50 percent of the voting power, the date upon which that proceeding was initiated. However, in either case the court may, upon the hearing of a motion by any party, and for good cause shown, designate some other date as the valuation date.

For all of the reasons discussed in Chapter 8, in the absence of a pre-existing buy-sell agreement to govern the issues of valuation, and procedures for accomplishing the buyout, the statutory buyout provisions are expensive, time consuming and unpredictable. The valuation formula is fundamentally unclear and there is no way of predicting if the appraisers will use a liquidation value or a going concern value. Each side, initiating and purchasing, is put at risk. If the appraised cost is too high, the purchasing side will back out but have to pay for attorneys fees and other expenses of the initiating parties. If the appraised cost is too low (if its fixed only at liquidation value), the initiating parties will be forced to accept a value for their shares that may be far below the true market value. There is nothing in the statute that restricts the court to the values submitted by the appraisers. Consider the case of *Dickson v. Remake*,[37] where three appraisers found the value of the interest of the party initiating the dissolution to be $0, $156,000, and $286,000. The purchasing

---

[37] 164 Cal. App. 4th 469 (2008). *Dickson* concerned the dissolution of a limited liability company. The statutory provisions in California governing LLC dissolution are similar to the provisions governing dissolution of corporations. In *Dickson* the company was owned by two members who were deadlocked regarding the operations of the business. Under provisions similar to § 2000, one owner moved for dissolution and the other owner responded by moving for a statutory buyout. *See*, Cal. Corp. Code § 17351, set out in relevant part, in Section C.3 of this chapter.

party convinced the court to use a "mean" value of $147,333.33 and the purchaser bought out his co-owner based on one-half this amount.

Once again, we see the importance of pre-planning for a buyout in the event of a dispute among the co-owners regarding the operation, or dissolution, of the company. Consider the following case:

MART v. SEVERSON
California Court of Appeal
115 Cal. Rptr. 2d 717 (2002)

I. INTRODUCTION

Bradley C. Mart (Mart) and Leland Severson (Severson) are the sole shareholders of Bay World Trading Ltd. (Bay World). Mart appeals from a decree which provides that Bay World will be dissolved unless Bay World and/or Severson elects to buy out Mart's shares in the corporation. Mart argues that the superior court's determination of the "fair value" of his Bay World shares was erroneous as a matter of law. We agree and, therefore, reverse the trial court's order.

II. CORPORATIONS CODE SECTION 2000

This appeal is from a special proceeding conducted pursuant to section 2000 of the Corporations Code[38] and is expressly authorized by that statute. (§ 2000, subd. (c)) Therefore, we begin by reviewing the statutory procedure.

The present case involves a voluntary dissolution proceeding. Shareholders of a corporation who represent 50 percent or more of the voting power may elect to wind up and dissolve that corporation by initiating a voluntary dissolution proceeding. (§§ 1900–1903) The special proceeding established by section 2000 "enable[s] a 50 percent shareholder to avoid dissolution of the corporation by purchasing the stock of the shareholder(s) seeking to dissolve the corporation." (*Abrams v. Abrams-Rubaloff & Associates, Inc.* (1980) 114 Cal. App. 3d 240, 247 [170 Cal. Rptr. 656] (*Abrams*)) This procedure, which also applies in involuntary proceedings, reflects the Legislature's "interest [in] preserving the corporate enterprise as a going concern if desired by the majority or by the other 50 owners" and is intended to be a "meaningful alternative to termination of the enterprise." (Legis. Com. com., 23E West's Ann. Corp. Code, § 2000 (1990 ed) pp. 514, 516–517)

Section 2000 states that, when a voluntary proceeding has been initiated by the vote of shareholders representing only 50 percent of the voting power (the moving parties), the corporation or the holders of the other 50 percent of the voting power (the purchasing parties) "may avoid the dissolution of the corporation and the appointment of any receiver by purchasing for cash the shares owned by the [moving parties] at their fair value." (§ 2000, subd. (a))

"Fair value" is defined in section 2000 as "the liquidation value as of the valuation date[39] but taking into account the possibility, if any, of sale of the entire

---

[38] [1] Unless otherwise indicated, all statutory references are to the Corporations Code.

[39] [2] The valuation date in the case of a voluntary dissolution proceeding is the date upon which that proceeding was initiated unless the court, for good cause, designates some other date. (§ 2000, subd. (f))

business as a going concern in a liquidation." (§ 2000, subd. (a)) In other words, section 2000 expressly requires that the going concern value of the corporation be reflected in the fair value price. The reason for this requirement is that "a liquidation does not necessarily contemplate that the assets will be sold piecemeal and the goodwill of the business sacrificed by a termination of the business." (2 Marsh et al., Cal. Corporation Law (4th ed. 2001 supp) § 21.08[C], p. 21-45) It may be possible to sell the entire business as a going concern in liquidation. "If that is true, then the moving parties should be entitled to a value which takes into account that possibility, since such a sale of the entire business as a going concern could be made in the liquidation if the dissolution were permitted to proceed." (*Ibid*)

Anticipating that opposing parties in a dissolution proceeding may not agree as to the "fair value" of the moving parties' shares, the Legislature established a procedure for determining that fair value. If the purchasing parties elect to purchase the shares of the moving parties but the parties cannot agree upon the fair value of those shares, the purchasing parties may apply to the superior court to stay the dissolution proceeding and "ascertain and fix the fair value of the shares owned by the moving parties." (§ 2000, subd. (b)) In such an event, the court "shall appoint three disinterested appraisers to appraise the fair value of the shares owned by the moving parties, and shall make an order referring the matter to the appraisers so appointed for the purpose of ascertaining such value. . . . The award of the appraisers or a majority of them, when confirmed by the court, shall be final and conclusive upon all parties." (§ 2000, subd. (c))

The court must then "enter a decree which shall provide in the alternative for winding up and dissolution of the corporation unless payment is made for the shares within the time specified by the decree." (§ 2000, subd. (c)) "If the purchasing parties desire to prevent the winding up and dissolution, they shall pay to the moving parties the value of their shares ascertained and decreed" within the time specified in the decree or fixed on appeal. Upon receiving such payment, "the moving parties shall transfer their shares to the purchasing parties." (§ 2000, subd. (d)) In other words, once the fair value is set pursuant to section 2000, the purchasing parties have the right, but no corresponding obligation, to purchase the moving parties' shares at the fair value price. (§ 2000, subd. (d))

With this statutory framework in mind, we turn to the facts which led to this appeal.

III. STATEMENT OF FACTS AND PROCEDURAL BACKGROUND

Bay World is a California corporation that sells and exports meat and meat by-products. Mart and Severson are each 50 percent shareholders and are both directors of the corporation.

On February 24, 2000, Mart signed a "Written Consent of Shareholders to the Election to Wind Up and Dissolve" Bay World. Mart delivered this written consent to Severson the following day at a meeting of Bay World's board of directors. That same day, Severson gave Mart notice of his intent to sue Mart for breach of fiduciary duty because Mart was allegedly attempting to establish a business that would compete with Bay World.[40]

---

[40] [3] On February 29, 2000, Severson filed an individual and derivative lawsuit against Mart.

On February 28, 2000, Mart filed a petition in the superior court pursuant to section 1904 requesting court supervision of the voluntary winding up of Bay World. According to the petition, court supervision was necessary because the shareholders were "divided into factions and the board of directors [was] deadlocked with regard to management and direction of the corporation." The directors could not agree on a plan of dissolution or liquidation and internal dissention threatened to substantially delay completion of the dissolution process absent court assistance.

On March 16, 2000, Severson exercised his right under section 2000 to have Bay World purchase Mart's shares at their "fair value" in order to avoid corporate dissolution. On April 6, 2000, the Honorable Ronald Quidachay stayed dissolution of Bay World and initiated the process of selecting a panel of three disinterested appraisers to value Mart's shares.[41] Thereafter, the court appointed one appraiser selected by Mart and one selected by Severson and then ordered those two to select a third who was then confirmed by the court. The three appraisers, KPMG Consulting, LLC, Sierra Capital Advisors, LLC, and Law and Economics Consulting Group, LLC, submitted a joint report dated November 30, 2000 (November 30 report). According to the November 30 report, the appraisers worked together to determine the fair value of Bay World, all understood their study was being made pursuant to section 2000, and the opinions expressed in the report were the consensus opinions of all three appraisers.

The appraisers defined fair value as it is defined in section 2000, i.e., "[t]he liquidation value as of the valuation date but taking into account the possibility, if any, of sale of the entire business as a going concern in a liquidation." The appraisers expressly stated that "we believe the Company would be sold as a going concern." Therefore, they concluded that a "cost approach" valuation method, which focuses exclusively on the assets and liabilities of the corporation, was not applicable. Instead, the appraisers employed two alternate valuation methods, the "income approach" and the "market approach" because these approaches "provide a more realistic indication of what [Bay World] would be sold for as a going concern . . . ." The November 30 report sets forth the following ultimate conclusion: "Based on our analysis, which relied in part on information and data supplied by the Company, our conclusion of the fair value of 100 percent of the common stock of Bay World . . . as of February 25, 2000 is: $5.6 Million Dollars ($5,600,000)."

On December 5, 2000, Severson filed a motion to remand the November 30 report. Severson argued the appraisers' valuation methods were erroneous because they resulted in a calculation of Bay World's fair market sale value rather than its liquidation value as required by California law. A hearing on Severson's motion was held on January 4, 2001, before the Honorable A. James Robertson. Initially, the court expressed the opinion that the appraisers' analysis was proper. However, Severson's counsel maintained that the report was ambiguous as to whether the appraisers had calculated a liquidation value. Ultimately, the court decided to request clarification from the appraisers.

Severson alleged causes of action for breach of fiduciary duty and wrongful dissolution and sought to remove Mart as a director of Bay World . . .

[41] [4] The superior court also appointed a provisional director to resolve any deadlock on the board of directors.

On January 9, 2001, the court filed an order instructing the appraisers to submit a supplemental letter further explaining their November 30 valuation of Bay World. The order inquired whether the appraisers calculated the liquidation value of Bay World or its sale value as a going concern in liquidation. The term "liquidation value" was not defined in the order. The order set forth several additional questions, including (1) whether the appraisers adjusted their valuation to reflect a forced sale under court supervision, (2) how the valuation differed from a standard fair market valuation, and (3) whether the appraisers considered threatened litigation against the corporation. Finally, the appraisers were asked whether they considered the effect of potential competition when calculating Bay World's value and specifically whether they "assumed a covenant not to compete on the part of the shareholders and directors in determining fair value."

On January 12, 2001, the appraisers sent a detailed (and again unanimous) letter to the court responding to the inquiries in the January 9 order (January 12 letter). The appraisers equated the "liquidation value" method referred to in the court's order to the "cost approach" which, as was stated in the November 30 report, was not applicable. Under this approach, "the fixed and other tangible assets of the Company are sold piecemeal, the liabilities are retired, and the remaining equity after expenses, if any, is distributed to the shareholders." According to the appraisers, this approach is used to value companies that are insolvent or incapable of earning a return adequate to support the value of the assets. Each of the appraisers considered the piecemeal liquidation value of Bay World, but all three independently concluded that value was irrelevant in light of Bay World's historical earnings record and future earnings capability.

The appraisers repeated their unanimous opinion that Bay World "would be sold as a going concern in liquidation." They explained that, as of the valuation date, a seller simply would not accept the piecemeal liquidation value as valid because it "would not reflect the value of the intangible assets of the business, such as the brand name and client relationships, which is best reflected through going concern, earnings-based approaches." The appraisers advised that they did interpret "fair value" to mean the price that would be received for the corporation in a liquidation sale under court supervision, assuming a "tainted" sale environment and a "forced seller." The appraisers took these liquidation-related factors into account when conducting their analysis.

The appraisers also advised the court that they had considered whether actual or threatened litigation against Bay World affected its value, but concluded it did not. The appraisers expressly found that Severson's lawsuit against Mart did not affect Bay World's value as of the valuation date for several reasons, including the facts that the litigation was "primarily personal in nature" and that Bay World's "operations had not been materially impacted by Mr. Mart's activities previous to the Date of Value."

Finally, the appraisers explained that they did not adjust their valuation to account for potential competition on the part of the shareholders. Relying on California authority construing section 2000, the appraisers "assumed hypothetical covenants not to compete would be executed by both shareholders and key employees in a sale of the Company on the Date of Value." The appraisers also explained that, although they had not attempted to estimate the impact on value if such agreements were not signed, it was their opinion that "a sale of the Company as a going concern would be very difficult, if not impossible, in such a circumstance."

A continued hearing was scheduled for February 9, 2001. Prior to that hearing, the court issued a tentative ruling requiring Mart to submit a noncompetition agreement as a condition for the court's approval of the appraisers' valuation of Bay World. At the hearing, the court continued the matter to give Mart time to prepare such an agreement.

The hearing was continued to February 27, 2001. At the hearing, the court expressed the view that Bay World could be valued as a going concern business only if Mart executed a valid covenant not to compete with Bay World. The court also expressed concern that such a covenant was not in place as of the valuation date. Mart's counsel produced a noncompetition agreement that Mart had signed. Severson's counsel objected to the agreement as untimely. The court concluded that the proffered agreement was too narrow but suggested that Mart attempt to draft an alternative agreement that would afford Bay World more protection. In the meantime, the court would request that the appraisers calculate a piecemeal liquidation value for Bay World.

In an order filed February 28, 2001, the court remanded the appraisers' November 30 report and instructed the appraisers to calculate the piecemeal liquidation value of Bay World as of February 25, 2000. The order also granted Mart leave to submit an alternative covenant not to compete, which the court would consider at the next hearing.

On March 19, 2001, the appraisers submitted their "Liquidation Value Analysis" which set forth the following conclusion: "Based on our study, our opinion of the liquidation value of Bay World . . . as of the Valuation Date is: One Million Four Hundred Eighty Thousand Dollars ($1,480,000)."

At a hearing on April 4, 2001, the court concluded that "the 1.48 million liquidation value was to be used rather than the greater sum." The court found that a revised noncompete agreement Mart had submitted prior to the hearing was not "fully effective" and did not give an "absolute guarantee" that Mart would not compete with Bay World. The court found that, even if such a guarantee could be provided now, it was too late because such an agreement did not exist as of the valuation date.

On April 17, 2001, the court filed a "Decree and Judgment Winding Up and Dissolving Bay World If Confirmed Value of Shares Is Not Paid And For Award of Expenses" (April 17 decree). The April 17 decree set forth the procedure pursuant to which Bay World and/or Severson could exercise their option to purchase Mart's shares of Bay World for a payment of $740,000, plus interest in order to prevent dissolution of the corporation. Among other things, the April 17 decree stated that "the appraisers March 19, 2001 supplementary report determining the piecemeal liquidation value of Bay World Trading to be $1,480,000 as of the February 25, 2000 valuation date is confirmed and is final and conclusive upon all parties." The decree further stated:

"The Court finds that the $5,600,000 award was premised upon the execution of an effective covenant not to compete by the parties and that no such covenant has been submitted to the Court. As the Court has doubts that any effective covenant not to compete could ever be executed, the

Court adopts the piecemeal liquidation value determined by the appraisers in their March 19, 2001 supplementary report."

On June 21, 2001, Mart filed a notice of appeal.

IV. DISCUSSION

Mart contends the April 17 decree must be reversed because the trial court's determination of the "fair value" of Bay World shares was erroneous as a matter of law. The factual aspects of the court's fair value determination are reviewed under the substantial evidence standard . . . However, the superior court's interpretation of the statutory standard set forth in section 2000 is subject to de novo review on appeal . . .

The trial court found that the fair value of Bay World's shares was its piecemeal liquidation value, i.e., $1.48 million. This conclusion is not supported by substantial evidence and resulted from an erroneous application of the section 2000 definition of "fair value."

The overwhelming evidence in this record indicates that the fair value of 100 percent of Bay World's shares as of the valuation date is $5.6 million. That was the unanimous conclusion of all three disinterested appraisers and that conclusion is supported by the appraisers' November 30 report and their January 12 letter to the court clarifying that report. Indeed, we find no contrary evidence in the appellate record. The trial court's conclusion that Bay World's fair value was $1.48 million is not supported by the evidence. The appraisers all agreed that this figure reflects Bay World's *piecemeal liquidation value*, but that value is not equivalent to its fair value because Bay World could have been sold as a going concern in liquidation on the valuation date.

The trial court rejected the appraisers' fair value determination of $5.6 million because it found that determination was "premised upon the execution of an effective covenant not to compete by the parties" and no such covenant had been or could be executed in this case. It is unclear to us whether the trial court concluded that (a) the appraisers made the execution of an effective covenant not to compete a precondition for their recommendation or (b) such a covenant was a legal prerequisite for finding that a corporation could be sold as a going concern in liquidation. In either case, the court was incorrect.

The appraisers did not condition their conclusions upon Mart's execution of a covenant not to compete. Rather, they concluded that Bay World could be sold as a going concern in liquidation and then calculated a monetary fair value by considering a hypothetical sale of Bay World on the valuation date. A reasonable and expected term of such a sale would be a sellers' covenant not to compete with the corporation after the sale. Therefore, the appraisers "assumed hypothetical covenants not to compete would be executed by both shareholders and key employees in a sale of the Company on the Date of Value." The appraisers did not consider whether Mart had already executed a covenant not to compete nor did they require that such a covenant be executed. Indeed, Mart was not the seller in the hypothetical they considered. The question the appraisers answered was whether the *entire corporation* could have been sold as a going concern in liquidation as of the valuation date, not whether Mart could have sold *his share* of the corporation to Severson under those circumstances.

The appraisers applied section 2000 properly by assuming that a hypothetical willing seller of Bay World would execute a covenant not to compete with the corporation after the sale. Section 2000 requires that the fair value determination reflect a corporation's value as a going concern if a sale of the corporation as a going concern in liquidation is possible. (§ 2000, subd. (a) ["fair value shall be determined on the basis of the liquidation value as of the valuation date but taking into account the possibility, if any, of sale of the entire business as a going concern in a liquidation"]) Thus, section 2000 necessarily requires that the appraisers contemplate a hypothetical sale scenario: *a sale of the entire corporation, in a liquidation setting, on the valuation date.* Further, since the corporation will almost always be closely held, "there will be no actual market value or any actual cash sales by which the market value could be determined. Therefore, the value to be determined must necessarily be a constructed or hypothetical market value at which the hypothetical willing seller would sell and the hypothetical willing buyer would purchase." (2 Marsh et al. Cal. Corporation Law, *supra,* § 21.08[C], p. 21–45)

California case law construing section 2000 approves the use of a hypothetical sale model, like the one employed by the appraisers in this case, to calculate the fair value of a corporation that can be sold as a going concern in liquidation. (*Abrams, supra,* 114 Cal. App. 3d at pp., 248–249) In *Abrams,* the court held that appraisers who conducted a section 2000 fair value determination acted properly by assuming that the owners of the corporation would have agreed not to compete with the corporation after it was sold as a going concern in liquidation. (*Abrams, supra,* 114 Cal. App. 3d 240) The court reasoned that "[s]ection 2000 states that the appraisers should consider the 'possibility of a sale as a going concern in a liquidation.' Under the statute, the appraisers are not only entitled, but are required, to consider the manner in which the parties to such a hypothetical sale are most likely to maximize their return." (*Id.* at p. 249)

Case law also confirms that the potential threat of future competition by the current shareholders should not affect the fair value analysis. (*Brown v. Allied Corrugated Box. Co.* (1979) 91 Cal. App. 3d 477 [154 Cal. Rptr. 170] (*Brown*)) *Brown* involved a fair value determination conducted pursuant to former section 4659, the predecessor statute to section 2000. (*Brown, supra,* 91 Cal. App. 3d at p. 480, fn. 2) The *Brown* court found that the appraisers who conducted that determination erred by considering the negative impact of the fact that the shareholder who was primarily responsible for developing the corporation's goodwill had not entered into a noncompete agreement with the corporation. (*Id.* at pp. 487–488) The *Brown* court reasoned that the goodwill of a business is the indivisible property of the corporation and the value of that asset must be reflected in the fair value determination. In other words, discounting the value of the corporation because of the threat of future competition by one of its shareholders unfairly deprives the moving party of the true value of his stock.

In the present case, the trial court misinterpreted section 2000. That statute contains a procedure for establishing a fair value price for the moving party's stock. However, the section does not govern or even address covenants not to compete or any other term of the sale pursuant to which the purchasing party can buy out the shares of the moving party. Nor does it authorize the trial court to dictate any of the terms of that sale *other than price.* In the present case, the trial court required that Mart submit executed covenants not to compete and then it found those proposed agreements were inadequate. Section 2000 does not give the trial court authority to require a party to execute a covenant not to compete or to evaluate the validity of such a covenant. The trial court should not have become involved in negotiations pertaining to that sales term.

Ignoring the flaws in the trial court's reasoning, Severson claims the April 17 decree must be affirmed because substantial evidence supports the finding that Bay World could not have been sold as a going concern in liquidation on the date of value. But the trial court made no such finding. Rather, it erroneously concluded that Mart had to execute a covenant not to compete in order to obtain fair value for his Bay World shares. As explained above, neither the appraisers nor section 2000 imposed any such precondition.

Furthermore, the "substantial evidence" upon which Severson relies is his subjective version of the dispute between himself and Mart which culminated in these dissolution proceedings including, in particular, evidence that Mart allegedly refused to agree not to compete with Bay World prior to the institution of the voluntary dissolution proceeding. The trial court did not rely on or even allude to this evidence (which Mart objected to) as supporting its fair value determination. Nor should it have done so because such evidence is not relevant to the fair value analysis.

Section 2000 establishes an objective process for valuing a corporation after dissolution proceedings have commenced. The fair value is the liquidation value. But liquidation value can mean going concern value if the corporation could be sold as a going concern in liquidation. Thus, the hypothetical question posed by section 2000 is whether the entire corporation could have been sold as a going concern in liquidation on the valuation date. To answer that question, the appraisers considered hypothetical reasonable sellers, hypothetical reasonable buyers, and a hypothetical forced sale liquidation environment. Evidence that Mart would not actually give Severson a covenant not to compete prior to the valuation date is simply not relevant to the hypothetical scenario the appraisers considered.

When determining fair value under section 2000, the only relevant issue with respect to Mart's allegedly competitive activities was whether they affected the value of Bay World *as of the date of value.* If Mart's activities had destroyed the value of Bay World or prevented it from being sold as a going concern in liquidation, then the court should have concluded that the piecemeal value was the fair value. But the trial court made no findings to support such a conclusion. Nor did the court reject or even question the independent appraisers' express conclusion that the conflicts between Severson and Mart, including Mart's activities prior to the valuation date, did not diminish Bay World's value. In their January 12 letter, the appraisers explained why Mart's alleged activities did not affect Bay World's value. The dispute between Mart and Severson was "primarily personal in nature" and, in any event, Bay World's "operations had not been materially impacted by Mr. Mart's activities previous to the Date of Value."

Severson contends that *Abrams, supra,* 114 Cal. App. 3d 240, does not require that appraisers assume a hypothetical seller's covenant not to compete in every section 2000 case and that the trial court "properly found that it would have been error to impute a hypothetical covenant not to compete in fixing 'fair value' in this case." Again, the trial court made no such finding. Nor did it even address *Abrams,* a case that expressly supports the use of a hypothetical sale model in order to conduct a section 2000 fair value analysis. Rather, the court erroneously concluded that Mart's actual covenant not to compete was required by either the appraisers or section 2000.

Furthermore, when making a section 2000 fair value determination, appraisers should always assume a hypothetical seller's covenant not to compete just as they should assume that the parties to the hypothetical sale will negotiate the other requisite terms to a sales agreement. Indeed, without these assumptions, it would be impossible to construct a hypothetical sale pursuant to which a fair value could be determined. All of the sale terms other than price are assumptions based on the reasonable person's conduct. These fixed assumptions permit the appraisers to calculate a fair value price that reflects the actual health of the corporation. Once the fair value is determined, the superior court's job is done. Section 2000 authorizes the court to set only one term of the contemplated sale — the price. Once the fair value price for the corporation is set, the parties must negotiate the remaining sales terms.

At oral argument, Severson's counsel asserted that the only reason Mart is now willing to sign a noncompete is because the competing business Mart was attempting to establish when he initiated the dissolution proceeding has now failed. Again, whether true or not, Severson's contention is not relevant. *Section 2000 results in the establishment of a fair value price as of the valuation date.* It does not result in an actual sale as of that date. The covenant not to compete is a term of the sale. Aside from the price, which is governed by section 2000, negotiations pertaining to the terms of the sale must be conducted by the parties themselves *after* the fair value is determined.

Furthermore, Severson's plea for fairness actually undermines his position. If we affirm the trial court's holding, a purchasing party could always deprive a moving party of the going concern value of his or her corporate shares simply by rejecting the moving party's proposed covenant not to compete (as Severson repeatedly did in this case). Under the trial court's reasoning, the absence of such a covenant would always result in a fair value price based exclusively on piecemeal liquidation value. Such a result flies in the face of the statutory definition of fair value, which expressly requires that the possibility of a sale of the entire corporation as a going concern in liquidation must be reflected in the fair value price. (§ 2000)

In contrast, when the covenant not to compete is properly viewed as a sales term outside the scope of section 2000, the moving party has a strong incentive to agree to give an effective covenant not to compete. Since the purchasing party has the right but no obligation to proceed with the buyout once the fair value is set, he may use his option of permitting the corporation to be liquidated as a bargaining tool for obtaining the moving party's covenant not to compete. In other words, if Mart refuses to execute a reasonable covenant not to compete, Severson can elect to proceed with a piecemeal liquidation and not pay Mart the fair value price. In that event, the price Mart would obtain for his shares would be substantially lower than their value.

* * *

Finally, Severson argues that the trial court had the power and the obligation to correct the allegedly erroneous November 30 report. We agree that when "the determination of the fair value of the shares by the appraisers, or a majority of them, is erroneous, it is 'the duty of the trial court to examine the matter de novo and to fix a proper value. . . . ' [Citation.]" (*Ronald v. 4- C's Electronic Packaging,*

Inc. (1985) 168 Cal. App. 3d 290, 301 [214 Cal. Rptr. 225]) However, in the present case, the trial court *did not* conclude that the appraisers' determination of Bay World's fair value was erroneous. Rather, it concluded that Mart was entitled only to the piecemeal liquidation value of his Bay World shares. That conclusion is erroneous in light of (a) the appraisers' unanimous conclusion that Bay World could have been sold as a going concern in liquidation on the valuation date and (b) the section 2000 requirement that the fair value determination must take into account the possibility that a corporation can be sold as a going concern in liquidation.

In summary, the trial court's conclusion that the fair value of Bay World is $1.48 million is not supported by substantial evidence and is based on an erroneous application of section 2000. Therefore, that ruling is reversed and the superior court is instructed to confirm the fair value determination set forth in the November 30 report.

V. DISPOSITION

The April 17 decree is reversed, and this case is remanded to the trial court for further proceedings consistent with this opinion. Costs on appeal are awarded to appellant.

NOTES AND QUESTIONS

1.   What formula did the appraisers use to unanimously agree that the company had a value of $5.6 million? Was this the "fair market value" of the company or some other "fair value." Pay close attention to the following excerpt from the opinion:

> The appraisers repeated their unanimous opinion that Bay World "would be sold as a going concern in liquidation." They explained that, as of the valuation date, a seller simply would not accept the piecemeal liquidation value as valid because it "would not reflect the value of the intangible assets of the business, such as the brand name and client relationships, which is best reflected through going concern, earnings-based approaches." The appraisers advised that they did interpret "fair value" to mean the price that would be received for the corporation *in a liquidation sale under court supervision, assuming a "tainted" sale environment and a "forced seller." The appraisers took these liquidation-related factors into account when conducting their analysis.* [Emphasis added.]

2.   The three appraisers were appointed by the court in April and delivered their report concerning the value of the company on November 30th. The appraisers were: (i) KPMG Consulting, LLC; (ii) Sierra Capital Advisors, LLC; and (iii) Law and Economics Consulting Group, LLC. These appraisers are national and global companies that charge large amounts for their services. What do you estimate were the costs of the appraisal process, particularly in view of the trial court's remand to the appraisers and additional valuation requests?

3.   Bradley Mart initiated the dissolution proceeding and filed a motion for court supervision of the winding up of Bay World, Inc., which was granted. Shortly thereafter, Leland Severson exercised his right under section 2000 to have Bay World purchase Mart's shares at their "fair value" in order to avoid corporate dissolution but the two 50% owners could not agree on a fair value. The appraisers chose a going concern liquidation value of $5.6 million. Nevertheless, Severson

convinced the trial court to use a piecemeal liquidation value (where each asset is sold individually) of $1.48 million, which excludes any going concern value. For reasons discussed in the opinion, the California Court of Appeals reversed and remanded, directing the trial court to use the $5.6 million value, which would require Severson to pay one-half of that amount ($2.8 million). If Severson refused to make the payment and the corporation proceeded to liquidate and wind up, how much would the two shareholders receive? In view of the discord between them, do you think they could succeed in winding up the corporation by a sale of the entire business as a going concern, or would they be lucky to get the lower liquidation value? A good guess would be that they would probably get only the lower liquidation value.

4.   Would a properly drafted buy-sell agreement have avoided such an undesirable outcome? Also, could a buy-sell agreement have avoided the enormous expense of the court-supervised dissolution and the expensive use of appraisers?

C.   LIMITED LIABILITY COMPANY DISSOLUTIONS

How is the dissolution of a limited liability company different from the dissolution of a corporation? A central feature of both types of entities is the limited liability for entity debts that is afforded to the equity holders. Because of this insulating quality of LLC's, creditor claims should be paid or provided for in full before equity holders are entitled to participate in distributions from the dissolution. It makes sense that, similar to the dissolution of corporations, LLC statutory provisions focus on the protection of creditors as the first priority in a state law dissolution of an LLC. Only after creditors have been fully satisfied, or adequate provisions made for payment to them, can distributions be made to members in their capacity as equity holders.[42]

It is worth repeating that when the owners of *any* business entity agree to dissolution, or the formation documents require dissolution, it is often in the best interests of all owners to cooperate in realizing the greatest value for the business, either as a going concern, if that's possible, or through a piecemeal liquidation. If the company has a positive net worth, then the owners can maximize the value received for assets, and reduce administrative costs by cooperating, thereby increasing the *pro rata* distribution they will receive. On the other hand, in the case of an LLC with a negative net worth, it is unlikely that the members will pursue a state-law based dissolution. If there will be no value remaining after the payout to creditors, then federal bankruptcy law serves as a much cheaper and efficient forum for the liquidation of the company and the maximization of the amounts paid to creditors.[43] There is no economic incentive for a member of a company with a negative net worth to force the LLC into dissolution under state law — unless the process is being initiated in a judicial proceeding to create a possible incentive for the non-moving member(s) to buyout the member initiating the judicial dissolution.[44] From a practical perspective, the provisions for LLC dissolution are really intended for positive-net-worth companies where there will be funds available for distribution to members after the debts of the LLC are paid or provided for.

---

[42]   Members who are creditors are generally entitled to distributions as creditors unless their loans are equitably treated as equity contributions. *See* Re-ULLCA § 708(a).

[43]   See the discussion of federal bankruptcy law later in this chapter.

[44]   Buyout rights in LLC dissolutions are discussed later in this chapter.

1.   LLC Dissolution Procedures

As an entity created by state statute, an LLC can *only* be dissolved in accordance with state statutory requirements. We will be using primarily the Revised Uniform Limited Liability Company Act ("Re-ULLCA" or "2006 ULLCA"). There is an earlier version, the 1996 Uniform Limited Liability Company Act ("ULLCA" or "1996 ULLCA"). When referring to both acts, we will use the term "ULLCA". States that have adopted neither the 1996 nor 2006 ULLCA have adopted limited liability company acts that are similar to either the 1996 and 2006 versions of the ULLCA.[45] Despite some differences between the two versions of ULLCA, both the 1996 and 2006 ULLCA place the priority of creditors above the rights of members in the event of the winding up of an LLC. Review the following provisions from the 2006 ULLCA dealing with the priority of creditors in LLC dissolutions:

§ 702.   Winding Up

(a)   A dissolved limited liability company shall wind up its activities, and the company continues after dissolution only for the purpose of winding up.

(b)   In winding up its activities, a limited liability company:

(1)   shall discharge the company's debts, obligations, or other liabilities, settle and close the company's activities, and marshal and distribute the assets of the company; and

. . .

§ 703.   Known Claims Against Dissolved Limited Liability Company.

(a)   Except as otherwise provided in subsection (d), a dissolved limited liability company may give notice of a known claim under subsection (b), which has the effect as provided in subsection (c).

(b)   A dissolved limited liability company may in a record notify its known claimants of the dissolution. The notice must:

(1)   specify the information required to be included in a claim;

(2)   provide a mailing address to which the claim is to be sent;

(3)   state the deadline for receipt of the claim, which may not be less than 120 days after the date the notice is received by the claimant; and

(4)   state that the claim will be barred if not received by the deadline.

(c)   A claim against a dissolved limited liability company is barred if the requirements of subsection (b) are met and:

(1)   the claim is not received by the specified deadline; or

(2)   if the claim is timely received but rejected by the company:

---

[45] The 1996 and 2006 versions of the ULLCA are significantly different with respect to *some* aspects of dissolution, discussed later in this chapter. However, with respect to the priorities and rights of creditors, there are no substantive differences between the two versions. The 1996 Act was been adopted in Alabama (1997), Hawaii, (1996), Illinois (1997), Montana (1999), South Carolina (1996), South Dakota (1998), Vermont (1996), Virgin Islands (1998), and West Virginia (1996). The 2006 Act has been adopted in Idaho (2008) and Iowa (2008). See the web site of the National Conference of Commissioners on Uniform State Laws (NCCUSL) for updates at www.nccusl.org.

(A)   the company causes the claimant to receive a notice in a record stating that the claim is rejected and will be barred unless the claimant commences an action against the company to enforce the claim within 90 days after the claimant receives the notice; and

(B)   the claimant does not commence the required action within the 90 days.

(d)   This section does not apply to a claim based on an event occurring after the effective date of dissolution or a liability that on that date is contingent.

Section 703 provides a clear procedure for assuring that the rights of *known* creditors are resolved and paid prior to the winding up of the company and distribution of any assets to the members. This would include most, if not all, contract creditors and some civil claimants with tort or other claims pending against the LLC. What about creditors who are not known to the LLC or with contingent claims? § 703(d) specifically exempts the claims of creditors with contingent claims from the necessity of filing a claim under § 703. Contingent and unknown claims are provided for in § 704:

§ 704.   Other Claims Against Dissolved Limited Liability Company.

(a)   A dissolved limited liability company may publish notice of its dissolution and request persons having claims against the company to present them in accordance with the notice.

(b)   The notice authorized by subsection (a) must:

(1)   be published at least once in a newspaper of general circulation in the [county] in this state in which the dissolved limited liability company's principal office is located or, if it has none in this state, in the [county] in which the company's designated office is or was last located;

(2)   describe the information required to be contained in a claim and provide a mailing address to which the claim is to be sent; and

(3)   state that a claim against the company is barred unless an action to enforce the claim is commenced within *five years after publication of the notice.* [Emphasis added.]

(c)   If a dissolved limited liability company publishes a notice in accordance with subsection (b), unless the claimant commences an action to enforce the claim against the company within five years after the publication date of the notice, the claim of each of the following claimants is barred:

(1)   a claimant that did not receive notice in a record under Section 703;

(2)   a claimant whose claim was timely sent to the company but not acted on; and

(3)   a claimant whose claim is contingent at, or based on an event occurring after, the effective date of dissolution.

(d)   A claim not barred under this section may be enforced:

(1)   against a dissolved limited liability company, to the extent of its undistributed assets; and

(2)   if assets of the company have been distributed after dissolution, against a member or transferee to the extent of that person's proportionate share of the claim or of the assets distributed to the member or transferee after dissolution, whichever is less, but a person's total liability for all claims under this paragraph does not exceed the total amount of assets distributed to the person after dissolution.

Similar to the California Corporations Code provisions dealing with corporate dissolutions, the 2006 ULLCA imposes a time limitations on the right of creditors who have contingent or unknown claims at the time of dissolution of the liability-insulating business entity. Unpaid creditors have a maximum of five years (after publication of the statutory notice) to bring their claims — or less time if the claim is barred by statutes of limitation on the underlying claim. In the event that a creditor with a contingent or unknown claim makes a timely filing following the distribution of assets to the equity holders under § 704, members who received distributions will have to return the amount distributed to them (but no more than that amount) to help satisfy the LLC debt. This makes sense since the members should not receive distributions at the expense of the creditors of the LLC entity, so long as claims are brought by the creditors within some reasonable period of time. Just as with corporations, this is a fair balance between the rights of creditors to be paid and the interests of the members in obtaining a final closure to the dissolution of the entity.

2.   Commencement of an LLC Dissolution

Limited liability companies are inherently more flexible than traditional corporations. To a substantial degree, the rights of members to all aspects of the LLC's life, or dissolution, can be governed by the LLC articles and operating agreement, with the statute providing default rules that operate in the absence of controlling provisions in the LLC documents.[46] However, some statutory provisions dealing with dissolution cannot be altered. For instance, the rights of creditors to priority of payment under §§ 702(a) and (b)(1) cannot be altered by the articles or operating agreement.[47] With regard to commencement and conduct of

---

[46] The 2006 ULLCA § 110 provides:

    (a) Except as otherwise provided in subsections (b) and (c), the operating agreement governs:

        (1) relations among the members as members and between the members and the limited liability company;

        (2) the rights and duties under this [act] of a person in the capacity of manager;

        (3) the activities of the company and the conduct of those activities; and

        (4) the means and conditions for amending the operating agreement.

    (b) To the extent the operating agreement does not otherwise provide for a matter described in subsection (a), this [act] governs the matter.

[47] Section 110(c)(7) states:

    An operating agreement may not:

       . . .

       (7) vary the power of a court to decree dissolution in the circumstances specified in Section 701(a)(4) and (5);

Although § 110 does not specifically refer to the procedural rights of creditors under § 703 (procedural rights of known creditors) and § 704 (procedural rights of creditors with unknown and contingent

the dissolution, the statute operates primarily as a default handbook except that two of the grounds for commencement of a dissolution proceeding (subsections (a)(4) and (a)(5)).[48] Why are those two grounds restricted from modification in the articles and operating agreement?

§ 701. Events Causing Dissolution

(a)   A limited liability company is dissolved, and its activities must be wound up, upon the occurrence of any of the following:

(1)   an event or circumstance that the operating agreement states causes dissolution;

(2)   the consent of all the members;

(3)   the passage of 90 consecutive days during which the company has no members;

(4)   on application by a member, the entry by [appropriate court] of an order dissolving the company on the grounds that:

(A)   the conduct of all or substantially all of the company's activities is unlawful; or

(B)   it is not reasonably practicable to carry on the company's activities in conformity with the certificate of organization and the operating agreement; or

(5)   on application by a member, the entry by [appropriate court] of an order dissolving the company on the grounds that the managers or those members in control of the company:

(A)   have acted, are acting, or will act in a manner that is illegal or fraudulent; or

(B)   have acted or are acting in a manner that is oppressive and was, is, or will be directly harmful to the applicant.

What is meant by the phrase is subsection (4)(B) that judicial dissolution is available when "it is not reasonably practicable to carry on the company's activities in conformity with the certificate of organization and the operating agreement." Consider the following South Dakota case.[49]

---

claims), these procedural rights are derived from the mandate in § 702(b)(1) that the LLC "shall discharge the company's debts, obligations, or other liabilities . . . " Of course, creditors can always agree with the LLC to the terms under which the LLC will discharge its obligations to creditors.

[48]   Section 110(c)(8) states: "(8) vary the requirement to wind up a limited liability company's business as specified in Section 702(a) and (b)(1)."

[49]   South Dakota has adopted the 1996 ULLCA.

KIRKSEY v. GROHMANN
South Dakota Supreme Court
754 N.W.2d 825 (2008)

KONENKAMP, J.

Four sisters inherited equal ownership in their family's land. They formed a limited liability company, conveying their property interests to the company in exchange for equal ownership in the LLC. One sister lives on the land and manages the LLC, and another sister leases the land for livestock grazing. Two other sisters live a great distance from the land. These sisters, who once agreed, are now divided. They speak only through their lawyers. Two sought to terminate the lease and dissolve the LLC; the other two opposed it. A majority vote is required, but the sisters are deadlocked. Judicial dissolution was sought and the circuit court granted summary judgment against it. On appeal, we conclude that it is not reasonably practicable for the company to continue and the economic purpose of the LLC is being unreasonably frustrated. We reverse and remand for an order of judicial dissolution.

Background

On July 10, 2001, Grace Kirksey died. She had four daughters: Lucille Ruby, Lorraine Kirksey, Dorothy Grohmann, and Eileen Randell. Grace left her four daughters equal ownership interest in 2,769 acres of land in Butte County, South Dakota, and 401 acres in Crook County, Wyoming. These tracts composing the Kirksey land have been in the family for over 100 years. Grohmann lives on and manages this land, and Randell lives in Rapid City, South Dakota. Kirksey lives in California, and Ruby lives in Colorado.

On October 7, 2002, the four daughters formed a limited liability company, Kirksey Family Ranch, LLC, to hold title to the land. Each sister conveyed her one-quarter interest in the property to the LLC in exchange for a 25% ownership in the company. Grohmann would serve as the manager. They formed the LLC (1) to avoid paying certain estate taxes by employing a special use valuation, (2) to keep the land in the family, and (3) to keep ownership interest in the real property with the sisters and not their spouses.

At the time of their mother's death, the land was valued at $550,000. With the special use valuation, it was reported to be valued at $215,000. To obtain the benefit of this valuation certain family members were required, among other things, to retain ownership in the land for ten years, and it was to be used for agricultural purposes. The eldest sister, Grohmann, had lived on the Kirksey land as a hired hand before their mother's death. Grohmann, Kirksey, and Randell each owned grazing livestock on the land. To continue the agricultural operation, the sisters decided that the LLC would lease the land to Grohmann, Kirksey, and Randell.

A lease agreement was executed in October 2002, effective September 1, 2002. It provided for an initial term of five years, to be automatically renewed for another year unless either party gave written notice of intent to terminate within ninety days before the termination of the lease. The annual rental rate was set at $14,263.20. The LLC, as the landlord, was responsible for all the real estate taxes and insurance.

Not long after the formation of the LLC, relations deteriorated. According to Kirksey, Grohmann and Randell "failed or refused to share information" with her on the operation of the ranch, on which she owned livestock as a tenant to the lease. She claimed that she wrote Grohmann "dozens of pages of letters" to resolve disagreements and requested information about livestock and other issues. She insisted that Grohmann did not provide the requested information and, if she did, it was either inaccurate or unreliable. Also, according to Kirksey, Grohmann and Randell subleased 401 acres of the land without notice to the LLC, as required by the lease agreement.

Grohmann, on the other hand, said that she always gave Kirksey necessary information. She further contended that the LLC was given notice of the sublease because the members of the LLC, the sisters, were aware of the sublease arrangement when Grohmann initially divided up the sublease payments equally and attempted to share them with all the LLC members. Grohmann said that Kirksey accepted the payment, but Ruby did not as she was not a tenant to the lease.

Because of her continued frustrations with Grohmann and Randell, Kirksey sold them her interest in the livestock in 2003. Grohmann and Randell were then the only tenants on the lease agreement. This, however, did not end the contentious relationship between the sisters. Kirksey and Ruby hired a real estate agent to value the Kirksey land. It was estimated to be worth in excess of $3.2 million. Kirksey and Ruby then sought to terminate the lease agreement, dissolve the LLC, and partition the land.

A meeting of the LLC was held on May 30, 2006. Ruby moved and Kirksey seconded a motion to terminate the lease agreement. Grohmann and Randell opposed, and the motion failed. Thereafter, Ruby moved and Kirksey seconded a motion to dissolve the LLC. This motion also failed when Grohmann and Randell opposed. All major actions taken by the LLC required a majority vote of its members. Because Grohmann and Randell had no desire to terminate the lease or dissolve the LLC, the parties remained deadlocked.

Kirksey and Ruby petitioned the circuit court for relief. Citing SDCL 47-34A-801, Kirksey and Ruby requested that the court dissolve the LLC because its economic purpose was unreasonably frustrated and it was not reasonably practicable to carry on the company's business in conformity with the articles of organization and the operating agreement. According to Kirksey, the strained relationship between the sisters made it impossible for any major decision making. Moreover, Kirksey claimed that "Grohmann and Randell have a personal financial interest in continuing the lease agreement and preventing dissolution of the LLC," all to her and Ruby's detriment.

On cross motions for summary judgment, the circuit court denied Kirksey and Ruby's petition and granted Grohmann and Randell's motion for summary judgment. Kirksey and Ruby appeal, asserting that the court erred when it granted summary judgment against judicial dissolution of the LLC.

Analysis and Decision

* * * Several facts are undisputed. Kirksey Family Ranch, LLC is a family enterprise, created to keep title to land held in the family for over a century and to

maintain ranching operations. Each sister invested in the company her one-quarter interest in the land with the understanding that she would have an equal say in the company's operations and equal ownership in its assets. When the sisters formed the LLC, they provided no way to break a tie vote between them and no way to end a deadlock. Today, the sisters are divided and speak only through their legal counsel. There being no avenue for relief in the operating agreement, two sisters ask the courts to intervene.

Through SDCL 47-34A-801, the Legislature provided courts with the limited power to order dissolution of an LLC if certain statutory standards are met. Under SDCL 47-34A-801(a)(4)(i) and SDCL 47-34A-801(a)(4)(iii), a court may judicially dissolve an LLC if "the economic purpose of the company is likely to be unreasonably frustrated" or "it is not otherwise reasonably practicable to carry on the company's business in conformity with the articles of organization and the operating agreement[.]"

How these statutory standards may be satisfied has not yet been detailed by this Court. A consistent view in other jurisdictions is that a limited liability company is governed by its articles of organization and operating agreement. *See, Horning v. Horning Constr., LLC*, 12 Misc. 3d 402, 816 N.Y.S.2d 877, 881 (NYSupCt 2006); *Historic Charleston Holdings, LLC v. Mallon*, 365 S.C. 524, 617 SE2d 388, 393 (SCCtApp 2005); *Dunbar Group, LLC v. Tignor*, 267 Va. 361, 593 SE2d 216, 219 (Va 2004). Beyond this, however, there is no prevailing interpretation of the terms "not reasonably practicable" and "economic purpose . . . unreasonably frustrated" in relation to dissolution of limited liability companies. *See* SDCL 47-34A-801.

Nevertheless, the cases interpreting language similar to our statutory terminology, whether involving a partnership or a limited liability company, are instructive. In defining what it means for it to "not be reasonably practicable" for a company to continue, one court consulted a dictionary to apply a plain and ordinary meaning. *Taki v. Hami*, 2001 Mich. App. LEXIS 777, 2001 WL 672399 (MichCtApp) (unpublished) (dissolution of a partnership). The *Taki* court held that " 'reasonably practicable' may properly be defined as capable of being done logically and in a reasonable, feasible manner."[50] 2001 Mich. App. LEXIS 777, [WL] at 3. Another court emphasized that "[t]he standard set forth by the Legislature is one of reasonable practicability, not impossibility." PC Tower Ctr., Inc. v. Tower Ctr. Dev. Assoc., L.P., 1989 Del. Ch. LEXIS 72, 1989 WL 63901, 6 (DelCh) (unpublished) (dissolution of a partnership). Under this view, the standard does not require that the purpose of the company, as set out in the operating agreement, be completely frustrated to warrant judicial dissolution.[51] Rather, the term "reasonably practicable" signifies a company's ability to continue the purpose identified in the operating agreement.

---

[50] [1] The court found that "it was not possible to complete the business of the partnership in a logical, reasonable and feasible manner." *Taki*, 2001 Mich. App. LEXIS 777, 2001 WL 672399, at 3. The members had not spoken to each other in years and filed three lawsuits against each other. There were also allegations of violence and attempted expulsion.

[51] [2] The purpose of the company was to use the property for profit and as an investment. *PC Tower Ctr., Inc.*, 1989 Del. Ch. LEXIS 72, 1989 WL 63901, at 5. Because the company was operating at a considerable loss and the prospect of future profits did not exist, the court found that it was not reasonably practicable for the company to continue. Id. at 6.

One approach, taken by several courts, is to examine the circumstances in light of the company's purpose and then determine if it is reasonably practicable to continue the business. Under this test, the Virginia Supreme Court reversed a lower court's order dissolving a limited liability company. *Dunbar Group, LLC*, 593 SE2d at 219. According to the *Dunbar* court, only when a business cannot continue "in accord with its articles of incorporation and any operating agreement" can dissolution be ordered. Despite one member of a two-member company being expelled, the court held that the company could continue, and, therefore, dissolution was not warranted.[52] *Dunbar Group, LLC*, 593 SE2d at 218. A court order had been entered finding that one member commingled the company's funds. Nevertheless, the court concluded that it was reasonably practicable for the company to continue and denied dissolution.

The Louisiana Court of Appeals similarly examined a company's operating agreement to determine if it was reasonably practicable for the business to continue. *Weinmann v. Duhon*, 818 So2d 206, 208–09 (LaCtApp 2002). The members of the company had no desire to continue their business relationship and began making side agreements that, in the court's view, made continued operation of the company not reasonably practicable.

A Massachusetts Superior Court required that "specific provisions of the partnership agreement" be shown to establish "impracticability to carry on the business in conformity with the partnership agreement."[53] *Houser v. River Loft Assocs. Ltd. P'ship*, 1999 Mass. Super. LEXIS 64, 1999 WL 33594570, 2 (MassSupCt) (unpublished) (dissolution of a partnership).[54] In *Houser*, the plaintiff alleged that the members engaged in self dealing. The court, nonetheless, found that the company operated for its stated purpose and denied dissolution.

Finally, in *Spires v. Casterline*, a New York court engaged in a detailed analysis of the company's articles of organization and operating agreement. 4 Misc. 3d 428, 778 NYS2d 259, 263 (NY Sup Ct 2004). It found no basis to dissolve the company based on the terms of the articles of organization. However, because the operating agreement mandated that dissolution occur before withdrawal of a member, and a member withdrew pre-dissolution, the court ordered that the company be judicially dissolved.

Another consideration, expressed by two courts, is the financial state of the company. In *Klein v. 599 Eleventh Ave. Co. LLC* the court dismissed a petition for judicial dissolution because the plaintiff "failed to articulate facts establishing why it was not reasonably practicable for [the company] to continue to carry on its business [and] failed to demonstrate that [the company] is failing financially[.]"

---

52 [3] One member asserted that "'serious differences of opinion as to company management have arisen between the members and managers' . . . and that the company was 'deadlocked' in its ability to conduct its business affairs. . . . "

53 [4] The plaintiff sought dissolution asserting "that the general partners have carried out a systematic course of self-dealing in which they refuse to liquidate the partnership in accordance with its investment objectives." *Houser*, 1999 Mass. Super. LEXIS 64, 1999 WL 33594570, at 2. The court held that the partnership was meeting its stated purpose, and therefore, denied dissolution.

54 [5] A Massachusetts Superior Court ordered dissolution of an LLC when the company was "not able to function in the manner intended and there is a clear and total deadlock between the sole two manager members thereof." *Rapoza v. Talamo*, 2006 Mass. Super. LEXIS 531, 2006 WL 3292632, 4 (MassSuperCt) (unpublished). The company in *Rapoza*, however, did not have an operating agreement and the members had ceased attempting to operate their businesses. *Id.*

2006 N.Y. Misc. LEXIS 3937, 14 Misc. 3d 1211A, 836 N.Y.S.2d 486, 2006 WL 3849059, 4 (NY Sup Ct) (unpublished). Similarly, a Delaware court declined to order dissolution because the company was serving its stated purpose from the operating agreement and producing returns for its investors. *Cincinnati Bell Cellular Sys. Co. v. Ameritech Mobile Phone Serv. of Cincinnati, Inc.*, 1996 Del. Ch. LEXIS 116, 1996 WL 506906 (Del Ch Ct) (unpublished) (regarding a partnership).

Two courts have held that a strict standard applies to judicial dissolutions. In *Dunbar Group, LLC*, the Virginia Supreme Court ruled that a strict standard reflects "legislative deference to the parties' contractual agreement to form and operate a limited liability company." 593 SE2d at 219. Also holding to an exacting standard, the court in *Horning* noted that this strictness might leave some members at the mercy of other members, but a company cannot be dissolved as long as it is thriving.

Yet another approach to interpreting the statutory language is to analogize dissolution of a limited liability company to dissolution of a corporation or partnership. One such instance occurred in *Haley v. Talcott*, 864 A2d 86, 94 (Del 2004). The court used its corporate dissolution law and required three prerequisites to judicial dissolution of a limited liability company. According to the *Haley* court, if (1) the company had "two 50% stockholders," who (2) "engaged in a joint venture," and (3) were "unable to agree upon whether to discontinue the business or how to dispose of its assets," judicial dissolution was warranted.[55] *Haley*, 864 A2d at 94–95. Although "the LLC can and does continue to function for its intended purpose and in conformity with the agreement," the court held that "this operation is purely a residual, inertial status quo that just happens to exclusively benefit one of the 50% members. . . . " Id. at 96. The parties could not function together and could not decide what to do with the LLC's assets or take any important actions that required a majority vote. Dissolution was further warranted because without relief the dissociated member would still be personally liable on the company's mortgage.

Also in Delaware, a chancery court distinguished *Haley* and instead compared the statutory language to that of a limited partnership dissolution. *In re Silver Leaf*, 2005 Del. Ch. LEXIS 119, 2005 WL 2045641, 10 (Del Ch Ct) (unpublished). The court ordered dissolution, finding that the sole asset of the company no longer existed, and therefore, continued operation of the company was not reasonably practicable. The court also took into account that the members were deadlocked and the operating agreement provided no means to end the deadlock. 2005 Del. Ch. LEXIS 119 [WL] at 11.

Another court, in dicta, noted that dissolution might be warranted when " 'it clearly appears that the business for which the partnership was formed is impracticable, or cannot be carried on except at a loss,' " and "where 'all confidence between the parties has been destroyed so that they cannot proceed together in prosecuting the business for which it was formed.' "[56] *Percontino v. Camporeala*, 2005 WL 730234, 3 (NJSupCt) (unpublished).

---

[55] [6] The court ordered judicial dissolution. . . .

[56] [7] Dissolution was not warranted in this case because the court ordered an alternative form of relief. Percontino, 2005 WL 730234, at 4.

Here, the operating agreement for the Kirksey Family Ranch, LLC states:

> The purpose for which this organization is created is to engage in a general livestock and ranching business; to feed, range, graze, herd, control, brand, care for, purchase, market and sell livestock of every kind, both on its own account and as an agent for other persons, organizations or corporations; to buy, lease, cultivate, manage, operate and sell ranch properties and products therefrom both on its own account and as an agent for other persons, organizations or corporations; and, take, buy, exchange, lease or manage and develop such property and interests in any manner that may be necessary, useful or advantageous for the purposes of this organization.

(Emphasis added). From this language, it is clear that the intended business was a "livestock and ranching" operation.

There is no dispute that the ranching and livestock operation, as a business, can continue despite the sisters' dissension. However, the question is whether it is reasonably practicable for the company to continue in accordance with the operating agreement. The sole asset of the company is the Kirksey land. This land is currently leased to only two sisters. Kirksey and Ruby contend that the lease is no longer beneficial to the company. The rental rate was set when the land was worth considerably less, and the company, no matter the extent of profits, is required to pay the taxes and insurance. Grohmann and Randall, however, assert that Kirksey and Ruby were aware of the nominal profit margin when the company was formed and that nothing has changed to make it impracticable for the company to continue.

The sisters created their company with the understanding that they would have relatively equal say in its overall management and operation. Although each sister has an equal vote, there no longer exists equality in the decision making. Grohmann and Randell have all the power with no reason to change the terms of a lease extremely favorable to them. Leaving two sisters, half the owners, with all the power in the operation of the company cannot be a reasonable and practicable operation of a business. Moreover, their deadlock certainly impedes the continued function of the business in conformity with its operating agreement. No procedure exists in the company's documentation to break a tie vote and protect the company in the event of changed conditions. As long as the company remains in control of, and favorable only to, half its members, it cannot be said to be reasonably practicable for it to continue in accord with its operating agreement.

Another statutory standard Kirksey and Ruby rely on is found in SDCL 47-34A-801(a)(4)(i): "[t]he economic purpose of the company is likely to be unreasonably frustrated." What it means for the economic purpose of a company to be unreasonably frustrated has not been clearly delineated. There are few cases on the subject. Two decisions have ordered judicial dissolution when extreme dissension between the members was present. *Navarro v. Perron*, 122 Cal. App. 4th 797, 19 Cal.Rptr. 3d 198, 200–01 (CalCtApp 2004) (dissolution of a partnership); *Pankratz Farms, Inc. v. Pankratz*, 322 Mont. 133, 2004 MT 180, 95 P3d 671 (Mont 2004) (dissolution of a partnership). However, those cases had other factors that led the court to dissolve the companies. *Navarro*, 19 Cal.Rptr. 3d at 200–01 (in addition to the dissension the parties filed multiple lawsuits and restraining orders); *Pankratz*, 95 P3d at 680–81 (the business of the partnership was effectively transferred).

Here, we have two members of an LLC that hold all the power, with the other two having no power to influence the company's direction. We recognize that forced dissolution is a drastic remedy and may produce financial repercussions for the sisters, but how can one reasonably conclude that the economic purpose of this company is not reasonably frustrated? The members cannot communicate regarding the LLC except through legal counsel. The company remains static, serving the interests of only half its owners. They neither trust nor cooperate with each other. The sisters formed their company contemplating equal ownership and management, yet only an impenetrable deadlock prevails.

We conclude that the economic purpose of the Kirksey Family Ranch, LLC is being unreasonably frustrated, and it is not reasonably practicable to carry on the LLC's business in conformity with its articles of organization and operating agreement. The circuit court erred when it granted Grohmann and Randell summary judgment. We remand for an order of judicial dissolution and winding up of the company's business under SDCL 47-34A-806.

Reversed and remanded.

NOTES AND QUESTIONS

1.   Once again we see that the failure of the parties to negotiate a buy-sell agreement at the time of formation of the business entity led to an expensive and time consuming court battle regarding the appropriate way to deal with a deadlock between the four owners. This decision holds that grounds exist for the court to order a dissolution of the LLC when a deadlock has occurred. Will the two sisters who opposed dissolution be able to buy out the two sisters who initiated the dissolution proceeding? The answer is maybe. South Dakota does not follow the 1996 segments of the ULLCA regarding the buy out of dissociated members, nor is there a statutory buyout right triggered by the initiation of a judicial dissolution proceeding. The two sisters who want to continue to operate the LLC will have to bargain privately to buy out their other two sisters.

2.   The two sisters seeking dissolution, Kirksey and Ruby, hired a real estate agent who estimated that the sole asset of the LLC (the land) was worth in excess of $3.2 million. The two sisters opposing dissolution, Grohmann and Randell, were leasing the land from the LLC for their private ranching and subleasing purposes at the astonishingly low rate of $14,263.20, while the LLC, as the landlord, was responsible for all the real estate taxes and insurance (leaving the LLC with far less in net profit). If, on the other hand, the land was sold and the money invested at a modest interest rate of 5%, the annual return would be $160,000 per year! The four sisters were deadlocked for obvious reasons. Grohmann and Randell received a windfall benefit of using valuable land for their own purposes for only $14,263.20 per year, while Kirksey and Ruby were foregoing a possible return of 50% of $160,000 and, perhaps, far more if the money from a sale of the land was invested in higher yield investments. Was the court correct in concluding that: (i) the economic purpose of the LLC was being unreasonably frustrated; and (ii) it was not reasonably practicable to carry on the LLC's business in conformity with its articles of organization and operating agreement?

3.   In the absence of a negotiated buyout, what will the final outcome be in this case? Kirksey and Ruby were seeking to terminate the lease agreement, dissolve the LLC, and partition the land. If the four sisters were acting rationally, would

they all agree to use real estate agents to sell the land and split the proceeds rather than continue with the *judicial* dissolution?

4.   The South Dakota court mentions the Delaware case of *Haley v. Talcott*.[57] In *Haley*, there were two members of the LLC, which owned land leased to one of the owners for operation of a successful restaurant. The lease rental of $6,000 was far below fair market rental value. The owner of the restaurant business, Talcott, then employed the other LLC member, Haley, to manage the restaurant operations. Rather than granting a 50% ownership interest in the business to Haley, the parties structured a complicated set of employment and related agreements that essentially resulted in splitting the profits of the restaurant 50/50. Therefore, they both enjoyed the benefit of the low rent and the profits from the successful restaurant. In a series of deteriorating events between Talcott and Haley, Talcott fired Haley and terminated Haley's interest in profits from the restaurant, leaving Haley with only a 50% interest in the LLC which was receiving only $6,000 per month under the lease arrangement with Talcott. The lease to the restaurant expired. Haley wanted to renegotiate or terminate the lease and relet the LLC's land at its true market value — a move that Talcott opposed. The LLC remained deadlocked and Talcott continued to operate the restaurant and pay only $6,000 per month to the LLC. As the court stated, "Haley and Talcott have suffered, to put it mildly, a falling out." Haley moved for a judicial dissolution under the applicable grounds stated in the Delaware limited liability company act:[58]

> On application by or for a member or manager the Court of Chancery may decree dissolution of a limited liability company whenever it is not reasonably practicable to carry on the business in conformity with a limited liability company agreement.

Talcott opposed the dissolution on the basis that the parties had included an "exit" provision in the LLC's operating agreement that allowed Haley to sell his interest to Talcott, which meant that it was "reasonably practicable" to continue the LLC business in conformity with the operating agreement:

> Talcott stresses that the LLC Agreement provides an alternative exit mechanism that allows the LLC to continue to exist, and argues that Haley should therefore be relegated to this provision if he is unhappy with the stalemate. In other words, Talcott argues that it is reasonably practicable for the LLC to continue to carry on business in conformity with its LLC Agreement because the exit mechanism creates a fair alternative that permits Haley to get out, receiving the fair market value of his share of the property as determined in accordance with procedures in the LLC Agreement, while allowing the LLC to continue. Critically, the exit provision would allow Talcott to buy Haley out with no need for the LLC's asset (i.e., the land) to be sold on the open market. The LLC could continue to exist and own the land (with its favorable mortgage arrangement) and Talcott, as owner of both entities, could continue to offer the [restaurant] its favorable rent.[59]

---

[57]   864 A.2d 86 (Del. Ch. 2004). For some further thoughts on these issues, see Note: *Delaware's Answer to Management Deadlock in the Limited Liability Company: Judicial Dissolution*, 32 Iowa J. Corp. L. 641 (2007).

[58]   6 Del. C. § 18-802

[59]   864 A.2d at 88.

The court noted that such an exit strategy was an important factor in determining whether *judicial* dissolution was appropriate. However, the exit provisions in the operating agreement had a significant flaw. Both Haley and Talcott had personally guaranteed a $720,000 mortgage. Even if Talcott bought out Haley under the terms of the operating agreement, Haley would remain liable for 50% of the mortgage. This was an exit strategy that no rational member would elect unless the purchase price of that member's interest included an additional $360,000 to cover the possible liability on the mortgage. Therefore, the court held, the exit strategy was not really available and the court ordered the LLC dissolved. Note the following excerpts from the court's opinion:

> Here, the key facts about the parties' ability to work together are not rationally disputable. Therefore, my decision on the motion largely turns on two legal issues: 1) if the doctrine of corporate deadlock is an appropriate analogy for the analysis of a § 18-802 claim on these facts; and 2) if so, and if action to break the stalemate is necessary to permit the LLC to function, whether, because of the contract-law foundations of the Delaware LLC Act, Haley should be relegated to the contractual exit mechanism provided in the LLC Agreement.

> * * * [I]f the LLC were a corporation, there would be no question that Haley's request to dissolve the entity would be granted. But this case regards an LLC, not a corporation, and more importantly, an LLC with a detailed exit provision. That distinguishing factor must and is considered next. * * *

> The Delaware LLC Act is grounded on principles of freedom of contract. For that reason, the presence of a reasonable exit mechanism bears on the propriety of ordering dissolution under 6 Del. C. § 18-802. When the agreement itself provides a fair opportunity for the dissenting member who disfavors the inertial status quo to exit and receive the fair market value of her interest, it is at least arguable that the limited liability company may still proceed to operate practicably under its contractual charter because the charter itself provides an equitable way to break the impasse.

> * * * [F]orcing Haley to exercise the contractual exit mechanism would not permit the LLC to proceed in a practicable way that accords with the LLC Agreement, but would instead permit Talcott to penalize Haley without express contractual authorization.

> Why? Because the parties agree that exit mechanism in the LLC Agreement would not relieve Haley of his obligation under the personal guaranty that he signed to secure the mortgage . . . Haley would still be left holding the bag on the guaranty. It is therefore not equitable to force Haley to use the exit mechanism in this circumstance. While the exit mechanism may be workable in a friendly departure when both parties cooperate to reach an adequate alternative agreement with the bank, the bank cannot be compelled to accept the removal of Haley as a personal guarantor. Thus, the exit mechanism fails as an adequate remedy for Haley because it does not equitably effect the separation of the parties. Rather, it would leave Haley with no upside potential, and no protection over the considerable downside risk that he would have to make good on any future

default by the LLC (over whose operations he would have no control) to its mortgage lender. * * *

For the reasons discussed above . . . it is not reasonably practicable for the LLC to continue to carry on business in conformity with the LLC Agreement. The parties shall confer and, within four weeks, submit a plan for the dissolution of the LLC. The plan shall include a procedure to sell the Property owned by the LLC within a commercially reasonable time frame. Either party may, of course, bid on the Property.[60]

In both cases, *Kirksey v. Grohmann* and *Haley v. Talcott*, the courts focused on the issue of whether or not continuation of the business of an LLC was practicable when the members were deadlocked and there was no fair and reasonable "exit" strategy that was contractually available to parties who were frustrated by the deadlock. It's interesting to note that in both cases there were 50% equity holders who were taking advantage of favorable deals with the LLC to advance their private business interests at the expense of the other 50% holders. Consider the following questions. In each case 50% of the members desire the liquidation of the LLC and 50% oppose the liquidation. Would the courts in *Kirksey v. Grohmann* and *Haley v. Talcott* have reached a different outcome and refused to compel a judicial dissolution?

a.   The leases of the LLC land were at fair market rental values to *non-members*?

b.   The LLC land was being leased to 50% of the members for their own personal businesses but the rent being charged was fair market rental value?

c.   Would your answer change in either or the above hypotheticals if land owned by the LLC was worth $5 million and was being leased for $100,000 per year (keep in mind that investing $5 million at a modest interest rate of 5% would yield $250,000 per year).

The 1996 ULLCA takes a substantially different approach to one ground for dissolution. Under the 1996 ULLCA (which is more widely adopted than the 2006 ULLCA), a dissociated member had a statutory right to be bought out by the remaining members or, if not bought out, that member could force a liquidation of the LLC. The applicable sections of the 1996 Act are set forth below:

§ 801.   Events Causing Dissolution and Winding up of Company's Business.

A limited liability company is dissolved, and its business must be wound up, upon the occurrence of any of the following events:

. . .

(4)   on application by a member or a dissociated member, upon entry of a judicial decree that:

. . .

(iv)   the company failed to purchase the petitioner's distributional interest as required by Section 701; . . .

---

[60] *Id.* at 93, 96, 97–98.

Section 801 imposes a default rule that the LLC *must* buy out any member who dissociates from the company if the remaining members desire the continuation of the business. Considering the many causes of dissociation,[61] the dissociation of one or more members during the lifetime of the LLC is going to be a common occurrence. Even a wrongful, at-will dissociation would initiate the buyout obligation, as you will see in ULLCA § 701 (1996) below.

While the mandatory statutory buyout right could not be waived in the operating agreement,[62] the *terms* of the buyout could be controlled in the operating agreement by incorporating contractual buy-sell provisions. Pay close attention to § 701(c) as you read the provisions of the 1996 ULLCA. The existence of the mandatory *statutory* buyout obligation upon dissociation of any member made the importance of a *contractual* buy-sell agreement essential to assure that the terms of the buyout were pre-determined by the buy-sell provisions in the operating agreement rather than based on the statutory default buyout rules of ULLCA § 701 (1996).

§ 701. Company Purchase of Distributional Interest.

(a)   A limited liability company shall purchase a distributional interest of a:

(1)   member of an at-will company for its fair value determined as of the date of the member's dissociation if the member's dissociation does not result in a dissolution and winding up of the company's business under Section 801; or

(2)   member of a term company for its fair value determined as of the date of the expiration of the specified term that existed on the date of the member's dissociation if the expiration of the specified term does not result in a dissolution and winding up of the company's business under Section 801.

———

Section 701(a) above grants a dissociated member the right to be bought out if the LLC is not dissolved. What is the difference between subsections (1) and (2)? Will the timing, and/or price, of the buyout be affected by whether the LLC is "at-will" or for a fixed term. Does the statutory right of the member to be bought out depend on whether the member dissociates wrongfully in contravention of the operating

———

[61] The 1996 ULLCA § 601 provides for many causes of dissociation, including the following: by the member's express will; by an event agreed to in the operating agreement; by the voluntary or involuntary transfer of all of a member's distributional interest; by the member's expulsion; if it is unlawful to carry on the company's business with the member; the dissolution of an entity-member or suspension of the entity's right to do business; the filing of a bankruptcy petition by or against a member; state law insolvency proceedings by a member such as an assignment for the benefit of creditors or the appointment of a trustee or receiver for all or substantially all of the member's property; an individual member's death; appointment of a guardian or general conservator for an individual member; or, a judicial determination that an individual member has otherwise become incapable of performing the member's duties under the operating agreement.

[62] § 103. Effect of Operating Agreement; Nonwaivable Provisions.

    . . .

(b) The operating agreement may not:

    . . .

(6) vary the requirement to wind up the limited liability company's business in a case specified in Section 801(3) or (4); . . .

agreement? Once you've answered these questions, read the following provisions, beginning with § 701(b) which deal with the procedures to be followed and valuation of the member's interest:

§ 701. Company Purchase of Distributional Interest.

. . .

(b) A limited liability company must deliver a purchase offer to the dissociated member whose distributional interest is entitled to be purchased not later than 30 days after the date determined under subsection (a). The purchase offer must be accompanied by:

(1) a statement of the company's assets and liabilities as of the date determined under subsection (a);

(2) the latest available balance sheet and income statement, if any; and

(3) an explanation of how the estimated amount of the payment was calculated.

(c) *If the price and other terms of a purchase of a distributional interest are fixed or are to be determined by the operating agreement, the price and terms so fixed or determined govern the purchase unless the purchaser defaults.* If a default occurs, the dissociated member is entitled to commence a proceeding to have the company dissolved under Section 801(4)(iv). [Emphasis added.]

(d) If an agreement to purchase the distributional interest is not made within 120 days after the date determined under subsection (a), the dissociated member, within another 120 days, may commence a proceeding against the limited liability company to enforce the purchase. The company at its expense shall notify in writing all of the remaining members, and any other person the court directs, of the commencement of the proceeding. The jurisdiction of the court in which the proceeding is commenced under this subsection is plenary and exclusive.

(e) The court shall determine the fair value of the distributional interest in accordance with the standards set forth in Section 702 together with the terms for the purchase. Upon making these determinations, the court shall order the limited liability company to purchase or cause the purchase of the interest.

(f) Damages for wrongful dissociation under Section 602(b), and all other amounts owing, whether or not currently due, from the dissociated member to a limited liability company, must be offset against the purchase price.

§ 702. Court Action to Determine Fair Value of Distributional Interest.

(a) In an action brought to determine the fair value of a distributional interest in a limited liability company, the court shall:

(1) determine the fair value of the interest, considering among other relevant evidence the going concern value of the company, any agreement among some or all of the members fixing the price or specifying a formula for determining value of distributional interests for any other purpose, the recommendations of any appraiser appointed by the court, and any legal constraints on the company's ability to purchase the interest;

(2) specify the terms of the purchase, including, if appropriate, terms for installment payments, subordination of the purchase obligation to the rights of the company's other creditors, security for a deferred purchase price, and a covenant not to compete or other restriction on a dissociated member; and

(3) require the dissociated member to deliver an assignment of the interest to the purchaser upon receipt of the purchase price or the first installment of the purchase price.

(b) After the dissociated member delivers the assignment, the dissociated member has no further claim against the company, its members, officers, or managers, if any, other than a claim to any unpaid balance of the purchase price and a claim under any agreement with the company or the remaining members that is not terminated by the court.

(c) If the purchase is not completed in accordance with the specified terms, the company is to be dissolved upon application under Section 801(b)(5)(iv). If a limited liability company is so dissolved, the dissociated member has the same rights and priorities in the company's assets as if the sale had not been ordered.

(d) If the court finds that a party to the proceeding acted arbitrarily, vexatiously, or not in good faith, it may award one or more other parties their reasonable expenses, including attorney's fees and the expenses of appraisers or other experts, incurred in the proceeding. The finding may be based on the company's failure to make an offer to pay or to comply with Section 701(b).

(e) Interest must be paid on the amount awarded from the date determined under Section 701(a) to the date of payment.

The above provisions are both similar to, and different from, the California Corporations Code provisions dealing with a statutory buyout in the case of *corporations* discussed earlier in this chapter. The primary distinction is that the obligation to buy out a shareholder in a corporate dissolution under California law arises only *after* a stockholder has initiated a dissolution proceeding based on some legitimate ground for dissolution rather than the simple voluntary or involuntary departure of the stockholder. Compare the 1996 ULLCA, where the mere voluntary or involuntary *dissociation* of a member is itself both a *grounds* for dissolution and the trigger for a mandatory buyout.

The provisions are similar in shifting the burden of valuation to the court if the parties can't agree on the value of the selling member's interest. The 1996 ULLCA and the California Corporations Code both use the phrase "fair value" rather than "fair market value," leaving the courts to develop case law as to exactly what this phrase "fair value" means.[63] Once again, we can see that the importance of drafting contractual buy-sell provisions is essential to the health and vitality of an LLC, particularly one in a state that has adopted the 1996 ULLCA or similar provisions granting a buyout right to a dissociated member.

One interesting distinction between the California Corporations Code and the 1996 ULLCA is that under § 702 there is no *obligation* to refer the valuation issue to independent appraisers. The court is granted independent authority to assess the

---

[63] Surprisingly, the California Corporations Code uses the phrase "fair *market* value" with regard to the buyout of an LLC membership interest. *See* Cal. Corp. Code § 17351.

"fair value" of the share of the dissociated member, although the court has the authority to use one or more appraisers if the court so decides.

3. Elimination of the Mandatory Buyout in the 2006 ULLCA

One of the major revisions in the 2006 ULLCA was the elimination of the mandatory buyout of a dissociated member. Why would the National Conference of Commissioners on Uniform State Laws eliminate the obligation to buyout dissociated members? A short statement in the Summary accompanying the 2006 ULLCA includes a truncated explanation:

> 9. In the 1996 Act dissociation (resigning from membership) of a member by express will triggers an obligation to buy the interest of that member in an at-will or term company. Failure to buy may subject the company to a judicial dissolution and winding up of the business. The 2006 Act provides no obligation to buy out a dissociating member, nor a ground based upon failure of a buyout for judicial dissolution. The company has greater stability under the 2006 Act, notwithstanding any dissociation of a member.

Imposing an obligation to buy out a dissociated member, which was the case under the 1996 ULLCA, truly creates potential instability in the affairs of an LLC. Especially in "at-will" LLCs, the business could be unintentionally forced into dissolution at any time by the unanticipated dissociation of a member. This is a problem that requires careful drafting of buy-sell provisions in the operating agreement to disable or delay the impact of the mandatory statutory buyout. Knowledgeable attorneys could circumvent the buyout obligation by drafting appropriate buy-sell provisions to comply with the edict in the 1996 ULLCA § 701(c) that: "(c) If the price and other terms of a purchase of a distributional interest are fixed or are to be determined by the operating agreement, the price and terms so fixed or determined govern the purchase unless the purchaser defaults." This seems to allow attorneys the freedom to draft all of the terms of the mandatory buyout, including a price of $0 in the case of certain causes of dissociation, or other terms that disembowel the mandate that any and all dissociated members *must* be bought out.

In view of the inherent flexibility of LLCs, and the ability of knowledgeable drafters to disable a mandatory buyout, it makes sense to simply leave the consequences of a dissociation to the terms of the operating agreement, rather than forcing a dissolution in the event of a dissociation — unless the operating agreement requires a buyout. Under the 2006 ULLCA, the dissociated member is still entitled to participate in *distributions* and is economically unharmed by the dissociation:

§ 603. Effect of Person's Dissociation as Member

(a) When a person is dissociated as a member of a limited liability company: (1) the person's right to participate as a member in the management and conduct of the company's activities terminates; (2) if the company is member-managed, the person's fiduciary duties as a member end with regard to matters arising and events occurring after the person's dissociation; and (3) subject to Section 504 and

[Article] 10, any transferable interest owned by the person immediately before dissociation in the person's capacity as a member is owned by the person solely as a transferee.

§ 502.   Transfer of Transferable Interest

. . .

(b)   A transferee has the right to receive, in accordance with the transfer, distributions to which the transferor would otherwise be entitled.

(c)   In a dissolution and winding up of a limited liability company, a transferee is entitled to an account of the company's transactions only from the date of dissolution.

The consequences of a dissociation *should* be governed by the operating agreement. The 2006 ULLCA leaves the parties free to decide which types of dissociations will lead to a buyout and which will not. For instance, the death of a member may lead to an obligation to buyout the deceased member's interest, while an at-will dissociation will give the remaining members an option, but not an obligation, to buyout the departing members. The freedom of contract regarding buyouts idealized in the 2006 ULLCA revisions makes far more sense then the provisions of the 1996 ULLCA.

4.   Non-ULLCA Buyout Rights

We have seen that there is a major difference between the 1996 and 2006 ULLCA with regard to the obligation of members to buyout the interest of a dissociated member. The 2006 ULLCA leaves the matter entirely to the buy-sell provisions, if any, in the operating agreement, while the 1996 ULLCA imposes a statutory obligation. There is a third alternative available in some states, such as California, which follow the same procedure for LLC's that are followed for corporations. The statutory *grounds* for dissolution do *not* include the mere dissociation of a member. However, in *judicial* dissolutions, members who desire to continue the business of the LLC are given the statutory right to buyout the members who initiated the judicial dissolution proceeding. Read the following provisions and compare them to the statutory buyout right in the case of California corporate dissolutions, discussed earlier in this chapter.

CALIFORNIA CORPORATIONS CODE

§ 17350.   Occurrence of dissolution upon specified event

A limited liability company shall be dissolved and its affairs shall be wound up upon the happening of the first to occur of the following:

(a)   At the time specified in the articles of organization, if any, or upon the happening of the events, if any, specified in the articles of organization or a written operating agreement.

(b)   By the vote of a majority in interest of the members, or a greater percentage of the voting interests of members as may be specified in the articles of organization or a written operating agreement.

(c)   Entry of a decree of judicial dissolution pursuant to Section § 17351.

The above provisions focus on the grounds for *non*-judicial, voluntary dissolution of an LLC. The following section focuses on judicially supervised dissolutions. Subsection (a) lays out the grounds for initiating a judicial dissolution, while subsection (b) sets for the statutory buyout rights of non-initiating members. You will notice that the grounds are similar to the grounds for involuntary dissolutions of corporations under California law, and that the statutory buyout right is highly analogous to the corporate buyout right. It is interesting to note with regard to the valuation question that, unlike the corporate buyout provisions which use the phrase "fair value," the LLC provisions use the phrase "fair market value." Will this make a difference in the value ascertained by appraisers?

§ 17351.   Decree of dissolution upon specified event; Avoidance of dissolution

(a)   Pursuant to an action filed by any manager or by any member or members, a court of competent jurisdiction may decree the dissolution of a limited liability company whenever any of the following occurs:

(1)   It is not reasonably practicable to carry on the business in conformity with the articles of organization or operating agreement.

(2)   Dissolution is reasonably necessary for the protection of the rights or interests of the complaining members.

(3)   The business of the limited liability company has been abandoned.

(4)   The management of the limited liability company is deadlocked or subject to internal dissention.

(5)   Those in control of the company have been guilty of, or have knowingly countenanced persistent and pervasive fraud, mismanagement, or abuse of authority.

(b)(1)   In any suit for judicial dissolution, the other members may avoid the dissolution of the limited liability company by purchasing for cash the membership interests owned by the members so initiating the proceeding (the "moving parties") at their fair market value. In fixing the value, the amount of any damages resulting if the initiation of the dissolution is a breach by any moving party or parties of an agreement with the purchasing party or parties, including, without limitation, the operating agreement, may be deducted from the amount payable to the moving party or parties; provided, that no member who sues for dissolution on the grounds set forth in paragraph (3), (4), or (5) of subdivision (a) shall be liable for damages for breach of contract in bringing that action.

(2)   If the purchasing parties (A) elect to purchase the membership interests owned by the moving parties, (B) are unable to agree with the moving parties upon the fair market value of the membership interests, and (C) give bond with sufficient security to pay the estimated reasonable expenses, including attorneys' fees, of the moving parties if the expenses are recoverable under paragraph (3), the court, upon application of the purchasing parties, either in the pending action or in a proceeding initiated in the superior court of the proper county by the

purchasing parties, shall stay the winding up and dissolution proceeding and shall proceed to ascertain and fix the fair market value of the membership interests owned by the moving parties.

(3)   The court shall appoint three disinterested appraisers to appraise the fair market value of the membership interests owned by the moving parties, and shall make an order referring the matter to the appraisers so appointed for the purpose of ascertaining that value. The order shall prescribe the time and manner of producing evidence, if evidence is required. The award of the appraisers or a majority of them, when confirmed by the court, shall be final and conclusive upon all parties . . .

(5)   For the purposes of this section, the valuation date shall be the date upon which the action for judicial dissolution was commenced. However, the court may, upon the hearing of a motion by any party, and for good cause shown, designate some other date as the valuation date.

These provisions are sufficiently similar to the corporate buyout provisions in the California Code to allow the courts to rely on corporations cases to interpret § 17531.[64] Consequently, all of the issues discussed earlier in this chapter regarding the statutory buyout right as it applies to corporations arise once again with regard to the statutory buyout rights granted to LLC members in § 17351.

5.   Summary — Dissolution of LLCs

As a liability-insulating entity, the foremost objective in LLC dissolutions is to assure that creditors of the entity are paid before distribution of assets to members. The right of creditors to priority extends to recovery of assets from members *after* distribution, with regard to unknown or contingent claims that are commenced within the statutory time limits but only to the extent of actual distributions to members.

Many operating agreements will carefully lay out the conditions under which dissolution will occur and how the dissolution is to be conducted. It's also possible that during the lifetime of an LLC, all of the members (or less than all if provided for in the operating agreement) may vote to dissolve the company. So long as the rights of creditors are respected, there is considerable freedom to structure the dissolution in a manner that maximizes the sale or liquidation of the business and enhances the distributions to members. When the dissolution is a voluntary one agreed to by the members, or conducted in accordance with the operating agreement, it is in the interests of all members to cooperate in the liquidation and winding up of the affairs of the LLC so as to yield the greatest possible distribution to members.

There may also be times where *judicial* intervention is warranted notwithstanding the objections of some members, based upon the grounds set forth in the LLC statutes. Such grounds often include: (i) the conduct of all or substantially all of the company's activities is unlawful; (ii) it is not reasonably practicable to carry on the company's activities in conformity with the certificate of organization and the operating agreement; (iii) the managers or members in

---

[64] *See Dickson v. Rehmke, supra.*

control of the company are acting in a manner that is illegal or fraudulent; or (iv) the managers or members in control are acting in a manner that is oppressive and directly harmful to the member(s) seeking dissolution. With the exception of grounds based upon illegality of the LLC's activities, courts may be reluctant to exercise the power to compel dissolution of an LLC unless there is no fair and reasonable "exit" strategy for the disgruntled members who initiate the judicial dissolution proceeding.

D. GENERAL PARTNERSHIP DISSOLUTIONS

How is the dissolution of a general partnership different from the dissolution of a corporation or LLC? Even though general partnerships lack the insulating quality of limited liability for partners, there are surprising similarities. Under the entity theory of partnerships that pervades the Revised Uniform Partnership Act, the first and dominant similarity is the requirement that creditors be paid before any distributions to partners in their capacity as equity holders. Only after creditors have been fully satisfied, or adequate provisions made for payment to them, can distributions be made to partners.

Another similarity is the importance of cooperation among the partners if the partnership has a positive net worth. The partners can maximize the value received for assets, and reduce administrative costs, by cooperating in a dissolution and winding up, thereby increasing the *pro rata* distribution they will receive.

However, unlike limited-liability entities, there is a *strong* incentive to cooperate in dissolution even when the partnership has a *negative* net worth. This incentive arises from the fact that the partners remain liable to creditors notwithstanding the dissolution of the partnership. To the extent that the dissolution is handled inefficiently, there will be an increase in the amount of unsatisfied creditors claims that partners must pay. For failing, negative-net-worth partnerships, federal bankruptcy liquidation will often be far more appealing than state law dissolution. This is because of procedures and powers that enable the bankruptcy trustee to conduct a liquidation more efficiently than under state law and enable a greater distribution to creditors, thereby diminishing the obligations of the partners for any remaining debts of the partnership.[65]

We will take a look at the widely adopted Revised Uniform Partnership Act of 1997[66] ("RUPA") to study how general partnerships are dissolved under state law and the rights and obligations of general partners in the dissolution process.

---

[65] See the discussion of federal bankruptcy law later in this chapter.

[66] RUPA was adopted in 1994. The act was amended in 1997 to provide limited liability for partners in a limited liability partnership. RUPA has been adopted in substantially similar form in the following 39 jurisdictions: Alabama, Alaska, Arizona, Arkansas, California, Connecticut, Colorado, Delaware, District of Columbia, Florida, Hawaii, Idaho, Illinois, Iowa, Kansas, Kentucky, Maine, Maryland, Minnesota, Mississippi, Montana, Nebraska, Nevada, New Jersey, New Mexico, North Dakota, Ohio, Oklahoma, Oregon, Puerto Rico, South Dakota, Tennessee, Texas, U.S. Virgin Islands, Vermont, Virginia, Washington, West Virginia, Wyoming.

1.   The Revised Uniform Partnership Act

RUPA introduced significant changes to the former Uniform Partnership Act of 1914 ("UPA") that are important for understanding how dissolutions are handled under RUPA. Under UPA there was a long standing confusion over whether or not a general partnership should be considered an aggregation of individuals, or as an entity with legal rights independent of its general partners. Could the partnership sue or be sued in its own name? Does a partner's departure from the partnership dissolve the partnership? Does each partner have an interest as a co-owner in the property of the partnership, or can the partnership own property independently? Do partners have the capacity to do business for the partnership?

Under the dual-personality approach of the UPA, the answer was "yes" — sometimes the partnership was viewed as a separate legal entity and sometimes it was viewed as merely an aggregation of the general partners.

This dual-personality approach had a significant impact on the UPA's approach to dissolution. *Any* departure of an owner for any reason, rightful or wrongful (at will, death, withdrawal, retirement, expulsion, bankruptcy, etc.), was considered to dissolve the partnership, leading to the automatic winding up of the partnership. While the non-departing owners might have a contractual or statutory right to terminate the dissolution and resurrect the partnership under some circumstances, the continuing business was technically a new partnership. Under the UPA, there was an inherent lack of stability in the continuity of life of a partnership. This instability, caused by the concept that "departure equals dissolution," was disruptive and problematic.

RUPA adopted an *entity* theory of partnerships, eliminating the long-standing concerns about whether the partnership was an entity or aggregation of partners. This newly conceived notion was paired with the reasonable idea that the mere departure of a partner does not necessarily cause a dissolution of the *entity*. Instead, RUPA introduced the concept of "dissociation" to describe the departure of a partner, regardless of whether that departure is voluntary, involuntary, rightful or wrongful. The entity theory of partnership provides a conceptual basis for continuing the partnership despite a partner's departure from the entity. Under RUPA, the *entity* continues to exist, and the remaining partners can *continue* the partnership business, although the dissociated partner may have some rights that the continuing partners may be obligated to honor. Only under certain circumstances does dissociation lead to dissolution of the partnership entity. A cryptic explanation of the changes is set forth in the Summary accompanying the 1994 version of RUPA:

> Automatic dissolution of the partnership after dissociation of a partner does not take place under [RUPA]. In a partnership at will only a partner who dissociates with notice of "express will" to dissolve causes the dissolution of the partnership. Thus, if a partner is simply bought out, there is not automatic dissolution.
>
> In a partnership for a term or for a particular purpose, dissolution and winding up are required unless a majority in interest of the remaining partners agree to continue the partnership within 90 days after a partner's triggering dissociation before the expected expiration of the term of the partnership. Again, a dissociation that triggers a buy out of the dissociating partner's interest does not imperil the partnership with dissolution.

Of the changes that [RUPA] makes over the 1914 Act, these rules may be the most significant. The ordinary dissociation of a partner does not mean the dissolution of the entity. It takes something more under [RUPA].

Dissociation normally entitles the partner to have his or her interest purchased by the partnership, and terminates his or her authority to act for the partnership and to participate with the partners in running the business. Otherwise the entity continues to do business without the dissociating partner. No other characteristic of a partnership under [RUPA] better illustrates the adoption of entity theory.

We can generally state the dissociation/dissolution rules under RUPA as follows:

— <u>At will partnerships</u>: A partnership may buy out the interest of a partner who leaves an at-will partnership *without dissolving the partnership*.
— <u>Partnerships for a particular purpose or for a particular term</u>: Term partnerships or partnerships for a particular purpose will not dissolve despite the departure of a partner, if least one-half of the partners choose to continue the partnership.
— <u>Dissociations that lead to dissolution</u>: When a partner's dissociation causes a dissolution, partners may *subsequently* vote (following the dissolution) to continue the partnership notwithstanding the dissolution.

Below we take a closer look at the causes and impact of dissociation, the triggers and procedures for dissolution, and the statutory buyout rights of partners under RUPA.

2. Dissociation

A good starting point for the discussion of dissociation is the edict of RUPA § 602(a) that: "A partner has the power to dissociate at any time, rightfully or wrongfully, by express will pursuant to Section 601(1)." Although many of the rules relating to dissociation and dissolution can be varied by the partnership agreement,[67] RUPA § 602(a) is *not* one of those rules.[68] The rule that any partner can dissociate at any time, rightfully or wrongfully, is a core concept of modern partnership law. Partnerships are a *voluntary* association of partners. Although the entity may continue under the revised rules of RUPA and there may be adverse economic consequences for a partner who wrongfully dissociates, the elemental power to dissociate from the partnership is preserved in RUPA.

The events causing a dissociation under RUPA are familiar ones that we discussed at length in Chapter 8. It is best to simply review § 601 of RUPA (following this paragraph), which lays out the usual grounds for dissociation. Keep

---

[67] RUPA § 103(a) states: "(a) Except as otherwise provided in subsection (b), relations among the partners and between the partners and the partnership are governed by the partnership agreement. To the extent the partnership agreement does not otherwise provide, this [Act] governs relations among the partners and between the partners and the partnership."

[68] RUPA § 103(b) states:

(b) The partnership agreement may not: * * * (6) vary the power to dissociate as a partner under Section 602(a), except to require the notice under Section 601(1) to be in writing; (6) vary the power to dissociate as a partner under Section 602(a), except to require the notice under Section 601(1) to be in writing; (7) vary the right of a court to expel a partner in the events specified in Section 601(5); (8) vary the requirement to wind up the partnership business in cases specified in Section 801(4), (5), or (6); . . .

in mind the list of dissociation triggers in RUPA § 601 are subject to modification by the partnership agreement under § 103(a)–(b) of RUPA, with the exception of dissociation by express will under § 601(1) and judicial expulsion under § 601(5).

§ 601. Events Causing Partner's Dissociation.

A partner is dissociated from a partnership upon the occurrence of any of the following events:

(1)   the partnership's having notice of the partner's express will to withdraw as a partner or on a later date specified by the partner;[69]

(2)   an event agreed to in the partnership agreement as causing the partner's dissociation;

(3)   the partner's expulsion pursuant to the partnership agreement;

(4)   the partner's expulsion by the unanimous vote of the other partners if:

(i)   it is unlawful to carry on the partnership business with that partner;

(ii)   there has been a transfer of all or substantially all of that partner's transferable interest in the partnership, other than a transfer for security purposes, or a court order charging the partner's interest, which has not been foreclosed;

(iii)   within 90 days after the partnership notifies a corporate partner that it will be expelled because it has filed a certificate of dissolution or the equivalent, its charter has been revoked, or its right to conduct business has been suspended by the jurisdiction of its incorporation, there is no revocation of the certificate of dissolution or no reinstatement of its charter or its right to conduct business; or

(iv)   a partnership that is a partner has been dissolved and its business is being wound up;

(5)   on application by the partnership or another partner, the partner's expulsion by judicial determination because:[70]

(i)   the partner engaged in wrongful conduct that adversely and materially affected the partnership business;

(ii)   the partner willfully or persistently committed a material breach of the partnership agreement or of a duty owed to the partnership or the other partners under Section 404; or

(iii)   the partner engaged in conduct relating to the partnership business which makes it not reasonably practicable to carry on the business in partnership with the partner;

(6)   the partner's:

(i)   becoming a debtor in bankruptcy;

(ii)   executing an assignment for the benefit of creditors;

---

[69] [The right of a partner to withdraw by express will under this subsection cannot be altered by agreement, except to require the notice under § 601(1) to be in writing. *See* RUPA §§ 103(b)(6), 602(a).—Eds.]

[70] The right of a court to expel a partner under this subsection cannot be altered by agreement. *See* RUPA § 103(b)(7).

(iii)   seeking, consenting to, or acquiescing in the appointment of a trustee, receiver, or liquidator of that partner or of all or substantially all of that partner's property . . .

(7)   in the case of a partner who is an individual:

(i)   the partner's death;

(ii)   the appointment of a guardian or general conservator for the partner; or

(iii)   a judicial determination that the partner has otherwise become incapable of performing the partner's duties under the partnership agreement;

. . .

(10)   termination of a partner who is [a business entity]

The important question that arises under RUPA is what *happens* following a partner's dissociation? Will the dissociation lead to dissolution? If not, what are the rights and obligations of the parties.

To start to answer these questions we note that RUPA retains the concept that a partner's exit from the partnership may be "rightful" or "wrongful." Whether the dissociation is rightful or wrongful is an independent concept from the *power* to dissociate. For instance, a partner can never be denied the power to dissociate at will but if that dissociation is in contravention of the partnership agreement, it will be wrongful, leading to: (i) adverse economic consequences for the dissociating partner; and (ii) consequences with regard to dissolution of the partnership and the statutory buyout obligations of continuing partners. When is a dissociation wrongful? The answer is in RUPA § 602(b):

§ 602   Partner's Power to Dissociate; Wrongful Dissociation.

(b)   A partner's dissociation is wrongful only if:

(1)   it is in breach of an express provision of the partnership agreement; or

(2)   in the case of a partnership for a ***definite term*** or ***particular undertaking***, before the expiration of the term or the completion of the undertaking: [Emphasis added.]

(i)   the partner withdraws by express will, [unless the withdrawal follows within 90 days after another partner's dissociation by death or otherwise under Section 601(6) through (10) or wrongful dissociation under this subsection[71]];

(ii)   the partner is expelled by judicial determination under Section 601(5);

(iii)   the partner is dissociated by becoming a debtor in bankruptcy; or

(iv)   in the case of a [business entity] the partner is expelled or otherwise dissociated because it willfully dissolved or terminated.

(c)   A partner who wrongfully dissociates is liable to the partnership and to the other partners for damages caused by the dissociation. The liability is in addition to any other obligation of the partner to the partnership or to the other partners.

---

[71] For an explanation of the bracketed material, see the text following this excerpt.

Dissecting § 602, we can see that subsection (b)(1) respects the primacy of the partnership agreement and makes an important distinction between partnerships at will and partnerships for a definite term or a particular undertaking. In the case of at-will partnerships, there is no default statutory rule making *any* cause of dissociation wrongful. The RUPA default rules limit wrongful dissociation to partnerships that have been formed for a definite term or particular purpose *and* the partner dissociates for one of the four reasons listed: (i) at will; (ii) judicial expulsion; (iii) bankruptcy; or (iv) a business entity partner that is expelled or that willfully terminates or dissolves.

The exception in the bracketed language in § 602(b)(i) protects a *reactive* withdrawal by a subsequent partner after the earlier, premature departure of another partner in the case of a partnership for a definite term or a particular purpose under circumstances that may lead to dissolution of the partnership. For instance, an *essential* partner (a figurehead partner, moneyed partner, client-connected partner) may, dissociate from the partnership by express will, death, bankruptcy or other cause that under RUPA may lead to dissolution and winding up under § 801(2), discussed below. The subsequent at-will dissociation of another partner under such circumstances is not "wrongful" under the RUPA default rules.

Keep in mind that the partnership agreement can add other causes of "wrongful" dissociation. Alternatively, the partnership agreement can eliminate all or some of the causes of wrongful termination under § 602(b).

Why does it matter if the dissociation is "wrongful" or not? First, under § 602(c) the partner who wrongfully dissociates is liable to the partnership for any damages caused by the dissociation. These damages can be offset against any amounts owing to the dissociated partner in the event of a buyout or upon winding up of the partnership, as discussed below. Damages might include the costs of replacing the partner, obtaining new financing and complying with the statutory dissociation and dissolution requirements, as well as any other proximately caused damages.

Under pre-RUPA law, the UPA *punished* the wrongfully departing partner by denying the partner a share of the going concern value of the partnership when determining the value of the partnership interest of the departing partner. Under RUPA, this punishment scheme is revised to reflect the *actual* loss suffered by wrongful dissociation. The going concern value will be included in the valuation process, *unless* the departing partner's wrongful dissociation causes a decrease in the going concern value.

Additionally, wrongfully dissociating partners are denied certain rights or privileges:

— In dissolution cases, the partner's vote will not be counted in a vote by other partners to continue the partnership business.[72]
— The right to participate in the winding up of the partnership if the dissociation leads to a dissolution and winding up.[73]
— The right to file a Statement of Dissolution.[74]

---

[72] RUPA § 802(b).

[73] RUPA § 803(a).

[74] RUPA § 805(b).

3.   Dissolution

Dissolution is the cessation of the partnerships business except for the winding up of its affairs.[75] Under RUPA default rules, dissolution will not always lead to winding up of the partnership. Nevertheless, dissolution will have an impact on the *authority* of the partners, the *liability* of the partners and the *affairs of the partnership*. Although the partnership continues as an entity during the period between dissolution and winding up, the general authority of partners to bind the partnership under RUPA § 301 is altered:

§ 802.   Partnership Continues after Dissolution.

(a)   Subject to subsection (b), a partnership continues after dissolution *only* for the purpose of winding up its business. The partnership is terminated when the winding up of its business is completed. [Emphasis added.]

§ 804.   Partner's Power to Bind Partnership after Dissolution.

Subject to section 805, a partnership is bound by a partner's act after dissolution that:

(1)   is appropriate for winding up the partnership business; or

(2)   would have bound the partnership under Section 301 before dissolution, if the other party to the transaction did not have notice of the dissolution.

§ 805.   Statement of Dissolution.

(a)   After dissolution, a partner who has not wrongfully dissociated may file a statement of dissolution stating the name of the partnership and that the partnership has dissolved and is winding up its business.

. . .

(b)   A statement of dissolution cancels a filed statement of partnership authority for the purposes of Section 303(d) and is a limitation on authority for the purposes of Section 303(e).

(c)   For the purposes of Sections 301 and 804, a person not a partner is deemed to have notice of the dissolution and the limitation on the partners' authority as a result of the statement of dissolution 90 days after it is filed.

Together, these provisions "wind down" the mutual agency and authority of the partners to bind the partnership except in connection with the winding up of the entity, or acts that would have been authorized in the absence of dissolution, if the other party does not have actual or constructive notice of the dissolution.[76] While the dissolution is pending, the partners lack the authority to bind the partnership to new transactions that further the general continuation of the business of the partnership — unless those actions are in furtherance of the winding up of the business.

---

[75] RUPA § 802(a)

[76] The rights of creditors and the authority of the partners to bind the partnership following dissolution are discussed in greater detail later in this chapter.

In other words, dissolution is a problematic and dramatic event that needs to be controlled and, if possible, avoided — if doing so is in the best interests of the non-dissociating partners. We will take a look at four aspects of dissolution: (i) When is dissolution triggered? (ii) What rights do the partners have to prevent winding up and continue the business of the partnership? (iii) What, if any, are the statutory buyout rights of dissociated partners? and (iv) What are the rules and procedures for distribution of partnership assets when partnerships are wound up?

a.   Dissolution Triggers — When Will Dissolution Occur?

Dissociation is far less likely to lead to dissolution under RUPA than under UPA. Nevertheless, dissolution can be triggered by dissociation in some cases, and by other events unrelated to dissociation of a partner. We will take a look at RUPA § 801, which gives us a list of triggering events, then evaluate the three different groups of triggers arising under § 801: (i) triggers for partnerships at will; (ii) triggers for partnerships for a definite term or particular purpose; and, (iii) triggers for all partnerships.

§ 801.   Events Causing Dissolution and Winding up of Partnership Business.

A partnership is dissolved, and its business must be wound up, only upon the occurrence of any of the following events:

(1)   in a partnership at will, the partnership's having notice from a partner, other than a partner who is dissociated under Section 601(2) through (10), of that partner's express will to withdraw as a partner, or on a later date specified by the partner;

(2)   in a partnership for a *definite term* or *particular undertaking*: [Emphasis added.]

(i)   within 90 days after a partner's dissociation by death or otherwise under Section 601(6) through (10) or wrongful dissociation under Section 602(b), *the express will of at least half of the remaining partners to wind up the partnership business, for which purpose a partner's rightful dissociation pursuant to Section 602(b)(2)(i) constitutes the expression of that partner's will to wind up the partnership business*; [Emphasis added.]

(ii)   the express will of all of the partners to wind up the partnership business; or

(iii)   the expiration of the term or the completion of the undertaking;

(3)   an event agreed to in the partnership agreement resulting in the winding up of the partnership business;

(4)   an event that makes it unlawful for all or substantially all of the business of the partnership to be continued, but a cure of illegality within 90 days after notice to the partnership of the event is effective retroactively to the date of the event for purposes of this section;[77]

(5)   on application by a partner, a judicial determination that:

---

[77] RUPA § 103(b) states: "The partnership agreement may not: . . . (8) vary the requirement to wind up the partnership business in cases specified in Section 801(4), (5), or (6)."

(i)   the economic purpose of the partnership is likely to be unreasonably frustrated;

(ii)   another partner has engaged in conduct relating to the partnership business which makes it not reasonably practicable to carry on the business in partnership with that partner; or

(iii)   it is not otherwise reasonably practicable to carry on the partnership business in conformity with the partnership agreement;[78] or

(6)   on application by a transferee of a partner's transferable interest, a judicial determination that it is equitable to wind up the partnership business:

(i)   after the expiration of the term or completion of the undertaking, if the partnership was for a definite term or particular undertaking at the time of the transfer or entry of the charging order that gave rise to the transfer; or

(ii)   at any time, if the partnership was a partnership at will at the time of the transfer or entry of the charging order that gave rise to the transfer.[79]

i.   Triggers — partnerships at will

Subsections (1) and (2) of § 801 deal with the distinctions between a partnership at will and partnerships for definite terms or particular purposes, while subsections (3)–(6) are applicable to *all* forms of general partnerships.

Note the careful wording of § 801(1), which governs only partnerships at will. A partnership at will is dissolved when a partner dissociates by express will to withdraw as a partner — provided that none of the other dissociation triggers in § 601, such as death, expulsion, bankruptcy, etc., have already occurred. The possibility that a single withdrawal by express will can throw an at-will partnership into dissolution and winding up is a serious matter. Just imagine a partnership with 20 or 30 partners. It's inevitable that one or more partners will, from time to time, dissociate by express will. As discussed above, § 103(b) prohibits the partnership agreement from eliminating the *right to dissociate* by express will from a partnership at will. However, § 103(b) does not prohibit a partnership provision that disables § 801(1). The partnership agreement can (and should) deal with this possibility. The impact of § 801(1) can be completely disabled (and often is) by the partnership agreement so that the dissociation does not cause a *dissolution* of the partnership. Or, the partnership agreement can allow dissolution to occur but provide for continuation based on a majority (or some other percentage) vote of the partners.

What happens in the absence of a provision in the partnership agreement that disables the dissolution trigger of § 801(1) or otherwise provides for the post-dissolution continuation of the business by the other partners? The answer is in § 802(b) which we discuss below. At this point we can state a simple answer — the partners (except for wrongfully dissociated partners) can unanimously vote to waive the winding up of the business, terminate the dissolution and continue the business of the partnership.

---

[78] *Id.*

[79] *Id.*

ii.   Triggers — partnerships for a definite term or particular purpose

The statutory dissolution triggers for partnerships for a definite term or particular purpose under § 801(2) are far less likely to cause a dissolution. First, it's only certain types of *dissociations* that trip the trigger that possibly lead to *dissolution*: (i) death or the types of dissociation listed in § 601(6)-(10); or (ii) wrongful dissociation under Section 602(b). Second, even if the dissociation is the type that triggers dissolution, the dissolution will not occur unless it is the express will of at least half of the remaining partners to wind up the partnership business.[80] Note that the partnership will continue *unless* there is a majority vote of the partners (other than wrongfully dissociated partners) to voluntarily dissolve following the dissociation.

There are two other triggers for dissolution of partnerships for a definite term or particular purpose under § 801(2). One, of course, is the express will of all of the partners to wind up the partnership business. The second is the expiration of the term or the completion of the undertaking — although partners wishing to continue the business might have some rights to buy out their co-owners and continue the business under certain circumstances.

iii.   Triggers — all partnerships

RUPA § 801(3)-(6) set out some additional dissolution triggers for *any* form of general partnership. The primacy of the partnership agreement is reiterated in § 801(3) which provides that the partnership agreement can specify other events that result in the dissolution and winding up of the partnership. Subsections (4)–(6) restate provisions that were discussed earlier in this chapter with regard to limited liability companies, such as uncured events that makes it unlawful for the business to be continued, or a judicial determination that the economic purpose of the partnership is likely to be unreasonably frustrated, or it is not reasonably practicable to carry on the partnership business in conformity with the partnership agreement.

b.   Summary — Triggers for Dissolution and Winding Up

If the partnership agreement is well drafted, an unintended dissolution caused by the dissociation of a partner should never occur. If the partners anticipate that they are likely to want to continue the partnership without interruption despite the dissociation by express will, death, disability, bankruptcy or any other cause, they should structure the partnership agreement to deal with the situation. The agreement should, at the very least, give the non-dissociating parties the option to continue the business without dissolution in those situations where it is likely that the remaining partners may desire continuation of the business. So long as there are fair buyout rights for the departing partner, there is simply no reason for the partnership to dissolve unless the *remaining* partners desire to do so. A well-drafted partnership agreement will specify which events, if any, lead to dissolution and which events give the remaining partners the option to continue the business without further action or, perhaps, vote on whether or not to continue the business.

---

[80] A wrongful partner's vote does not count but the vote of a partner who's dissociation is rightful constitutes the expression of that partner's will to wind up the partnership business.

The vote, if any, can be structured to require only a majority to approve continuation, or a super-majority, or a unanimous vote, depending on the event that occurs.

In the absence of provisions in the partnership agreement, RUPA significantly deviates from the earlier UPA by limiting the impact of partner departures. Dissociation of a partner leads to dissolution only under limited circumstances.

c. Stopping Dissolution and Winding Up

Even if dissolution has been triggered by a rightful or wrongful dissociation, the "bullet" that leads to winding up can be halted before there are adverse consequences. RUPA § 802(b) states:

§ 802. Partnership Continues after Dissolution.

. . .

(b) At any time after the dissolution of a partnership and before the winding up of its business is completed, all of the partners, including any dissociating partner other than a wrongfully dissociating partner, may waive the right to have the partnership's business wound up and the partnership terminated. In that event:

(1) the partnership resumes carrying on its business as if dissolution had never occurred, and any liability incurred by the partnership or a partner after the dissolution and before the waiver is determined as if dissolution had never occurred . . .

(2) the rights of a third party accruing under Section 804(1) or arising out of conduct in reliance on the dissolution before the third party knew or received a notification of the waiver may not be adversely affected.

Note that § 802(b) allows a resurrection of the partnership as though dissolution had never been triggered but it requires a unanimous vote of all partners, even dissociated ones, with the exception of partners who wrongfully dissociated. This resurrection provision is primarily of use when there has been a wrongful dissociation and the remaining partners desire to continue the business. They can vote to continue a successful business without having to worry about obtaining the consent of a departing partner who has wrongfully dissociated.

It's important to note that the partnership agreement can govern such a post-dissolution resurrection and adjust the voting scheme so that there is less than a unanimous requirement for continuation. At the very least, the agreement could exclude the vote of *any* dissociated partner (not just wrongful ones) from the vote count.

Waiver of the winding up reinstates the business of the partnership, as though it was never dissolved and the partners' authority is restored. Of course, § 802(b) reinforces the concept that acts related to *winding up* that were authorized are ratified, notwithstanding the fact that the process of winding up was waived. In addition, the partnership remains liable for post-dissolution acts and obligations that would have been authorized if the business was *continued* and the third party did not have notice of the dissolution.[81]

4.   Buyout Rights

In this chapter and in Chapter 8 we have seen that it is common to afford buyout rights, by agreement or by statute, to departing owners. It's only fair that departing owners be entitled to their share of the worth of a co-owned legal entity, regardless of the cause of their departure. Of course, if their departure causes damages, those costs should be deducted from their share. The buyout of a departing partner *should* be well thought out and carefully scripted in the partnership agreement or a related buy-sell agreement.

For partnerships formed without the benefit of carefully negotiated and drafted buyout provisions, RUPA offers a statutory buyout right that is similar to the statutory buyouts in California Corporations Code § 2000 and the 1996 ULLCA.[82] The terms of the buyout will seem familiar and have been discussed in connection with corporation and LLC statutory buyouts:

RUPA

§ 701.   Purchase of Dissociated Partner's Interest.

(a)   If a partner is dissociated from a partnership without resulting in a dissolution and winding up of the partnership business . . . , the partnership shall cause the dissociated partner's interest in the partnership to be purchased for a buyout price determined pursuant to subsection (b).

(b)   The buyout price of a dissociated partner's interest is the amount that would have been distributable to the dissociating partner under Section 807(b)[83] if, on the date of dissociation, the assets of the partnership were sold at a price equal to the greater of the liquidation value or the value based on a sale of the entire business as a going concern without the dissociated partner and the partnership were wound up as of that date. Interest must be paid from the date of dissociation to the date of payment.

(c)   Damages for wrongful dissociation under Section 602(b), and all other amounts owing, whether or not presently due, from the dissociated partner to the partnership, must be offset against the buyout price. Interest must be paid from the date the amount owed becomes due to the date of payment.

(d)   A partnership shall indemnify a dissociated partner whose interest is being purchased against all partnership liabilities, whether incurred before or after the dissociation, except liabilities incurred by an act of the dissociated partner under Section 702.[84]

(e)   *If no agreement for the purchase of a dissociated partner's interest is reached within 120 days after a written demand for payment, the partnership shall pay, or cause to be paid, in cash to the dissociated partner the amount the*

---

[81] See the discussion of creditors rights later in this chapter.

[82] The statutory buyout right for limited liability companies was eliminated in the 2006 version of the ULLCA.

[83] UPA § 807 deals with the final distribution to partners following the liquidation of partnership assets and payoff of creditors.

[84] [UPA § 702 refers to acts of the dissociated partner following dissolution that creates a partnership liability.—Eds.]

partnership estimates to be the buyout price and accrued interest, reduced by any offsets and accrued interest under subsection (c). [Emphasis added.]

(f)   If a *deferred payment* is authorized under subsection (h), the partnership may tender a written offer to pay the amount it estimates to be the buyout price and accrued interest, reduced by any offsets under subsection (c), stating the time of payment, the amount and type of security for payment, and the other terms and conditions of the obligation. [Emphasis added.]

. . .

(h)   A partner who *wrongfully dissociates* before the expiration of a definite term or the completion of a particular undertaking is *not entitled to payment* of any portion of the buyout price *until the expiration of the term or completion of the undertaking*, unless the partner establishes to the satisfaction of the court that earlier payment will not cause undue hardship to the business of the partnership. *A deferred payment must be adequately secured and bear interest.* [Emphasis added.]

(i)   A dissociated partner may maintain an action against the partnership, . . . to determine the buyout price of that partner's interest, any offsets under subsection (c), or other terms of the obligation to purchase . . . after the partnership has tendered payment or an offer to pay or within one year after written demand for payment if no payment or offer to pay is tendered. The court shall determine the buyout price of the dissociated partner's interest, any offset due under subsection (c), and accrued interest, and enter judgment for any additional payment or refund. If deferred payment is authorized under subsection (h), the court shall also determine the security for payment and other terms of the obligation to purchase. The court may assess reasonable attorney's fees and the fees and expenses of appraisers or other experts for a party to the action, in amounts the court finds equitable, against a party that the court finds acted arbitrarily, vexatiously, or not in good faith. The finding may be based on the partnership's failure to tender payment or an offer to pay . . .

————

What do you notice about RUPA's statutory buyout provisions that are different from earlier provisions we have looked at? Take a close look at subsections (e) and (f). If the parties can't agree on the value of the departing partner's interest, or the amount of damages caused by a wrongful dissociation, the partnership can simply estimate these amounts in good faith, pay off the departing partner, and continue the business without having to *first* go to court. This makes much sense. The business of the partnership continues unabated by the dissociation, without the pall of a law suit dragging on for months before the payoff is made. In addition, the partner's interest is quickly acquired by the partnership, thereby terminating any of the dissociated partner's rights under the partnership agreement or RUPA.

The partnership has the incentive to exercise good faith in making its determinations of value. Under subsection (i), the question of valuation and terms of the buyout can be dragged into court if the dissociated partner disagrees with the valuations reached by the partnership but only *after* the partnership has ousted the partner and acquired the partner's interest (or neglected to do so). The court is authorized to assess attorney's fees and expenses of appraisers or experts against a party that the court finds acted arbitrarily, vexatiously, not in good faith or if the partnership's fails to tender payment or an offer to pay the departing partner.

Subsections (f) and (h) allow the partnership in most cases to *defer* payment in the event that the departing partner wrongfully dissociates before the expiration of a definite term or the completion of a particular undertaking. This makes sense since all partners of such a partnership have tacitly agreed to remain in the partnership until completion. Of course, the deferred payment must be secured and bear interest.[85] It's also interesting to note that § 701 uses the language "cause to be purchased." This allows for an entity buyout by the partnership, or a cross-purchase type buyout, or even a buyout by a third person. So long as the departing partner is paid the good faith value of the partner's ownership interest, the partnership's obligations under § 701 are satisfied.

What is the "value" of the departing member's interest? Subsection (b) dispenses with the valuation terms that we have seen with regard to corporations and LLC's: "fair value" and "fair market value." Instead, § 701(b) uses the term "buyout price" and then cross refers to § 807(b) for more information about how to value the interest. That section deals with the ultimate distribution of the assets of a wound up partnership, after creditors have been paid. The comment accompanying § 701(b) states:

> 3. . . . The terms "fair market value" or "fair value" were not used because they are often considered terms of art having a special meaning depending on the context, such as in tax or corporate law . . .

> Under subsection (b), the buyout price is the amount that would have been distributable to the dissociating partner under Section 807(b) if, on the date of dissociation, the assets of the partnership were sold at a price equal to the greater of liquidation value or going concern value without the departing partner. Liquidation value is not intended to mean distress sale value. Under general principles of valuation, the hypothetical selling price in either case should be the price that a willing and informed buyer would pay a willing and informed seller, with neither being under any compulsion to deal. The notion of a minority discount in determining the buyout price is negated by valuing the business as a going concern. Other discounts, such as for a lack of marketability or the loss of a key partner, may be appropriate, however.

Is this "buyout price" formula for determining value differ significantly from the "fair value" and "fair market value" formulas we studied earlier in this chapter and in Chapter 8? Despite the comment, it doesn't appear that the "buyout price" formula offers much to distinguish it from "fair value" or "fair market value."

Of course, RUPA § 701(c), as well as § 602(c), allows the damages caused by the wrongful dissociation of a partner to be deducted from the value of the partner's share when computing the final "buyout price" to be tendered by the partnership to the dissociated partner. As mentioned earlier, a wrongfully dissociating partner is not to be *punished* by the withdrawal other than the offset for actual damages

---

[85] The requirement for security is discussed in depth in Chapter 8. Once the partner is bought out, the partner will have no ability to control the affairs of the partnership and the partnership's ability to make future payments that have been deferred. If the non-dissociating partners want to continue the business without winding up, the dissociated partner is *entitled* to the value of that partner's ownership interest at the time of dissociation, even though payment of that value, plus interest is being deferred. See the discussion in Chapter 8.

caused by the dissociation.[86] This means that the dissociating partner, whether rightful or wrongful, gets to participate in the full value of the partnership, including going concern value if the winding up of the company could be accomplished by a sale as a going concern in a non-forced-sale environment.

RUPA's statutory buyout provisions establish two interesting requirements. Let's take a look at them and see if they make sense — with the ultimate test of sensibility being whether or not you would include these requirements in a well-drafted buyout:

(i) RUPA sets the valuation *date* as the date of the dissociation rather than the date of the completion of the undertaking or expiration of the term.

(ii) RUPA § 701(d) requires that the continuing partnership indemnify the *departing* partner for any debts incurred before or after the dissociation.[87]

These provisions are reasonable. A partnership is a voluntary association of partners who share in the profits, losses and value of the business. The departing partner is exiting the partnership and *if the partnership was dissolved at that point* is entitled to the amount that would be distributed at the time of dissolution. That amount would be the value of the business (sold under normal winding up conditions), less payments to creditors, less any damages assessed to the departing partner if the dissolution was caused by a wrongful dissociation. If the remaining partners want to avoid dissolution and continue the business, they must pay the departing partner his/her/its fair share. If a well-drafted buy-sell agreement was prepared, this value would be the value that fair parties with equal negotiating power would agree to.

The indemnity provisions are also sensible. The departing partner is technically liable for all of the debts of the partnership prior to the partner's departure from the partnership. If the partnership was dissolved, these debts would be paid off prior to distribution, leaving the departing partner with a cash payment and no liability for outstanding debts of the partnership. However, if the partnership continues, the relative proportion of debt will be deducted from the payout to the the departing partner, receives the same cash amount as a dissolution — but the debts have *not* been paid off since the partnership is continuing. Unless the creditor agrees to release the departing partner (an unlikely event), this leaves the departing partner saddled with debt that has *already* been deducted from the partner's payout, subjecting that partner to double liability. For instance, suppose that a partnership with four partners is valued at $5 million and has debt of $1 million. Assuming equal capital accounts and equal rights to profits and losses then, upon dissolution, each partner would end up with $1 million in final distribution and no liability for debt, which has been paid. Now suppose that, instead of dissolution following a dissociation by one of the partner's, Danielle, the remaining three partners continue the business and buyout Danielle for $1 million ($5 million in value, less $1 million in debt, divided by four). Even though Danielle has $1 million

---

[86] Prior to adoption of RUPA in 1994, UPA § 38(2)(c)(II) punitively excluded the going concern value of the partnership from the valuation of the dissociating partner's interest.

[87] However, the continuing partners need not indemnify the departing partner for "liabilities incurred by an act of the dissociated partner under Section 702." UPA § 702 refers to acts of the dissociated partner following dissolution that creates a partnership liability.

in cash, she remains jointly and severally liable to the third-party creditors for the outstanding partnership debt of $1 million. In the absence of an indemnity agreement, Danielle could lose all of the buyout amount.

Is an indemnity agreement enough to fully protect the departing partner? What if two years after the statutory buyout, the partnership dissolves and the $1 million debt owed to creditors prior to Danielle's departure remains unpaid? The other three partners are judgment proof (they filed personal bankruptcy) and the creditors come after Danielle for the full $1 million. What good is the indemnity agreement? It's not any good at all. If the other partners are judgment proof, then Danielle won't be able to collect contributions from them under the indemnity agreement.

Certainly RUPA's default buyout provisions provide reasonable procedures for the buyout of a departing partner. However, once again, to fully protect the interests of all parties, it's clear that a well-drafted buy-sell agreement is required to properly protect the interests of the parties.

EXERCISE 10-1

As attorney for a potentially departing partner how would you handle Danielle's possible departure in a well-drafted buy-sell agreement to protect Danielle? What are some possible provisions you might draft with regard to outstanding debts of the partnership if Danielle departs? Consider the following possibilities when drafting the provisions:

(i) An escrow fund could be set aside for the payment of the debts.

(ii) The partnership or partners execute a security agreement providing sufficient collateral to secure Danielle in the event that the creditors are not paid and seek recovery from her?

Be creative. What are some other possible ways of protecting Danielle with regard to outstanding debt obligations?

5.   Winding Up

If the general partnership is dissolved and moves towards winding up, rather than continuation, what are the procedures and rules governing the process of liquidating assets, paying off creditors, making distributions to partners, and balancing the capital accounts of the partners?

a.   Post-Dissolution Authority

RUPA

§ 803.   Right to Wind up Partnership Business.

(a) After dissolution, a partner who has not wrongfully dissociated may participate in winding up the partnership's business, but on application of any partner, partner's legal representative, or transferee, the [designate the appropriate court], for good cause shown, may order judicial supervision of the winding up.

(b) The legal representative of the last surviving partner may wind up a partnership's business.

(c)   A person winding up a partnership's business may preserve the partnership business or property as a going concern for a reasonable time, prosecute and defend actions and proceedings, whether civil, criminal, or administrative, settle and close the partnership's business, dispose of and transfer the partnership's property, discharge the partnership's liabilities, distribute the assets of the partnership pursuant to Section 807, settle disputes by mediation or arbitration, and perform other necessary acts.[88]

§ 804.   Partner's Power to Bind Partnership after Dissolution.

Subject to section 805, a partnership is bound by a partner's act after dissolution that:

(1)   is appropriate for winding up the partnership business; or

(2)   would have bound the partnership under Section 301 before dissolution, if the other party to the transaction did not have notice of the dissolution.

Note that RUPA specifically authorizes the partner(s) winding up the affairs of the entity to continue the partnership as a going concern for a *reasonable* time if that will enhance the value received during the winding up process. All acts of the winding up partners in furtherance of the winding up, including continuation of the business as *part* of the winding up process, are specifically authorized by § 804(a). However, post-dissolution acts by *any* partner may bind the partnership, even if they are *not* part of the winding up process if those acts would have been authorized under § 301 (apparent authority) in the normal course of the affairs of the non-dissolved partnership, if the other party does not have notice of the dissolution.[89] To partially deal with this problem of binding but unauthorized acts, § 805 allows the partnership to file a statement of dissolution that creates an irrefutable presumption of notice 90 days after the filing:

§ 805.   Statement of Dissolution.

(a)   After dissolution, a partner who has not wrongfully dissociated may file a statement of dissolution stating the name of the partnership and that the partnership has dissolved and is winding up its business.

. . .

---

[88]   This subsection is based on Delaware Laws, Title 6, § 17-803 and is intended to clearly enumerate the broad scope of powers granted to the persons winding up the affairs of the partnership by listing some examples of the scope of powers.

[89]   Notice is defined in RUPA § 102 which generally provides:

§ 102. Knowledge and Notice.

(a) A person knows a fact if the person has actual knowledge of it.

(b) A person has notice of a fact if the person:

(1) knows of it;

(2) has received a notification of it; or

(3) has reason to know it exists from all of the facts known to the person at the time in question.* * *

(c)   For the purposes of Sections 301 and 804, a person not a partner is deemed to have notice of the dissolution and the limitation on the partners' authority as a result of the statement of dissolution 90 days after it is filed.

———————

We have carefully looked at the triggers that cause dissolution. It's quite possible that dissolution might be triggered (such as by a partner's dissociation by express will) without much change that is noticeable to the outside world, or even the partners. Considering the fact that many creditors won't know that dissolution has occurred, the potential for binding the partnership to obligations unrelated to winding up is a substantial possibility. If the business is continued, rather than wound up, it's unimportant, since those actions will be automatically ratified by the continuation of the partnership pursuant to § 802(b)(2) discussed earlier in this chapter. However, what if the partnership is wound up and remains liable for the post-dissolution unauthorized act of the partner?

§ 806.   Partner's Liability to Other Partners after Dissolution.

(b)   A partner who, with knowledge of the dissolution, incurs a partnership liability under Section 804(2) by an act that is not appropriate for winding up the partnership business is liable to the partnership for any damage caused to the partnership arising from the liability.

———————

A partner who commits an unauthorized but binding post-dissolution act may incur liability for the entire obligation that the partner incurred ostensibly on the part of the partnership — if that partner had "knowledge of the dissolution." As used in RUPA, knowledge is a different standard than notice, since actual knowledge of the fact is required.[90] Thus, the incurring of the post-dissolution, unauthorized debt will become the liability of the partnership and all of its partners, unless the partner incurring the obligation had actual knowledge of the dissolution. This distinction makes it imperative that information about the dissolution be quickly disseminated to all partners following an event that triggers dissolution. As mentioned earlier, the occurrence of dissolution is a destabilizing and dramatic event that requires quick action by the partnership and its partners to either waive winding up and proceed with continuation, or enter the winding up process quickly and responsibly. Keep in mind that, ultimately, many of the provisions in RUPA dealing with dissolution and winding up are *default* rules that can be handled differently in a well-drafted partnership agreement. Preventing an unintended dissolution (and the issues that arise as a result) is a high-priority in the drafting of the partnership agreement

b.   Creditors Rights

What happens following the sale of the partnership assets if the partnership proceeds with winding up, rather than waiver of dissolution and continuation? Suppose that the business is sold as a going concern, or liquidated on an asset-by-asset basis and yields $2 million. What will happen to the cash that has been

———————

[90] *Id.*

accumulated as part of the winding up process? The answer is contained in RUPA §§ 801, 806 and 807. It should come as no surprise that the first priority with regard to the distribution of assets is the payment of creditors. Despite the fact that general partners remain personally liable for the debts of the partnership, RUPA requires that assets first be used to satisfy creditors, rather than be distributed to the owners of the partnership.

The rights of creditors to priority of distribution are contained in § 807(a), which contains the rules for distributions to both creditors and partners:

§ 807. Settlement of Accounts and Contributions among Partners.

(a) In winding up a partnership's business, the assets of the partnership, including the contributions of the partners required by this section, must be applied to discharge its obligations to creditors, including, to the extent permitted by law, partners who are creditors. Any surplus must be applied to pay in cash the net amount distributable to partners in accordance with their right to distributions under subsection (b).

This priority scheme, at least as it relates to creditors, is one of the statutory rules that cannot be altered by the partnership agreement.[91] As we have seen with regard to other entities, the creditors of the entity are entitled to be paid before the equity holders receive distributions *as equity holders*. However, partners who have loaned money to the partnership or incurred debts on behalf of the partnership are creditors for purposes of § 807(a) and also entitled to be paid before distributions of any surplus to equity holders.[92] What if there are insufficient funds to from the liquidation of the partnership's assets to pay all third party creditors the full amount of their claims. Should partners who are creditors share equally with third party creditors in the distribution? If the creditor-partners are truly creditors of the partnership, then there is no reason to exclude them from the distribution to creditors if there are sufficient proceeds in distribution. However, when there are insufficient funds to fully pay all creditors at the time of liquidation, it seems unfair to reduce the percentage distribution to outside creditors, particularly when the creditor-partner has made a large loan to the partnership that is really in the nature of an equity contribution. Prior to 1994 and the adoption of RUPA, UPA expressly provided for the subordination of the claims of creditor partners to outside creditors.[93] According to the comments to RUPA § 806, this subordination rule was abolished when RUPA was adopted, although there is no express language in

---

[91] See § 103(b)(10) which states: "(b) The partnership agreement may not: . . . (10) restrict rights of third parties under this [Act]."

[92] RUPA § 404(f) states: "A partner may lend money to and transact other business with the partnership, and as to each loan or transaction the rights and obligations of the partner are the same as those of a person who is not a partner, subject to other applicable law."

[93] UPA § 40(b) stated: "(b) The liabilities of the partnership shall rank in order of payment, as follows: I. Those owing to creditors other than partners, II. Those owing to partners other than for capital and profits, III. Those owing to partners in respect of capital, IV. Those owing to partners in respect of profits." Section 40(c) added: "(c) The assets shall be applied in the order of their declaration in clause (a) of this paragraph to the satisfaction of the liabilities."

RUPA making clear that the subordination rule is overturned.[94] As the Comment correctly points out, if there are insufficient proceeds to pay all creditors fully, then if the creditor-partners are paid on a *parity* with outside creditors, then the portion of outside creditor debt that is *not* repaid becomes a partnership obligation that must be paid by all partners, including the creditor-partners, thereby indirectly subordinating the debt of the creditor-partner anyway. It makes more sense to simply subordinate creditor-partner debt to outside creditor debt as was the case under UPA and remains the case under the Uniform Limited Partnership Act.[95] Under the preemptive powers of federal bankruptcy law, the bankruptcy courts have the authority to subordinate debt owed to partners to the debt owed to creditors, assuring that when equity requires, outside creditors are paid first.[96] Nevertheless, even if a creditor-partner's claim is subordinated to the claims of third party creditors, creditor-partners are entitled to be paid before distributions to *other* partners who are equity holders.

It's interesting to note that unlike the statutory rules regarding dissolution of corporations and LLCs, which insulate equity holders from liability, RUPA does not provide any additional rules regarding the rights of creditors in the event that the partners in charge of winding up improperly make distributions to *partners* before fully compensating known, or unknown, creditors. In the case of corporations and LLCs we've studied special statutory provisions that guarantee creditors the right to seek post-dissolution recoveries from stockholders of corporations and members of LLCs. The absence of similar provisions in RUPA reflect the underlying nature of general partnerships. Since the partners remain jointly and severally liable for the debts of the partnership, there is no need to grant creditors extra post-dissolution collection rights. If the distributions to creditors from liquidation or sale of the partnership assets does not satisfy their claims, then following dissolution the creditors can simply pursue all of the partners, or their estates, for the unpaid portions of their claims to the extent that those claims are enforceable under state or federal law.

c. Distributions to Partners and Balancing Partner's Accounts

RUPA § 807(a) states that, after payment to creditors, "[a]ny surplus must be applied to pay in cash the net amount distributable to partners in accordance with their right to distributions under subsection (b)." In the case of losses, § 807(b) states:

> In settling accounts among the partners, profits and losses that result from the liquidation of the partnership assets must be credited and charged

---

[94] The comment to RUPA § 807 states in part:

> The partnership must apply its assets to discharge the obligations of partners who are creditors on a parity with other creditors. See Section 404(f) and Comment 6. In effect, that abolishes the priority rules in UPA § 40(b) and (c) which subordinate the payment of inside debt to outside debt . . . Ultimately, however, a partner whose "debt" has been repaid by the partnership is personally liable, as a partner, for any outside debt remaining unsatisfied, unlike a limited partner or corporate shareholder. Accordingly, the obligation to contribute sufficient funds to satisfy the claims of outside creditors may result in the equitable subordination of inside debt when partnership assets are insufficient to satisfy all obligations to non-partners.

[95] RULPA § 804.

[96] 11 U.S.C. § 510.

to the partners' accounts. The partnership shall make a distribution to a partner in an amount equal to any excess of the credits over the charges in the partner's account. A partner shall contribute to the partnership an amount equal to any excess of the charges over the credits in the partner's account . . .

Keep in mind that the remainder of our discussion is about the *default* distribution rules under RUPA. The partnership agreement may alter the distributions available to partners.

RUPA § 807(b) contains a potentially dangerous default rule. To understand why, we need to understand how any surplus — or any deficiency — is shared by and among partners in the absence of some other agreement to the contrary. Suppose that Anita, Ben and Cedric agreed to start a general partnership. Anita and Ben were the monied partners. They each contributed $2 million and took no active role in the management or operations of the partnership. Cedric was the "workhorse" partner, contributing only $100,000 in cash. They agreed in the partnership agreement to share profits and losses equally. Cedric received a salary in addition to his interest in the partnership. During the life of the partnership, all profits were distributed equally to the partners. What is the result under RUPA default rules if the partnership dissolves and: (i) the business is profitable and there is a surplus of $5 million after paying creditors; or, (ii) the business was unprofitable and there was a deficit of $1.9 million? Read the default rules and determine what the outcome should be:

§ 807.   Settlement of Accounts and Contributions among Partners.

(a)   In winding up a partnership's business, the assets of the partnership, including the contributions of the partners required by this section, must be applied to discharge its obligations to creditors, including, to the extent permitted by law, partners who are creditors. Any surplus must be applied to pay in cash the net amount distributable to partners in accordance with their right to distributions under subsection (b).

(b)   Each partner is entitled to a settlement of all partnership accounts upon winding up the partnership business. In settling accounts among the partners, profits and losses that result from the liquidation of the partnership assets must be credited and charged to the partners' accounts. *The partnership shall make a distribution to a partner in an amount equal to any excess of the credits over the charges in the partner's account. A partner shall contribute to the partnership an amount equal to any excess of the charges over the credits in the partner's account* but excluding from the calculation charges attributable to an obligation for which the partner is not personally liable under Section 306. [Emphasis added.]

. . .

(e)   The estate of a deceased partner is liable for the partner's obligation to contribute to the partnership.

. . .

(f)   An assignee for the benefit of creditors of a partnership or a partner, or a person appointed by a court to represent creditors of a partnership or a partner, may enforce a partner's obligation to contribute to the partnership.

§ 401.   Partner's Rights and Duties.

(a)   Each partner is deemed to have an account that is:

(1)   credited with an amount equal to the money plus the value of any other property, net of the amount of any liabilities, the partner contributes to the partnership and the partner's share of the partnership profits; and

(2)   charged with an amount equal to the money plus the value of any other property, net of the amount of any liabilities, distributed by the partnership to the partner and the partner's share of the partnership losses.

(b)   Each partner is entitled to an equal share of the partnership profits and is chargeable with a share of the partnership losses in proportion to the partner's share of the profits.

Under the RUPA default rules, partners share *profits* equally — not in proportion to their capital contribution. If there's a profit after paying off creditors, the net result of §§ 807 and 401 is that the partners will be repaid their capital contributions and then the profits will be distributed equally. In part (i) of our hypothetical we asked what the result would be under RUPA if "the business is profitable and there is a surplus of $5 million after paying creditors." The answer is that the capital contributions of Anita and Ben ($2 million each) would be repaid, as would Cedric's contribution of $100,000. This would leave $900,000 to split evenly among the partners. The outcome under the RUPA default rules makes sense and is most likely what the three partners intended when they formed the partnership.

But what is the result under part (ii) of our hypothetical, if there's a net loss of $1.9 million? RUPA § 807 (which is no different than the rules under UPA) states that: "A partner shall contribute to the partnership an amount equal to any excess of the charges over the credits in the partner's account . . . " The *total* loss suffered by this partnership was $6 million. The capital contributions of $4.1 million are gone, and the partners remain liable for $900,000 in outstanding debt. Since the three partners share the loss equally, they should each contribute one-third of the $6 million loss. Each is responsible for $2 million of the *total* loss ($6 million ÷ 3). Since Anita and Ben have already contributed $2 million in the form of their original capital contributions, Ben is liable to contribute the entire $1.9 million since his initial contribution was only $100,000 and he is responsible for a $2 million share of the loss. This result is consistent with the concept that Anita, Ben and Cedric agreed to share losses equally and, so far, Cedric has only paid $100,000 of his share of the loss.

This result is a trap for the poorly informed partners who make uneven financial contributions to the equity of the partnership. It's probably *not* what Anita, Ben and Cedric intended at the startup of the partnership. The moneyed partners expected to have more money at risk in this venture than Cedric, who was contributing time and expertise instead. Do you think Cedric expected that, if there was a loss, he would have to contribute the lion's share towards payment of that loss? The comment to RUPA § 807 recognizes this potentially unfair result:

It may seem unfair that the contributor of services, who contributes little or no capital, should be obligated to contribute toward the capital loss of the large contributor who contributed no services. In entering a partnership with such a capital structure, the partners should foresee that application of the default rule may bring about unusual results and take advantage of their power to vary by agreement the allocation of capital losses.

How would you use the partnership agreement to alter the *default* RUPA contribution rules if you were Cedric's attorney? Would you try to assure that all three partners shared equally in any losses in excess of the total capital contributions, rather than equalizing their capital accounts? Could you draft such a provision?

E. BANKRUPTCY

1. Introduction to the Bankruptcy Code

The bankruptcy laws of the United States are contained in 11 U.S.C. § 101 *et seq.* (the "Bankruptcy Code"). There are five different types of bankruptcy cases that can be filed under the Bankruptcy Code: (i) *liquidation* of individuals and entities under chapter 7; (ii) *municipal reorganizations* under chapter 9; (iii) *reorganization of individuals or business entities* under chapter 11; (iv) *adjustment of debts of family farmers* under chapter 12; and (v) *adjustment of debts of individuals with regular income* under chapter 13.[97] Some of the differences between the chapters will be discussed in this section. It is helpful to first gain some perspective on the origins and objectives of the bankruptcy laws.

The vast majority of bankruptcy filings are chapter 7's, where the aim is to liquidate the estate of the debtor by gathering the debtor's assets, selling them, and distributing the proceeds to creditors. Chapter 9 is designed for a bankruptcy proceeding by a municipality and is rarely used, nor is it relevant to a business planning course. Chapter 11 provides for "reorganization" rather than "liquidation" of a debtor. Chapter 11 is used mostly by business enterprises, in order to continue the debtor's business and maximize the distribution of value to the debtor's creditors. This goal is accomplished by allowing the business enterprise to "reorganize" — to reduce the amount of, and extend time for, payment of its outstanding debts and obligations. It probably occurs to you to question the fairness of allowing a debtor to continue in business while diminishing creditors' claims. However, upon closer examination, it becomes clear that reorganization often significantly improves the position of many of the debtor's creditors and does not diminish the rights of any of them when compared to a chapter 7 liquidation. How is additional value generated in a chapter 11, as compared to a chapter 7 liquidation? First, the value of a going business concern is often more than its liquidation value. By continuing to operate the business, this excess value can be tapped and distributed to creditors. Second, liquidation bankruptcies distributes only those assets in which the debtor has an interest at the time of the filing of the bankruptcy petition. A reorganization plan permits the debtor to stay in business, retain assets and use *future* earnings to pay a larger percentage of creditors' claims then the would receive in a chapter 7 liquidation. When compared to liquidation, a reorganization plan can substantially increase the

---

[97] There is also a sixth type of bankruptcy dealt with in chapter 15 dealing with "cross-border" international cases, which we will not be covering.

pro rata portion of creditors' claims that are repaid by the debtor. Chapter 11 creates a system whereby the debtor and the debtor's creditors can formulate and institute a plan of reorganization which, when compared to liquidation, makes some creditors better off by increasing the *pro rata* distribution, while making no creditors worse off.

Chapter 13 provides a type of reorganization for individual debtors with a regular stream of income. For many reasons, liquidation may often be unacceptable, or at least distasteful, for individual debtors. Chapter 13 creates a procedure (which is much simpler than the procedure in Chapter 11) whereby individual debtors can avoid the stigma of liquidation bankruptcy, avoid disruption and loss of their assets, and yet still obtain a discharge of their debts. Chapter 12 (established in 1986) provides similar opportunities for "family farmers" with a regular annual income but, as you will see, it is rarely used.

Players in the Bankruptcy System

There are certain parties that appear in bankruptcy cases:

1. The "debtor."[98] Simply stated, the debtor is the individual or entity that files a bankruptcy petition, seeking relief from creditors.
2. The "creditors."[99] Any person[100] with a claim against the debtor, whether that claim is fixed, contingent, liquidated, unliquidated, matured, unmatured, etc.
3. The "trustee." A trustee is appointed in every chapter 7 case. The role of the trustee is to gather the non-exempt assets of the debtor, liquidate those assets and use the proceeds to pay the debtors creditors. The trustee also manages many aspects of the chapter 7 case and can bring legal actions regarding matters such as: the recovery of property from third parties; the exemptions of the debtor; the avoidance of pre-petition or post-petition transfers; the debtor's entitlement to a discharge; etc. In chapter 12 and 13 cases, each federal district has one or more "standing" trustees who oversee the administration of chapter 12 and 13 cases.
4. The "debtor in possession." In chapter 11 reorganization cases, it makes sense to let the debtor continue to operate the business while a reoganization plan is proposed and confirmed. Unless a creditor or other party moves for appointment of a trustee to take over the operations of the debtor, the individual or business entity in a chapter 11 case becomes the "debtor in possession" and is vested with the rights, powers, functions and duties of the trustee.[101]
5. The "United States Trustee". The United States Trustee Program ("USTP") is a component of the Department of Justice. According to the Mission Statement of the USTP:

The United States Trustee Program acts in the public interest to promote the efficiency and to protect and preserve the integrity of the bankruptcy system. It works to secured the just, speedy, and economical resolution of

---

[98] *See* 11 U.S.C. § 101(13).

[99] See § 101(10) for the definition of creditor and § 101(5) for the definition of "claim."

[100] *See* 11 U.S.C. § 101(41).

[101] See the discussion of "debtor in possession" later in this section.

bankruptcy cases; monitors the conduct of parties and takes action to ensure compliance with applicable laws and procedures; identifies and investigates bankruptcy fraud and abuse; and oversees administrative functions in bankruptcy cases to promote and defend the integrity of the federal bankruptcy laws.

The U.S. Trustee in each district appoints chapter 7 trustees, appoints standing trustees, oversees § 341(a) meetings (a required meeting between the debtor and any creditors who want to attend), reviews chapter 11 reports, and many other activities. The U.S. trustee acts to represent the public interest in bankruptcy cases.

6.   The "judge."[102] Bankruptcy judges are federal judges appointed for 14 year terms. They serve the judicial role in bankruptcy as neutral arbiters of disputes between parties, and oversee the application of the bankruptcy laws to debtors and creditors.

2.   History and Sources of Bankruptcy Law

The Bankruptcy Code is a comprehensive, federal statutory scheme that has significant consequences for virtually all people and business entities, whether they are debtors or creditors. Bankruptcy proceedings are inherently equitable proceedings where the state law rights of creditors are subject to modification and/ or elimination.[103] Even the rights of secured creditors may be subject to some delay or modification in bankruptcy, although the underlying security interest cannot be adversely affected by that modification or delay. While it might seem unfair to allow debtors to use the bankruptcy system to modify or eliminate the state-law rights of creditors, we will see that there are fundamental justifications that support the objectives of the bankruptcy code, including objectives that benefit creditors, as well as debtors.

Bankruptcy laws can be traced back to the Italian city-states of the 14th century. The first English legislation appeared in the 16th century and by the late 1700s bankruptcy law became sufficiently entrenched to warrant a lengthy discussion in Blackstone's Commentaries. The need for bankruptcy legislation was important to the drafters of the U.S. Constitution, which lists the creation of bankruptcy laws as one of only 18 enumerated powers granted to Congress in Article 1. Section eight, Clause four of Article 1 states that Congress shall have the power to pass "uniform Laws on the subject of Bankruptcies." As early as 1800, a comprehensive Bankruptcy Act was enacted by the U.S. Congress. The 1800 Act was followed by three other comprehensive bankruptcy acts in the 19th century, those of 1841, 1867, and 1898. The Bankruptcy Act of the 1998 remained the law for the next 80 years and was applicable only to business debtors. In 1938, in the wake of the Great Depression, congress adopted the Chandler Act,[104] which brought the benefits of bankruptcy laws to individual consumers.

In 1978, following ten years of study, the bankruptcy laws were completely revised and replaced by the *Bankruptcy Reform Act of 1978*, which repealed prior bankruptcy provisions and enacted a brand new Title 11 of the United States Code,

---

[102] *See* 28 U.S.C. §§ 152, § 157.

[103] *See* Heiser v. Woodruff, 327 U.S. 726 (1946); S.E.C. v. United States Realty & Improvement Co., 310 U.S. 434 (1940); Pepper v. Litton, 308 U.S. 295 (1939).

[104] Chandler Act, June 22, 1938, ch. 575, 52 Stat. 883.

effective October 1, 1979.[105] Since 1978 there have been many minor revisions and four large-scale revisions: (i) The Bankruptcy Amendments and Federal Judgeship Act of 1984; (ii) The Bankruptcy Judges, U.S. Trustee & Family Farmer Bankruptcy Act of 1986; (iii) The Bankruptcy Reform Act of 1994; and (iv) Bankruptcy Abuse Prevention and Consumer Protection Act of 2005.

The most substantial changes in the Bankruptcy Code were implemented by the Bankruptcy Abuse Prevention and Consumer Protection Act of 2005 ("BAPCA"). The impetus behind BAPCA was a ten year long lobbying effort (mostly by consumer lenders) focused on alleged "abuse" of the bankruptcy laws by consumers. The end product, BAPCA, contained many provisions calculated to make it expensive, time-consuming and difficult for consumers to take advantage of the bankruptcy laws. Nevertheless, BAPCA made some sensible changed to the way that business reorganizations and liquidations are conducted. BAPCA became effective on October 17, 2005.

One of the changes implemented by BAPCA was the creation of administrative and substantive obstacles to consumer filings, especially chapter 7 liquidations. At the heart of BAPCA is a "means test" that restricts consumers from filing chapter 7 liquidations if they have the "means" to file a chapter 13 reorganization. Interestingly, the pre-BAPCA factual evidence presented by most academics, lawyers, consultants and the congressionally created National Bankruptcy Review Commission,[106] was that abuse occurred in less than 5% of consumer cases — and there were adequate provisions in the Code to handle those abuses and assure the integrity of the bankruptcy system. Nevertheless, the lobbyists were successful and BAPCA created some serious barriers to *all* consumers (whether "abusive" or not) and has substantially increased the cost of filing bankruptcy. Whether or not BAPCA has succeeded in preventing the small amount of abuses that occurred prior to its implementation remains unclear.

3. Why is Understanding Federal Bankruptcy Important for Business Planning Lawyers?

How pervasive is bankruptcy in the United States? Since the adoption of the modern bankruptcy code in 1978, approximately 27 *million* debtors have filed bankruptcy and *hundreds of billions* of dollars in wealth has been funneled through the bankruptcy system.

a. Bankruptcy Filing Trends

The number of bankruptcy cases filed provide us with an excellent indicator of the availability of credit in our economy, as well as the health of the economy. In 1980, there were 331,264 bankruptcy filings. Following the effective date of the Bankruptcy Code (October, 1979), records were set in each of the next 10 years —

---

[105] 11 U.S.C. § 101 *et. seq.*, often referred to as the "Bankruptcy Code," or "Code."

[106] The National Bankruptcy Review Commission was created by Public Law 103-394 (1994). The Commission ceased to exist on November 19, 1997. The purposes of the Commission were to: (1) investigate and study issues and problems relating to title 11, United States Code; (2) evaluate the advisability of proposals and current arrangements with respect to such issues and problems; (3) prepare and submit to the Congress, the Chief Justice, and the President a report; and (4) solicit divergent views of all parties concerned with the operation of the bankruptcy system. *See Bankruptcy: The Next Twenty Years*, National Bankruptcy Review Commission Final Report, Oct. 20, 1997.

from 360,329 for the year ending June 1981 to 880,399 in the year ending June 1991. In 1991, bankruptcies in the Los Angeles area were being filed at a rate of more than 6,500 a month — a reflection of the recession that hit Southern California during that time. From 1995 to 1997 filings increased a stunning 52% over a two year period. With the recession of the late 1980's and early 1990's, it was no surprise that bankruptcy filings would rise steadily to the point that filings exceeded one million from 1996–2005, with an all-time high of over two million in 2005, followed by a sharp decline in 2006. The reasons for the sudden rise in 2005, and decline in 2006, are discussed below. Consider the following chart which shows bankruptcy filings during the seven year period from 2001–2007:[107]

2001–2007 Filing Comparisons							
	Total Filings	Chap. 7	Change from Prior year	Chap. 11	Change from Prior year	Chap. 13	Change from Prior year
2001	1,386,606	972,659	—	10,272	—	403,418	—
2002	1,505,306	1,053,230	8.28%	11,401	10.99%	440,231	9.13%
2003	1,650,279	1,165,993	10.71%	10,602	-7.01%	472,811	7.40%
2004	1,597,462	1,137,958	-2.40%	10,132	-4.43%	449,129	-5.01%
2005	2,078,415	1,659,017	45.79%	6,800	-32.89%	412,130	-8.24%
2006	617,660	360,890	-78.25%	5,163	-24.07%	251,179	-39.05%
2007	751,056	450,332	24.78%	5,586	8.19%	294,693	17.32%

Why the huge increase in filings in 2005? There was an abnormally high number of filings as consumers rushed to avoid the restrictive provisions of BAPCA which became effective in October 2005. In 2006, there was a related decline in consumer filings as access to use of the bankruptcy system was impeded by the anti-consumer BAPCA provisions (discussed below) and lawyers wrestled with the confusing and myriad administrative requirements for the filing of consumer bankruptcy petitions.

Where did all the debtors *go* during 2006? Were their debts resolved? Were their creditors satisfied? Probably not. By 2007, the number of consumer filings began to increase again at the astonishing rate of 66% and the same looks true for 2008, with a projected increase in filings of at least 27%, edging the total number of filings close to the million-filing mark again.[108] The likely explanation is that attorneys and consumers have begun to understand the provisions of BAPCA and "gear up" to handle the challenging administrative hurdles that BAPCA placed in the way of consumer filings.

Consumer bankruptcies account for approximately 95% of all bankruptcy filings. The availability of easy credit from banks, and concomitant spending by consumers during times of easy credit, tends to lead to bankruptcy filings in subsequent years. Individuals are prone to spend beyond their means when credit is available and the

[107] Based on calendar year filings. Data from the Administrative Office of the United States Courts, *available at* http://www.uscourts.gov/bnkrpctystats/bankruptcystats.htm. Chapter 9 (municipal) bankruptcies have been excluded from the chart because they are very small in number and play an insignificant role in the bankruptcy system. Chapter 12 (family farmer reorganizations) have been excluded for the same reasons, with only 2,568 filings over an seven year period — an average of less than 367 per year.

[108] First quarter filings for 2008 were 245,695 compared to 2007 first quarter filings of 193,641 — an increase of 27%. If that trend continues throughout 2008, the total number of filings will be approximately 953,841.

economy is healthy and, eventually, find themselves unable to cover their increasingly overwhelming debts in subsequent years when job losses, divorces, health issues, credit unavailability, or downturns in the economy impede their abilities to repay debt.

b.   Business Filings

Although far fewer *business* bankruptcy cases are filed, they are bigger, more complex and involve much greater amounts of assets. In 1980, $1.7 billion in assets held by 62 bankrupt public companies were administered through the bankruptcy system. By 1990, there were 116 public companies with assets of $82.8 billion in bankruptcy. Below is a chart for the period from 2000–2008 showing the numbers and amounts of bankruptcies of publicly traded companies during the first eight years of the 21st century.[109] Note the small number of filings but the large amounts of money involved. The chart does not include filings by non-publicly traded business entities, which adds tens of billions more to the total amount of business related filings:[110]

Public Company Bankruptcy Filings Through February 2008

Year	Number	Assets
2000	28	$21,887,000,000
2001	35	$13,698,000,000
2002	54	$67,707,000,000
2003	35	$6,192,000,000
2004	20	$7,097,000,000
2005	19	$9,064,000,000
2006	10	$1,978,000,000
2007	11	$691,000,000
2008	16	$8,708,000,000
Totals	**228**	**$137,022,000,000**

Over the eight year period ending March 2008, there were 228 publicly traded companies that filed bankruptcy, with a total of $137 billion in assets. There is likely to be a much larger number of public company filings in 2008 and 2009 as the gasoline crisis, mortgage crisis and economic downturn impacts the economy of the U.S.

These statistics give us some perspective on the role that federal bankruptcy laws play in the resolution of debtor-creditor relationships in the United States. With such an enormous impact on the economy, we need to fully understand the impact of bankruptcy on business entities, whether they are healthy or in trouble. Healthy companies will be affected by the bankruptcy system because they will hold equity interests in, or be creditors of, business debtors that end up in bankruptcy. On the other hand, many troubled companies will use the bankruptcy system to liquidate or reorganize.

---

[109] The 2008 filings were only as of August 2008

[110] The amounts in the chart are from, Reuters UK, *U.S. Bankruptcy Filings in 2008*, Feb. 29, 2008, *available at* http://www.reuters.com/article/rbssFinancialServicesAndRealEstateNews/idUSN2742137720080229.

4.   Objectives of Bankruptcy

There are two fundamental objectives that are implemented by the Bankruptcy Code. The first objective is to relieve honest and cooperative debtors from the burden of overwhelming, long term debt. The second is to satisfy the claims of the debtor's creditors in a manner that is efficient, maximizing and inexpensive, when compared to alternatives under state debtor-creditor law. In the case of business entities that have reached the end of the line, and cannot continue to operate and pay outstanding debts, bankruptcy is a place where the liquidation of the entity can be handled in an inexpensive and creditor-maximizing manner in chapter 7. It's also a forum where business debtors who are in financial trouble may use chapter 11 of the bankruptcy code to "reorganize" and create a plan for the *continuation* of the company — if that plan pays creditors more than they would receive in a liquidation.[111]

We will take a look at the application of the two fundamental bankruptcy objectives as they relate to both individual debtors and business debtors. The following excerpt from Sir William Blackstone's Commentaries, written over 225 years ago, helps to provide some insights into the objectives of bankruptcy, which continue to apply to bankruptcy laws in modern times.[112]

Sir William Blackstone, Commentaries on the Laws of England
Book the Second (9th ed. 1783)

CHAPTER THE THIRTY-FIRST: OF TITLE BY BANKRUPTCY

The preceding chapter having treated pretty largely of the acquisition of personal property by several commercial methods, we from thence shall be easily led to take into our present consideration a tenth method of transferring property, which is that of:

X. BANKRUPTCY; a title which we before lightly touched upon, so far as it related to the transfer of the real estate of the bankrupt. At present we are to treat of it more minutely, as it principally relates to the disposition of chattels, in which the property of persons concerned in trade more usually conflicts, than in lands or tenements. Let us therefore first of all consider, 1. *Who* may become a bankrupt: 2. What *acts* make a bankrupt: 3. the *proceedings* on a commission of bankrupt: and 4. In what manner an estate in goods and chattels may be *transferred* by bankruptcy.

1. Who may become a bankrupt. A bankrupt was before defined to be "a trader, who secretes himself", or does "certain other acts, tending to defraud his creditors". He was formerly considered merely in the light of a criminal or offender; and in this spirit we are told by sir Edward Coke, that we have fetched as

---

[111] Chapter 11 plans may also provide for liquidation of the company but, if that's the case, the company business will probably continue while the liquidation plan is executed, rather than grind to a halt, as it would in chapter 7.

[112] We have taken the liberty of converting some of the antiquate English into more readable form. For instance, changing "ſ" to the modern "s" and terms such as "gaol" to "jail." We've also removed some Latin phrases.

well the name, as the wickedness of bankrupts from foreign nations.[113] But at present the laws of bankruptcy are considered as laws calculated for the benefit of trade, and founded on the principles of humanity as well as justice; and to that end they confer some privileges, not only on the creditors, but also on the bankrupt or debtor himself. On the creditors; by compelling the bankrupt to give up all his effects to their use, without any fraudulent concealment: on the debtor; by exempting him from the rigor of the general law, whereby his person might be confined at the discretion of his creditor, though in reality he has nothing to satisfy the debt: whereas the law of bankrupts, taking into consideration the sudden and unavoidable accidents to which men in trade are liable, has given them the liberty of their persons, and some pecuniary emoluments, upon condition they surrender up their whole estate to be divided among their creditors.

In this respect our legislature seems to have attended to the example of the Roman law. I mean not the terrible law of the twelve tables; whereby the creditors might cut the debtor's body into pieces, and each of them take his proportionable share: if indeed the law . . . is to be understood in so very butcherly a light; which many learned men have with reason doubted. Nor do I mean those less inhuman laws (if they may be called so, as *their* meaning is indisputably certain) of imprisoning the debtor's person in chains; subjecting him to stripes and hard labor, at the mercy of his rigid creditor; and sometimes selling him, his wife, and children, to perpetual foreign slavery *trans Tiberim*:[114] an oppression, which produced so many popular insurrections, and secessions to the *mons facer.* But I mean the law of *cession,* introduced by the Christian emperors; whereby, if a debtor *ceded,* or yielded up all his fortune to his creditors, he was secured from being dragged to a jail . . . Thus far was just and reasonable: but, as the departing from one extreme is apt to produce it's opposite, we find it afterwards enacted, that if the debtor by any unforeseen accident was reduced to low circumstances, and would swear that he had not sufficient left to pay his debts, he should not be compelled to cede or give up even that which he had in his possession: a law, which under a false notion of humanity, seems to be fertile of perjury, injustice, and absurdity.

The laws of England, more wisely, have steered in the middle between both extremes: providing at once against the inhumanity of the creditor, who is not suffered to confine an honest bankrupt after his effects are delivered up; and at the same time taking care that all his just debts shall be paid, so far as the effects will extend. But still they are cautious of encouraging prodigality and extravagance by this indulgence to debtors, and therefore they allow the benefit of the laws of bankruptcy to none but actual *traders;* since that set of men are, generally speaking, the only persons liable to accidental losses, and to an inability of paying their debts, without any fault of their own. If persons in other situations of life run in debt without any fault of their own. If persons in other situations of life run in debt without the power of payment, they must take the consequences of their own

---

[113] [1] The word itself is derived from the word *bancus* or *banque,* which signifies the table or counter of tradesmen and *ruptus,* broken; denoting thereby one whose shop or place of trade is broken and gone; though others rather choose to adopt the word route, which in French signifies a trace or track, and tell us that a bankrupt is one who hath removed his banque, leaving but a trace behind. And it is observable that the title of the first English statute concerning this offense 34 Hen. VIII. "against " such persons as do make bankrupt," is literal translation of the French idiom, *qui font banque route.*

[114] [2] In Peru, and the adjacent countries in East India, the creditor is entitled to dispose of the debtor himself, and likewise of his wife and children; insomuch that he may even violate with impunity the chastity of the debtor's wife; but then, by doing, the debt is understood to be discharged.

indiscretion, even though they meet with sudden accidents that may reduce their fortunes: for the law holds it to be an unjustifiable practice, for any person but a trader to encumber himself with debts of any considerable value. If a gentleman, or one in a liberal profession, at the time of contracting his debts, has a sufficient fund to pay them, the delay of payment is a species of dishonesty, and a temporary injustice to his creditor: and if, at such time, he has no sufficient fund, the dishonesty and injustice is the greater. He cannot therefore murmur, if he suffers the punishment which he has voluntarily drawn upon himself. But in mercantile transactions the case is far otherwise. Trade cannot be carried on without mutual credit on both sides: the contacting of debts is therefore here not only justifiable, but necessary. And if by accidental calamities, as by the loss of a ship in a tempest, the failure of brother traders, or by the non-payment of persons out of trade, a merchant or trader becomes incapable of discharging his own debts, it is his misfortune and not his fault. To the misfortunes therefore of debtors, the law has given a compassionate remedy, but denied it to their faults: since, at the same time that it provides for the security of commerce, by enacting that every considerable trader may be declared a bankrupt, for the benefit of his creditors as well as himself, it has also (to discourage extravagance) declared, that no one shall be capable of being made a bankrupt, but only a trader, nor capable of receiving the full benefit of the statutes, but only an *industrious* trader.

* * *

3. The *proceedings* on commission of bankrupt, so far as they affect the bankrupt himself. And these depend entirely on the several statutes of bankruptcy; all which I shall endeavor to blend together, and digest into a concise methodical order.

* * *

When the bankrupt appears, the commissioners are to examine him touching all matters relating to his trade and effects. They may also summon before them, and examine, the bankrupt's wife and any other person whatsoever, as to all matters relating to the bankrupt's affairs. And in case any of them shall refuse to answer, or shall not answer fully, to any lawful question, or shall refuse to subscribe such their examination, the commissioners may commit them to prison without bail, till they submit themselves and make and sign a full answer; the commissioners specifying in their warrant of commitment the question to refused to be answered. Any jailer, permitting such person to escape, or go out of prison, shall forfeit 500£ to the creditors.

The bankrupt, upon this examination, is bound upon pain of death to make full discovery of all his estate and effects, as well in expectancy as possession, and how he has disposed of the same; together with all books and writings relating thereto; and is to deliver up all in his own power to the commissioners; (except the necessary apparel of himself, his wife, and his children) or, in case he conceals or embezzles any effects to the amount of 20£ or withholds any books or writings, with intent to defraud his creditors, he shall be guilty of felony without benefit of clergy; and his goods and estate shall be divided among his creditors. And unless it shall appear, that his inability to pay his debts arose from casual loss, he may, upon conviction by indictment of such gross misconduct and negligence, be set upon the pillory for two hours, and have one of his ears nailed to the same and cut off.

* * *

Hitherto every-thing is in favor of the creditors; and the law seems to be pretty rigid and severe against the bankrupt; but, in case he proves honest, it make him full amends for all this rigor and severity. For if the bankrupt hath made an ingenuous discovery, (of the truth and sufficiency of which there remains no reason to doubt) and hath conformed in all points to the directions of the law; and if, in consequence thereof, the creditors, or four parts in five of them in number and value, (but none of them creditors for less than 20£) will sign a certificate to that purport; the commissioners are then to authenticate such certificate under their hands and seals, and to transmit it to the lord chancellor: and he, or two of the judges whom he shall appoint, on oath made by the bankrupt that such certificate was obtained without fraud, may allow the same; or disallow it, upon cause shown by any of the creditors of the bankrupt.

If no cause be shown to the contrary, the certificate is allowed of course; and then the bankrupt is entitled to a decent and reasonable allowance out of his effects, for his future support and maintenance, and to put him in a way of honest industry. This allowance is also in proportion to his former good behavior, in the early discovery of the decline of his affairs, and thereby giving his creditors a larger dividend. For, if his effects will not pay one half of his debts, or ten shillings in the pound, he is left to the discretion of the commissioners and assignees, to have a competent sum allowed him, not exceeding *three per cent*; but if they pay ten shillings in the pound, he is left *five per cent*; if twelve shillings and six-pence, then *seven and a half per cent*; and if fifteen shillings in the pound, then the bankrupt shall be allowed *ten per cent*: provided, that such allowance do not in the first case exceed 200£ in the second 250£ and in the third 300£.

Besides this allowance, he has also and indemnity granted him, of being free and discharged for ever from all debts owing by him at the time he became a bankrupt; even though judgment shall have been obtained against him, and he lies in prison upon execution for such debts; and, for that amount other purposes, all proceedings on commissions of bankrupt are, on petition, to be entered of record, as a perpetual bar against actions to be commenced on this account: though, in general, the production of the certificate properly allowed shall be sufficient evidence of all previous proceedings. Thus the bankrupt becomes a clear man again; and, by the assistance of his allowance and his own industry, may become a useful member of the commonwealth: which is the rather to be expected, as he cannot be entitled to these benefits, unless his failures have been owing to misfortunes, rather than to misconduct and extravagance.

a.   The Fresh Start for Honest and Cooperative *Individual* Debtors

The U.S. Supreme Court concisely stated the fresh start objective of the bankruptcy laws in 1934:

> [The bankruptcy discharge] gives to the honest but unfortunate debtor . . . a new opportunity in life and a clear field for future effort, unhampered by the pressure and discouragement of preexisting debt.[115]

---

[115] Local Loan Co. v. Hunt, 292 U.S. 234, 244 (1934).

Chapter 7 liquidations allow individual debtors a "fresh start" in the form of a discharge from all pre-petition debt, with some exceptions.[116] The discharge releases debtors from *personal liability* for pre-petition[117] debts and prohibits pre-petition creditors from taking action against the debtor, the debtor's property, or the debtor's post-petition earnings to collect those debts.[118] Individuals can file for relief from creditors under chapters 7 (liquidation), 11 (reorganization),[119] 12 (family farmer reorganization) or 13 (wage earner reorganization. In any of these chapters, the debtor will be seeking a discharge of pre-petition debt and a "fresh start" free of that debt.[120] By far, most individual debtors elect chapter 7 liquidation, although changes brought about by BAPCA have caused a slight shift of consumer debtors from chapter 7 to chapter 13. Later in this chapter we will see that individual debtors must fully cooperate in the handling of the bankruptcy case, or risk having their discharge denied or, in a worst case scenario, face fines and imprisonment if they knowingly and fraudulently abuse the bankruptcy system.

i.   The mechanics of bankruptcy for individual debtors

In a chapter 7 liquidation, an individual debtor must turn over all of his or her non-exempt assets[121] and, in turn, the debtor will be granted a discharge that is effective as of the date of the filing of the petition. Most individual chapter 7 cases are "no asset" cases, meaning that there are no assets available for distribution to creditors once secured claims and the debtor's exemptions are taken into account. To understand why no asset cases are so prevalent, we need to get a snapshot of the average chapter 7 debtor.[122]

Distribution of Income, Assets, and Debts for Bankruptcy Petitioners in 1981 and 1991, adjusted to 1991 dollars

1991 Distribution	Family Income	Total Assets	Total Debt	Secured Debt	Unsecured Debt
Mean	20,535	38,553	50,783	29,879	20,706
25th Percentile	12,078	3,200	15,963	732	7,239
Median	18,000	16,765	31,077	10,953	13,023
75th Percentile	26,622	60,130	65,752	50,479	23,021

---

[116] Section 523(a) contains a list of certain debts that are excluded from the discharge.

[117] Under the Code, the date of the filing of a bankruptcy petition constitutes an important point in time and serves as a dividing line between debt owed prior to the petition, which is subject to discharge or rearrangement, and debt incurred after discharge, which is not. The term "pre-petition" takes on significant meaning under the Code.

[118] Creditors are, however, free to pursue other persons who are liable for those same debts. Secured parties will be allowed, eventually, to pursue repossession and foreclosure of their collateral, although they may be temporarily stopped from doing so by the automatic stay, discussed later in this chapter.

[119] It's possible but uncommon for individuals to elect chapter 11 reorganization.

[120] The effect of the discharge for chapter 7 cases is set forth in § 727(b) which states: "(b) Except as provided in section 523 of this title, a discharge . . . discharges the debtor from all debts that arose before the date of the order for relief under this chapter . . . " Provisions for discharges for individuals in chapters 11, 12 and 13 are contained in §§ 1141, 1228 and 1328.

[121] Exemptions are discussed later in this chapter.

[122] The chart is from Teresa A. Sullivan, Elizabeth Warren & Jay Lawrence Westbrook, *Consumer Debtors Ten Years Later: A Financial Comparison of Consumer Bankrupts 1981–1991*, 68 AM. BANKR. L.J. 121 (1994). Although the chart reports on data collected in 1991, the relative positions of individual debtors have not changed for the better since that time.

What can we learn from this chart? First, it's clear that individuals filing bankruptcy are deeply in debt, without the capacity to repay that debt from the incomes available to them. Even the wealthiest of these debtors (at the 75th Percentile) had average annual incomes of only $26,622. For the average family living at the poverty level, there would be no funds available to pay for other than rent/mortgage, food, transportation, clothing and other basic life necessities. These debtors were in debt way over their heads, without any reasonable means of repaying that debt.

Second, even debtors *with* assets lacked sufficient equity in those assets to repay any meaningful portion of their unsecured debt, even if they sold everything they owned. For instance, look at the "75th Percentile" line. These debtors averaged $60,130 in assets but had $50,479 in *secured* debt. Since secured creditors are entitled to use their collateral to satisfy their claims, secured debts must be paid off if the assets are sold, leaving the debtor with equity of only $9,651 to pay the remaining *unsecured* debt of $23,021.[123] Keep in mind that if a debtor did this, the debtor would be left asset-less, with no home, no car, no clothes, no appliances, no furniture and no food. Even so, after using the $9,651 to pay part of the unsecured debt of $23,021, the debtor would still owe unsecured creditors over $13,000 — an amount that can't possibly be repaid by a family of four earning an annual pre-tax income of only $26,622. In other words, it just doesn't make sense to force this debtor to sacrifice this meager amount of equity, and then leave the debtor destitute, hungry and without essential belongings to earn a living.

In every state, debtors are entitled to a certain amount of "exempt" property in the debtor's equity (the value of assets in excess of secured claims). Exempt property may not be seized by an unsecured judgment creditor to satisfy the creditor's claim. In the absence of exemptions, debtors could be left naked, destitute and homeless. Exemptions are meant to protect against *unsecured* creditors. Secured creditors with lien interests are entitled to use the property to satisfy their claims regardless of the debtor's exemptions, since the debtor voluntarily transferred a property right to such secured creditors. Exemptions are governed primarily by *state* law which is respected in bankruptcy when determining the debtor's exemptions.[124] The amounts of exemptions and the types of property entitled to be exempted varies from state to state. However, the federal list of exemptions in § 522(d) of the Code gives us a good idea of common exemption provisions. The federal bankruptcy list of exemptions is not overly generous when compared to many states exemption laws. Nevertheless, you will see that a fairly large amount of property is exempt:

[123] Under state law of secured transactions, a creditor with a valid lien is entitled to have the property sold at foreclosure to satisfy the creditor's claim. A buyer of the property takes it subject to the lien. In order to sell the property free of the lien, the secured creditor must be paid. See the discussion of secured creditors in Chapter 1.

[124] Bankruptcy Code § 522 gives the debtor the option to choose between the debtor's available state law exemptions or, alternatively, a list of federal exemptions. However, out of respect for state autonomy, states may "opt out" and limit bankruptcy debtors to use of state law exemptions only. Over 40 states have "opted out" of the federal bankruptcy exemptions.

§ 522. Exemptions

(d)   The following property may be exempted . . .

(1)   The debtor's aggregate interest, not to exceed $20,200 in value,[125] in real property . . . the debtor uses as a residence . . .

(2)   The debtor's interest, not to exceed $3,225 in value, in one motor vehicle.

(3)   The debtor's interest, not to exceed $525 in value in any particular item or $10,775 in aggregate value, in household furnishings, household goods, wearing apparel, appliances, books, animals, crops, or musical instruments, that are held primarily for the personal, family, or household use of the debtor or a dependent of the debtor.

(4)   The debtor's aggregate interest, not to exceed $1,350 in value, in jewelry held primarily for the personal, family, or household use of the debtor or a dependent of the debtor.

(5)   The debtor's aggregate interest in any property, not to exceed in value $1,075 plus up to $10,125 of any unused amount of the exemption provided under paragraph (1) of this subsection.[126]

(6)   The debtor's aggregate interest, not to exceed $2,025 in value, in any implements, professional books, or tools, of the trade of the debtor or the trade of a dependent of the debtor.

. . .

(8)   The debtor's aggregate interest, not to exceed in value $10,775 . . . in any accrued dividend or interest under, or loan value of, any unmatured life insurance contract owned by the debtor under which the insured is the debtor or an individual of whom the debtor is a dependent.

(9)   Professionally prescribed health aids for the debtor or a dependent of the debtor.

(10)   The debtor's right to receive —

(A)   a social security benefit, unemployment compensation, or a local public assistance benefit;

(B)   a veterans' benefit;

(C)   a disability, illness, or unemployment benefit;

(D)   alimony, support, or separate maintenance, to the extent reasonably necessary for the support of the debtor and any dependent of the debtor;

(E)   a payment under a stock bonus, pension, profitsharing, annuity, or similar plan or contract on account of illness, disability, death, age, or length of service, to the extent reasonably necessary for the support of the debtor and any dependent of the debtor,

(11)   The debtor's right to receive, or property that is traceable to —

---

[125] The dollar amounts in this section are subject to adjustment every three years, in April, based on the Consumer Price Index. *See* § 104. The amounts listed here are as of April 2007.

[126] This is a catch-all exemption that the debtor can use for any property, even a cash bank account. Notice that a debtor who does not use all of the homestead exemption in subsection (d)(1) can add up to $10,125 to the $1,075 listed in (d)(5) for a possible total catch-all exemption of $11,200.

(A)   an award under a crime victim's reparation law;

(B)   a payment on account of the wrongful death of an individual of whom the debtor was a dependent, to the extent reasonably necessary for the support of the debtor and any dependent of the debtor;

(C)   a payment under a life insurance contract that insured the life of an individual of whom the debtor was a dependent on the date of such individual's death, to the extent reasonably necessary for the support of the debtor and any dependent of the debtor;

(D)   a payment, not to exceed $20,200, on account of personal bodily injury, not including pain and suffering or compensation for actual pecuniary loss, of the debtor or an individual of whom the debtor is a dependent; or

(E)   a payment in compensation of loss of future earnings of the debtor or an individual of whom the debtor is or was a dependent, to the extent reasonably necessary for the support of the debtor and any dependent of the debtor.

(12)   Retirement funds to the extent that those funds are in a fund or account that is exempt from taxation under section . . . of the Internal Revenue Code . . .

In addition to these exemptions, the debtor may also exclude from the bankruptcy estate (and thereby indirectly exempt the property from distribution to creditors) certain ERISA retirement plans and a few other assets that meet certain requirements.[127]

It should be apparent why so many individual chapter 7 cases are "no-asset" cases, without funds available to creditors.

For chapter 7 debtors with assets that *exceed* the combined amount of security interests plus the debtor's exemption entitlements ("asset cases"), chapter 7 is, potentially, a highly-disruptive proceeding. The debtor must turn over the debtor's non-exempt assets to the bankruptcy trustee, who will liquidate them for the benefit of the debtor's creditors. In turn, if the debtor is cooperative and honest, the debtor's pre-petition debts will be discharged. The debtor will be allowed to keep property in which there is no equity, as well as property which is exempted. However, property that is not exempt and not subject to a security interest will be sold by the trustee. In addition, property that exceeds the value of *both* a security interest and the debtor's exemptions will also be sold so that the debtor's non-exempt equity can be used to satisfy the debtor's unsecured creditors. For instance, suppose a debtor has non-exempt equity in some assets and $95,000 in unsecured debt. Here's a picture of the debtor's assets, security interests and exemptions:

---

[127]   *See* § 541(b)(7), (c)(2); Patterson v. Shumate, 504 U.S. 753 (1992).

Asset	Value	Secured Lien	Exemption	Equity available for unsecured creditors
Bank Account	$20,000	$0	$0	$20,000
House	$200,000	$150,000	$35,000	$15,000
Furnishings & appliances	$15,000	—	$15,000	$0
Auto	$22,000	$17,000	$2,700	$2,300
Clothing & Household Goods	$12,000	$0	$12,000	$0
Total Assets Available to Unsecured Creditors				$37,300

There is $37,300 in non-exempt, unsecured equity in the debtor's assets available to pay off the $95,000 in unsecured debts. That's enough for a 39% repayment to the debtor's unsecured creditors. However, in this asset case, the individual debtor would be reluctant to file chapter 7. Can you see why? The debtor would have to turn over the house and automobile, which will be sold by the trustee so that the equity in excess of the combined security interest and exemption amounts can be used to satisfy creditors.

Individual debtors have an alternative available to prevent such a disruptive liquidation. Under chapter 13, an individual debtor can keep his creditors from collection activities while the debtor *voluntarily* agrees to use all or a part of the debtor's *future disposable income* (usually over a five year period) to repay the debtor's pre-petition creditors, rather than liquidating some or all of the debtor's assets.[128] For instance, if our hypothetical debtor earns $50,000 per year (after taxes and other payroll deductions) and has basic living expenses of $35,000 per year, that leaves $15,000 per year of disposable income that can be used to pay pre-petition creditors. Over a five year period following the filing of the bankruptcy petition that adds up to $75,000, which is a far greater amount than the creditors would receive under chapter 7 ($37,300), even taking into account the delay in payment.[129] Such a repayment plan offers both the debtor and the unsecured creditors an optimizing agreement that preserves the debtor's assets from disruption and gives the creditors far more than they would get in chapter 7. Following the debtor's completion of the chapter 13 repayment plan, the debtor will be granted a discharge.

---

[128] The rarely-used chapter 12 provides similar opportunities to "family farmers" to take advantage of a plan similar to chapter 13, even though they have assets that exceed the chapter 13 limitations or lack the type of regular wage income required for chapter 13. Chapter 11 is also available for individuals who do not qualify for chapter 13. Although individuals can use chapter 11 to come up with a repayment plan, it is rarely done due to the cost and complexity of chapter 11, which requires the informed consent of the debtor's creditors. Nevertheless, a properly motivated individual debtor with substantial equity in assets who wants to avoid liquidation under chapter 7, can use chapter 11 to propose a plan to repay more than the creditors would receive in chapter 7 liquidation and obtain the necessary votes from creditors, and confirmation by the court, to effectuate a chapter 11 plan that leads to a discharge.

[129] It might help to know that the chapter 13 plan *must* pay creditors at lease as much as they would have received in a chapter 7 liquidation *plus* interest as of the effective date of the plan.

ii. The logic behind the fresh start discharge for individuals

Whether the individual debtor files a chapter 7 "no-asset" petition, a chapter 7 "asset" petition, a chapter 13 repayment plan, or a more complex and difficult chapter 11 plan, the honest and cooperative debtor will be granted a discharge upon completing the debtor's obligations under the Bankruptcy Code. All of the chapters allow individuals to emerge from the burden of life-long, overwhelming debt and restart their economic lives, notwithstanding the low payments to creditors, or no payments to creditors in no-asset chapter 7 cases.

Why would the drafters of the U.S. Constitution contemplate, and the U.S. Congress implement, bankruptcy laws that allow debtors a "fresh start" despite the fact that creditors are left with partial or no payment of their claims? There are important reasons for allowing individual debtors a fresh start at the expense of their creditors.

One justification is that these creditors are unlikely to obtain payment of their claims under state law in the absence of bankruptcy. As the saying goes, "you can't squeeze blood out of a stone." The vast majority of debtors are, simply, judgment proof. They lack sufficient income or assets that unsecured creditors can seek to satisfy their claims. It's senseless for creditors to spend the time, money and energy to pursue collection of these claims against debtors who are incapable of paying them. It's equally senseless to leave these debtors at the mercy of never-ending harassment and collection attempts.

A second and, perhaps more important, justification is that the *availability* of a discharge has a positive impact on our economy. Financial setback is a fact of life in any commercial society — particularly in our modern, credit-reliant economy. The availability of credit fuels the purchases made by consumers which, in turn, constitutes the largest proportion of the gross domestic product, encourages business and generates wealth. Credit also fuels the ventures undertaken by individuals who start businesses, build real estate improvements, startup software companies or other business enterprises. While business-oriented individuals may try to protect themselves from the risks of debt associated with new ventures by using limited liability entities such as corporations and LLC's, they will often be required to personally guarantee the obligations of the entity.

Part of the psychology of our credit dependent society, whether individuals act as consumers or business investors, is that there has to be some relief from the specter of life-long debt if there is a failure in the transactions that, unfortunately, lead to a debt load the debtor can't handle. Individuals simply wouldn't take the credit risks that they do without some *possibility* of relief from debt in the event that the debt load turns out to be more than they can repay. In other words, the *availability* of a bankruptcy discharge *later* in time, helps to encourage individuals to borrow money on credit today and contribute to the growth and well being of our economy. An example helps to understand the incentives provided by the availability of a discharge of debts in bankruptcy.

Suppose you earn $125,000 per year. You have saved about $200,000 and want to invest in a software venture (or retail store) that is risky but, if it succeeds, there is a potential for earning millions. On the other hand, if the venture fails, there is a potential for millions of dollars in liability.[130] Would you make the investment knowing that, if the venture fails, you face the possibility of $5 million in debt that could *never* be discharged — nor could it ever be repaid. Even assuming that your creditors agreed to a repayment plan, to pay off that much debt over a ten year period at 7.5% interest would take $59,350.88 *per month* ($712,000 per year). However, after taxes, your income of $125,000 would yield well under $100,000 per *year*.

What would you do? You couldn't possibly pay this amount, ever. In the meantime, your creditors would be hounding you to make payments, commencing collection actions, garnishing your salary and seizing non-exempt assets for the rest of your life. How would you provide for your family? What would happen to your non-exempt assets, including the portions of your monthly paycheck that are subject to garnishment?[131] Would you continue working if a substantial portion of every paycheck was seized by your creditors and those creditors relentlessly seized any non-exempt assets you acquired?

If all, or a substantial portion, of a debtor's future income and assets are subject to seizure by creditors, the debtor will obviously have a diminished incentive to produce. On a broad, societal scale, the social cost of sentencing debtors to a non-productive netherworld of continuing debt obligation is far too high when compared to the alternative — compelling creditors to release their claims for less than full payment by the debtor.

In the absence of the *availability* of a discharge from such impossible debt, would you have made the $200,000 investment and start up that new, risky business? Probably not. Can you see that the availability of a discharge encourages both consumers and business debtors to take credit risks by reducing the Draconian impact of a risk failure?

So long as goods and services are sold on credit, there will be individual consumer and business debtors who cannot repay their debts. Who should bear the risk of such a setback? If we place the risk on the individual debtor, we create tremendous disincentives to consumer spending. We also created disincentives to business ventures which are not highly conservative and, consequently, we impede industrial/technological growth and discourage competition. On the other hand, if we *spread* the risk of financial setback by allowing a debtor to transfer the setback to and among his or her creditors, then we create a medium in which good faith business risks can be taken without fear of the consequences. These objectives were well-recognized over two hundred years ago in the Blackstone excerpt set forth earlier in this chapter and worth repeating here:[132]

---

[130] You plan to borrow and purchase goods and services on credit in the amount of $5 million dollars over the first 3 years of the venture. All of the lenders and creditors will require that you sign personal guarantees.

[131] Federal law protects some portion of wages from seizure by creditors. The maximum amount that can be garnished is limited to 25% of the debtor's disposable earnings (the part of the earnings remaining after deduction of amounts required by law to be withheld), or a lesser amount for lower income earners. 15 U.S.C. § 1673. Although the wage garnishment laws protect *direct* seizure of wages, as soon as those wages are converted into non-exempt assets, the assets remain subject to seizure by writ of execution. The Federal Wage Garnishment Act is contained in Title III of the Consumer Credit Protection Act, Pub. L. 90-321, May 29, 1968, 82 Stat. 146 (15 U.S.C. § 1601 *et seq.*)

[132] These excerpts refer to traders only. At the time there was no such thing as consumer credit as

But at present the laws of bankruptcy are considered as laws calculated for the benefit of trade, and founded on the principles of humanity as well as justice; and to that end they confer some privileges, not only on the creditors, but also on the bankrupt or debtor himself. On the creditors; by compelling the bankrupt to give up all his effects to their use, without any fraudulent concealment: on the debtor; by exempting him from the rigor of the general law, whereby his person might be confined at the discretion of his creditor, though in reality he has nothing to satisfy the debt: whereas the law of bankrupts, taking into consideration the sudden and unavoidable accidents to which men in trade are liable, has given them the liberty of their persons, and some pecuniary emoluments, upon condition they surrender up their whole estate to be divided among their creditors.

Trade cannot be carried on without mutual credit on both sides: the contacting of debts is therefore here not only justifiable, but necessary. And if by accidental calamities, as by the loss of a ship in a tempest, the failure of brother traders, or by the non-payment of persons out of trade, a merchant or trader becomes incapable of discharging his own debts, it is his misfortune and not his fault.

[T]he bankrupt is entitled to a decent and reasonable allowance out of his effects, for his future support and maintenance, and to put him in a way of honest industry . . .

Besides this allowance, he has also and indemnity granted him, of being free and discharged for ever from all debts owing by him at the time he became a bankrupt; . . .

b.   Liquidation and Reorganization of Business Debtors

i.   Business entity liquidations

Why would a corporation, partnership or LLC choose to file a chapter 7 liquidation case in bankruptcy, rather than pursue state law dissolution? The answer is twofold. First, chapter 7 is a cheap and efficient way to liquidate the assets of an insolvent and failing business when compared to the state law alternative. Second, bankruptcy will almost always produce a greater distribution to creditors than state law dissolution proceedings.

Once the petition is filed, all of the assets of the entity *immediately* become property of the bankruptcy estate,[133] which will be managed by a bankruptcy trustee who specializes in chapter 7 cases. This will be true regardless of where the assets are located and who is in possession or control of the assets. The jurisdictional power of the federal district courts over the debtor's property is exclusive and absolute:

---

we know it today. Nevertheless, Blackstone's points are equally applicable to both modern consumer and business debtors.

[133] Section 541(a) states: "(a) The commencement of a case . . . creates an estate. Such estate is comprised of all the following property, wherever located and by whomever held . . . " The list of property is exhaustive, and includes "all legal or equitable interests of the debtor in property as of the commencement of the case."

§ 1334.   Bankruptcy cases and proceedings

(e)   The district court in which a case under title 11 is commenced or is pending shall have exclusive jurisdiction —

(1)   of all the property, wherever located, of the debtor as of the commencement of such case, and of property of the estate; . . .[134]

Once the petition is filed, an automatic stay will halt the collection activities of both unsecured and secured creditors, including any pending litigation, repossessions, foreclosures and writ enforcement proceedings.[135] The chapter 7 trustee will use the power of the automatic stay to maintain the status quo while the trustee seeks to maximize the distribution to the unsecured creditors of the estate. During the pendency of the case, the trustee will:

(1) Collect the property of the estate, and, if there is equity worth selling, sell the property for cash.[136] The trustee is aided in his or her collection efforts by powerful "turnover" provisions that compel persons in custody, control or possession of assets of the estate to turn them over to the trustee.[137] When selling the property, bankruptcy trustees are not limited to auctions or foreclosure-type sales. They can sell assets in the regular marketplace or by any means that enhances the value received for the asset.

(2) Avoid liens that impair the value of some assets. The bankruptcy trustee is given extraordinary powers to avoid some pre-petition transfers, including the transfer of liens and security interests that, if avoided, will increase the overall distribution to unsecured creditors.[138] This may be of tremendous value to the unsecured creditors of the estate in cases where there have been large-scale preferential transfers or fraudulent conveyances prior to bankruptcy. While most properly perfected security interests will be unavoidable, certain types of liens, including unperfected security interests or untimely perfected security interests, will be subject to avoidance in bankruptcy. These powerful avoidance powers can be used by the trustee to vastly increase the distribution to creditors. The trustee's avoidance powers will be discussed in greater detail later in this chapter.

(3) Determine the validity of the claims against the debtor. Every creditor who wants to participate in bankruptcy distribution will have to file a proof of claim, with supporting documentation. For good and fair reasons (such as the unenforceability of the claim under state law) some of the unsecured claims may not be allowed to participate in distribution of the assets of the estate, thereby increasing the overall distribution to creditors with allowable claims.[139]

---

[134]   28 U.S.C. § 1334(e).

[135]   The automatic stay is contained in § 362 and discussed in greater detail later in this chapter.

[136]   11 U.S.C. § 363.

[137]   11 U.S.C. §§ 542–43, 550.

[138]   11 U.S.C. §§ 544–48.

[139]   Section 726(a)(2) requires all unsecured creditors timely file a "proof of claim." The notice to creditors of the bankruptcy filing, Official Form 9C, contains a clear notice of the need to timely file a proof of claim. Section 502 provides a list of claims which are only partially allowable, or not allowed in their entirety.

(4) Fairly distribute the cash from liquidation of the estate to the debtor's pre-petition creditors. There is a list of *priority* creditors who, as a matter of public policy, must be paid first. Priority creditors include the bankruptcy trustee and others who participate in administering and liquidating the debtor's estate (for obvious reasons), employees and taxing authorities, and others.[140] Once the priority creditors have been paid, the remainder of the cash will be fairly and evenly to the *general* (non-priority) unsecured creditors of the estate, *pro rata*.

How does liquidation of a business entity under federal bankruptcy law compare to the state law dissolution provisions we studied earlier in this chapter? There are many advantages to the federal system:

(1) There is no need to find one or more directors (in the case of corporations), partners (in the case of partnerships) or members (in the case of LLC's) to take responsibility for the dissolution and liquidation of the debtor. Often, in the case of a failed and insolvent business, none of the owners are economically motivated to handle the dissolution, since all the proceeds will be paid to creditors. By placing the liquidation of the business in chapter 7, trained professionals will represent the interests of creditors. Unlike former equity owners, chapter 7 trustees are highly motivated to efficiently process the liquidation and maximize the distribution to creditors. The chapter 7 trustees are appointed to panels by the U.S. Trustee for their federal district, who periodically evaluate the effectiveness of all of the trustees on the panel. Those that perform poorly will be removed from the panel. Interestingly, chapter 7 trustees are paid only $60 from the filing fee for each chapter 7 case. However, when an asset-based business case is assigned to them, they also are paid a percentage interest of the value that they bring in from the sale of assets. Currently, the percentage is 25% of the first $5,000, plus 10% of amounts over $5,000 to $50,000, plus 5% of amounts over $50,000 to $1,000,000, plus 3% of amounts above $1,000,000. Consider a business case with $800,000 in unsecured assets and $4 million in debt. In a state law dissolution, the owners lack any motivation to conduct the dissolution, since all of the proceeds of the dissolution will be paid to creditors. However, in bankruptcy, the trustee will be working hard to maximize the amounts received for the assets of the business, yielding the trustee a potentially large fee.

(2) The cost of chapter 7 liquidation is far less than a court supervised dissolution under state law. Using the state law system is time-consuming and extremely expensive once the jurisdiction of the state courts is invoked. Overworked and non-specialized trial judges will oversee many aspects of the dissolution and there may be extensive litigation regarding the conduct of the dissolution and the disputes that arise. Trial judges in most states may handle a panoply of cases, from marital dissolutions, to criminal matters, to landlord tenant matters, to property cases, etc. Very few have any specialized expertise in business entity dissolution. On the other hand, in bankruptcy, most of the process is handled by the trustee, who is invested with powers to quickly collect, liquidate and distribute the property of the estate, as well as resolve the allowability of creditor claims. When disputes arise in bankruptcy, or court orders are needed, the matters will be heard before specialized bankruptcy judges with experience and knowledge of bankruptcy liquidations.

---

[140] The priority scheme is set forth in §§ 726(a) and 507(a).

(3) The automatic stay halts virtually all creditor collection activities, giving the person conducting the liquidation the time to collect and maximize the liquidation of assets on behalf of the unsecured creditors. To obtain the equivalent stasis under state law, law suits would have to be commenced by the person conducting the dissolution, seeking preliminary injunctions or other relief. The cost would be stunningly high, the timing difficult since state law cases take weeks-to-months to resolve, and there is no guarantee that the injunctions or other relief will be obtained.

(4) The bankruptcy trustee is given powerful rights to avoid certain pre-petition transfers that depleted the estate. While some of those rights (such as the right to avoid fraudulent conveyances) exist under state law, those given to the trustee under the federal bankruptcy laws are far more extensive and will be litigated in front of bankruptcy judges.

(5) The jurisdictional grant over the bankruptcy case, proceedings related to the case, and the property of the estate is centralized in a single federal district.[141] The entire case and all the related proceedings will be conducted in a single court, before a single judge, intimately familiar with the case.

(6) In state law dissolution proceedings, there is likely to be litigation regarding the conduct of the dissolution among the equity holders of the entity, as they vie for control of the dissolution or object to the conduct of the dissolution. In bankruptcy, that is not the case. The liquidation will be handled by the chapter 7 trustee, in accordance with the detailed and powerful provisions of the bankruptcy code.

For all of these reasons, it is highly unusual to see a business entity liquidation conducted under state law dissolution statutes. If the business is failing and insolvent, with no assets available for the owners, the company will invariably be *voluntarily* liquidated in chapter 7 bankruptcy. One of the owners, directors or managers will take responsibility for filing a chapter 7 petition.[142] Once the petition is filed, the owners, directors and managers can simply walk away, leaving the liquidation in the hands of the chapter 7 trustee.

ii.   The problem of partner, guarantor and joint liability

An issue arises concerning the chapter 7 liquidation of partnerships, as well as other entities where the equity holders may have signed personal guarantees or otherwise face liability for the debts of the entity. The filing of a bankruptcy petition by the *entity* will not eliminate the independent liability of general partners or, in the case of corporations or LLCs, persons who have guaranteed contractual debts (or fact joint liability for non-contractual debts). Is it still worth it to use chapter 7 to liquidate an insolvent and failing business entity if some or all of the equity holders will remain liable for any debts of the entity that aren't fully paid in bankruptcy?

The answer is probably yes, unless the business can be sold as a going concern. If, before bankruptcy, the equity holders can find a buyer for the business as a going concern, they might be able to produce a greater value for the assets of the company than if they liquidated the company in bankruptcy. However, if the

---

[141] *See* 28 U.S.C. § 1334.

[142] 11 U.S.C. § 301.

company is insolvent and failing, the chance of a knight on horseback riding in to buy the company as a going concern is highly unlikely. In the absence of a rescuing knight, it's well worth it for partnerships (and entities with jointly liable owners) to choose chapter 7 bankruptcy, rather than state law dissolution, to liquidate the assets of the business. There is, simply, a greater cost savings if the liquidation is conducted in the bankruptcy system. The more that is repaid to creditors as a consequence of the liquidation, the less the amount that general partners, guarantors or other jointly liable parties will have to pay. Indeed, the Code allows *less* than all of the general partners to file a bankruptcy petition notwithstanding a contrary agreement between the partners or state law.[143] Thus, if there is discord among the general partners or impending actions by other partners that might produce potential liability for the petitioning partner(s), the filing of a petition can suspend the activities of the partnership and provide for a maximizing liquidation.

iii. Business entity reorganizations

There is an incentive for *both* creditors and business debtors in attempting a reorganization under Chapter 11 rather than a liquidation under Chapter 7. In a liquidation case the creditors are limited to repayment from the debtors equity in assets at the time of the filing of the chapter 7 petition. In chapter 11, rather than liquidating the debtor's pre-petition assets and distributing the cash proceeds, the assets are retained by the debtor and the business continues to operate.[144] By allowing the debtor to continue operations, the debtor can come up with a plan to pay creditors *more* than they would receive in a liquidation case. By participating in a reorganization plan, the creditors will be entitled to increased payment of their pre-petition claims. It's worth noting that creditors get to *vote* on the reorganization plan and, in addition, the bankruptcy court plays an active role in confirming the plan. A debtor can successfully utilize chapter 11 only if the plan is appealing to the creditors — and that will be true only if the plan pays them more than they would receive in chapter 7.[145]

From the viewpoint of a business entity debtor, there is a significant advantage to electing chapter 11 rather than chapter 7. In chapter 7, the equity interests of

---

[143] 11 U.S.C. § 303(b)(3). A filing by less than all of the general partners is considered an "involuntary" bankruptcy petition. This means that a general partner who did not agree to the filing may object to the filing and seek to have the case dismissed from bankruptcy court. If there is such an objection, the petitioning partners must show either: (1) the partnership is generally not paying its debts as they debts become due; or, (2) within 120 days before the date of the filing of the petition, substantially all of the assets of the partnership were transferred to a custodian or trustee under state law.

[144] In some chapter 11 cases, the plan calls for a liquidation of the company. Nevertheless, unlike chapter 7, the business will continue to operate and the company will be liquidated in a manner that enhances the distribution to creditors.

[145] There are various requirements in the Code for the proposal, voting and confirmation of a plan which will sometimes allow the equity holders to participate in the reorganization and sometimes they will be foreclosed from doing so. A successful plan will require the cooperation and approval of at least one class of creditors, and, often, the cooperation and approval of several classes. Although creditors generally have an opportunity to vote for or against the confirmation of the plan, a negative vote can sometimes be neutralized under provisions in § 1126. A reorganization plan may be confirmed even in those circumstances where some of the debtor's creditors do not agree to the plan. However, that will only be true in cases where the plan pays creditors more than they would receive in chapter 7 and, if an entire class objects, the equity holders cannot force the confirmation of a plan unless junior classes (including the equity holders) receive no distributions from the reorganization plan.

the equity holders will be wiped out.[146] In chapter 11, the plan *may* provide that the equity holders are entitled to retain some interest in the *post*-petition business assets.[147] Keep in mind that the creditors must vote to approve such a plan.

How does this happen? Where does the extra value come from in a chapter 11 that allows creditors to be paid more than a liquidation case and still allow the equity holders some participation interest in the reorganized debtor?

There are several sources of additional value in a chapter 11 reorganization.

First, the value of a reorganized debtor that continues in business as a going concern is often in excess of its liquidation value. Many airlines have successfully used chapter 11 to manage their debt and stay in business. The compelling factor for creditors to agree to airline reorganization plans is the low liquidation value of an airline, compared to its going concern value. If liquidated, most airlines would yield very low value. Their assets consist primarily of highly-leveraged airplanes (there are security interests that eat up most of the value of the planes, leaving little equity for unsecured creditors). The remainder of their assets are their trained pilots and crews, and the "good will" name recognition of the airline. None of these assets are of much value in a liquidation. However, by reorganizing, many airlines have been able to renegotiate labor contracts, cancel unprofitable routes, eliminate or sell subsidiary regional airlines and otherwise "slim down" to a more efficient and profitable business, thereby creating additional value for their pre-petition creditors.

A second source of additional value is the ability of a reorganized debtor to use *future* income to pay off pre-petition debt. In a chapter 7, the sole source of creditor payment is the liquidation value of the debtor's assets. In a chapter 11, the debtor will stay in business and use future earnings from operations, or the future sale of assets, to pay a larger percentage of the pre-petition debt.

A third source of value is the power given to the chapter 11 debtor in possession to reject *burdensome* contracts and leases. A business entity may be weighted down by contracts and leases that make the company non-competitive. For instance, suppose that the debtor is a company with a contract for the delivery of 100,000 manufactured computer chips to a buyer at $15 per chip (a total sales price of $1.5 million). However, recent shortages of materials have driven the cost of manufacturing the chips to $20 per chip. If the contract is performed, the debtor will *lose* $500,000. Under § 365 of the Code, this type of burdensome contract can be rejected. The resulting claim of the buyer for breach of contract is converted into a pre-petition unsecured claim.[148] Rejection might also be justified for contracts where the debtor is the *buyer* and is obligated to pay a price for goods that exceeds the current market value of the goods. For instance, the debtor might be obligated to buy 100,000 computer chips at $25 per chip but market prices have dropped and the chips are readily available from other suppliers for $10 per chip.

---

[146] Under § 726 (priority of distribution in chapter 7) the equity holders are entitled to distribution only when all of the creditors' claims and all of the administrative expenses have been paid, including interest from the date of the bankruptcy petition to the date of claim payment. It is extremely unlikely that the equity holders will ever participate in distribution under chapter 7. To participate would mean that the debtor was solvent at the time of the filing of the bankruptcy petition.

[147] Many reorganizations do not yield significant value for the equity holders, particularly in the case of publicly traded business entities.

[148] This result is dictated by §§ 365(g) and 502(g).

It makes sense to reject such a burdensome contract. Many airlines have used the power to reject executory contracts to force renegotiation of labor union contracts with pilots, flight attendants and mechanics that were unsustainable. The contracts may have been agreed to during economic times when airfares were high, fuel was cheap and competition from other airlines a minor issue. However, as losses mounted, the airlines needed to reject those contracts and renegotiate them to keep the airline competitive and prevent liquidation. It was in the best interests of *both* the airlines and their labor forces to agree to a new contract that lets the company stay in business and effectively compete. The alternative is liquidation, which leaves the employees without jobs.[149]

Similarly, burdensome *leases* may be rejected as well. Many retail store chains such as K-Mart, Macy's, Bloomingdales and Federated Department Stores have successfully used chapter 11 to stay in business and flourish following their emergence from a chapter 11 plan. One of the strategic elements of their reorganization plans included the rejection of real property leases for their less profitable locations.[150]

An essential requirement of the confirmation process for approval of a chapter 11 reorganization plan is obtaining the consent of the unsecured creditors. Therefore, when designing the plan, the debtor must be careful to propose a *feasible* reorganization plan that offers the creditors more than they would receive in a chapter 7. If such a plan is proposed, the creditors would be acting against their own economic interests if they refused to consent to the plan. In fact, there should be no need to use chapter 11 to accomplish such a consensual "workout" among the debtor and its creditors. In a perfect world, the debtor and its creditors could reach the same result by executing an agreement under state law. Why doesn't that

---

[149] The first airline to reject a labor union contract was Continental Airlines in 1983 when the airline filed bankruptcy and terminated its labor contract with its pilots. In re Continental Airlines Corp., 38 B.R. 67 (S.D. Tex. 1984). In response, the pilots called a strike that lasted for more than 2 years. The strike was acrimonious, with incidents of violence and the filing of lawsuits, charges, and countercharges. Although most of the approximately 2,000 pilots originally supported the strike, about 600 of them were working by August 1985, along with about 1,000 replacement workers hired by the airline. In 1984, the U.S. Supreme Court held unanimously that collective bargaining agreements were executory contracts capable of being rejected if the agreement burdens the estate. NLRB v. Bildisco & Bildisco, 465 U.S. 513 (1984). Soon thereafter, Congress adopted § 1113, which places some limits on the ability of companies to reject labor union contracts. Although the contracts may still be rejected if burdensome, some obligations are placed on the debtor to negotiate in good faith with the labor representatives, and the bankruptcy court must confirm that "the balance of the equities clearly favors rejection of such agreement.

[150] The K-mart Disclosure Statement summarized a major element of its reorganization plan as follows:

> Chapter 11 would afford the Company the best opportunity for restructuring its affairs and for developing and implementing a long term, go forward, retail business strategy. To this end, Kmart has worked to implement a number of key initiatives . . . including, among other things, elimination of unprofitable stores and leases . . . A primary focus of Kmart and its constituents . . . has been on rationalizing and optimizing the Company's store and lease portfolio. to this end, Kmart will have reduced its total number of stores from 2,114 as of the Petition Date to 1,514 as of emergence from Chapter 11, which constitutes a total reduction of 600 stores . . . Kmart has also obtained substantial value through the renegotiation and/or assumption of significant executory contracts, including licensing agreements with its key brand partners . . .

Case No. 02–02474, U.S. Bankruptcy Court, N.D. IL, Disclosure Statement, page v. The full K-Mart Reorganization Plan and Disclosure Statement can be found on the SEC EDGAR site at http://www.sec.gov (search EDGAR for CIK# 0000056824, then open the 8-K statement dated 2003-03-07).

happen more often? The problem is that the *costs* of obtaining consents from *all* creditors and the possibility of *holdouts* (creditors who refuse to agree or who will agree only if given a larger share) will diminish or eliminate the possibility of success in obtaining such an agreement under state law. Just think of the cost of contacting and negotiating an agreement with thousands of creditors, each with a different claim and a different point of view. Chapter 11 serves as a *forum* where these *costs* and *holdout* problems can be eliminated or reduced.

When newspapers, radio and television media announce the chapter 11 filing of a well known company, they often use a phrase similar to the following: "Today, Federated Department Stores, filed for relief from its creditors." Its true that filing of the chapter 11 petition will invoke the power of the automatic stay to halt creditor collection activities. However, the stasis created by the automatic stay is actually for the benefit of the *creditors*. By halting lawsuits, repossessions, foreclosures and other collection activities by *some* creditors, the debtor can continue operations, preserve assets and enforce a period of calm, while the debtor comes up with a reorganization plan that self-maximizing creditors should agree to as an alternative to liquidation.

The key element in a chapter 11 reorganization is the plan. When a Chapter 11 petition is filed the debtor is given an opportunity (currently 180 days) to propose a plan for reorganization. If the debtor fails to prepare such a plan or if the plan is not approved by creditors, the *creditors* then have an opportunity to propose an alternate plan. Assuming that a plan will be confirmed, what will its contents be? The types of arrangements for reorganizing debtors are virtually limitless. The plan will provide that some creditors are paid cash immediately, that others receive future periodic payments in satisfaction of their claim, that others extend time for repayment by the reorganized debtor, and that some creditors receive an equity interest in the reorganized debtor.

It must be remembered that rational creditors will often desire a reorganization rather than a liquidation case. So long as they receive some repayment of their pre-petition claims in excess of what they would receive in a chapter 7 liquidation, it is certainly in their interest to seek a successful reorganization.

iv.   The debtor-in-possession

Since the purpose of most chapter 11's is to rehabilitate and continue the debtor's business, it is important that the business be operated as seamlessly as possible during the pendency of the bankruptcy case. For instance, in airline or department store bankruptcies, it is essential to the success of the reorganization effort that the airline or store continue to operate as though bankruptcy has not occurred at all. Otherwise, in the case of airlines, passengers will cancel their reservations and move to other airlines. In the case of department stores, customers will abandon the stores and move to competitors to do their shopping. In both cases, suppliers, employees, and others who do business with the debtor would quickly cease their relationships with the debtor if it looks like the business is going to quickly come to a halt. For these reasons, a trustee is normally *not* appointed in a chapter 11 case. The debtor will continue to operate the business as a "debtor in possession."[151] With some minor exceptions, wherever the word "trustee" appears in the Code, the debtor in possession *is* the trustee. In every

---

[151] *See* 11 U.S.C. § 1107. The legislative comment accompanying the enactment of § 1107 stated:

chapter 11, the "trustee" (i.e., the debtor in possession) is automatically authorized under to operate the debtor's business.[152] The debtor in possession is also vested with the usual duties of collecting the property of the estate under § 541, avoiding pre-petition transfers under §§ 544–548, and assuming or rejecting executory contracts and leases. The debtor-in-possession is the same corporate or other business entity as the debtor but operates in a fiduciary capacity as the trustee.

The norm is that the debtor will continue as the debtor-in-possession. A trustee will be appointed only in those cases where there has been fraud, dishonesty or other good cause for appointment of a trustee — or if the court finds that it's in the best interest of creditors or equity security holders.[153]

v.   BAPCA and "small business reorganizations"

The Bankruptcy Abuse Prevention and Consumer Protection Act of 2005 added new provisions to chapter 11 to move *small* business cases through the chapter 11 process with greater speed and less cost. This makes sense when the entity is small and lacks the resources to fulfill the requirements of a normal chapter 11. The changes also assure that small business debtors are not using chapter 11 merely to postpone an inevitable liquidation.

The provisions apply only to individuals or entities engaged in commercial or business activities (but not if the primary activity is not owning or operating real estate). If the aggregate debts of such a business, both secured and unsecured, are less than $2 million,[154] special provisions apply in the chapter 11 reorganization. The case is put on a faster track than a larger chapter 11 and procedures for proposal, voting on and confirmation of the reorganization plan, are more streamlined. Among the benefits and burdens for the small business debtor are the following:[155]

— The time periods for filing a reorganization plan and obtaining confirmation are shortened. If the time periods are not met, the case is converted to a chapter 7 liquidation

— Small business debtors are required to file periodic financial statements and reports regarding:

(1) the debtor's profitability;

(2) reasonable approximations of the debtor's projected cash receipts and cash disbursements over a reasonable period;

"This section places a debtor in possession in the shoes of a trustee in every way . . . He is required to perform the functions and duties of a chapter 11 trustee (except the investigative duties). He is also subject to any limitations on a chapter 11 trustee, and to such other limitations and conditions as the court prescribes, cf. *Wolf v. Weinstein*, 372 U.S. 633, 649–650 (1963)." S. Rep. 95-989, 95th Cong., 2d Sess. 35 (1978).

[152] 11 U.S.C. § 1108.

[153] Section 1104 allows creditors, or the U.S. Trustee, to seek appointment of a trustee for several reasons, such as: "(1) for cause, including fraud, dishonesty, incompetence, or gross mismanagement of the affairs of the debtor by current management . . . , (2) if such appointment is in the interests of creditors . . . "

[154] 11 U.S.C. § 101(51D). Debts to affiliates and insiders are not included in determining whether or not the business is a small business debtor. The provisions are intended for businesses with outside debts of under $2 million.

[155] The list is derived from §§ 308, 1102, 1116, 1125(f) and 1129.

(3) comparisons of actual cash receipts and disbursements with projections in prior reports;

(4) whether the debtor is in compliance in all material respects with requirements imposed by the Code and the Federal Rules of Bankruptcy Procedure; and

(5) whether the debtor has timely filed tax returns, other required government filings and is paying taxes and other administrative expenses when due.

— Upon court order, there is no requirement for the appointment of a creditor's committee.[156]

— The debtor must attend meetings scheduled by the court and the US Trustee

— The debtor must maintain insurance customary and appropriate to the industry

— The debtor must allow inspection of books and records upon receipt of reasonable notice by the United States Trustee or designated representative

— The need for a disclosure statement and the process for approval of a disclosure statement, if one is required, are dramatically reduced.[157] The court may determine that the *plan* itself provides creditors with adequate information, eliminating the need for a disclosure statement. If a disclosure statement is required, the small business debtor may use standard forms approved.

— The disclosure statement hearing and the confirmation hearing may be combined.

c. Fair, Efficient and Maximizing Distribution to Creditors

To fully understand the power and fairness of the bankruptcy system with respect to *creditors*, it's important to first understand how unsecured creditors get paid under *state* law.

We are not too concerned about satisfaction of debts owed to *secured* creditors. In the absence of bankruptcy, secured creditors with adequate collateral will use state law proceedings to repossess the collateral and have it sold to at a foreclosure sale to satisfy their claims.[158] *Over*secured creditors, with collateral that exceeds the amount of their claims have little to worry about. For instance, a secured creditor may have loaned the debtor $100,000 and, in return, the debtor granted the secured creditor a security interest in equipment with a liquidation value of $150,000. In the security agreement, the debtor agreed that the security interest would secure payment of the principal, interest, and costs of collection. Suppose

---

[156] Normally, in a chapter 11, a creditor's committee is appointed, usually consisting of the debtor's seven largest creditors willing to serve on the committee. The costs of the committee and its lawyers are borne by the estate.

[157] In a regular chapter 11, the debtor must prepare a disclosure statement tailored to the case, then submit the disclosure statement for formal court approval. Only after approval may the debtor distribute the disclosure statement and solicit votes in favor of a proposed plan of reorganization. The process is expensive and time consuming.

[158] There are, of course, procedures for the foreclosure of intangible property as well.

the debtor defaults and the secured creditor exercises its rights? The secured creditor will seize the equipment and have it sold at a public foreclosure sale (for its liquidation value of $150,000). On the day of foreclosure, assume that the principal balance of the loan is still $100,000 and that accrued but unpaid interest has accumulated in the amount of $4,000. If the costs of repossession and foreclosure were $3,000, the total debt owed to the secured creditor would be $107,000. The proceeds of the foreclosure sale will first be used to satisfy the secured party for principal and interest and costs of foreclosure, leaving a surplus of $43,000, which will be returned to the debtor.

The outcome will be the same in a bankruptcy proceeding. The Bankruptcy Code respects the property rights and expectations of secured creditors with validly created and perfected security interests.[159] Although the automatic stay may *temporarily* prevent the secured party from seizing the collateral and having it sold, the security interest will "ride through" the bankruptcy proceeding and, if endangered, the secured creditor can move for relief from the stay to adequately protect its security interest.

How do *unsecured* creditors get paid under state law? In the event that a debtor is unable, or unwilling, to pay debts, unsecured creditors are in a difficult position. To obtain satisfaction of a claim, an unsecured creditor must commence a law suit in state or federal court, obtain a judgment and then, if the judgment remains unpaid, find valuable assets of the debtor that can be seized to satisfy the claim. If there is property available, the judgment creditor will use a lien creation mechanism (such as a writ of execution, writ of garnishment or a judgment lien) to establish an involuntary lien in property of the debtor. At some point, if the creditor remains unpaid, the lien can enforced by foreclosure. The process is expensive, time-consuming and inherently unreliable. Even if the creditor rigorously pursues relief, the creditor must compete with many other unsecured creditors who are also seeking to obtain satisfaction of their claims. Each unsecured creditor will be racing to the courthouse to be the first to obtain a judgment and seize any of the entity's available assets. Unfortunately, even the winner of this race often finds that the debtor has no any assets worth seizing. In the case of individual debtors, many of the debtor's assets may be exempt from creditor attachment. In the case of all debtors, there simply may be no equity in the debtor's assets. For a debtor in trouble, available assets will be used or borrowed against to keep the business operating. Any cash will be used to pay employees, providers of goods and services and other parties who are essential to keeping the business operating. Troubled debtors are likely to already have borrowed against any equity they have in assets, granting security interests to obtain loans. For the unsecured creditor who succeeds in getting a judgment, there simply may be no property worth seizing.

If there *are* assets available to satisfy judgment creditors, the state law "race" system is inherently unfair, expensive and wasteful. State law rewards only those unsecured creditors who race to the courthouse, obtain judgments and then establish judgment liens against the debtor's property. The "race" system of creditor satisfaction rewards only the quickest creditor-litigants, while denying

---

[159] There are times that security interests can be avoided in bankruptcy as preferential or unperfected transfers but properly created and perfected security interests will be fully respected in bankruptcy. An amalgam of Code sections assure secured creditors full protection of their security interests. *See* §§ 101(30), 101(43), 361, 362(d), 363(d)–(f), 506(a)–(b), 507(b), 522(f), 552, 554, 722.

other unsecured creditors a share of the debtor's property. Consequently, if the creditors of the debtor sense a financial reversal in the debtor's business or income, *all* of the debtor's unsecured creditors will be racing to the court house to be the first in time to establish a lien interest in the debtor's assets. Think of the aggregate cost to all creditors, and the debtor. Assume there are ten major unsecured creditors, each with a $75,000 claim against the debtor. The debtor has only $75,000 in equity available for creditor lien seizure. The ten creditors have aggregate claims of $750,000. Only the first creditor to succeed in obtaining a judgment and lien will achieve satisfaction of the creditor's claim. Yet, all ten of the creditors will each be spending thousands (probably tens of thousands) of dollars racing to be the first judgment lienor. The *aggregate* cost of attempting collection by these ten creditors is likely to exceed the $75,000 value of the assets available for distribution to unsecured creditors.

It would make far more sense for the creditors to simply agree to act together to minimize the costs of collection and *share* the $75,000. This is the objective of the federal bankruptcy laws. In liquidation cases, rather than leaving the creditors to the preferential, wasteful, expensive and unreliable state law system of debt collection, the Bankruptcy Code imposes mechanisms to eliminate litigation, reduce costs, speedily collect and liquidate the property of the estate, and distribute the assets *pro rata* to similarly situated general unsecured creditors.[160] In asset-based chapter 7 liquidations, the Code gives the bankruptcy trustee powerful tools to collect the property of the debtor and liquidate it on behalf of *all* of the unsecured creditors. If there is equity in the debtor's property available in excess of secured liens (and exemptions in individual cases), that equity will be equally divided among unsecured creditors.

Can you see how superior federal bankruptcy is to the state law system? In the absence of bankruptcy, it is possible that whatever assets an insolvent debtor has might be unfairly distributed (voluntarily or involuntarily) among creditors, favoring some while disfavoring others. It is often difficult for unsecured creditors to locate and attach, or obtain a lien upon, the diffuse assets of the debtor. Bankruptcy provides a mechanism whereby the debtor's assets can be quickly determined, collected, and then distributed equitably among the debtor's creditors. In a sense, bankruptcy merely serves as a centralized forum for the equitable distribution of an insolvent debtor's assets among existing creditors, or the working out of a reorganization plan where the debtor agrees to pay a larger amount to the debtor's creditors.

In reorganization cases, the debtor will be allowed to stay in business (or keep his or her assets in individual cases) while the debtor designs a reorganization plan that uses the retained assets, and/or post-petition earnings, to pay unsecured creditors on a *pro rata* basis at least as much as they would have received in chapter 7 and, often, much more. The beauty of a reorganization plan is that it costs the creditors nothing, yet they will be receiving more than they would if the debtor liquidated *and* the debtor gets to stay in business (if a business debtor) and retain current assets. For individual debtors using chapter 13, this means they can retain their house, car and personal property, so long as they can use post-petition

---

[160] 11 U.S.C. § 726(a)–(b). The distribution of assets in a liquidation will be made to all unsecured claimants with valid and timely filed claims. However, some creditors will be entitled to priority of distribution under § 507.

earnings to pay a larger share to their unsecured creditors then would be paid in a chapter 7 liquidation.

5.   Some Essential Bankruptcy Mechanisms

What are the mechanisms that the federal bankruptcy laws use to accomplish the lofty objectives of providing debtors with a fresh start, while efficiently maximizing the distribution to creditors?

a.   The Automatic Stay

The filing of a bankruptcy petition gives rise to an "automatic stay"[161] which immediately halts virtually all types of creditor collection activities against the debtor, the debtor's property, and the debtor's post-petition earnings or business operations. The stay also halts collection activities against the property of the debtor that passed to the bankruptcy estate. There are two purposes served by the automatic stay.

First, the stay protects the debtor. In the case of an individual debtor, collection activities will cease while the individual debtor pursues a discharge. Since the pre-petition unsecured debts will, eventually, be discharged, the stay serves to protect the debtor's post-petition fresh start. In the case of business entities, the stay halts collection activities while the entity pursues liquidation or reorganization in an orderly and creditor maximizing way.

Second, the automatic stay serves to protect *creditors* by assuring that assets of the debtor, and the bankruptcy estate, won't be grabbed by overzealous creditors seeking to enforce their claims. In the absence of the automatic stay, unsecured creditors would be commencing and continuing legal actions, obtaining writs to establish liens in property (including writs of garnishment that grab the debtor's post-petition earnings) and, eventually, foreclose on those liens. With regard to secured creditors, if there was no stay, the secured creditors would be seizing assets as a prelude to foreclosure. In a liquidation case, these seizures would interfere with the trustees efforts to collect and sell the assets of the estate which have equity. To the extent that there is equity over and above the amount of the secured claim, that equity should be liquidated for the benefit of the estate. In reorganization cases, seizures and foreclosures by secured creditors would deny the debtor assets that might be essential to the debtor's ability to operate a business or earn post-petition income. The automatic stay keeps secured creditors from seizing assets, so long as the underlying property interest of the secured creditor can be adequately protected.[162]

---

[161] 11 U.S.C. § 362.

[162] *See* 11 U.S.C. §§ 362(d), 363(d)–(e). See also *U.S. v. Whiting Pools, Inc.*, 462 U.S. 198 (1983), where the Internal Revenue Service was precluded from repossessing and foreclosing on collateral in which the IRS had a perfected lien interest. The court held that, so long as the underlying security interest of the IRS was adequately protected, the assets should be retained by the chapter 11 debtor so that the business could be reorganized and a higher payout made to unsecured creditors. In *Whiting*, the debtor owed $92,000 federal trust fund taxes withheld from its employees but not paid over to the IRS. As a consequence, a tax lien in that amount attached to all of Whiting's property. The IRS seized all of Whiting's tangible equipment, vehicles, inventory, and office supplies to enforce the lien. The seizure put Whiting out of business. The estimated liquidation value of the property was, at most, $35,000 but its estimated going-concern value in Whiting's hands was $162,876. The bankruptcy court held that the IRS must return the assets to the debtor so that the debtor could pursue a viable chapter 11 plan.

The automatic stay saves creditors, the debtor and the bankruptcy trustee large sums of money that would otherwise be spent pursuing and defending against state law based collection activities. Instead, the stay serves to create a *stasis* while the trustee (in chapter 7 cases) or debtor (in reorganization cases) attempts to maximize the distribution to creditors. The stay is so powerful that it is sometimes used by positive-net-worth companies to halt litigation, while a solution is worked out with the claimants.

b.   Subject Matter Jurisdiction of the Federal Courts

Congress has granted to the District Courts of the United States powerful jurisdiction over bankruptcy cases and proceedings arising in, or related to, bankruptcy cases. It's worth reading 28 U.S.C. § 1334 to recognize the extraordinary breadth of the jurisdictional grant:[163]

§ 1334.   Bankruptcy cases and proceedings

(a)   Except as provided in subsection (b) of this section, the district courts shall have original and exclusive jurisdiction of all cases under title 11.

(b)   Except as provided in subsection (e)(2), and notwithstanding any Act of Congress that confers exclusive jurisdiction on a court or courts other than the district courts, the district courts shall have original but not exclusive jurisdiction of all civil proceedings arising under title 11, or arising in or related to cases under title 11.

. . .

(e)   The district court in which a case under title 11 is commenced or is pending shall have exclusive jurisdiction —

(1)   of all the property, wherever located, of the debtor as of the commencement of such case, and of property of the estate; . . .

Section 1334 is the *jurisdictional* grant of power by Congress to the *district courts* of the United States. Subsection (a) grants *original and exclusive*[164] jurisdiction over the bankruptcy case to the district courts. The term "case" refers to the entire bankruptcy case for a particular debtor, rather than any specific controversy or matter. Subsection (b) grants *original*, but not exclusive, jurisdiction over all civil proceedings arising under title 11, arising in title 11 or related to cases under title 11. Nevertheless, the automatic stay will halt the exercise of jurisdiction by any other state or federal court.

This jurisdictional grant is virtually unlimited in its expansiveness. It effectively grants the federal district courts power over disputes between the debtor and others, even though such disputes involve state law matters such as contract, family

---

[163] 28 U.S.C. § 1334 is one of several jurisdictional grants to the District Courts, some of which you undoubtedly studied in Civil Procedure: § 1331 (federal question jurisdiction), § 1332 (diversity jurisdiction), § 1333 (admiralty jurisdiction), § 1334 (bankruptcy jurisdiction) § 1335 (interpleader jurisdiction).

[164] Because such jurisdiction is exclusive, no other court has jurisdiction to adjudicate the bankruptcy case.

law, tort or other civil liability. However, even though the grant of jurisdiction to the district courts is expansive, the courts may voluntarily abstain, or in rare cases, *must* abstain from exercising that jurisdiction.[165] Can you imagine why such a broad grant of jurisdiction was created? The answer is that the objectives of bankruptcy require that a single court have authority over all of the many debtor-creditor claims, privileges, obligations and disputes that typically arise in a bankruptcy case. Could you imagine adjudicating a large chapter 11 case involving a department store chain with tens of thousands of creditors, hundreds of real property leases, thousands of supply and employment contracts in dozens of different state courts that, in the absence of bankruptcy, would adjudicate the matters? The reorganization would take decades to accomplish. Obviously, for both liquidations and reorganizations to function effectively and efficiently, there needs to be a central forum where the case, and all the proceedings related to the case, can be resolved.

c.   Delegation of Authority to Bankruptcy Judges

Section 1334 grants jurisdictional authority to the *district courts* of the United States. District court judges are "Article III" judges appointed under the constitutional mandate, contained in Article III, that judges be appointed for life, with undiminishable salaries, and protection from removal by office except by impeachment. These essential attributes of judicial power are essential to the existence of an independent judiciary in our tripartite system of government.

Unlike district court judges, bankruptcy judges are appointed for 14 year terms, are subject to removal for cause and Congress has the ability to diminish their salaries. Therefore, bankruptcy judges lack the independence of Article III judges. The bankruptcy courts are creations of Congress and sometimes referred to as "Article I" courts, staffed by "Article I" judges.

The bankruptcy courts are "units" of the district courts and 28 U.S.C. § 157 provides for the *delegation* of judicial power[166] from the district judges to the bankruptcy judges of the district, who have authority to hear only those matters which are delegated to them. Every district court in the U.S. has adopted a general order, referring all bankruptcy cases and proceedings to the bankruptcy courts, with one exception discussed below. § 157 also gives the district judges the authority to withdraw the case, or any particular proceedings, from the bankruptcy

---

[165] Although the federal courts have the jurisdiction to hear most state law proceedings, they also have the option, or mandate, to abstain from matters that are best resolved by state courts. Section 1334(c) provides:

(1) [N]othing in this section prevents a district court in the interest of justice, or in the interest of comity with State courts or respect for State law, from abstaining from hearing a particular proceeding arising under title 11 or arising in or related to a case under title 11.

(2) Upon timely motion of a party in a proceeding based upon a State law claim or State law cause of action, related to a case under title 11 but not arising under title 11 or arising in a case under title 11, with respect to which an action could not have been commenced in a court of the United States absent jurisdiction under this section, the district court shall abstain from hearing such proceeding if an action is commenced, and can be timely adjudicated, in a State forum of appropriate jurisdiction.

[166] There is one exception to the authority to delegate civil bankruptcy proceedings to the bankruptcy courts. Personal injury and wrongful death claims must be heard in the district courts and cannot be delegated to bankruptcy judges.

courts.[167] Why have all district courts generally referred bankruptcy cases and proceedings to the bankruptcy judges? The answer is that bankruptcy judges are experts in the field and have the specialized experience in debtor-creditor law to quickly and effectively move cases and proceedings through the bankruptcy system, increasing the efficiency of the liquidation or reorganization and assuring greater distributions for creditors, as well as preserving the fresh start for individual debtors.

Although the power to hear the case and proceedings related to the case have been delegated, the authority of the bankruptcy courts to render final judgments and orders is limited. In *Northern Pipeline Construction Co. v. Marathon Pipe Line Co.*,[168] the U.S. Supreme Court held that the "essential attributes" of judicial power over Article III type actions and proceedings must be held by judges vested with Article III protections. While Congress might be free to create Article I courts to hear special matters that arise out of a legislatively created scheme, such as bankruptcy, disputes that exist independently of that legislative scheme must be overseen by Article III judges. For instance, Congress could create Article I courts (such as the bankruptcy court) and vest its judges with authority to adjudicate and issue orders and judgments regarding matters that arise only in the context of bankruptcy — such as the granting or denial of a discharge; or the applicability of the automatic stay; or the confirmation of a chapter 11 plan.

However, if the dispute involves resolution of rights that arise independently of bankruptcy, such as a contract claim by a creditor, the essential attributes of judicial power over such a dispute must be in the hands of an Article III judge.

As the result of the decision in *Northern Pipeline*, we have a bifurcated system of adjudication for matters heard before bankruptcy judges. Under 28 U.S.C. § 157(b)(1), bankruptcy judges may issue "final judgments and orders" with regard to "core" matters — those matters that arise only under the legislative bankruptcy scheme created by Congress. Under 28 U.S.C. § 157(c), as to all other "non-core" matters, the bankruptcy judges can issue only proposed findings of fact and conclusions of law, with the district judge issuing the final order in the matter (unless the parties consent to a final judgment by the bankruptcy court).

d.   Involuntary Petitions

Virtually all bankruptcy cases are initiated with *voluntary* petitions, filed by the debtor. However, creditors are given the power under § 303 of the Code to commence an *involuntary* case against a debtor under certain circumstances. Why would such power be given to creditors? The answer lies in one of the two fundamental objectives of bankruptcy law — a fair and maximizing distribution to the creditors of the debtor. Involuntary petitions are a remedy for creditors who decide, *as a group*, that bankruptcy is the appropriate forum to maximize the distribution to them when they are not being paid. The requirements for successfully filing an involuntary petition can be summarized as follows:

---

[167] 28 U.S.C. § 157(d) provides: "The district court may withdraw, in whole or in part, any case or proceeding referred under this section, on its own motion or on timely motion of any party, for cause shown . . . "

[168] 458 U.S. 50 (1982).

1.	There must be three or more creditors with claims exceeding $13,475,[169] and the claims must not be contingent as to liability nor the subject of a bona fide dispute as to liability or amount.[170]

2.	If the debtor does not timely object to the involuntary petition, it will be granted. However, if the debtor objects, the creditors filing the petition must prove either (a) the debtor is generally not paying debts as they become due (unless such debts are the subject of a bona fide dispute as to liability or amount); or (b) within 120 days before the date of the filing of the petition, an assignee, trustee or custodian was appointed under non-bankruptcy law to take control and/or possession of substantially all of the assets of the debtor.[171]

The requirements assure that creditors can move the resolution of their claims against the debtor into the federal bankruptcy system in the event that the debtor is *generally* not paying debts as they come due, or the debtor has already voluntarily or involuntarily gone out of business by transferring substantially all of the debtor's assets to a non-bankruptcy trustee who is administering the liquidation of the debtor's assets. This gives the creditors the option of moving the resolution of their claims to the federal bankruptcy forum, where there is a likelihood of enhancing the amounts they receive from the debtor's liquidation.

There is one other important function of § 303 involuntary petitions. In the event that the debtor, while generally not paying debts, is dissipating assets, or preferring some creditors over others, the remaining unsecured creditors have the power to initiate a bankruptcy case which automatically stays any further dissipation or preferential transfers *and* vests the trustee with the power to avoid many of the improper pre-petition transfers as voidable preferences or fraudulent conveyances.

While involuntary petitions account for less than one percent of all bankruptcy cases, the availability of an involuntary petition is a powerful tool in the arsenal of creditors seeking to get paid from a failing debtor for two reasons. First, creditors can transfer the resolution of their claims to federal bankruptcy court, stop loss of assets, recover voidable pre-petition transfers and maximize the distributions to unsecured creditors. Second, the *threat* of an involuntary petition can often serve to motivate a debtor to pay the debtor's debts or, at least, agree to a payment plan.

EXERCISE 10-2

Imagine for a moment that a debtor, Deb Boat Manufacturing, Inc. ("DBI"), owes its five unsecured creditors $1 million. DBI has $2 million in assets, with about $1.5 million in secured loans, leaving $500,000 in equity. DBI has *net* income each month of $50,000. DBI is generally not paying its current debts, although there is sufficient cash flow to pay at least *part* of the outstanding debts. The reason is that DBI is hoping to introduce a new product line and is using the cash

---

[169] This amount is subject to adjustment every three years under § 104.

[170] 11 U.S.C. § 303(b)(1). The claims must be current claims held by creditors who have a right to payment. The remedy of an involuntary petition is intended for creditors who decide, as a group, that bankruptcy is the best path to satisfaction of their claims. Involuntary petitions are not intended for creditors with contingent claims or claims that are the subject to a bona fide dispute that needs to be resolved in litigation.

[171] 11 U.S.C. § 303(h).

flow to gear up for production and advertising. Under state law, what can the three unsecured creditors do? If they act individually, they are limited to pursuing judgments (which may take years), then obtaining judgment liens on any property in which DBI has equity at the time the lien is established. The process is expensive and unreliable, since there may be no equity in DBI's assets when the judgment is finally obtained. Yet, all three creditors will be pursuing the same path, each spending tens of thousands of dollars to obtain a judgment and hoping that there will be property to satisfy their claims. Do these creditors have a right to commence an involuntary case under § 303? Should the creditors commence a case? Can the *threat* of an involuntary petition help these creditors in their negotiations with the debtor?

e.   Bankruptcy Fraud

The success of the bankruptcy system depends to a substantial degree on the honesty and cooperativeness of debtors and other parties who participate in the system. In addition to signing the petition, substantial burdens are placed on debtors to fill out extensive *lists and schedules* relating to the debtors assets, debts, financial affairs, income, expenses and many other matters.[172] The lists and schedules are comprehensive and require an honest exposé of the debtor's financial life. An individual debtor who knowingly or recklessly makes material representations or omissions in the petition, lists or schedules may be denied a discharge.[173] In addition, a debtor or other party who participates in bankruptcy fraud is subject to *criminal* prosecution — with a penalty of up to five years in prison for each offense:

18 U.S.C. § 152.   Concealment of assets; false oaths and claims; bribery

A person who —

(1)   knowingly and fraudulently conceals from a custodian, trustee, marshal, or other officer of the court charged with the control or custody of property, or, in connection with a case under title 11, from creditors or the United States Trustee, any property belonging to the estate of a debtor;

(2)   knowingly and fraudulently makes a false oath or account in or in relation to any case under title 11;

(3)   knowingly and fraudulently makes a false declaration, certificate, verification, or statement under penalty of perjury . . . in or in relation to any case under title 11;

(4)   knowingly and fraudulently presents any false claim for proof against the estate of a debtor, or uses any such claim in any case under title 11, in a personal capacity or as or through an agent, proxy, or attorney;

(5)   knowingly and fraudulently receives any material amount of property from a debtor after the filing of a case under title 11, with intent to defeat the provisions of title 11;

---

[172] *See* Fed. R. Bank. Proc., Official Forms 1, 4, 6, 6A–6J, 7, 8, 22, 23.

[173] 11 U.S.C. § 727(a).

(6)   knowingly and fraudulently gives, offers, receives, or attempts to obtain money or property, remuneration, compensation, reward, advantage, or promise thereof for acting or forbearing to act in any case under title 11;

(7)   in a personal capacity or as an agent or officer of any person or corporation, in contemplation of a case under title 11 by or against the person or any other person or corporation, or with intent to defeat the provisions of title 11, knowingly and fraudulently transfers or conceals any of his property or the property of such other person or corporation;

(8)   after the filing of a case under title 11 or in contemplation thereof, knowingly and fraudulently conceals, destroys, mutilates, falsifies, or makes a false entry in any recorded information (including books, documents, records, and papers) relating to the property or financial affairs of a debtor; or

(9)   after the filing of a case under title 11, knowingly and fraudulently withholds from a custodian, trustee, marshal, or other officer of the court or a United States Trustee entitled to possession, any recorded information (including books, documents, records, and papers) relating to the property or financial affairs of a debtor,

shall be fined not more than $5,000, imprisoned not more than 5 years, or both.

F.   CONCLUSION — DISSOLUTIONS AND BANKRUPTCY

We have seen that both state and federal law provide mechanisms for the end-stage of a business entity. The path the owners will take to implement dissolution will depend on whether or not the entity has a positive or negative net worth. In a positive-net-worth company it is in the best interests of *all* of the owners to cooperate in the dissolution. If the owners have been well-advised, they have pre-drafted buyout agreements and dissolution agreements that make the dissolution efficient and maximizing. Even where they have not done so, state law dissolution statutes give the equity holders the opportunity to cooperate in optimizing the dissolution. Regardless of variations among state dissolution statutes, the primary tasks of the equity holders in such cases is to: (i) selling the assets of the company for the greatest possible value in an efficient and timely manner; (ii) determine and pay off the company debts (or providing for their future payment); and, (iii) distribute the remaining proceeds in accordance with the distribution scheme set forth in the formation documents or in accordance with statutory default rules for distribution if the formation documents are unclear.

However, in the case of a company with a *negative* net worth, it is relatively unusual for business entities to use state law dissolution proceedings. It simply may not be in the interests of the equity holders to oversee and cooperate in the dissolution. To protect creditors and simplify the liquidation of failed businesses, the federal Bankruptcy Code provides a streamlined and comparatively easy way for companies to liquidate. The simple filing of a chapter 7 petition will transfer control of the liquidation to the bankruptcy trustee, who is vested and supported by statutory powers to enhance the trustee's ability to collect the property of the debtor, liquidate it and fairly distribute the property to creditors.

In addition, the federal bankruptcy laws allow business entities to seek reorganization under chapter 11. When the company is suffering from financial adversity, it can use chapter 11 to temporarily stay creditor enforcement and collection activities while it proposes a plan to responsible handle its debt and then submit that plan for creditor approval.

TABLE OF CASES

[References are to page numbers. Principal cases are in capital letters.]

[References are to page numbers. Principal cases are in capital letters.]

[References are to page numbers. Principal cases are in capital letters.]

INDEX

[References are to pages.]

I-1

[References are to pages.]

[References are to pages.]

[References are to pages.]

[References are to pages.]

[References are to pages.]

[References are to pages.]

[References are to pages.]

[References are to pages.]